PENGUIN BOOKS

THE HOLY GRAIL

'Barber's sensitivity to the diversity of nuances in each of his many sources ensures that each one he looks at affords him some fresh insight. The result is a fascinating compendium of theology, literary criticism and cultural history' Lucy Hughes-Hallett, *Sunday Times*

'Thoroughly refreshing and rewarding . . . An elegantly argued and immensely readable study of medieval religious symbolism and literature' S. B. Kelly, *Scotland on Sunday*

'Scholarly and comprehensive . . . Barber is an Arthurian expert whose purpose is to hack a path through the muddled, corrupted and conflicting versions of the Grail story . . . the result is admirably thorough, sane and sceptical' Nicholas Shakespeare, *Daily Telegraph*

'A valuable account of the literary origins of the Grail legend, as well as its subsequent fortunes' Jonathan Sumption, *Guardian*

'Not only does Barber give thorough consideration to a number of conspiracy theories about "the secret of the Grail", most notably the idea that Christ survived the Crucifixion and begat a line of kings with Mary Magdalene, he also summarizes the Grail's role in alchemical, Rosicrucian, Templar and Gnostic tradition . . . This is a humane and serious book' Carolyne Larrington, *The Times Literary Supplement*

'Masterly . . . Barber's book, which restores all [the Grail's] gravitas, gives it an exciting new lease of life' Christina Hardyment, *Independent*

'The origins, nature and significance of the Holy Grail and why it has exerted such a hold on the Western imagination are the themes that Barber explores in this fascinating and comprehensive account . . . a stimulating study' Michael Arditti, *Daily Mail*

'Richard Barber's splendid new book presents a comprehensive survey of the search for the Holy Grail from the twelfth century to the present day' Juliette Wood, *The Times*

'Fascinating . . . Barber does a dexterous job of conveying the mood and texture of these variations on Grail story, while at the same time illuminating the religious and political dramas that informed their creation . . . engaging reading as both literary creation and cultural history, thanks largely to the author's fluency and aplomb as a writer' Michiko Kakutani, *The New York Times*

'A serious and useful history of the Grail legend, which should dispel some of the more lunatic theories' Karen Armstrong, *New Statesman*

'[A] quest to disentangle the numerous myths and meaning that have grown up around the Holy Grail . . . Not only has Richard Barber dealt skilfully with the original medieval evidence; he has also traced the long after-life of the Grail legend, above all in its various nineteenth- and twentieth-century avatars' Noel Malcolm, *Sunday Telegraph*

'Fascinating reading . . . Barber offers a fine interpretation of an inspiring legend' Ronald Blythe, *Oldie*

ABOUT THE AUTHOR

Richard Barber has been writing and publishing in the field of medieval history and literature ever since his student days. His first and most recent books both concern the Arthurian legend. He started with a general survey, *Arthur of Albion*, in 1961, which is still in print in a revised edition; his second book, *Henry Plantagenet* (1964) has just been reissued in paperback. He has also written on chivalry, and won the Somerset Maugham award in 1970 for *The Knight and Chivalry*. Other books include the standard biography of Edward the Black Prince, *Edward Prince of Wales and Aquitaine*, *The Penguin Guide to Medieval Europe*, an edition of John Aubrey's *Brief Lives*, and anthologies of medieval literature (*Myths and Legends of the British Isles*, *Legends of Arthur*).

Richard Barber has also been a successful publisher. In 1969 he helped to found the Boydell Press, which later became Boydell & Brewer Ltd, one of the leading publishers in medieval studies, and he has been managing director since the outset.

RICHARD BARBER

The Holy Grail

THE HISTORY OF A LEGEND

PENGUIN BOOKS

PENGUIN BOOKS

Published by the Penguin Group
Penguin Books Ltd, 80 Strand, London WC2R ORL, England
Penguin Group (USA) Inc., 375 Hudson Street, New York, New York 10014, USA
Penguin Group (Canada), 10 Alcorn Avenue, Toronto, Ontario, Canada M4V 3B2
(a division of Pearson Penguin Canada Inc.)
Penguin Ireland, 25 St Stephen's Green, Dublin 2, Ireland
(a division of Penguin Books Ltd)
Penguin Group (Australia), 250 Camberwell Road, Camberwell, Victoria 3124, Australia
(a division of Pearson Australia Group Pty Ltd)
Penguin Books India Pvt Ltd, 11 Community Centre, Panchsheel Park, New Delhi – 110 017, India
Penguin Group (NZ), cnr Airborne and Rosedale Roads, Albany, Auckland 1310, New Zealand
(a division of Pearson New Zealand Ltd)
Penguin Books (South Africa) (Pty) Ltd, 24 Sturdee Avenue, Rosebank 2196, South Africa

Penguin Books Ltd, Registered Offices: 80 Strand, London WC2R ORL, England

www.penguin.com

Published by Allen Lane 2004
Published in Penguin Books 2005
6

Copyright © Richard Barber, 2004
Postscript © Richard Barber, 2005

All rights reserved
The moral right of the author has been asserted

Typeset by Rowland Phototypesetting Ltd, Bury St Edmunds, Suffolk
Printed in England by Clays Ltd, St Ives plc

Except in the United States of America, this book is sold subject
to the condition that it shall not, by way of trade or otherwise, be lent,
re-sold, hired out, or otherwise circulated without the publisher's
prior consent in any form of binding or cover other than that in
which it is published and without a similar condition including this
condition being imposed on the subsequent purchaser

For Helen

Contents

List of Illustrations

Acknowledgements

It is almost impossible to do justice to the many debts I have incurred in writing a book like this. First and foremost in the list must be the libraries which have provided the often esoteric material on which the text draws so heavily. They have been principally the London Library, that invaluable resource for those who are bad at working in libraries, Cambridge University Library, and the British Library.

I am particularly grateful to two readers, one without specialist knowledge, and the other an experienced Arthurian scholar, who have read the entire work in draft and have made invaluable comments. If the general reader, that mythical beast which all authors hope to pursue, can follow my arguments, it is largely due to Fionnuala Jervis's acute comments. Linda Gowans has both spotted egregious errors in my Arthurian knowledge and made most helpful scholarly suggestions, to the benefit of the book. I am also most grateful to Douglas Matthews for providing an invaluable index, and in the process helping me to clear up the remaining problems in the text.

But the present book is also the result of conversations over the years, even over decades, with fellow-scholars. The Grail in all its forms is perhaps a subject best left to someone who does not have an academic reputation to worry about, and the encouragement and help from friends and colleagues has been all the more generous given the unorthodox nature of the subject. I am indebted on various counts, whether for advice on individual topics or for a general reading of all or parts of the text, to a wide group of scholars; I hope that I have remembered them all in the following list, given that this project has taken a number of years: Norris Lacy, Derek Brewer, Ceridwen Lloyd-Morgan, Michael Lapidge, Nicolas Barker, James Carley, Bernard Hamilton, Jim Hardin, Harry Jackson, Felicity Riddy, Tom Shippey, Maureen Boulton and Jonathan Boulton, and Robert Dunning. I am particularly grateful to Cyril Edwards, whose new translation of *Parzival* will appear shortly after this book, for the lengthy discussions over points of detail, and for the use of his new version of Wolfram's poem, and to John Marino, whose study of the twentieth-century Grail romances will also be published at about the same time.

For help of quite another kind, in terms of generous hospitality at Racalía in Sicily which enabled me to complete the book away from the distractions of the business world, my thanks to Will and Val Richards.

This is the first of my books to carry a dedication, but it rectifies an omission of some thirty years' standing.

Excerpts from the following works are reprinted by permission of Boydell & Brewer Ltd.

Nigel Bryant, *The High Book of the Grail*; *Perceval: The Story of the Grail*; *Merlin and the Grail*.

Cyril Edwards, *Parzival*.

Excerpts from *Lancelot-Grail*, edited by Norris Lacy, are reprinted by permission of Taylor & Francis Ltd.

Excerpts from *The Quest of the Holy Grail*, translated by Pauline Matarasso, are reprinted by permission of Penguin Books Ltd.

Excerpts from John Cowper Powys, *A Glastonbury Romance* are reprinted by permission of Christopher Sinclair-Stevenson.

Excerpts from *The Mabinogion*, translated by Gwyn Jones and Thomas Jones, are reprinted by permission of Everyman Books Ltd.

Excerpts from Adolf Muschg, *Der rote Ritter* are translated by permission of Suhrkamp Verlag.

A Note on Names

The spelling of the names of Arthurian characters in the Grail stories has been standardized, even though this leads to some anomalies in the context of romances in different languages. The only exception is Perceval, whose character changes much more substantially between the various retellings of his story. I have retained the spelling Parzival in connection with the German medieval romances and later versions. Parsifal is used to refer to Wagner's depiction of the same character.

Introduction

This book is a journey that begins in territory that may seem strange and remote today. How many modern writers would begin a work of fiction with the following prologue?

The high book of the Grail begins in the name of the Father, Son and Holy Spirit. These three are one substance, and that substance is God, and from God comes the noble story of the Grail; and all those who hear it must be attentive and forget all their baseness, for those who hear it with their hearts will find it most profitable . . .[1]

The Grail is a mysterious and haunting image, which crosses the borders of fiction and spirituality, and which, for eight centuries, has been a recurrent ideal in Western literature. What follows is an attempt to trace what we know about the Grail: it is, in all its forms, a construct of the creative imagination, but one which lays claim to the highest of religious ideals and experience. Even when it has been neglected for centuries, it has reappeared to appeal with renewed vigour to artists and writers; and from its first shape as a Christian symbol it has been recreated in a multitude of different forms.

Such a topic exerts an extraordinary attraction for lovers of historical conundrums and enthusiasts for the esoteric and mysterious, particularly because we cannot give an answer to the question 'What is the Holy Grail?' The very first writer to mention it, who probably invented the idea, makes his story hinge on a similar question – 'What is the Grail for?' – and because he never provided the answer to his own riddle, the question continues to be asked. The initially mysterious and undefined 'Grail' had extraordinary repercussions: in a brief time span half a dozen major writers tried their hands at either completing the original stories or creating new ones, and in the process virtually invented a new art form, the prose romance, which many centuries later became the modern novel. As if this was not enough, the concept of the Grail was the unexpected product of the latest theological debate: something which was not abstruse and remote, but which arose out of the most dramatic event that ordinary people would witness, the Christian celebration of Mass. And from this blend of poetic imagination and religious belief come pages which rival in their intensity the closing scenes of Dante's *Paradiso* and the transcendent finale of Goethe's *Faust*.

These are large issues, and large claims. Where then do we begin our quest for the Holy Grail? In strictly physical terms, we will find the first evidence in the pages of a medieval manuscript, an object so unfamiliar that we need to describe it as if it were something found on an archaeological dig. All that it has in common with the modern book is its physical structure: it is made of sections bound in the same way, but everything else about it is different. Manuscripts were written by hand on parchment, the skin of sheep or calves, which had been prepared by curing it and scraping it smooth. The scribes who wrote on it used a script which is almost unreadable today except to the trained eye; the difficulty is compounded by the frequent use of abbreviations, because writing was such a laborious process that a scribe saved valuable time by using these signs. We very rarely possess the original manuscript of a medieval work, and copying by hand inevitably produces minor changes and, sometimes, major errors; so the texts we have are often at second or third hand. All this must be unravelled by patient editors if it is to appear in modern printed form. And then, if anyone except a handful of specialists is to know what the medieval author had to say, the text must be translated. The medieval books about the Grail range from the elegantly simple to poems which have moments of verbal anarchy of which James Joyce would have been proud, so a further layer of distance is added to our chances of responding directly to the author's original intentions.

Furthermore, manuscripts were fragile objects, prone to destruction by fire or flood, or by the depredations of mice or men. Even before the end of the Middle Ages, library catalogues recorded decayed manuscripts in a script no one could read, and at the Reformation and in the French Revolution monastic libraries were destroyed wholesale. In England, John Aubrey, the seventeenth-century antiquary, lamented the loss of the manuscripts of Malmesbury Abbey, near his home: 'in my grandfather's days, the manuscripts flew about like butterflies'. They were used to stop the rector's beer barrels, to cover books or to wrap the gloves which were the town's speciality. So there is always the lurking question in any discussion of medieval literature of what has been lost. This is aggravated and complicated by the extreme respect for tradition in the Middle Ages: originality was suspect and writers therefore often claimed to be working from an earlier text which was actually a figment of their imagination, as much an invention as the tale they had to tell. Perhaps, in the end, we have not lost very much.

There are famous examples, like the work of the Greek philosopher Aristotle on comedy, counterpart to his surviving book on tragedy; the fictional destruction of the unique copy of the book on comedy forms the denouement of Umberto Eco's *The Name of the Rose*. But for all the havoc wreaked at Malmesbury in John Aubrey's day, we can still positively identify twenty-five manuscripts as coming from that abbey. And of the two dozen texts listed by a visitor to Malmesbury shortly before the Reformation, almost all survive in copies from elsewhere. Indeed, a scholar who devoted an entire book to the lost literature of medieval England concluded that 'in the Middle English period little seems to have been lost from the three great Matters of Romance'.[2] So, however remote the original texts may be, we have to be careful about claiming that the answer to all the problems raised by the Grail lies in a missing manuscript.

The next obstacle is that even if we can get close to the medieval originals after they have been edited and translated, we still have to understand the mindset and culture which produced them. French historians have specialized in the study of *mentalités*, and we must at least attempt a sketch in that vein if we are to approach our medieval texts with some hope of understanding the driving forces behind them.

Fortunately, we will be looking at a handful of romances written in a very short time span: so we can begin to define certain aspects of the society for which they were produced. The moment in history when the Grail is created and re-created is the end of the twelfth century and the beginning of the thirteenth, from about 1190 to about 1240. The stories are written for a new social class, the knights, warriors whose influence and wealth depend on the lands they hold in return for their military service. The writers of the time, anxious to please their audience, have just developed new literary forms designed to appeal to them, the romances, and have imagined a new set of ideals to create a knightly culture. The Church, too, has seen the opportunity to secure its influence over these powerful and potentially disruptive men, and has begun to develop a religious version of these secular ideals. And we can add to this a previously unknown degree of political stability and an economy which enabled the knights to enjoy increasing leisure and even luxury. Against this background, the convergence of literary imagination and religious ideals made the stories about the Grail possible.

There is a further element, easily overlooked, namely the visual culture of the period. Here, we have lost an enormous amount, in contrast to the high survival rate for literature. Hundreds of churches which were once painted with elaborate frescoes illustrating the Bible have lost their decoration, medieval stained glass has only survived in relatively small quantities, and only mosaics, rare in Western Europe, have been relatively proof against destruction and decay. These images were part of the common knowledge of the period, and were how most people knew the Bible; those with good Latin would understand the readings of the Bible during church services, but for an individual to read the Bible, unless they were a member of a religious order or of the clergy, would bring a suspicion of heresy. The Church kept a strict rein on the interpretation of the Bible, and these visual images were in a sense one of its ways of propagating the message that it wanted to put across, serving as an aide-memoire for preachers and as instruction for the congregation. We shall see their particular importance in the context of the Grail romances.

But this is only a broad and simplistic outline of a hugely complex interaction of learning, theology and creativity. Even the problems of how we should read the texts are intricate and difficult: were the poets themselves scholars, writing with half an eye on their fellow-scholars and practising the subtleties of the classical learning which they had inherited from Greek and Roman writers? Or do we read their lines at face value, as intended for a relatively unsophisticated audience, on whom subtleties of style would be lost? And if this simplicity is true at the outset, the later Grail romances can only be understood if we explore contemporary medieval Christian theology, a highly elaborate and recondite subject, but one which is essential to our understanding of what the Grail became – and indeed, what it originally may have been.*

The background to the Grail romances, then, is a time of huge innovations in a society where tradition was highly valued, a moment both exciting and disturbing in terms of new ideas, new art forms, and new social culture. The Grail reflects, in addition, a heated debate about the central mysteries of the Christian faith, and its existence owes much to the shadowy borderland between imagination and belief, which are the two recurrent influences on its development. It never fitted into the orthodox scheme of things, and it produces questions and contradictions which seem strange to us today: how can medieval romances apparently invade the province of medieval religion, and how can secular authors write about the highest mysteries of the Church? Why, when the medieval Church never officially recognized the Grail stories, did the Grail become a powerful religious icon, but only to non-clerics? How did the Grail acquire its aura of perfection?

*

* Definitions of the theological terms used are provided in Appendix 3.

If the history of the Grail had been no more than this astonishing interaction at the beginning of the thirteenth century, it would be exciting enough; yet the story does not end there. The Grail stories were read and retold for the next two centuries, until the religious concept at their heart became a matter of bitter and violent controversy at the Reformation. But in the eighteenth century scholars began to study the literary past, and the great canvases of medieval romance were once more uncovered. The Grail found new enthusiasts in the early nineteenth century, who refashioned it in images current at the time. And, as literary criticism and literary history developed as disciplines, we find an obsession with discovering the origins of the Grail legends. At the other extreme, the new mystics of the late nineteenth and twentieth centuries have taken the Grail to heart, and imagined a new Grail, symbol of whatever spiritual nirvana takes their fancy, all-embracing and often ill-defined. It is a trend paralleled in the popular image of the Grail, as found in journalism, where it has become a shorthand expression; but what exactly does it now imply? And finally, why, in the twenty-first century, are we unable to face uncertainty about the past? Many of us are not content with possibilities as the answer to historical problems, but are driven to see questions like these as secrets locked from us by some vast conspiracy, for which a key must be found. The nature of this form of imagination is best defined by a demonstration of how such keys can be created from a few carefully selected striking facts.

Finally, after all these different avatars of the Grail, we return to the ideal. Even if we can trace the different ways in which it has been envisaged over the centuries, the Grail functions ultimately as something beyond the reach of the ordinary world. Whatever shape or form we may attribute to it, the Holy Grail offers us, in imagination, the possibility of perfection.

PART ONE

Creating the Grail

Authors and Texts

The enigmas of the Grail . . . expose today's reader to plenty of illusions and temptations: through a web of highlights and shadows, to recon-struct, come what may, the original myth; or to attribute to the author, in the name of a symbolism which is complaisantly pliable, hidden intentions, unconnected to reality, if not in direct contradiction of it. It is by no means the case that the text does not have deeper meanings, but before venturing into these hidden depths and yielding to the seductions of uncontrollable exegesis, we must scrutinise the text itself, analyse it minutely, adding nothing to it, taking nothing away, refusing to distort it for the sake of a preconceived or over-hasty interpretation: in short, we must ensure that we understand it exactly. Jean Frappier[1]

Within a given story any object, person or place is neither more nor less nor other than what the story effectively shows it to be. C. S. Lewis[2]

I

Imagining the Grail:
Chrétien de Troyes

In the room, a man is writing. We cannot see the room clearly, nor do we know where it is: a private house, a monastery, a castle? It may be somewhere in north-east France. Perhaps someone is dictating to him; perhaps he is alone. There is parchment, certainly, made from sheepskin; a blackish-brown ink, coloured by oak-galls; and a feather shaped into a writer's quill. With it, a story is being written down, a story in the new fashion, called 'romance' by some; the French word is *roman*, a story told in *romanz*, the ordinary language of everyday life, rather than in Latin, the formal language of law and learning. It is a work of the imagination, a *conte* or tale. Imagining stories is one of man's oldest skills, one of his most distinctive steps on the ladder of evolution. Tales had once been sacred, magical; they had been woven round past events or stories; but in those days they had been remembered and recited. Now, the products of the imagination were being written down as they were composed. It had happened before, in the civilizations of Rome and Greece, and there were writers of romances in the eastern Empire of Byzantium; so it was indeed possible to imagine and to write almost simultaneously. But to write a tale was to expect to be read, perhaps aloud, perhaps silently: the phrase 'to hear and to read' is used by writers of the time, implying that their audiences might approach their work in either way. The reader saw the tale on the page, the hearer could only listen; the inflections of the voice were replaced by new patterns and new subtleties on the page. Public recital co-existed with this private reading: William of Malmesbury tells us that earl Robert of Gloucester used his leisure to read or to hear others reading.[1]

The teller of tales could draw only on his memory to fire his imagination. It may be that in the room we are looking at there is another book, or perhaps several books; the writer may be copying one closely, or, if there are several, he may occasionally open one and read something before taking up his pen again. In either case his work will echo not only remembered stories but other written sources. He may have noted down a brief outline of how his story is to proceed, or he may simply rely on his skills of improvisation to carry him along.

It is time to name our imagined figure: he is Chrétien de Troyes, probably a native of the French town of that name. The year is towards the end of the twelfth century. We can only guess at his age, but it may be between forty and sixty. He has entitled the work before him *The Story of the Grail*, and this is where our story of the Grail begins.

We know little enough about Chrétien himself, other than his works; and while he says something of his literary career in his writings, there is no personal information. Even a possible nickname, 'li Gois',[2] which is quoted in one poem, is obscure. The dedications of his works tell us that he moved among the courts of north-east France and Flanders, and give us some clue as to time and place. He may have written one work for Marie, countess of Champagne, before her marriage in 1159; and his strongest associations are with her court. His last work was written for Philip, count of Flanders, and was probably started before Philip went on crusade in 1191. There may be indications in his stories that he knew England a little, and one of his romances may have been produced for the Anglo-Norman court of Henry II.[3]

He also tells us that he had translated from Ovid, and he was evidently well educated; he seems to know the classical poets in a way that would have been unthinkable a century earlier. For Chrétien was writing in a world full of intellectual excitement, of new ideas and new ideals. How far he was involved in the rediscovery of classical literature and philosophy in the schools of Paris at this time is hard to say; it is possible to read him as a master of irony, subtly disguising his true meaning, but this seems to me to be at odds with the substance of his work. Chrétien was not a member of some inward-looking scholarly circle, but the chronicler of the world of the newly emerging class of knights, whose praises he sang and whose ideals he to some extent invented. He celebrates the peacetime heroics of chivalry, tournaments rather than war, and in this differs sharply from the contemporary *chansons de geste* (songs about deeds), whose subject matter is war of any kind, whether against the Saracen or against one's neighbour. These hark back to the anarchy of the previous century, and have a strong political agenda: they glorify the great barons as the defenders of Christianity, and emphasize their status as mighty vassals whom the king tries to control at his peril.

To the novelty of his subject matter, we must add the novelty of Chrétien's approach. His favourite study is love in all its moods; even if he tells us that he shied away from the greatest love story of all, that of Tristan and Iseult, because it was beyond the moral pale, and failed to complete the story of Lancelot and Guinevere because he was uneasy about its morality, it is for his deft portrayal of the relationships between lover and beloved, and particularly his acute perception of feeling, as expressed in the lover's monologues when alone, that we remember him. The thread of all his stories is the development of a relationship or character, and the marvels and adventures along the way are simply devices to move the story on and engage the audience's attention.

For marvels and adventures there are in plenty. If the psychology may be inherited from his reading of the classical poets, and the pavilions and courts may reflect his own contemporary world, there is yet another new strand in Chrétien's tales. With the Norman conquest of England, there was for the first time direct political contact between the Latin world and that of the remaining independent Celtic principalities. In the late eleventh century, the Normans overran the ancient border between Celt and Saxon lands, which had remained much the same for five centuries, and established lordships in south Wales; by Chrétien's day, they had ventured as far as Ireland. In Wales, they came into contact with the local lords, and inter-married with their kin; so a bridge between the two cultures was created. Out of the Celtic past came tales and wonders of a magical heroic time. The Norman lords, descendants of the Vikings, had never encountered such spell-binding tales; and within a few decades these tales – by what means we cannot say – became known to a wider circle in Britain and on the Continent. Shadowy figures such as Bledri or Bledhericus, said to be a translator of such stories, elude us when we try to approach them, and we can only guess at some wildfire fashion for the new-found stories which carried them as far as Italy and Sicily within less than a century of the Norman invasion of England. The problem is that the stories themselves have vanished, leaving only mysterious traces for which the Celtic tellers of tales may or may not have been ultimately responsible. There is a frieze above a doorway at Modena Cathedral on which inscriptions name the figures as Arthur and his knights, dating from the first or second quarter of the twelfth century; there is a pavement in Otranto Cathedral, of much the same date, showing Arthur riding a goat. And there is a folktale, collected at the end of the twelfth century, which claimed that Arthur was still alive and living under Mount Etna.

These legendary tales were also part of Chrétien's intellectual world, but they were only one element among several; indeed, they were perhaps the least interesting part of his material as far as he was concerned. Chrétien has his feet planted firmly in the real world; as we have seen, his focal point is the realistic depiction of characters and the study of love – all his romances have as central figures a hero and heroine, except perhaps the last. The theme of each story is the progress of their love, which Chrétien analyses in monologues depicting the state of the character's feelings. Indeed, he at one point creates a situation where the heroine holds an imaginary debate with her beloved in order to establish the true state of her emotions; Laudine, in *Yvain*, argues with the absent hero, who is also her husband's slayer, as to whether he has deliberately done her harm, and is therefore unworthy of her love. Such a device is the key to Chrétien's art. He sets his tales in what passes for the distant past, but is in fact a tolerably accurate representation of contemporary court life. All the stories are set in the context of the court of king Arthur, with the exception of an early romance, *Cligés*; and even this has an interlude at Arthur's court, during which Perceval, whom we shall shortly meet as hero of Chrétien's Grail romance, makes his first appearance in literature.*

The chief business of the court, however, is not that of royal government, but of courtly entertainments on the grand scale, particularly tournaments. We know from historical sources that the tournament evolved from a kind of mock warfare, a training for the real thing, into something more formalized at exactly the time and place where Chrétien was writing. Equally, war – also the business of the king's court – does not enter into the stories, except in a minor and incidental way. Even the most improbable element of his heroes' exploits, the idea of setting out at random in search of adventures, is documented in real life: a Norman knight at Byzantium with the men of the First Crusade told the Emperor how

at a crossroads in the country where I was born is an ancient shrine; to this anyone who wishes to engage in single combat goes, prepared to fight; there he prays to God for help and there he stays awaiting the man who will dare to answer his challenge. At that crossroads I myself have spent time, waiting and longing for the man who would fight – but there was never one who dared.[4]

But for all Chrétien's realism, he needed material which clothed his ideas in a garb suitable for the time in which they were supposed to be set. Such stories about Arthur as he may have known drew on a world of magical adventures, and it is these that he intersperses between the encounters of the lovers and the heroic victories in tournaments. A real knight errant would probably have had a dull enough time of it between tournaments. The

---

* He is named, but no more, in a list of knights in Chrétien's earlier romance *Erec and Enide*.

nearest equivalent that we have is William Marshal, whose autobiography describes his chivalric career; and his exploits are often portrayed humorously rather than romantically. Chrétien escapes from the prosaic realities of knightly life by interspersing fantastic episodes which give his stories their tension and narrative drive, a 'now read on' or 'to be continued in our next' quality which is generally lacking in the *chansons de geste* with their interminable battles and technical squabbles about feudal rights. For instance, in *Yvain*, the hero has promised to rescue a girl who has been unjustly accused and is to be burnt at the stake the next day. He finds lodging for the night nearby, only to be faced in the morning with the host's urgent request for help against a giant who is threatening to carry off his daughter. Yvain can hardly refuse, though he tries to plead that he may not arrive in time to fulfil his promise to the girl. Chrétien is deliberately inventing a 'cliffhanger', in which the audience waits with bated breath to see whether Yvain can succeed in killing the giant in time to rescue the girl. In *Erec and Enide*, where the hero has compelled his wife to silence as he rides with her in search of adventures, she sees that Erec is threatened by an enemy whom he has not noticed, and the tension is built up by her choice between breaking her oath in order to save him, or obediently staying silent, in which case he may be killed. And the famous moment in *Lancelot*, or *The Knight of the Cart*, when Lancelot, having lost his horse as he rides to rescue Guinevere, sees a cart passing, has the same element of suspense: will he ride in the cart, to his undying shame, like a knight who is being taken to execution, or will he stand on his pride and risk reaching Guinevere too late?

But what is the audience whom Chrétien keeps so adeptly in suspense? We have no firm evidence as to who they were; indeed, we do not know for certain whether his works were recited or read as we read books today. He is at the watershed between a predominantly oral culture, where stories were recorded only occasionally in manuscripts, and a world where the written word is the normal format of communication between the author and his public. It is reasonable to assume that the *chansons de geste* were recited, and any narrative with distinctive internal crisis-points such as we have noted above is likely to have been presented in instalments, which would imply recital rather than reading. This, together with Chrétien's subject matter, points strongly to a knightly audience, not particularly sophisticated but not totally out of touch with the intellectual world. It seems much less likely that Chrétien was addressing fellow-clerics or scholars, and this has important implications for our understanding of his tales. Unlike the treatise on the art of courtly love by Andreas Capellanus, which is contemporary with Chrétien's romances, and which has been unmasked as an exercise in philosophical argument, probably from the pen of a member of the university of Paris,[5] I would argue that Chrétien's work needs to be taken at face value; beyond some gentle flattery of his patrons, he is not writing for initiates or conducting subtle propaganda campaigns.

The Story of the Grail – the phrase is Chrétien's own, in the prologue to the poem – was his last romance, and remained unfinished at his death. It was also known by the name of its hero, Perceval, by the first scribes who copied it.

It represents a new departure for Chrétien, because his theme is not the customary love story, but instead the development of a knight's character. The title he chooses, like that which he gave to his romance about Lancelot,* does not necessarily indicate the topic of the story, but simply the object on which the plot hinges – Hitchcock's MacGuffin, in effect. For Lancelot, it was the cart into which he hesitated to climb, proving himself a less than perfect lover because he put his own honour before his duty to his love. For Perceval, it is the Grail, about which he fails to ask, proving himself an imperfect knight, because he observes the letter of the instruction he has received, but not the spirit, and shows himself lacking in true sympathy.

Perceval's story begins in a world isolated from courtly life and knighthood; his mother, having lost her husband and elder sons through their pursuit of knightly glory, has done all she can to keep Perceval from the same fate. But one day, hunting in the forest, Perceval encounters knights for the first time: overwhelmed, he takes them for angels, and, dazzled, asks their leader 'Are you God?' They gently disabuse him of such notions, and explain something of knighthood. Perceval is at once seized by enthusiasm and determines to become a knight; despite his mother's pleas, he sets out in search of king Arthur, to demand knighthood at his hands. His mother offers him good advice on manners and on how to behave towards women, and instructs him briefly in matters of religion. Most of this advice he misunderstands, as his subsequent adventures show: but Chrétien uses this scene to underline the fact that Perceval starts out from a basis of almost total ignorance. He is a child of nature; but it is his own nature which is to lead him inexorably to great knightly deeds.

At first, everything goes badly. He finds a girl alone in a tent, compromises her by stealing a kiss from her and taking her ring as a memento, and leaves her to face the fury of her lover. When he reaches Arthur's court, he is mocked by Kay the seneschal, and even the king does not try to hold him

---

* *Li chevalier de la charrete* – the knight of the cart.

back when he refuses to wait to be knighted. Instead he sets out in pursuit of a knight who has just seized the queen's cup, and whose fine red armour Perceval covets. He kills the knight with a lucky cast of his javelin when he fails to get the armour by threats, and has to be shown how to put it on by a squire who has watched the combat. The squire rides back to the court with a message from Perceval to Kay promising vengeance for his mockery, while Perceval departs in the other direction.

In his next encounter, he heeds his mother's advice correctly for once, and takes instruction from an older knight, Gorneman, to whose castle he comes. He is taught to handle knightly weapons, and his instructor finds him a quick and skilful learner; Perceval is knighted by his host, who begs him to stay for longer, but now that he has achieved his immediate objective, Perceval, with the impatience of youth, insists on leaving the next morning. His path, however, does not lead him home, but to the beginning of his adventures, and to love.

He finds his way to a castle half in ruins, whose ruler is a beautiful girl, Blancheflor; she and her meagre retinue are defending it against her unwelcome suitor, Clamadeus of the Isles, who has sent his seneschal to besiege her. She comes to Perceval in the middle of the night to pour out her sorrows; they embrace and he shelters her chastely in his bed that night before going out to overthrow her enemy the next day. Clamadeus comes to avenge the seneschal, but he too is overthrown, and, like the seneschal, is sent to Arthur to yield as his prisoner. But once Perceval has rescued Blancheflor, he remembers his mother, and insists on setting out at once in search of her, comforting his new-found love with a promise of almost instant return, which, this being a romance, he of course fails to fulfil.

He comes to a river, which is so swift and deep that he is unable to cross it. He sees a boat with two men in it, one of whom is fishing; he asks them if there is any bridge over the river, and the fisherman replies:

'No indeed, brother, by my faith; nor is there any boat, I think, bigger than the one we're in, which wouldn't carry five men. You can't cross on horseback for twenty leagues upstream or down, for there's no ferry or bridge or ford.'

'Then tell me, in God's name,' he said, 'where I could find lodging.'

And the man replied:

'You've need of that and more besides, I think. I will give you lodging tonight. Ride up through the cleft in that rock, and when you come to the top you'll see a house in a valley ahead of you where I live, near the river and the woods.'

So he climbed up on to the rock; but when he reached the top he looked all around him and saw nothing but sky and earth; and he said:

'What did I come up here to find? Foolishness and nonsense! God bring disgrace on the one who sent me here! What fine guidance he gave me, telling me I'd find a house when I reached the top! Fisherman who told me so, you did a most unworthy deed, if you said it to do me harm.'

But just then, in a valley nearby, the top of a tower caught his eye. From here to Beirut you would not have found a more handsome one or one more finely placed. It was square and built of grey rock, flanked by two smaller towers. The hall stood before the tower, and lodges before the hall. The boy rode down towards it, saying that the one who had sent him there had guided him well, and he praised the fisherman, no longer calling him treacherous or dishonest or untruthful, now that he had found a place to lodge. He headed towards the gate; and before the gate he found a drawbridge, and it was lowered. He rode in over the bridge, and four boys came to meet him; two of them disarmed him, while the third led away his horse and gave it hay and oats; the fourth dressed him in a fresh and brand new mantle of scarlet cloth. Then they led him to the lodges; . . . [where] the boy stayed . . . until he was summoned to go to the lord, who sent two servants to him. He returned with them to the hall, which was square, being as long as it was wide. In the middle of the hall he saw, sitting in a bed, a most handsome nobleman with greying hair; on his head he wore a hat of sable, dark as mulberry, covered in a deep rich cloth on top, and his whole gown was the same. He was leaning on his elbow, and before him was a huge fire of dry logs, blazing brightly, surrounded by four columns. Four hundred men could easily have sat around that fire and each would have had an excellent place. The columns were very strong, supporting a tall, wide chimney of heavy bronze. The two servants who were escorting the boy, one on each side of him, came before their lord. When the lord saw him coming he greeted him at once, and said:

'My friend, don't be upset if I don't get up to meet you, for I'm unable to.'

'In God's name, sir,' said the boy, 'say no more about it; may God give me joy and health, it doesn't upset me at all.'

But the worthy man so exerted himself for the boy's sake that he struggled up as much as he could; then he said:

'Come here, my friend. Don't be afraid of me: sit down here beside me, you're quite safe. I command you.'

The boy sat down at his side, and the nobleman asked him:

'Where have you come from today, my friend?'

'Sir,' he said, 'I rode this morning from Beaurepaire – that was its name.'

'God help me,' said the nobleman, 'you've travelled a very long way today. You must have left before the watch blew the dawn signal this morning.'

'No indeed,' said the boy. 'The first hour had already been sounded, I promise you.'

While they were talking thus, a boy came in through the door; he was carrying a

16

sword hung round his neck, and presented it to the nobleman. He drew it half out of its scabbard, and saw clearly where it was made, for it was written on the sword. And he also learned from the writing that it was of such fine steel that there was only one way it could ever be broken, which no one knew except the one who had forged and tempered it. The boy who had brought it to him said:

'Sir, the beautiful fair-haired girl, your niece, has sent you this present; you never saw a finer sword as long and as broad as this. You may give it to whoever you like, but my lady would be most happy if it were put to good use where it's bestowed. The one who forged the sword has only ever made three, and he's about to die, so this is the last he'll ever make.'

And straight away the lord girded his guest with the sword by its straps, which themselves were worth a fortune. The sword's pommel was made of the finest gold of Arabia or Greece, and the scabbard was of golden thread from Venice. With all its rich decoration, the lord presented it to the boy and said:

'Good brother, this sword was intended and destined for you, and I very much want you to have it; come, gird it on and draw it.'

The boy thanked him, and girded it on so that it was not restricting, and then drew it, naked, from the scabbard; and after gazing at it for a while, he slid it back into the sheath. And truly, it lay splendidly at his side, and even better in his hand, and it seemed indeed that in time of need he would wield it like a man of valour. Behind him he saw some boys standing around the brightly burning fire; he noticed the one who was looking after his arms, and he entrusted the sword to him, and he kept it for him. Then he sat down again beside the lord, who treated him with the greatest honour. And no house lit by candles could ever provide a brighter light than there was in that hall.

While they were talking of one thing and another, a boy came from a chamber clutching a white lance by the middle of the shaft, and passed between the fire and the two who were sitting on the bed. Everyone in the hall saw the white lance with its white head; and a drop of blood issued from the tip of the lance's head, and right down to the boy's hand this red drop ran. The lord's guest gazed at this marvel that had appeared there that night, but restrained himself from asking how it came to be, because he remembered the advice of the nobleman who had made him a knight, who had taught and instructed him to beware of talking too much; he feared it would be considered base of him if he asked, so he did not. Just then two other boys appeared, and in their hands they held candlesticks of the finest gold, inlaid with black enamel. The boys who carried the candlesticks were handsome indeed. In each candlestick burned ten candles at the very least. A girl who came in with the boys, fair and comely and beautifully adorned, was holding a grail between her hands. When she entered holding the grail, so brilliant a light appeared that the candles lost their brightness like the stars or the moon when the sun rises. After her came another girl, holding a silver trencher. The grail, which went ahead, was made of fine, pure gold; and in it were set precious stones of many kinds, the richest and most precious in the earth or the sea: those in the grail surpassed all other jewels, without a doubt. They passed before the bed as the lance had done, and disappeared into another chamber. The boy saw them pass, but did not dare to ask who was served from the grail, for he had taken the words of the wise nobleman to heart. I fear he may suffer for doing so, for I have heard it said that in time of need a man can talk too little as well as too much. I don't know whether it will bring him good or ill, but he asked nothing.

The lord commanded the boys to bring them water and to lay the cloths. Those whose job it usually was did as they were bidden, and the lord and the boy washed their hands in warm water. Two boys brought in a wide table of ivory – according to my source-book it was all one solid piece – and they held it for a moment in front of their lord and the boy until two other boys came with two trestles. The wood of which the trestles were made had two fine qualities: they would last forever, for they were made of ebony, a wood which need never be expected to rot or burn – it is proof against both. The table was set upon these trestles and the cloth was laid. And what should I say about the cloth? No legate or cardinal or pope ever dined at one so white. The first dish was a haunch of venison, seasoned with hot pepper and cooked in fat. There was no shortage of clear, delicious wine to drink, from golden cups. Before them a boy carved pieces from the peppered haunch of venison, drawing the haunch to him with the silver trencher, and presented the pieces to them on a slice of perfectly baked bread. And meanwhile the grail passed before them once again, but the boy did not ask who was served from it: he refrained because of the nobleman's well-meaning warning not to talk too much – he had taken it to heart and remembered it constantly. But he held his tongue more than he should have done, for each time a course was served, he saw the grail pass before him, right before his eyes, and he did not know who was served from it and he longed to know. But he said to himself that before he left he would certainly ask one of the boys of the court, but he would wait till the morning when he took his leave of the lord and the rest of the household. And so he put it off till a later time, and concentrated on eating and drinking.

They were not mean with the wines and dishes, and they were delicious and most agreeable. The food was fine and good: the worthy man and the boy were served that night with all the dishes befitting a king or a count or an emperor. And after they had dined they stayed up together and talked, while the boys prepared the beds and provided fruit to eat – and there was fruit of the dearest kind: dates, figs and nutmegs, and cloves and pomegranates, and to finish there were electuaries and ginger from Alexandria ... Then there were many different drinks to taste: sweet, aromatic wine, made with neither honey nor pepper, and old mulberry wine and clear syrup. The boy, who had no knowledge of these, was filled with wonder. Then the nobleman said:

'Good friend, it's time to take to our beds for the night. I'll go now, if you don't mind, and sleep there in my chambers, and whenever you wish you can go to sleep in here. I have no strength in my body: I shall have to be carried.'

Then four servants, strong and hearty, came from the chamber, and taking hold of the four corners of the blanket that was spread across the bed on which the nobleman was sitting, they carried him where they were told. Other boys stayed with his guest and served him and fulfilled his every need: when he wished they took off his shoes and clothes and bedded him in sheets of fine white linen.

He slept until the morning when day had broken and the household had risen; but he could see no one as he looked about him, and he had to get up alone whether he liked it or not. Seeing that he had no choice he did the best he could, and put on his shoes without waiting for help; then he went to don his arms again, finding that they had been brought and left at the head of a table. When he had fully armed his limbs he headed for the doors of the chambers which he had seen open the night before; but the move was fruitless, for he found them shut tight. He called and beat and barged a good deal. Nobody opened up for him or said a word. After calling out for quite a while he turned back to the door of the hall. He found it open, and went down the steps to find his horse saddled, and saw his lance and shield leaning against a wall. He mounted and went looking everywhere, but did not find a living soul and could not see a squire or boy. So he came straight to the gate and found the drawbridge lowered: it had been left like that so that, at whatever time he came to leave, nothing should stop him passing straight across. Seeing that the bridge was down he thought the boys must all have gone into the woods to check their traps and snares. He had no wish to stay any longer, and decided to go after them to see if any of them would tell him why the lance bled, if perhaps there were something wrong, and where the grail was carried. And so he rode out through the gate; but before he had got across the bridge, he felt his horse's hooves rise high into the air. The horse made a great leap; and if he had not jumped so well both horse and rider would have been in a sorry plight. The boy looked back to see what had happened, and saw that the bridge had been raised. He called out, but no one replied.

'Hey!' he cried. 'Whoever raised the bridge, talk to me! Where are you? I can't see you. Come out and let me look at you: there's something I want to ask you.'

But he was wasting his time calling out like this, for nobody would answer him.[6]

I have quoted this at length, because it is the original of all subsequent descriptions of the Grail and its surroundings, and we shall see how the least detail becomes critical to our investigation. The adventure is told in a series of pictures, and we see these pictures through Perceval's eyes. He looks, apparently in vain, for the house, suffering from a visual deception, until he sees it half-hidden in a valley. Once he is inside the house, the strongly visual descriptions continue, culminating in the procession bearing the lance and Grail. Everything here is described simply as Perceval sees it, and it is only his emotions, not those of the other participants, which are described. We both see and experience the procession as Perceval saw and experienced it. Chrétien's purpose is twofold: to summon up the impact of something unbelievably rich and strange on a naïve young man, and to create a curiosity in his audience about this unexplained and hence mysterious scene, which will whet their appetite for the continuation of the story. It is, as befits a master storyteller, both a narrative device and an acutely observed psychological sketch.

At the point when Perceval rides out into the grey and empty dawn from the deserted castle, we are two-fifths of the way through Chrétien's work in its unfinished form. Perceval learns first that his lack of compassion and interest in the fate of the wounded king has condemned the latter to continued pain and grief, and next that his thoughtless departure has caused his mother's death. This is the nadir of his fortunes, however; his redemption is beginning, for he now encounters the girl whose ring he had stolen soon after he set out, and reconciles her with her lover, confessing that he had been at fault. Arthur and all his court go in search of Perceval, who has his revenge on Kay by unhorsing Kay when the latter disturbs him as he sits entranced, contemplating three drops of blood on the snow which remind him of his beloved's colouring.

But once again, Chrétien draws us back to the unsolved mystery of the castle: a hideous girl rides up and denounces Perceval for failing to ask the crucial question and end the suffering of the Fisher King, the lord of the Grail castle. The king will be unable to rule his land, and as a result the horrors of war will ensue: 'Ladies will lose their husbands, lands will be laid waste, girls will be left in distress and orphaned, and many knights will die; all these evils will happen because of you.'[7] There is no hint of magic, merely the stark reality of a land left prey to marauders. The Fisher King got his wound in battle: his enemies are presumably still at large, and because he cannot lead his army to fight them, his land is open to attack.[8] As she leaves, she challenges Arthur's knights to undertake the adventure of the rescue of the lady of Montesclaire; and almost at once another messenger appears, a knight who accuses Gawain, Arthur's nephew and the greatest hero of his court, of the treasonable slaying of his lord. The knights disperse in quest of the lady of Montesclaire, while Gawain sets out to meet his challenger at the court of king Escavalon. In contrast, Perceval, who has been deeply shocked by the curses of the first messenger, abandons these knightly exercises, swearing that

as long as he lived he would not lodge in the same place for two nights together, nor hear word of any perilous passage but he would go and attempt it, nor would he hear of a knight greater than any other – but he would go and do combat with him, until he knew who was served from the Grail and had found the bleeding lance, and learned the certain truth about why it bled; he would never give up, whatever happened.[9]

Chrétien now uses a narrative technique which was to become a commonplace of Arthurian romance, that of interweaving two series of adventures, and moving the focus from one hero to another, until they eventually meet and the story is resolved. He follows Gawain until he finds his challenger, and the battle is postponed for a year while Gawain is sent in search of 'the lance whose head sheds tears of the clearest blood', in other words, the lance which Perceval had seen at the Fisher King's castle. The two heroes are now on a converging path; at this, 'the story leaves Sir Gawain here, and begins to tell of Perceval'. Perceval's reappearance is brief: but once again the episode is so crucial to our knowledge of the Grail that it must be quoted in full:

Perceval, my source-book tells us, had lost his memory to such a degree that he no longer remembered God. April and May passed by five times – that's five whole years – without him entering a church or worshipping God or His cross: he lived like this for five years. That's not to say that he stopped seeking deeds of chivalry: he went in search of strange, hard and terrible adventures, and encountered so many that he tested himself well. In five years he sent sixty worthy knights as prisoners to King Arthur's court. That was how he spent five years, without a thought for God.

At the end of these five years it so happened that he was riding across a wilderness, fully armed, as always, when he met three knights and as many as ten ladies with them, their heads hidden in their hoods, all on foot, in hair-shirts and bare-footed. The ladies, for the salvation of their souls, were doing their penance on foot for the sins they had committed, and were astonished to see him coming in armour, holding a lance and a shield. And one of the three knights stopped him and said:

'My good, dear friend, don't you believe in Jesus Christ, who laid down the New Law and gave it to the Christians? Truly, it's neither right nor good, but very wrong, to carry arms on the day when Jesus Christ died.'

And he who had no sense of day or hour or time, so tormented was his heart, replied:

'What day is it, then?'

'What day, sir? Don't you know? It's Good Friday, the day when a man should worship the cross and weep for his sins, for on this day the one who was sold for thirty pieces of silver was nailed to the cross. He who was clean of all sins saw the sins with which the whole world was stained and bound, and became a man to save us from them. It's true that He was God and man, for the Virgin bore a son conceived by the Holy Spirit, in whom God assumed flesh and blood, so that the Deity was housed in the flesh of man: that's certain. And those who will not believe it will never see Him face to face. That son born of the Virgin Lady, who assumed the form and the soul of man with His holy deity, truly, on such a day as today He was nailed to the cross and freed all His friends from Hell. It was a most holy death, which saved the living and brought the dead from death to life. With their spite the false Jews, who should be put down like dogs, did themselves great harm and us great good when they raised Him to the cross; for they damned themselves and saved us. All who believe in Him should be spending today in penitence. No man who believes in God should be carrying arms today, either in the field or on the road.'

'Where have you just come from?' said Perceval.

'From over there, sir; from a worthy man, a holy hermit who lives in this forest. He is such a holy man that he lives solely by the glory of God.'

Perceval, overcome with remorse for his lack of faith in God's mercy, goes at once in search of the hermit:

He rode on, weeping, right through the wood.

When he came to the hermitage he dismounted and disarmed and tethered his horse to an elm tree. Then he entered the hermit's cell. In a little chapel he found the hermit and a priest and a clerk – this is the truth – who were beginning the highest and sweetest service that can be held in a holy church. Perceval went down on his knees as soon as he entered the chapel, and the good man, seeing him so humble and weeping, with tears streaming from his eyes to his chin, called him to him. And Perceval, who deeply feared that he had sinned against God, clung to the hermit's foot and bowed down before him, and then, with joined hands, he begged him to give him guidance, for he had great need of it. The good man told him to make confession, for he would never have remission if he did not confess and repent.

'Sir,' said Perceval, 'fully five years ago I lost my bearings, and stopped loving God and believing in God; and since then I've done nothing but ill.'

'Oh, good friend,' said the worthy man, 'tell me why you did this, and pray to God to have mercy on His sinner's soul.'

'Sir, I was once at the house of the Fisher King, and I saw the lance with the head that most certainly bleeds, but I asked nothing about the drop of blood I saw hanging from the tip of that white head. And truly, I've done nothing since then to make amends. Nor do I know who was served from the Grail that I saw there, and I've since suffered such grief that I would gladly be dead; for I've forgotten God because of it, and not once since then have I asked Him for mercy – and I don't think I've done anything to earn it.'

'Oh, my dear friend,' said the worthy man, 'tell me your name.'

And he said:

'Perceval, sir.'

At that the worthy man gave a sigh, for he recognised the name, and said:

'My brother, a sin of which you know nothing has done you great harm: it's the grief you caused your mother when you left her.[10] She fell to the ground in a faint at the foot of the bridge outside the gate, and she died of that grief. It was because of the sin you committed there that you came to ask nothing about the lance and the Grail, and many misfortunes have befallen you because of that. And I tell you this: you wouldn't have survived this long if she hadn't commended you to God. But her prayer had such power that God has watched over you for her sake, and kept you from being killed or captured. It was sin that stopped your tongue when you saw the lance-head that never staunched its flow of blood, so that you didn't ask the reason; and folly seized you when you failed to learn who was served from the Grail. The one who is served from it is my brother. My sister, and his, was your mother. And I believe the rich Fisher King is the son of the king who is served from the Grail. And don't imagine that he's given pike or lamprey or salmon; he's served with a single host which is brought to him in that Grail. It comforts and sustains his life – the Grail is such a holy thing [*tante sainte chose*]. And he, who is so spiritual that he needs no more in his life than the host that comes in the Grail, has lived there for twelve years without ever leaving the chamber which you saw the Grail enter. Now I want to direct you and give you penance for your sin.'

'I want that with all my heart, good uncle,' said Perceval. 'And since my mother was your sister, you ought to call me nephew and I should call you uncle and love you the more.'

'That's true, good nephew, but listen now: if pity has taken hold of your soul, repent in all truthfulness, and go in the name of penitence to church each morning before anywhere else, and you'll benefit greatly: don't fail to do so on any account. If you're in a place where there's a minster, a chapel or a parish church, go there when you hear the bell ring, or sooner if you're awake; it won't be to your disadvantage but very much to your soul's improvement. And if mass is begun there'll be even more profit in being there: stay there until the priest has said and sung everything. If you do this with a will, you may come to redeem yourself and win honour and a place in Paradise. Love God, believe in God, worship God; honour worthy men and women; and stand up before priests – it's a service that costs little, and God truly loves it as a sign of humility. And if a girl or a widow or an orphan requests your help, grant it, and it'll be the better for you; it's a most worthy charity, so you'll do well to give them your aid: make sure you do so, without fail. I'd have you do this for your sins, if you want to recover all the virtues that you used to have. Now tell me if you'll do so.'

'Yes, sir, most gladly.'

'Then stay here with me, please, for two whole days, and in penitence eat such food as I eat.'

Perceval agreed to all of this, and the hermit whispered a prayer in his ear, repeating it to him until he had learnt it. Many of the names of Our Lord appeared in this prayer, including the greatest ones, which the tongue of man should never utter except in fear of death. And when he had taught him the prayer he forbade him ever to utter those names except in times of great peril.

'I shan't, sir,' said Perceval.

And so he stayed there and heard the service, which delighted him. And after the service he worshipped the cross and wept for his sins. That night he ate as the holy hermit pleased; but there were only beets, chervil, lettuces and cress and millet, and bread made of barley and oats, and water from a clear spring. And his horse had straw and a full trough of barley.

Thus Perceval came to recognise that God received death and was crucified on the Friday. And at Easter, most worthily, Perceval received communion.

The story says no more about Perceval for now. You'll have heard a great deal about Sir Gawain before I tell of him again.[11]

Chrétien, as far as we know, never told of Perceval again. The adventures of Gawain take up the remainder of his text, to the point where other hands began their continuation of his work.

If the first Grail scene proposes a mystery, the second episode in which it appears gives answers which prove to be just as puzzling as the questions. What is a scene of religious instruction, a sermon from a hermit, doing in a romance? There is one precedent, in the romance of *Tristan*, for such an intervention, but that is directly related to the adultery of Tristan and Iseult, not to the state of mind of the hero; so what is Chrétien doing? Why have we heard nothing of Perceval's 'strange, hard and terrible adventures', but are instead confronted by an heroic figure who is also a lost soul? The transition is so abrupt and the scene so unexpected, that we might suspect that it has been introduced into the story by another writer. But if we look closer, there is a pattern and logic behind all this. Perceval has passed through the first stages of the ideal knightly life; he has proved his skill in arms, and he has won his lady. Now he must move from the earthly to the spiritual, just as his mother's counsel had begun with earthly matters and had ended with an admonishment to be true to the Christian faith. Perceval is first reminded of his spiritual duty, not by a man of religion but by another knight, who directs him to the hermit. Only a priest can hear his confession and absolve him; but the hermit also proves to be his equal in knightly lineage, for he is Perceval's uncle. Perceval is discovering the next stage on his journey towards chivalric perfection – the part that religion should play in the life of a true knight. The lesson he learns is that of the power of the Mass and of the consecrated Host: the father of the Fisher King is sustained by the Host, just as Perceval himself will be sustained by daily attendance at Mass. The climax of the scene is the moment when 'at Easter, most worthily, Perceval received communion'.

And with that image, we see Chrétien's Perceval for the last time. We can see the thrust of Chrétien's story, and the way in which he is developing the character of Perceval, but because he left his work unfinished, there are unanswered questions, and it is these that have come to provide the dominant interest in the story. It is as if the story of Lancelot had been broken off after he mounts the cart on his way to rescue Guinevere, but before we can see the place of this episode in their relationship, leaving the cart to appear as some magical means of transport: it is easy to imagine the possibilities. Every detail of the Grail and lance have been minutely scrutinized, while other curious features, such as the magical prayer which the hermit teaches Perceval, have been ignored by later readers. For this unfinished tale has aroused endless curiosity over the last eight centuries: and never more so than in the two decades after it was written.

The Story of the Grail was immediately popular, and we have a number of copies of the manuscript – fifteen and four fragments – mostly from about fifty years after the poem was written.[12] But, unusually, they do not divide into groups copied from one or two originals, but are quite diverse. Usually patterns of errors or the idiosyncrasy of a given scribe will help us to trace the pedigree of the text, but in this case what the evidence implies is that the text was widely copied soon after it was written. As we might expect of an unfinished masterpiece by a famous writer, it aroused instant attention.

This is borne out by the reaction of other writers. Within twenty years of the date at which Chrétien broke off his work on *The Story of the Grail*, there were two attempts to continue his story, as well as two new and almost totally different versions of the Grail history which placed it firmly in the Christian tradition, and a German version which introduced a host of new ideas into the story. Even the first attempt to complete Chrétien's work exists in three often very different versions, spread across thirteen surviving manuscripts.[13] The Grail had fired the imagination of writers and readers alike.

2

Completing the Grail: Chrétien continued

In 1180, as far as we can tell, no one would have known anything of the 'holy thing' called the Grail. Thirty years later, romances which took up Chrétien's unfinished tale were widespread. Chrétien's great reputation as a storyteller would in itself have ensured that the Grail became famous, but the spread of the Grail romances was undoubtedly helped by the fascination which always surrounds an incomplete masterpiece. For an imaginative writer, it offered an opportunity to create not only an ending for the tale of Perceval, but also to define the mystery at the centre of the romance, the Grail itself.

The challenge was taken up by not one, but at least half a dozen writers, in very different ways. If we were talking about twentieth-century literature, we could set these writers in chronological order, and attempt to show how the idea of the Grail had developed as one writer succeeded another. But the surviving evidence simply does not allow us to do this with the Grail romances. All we can say is that they were written within a short span of time, three or four decades, and that any attempt to set them in sequence is purely notional. Dating a medieval romance is difficult at the best of times; we rarely have the original manuscript from the author's hand, and even then there may well be no date or name on it. If we do have an author's name, we may know nothing about him: Chrétien was famous in his time, and yet we have none of his personal history. So all we can do is to set out the different ways in which the story of the Grail was told about the beginning of the thirteenth century; and it seems logical to begin with the texts which attempt to continue and complete Chrétien's own text.

Most medieval readers would never have known *The Story of the Grail* in the form in which we now read it. They might have seen one of the few manuscripts which ended with the romance incomplete, of which three examples survive; or they might have known the point at which Chrétien stopped, as one or two manuscripts mark the division by a note reading

Here ends the old Perceval. But for most readers, the story of the Grail was a longer story, completed – or partially completed – by an anonymous author, by Wauchier de Denain, by Gerbert de Montreuil or by Manessier, according to which version lay before them.

These continuations of *The Story of the Grail* are not easy to disentangle, nor are they easy reading. All too often scholars have tended to plunder them for details to bolster their own pet theories rather than looking at them as a whole. But the authors of the continuations have important things to tell us, not least because they are the most direct evidence of how contemporaries read Chrétien himself. The majority of manuscripts contain the original text and three continuations; in these, the 9,000 lines of Chrétien's work are dwarfed by the additional contributions, which amount to between 37,000 and 42,000 lines. In two copies, there is real confusion: a fourth continuation is added, not at the end, but inserted between the *Second* and *Third Continuations*. This fourth continuation seems to have been an alternative to the *Third Continuation*, and to have provided a different conclusion. But a medieval scribe or editor has reshaped the ending so that it leads instead to the opening of the *Third Continuation*! The resulting 'complete' version of *The Story of the Grail*, in whichever form we read it, is not surprisingly prone to contradictions and confusions. Compared with Chrétien's tautly plotted poem, the finished version has become a baggy monster, which has swallowed not merely bits and pieces of other romances, but even, at one point in the *First Continuation*, a tale, the story of Carados, which is in effect a complete independent romance in its own right. And just as the continuators' approach to their material is different, so the content and emphasis are at odds with the original.

The Story of the Grail was written under the patronage of Philip, count of Flanders, and it seems likely that its continuations were particularly closely associated with his successors in Flanders. We have no name for the author of the *First Continuation*, and the evidence of the manuscripts points to an origin in Burgundy or Champagne; the earliest copies come from this area at the beginning of the thirteenth century, only reaching Picardy and Paris some decades later. This would make the connection between the Flemish rulers and the *First Continuation* possible but tenuous. However, Wauchier de Denain, the next to take up the story, very probably produced the *Second Continuation* for Jeanne, granddaughter of Philip, who was countess of Flanders from 1212 to 1244, since one of his other poems was commissioned by her, and he retold some of the lives of the early saints for her uncle, the count of Namur.[1] Apart from his literary works, Wauchier is a shadowy figure. The author of the *Third Continuation*, Manessier, is equally shadowy, and known only from what he tells of his own activities.[2] He, too, certainly worked for the countess and produced his completion of the story for her, for he tells us at the end:

so Manessier testifies, who brought this work to an end in the name of Countess Jehane, lady and mistress of Flanders . . . It was begun in the name of her ancestor, but no one subsequently set his hand to completing it. Lady, it is for you that Manessier has laboured to finish it – and accurately, according to the source.[3]

The Flemish court was notable for its literary patronage,[4] particularly in the field of romance, and it is arguable that *The Story of the Grail* was regarded as the property of the ruling family, with dynastic associations. If this is the case, Jeanne's patronage of Manessier was designed to emphasize her position as Philip of Flanders' rightful heir, since this had been challenged by an impostor claiming to be her father. And one manuscript survives with the prologue and last verses removed, perhaps produced for Jean II d'Avesnes, who claimed Flanders later in the century, but owed his allegiance to the German emperor rather than the king of France, unlike his predecessors whose names have been obliterated;[5] it is as if the scribe saw the romance as part of Jean's inheritance, but the associations with the French past were no longer deemed appropriate.

Gerbert de Montreuil, author of the *Fourth Continuation*, is a more substantial figure: his other work, *Le Roman de la Violette*, was written for the countess of Ponthieu in north-east France around 1227–29, and he may have known the French royal court. He is a more polished and learned writer than the other authors of the continuations, and seems to have had a foot in both the clerical world and that of the minstrels or *jongleurs*.[6] But we are still very close to the origins of the Grail story in Flanders and Champagne.

We cannot – as usual – absolutely prove the idea that the *Continuations* were written for the Flemish court, with Gerbert's work as a possible exception; but an ongoing patronage of the romance as a whole by the house of Flanders would make sense of one of the main problems that they present. Whatever the exact chronology of the early stories about the Grail, we have, on the one hand, a group of strikingly original romances by different hands, which develop the idea of the Grail very rapidly. On the other hand, we find the highly conservative *Continuations*, which continually hark back to Chrétien's original, and yet have some scenes and ideas in common with the other romances. Inventiveness is not their strong point, and it would make a great deal of sense to read them as a separate Grail tradition, developed from the original *Story of the Grail* but borrowing occasionally from the new stories. In other words, if we find a story in both the *Continuations* and the other romances, the *Continuations* are not the original source of that story. This is borne out by what we know of the chronology of the *Continuations*, and in the survey of these attempts to complete Chrétien's original which follows, I have left aside these common episodes for discussion in the context of the romances in which I believe they originated.

The First Continuation

The *First Continuation* is concerned with Gawain, who is the focus of attention when Chrétien's poem breaks off. But instead of returning at intervals to Perceval, as Chrétien does, the author virtually ignores him.[7] Gawain is in search of the lance which Perceval has seen at the Grail castle. This was a quest to which Chrétien had given some emphasis, but only as a parallel to Perceval's adventures. In the *First Continuation*, it is Gawain who visits the Grail castle; and he does so twice. This shows that for a contemporary audience the theme of the lance was potentially as important as that of the Grail. When Gawain, after a long series of adventures, comes to the Grail castle for the first time, he is offered a challenge which Perceval did not have to face, that of mending a broken sword, which becomes a kind of preliminary test of his ability to ask the crucial question about the Grail. At his first attempt, he fails to mend the sword, but not before he has seen the procession. As in Chrétien, the Grail is borne by a girl; but here, though she is 'of lovely appearance, most beautiful . . . she was grieving bitterly. Between her hands she held aloft the Holy Grail for all to see. Gawain saw it quite clearly, and longed to know why she was weeping so bitterly.'[8] Here, perhaps for the first time, the Grail assumes its full title; Chrétien had called it 'a holy thing' but had never used the actual phrase 'the Holy Grail'. It is far more frequently called 'the rich Grail', from the description in Chrétien's original text, where he portrays it as studded with the most precious of jewels. We shall see how and why the Grail earned its new epithet shortly.

Gawain returns a little later to the Grail castle, and despite the fact that he fails the test of the sword once more, he is able to ask his host about the history and significance of the bleeding lance; what he learns associates the lance with the Grail and with the crucifixion of Christ. Again, this is all taken from the new romances, but welded into Chrétien's original, where

1 *Gawain sees the bleeding lance and the Grail, followed by a bier with a sword on it, at the court of the Fisher King. The text specifies that the Grail maiden followed the bearer of the lance, but the artist has reversed the order. From a French manuscript of the* First Continuation, *c.1330–40.*

the lance is Gawain's particular quest. It means that we are faced with a paradox: Gawain, the most secular of Arthurian heroes, is involved here in an adventure which is unlike anything else that befalls him. It is a moment of deep spiritual resonance; but it comes oddly from the pen of the unknown writer, who prefers run-of-the-mill episodes of knight-errantry. This scene is in a different key, touching on the central mysteries of the Christian faith, and seems to be almost out of context here.

On the occasion of Gawain's second visit to the Grail castle, the Grail performs a miracle, and feeds the assembled company. Gawain marvels at how it comes and goes, without any sign of a seneschal or sergeant or valet; when all the courses are served, it vanishes. However, despite his curiosity, Gawain falls asleep from exhaustion and fails to aks the crucial question. The story then takes a different direction, and tells of Gawain's brother, Guerrehet, his defeat at the hands of a dwarf knight, and his subsequent revenge. On this note, far from the Grail theme, the anonymous author ends the *First Continuation*.

The Second Continuation

For Wauchier, the author of the *Second Continuation*, the hero of the romance is Perceval, but his adventures have little to do with the Grail: indeed we learn more about the Grail from the brief section in which Gawain gives an account of what happened to him at the castle of the Fisher King. Gawain concentrates on his own quest for the bleeding lance, but repeats the account of the Grail given in the *First Continuation*. Perceval encounters the Grail without knowing it when he sees five lights like candles in the forest at the dead of night, 'so bright and clear that it seemed that the great, dense forest was lit up and blazing with their light on every side'.[9] He learns the next day that this was a sign of the presence of the Grail:

'As for the light you saw, have you ever heard of the rich king fisherman? He lives near here beside a river, and he was in the forest last night because he's very fond of it. That's where the great light came from that you mentioned. Sir, the fire which burned so brilliantly is a sign that the Grail which is so beautiful and precious . . . was with the Fisher King in the forest, for the Devil cannot harm or lead to sin any man who sees its light.'[10]

It is only at the end of Wauchier's work that Perceval comes back to the Grail castle. Once again, he sees a light in the forest, an oak blazing with a thousand candles, which vanish as he approaches the tree. Other marvels follow, and he at last reaches the castle. He is welcomed by the king, and after Perceval has told him of his adventures, they sit down to dinner:

They had not long been seated when a girl, fairer than a flower in April upon a sapling's branch, appeared from a beautiful chamber. She was holding the Holy Grail in her hands, and passed before the table. A moment later another girl came – a fairer one was never seen – dressed in white, embroidered silk. She was carrying the lance which dripped blood from its tip. And a boy followed after her, carrying a naked sword which was broken clean in half across the middle. He laid it on the table, on the corner by the king.[11]

Perceval asks about the Grail and the lance, but the king's reply is about Perceval's adventures, though he promises to say more when they have eaten. Perceval presses him to tell him about the sword, which the king does, telling him that he hopes that Perceval will be able to mend it. If he can join the pieces, he will be answered about the Grail and the lance.

Perceval joins the sword, but a small notch in the edge remains. The king praises his prowess, and with this Wauchier's work ends: Perceval has neither learnt about the Grail, nor achieved his adventure.

The Third *and* Fourth Continuation

By the time we reach the *Third Continuation*, matters get really complicated. Two of the manuscripts insert the work of Gerbert de Montreuil, the longest continuation of all, running to some 20,000 lines, before picking up the last of the three usual continuations. This composite text has almost certainly been adapted from a version which had a conclusion, for the last few lines repeat the end of Wauchier de Denain's work so that Gerbert's continuation joins correctly to the following text.

We will take the orthodox *Third Continuation* first. Manessier, the author, begins his text by providing the answers to Perceval's questions: the king starts by explaining the history of the lance, beginning with the story as told in the *First Continuation*, adding more details from the other versions of the Grail story which had now appeared. But the theme of Manessier's story has to do not with the Grail, but with the broken sword which Perceval has repaired: he learns that it was used by a knight called Partinial to kill the Fisher King's brother by treachery, and he vows to avenge him. His search for Partinial occupies most of the romance; it ends with a duel in which Partinial is killed. Perceval returns to the Grail castle with Partinial's head,

2 *The Grail, in the form of a large covered chalice, is carried before Perceval. From a manuscript of Manessier's* Continuation *of Chrétien's poem.*

and is greeted joyfully by the Fisher King, who reveals that Perceval is his nephew.*

During these adventures, the Grail appears three times. On the first occasion, Perceval has unknowingly challenged and fought Ector, Lancelot's brother, and they have almost killed each other: when they regain consciousness, they see an angel bearing the Grail, and the presence of the Grail heals them.

The Grail's next appearance should be the crucial scene of the whole work, for it represents Perceval's achievement of the Grail, even though he has long since asked the necessary question about it – or as near an approximation to that question as the authors of the *Continuations* can manage, for the question as specified by Chrétien is never actually repeated.[12] Perceval has returned to the Grail castle with Partinial's head, and has just sat down to dinner with the Fisher King. All that we are given is an abbreviated version of Chrétien's original description, with the sole difference that the trencher is carried by a boy, and draped with red and grey samite cloths. As it passes, the tables 'were filled on every side with the most delectable dishes'. The question is forgotten, as on the previous occasions, even though one manuscript adds: 'and Perceval stared long at [the Grail] until finally it happened that the Grail came right up to him, freely and openly, and Perceval was filled with joy'.[13]

3 The Grail is taken up to heaven at the end of Manessier's Continuation *of* Chrétien's poem. *From a late thirteenth-century French manuscript.*

* The hermit had already told Perceval this in the original *Story of the Grail*.

Finally, the Grail appears after the Fisher King's death, at the great feast following Perceval's coronation, on the feast of All Saints. 'That day fourteen crowned kings were present in honour of him, and all were of high renown.' The gathering lasts for a month, and 'every day the Grail served them in its customary way'. The conclusion tells how Perceval rules his kingdom for seven years, and then becomes a hermit: Grail and lance and trencher follow him to his hermitage, and when he dies, the Grail vanishes, and no one will ever see it on earth again.

Gerbert de Montreuil's Continuation

Manessier writes in a fairly simple but not unattractive style: Gerbert de Montreuil, author of the alternative version which we only know from the text interpolated between the *Second* and *Third Continuation*, is an altogether more accomplished author. Instead of revealing the secrets of the Grail as soon as he picks up the narrative, he tells instead how the little notch in the sword which Perceval has just mended signifies that although he has made much spiritual progress, he is not yet ready to learn the secrets of Grail and lance because he has not yet expiated his sin towards his mother, who had died of grief the day he left her to become a knight. When he departs from the Grail castle, he comes to an enclosed garden, where he breaks his own sword by hammering on the gate to demand entrance: he is refused, and learns that within is the Earthly Paradise. As he rides on his way, he finds that the waste land around the Fisher King's castle has become green and pleasant once more, because he has asked the questions of the Fisher King. A series of adventures follow which involve demons and ghosts, and which each bear a spiritual significance: we are in a different world from that of Chrétien, a landscape and context that will shortly become familiar. But Gerbert has not forgotten the other half of Chrétien's story, and his poem also continues the adventures of Gawain. These, however, are entirely secular, and Gawain's quest for the lance is never mentioned. Gerbert then returns to the fortunes of Perceval. At the end of the tale, Perceval finally reaches the Grail castle again, where he mends the broken sword perfectly. Gerbert, who has refrained from bringing either Perceval or Gawain to the Grail castle again until this point (and therefore has nothing new to say about the Grail itself) probably concluded his story with the reappearance of the Grail and Perceval's succession to the Fisher King; but, as we have already noted, the text we have brings us back to the lines from the end of Wauchier's story which are repeated exactly, so that Manessier's *Continuation* can follow.

Prologues to The Story of the Grail

If the various attempts to complete *The Story of the Grail* seem confusing to us, they were equally so to contemporaries, despite their relative popularity. Even while these continuations were being written, two authors felt that a prologue was needed to explain the action. The results, the so-called *Bliocadran* and *Elucidation Prologues*, take very different views of the work. In *The Bliocadran Prologue*,[14] the emphasis is on the family and descent of Perceval, and this is indeed an important aspect of the romances about the Grail, which can be seen as the chronicle of the 'Grail family', much as other romances such as *Beves of Hampton* or *Guy of Warwick* were the imagined chronicles of the ancestors of real families. Bliocadran is Perceval's father, and the description of his adventures explains how Perceval and his mother find themselves in straitened circumstances deep in the forest at the beginning of *The Story of the Grail*. The theme of the prologue is that chivalry has its dark side, and that tournaments, so highly regarded in Chrétien's stories, can be brutal and destructive. Perceval's father and eleven of his brothers die in tournaments, and it is this that prompts his mother to flee to the forest, where she builds a manor in a remote spot. This account is at odds with Chrétien's own tale, where Perceval's father is portrayed – like other knights in Chrétien's romances – as having fallen on hard times: his sons are killed in an unspecified quarrel when they return home shortly after they are knighted, and he dies of grief as a result. In *The Bliocadran Prologue* we first meet the concept of using a knightly romance to emphasize the failure of knightly ideals and the dangers of the quest for glory; it is an idea which recurs in later Grail romances. But we learn relatively little about how the author saw Chrétien's work, and nothing at all about the concept of the Grail.

The Elucidation Prologue[15] is a much stranger piece, which begins with an apparently quite unrelated folktale, whose connection with the Grail story is never really explained. It is difficult to find any real link between this story, which tells of the girls who live near wells in the forest, and offer meat and drink to passers-by in golden cups, and that of the Grail itself; the theft of the cups and the rape of the girls by king Amangons and his knights are avenged by Arthur's knights, but even on its own terms the story is confused and contradictory. When the storyteller turns to the Grail, he portrays it in a quite different light. Firstly, he tells us the resolution of the story, that 'it was Perceval the Welshman who asked whom the Grail served, but he did not ask about the lance when he saw it, nor why it bled, nor about the sword of which one half was missing and the other half lay in the bier over a dead man, nor why all the castle vanished'. He both destroys the suspense of the story, and portrays Perceval's success as only partial: but this is not all. The Grail's appearance echoes that in the *First Continuation* very closely: it appears when the company at the Grail castle are seated at table: 'the Grail, without serving-man or seneschal, came through the door of a chamber and served everyone in royal fashion in rich dishes of gold that were worth a great treasure. The first food it set before the king, and then it served all the others round about; it was a miracle to see the food that it brought them and the meat that it gave them. And then came the greatest miracle of all, to which nothing else can be compared.'

This miracle, however, the author leaves for Perceval to recount; and he goes on to describe the seven branches of the story of the Court of the Rich Fisherman, 'which was found seven times in the seven guises of the story'. Like the rest of this prologue, it is a passage which raises more questions than it answers, both deliberately and through the author's often vague phrasing:

The seventh branch is the most pleasing, which is about the lance with which Longinus struck the King of holy majesty in the side. The sixth tells without fault of the great events of the toil. In the fifth I will tell you of the anger and loss of Huden. The Story of Heaven is the fourth: the knight Mors de Calan who came first to Glomorgan was no coward. The other is the third, about the goshawk of which Castrars was so frightened. Pecorins the son of Amangons always bore the scar on his forehead. The second is nowhere to be found, say the good storytellers; it was the Story of Great Sorrow, how Lancelot du Lac came to the place where he lost his virtue. Then there is the last: as I have undertaken the task, I ought to tell it without delay. It is the adventure of the Shield, the best that ever was. These are the seven natural stories about the Grail.

Why this proposed romance in seven 'branches' should merely repeat Chrétien's work after such promises is a mystery. But what it tells us is that the author saw the Grail as simply another knightly adventure among many. We could read the story of the goshawk as in some way related to the *Joie de la Cort* episode in Chrétien's *Erec*, in which the prize of a goshawk brings many knights to their death, and the 'loss of Huden' might relate to Tristan's little dog Houdenc in the tale of Tristan and Iseult. But he also relates it to the tale of Longinus, from the New Testament and the Apocryphal Gospels. There is, too, an element of natural magic; in *The Elucidation Prologue*, it is simply the finding of the Court of the Rich Fisherman and of the Grail 'through which the land was repeopled; so that the streams which no longer ran and the fountains which did not spring up because they were dry once more flowed through the meadows; the fields were green and lovely, and the woods clothed in leaves . . .', images lifted almost verbatim from the *First Continuation*. And then we are back in the world of king Amangons; we learn of the emergence of the Order of the Peers of the Rich Retinue, who aim to rival Arthur's court and power, but are immoral and wicked. Arthur overthrows them after four years of war. *The Elucidation Prologue* does not deserve its name: it elucidates nothing, and seems to be a muddled and thoroughly amateur attempt, misunderstanding the episodes that it has copied from the *Continuations* and adding a completely unrelated adventure which is clumsily worked into the main story. Not surprisingly, it has been used as the basis for all kinds of speculative discussions on the origins of the Grail stories, but it is largely derivative where the Grail narrative proper is concerned, rather than harking back to older sources.

So the poets who, in their various ways, offered completions of Chrétien's original work undertook no great leap of the imagination, and we shall show in due course something of how they obtained their new material about the Grail. But the style and approach to the tale is relatively consistent, until the latter part of Gerbert's work. The mechanics of the story remain those of the predestined quest – Perceval is predestined to seek the Grail, Gawain the lance, and these are 'their' adventures. These themes may be similar to those of secular romance, but the religious connotations present in *The Story of the Grail* are reinforced: for just as Perceval is in search of the Grail, which now has a sacred history, the object of Gawain's quest is the lance of the Crucifixion; he, like Perceval, must find the Grail castle in order to achieve his goal.

3

Sanctifying the Grail Hero: Robert de Boron

We know a little more about our next author, Robert de Boron. He wrote his first poem for a lord named Gautier de Montbéliard; Boron, from which he took his name, is a village near Montbéliard. Gautier was a member of a noble family descended from the dukes of Burgundy; he was related to Thierry, archbishop of nearby Besançon, and was distantly connected by marriage to the counts of Champagne and Flanders, patrons of Chrétien de Troyes. Gautier set out on the Fourth Crusade in 1202, but joined a Burgundian contingent who sailed direct from Marseilles to the Holy Land, unlike most of the crusaders, who were diverted to a secular expedition which resulted in the scandalous capture and sacking of Constantinople in 1204.* In the Holy Land, Gautier married Burgundia, daughter of Amalric, king of Jerusalem and Cyprus. He became regent of Cyprus during the minority of his brother-in-law, who succeeded to the throne in 1205. Gautier was a just and competent ruler, but avaricious. When Hugh came of age in 1210, he demanded an account of the revenues during the regency. Fearing the king's displeasure, Gautier fled to Acre, where he accompanied his cousin the king of Jerusalem, Jean de Brienne, on campaigns against the Saracens; he may have died on such a campaign in 1212.[1] It is not impossible that Robert de Boron could have been in Cyprus with Gautier, and there are traces of Oriental influence on his work, such as apparent knowledge of a Georgian version of the legend of Joseph of Arimathea and names derived from the Greek.[2] Cyprus was a melting-pot of races and languages, and Greeks, Syrians and Franks worked side by side in the royal administration; there were links with Lydda, whose church Joseph of Arimathea was supposed to have founded, and the royal family of Jerusalem seem to have collected relics of Joseph.[3] But despite a mass of hints and details that might suggest Robert de Boron's presence in the East, there is nothing in all this that takes us beyond the realms of conjecture and possibilities, and he too

* See p. 46 below.

seems to come from the same fairly narrowly defined background as our other authors: that of north-east France and the Flemish border, with particular associations with the Flemish nobility and links with the crusading movement.

Robert de Boron is a major figure in the development of the story of the Grail, for he approaches the Grail story from a radically different standpoint. Chrétien's *The Story of the Grail* is focused on the Grail and lance, but only as they relate to Perceval and Gawain: the alternative title of *Perceval* is perfectly justifiable. The events take place within Perceval's lifetime, and the background of the adventures is Arthur's court. Within the story begun by Chrétien, even in the extended form of the *Continuations*, there is no history of the Grail, apart from a brief sketch in Manessier's *Continuation*, which is in fact borrowed from elsewhere. Robert de Boron imagines the subject in a totally different way. For him, the focal point is not Perceval, but the Grail itself, and he takes the story back to the time of Christ, relating the history of the Grail to the Gospel narrative and to the apocryphal gospels.

Robert de Boron's work does not read like a romance. Its whole tone is that of the saints' lives and versions of the apocryphal gospels which were retold in French verse during the twelfth century. Wace, one of the earliest writers to produce a poetic version of the story of Arthur, had written just such a poem, about the Virgin Mary, and it was a flourishing and popular genre, making accessible to an increasingly sophisticated devout lay audience material which only readers of Latin could hitherto access. A great deal of Robert's poem is to be found in the Apocrypha, but his stroke of genius – even if his poetry leaves something to be desired – is to see that this religious verse addressed to laymen could be linked with the newly fashionable knightly romances, particularly since Chrétien's last work had moved towards a more spiritual view of the knight's role. He specifically gives his book the title *L'Estoire dou Graal*, 'The History of the Grail', as if to claim more authority for it than Chrétien's work, which is merely a tale about the Grail, *Li Contes del Graal*.* This may seem a fine distinction to make, but it is nonetheless real, and affects the way in which we read Robert de Boron's text and the context to which it belongs.

As far as we can tell, Robert planned his work as a trilogy, beginning with the early history of the Grail (*Joseph of Arimathea*), the story of Merlin and of Arthur (*Merlin*), and the story of *Perceval*, finishing with the dispersal

---

* See p. 161 below on the question of 'estoire' as representing a true history.

of the knights of the Round Table and Arthur's death.[4] The original version of the work (which we shall call *The Romance of the History of the Grail*) was in verse;[5] only the first part, dealing with Joseph of Arimathea, and the first five hundred lines of the story of Merlin survive. It was then reworked in prose, and a number of copies of the first two parts, *Joseph of Arimathea* and *Merlin*, have come down to us. However, there are only two surviving texts of the prose *Perceval*, and these differ from each other in many details.

Robert de Boron begins and ends with the Grail; and though he takes in a wide range of adventures, and indeed the whole history of Arthur himself, into the story, it is the Grail that is always the central point of his narrative. He introduces a new 'Grail hero' in the shape of Joseph of Arimathea, and although there may have been legends which foreshadowed the association of Joseph with the dish of the Last Supper, Robert may well have chosen Joseph because of his portrayal in the New Testament as a *decurio*, a military title which later came to mean councillor. Translations of the Latin New Testament tend to mask this semi-military attribute, but Robert would of course have known the Latin rather than a vernacular version. He makes Joseph a *soudoier* or soldier, and hence a role model for the knightly class for whom the romances were written.

At the outset, we learn how the vessel in which Christ broke bread at the Last Supper was taken from the house where the disciples met by one of the Jews who took Christ prisoner. It was given to Pilate, who in turn, not wanting to keep anything that belonged to Jesus, gave it to Joseph of Arimathea. In it, Joseph collected the blood that flowed from Christ's wounds when he washed the body after taking it down from the Cross. When Christ's body disappeared from the tomb at the Resurrection, Joseph was thrown into prison: but Our Lord came to him, bearing the vessel, and told him that He had risen from the dead. He gave Joseph the vessel, and explained that he was to celebrate Mass in commemoration of His crucifixion:

'Joseph, you took me from the cross. And you know well that I took the Last Supper at the house of Simon the Leper, where I said that I was to be betrayed. As I said at that table, several tables will be established in my service, to make the sacrament in my name, which will be a reminder of the cross; and the vessel of the sacrament will be a reminder of the stone tomb in which you laid me, and the paten which will be placed on top will be a reminder of the lid with which you covered me, and the cloth called the corporal will be a reminder of the winding-sheet in which you wrapped me. And so your work will be remembered until the world's end. And all who see the vessel and remain in its presence will have lasting joy and fulfilment for their souls. And all who take these words to heart will be more gracious and admired both in this world and in the eyes of Our Lord, and will never be victims of injustice or deprived of their rights.'[6]

So far, Robert de Boron has simply referred to the dish of the Last Supper as 'the vessel', but he now names it as the Grail, in a way which emphasizes its power and sanctity:

Then Jesus spoke other words to Joseph which I dare not tell you – nor could I, even if I wanted to, if I did not have the high book in which they are written: and that is the creed of the great mystery of the Grail. And I beg all those who hear this tale to ask me no more about it at this point, in God's name, for I should have to lie. And from lies, you may be sure, they would gain nothing.[7]

When Joseph is released from prison, he gathers a group of disciples round him, and guards the holy vessel. However, some of his followers fall into sinful ways; despite all their efforts, their crops fail and there is a famine. Joseph is told to make a table like that of the Last Supper, and to place the vessel on it, covered with a cloth. Then he is to summon those who truly believe to sit at it:

Joseph did as Our Lord had commanded, and a great number of his people sat down at the table; but there were many more who did not . . . And when those who had sat down to eat sensed the sweetness and the fulfilment of their hearts, they very soon forgot the others. One who was seated at the table, whose name was Petrus, looked at those who were standing and said: 'Do you feel what we feel?'

'We feel nothing,' they replied; and Petrus said: 'Then you are guilty of the sin you discussed with Joseph, which has brought the famine upon us.'

It is only in this ecstatic context that Robert de Boron again refers to the Grail by name. The sinners ask:

'And what can we say about the vessel we have seen, which has so delighted us and delights us still, so that we forget all pain – what shall we call it?'

[Petrus replies] 'Those who wish to name it rightly will call it the Grail, which gives such joy and delight to those who can stay in its presence that they feel as elated as a fish escaping from a man's hands into the wide water.'

And hearing this, they said:

'This vessel should indeed be called the Grail.'[8]

The play on words between 'agreer' (to delight) and 'graal' – the sounds are more similar in medieval French – is lost in translation. This was to be the generally accepted explanation for the name, repeated in successive romances.

We learn how the next keeper of the vessel, Joseph's brother-in-law Bron, became known as the Fisher King, and from now on he and his fellows are called 'the company of the Grail'. When Merlin appears on the scene, he is particularly anxious to record the history of the Grail, which he dictates to his disciple, master Blaise: Blaise is charged with recording the deeds of both the company of the Grail and those of king Arthur and his court, and Merlin prophesies

'And I tell you, the story of no king's life will ever have been heard so eagerly as that of King Arthur and his court. When you've finished your work and told the story of their lives, you'll have earned a share in the rewards enjoyed by the company of the Grail . . . your book . . . [will] be called *The Book of the Grail*, and will be heard most gladly, for every word and deed therein will be good and beneficial.'[9]

It is at another solemn moment that the Grail is next named as such, when Merlin encourages Uther Pendragon, Arthur's father, to found the Round Table. This is the third of the three tables of the Grail to which Christ referred in his command to Joseph of Arimathea. The first was that of the Last Supper, and the second that of the Grail company. The Round Table will have one seat left vacant, and 'the one who will fill the empty seat needs to have been in the presence of the Grail'.[10] Merlin tells Arthur, once he is crowned, how the Round Table is intimately connected with the Grail, and that Arthur himself cannot fulfil his destiny, to become emperor of Rome,

until a knight of the Round Table has performed enough feats of arms and chivalry – in tournaments and by seeking adventures – to become the most renowned knight in all the world. When that knight has attained such heights that he's worthy to come to the court of the rich Fisher King, and has asked what purpose the Grail served, and serves now, the Fisher King will at once be healed. Then he will tell him the secret words of Our Lord before passing from life to death. And that knight will have the blood of Jesus Christ in his keeping. With that the enchantments of the land of Britain will vanish, and the prophecy will be fulfilled.[11]

These sparing, solemn references to the Grail build up its image, so that when the quest of the Grail is undertaken in the last part of the trilogy, we are already in awe of its holiness and power. The quest is undertaken not just by Perceval, but by the whole company of the Round Table, though it is only Perceval who reaches the castle of Bron, the Fisher King. He is directed there by his uncle, a hermit who lives near the castle, who warns him that he should 'behave with all honour' while he is there. At dinner, he sees the Grail procession, but fails to ask the fateful question which will bring healing; the description is much as in Chrétien, whom the author acknowledges[12] as his source:

And as they were sitting there and the first course was being served, they saw a damsel, most richly dressed, come out of a chamber: she had a cloth about her neck, and in her hands she carried two small silver platters. After her came a boy carrying a lance, which shed from its head three drops of blood. They passed before Perceval and into another chamber. After this came a boy bearing the vessel that Our Lord had given Joseph in prison: he carried it in his hands with great reverence. When the lord saw it he bowed and said the *mea culpa*, as did all the others in the house. And when Perceval saw it he was filled with wonder and would gladly have asked the question – but he was afraid of upsetting his host. He kept thinking about it all that night, but kept remembering how his mother had told him not to talk too much or to ask too many questions. And so he refrained from asking. The lord kept turning the conversation in such a way as to prompt the question, but Perceval said nothing: he was so exhausted from his two sleepless nights before that he was near to collapsing on the table. Then the boy returned carrying the Grail, and passed back into the chamber from which he had first come; and the boy bearing the lance did likewise; and the damsel followed after – but still Perceval asked nothing. When Bron the Fisher King realised no question was going to come he was most distressed. He had had the Grail presented to all the knights who had lodged there, because Our Lord Jesus Christ had told him he would never be healed until a knight asked what it was for, and that knight had to be the finest in the world. Perceval himself was destined to accomplish the task, and if he had asked the question, the king would have been healed.[13]

The consequences of Perceval's failure are also much as in *The Story of the Grail*; he wanders for seven years before he returns to the hermit's house and confesses. After this, he takes part in a great tournament; at the end of the day's jousting, Merlin, disguised as a reaper, catches his horse by the reins as he rides back to his lodgings, and reproves him sharply for taking part in the fighting, saying that he has forgotten his vow never to spend two nights in the same place until he has found his way back to the Fisher King's castle. Merlin sets him on his way, but tells him that it will be a year before he reaches the object of his quest. When Perceval does at last arrive, he sees the Grail procession again:

Two servants came to meet him and welcomed him heartily, and helped him to disarm and stabled his horse with the utmost care; then they led him to the hall where his grandfather the king lay. And as soon as he saw Perceval he did his best to rise, overjoyed at his coming; and Perceval sat down beside him, and they spoke together of many things. Finally the king called for the table to be set; it was no sooner said than done, and they sat down to dine.

Just after the first course had been served, the lance with the bleeding head came out of a chamber, and after it came the Grail, and the damsel carrying the little silver platters. And Perceval, who could not wait to ask the question, said to the king:

'Sire, by the faith you owe me and all men, tell me the purpose of these things I see.'

And as soon as he had said this, he looked up and saw that the Fisher King was utterly changed, cured of his sickness.[14]

Perceval becomes keeper of the Grail, and Bron departs from this world, having 'taught Perceval the sacred words that Joseph had taught him, which I cannot – and must not – tell you'.[15]

Merlin brings Blaise to join the company of the Grail, and returns to Arthur to tell him that the 'enchantments of the land of Britain are cast out'. The story then turns to Arthur's conquest of France, and his preparations to march on Rome itself, which are interrupted by the news of the treachery of his nephew Mordred, who has seized the throne of Britain. When Mordred has been slain, and Arthur has been taken to Avalon, Merlin returns to the Grail company, and dictates these events once more to Blaise. And the story ends with Merlin's retreat into his dwelling-place outside the Grail castle, which he calls his *esplumoir*, adding a final note of mystery, since this otherwise unknown word implies the shedding of feathers, and hence moulting, renewal, transformation.

4

The Old Law and the New Law: The High Book of the Grail

We only know Robert de Boron's poetic work in full from a prose version; the next romance, *Perlesvaus*, otherwise known as *The High Book of the Grail* seems to have been written in prose, with no verse predecessor, though it is just possible that there really was a Latin original, as the author claims.[1]

One of the three surviving manuscripts of *Perlesvaus* contains a colophon which tells us that it was written at the request of the lord of Cambrin, near Lille, for Jean de Nesle. Jean de Nesle was castellan of Bruges, one of the key cities of Flanders, and a leading figure in Flemish political life. He was also a leading figure in the Fourth Crusade in 1204; before he left, he had founded a Cistercian monastery at Noyou in Picardy. Jean de Nesle and Thierry of Flanders, son of count Philip, led a group of Flemish crusaders who sailed from Flanders itself, round the French coast, and through the Straits of Gibraltar. The majority of the crusaders assembled in Venice, where the Venetians provided ships. But their leaders were unable to pay the cost of the ships and the expedition was diverted against Venice's commercial rivals to settle the debt. The crusaders first sacked Zadar on the Dalmatian coast, and then Constantinople itself. The Venetians seized much of that city's fabled wealth, including the famous bronze horses now at San Marco. However, the Flemish, learning that the expedition had turned aside to attack Christians at Zadar, refused to join the other crusaders, and headed straight for the Frankish kingdom in Syria. Their stay in the Holy Land lasted some three years, but resulted in little action, because Amaury, king of Jerusalem, could not mount a campaign with the reduced number of knights at his disposal. Jean de Nesle returned home in 1206 to resume his political career. His connections with France were close, and in 1212 he was forced to leave Flanders because of this. At the great battle between Flanders and France at Bouvines in 1214, he fought on the French side, and after the French victory regained his former influence, particularly during the minority of Jeanne of Flanders, until 1222, when he seems to have fallen into disfavour. In 1226, we find him among the leaders of the crusade against the Albigensians.[2] He died at the end of 1239.[3]

Perlesvaus proclaims its intentions in the first sentence, defining its image of the Grail and the context to which it belongs:

Hear the story of that holy vessel which is called the Grail, in which the precious blood of the Saviour was gathered on the day when He was crucified to redeem mankind from Hell: Josephus recorded it at the behest of an angel, so that by his writing and testimony the truth might be known of how knights and worthy men were willing to suffer toil and hardship to exalt the Law of Jesus Christ, which He had aimed to renew by His death and crucifixion.[4]

The prologue then outlines the descent of the guardianship of the Grail through Joseph of Arimathea's family down to Arthur's times. The only mystery that is not revealed is the identity of the Good Knight, descendant of Joseph, 'of whose name and ways you soon will hear'. This is in much the same vein as Robert de Boron's work, but Robert de Boron only gradually reveals the power of the Grail: here it is proclaimed at once, as is the theme of the New Law of Christ against the Old Law of the pagans and Jews. In *Perlesvaus* there are no mysteries, no slow and subtle unfolding of the nature of the Grail; the theme is boldly set out, and the story proceeds in a series of dramatic tableaux, the work of a powerful and pictorial imagination.

The story proper opens in Arthur's court, where the king has 'lost his former passion for great deeds'. When the queen reproaches him for this, he sets out in search of adventures: in the course of these, he learns of Perlesvaus from a girl who also reproaches him for his lack of zeal in matters of chivalry but, as he returns, dejected by her accusations, he hears a voice commanding him to hold a great court, after which his fame will be restored. When the knights are assembled at dinner, a girl arrives with a cart in which there are the heads of 150 knights, sealed in silver and gold and lead. She tells Arthur that their deaths are the fault of the knight who came to the house of the Fisher King and failed 'to ask the question': as a result the king has 'fallen into a grievous languor'.[5] The girl rides off, but encounters Gawain, who is late for the court; he escorts her, and from her learns of the existence of the Good Knight who will ask the fateful question. Gawain comes within reach of the Fisher King's castle, but is told that he can only find it if God so wills. He begins to search for the Good Knight, at first without success; it is not until he comes by chance to the house of a hermit

4 The opening of The High Book of the Grail, *with a beautiful miniature of the Crucifixion in which Joseph of Arimathea collects Christ's blood in the Grail. Many manuscripts of the Grail story include a picture of the Crucifixion, but these often omit Joseph of Arimathea. From a manuscript written in 1405 and bought by Jean duc de Berry.*

near the Fisher King's castle that he gains news of him. He rides on to the Grail castle:

. . . soon he could see the great wall that surrounded it and the strong castle gate. And lying in the middle of the gateway he saw a lion, chained to the wall, and on either side of the gate stood two ghastly figures of copper, which by an ingenious device could fling forth crossbow-bolts with great strength and fury. Seeing the lion at the gateway and these dread figures, Sir Gawain did not dare go any nearer. He looked along the top of the walls and saw people who seemed to be of the holy life – priests dressed in albs, and old white-haired knights dressed like monks or clerics – and on each of the battlements there was a cross. A chapel stood on the wall, and people were passing thither from a great hall in the castle, and on top of the chapel were three crosses, with an eagle of gold on each one. The priests and the knights on the wall knelt towards the chapel, and from time to time they would look up at the sky, rejoicing, and it seemed as though they could see God and His mother on high. Sir Gawain sat watching from far off, not daring to approach the castle because of the figures that could shoot bolts with such fury that no armour could withstand them. But he could see no path to right or left: he would have to turn back or go on to the castle. He did not know what to do. But just then he looked ahead and saw a priest coming out of the gate.

'Fair sire,' he cried to Sir Gawain, 'what would you?'

'Sire, I pray you, tell me what castle this is.'

'Sire, this is the entrance to the land of the rich Fisher King, and inside the service of the Holy Grail is begun.'

'Then permit me to ride on,' said Sir Gawain, 'for I have been heading for the land of the Fisher King.'

'Sire,' said the priest, 'I tell you true, you cannot enter the castle or go any nearer the Grail, unless you bring the sword with which Saint John was beheaded.'[6]

Gawain's quest for the sword leads him into a series of adventures, at the end of which he succeeds in finding and winning the sword. But these are not simple heroics; for when he comes to the Castle of Enquiry, he learns that the events which have befallen him have a spiritual and symbolic meaning. For this is the innovation of the anonymous author of *Perlesvaus*; the story is now to be read as a medieval theologian might have read the Old Testament; events which apparently exist only on a chivalric plane have now acquired a deeper spiritual and symbolic meaning, which is expounded at intervals during the narrative.

Because Gawain has won the sword he is able to enter the Grail castle, and when he presents the sword to the Fisher King, he is welcomed and led in to dine.

At that moment there was brought in a loin of stag and other venison in great plenty, and rich golden plate adorned the table, with great lidded goblets of gold, and magnificent golden candlesticks bearing great candles. But the light of these was dimmed by the other light in the room. Just then two maidens appeared from a chapel: in her hands one was carrying the Holy Grail, and the other held the lance with the bleeding head. Side by side they came into the hall where the knights and Sir Gawain were eating. So sweet and holy a fragrance came forth that their feasting was forgotten. Sir Gawain gazed at the Grail and thought he saw therein a chalice, which at that time was a rare sight indeed; and he saw the point of the lance from which the red blood flowed, and he thought he could see two angels bearing two golden candlesticks with candles burning. The maidens passed before Sir Gawain and into another chapel. Sir Gawain was deep in thought, so deep in joyful thought that he could think only of God. The knights stared at him, all downcast and grieving in their hearts. But just then the two maidens came out of the chapel and passed once more before Sir Gawain. And he thought he saw three angels where before he had seen but two, and there in the centre of the Grail he thought he could see the shape of a child. The foremost knight cried out to Sir Gawain, but he, looking before him, saw three drops of blood drip on to the table, and was so captivated by the sight that he did not say a word. And so the maidens passed on by, leaving the knights looking at one another in dismay. Sir Gawain could not take his eyes off the three drops of blood, but when he tried to kiss them they moved away from him, and it grieved him deeply that he could not touch them with his hand or anything within his reach. Thereupon the two maidens passed once more before the table, and to Sir Gawain it seemed that there were three; and looking up it appeared to him that the Grail was high up in the air. And above it he saw, he thought, a crowned king nailed to a cross with a spear thrust in his side. Sir Gawain was filled with sorrow at the sight and he could think of nothing save the pain that the king was suffering. Again the foremost knight cried out to him to speak, saying that if he delayed longer, the chance would be lost forever. But Sir Gawain remained gazing upwards in silence, hearing nothing that the knight had said. The maidens disappeared into the chapel with the Grail and the lance, the knights cleared the tables, left the feast and moved off into another chamber, and Sir Gawain was left there alone.[7]

Gawain is shut out of the Grail service and leaves the castle. He meets Lancelot, and the story now focuses on Lancelot's exploits. It is only after this that we finally encounter Perlesvaus himself, but we learn little about him. It is Lancelot who next comes to the Grail castle: 'but the story assures us that the Grail did not appear at the feast. It did not appear, because Lancelot was not one of the three finest knights in the world, because of his sin with the queen;* his love for her he would not repent, for he thought more of her than of anything else, and could not keep his heart from her.'[8]

Perlesvaus is now being sought by his sister, who asks Gawain to find him, saying that Perlesvaus' mother also needs his help. He is engaged in fighting the evil King of Castle Mortal, his uncle and the brother of the Fisher King, who has been attacking the Grail castle. Perlesvaus defeats him, and he flees in a ship. Before Perlesvaus can rescue his mother, his sister has a terrifying vigil in a cemetery near the Grail castle, where evil spirits are engaged in a furious battle. At midnight a voice declares that the Fisher King is dead, and that the King of Castle Mortal has seized the Grail stronghold; the Grail has vanished, and only Perlesvaus can help.

Perlesvaus' sister finds him almost immediately, and tells him this news. He rescues his mother, and then returns to Arthur's court; but the girl with the cart laden with knights' heads who had begun the adventures appears to summon him to the Grail castle. On the way, he stays with his uncle the

* I.e. his illicit love for Guinevere.

hermit king, who explains to him the meaning of all that has happened to him, and tells him how he can capture the Grail castle. As he approaches the castle, he is followed by twelve hermits, whom the king of Castle Mortal is driving from their places in the forest. With the help of a friendly lion and Joseus, one of the hermits who had once been a knight, Perlesvaus overcomes the knights who guard the seven bridges that lead to the centre of the castle. Seeing that his defenders have been killed, the king of Castle Mortal climbs on to the battlements, stabs himself with his sword and falls into the river far below.

This high story tells us that when the castle had been conquered the Saviour of the world rejoiced and was greatly pleased. The Holy Grail reappeared in the chapel, and so did the lance with the bleeding head and the sword with which Saint John was beheaded . . . Joseus stayed at the castle with Perlesvaus as long as he wished, but the Good Knight went out once more to scour the land where the New Law was being neglected. He killed all those who would not believe in it, and the country was ruled and protected by him, and the Law of Our Lord exalted by his strength and valour.[9]

This, however, is not the end of the romance; the remainder of the tale is concerned with Arthur's attempts to maintain his rule and that of the New Law in the face of a rebellion by Brian of the Isles. Soon after this new sequence of adventures begin, Arthur comes on pilgrimage to the Grail castle, and stays with Perlesvaus. One day, sitting at the window, he sees a procession of people dressed in white approaching the castle; they sing as they walk. At their head is a man bearing a huge cross, and at the rear is a man with a bell and a clapper; they are the hermits of the forest who come to worship the Holy Grail. The king and Perlesvaus go to greet them, and lead them to the Grail chapel:

And as soon as they entered the chapel they took the bell from the one at the rear and offered it to the altar, and then laid it on the ground. Then the holy and glorious service began.

Now, the story tells us that at that time there was no chalice in the land of King Arthur. The Grail appeared at the consecration in five forms, but they should not be revealed, for the secrets of the sacrament none should tell save he whom God has granted grace. But King Arthur saw all the changes,[10] and last appeared the chalice; and the hermit who was conducting the mass found a memorandum upon the consecration cloth, and the letters declared that God wanted His body to be sacrificed in such a vessel in remembrance of Him. The story does not say that it was the only chalice anywhere, but in all of Britain and the neighbouring cities and kingdoms, there was none.

The king was filled with joy by what he had seen, and he bore in his heart the memory of the name and form of the holy chalice.[11]

Perlesvaus' final deed is to slay the Black Hermit, a figure of satanic evil, and at the very end, he is summoned to depart from the Fisher King's castle: a voice tells him as he is in the chapel of the Grail:

'Perlesvaus, you will not stay here much longer: God wishes you to divide the relics between the hermits of the forest, and with them His body is to be served and honoured. And the Holy Grail will appear here no more, but you will soon know where it is to be.'[12]

A ship comes for Perlesvaus, and when it leaves, 'angels rose from the castle and commended them to God and His sweet mother. Josephus tells us that Perlesvaus thus departed, and from that time forth no earthly man ever knew what became of him, and the story tells nothing more.'

What we have described so far is, in effect, three completed works dealing with the Grail: first, *The Story of the Grail* in its full version by various hands; secondly, the cycle of three poems attributed to Robert de Boron, and thirdly, *Perlesvaus*. They represent very varied approaches to the subject: the complete version of *The Story of the Grail* is the result of a backward-looking attempt to create the work that Chrétien might have written, while the other writers took up the Grail theme in order to create original works of their own. These draw on Chrétien for little more than the bare bones of the plot – the name of the hero and his association with the Grail. *Perlesvaus* is a highly dramatic rethinking of the whole Arthurian scenario, suffused with a fierce and elemental Christianity. Robert de Boron's work is much more orthodox in religious terms, but hugely ambitious in concept: he sets out to link the Grail of Arthur's time with the Gospels, and to create a history of the sacred object from the time of the Crucifixion onwards. It was this theme that was to be taken up by the author (or authors) of what was to become the nearest we have to a definitive version of the Grail story.

5

Creating the Grail Hero:
The Lancelot-Grail

In the room, a man has just finished writing, and is putting away his implements. In the quick darkness of an early winter evening, his figure is indistinct: it could be that he is wearing a monastic habit, and that we are in a monastic scriptorium or writing-room in northern France. But he is more likely to be only a cleric or even a devout layman; perhaps he has withdrawn from the world at the end of his life, and is housed and fed by the monks in return for the gift of his secular goods. He moves round the room closing books which he has evidently been using, and he replaces them on shelves in a recess closed by wooden shutters. Somewhere nearby the sound of chanting voices marks the start of Vespers. He straightens the loose quires of parchment which represent the sum of his work so far, and adds them to the books on the shelves. He takes a candle from the alcove by the door, and lights it before he goes down the stairs.

No more than forty years have passed since we watched Chrétien de Troyes creating the first of the Grail romances. What lies in the room which our new anonymous author has just left is a work on a much more ambitious scale than Chrétien's powerful yet simple fragment. Like the work of Robert de Boron, it will eventually begin far back in time, with the events surrounding the Crucifixion; but it is vastly more elaborate, for there are two great piles of quires already on the shelves, which dwarf the modest tome that contains the whole of the prose versions of Robert's work. The scope of the new work in hand, which we call the *Lancelot-Grail*,* is the same, telling the story of the Grail from its hallowed beginnings to its appearance at Arthur's court, and closing with the deaths of Arthur, Guinevere and Lancelot. But it springs from a very different topic: it is not yet about the Grail, or even really about Arthur. It takes as its central figure Lancelot, the hero of Chrétien's romance of the same name, in which Chrétien tells of

---

* The older title, 'the Vulgate Cycle', is unnecessarily technical; it is also referred to by scholars as the 'Prose *Lancelot*' or the 'Pseudo-Map Cycle'.

Lancelot's love for Guinevere. The first romance to be written, *Lancelot*, opens, not with the birth of Arthur, but with the lineage and birth of Lancelot himself. Lancelot's prowess, which Chrétien takes for granted, is demonstrated in a long series of adventures, which have no counterpart at all in the scheme of Robert de Boron's version. Lancelot joins Arthur's court when the Round Table is already established, and the marriage of Arthur and Guinevere has taken place.

Within the series of adventures, after Lancelot's status as the greatest champion of the Round Table has been established, and he and Guinevere have admitted their love for each other, there are marvellous episodes and mysterious events; but nothing really prepares us for what befalls Gawain, when, riding in search of adventures, he arrives at a small moated castle, where he is greeted by the king to whom it belongs. As they talk, a white dove bearing a gold censer in its beak flies in, and all the company kneel as it disappears into another room. Tables are laid, and everyone sits down in silence, praying as they do so. From the room into which the dove vanished a beautiful girl emerges,

carrying in her two hands the most splendid vessel that had ever been seen by earthly man, which was made in the semblance of a chalice; she held it above her head so that all those present saw it and bowed.

Sir Gawain looked at the vessel and admired it more than anything he had ever seen, but he was unable to learn what it was made of, for it was composed neither of wood nor of any kind of metal, nor of stone, nor was it of horn or bone, which amazed him . . . As the maiden passed in front of the dining table, each knight knelt before the holy vessel and the tables were at once replenished with all the delightful foods that one could describe; and the palace was filled with delicious odors as if all the spices in the world had been scattered there.[1]

Gawain is so bemused by the girl's beauty that he fails to pray; as she passes through the hall, the tables are filled with abundant food for everyone present save Gawain. When the meal ends, the others leave, but Gawain finds that he is locked in the room. A terrifying series of adventures ensues: Gawain is wounded by a flaming lance, and fights with monsters and an unknown knight. The girl bearing the vessel reappears, and he hears voices singing the most beautiful music imaginable; he is healed by the vessel's presence, but the next morning he is seized and bound, and taken from the castle in disgrace before being carried out of the town in a cart. All that he has learnt about the castle is that it is called Corbenic; but soon afterwards Gawain is told by a hermit that the vessel was 'the Holy Grail, where the blood of Our Lord was shed and gathered. Because you were not humble and simple, it is right that His bread should be refused to you . . .'[2]

The next knight to come to Corbenic is Lancelot himself. His adventures are more auspicious; we shall see that they are central to the story of the Grail as told in this romance. Before he enters the castle, his prowess as the best knight living enables him to slay a dragon hidden in a tomb in a chapel below the castle walls, and he is warmly welcomed by king Pelles. Once again, the dove appears, and the lovely girl appears from the room, bearing the vessel, 'the most precious that mortal man had ever seen, and it was in the shape of a chalice . . .'[3] This time, because Lancelot bows humbly before it and performs his devotions, the vessel provides food for him as for all the others. Pelles says to Lancelot afterwards that he feared that 'our Lord's grace might fail this time as it did the other day when Sir Gawain was here', and recognizes that Lancelot is the best knight in the world. Pelles knows that his daughter Helaine is destined to bear Lancelot's son, who will free his kingdom from a curse that has laid it waste; but because Lancelot is in love with Guinevere, Pelles has to enlist the help of Brisane, his daughter's tutor. Brisane gives Lancelot a magical drink which makes him believe that the king's daughter is Guinevere herself. Lancelot sleeps with Helaine, and their son is conceived. He discovers the deceit the next morning, and rides off, disconsolate and angry.

Bors de Ganis, Lancelot's cousin, is the next knight to reach Corbenic. He meets Helaine, who no longer carries the Grail now that she has lost her virginity; her cousin is now the Grail-bearer. Bors is miraculously fed by the Grail with the rest of the company, and goes on his way; but it is not long before he returns, and seeks to encounter the adventures which Gawain had endured in the castle, and about which he had learnt nothing on his previous visit. He meets Helaine, and sees her son by Lancelot, who is now ten months old. Once again he partakes of the Grail feast, and then undergoes the hazards of the Palace of Adventures: the encounters that befell Gawain are repeated, but at the end of them Bors

looked into the room and saw a silver table upon four wooden supports, splendidly decorated with gold and precious stones . . . Upon the silver table was the Holy Grail, covered with a piece of white samite, and before the table was a kneeling man, dressed like a bishop. After he had stayed there a long time, he stood up, went to the Holy Vessel, and removed the samite that covered it. At once the room was filled with the greatest brightness that I could describe.[4]

A voice warns Bors not to approach, as he is not worthy to come any closer. He retreats, dismayed, but is healed by the presence of the holy vessel of the wounds inflicted in the night's adventures. He is unable to learn much about the meaning of his experiences, for this will only be revealed 'when the last quest of the Grail is undertaken'.[5]

The Grail appears twice more before the end of *Lancelot*; in both cases the emphasis is on its healing powers, which have helped Gawain and Bors at Corbenic. It appears mysteriously, in an unspecified place, to Perceval and Ector, who have nearly killed each other by fighting without knowing the other's identity.

At the point when they were in such danger and anguish that they truly thought they would die, they saw a great brightness coming toward them, as if the sun were descending upon them, and they were mystified as to what this might be. They looked and saw a vessel made like a chalice and covered with white samite; it was preceded by two censers, and two others followed it, but they could not see who carried them or who was holding the vessel. Nevertheless, the vessel seemed to be a holy thing, and they hoped for so much virtue from it that they bowed down to it, despite all the pain they were suffering. And immediately ... they felt hale and hearty, recovered from their wounds.[6]

Soon afterwards, Lancelot, whose despondency on leaving the castle has turned to madness, is captured and brought to Corbenic, where the Grail restores him to sanity.[7]

The thread of the story so far, even where the Grail is concerned, is the history of Lancelot and his kind. Perceval is sidelined, and the stage is set for the emergence of a new Grail hero, created especially for that role. If the end of *Lancelot* is a preamble to the quest for the Grail, it sets up a very different set of circumstances from those with which we are familiar from earlier romances. In the closing pages, Lancelot's son, who is now named as Galahad, leaves his mother at Corbenic, and goes to an abbey in the forest of Camelot to be near his father. When he is fifteen he is prepared for knighthood, at the feast of Pentecost. The book ends with the words of a hermit who has befriended Galahad, telling Arthur that 'on this coming Pentecost there will be a new-made knight who will bring the adventures of the Holy Grail to an end'.[8]

And so *The Quest of the Holy Grail* begins, with Galahad's arrival at Arthur's court. He is in many ways a contrast to the innocent, clumsy Perceval of Chrétien's story: from the outset he is portrayed as physically and spiritually perfect, and there is no question of a progression from innocence to maturity. His birth, from the lineage of Lancelot and of the keepers of the Grail, gives him effortless spiritual and chivalric prowess; just as Lancelot's worldly prowess predestined him to achieve adventures such as that of the dragon in the tomb, so this prowess predestines Galahad to achieve the Grail itself. His entrance into the Arthurian world is heralded by portents: an inscription appears on the empty seat at the Round Table, the Siege Perilous in which no knight has ever sat without deadly consequences, foretelling that 'this seat shall find its master' that day; a sword floats down the river embedded in a stone, its inscription prophesying that the knight who draws it 'shall be the best knight in the world'. Arthur's knights try to draw it, and fail. And when Galahad finally makes his entrance to Camelot, all the doors and windows of Arthur's palace close of their own accord before he mysteriously appears, accompanied by an aged man who declares him to be of 'the noble house of king David and the lineage of Joseph of Arimathea'. The words on the Siege Perilous change: they now read 'This seat is Galahad's'; and he draws the sword from the stone, saying, 'I was so sure of this sword that I came to court without one, as you may have seen.' To crown the day's marvels, the Grail itself appears as Arthur and his knights sit down at table.

When they were all seated and the noise was hushed, there came a clap of thunder so loud and terrible that they thought the palace must fall. Suddenly the hall was lit by a sunbeam which shed a radiance through the palace seven times brighter than had been before. In this moment they were all illumined as it might be by the grace of the Holy Ghost, and they began to look at one another, uncertain and perplexed. But not one of those present could utter a word, for all had been struck dumb, without respect of person. When they had sat a long while thus, unable to speak and gazing at one another like dumb animals, the Holy Grail appeared, covered with a cloth of white samite; and yet no mortal hand was seen to bear it. It entered through the great door, and at once the palace was filled with fragrance, as though all the spices of the earth had been spilled abroad. It circled the hall along the great tables, and each place setting was furnished in its wake with the food its occupants desired. When all were served, the Holy Grail vanished, they knew not how or whither.[9]

To underline the religious nature of the experience, the author makes Arthur say 'we should be very happy that our Lord showed us a sign of such great love ... on such a solemn day as Pentecost'. The next day, Gawain leads the knights in vowing – rashly, as it transpires – to seek the Grail and its mysteries; and the quest begins. The adventures that they encounter are not the chance encounters of knights-errant, but are charged by symbolic meaning: Galahad himself is called 'the adventurous knight', as if to underline the connection between the adventures and the spiritual progress of

Il roy artus

Le liege ps illous

Lancelot du lac

5 *Arthur's court at Pentecost, with the empty Siege Perilous, in which only Galahad may sit. Woodcut from the edition of* Lancelot du Lac *printed at Rouen in 1488 by Jehan and Gaillard Le Bourgeois.*

6 The knights take an oath before setting out in search of the Grail. A North Italian miniature of about 1380–1440, from The Quest of the Holy Grail.

those involved in the quest. Gawain, the most sinful of the knights, is dismayed to find that nothing happens to him for months on end, 'having expected the Quest of the Holy Grail to furnish a prompter crop of strange and arduous adventures than any other emprise';[10] and what happens to him and the other knights who are not destined to achieve the quest is often misadventure rather than an adventure. However, even for the chosen knights, the Grail is notably absent from the account of what befalls them, and makes only one appearance before the final apotheosis: yet again the episode centres on Lancelot, and yet again it is the healing power of the Grail that is emphasized. Lancelot comes to a deserted chapel where, through a locked grille, he sees the Grail on a silver table. But, weary from his adventures, he falls asleep before he can see it properly, and as he sleeps, the Grail miraculously cures a sick knight who has been brought there on a litter. As the knight leaves, he comments on the sleeping Lancelot, who has seen nothing of all this, and his squire says that 'it is some knight who committed a grave sin, of which he was never shriven, and maybe so offended Our Lord thereby, that He would not have him witness this high adventure'.[11] The scene seems to foreshadow Lancelot's eventual failure to achieve the Grail, and to underline his replacement by Galahad as the shining exemplar among Arthur's knights.

As the quest draws to its end, it is Lancelot who is the first to reach Corbenic, and as he comes to the castle, a voice promises him that 'You'll find in part what you're seeking and have waited so long to see.' He finds the palace deserted, for it is midnight, and walks through it until he comes to a door which opens to reveal a brilliant light: 'it seemed as if all the candles in the world were burning there'. Again, a voice is heard, warning Lancelot that he must not approach any closer:

So he let his gaze run round the room and observed the Holy Vessel standing beneath a cloth of bright red samite upon a silver table. And all around were ministering angels, some swinging silver censers, others holding lighted candles, crosses and other altar furnishings, each and every one intent upon some service. Before the Holy Vessel was an aged man in priestly vestments, engaged to all appearances in the consecration of the mass. When he came to elevate the host, Lancelot thought he saw, above his outstretched hands, three men, two of whom were placing the youngest in the hands of the priest, who raised him aloft as though he were showing him to the people.*

Lancelot was more than a little amazed at what he saw; for he noticed that the celebrant was so weighed down by the figure he was holding that he seemed about to fall beneath the burden.[12]

Forgetting that he has been warned not to go any closer, Lancelot rushes to the priest's aid and is struck by a fiery blast; he falls unconscious, and lies in a trance for twenty-four days, representing the twenty-four years of his sinful love for Guinevere. When he awakes, he is told that the quest is over as far as he is concerned, 'for you should know that you will not see more of it than you have seen. May God now bring us those who are to see that more.'

The story now turns to those who are destined to see more. During the adventures of the quest three knights have been singled out as the future Grail companions: Galahad, Perceval and Bors, Lancelot's cousin. Perceval and Bors have already encountered the Grail in their earlier adventures at the end of *Lancelot*, and Galahad's primacy in the quest has been repeatedly proclaimed. As they approach Corbenic for the last time, Galahad performs a miracle similar to that which Lancelot accomplished on his first visit to the castle, but instead of slaying a dragon, he releases his ancestor Simeon from the flames of purgatory when he opens his tomb. Simeon tells him that

---

* This is an image of the Trinity (God the Father, God the Son and God the Holy Spirit).

7 Lancelot is struck down because he approaches the Grail too closely. From a manuscript of a version of the Lancelot-Grail *written by Michel Gantelet at Tournai in 1470.*

'the Holy Ghost, who works more powerfully in you than do the interests of the world, looked with compassion on me . . .' At Corbenic itself, they are joined by nine other knights, three from Gaul, three from Ireland, and three from Denmark – all countries which were subject to Arthur. Everyone save the chosen knights is told to leave the hall, and four angels bear in a bishop on a throne, who proves to be Josephus, whom Christ himself had consecrated as the first bishop of his Church. Next to him, the Holy Grail appears on a silver table, and the tale moves to its climax:

[Josephus] approached the silver table and prostrated himself on hands and knees before the altar; after a lengthy interval the sound of the chamber door flying suddenly open burst upon his ear. He turned his head towards it, as did the others too, to see the angels who had borne him thither were proceeding from the room; two had candles in their hands, the third bore a cloth of red samite, the fourth a lance which bled so freely that the drops were falling into a container which the angel held in his other hand. The first two placed the candles on the table, and the third laid the cloth beside the Holy Vessel; the fourth held the lance upright over the vessel so that the blood running down the shaft was caught therein. As soon as these motions had been carried out, Josephus rose and lifted the lance a little higher above the Holy Vessel, which he then covered with the cloth.

Next Josephus acted as though he were entering on the consecration of the mass. After pausing a moment quietly, he took from the Vessel a host made in the likeness of bread. As he raised it aloft there descended from above a figure like to a child, whose countenance glowed and blazed as bright as fire; and he entered into the bread, which quite distinctly took human form before the eyes of those assembled there. When Josephus had stood for some while holding his burden up to view, he replaced it in the Holy Vessel.

Having discharged the functions of a priest as it might be at the office of the mass, Josephus went up to Galahad and kissed him, bidding him to kiss his brethren likewise. Next he addressed them, saying:

'Servants of Jesus Christ, who have suffered and struggled and striven for some glimpse of the mysteries of the Holy Grail, be seated before this table and you shall be filled with the most sublime and glorious food that ever knights have tasted, and this at your Saviour's hand. You can justly claim to have laboured manfully, for you shall reap this day the highest recompense that ever knights received.'

When he had spoken thus, Josephus vanished from their midst, without their ever knowing what became of him. Fearfully they took their seats at the Table, their faces wet with tears of awe and love.

Then the companions, raising their eyes, saw the figure of a man appear from out of the Holy Vessel, unclothed, and bleeding from his hands and feet and side; and he said to them:

'My knights, my servants and my faithful sons, you who have attained to the spiritual life while still in the flesh, you who have sought me so diligently that I can hide myself from you no longer; it is right that you should see some part of my secrets and my mysteries, for your labours have won a place for you at my table, where no knight has eaten since the days of Joseph of Arimathea. As for the rest, they have had the servant's due: which means that the knights of this castle and many more beside have been filled with the grace of the Holy Vessel, but never face to face as you are now. Take now and eat of the precious food that you have craved so long and for which you have endured so many trials.'

Then he took the Holy Vessel in his hands, and going to Galahad, who knelt at his approach, he gave his Saviour to him. And Galahad, with both hands joined in homage, received with an overflowing heart. So too did the others, and to everyone it seemed that the host placed on his tongue was made of bread. When they had all received the holy food, which they found so honeyed and delectable that it seemed as though the essence of all sweetness was housed within their bodies, he who had fed them said to Galahad:

'Son, who art as cleansed and free from stain as any may be in this life, knowst thou what I am holding?'

'No,' Galahad replied, 'unless thou tell it me.'

'It is,' he answered, 'the platter in which Jesus Christ partook of the paschal lamb with His disciples. It is the platter which has shown itself agreeable to those whom I have found my faithful servants, the same whose sight has ever been most hurtful to the faithless. And because it has shown itself agreeable to all my people it is called most properly the Holy Grail.[13]

Christ then tells the knights that because the people of Logres have not respected the presence of the Grail in their midst, it is to be removed from Logres; they are to take it to Sarras, where, 'in the spiritual palace', they will see it fully. Before they leave, Galahad is to heal the Maimed King, who lies in the room where the Grail has appeared, by anointing him with the blood from the lance. 'And all but one of you will die in performing this service.' With these words he blesses them and ascends again into heaven.

When the knights arrive at Sarras, they find it in the hands of a pagan king, who throws them into prison. Here, like Joseph of Arimathea, they are fed by the Grail, until the king becomes mortally ill and releases them. Galahad is acclaimed king on his death: but when he first saw the Grail he had prayed that if he should ask for bodily death, he should at once receive the life of the soul and eternal joy, because the experience of the Grail had been of such spiritual intensity.

When the year was up and the self-same day that had seen Galahad crowned came round again, the three companions rose at crack of dawn and went up to the palace which men termed spiritual. Looking towards the Holy Vessel they saw a noble-looking man in the vestments of a bishop kneeling before the table reciting the Confiteor. After a long moment he rose from his knees and intoned the mass of the glorious Mother of God. When he came to the solemn part of the mass and had taken the paten off the sacred Vessel, he called Galahad over with the words:

'Come forward, servant of Jesus Christ, and look on that which you have so ardently desired to see.'

Galahad drew near and looked into the Holy Vessel. He had but glanced within when a violent trembling seized his mortal flesh at the contemplation of the spiritual mysteries. Then lifting up his hands to heaven, he said:

'Lord, I worship Thee and give Thee thanks that Thou hast granted my desire, for now I see revealed what tongue could not relate nor heart conceive. Here is the source of valour undismayed, the spring-head of endeavour; here I see the wonder that passes every other! And since, sweet Lord, Thou has fulfilled my wish to let me see what I have ever craved, I pray Thee now that in this state Thou suffer me to pass from earthly life to life eternal.'

As soon as Galahad had made his petition to Our Lord, the venerable man who stood in bishop's robes before the altar took the Lord's Body from the table, and tendered it to Galahad who received it humbly and with great devotion. When he had received it, the man of God said to him:

'Do you know who I am?'

'No, Sir, unless you tell me.'

'Learn then,' he said, 'that I am Josephus, son of Joseph of Arimathea, whom Our Lord has sent you for companion. And do you know why he has sent me rather than another? Because you have resembled me in two particulars: in that you have contemplated the mysteries of the Holy Grail, as I did too, and in that you are a virgin like myself; wherefore it is most fitting that I should keep my fellow company.'

When Josephus had finished speaking, Galahad went to Perceval and kissed him, and then to Bors and said to him:

'Bors, as soon as you see Sir Lancelot, my father, greet him from me.'

Returning then to the table he prostrated himself on hands and knees before it; and it was not long before he fell face downwards on the flagged floor of the palace, for his soul had already fled its house of flesh and was borne to heaven by angels making jubilation and blessing the name of Our Lord.

A great marvel followed immediately on Galahad's death: the two remaining companions saw quite plainly a hand come down from heaven, but not the body it belonged to. It proceeded straight to the Holy Vessel and took both it and the lance, and carried them up to heaven, to the end that no man since has ever dared to say he saw the Holy Grail.[14]

Perceval becomes a hermit, and Bors returns alone to Arthur's court to tell of the result of the quest. The last of the cycle of romances, *The Death of Arthur*, moves on to the tragedy of Arthur and his court or, rather, turns from the fate of Lancelot's son to that of Lancelot himself, the focal figure of the denouement. Just as his chivalry is the theme of the first part, so his spiritual failure and the success of his son is the theme of the quest. His betrayal of Arthur leads to the fatal rift between himself and the king, and the destruction of Arthur's court. The narrative ends, not with the death of Arthur, but with the deaths of Lancelot and Guinevere.

The problem of exactly how this lengthy work was composed is still much debated, but it is possible that the original was a purely secular work, concerned only with Lancelot, and that *The Quest of the Holy Grail* is a later interpolation by another hand. Yet the three sections of the story – *Lancelot, The Quest of the Holy Grail, The Death of Arthur* – nonetheless form a coherent whole with Lancelot as the central hero, even though other great themes have been drawn into his story. Only four of the surviving manuscripts preserve the *Quest* on its own. Once these themes, the Grail and the story of Arthur himself, had been added to the story of Lancelot, they seemed to demand a fuller treatment. As a result, two further sections were added at the beginning of the story, largely corresponding to the first two parts of Robert de Boron's work, *Joseph of Arimathea* and *Merlin*, but on a grander scale: these were the *History of the Holy Grail* and *Merlin*, which form a 'prequel' to the main Grail story. The new version of *Merlin* forms the second part of the cycle and tells the history of Britain from Merlin's birth to the birth of Arthur and the latter's victory over the power of Rome. However, it is the first part, the *History of the Holy Grail*, which concerns us here, for it is a greatly expanded version of the early history of the Grail, and although it has attracted less attention than the more familiar and dramatic books of chivalric romance, it is a remarkable narrative in its own right.

The *History of the Holy Grail* begins with an immensely elaborate prologue, a great flourish of trumpets and drums, which makes the highest possible claims for what follows. For this is a story written not only about sacred events but by the chief protagonist, Christ himself. In the year 717, a hermit living in a remote, unnamed place has a vision of Our Lord, who gives him a small book, 'no larger or wider than the palm of a man's hand', containing 'greater marvels than any mortal heart could conceive. Nor will you have any doubts that will not be set straight by this book. Inside are My secrets, which I myself put there with My own hand . . .'[15] A series of apocalyptic visions, of sudden light and sudden darkness, sweet scents and melodies, follows, and an angel shows the hermit marvels whose meaning links the theology of the Eucharist with that of the Trinity.

The hermit places the book under lock and key, but the next day he finds that it has vanished. A voice instructs him to go in search of the book; he will be guided by an animal 'such as you have never seen'; the written text of the romance itself becomes the object of a brief quest, a series of adventures such as any knight would have been glad to undertake. The book is found on the altar of a remote chapel, deserted save for a man possessed by the devil, and by the book's power the hermit is able to drive out the devil. The hermit returns home, and begins the work of copying the book, at which the tale begins.

The opening pages tell the story of Joseph of Arimathea very much as it is found in Robert de Boron. However, in this version, Joseph is not given the Grail by Pilate: when he sees Jesus crucified, Joseph 'thought he would do what he could to obtain some of the things He had touched when He

8 Christ's body is taken down from the cross and buried by Joseph of Arimathea. A picture like this would normally be found in a bible, but in fact this comes from the beginning of the Lancelot-Grail, The History of the Holy Grail, *where it forms an integral part of the romance. From a French manuscript of c. 1290.*

was alive'. He goes to the house in the upper room of which the Last Supper took place, and finds 'the dish from which the Son of God and two others had eaten, before he gave the twelve disciples His flesh and blood to take in communion'.[16]

It is in this dish that he collects Christ's blood when he takes the body down from the cross. The narrative then follows Robert de Boron's version in telling of Joseph's imprisonment, but once Joseph leaves Palestine we move into a quite different kind of narrative, best defined as the Old Testament of the Grail Bible. Joseph's wanderings with the Grail become the wanderings of the Israelites in the wilderness, and the Grail becomes the Ark of the Covenant. Joseph is specifically commanded to house the Grail in an ark by Our Lord: 'I am He who delivered your ancestors from the hand of Pharaoh with signs and portents. I had them cross the Red Sea on dry ground and led them to the desert where their hearts had everything they desired . . . Before you leave . . . you shall make an ark for My bowl, and you shall say your prayers to have the love of your God. And when you wish to speak to Me, open the ark, wherever you may be, so that only you and your son Josephus see the bowl.'[17] Joseph's followers are depicted as the chosen people of the New Testament; like their Jewish forebears, they go in search of the promised land where they will settle, but they also act as missionaries for the new faith as they proceed on their way.

They come first to Sarras, the city of the Saracens, where Joseph tries to convert the king, Evalach; a great theological debate over the Trinity and the virginity of Mary is the first of many such scenes, where a vision or a marvel is interpreted by Joseph or one of his followers to demonstrate in vivid pictorial terms the subtleties of theology. It is at Sarras that Josephus, Joseph of Arimathea's son, is commanded to open the door of the ark by Our Lord:

In dread and fear Josephus opened the door of the ark. Upon doing so, he saw a man dressed in a robe, a hundred times redder and more hideous than fiery lightning, and whose feet, hands, and face were exactly the same. Around this man were five angels all dressed in the same kind of robe and with the same appearance. Each of them had six wings that seemed to be made of burning fire, and each held in his left hand a bloody sword.

In their right hands, the angels hold the symbols of Christ's crucifixion, the so-called 'arms of Christ'. The fiery man has an inscription on his forehead, which declares that

'in this semblance I will come to judge all things on the cruel and terrible day'. And it seemed that red bloody dew flowed from his feet and hands all the way down to the ground.

It seemed to Josephus that the ark was four times wider than it had been before, for the man he saw was inside as well as the five angels. He was so astonished at the marvel he saw that he did not know what to say, so he bent his head toward the ground and began to think very intently. As he pondered with bowed head, the voice called him. He looked up and saw the man crucified on the cross that the angel held; the nails he had seen held by the other angel were on the man's feet and hands, while the sponge was pressed against His chin, and He seemed to be a man who was surely in the anguish of death.

After that Josephus saw that the lance he had seen in the hand of the third angel was embedded in the side of the crucified man; down the handle dripped a stream composed neither completely of blood nor of water, and yet it seemed to be of blood. Under the feet of the crucified man he saw the bowl that his father Joseph had placed in the ark; it seemed to him that the blood from the feet of the crucified man was dripping into this bowl, and that it was already nearly full. It appeared to Josephus that it was about to run over and that the blood would spill. Then it seemed to him that the man was about to fall to the ground . . .[18]

Like Lancelot at Corbenic, Josephus is so concerned that he tries to run in and support the figure in his vision, but the angels hold him back. Joseph joins him at the entrance to the ark, and they see Jesus in the robes of a priest. Our Lord then consecrates Josephus as the first bishop of the church, 'as sovereign pastor, after Me, to watch over My new sheep'. The ceremony of investiture and its symbolism is described in detail, for this is a crucial point in the establishment of Christianity. It is followed by the celebration by Josephus of the first ritual of communion, in which the sacrament is seen as the body of a child.

The tale now returns to Joseph's attempts to convert Evalach; he succeeds after Evalach has been helped to defeat his enemy Tholomer by a mysterious White Knight who performs miraculous feats of arms. Evalach and his brother are baptised, and take the names Mordrains and Nascien, and join Joseph and his followers. We now begin to encounter adventures of another kind, which are designed to prefigure the Grail quest: sometimes, even though the resolution of an adventure is promised at a future date, there is no corresponding conclusion, while in other cases a theme or motif recurs several times, for no very apparent reason. For instance, when Josephus converts Mordrains' people, some of them refuse baptism, and a devil attacks them. Josephus tries to rescue them, but an angel wounds him in the thigh as a punishment for interfering in the divine judgement. The same wound is inflicted on two other characters in the story, before we come to Pellehan, the Maimed King, who corresponds to the invalid king of Chrétien's original tale.

The Grail company divides: Josephus consecrates thirty-three bishops who are sent out as missionaries, while sixteen others are made priests and remain with him and the main body of his followers. Nascien asks to see the holy vessel, but when the ark is opened, he approaches too closely, and raises the paten which covers it; like Lancelot in *The Quest of the Holy Grail*, he is blinded, but remains conscious. He tells Josephus that he cannot describe what was within the bowl: 'I have seen the beginning of the bold endeavor, the occasion of the great exploits, the search for the great knowledge, the founding of the great religion, the separation of the great sins, the proof of the great marvels, the end of goodness and true kindness, the marvel of all marvels.' An angel cures his blindness with a lance which bleeds from its tip, and tells Josephus what the lance symbolizes:

'This is the beginning of the marvelous adventures that will take place in the land where God intends to lead you. There the great marvels will occur and the great deeds will be demonstrated . . . But when they are to begin, it will happen that this lance will bleed, as you have seen it just now. Not a single drop of blood will fall from now until the time when the adventures are to take place, just as you have heard. And then the marvels will begin to occur throughout all the lands where this lance is, and they will be so great and so frightening that everyone will be terrified. All these marvels will happen only because the good who will exist at this time will so desire knowledge of the Holy Grail and this lance that they will undertake to suffer the difficult burden of earthly exploits of chivalry in order to learn about the marvels of the Holy Grail and the lance . . . You may be sure that the marvels inside the Grail will be seen by only one mortal man, and he will be full of all the qualities that can or should be in man's body and heart.'[19]

Soon afterwards, a series of adventures begins, though these are not the main adventures of the Grail. They are announced by a voice which cries: 'Here begin the fears!' Nascien and Mordrains are caught up in a magical mist, and Mordrains vanishes. Nascien is accused of murdering him, and is imprisoned. Mordrains, meanwhile, finds himself on a rocky island, where his faith is tested by afflictions and temptations: the latter are offered by a richly dressed, beautiful lady who appears in a ship and offers to rescue him if he will abjure his faith. He is comforted by her husband, a Christian, and remains steadfast, even when he sees a ship in which it seems that Nascien is lying dead.

Nascien has also been magically transported to the mysterious Turning Isle, where he too sees a ship, which contains a bed on which there lies a sword: this proves to be the ship in which the heroes of the Grail quest, accompanied by Perceval's sister, will reach Sarras at the close of the high adventures. In *The Quest of the Holy Grail*, there is an elaborate description of the symbolism of the ship, and here this passage is largely repeated, telling how parts of the furnishing of the ship were made by Solomon from the Tree of Life, which grew from a branch of the Tree of Knowledge that Eve had brought with her when she and Adam were expelled from Eden. The ship is thus connected both with the primeval Fall, and with the establishment of the lineage of David, from whom Galahad is descended. The sword with the strange girdle which lies on the bed, covered in portentous inscriptions, has a part to play in *The Quest of the Holy Grail*. It is first mentioned in *The Story of the Grail* as part of an adventure which is never completed, and it corresponds to the sword in Gerbert de Montreuil's continuation, which Perceval broke beating on the gates of the Earthly Paradise, and which only the smith Triboet could mend. This time the sword breaks when Nascien defies the warning inscribed above it and uses it to defend himself from a giant: Mordrains joins the two pieces when he and Nascien next meet, but Nascien is magically wounded in the shoulder as a punishment.

Nascien and his son Celidoine are now commanded to go their separate ways: Celidoine is 'to go where chance takes him' aboard a small boat, and Nascien is to take ship once again to search for Joseph of Arimathea. He finds the ship of Solomon on the shore, and is tempted by a beautiful lady, who wants him to carry her aboard. But Nascien, wary of her, makes the sign of the cross, and she is transformed into a devil, who vanishes roaring and crying. Nascien sleeps on the bed in the ship, and dreams a vision of his descendants, ending with Galahad: all are symbolized by lions, save Lancelot, who, because of his sins, appears as a dog. Galahad also appears as a river, disturbed and muddy at its source, but eventually running clear and pure, prefiguring his sinful conception and pure life.

Meanwhile, Josephus has at last reached Britain, bearing the Grail: he and 150 of his disciples cross the sea by a miracle, walking on one of his garments. Nascien joins him, and they begin the task of converting the pagans whom they find in Britain. The first ruler they encounter, duke Ganor, becomes a Christian, and is able to defeat the Saxons with divine help. Josephus sets out to convert North Wales, but is imprisoned by its king, Crudel: Mordrains comes to his rescue and defeats Crudel. Mordrains goes to give thanks at the table of the Holy Grail for his victory, and approaches it too closely, despite the warning of a disembodied voice. The image here is that of the Ark of the Covenant in the Old Testament; to approach it, if you were not of the priesthood, was to invite divine punishment.[20] In this way, the Grail is equated with the central mystery of the faith in both the Old and New Testaments.[21]

Mordrains prays that despite his sin he may live until the knight who is to achieve the adventure of the Grail shall come; and a voice confirms that his wish will be granted. Josephus now comes to the city of Camelot, ruled by Agrestes. Agrestes pretends to be converted, but turns apostate and martyrs twelve of Josephus' companions. He is punished by divinely inflicted madness, and destroys himself. The citizens return to the Christian faith, and Josephus founds the church of St Stephen the Martyr.

Since the scenes at the outset of the romance, little of the narrative has borne any relation to that of Robert de Boron, but the tale now returns to the events which he describes; the episode of Moyses, who is struck down when he tries to occupy a seat at the Grail table reserved by divine command for the greatest of heroes, is related, as is the Grail's refusal to serve those of Joseph's companions who have sinned. A series of episodes follow which set up the adventures which Galahad or one of the other Grail heroes will accomplish. A sword is broken which Galahad will join together again; Moyses is seen burning in a fire which will only be quenched on Galahad's coming; and another sinner who attacks his own brother out of jealousy at his piety suffers the same fate. Josephus makes a cross with his own blood on a white shield which Mordrains had used in battle with the heathen, and the shield is placed in the abbey where Mordrains now lives, to await the arrival of the Grail knights.

The *History of the Holy Grail* closes with the death of Josephus and Alain's succession as keeper of the Grail. Alain's wanderings bring him to the Land Beyond, whose king, Alphasan, he converts. In recompense, Alphasan builds a beautiful stronghold to house the Grail; when it is finished, an inscription mysteriously appears, reading 'This castle should be called Corbenic'. The Grail is placed there for safe keeping. When Alphasan sleeps at his new castle, he has a vision of the Grail, but after this

a man who seemed to be enveloped in flames came to King Alphasan and said, 'King, no man should lie in this palace – neither you nor anyone else – for scarcely could any man, through a good life, be worthy of remaining in the place where the Holy Vessel was honoured as you saw. You did a very foolhardy thing in coming to sleep here; Our Lord wants vengeance taken.'[22]

He wounds Alphasan in the thighs with a lance, as a warning that no one save those who will achieve the Grail should attempt to stay in the Palace of Adventures.

The history of the descendants of Alain is briefly told: one of them, Lambor, is killed with the sword from the ship of Solomon, again in defiance of the dire warnings inscribed on it; and this 'Dolorous Blow' lays waste two kingdoms. We learn of the descent of Alain's branch to king Pelles and Elaine; and the story of the descendants of Nascien is then told. This culminates in the story of duke Lancelot, who is killed because of his love for the wife of his lord, even though he is innocent of sin. Lancelot's head is thrown into a spring, which immediately boils, and will continue to do so until Galahad's arrival. Lancelot's tomb is guarded by two lions, which let no one near the tomb until the second Lancelot, grandson of the dead man, appears there. And so, abruptly, the *History of the Holy Grail* ends, and the story 'returns to a branch called the Story of Merlin, which should be joined carefully to the History of the Holy Grail because it is a branch of it'. The transition is clumsy, for *Merlin* is only part of the Grail story in the original scheme of Robert de Boron, where the stories of the Grail and of Arthur's kingdom are much more closely intertwined. This awkwardness confirms the view that the *History of the Holy Grail* was added after the rest of the adventures in the *Lancelot-Grail* romances had already been written.

We hear only once more of the Grail before the first stirrings of the quest for the Grail at the end of *Lancelot*. Again, this is a passage which is almost certainly a later addition; it comes in the *Merlin* and tells how the news of the Grail came to Britain, and how the knights of the Round Table learned that only the best knight in the world could achieve it. Knightly quests, which until then were unknown, were instituted as a way of discovering who this knight might be. But the description of the Grail itself is curious:

It was true that news spread throughout the kingdom of Logres about the most holy Grail, in which Joseph of Arimathea had caught the blood that flowed from the side of Jesus Christ when he and Nicodemus took him down from the glorious Cross; about the most holy vessel that came down from heaven onto the ark in the city of Sarras in which He first sacrificed His holy body and His flesh through His bishop Josephus whom He consecrated with his own hand; and about the most holy Lance with which Jesus Christ was wounded.[23]

Even with the stories already told, the writer seems to be uncertain of the identity of the Grail, making it into two distinct objects, perhaps to form a trinity of Grail, vessel and lance. In the most consistently religious version of the Grail story, the Grail still appears in unexpected forms.

6

Visions of Angels, Versions of Men: Wolfram von Eschenbach's Parzival

In the room, a man is talking. Around him is a lively coming and going of knights and servants, ladies and their attendants, merchants and travellers; this is the court of count Hermann of Thuringia, and, renowned as he is for his patronage of the arts, there are poets among the knights, and men of learning among the travellers. Beside the man is a figure in distinctive dress, evidently from foreign parts; his clothing may indicate that he is Jewish or Arab by origin, and they are talking of abstruse matters, the lore of gem-stones or the properties of herbs, tales of strange beasts and the problems of astrology. The speaker is a knight, Wolfram von Eschenbach, whose small property is at Eschenbach in Franconia or Bavaria, some distance away. Hermann is not his lord, so he has evidently come here in search of literary patronage.

Unlike his near-contemporaries Chrétien de Troyes, who is very reticent about himself, and the anonymous author of the *Quest*, we know a good deal about Wolfram – or we think we do. He is imaginative, outspoken, and quite prepared to play sophisticated games with his listeners or readers. For a start, he claims that 'I don't know a single letter of the alphabet. There are plenty who take such as a starting-point – this adventure makes its way without books' guidance.'[1] He tells us that he was so poor at home that even the mice were hard put to it to find something to eat. And he can be scathing about his fellow-courtiers, telling his patron Hermann that he should employ someone like Keie, Arthur's notoriously bad-tempered seneschal, 'since true generosity has imposed upon you such a varied entour-age – now an ignominious throng, now a noble press of people'.[2] And elsewhere he says that he would never bring his wife to Arthur's court, because someone would soon be whispering sweet nothings in her ear, telling her that he was dying of love for her and if she would end his sufferings, he would serve her for evermore.[3]

This is a very different setting, a very different kind of writer. So it is no surprise that the image of the Grail, too, is very different. And yet, is there such a gulf between Wolfram's work and that of the French writers? And how much of it is due to him, and how much to a different tradition about the Grail? German writers of the period took the fashionable French romances and indeed lyrics and melodies – and translated, adapted and reinvented them. Wolfram's great predecessor, Hartmann von Aue, adapted two of Chrétien de Troyes' romances, *Erec* and *Yvain* (*Iwein* in German); his versions are masterly, but generally faithful to the shape and form of the originals. If the broad outline remains the same, the concepts of chivalry and social order are transmuted; we shall meet this kind of re-creation in Sir Thomas Malory's use of the French romances in the fifteenth century.

After Hartmann and Wolfram, the third great Arthurian writer in Germany at this time was Gottfried von Strassburg, who took the Anglo-Norman poems about Tristan and Iseult and reshaped them radically, infusing ideas about courtly love which are a world apart from the original fatalistic story of lovers united by a magic potion. What Gottfried does to his original is in terms of distance from the source not dissimilar to Wolfram's reworking, but the style is utterly different. Gottfried is classical, delicate, restrained; Wolfram is boisterous, exuberant and baroque. Gottfried attacks an unnamed poet whom he calls 'friend of the hare', and Wolfram is clearly intended.[4] His hostile characterization of Wolfram's work does nonetheless give us some clues as to what we are in for: 'Inventors of wild tales, hired hunters after stories, who cheat with chains and dupe dull minds, who turn rubbish into gold for children, and from magic boxes pour pearls of dust ... These same story-hunters have to send commentaries with their tales: one cannot understand them as one hears and sees them. But we for our part have not the leisure to seek the gloss in books of the black art.'

Today, in an age which loves magic, Wolfram is a more appealing writer than Gottfried, who takes Chrétien's interest in the psychology of his characters to its ultimate possibilities, at the expense of the action. But Wolfram, for all the exotic surface of his writing, is a match for Gottfried in just such matters as these. Beneath the flourishes and fantasies lies a powerful vision of the ideals by which society and knighthood should be governed: he has built on Chrétien's original concept of a romance, which depicts the development of a knight's mind and character, and made of it a resounding affirmation of the possibilities of the human spirit.

Parzival opens with a lengthy account of the events leading up to the original tale as told by Chrétien. In the French versions of the Grail stories, we learn relatively little of the family of Perceval, of his father's history and of why his mother came to be a widow living alone in a remote place with her son and daughter. Wolfram changes all this, and begins with the exploits of Gahmuret, Parzival's father. Gahmuret is the younger son of the king of Anjou, and on his father's death his elder brother inherits the Angevin lands, while he sets out to find fame and fortune in warfare. It would have been a familiar theme to Wolfram's audience, and it has been argued that the adventures of such younger sons were at the heart of the development of romance and courtly literature.[5]

Gahmuret's quest for fame and fortune takes him to the heathen world, to Babylon, to Arabia itself: Wolfram's exotic fancy is already at work. He becomes the lover of Belacane, the black queen of Zazamanc, by whom he has a son, Feirefiz, 'parti-coloured like a magpie', who grows up to become a great warrior. But by the time Feirefiz is born, Gahmuret has left in secret, in search of new adventures. He returns to the West, where he forsakes Belacane – his marriage to her is invalid in Christian eyes – and is won by Herzeloyde, queen of Waleis, whom he now marries, on condition that he may continue to go tourneying. His brother has died in his absence, so he is also lord of Anjou.

But a message comes from the East that his old ally, the Baruc of Baghdad, has been attacked by the Babylonians, and Gahmuret sets out to help him. The Babylonian leader Ipomedon is burning to avenge himself on Gahmuret, who had defeated him long ago; and one of his knights uses magic to soften Gahmuret's adamantine helmet. It offers no resistance to Ipomedon's spear, and Gahmuret dies on the battlefield. The news comes to Herzeloyde a fortnight before their son, Parzival, is born.

Herzeloyde, although she is ruler of three kingdoms, withdraws to the forest, 'fleeing the world's delights'. From this point onwards, Wolfram's story is, in outline at least, much the same as that told by Chrétien: of how Perceval is brought up in ignorance of the word 'knight', of how he meets three knights in the forest and at once desires to set out in search of knighthood. The emphasis and details may differ – Herzeloyde deliberately dresses her son in fool's clothing in the hope that he will be mocked and will return to her – but the underlying theme, of the innocent making his entrance into the world, is the same. Wolfram rearranges the sequence of the adventures, and adds a scene almost at the outset, in which Parzival encounters his cousin Sigune, who is bewailing the death of her beloved, Schionatulander: from her he learns the story of his family. Parzival rides on to Arthur's court, where he pursues and kills Ither; he rides off in Ither's armour, and comes to Gurnemanz's castle. Here he stays for a fortnight, before riding off in search of adventures, rather than, as in Chrétien, hastening off the next day. The meeting with Blancheflor follows, but Wolfram calls his heroine Condwiramurs, from the French 'conduire amours' – roughly, bringer of love; this is typical of Wolfram's exuberant playing with words.

Parzival now sets out in search of his mother, 'and also in search of adventure', as he tells Condwiramurs. He comes to the Grail castle, which Wolfram names as Munsalvaesche, which could mean either 'the savage mountain' or 'the mountain of salvation'. Parzival is welcomed, and when he has been disarmed, he joins his host, who is in a bed by the fire. No sooner has Parzival sat down than the conversation is interrupted:

There sat many an elegant knight, when sorrow was carried before them. A squire leapt in at the door, carrying a lance – a custom that furthered grief. From its blade blood gushed forth, running down the shaft to his hand, stopping at his sleeve. Then there was weeping and wailing all over the wide hall. The populace of thirty lands would be hard put to exact so much from their eyes! He carried the lance in his hands round to all four walls, and back again to the door. The squire leapt out through it.[6]

An elaborate procession begins: two dazzling ladies bear in golden candelabra, while another pair carry in ivory trestles. Then eight more ladies appear:

See now where other ladies have brooked no delay, four-times-two of them, acting to order. Four carried huge candles. The other four, without reluctance, carried a precious stone, through which by day the sun shone brightly. Its name was renowned: it was a garnet hyacinth, both long and broad. To make it light of weight, it had been cut thinly by whoever measured it for a table-top. At its head the host dined, displaying his opulence. They walked in correct procession straight up to the lord, all eight of them, inclining their heads in a bow. Four placed the table-top upon ivory, white as snow – the trestles that had arrived there before. They knew how to withdraw decorously, to stand by the first four.

On those eight ladies were dresses greener than grass, samite of Azagouc, well-cut, long and wide. About the middle they were squeezed together by belts, precious, slender and long. These eight discerning damsels all wore over their hair an elegant, flowery garland. Count Iwan of Nonel and Jernis of Ril – many a mile, indeed, their daughters had been brought to serve there. The two princesses were seen to approach in most lovely garments. Two knives, sharp-edged as fish-spines, they carried, to proclaim their rarity, on two towels, one apiece. They were of silver, hard and gleaming. Wondrous skill lay therein, such sharpening not spared that they could readily have sliced through steel. Before the silver came noble ladies, called upon to serve there, carrying lights to accompany the silver, four maidens free of reproach.

Thus they all six approached. Hear now what each does: they bowed. Two of them then carried the silver forward to the beautiful table, and laid it down. Then they decorously withdrew, immediately rejoining the first twelve. If I've checked the numbers right, there should be eighteen ladies standing here. *Âvoy!** Now six are seen to walk in clothing that had been dearly bought – half cloth-of-gold, the other half phellel-silk of Nineveh. These and the first six before them wore twelve dresses, of mixed material, bought at high price.

After them came the queen. Her countenance gave off such sheen that they all thought day wished to break. This maiden, they saw, wore phellel-silk of Araby. Upon a green achmardi she carried the perfection of Paradise, both root and branch. This was a thing that was called the Grail, earth's perfection's transcendence. Repanse de Schoye was her name, she by whom the Grail permitted itself to be carried. The Grail was of such a nature that her chastity had to be well guarded, she who ought by rights to tend it. She had to renounce falseness.

Before the Grail came lights. Those were of no small expense, six glasses, long, clear, beautiful, in which balsam burned brightly. When they had advanced from the door in fitting fashion, the queen bowed decorously, as did all the little damsels who carried balsam-vessels there. The queen, devoid of falsity, placed the Grail before the lord. The story tells that Parzival often looked at her and thought: she who was carrying the Grail there – he was wearing her cloak! Courteously, the seven went back to the first eighteen. Then they admitted the most noble amongst them – twelve on either side of her, they told me. The maiden with the crown stood there in great beauty.[7]

With the Grail in place, the company sits down to dinner, and pages 'carried meat and drink to table', while golden cups are handed to the knights.

Now hear a new tale: a hundred squires had been given their orders. Courteously they took bread in white towels from before the Grail. They walked over in unison and apportioned themselves to the tables. They told me – and this I tell upon the oath of each and every one of you! – that before the Grail there was in good supply – if I am deceiving anyone in this, then you must be lying along with me! – whatever anyone stretched out his hand for, he found it all in readiness – hot food, cold food, new food and old too, tame and wild. 'Never did anyone see the like!' – someone or other is about to say, but he'll have to eat his words, for the Grail was bliss's fruit, such sufficiency of this world's sweetness that it almost counterweighed what is spoken of the Heavenly Kingdom.

From elegant golden vessels they partook, as befitted each course, of sauces,

---

* 'Behold!' in medieval French.

pepper, verjuice. There the abstinent and the glutton both had plenty. With great decorum it was brought before them: mulberry juice, wine, red sinople. Whatever anyone reached out his goblet for, whatever drink he could name, he could find it in his cup, all from the Grail's plenty. The noble company was entertained at the Grail's expense. Parzival marked well the opulence and this great mystery, yet out of courtesy he disdained to ask questions, thinking: 'Gurnemanz advised me, in his great and limitless loyalty, that I ought not to ask many questions. What if my stay here turns out like that with him there? Without asking many questions, I'll learn how it stands with this household.'

As these thoughts passed through his mind, a squire approached, carrying a sword. Its scabbard was worth a thousand marks; its hilt was a ruby, and its blade, too, might well be the cause of great wonder. The host gave it to his guest, saying: 'Lord, I took this into extremity in many a place, before God afflicted my body. Now let this be your compensation, if you are not well treated here. You're well capable of carrying it along all roads. Whenever you test its mettle, you will be protected by it in battle.'

Alas that he did not ask then! I am still unhappy for him on that account, for when he took the sword into his hand, he was admonished to ask the question.[8]

When the meal ends, the Grail is withdrawn, and as the ladies go out, Parzival glimpses a very handsome silver-haired old man lying in bed in the chamber into which the Grail is taken.

The tale now reverts to the familiar story: Parzival meets Sigune again, who reproaches him for his failure to ask the question at Munsalvaesche. The adventures leading up to Parzival's encounter with Arthur and his knights follow; when the hideous damsel arrives, Wolfram names her as 'Cundrie the sorceress', and her condemnation of Parzival is couched in spirited and vivid language: but instead of warning of the dire consequences of his failure to ask the question for the Fisher King and his people, she dwells instead on the dishonour to Parzival himself and to his lineage. Parzival sets out despondently in search of the Grail, and when Gawain wishes that God may grant him success, Parzival replies:

'Alas, what is God? If He were mighty, He would not have given us both such scorn – if God could live in power. I served Him as His subject, hoping for favour from Him. Now I'll refuse him service. If He is capable of enmity, that I shall bear.'[9]

The story now turns to Gawain's adventures: he too eventually embarks on the quest for the Grail (not for the lance, as in Chrétien and his continuators). He undertakes this on behalf of king Vergulaht; the latter had been defeated by Parzival in a joust, and had been obliged to swear to win the Grail or to surrender to Condwiramurs in a year's time. Gawain, whom Vergulaht wrongly believes to have killed his father, is sent in his stead as a settlement of their quarrel.

When we meet Parzival again, it is at the hermitage to which his cousin Sigune has retreated: she asks him how he has fared with regard to the Grail, and he tells her of his intense longing to return to Munsalvaesche. She takes back her earlier reproaches, and tells him that Cundrie, who brings her food from the Grail each Saturday evening, has just left. If he is quick, he can follow her tracks back to the Grail castle. But he fails to find the hoofprints, and instead encounters one of the knights who guard the lands of Munsalvaesche, whom he unhorses in a joust. Some weeks later, he encounters a group of pilgrims, and they tell him that it is Good Friday. We are, for the last time, back with Chrétien's original tale, but in Wolfram's version, the exchange between Parzival and the pilgrims is much more intense:

'Sir, I do not know one way or the other how the year's juncture stands, nor how the weeks' count advances. How the days are named is all unknown to me. I used to serve one who is called God, before His favour imposed such scornful disgrace upon me – never did my mind waver from Him of whose help I had been told. Now His help has failed me.'

Then the grey-hued knight said: 'Do you mean God, whom the Virgin bore? If you believe in His humanity, what He on this very day suffered for our sake, as is commemorated on this day's occasion, then your armour ill becomes you. Today is Good Friday . . .'[10]

In Chrétien, Perceval follows the pilgrim's directions that lead him to his uncle the hermit, and 'set off along his path, sighing from the depths of his heart, for he felt he had wronged God, for which he was deeply repentant'.[11] In Wolfram, the mood is much darker:

'If He ever grew well-disposed towards a knight – if a knight ever earned His reward – or if shield and sword may prove so worthy of His help, and true manly valour, that His help may protect me from sorrows – if today is His helpful day, then let Him help, if help He may . . . If God's power is so sublime that it can guide both horses and beasts, and people, too, I will praise His power. If God's skill possesses such help, let it direct this Castilian of mine along the best road for my journey. Then His goodness will indeed make help manifest. Now go as God chooses!'[12]

But before Parzival's horse brings him to the hermit's cell, Wolfram turns to address his audience, and declares how the story came to him on the highest authority:

From him [Trevrizent] Parzival will now learn the hidden tidings concerning the Grail. Whoever asked me about this before and squabbled with me for not telling him about it has won infamy by it. It was Kyot who asked me to conceal it, for the adventure commanded him that no one should ever think of it until the adventure took it, through words, to meet the stories' greeting – so that now it *has*, after all, to be spoken of.

Kyot, the renowned scholar, found in Toledo, lying neglected, in heathen script, this adventure's fundament. The a b c of those characters he must have learned beforehand, without the art of necromancy. It helped that baptism dwelt with him, or else this tale would still be unheard. No heathen cunning could avail us to tell about the Grail's nature – how its mysteries were perceived.

A heathen, Flegetanis, had won high fame by his skills. That same visionary was born of Solomon's line, begotten of age-old Israelite stock, before baptism became our shield against hell-fire. He wrote about the Grail's adventure. He was a heathen on his father's side, Flegetanis, worshipping a calf as if it were his god. How can the Devil inflict such mockery upon such wise people, without Him who bears the Highest Hand parting them, or having parted them from it – He to whom all marvels are known?

Flegetanis the heathen knew well how to impart to us each star's departure and its arrival's return – how long each revolves before it stands back at its station. By the stars' circuit's journey all human nature is determined. Flegetanis the heathen saw with his own eyes – modestly though he spoke of this – occult mysteries in the constellation. He said there was a thing called the Grail, whose name he read immediately in the constellation – what it was called: 'A host abandoned it upon the earth, flying up, high above the stars. Was it their innocence drew them back? Ever since, baptised fruit has had to tend it with such chaste courtesy – those human beings are always worthy whose presence is requested by the Grail.'

Thus Flegetanis wrote of it. Kyot, that wise scholar, began to seek for that tale in Latin books, of where there might have been a people fitting to tend the Grail and embrace such chastity. He read the chronicles of the lands, those of Britain and elsewhere, of France and Ireland. In Anjou he found the tidings.[13]

Parzival reaches Trevrizent's cell, where he is warmly welcomed. He confesses his woes and his sin in failing to worship God; and the hermit's reply dwells on the familiar themes of the fall of man and the redemption through the virgin birth and the grace bestowed by God on mankind. The story of the Grail which follows, however, is entirely unexpected. When Parzival tells Trevrizent of his longing to see the Grail, the hermit answers:

'It is well known to me that many a valorous hand resides by the Grail at Munsalvaesche. In search of adventure they constantly ride many a journey. Those same templars – wherever they meet with grief or fame, they count it against their sins. A combative company dwells there. I will tell you of their food: they live by a stone whose nature is most pure. If you know nothing of it, it shall be named to you here: it is called *lapsit exillis*. By that stone's power the phoenix burns away, turning to ashes, yet those ashes bring it back to life. Thus the phoenix sheds its moulting plumage and thereafter gives off so much bright radiance that it becomes as beautiful as before. Moreover, never was a man in such pain but from that day he beholds the stone, he cannot die in the week that follows immediately after. Nor will his complexion ever decline. He will be averred to have such colour as he possessed when he saw the stone – whether it be maid or man – as when his best season commenced. If that person saw the stone for two hundred years, his hair would never turn grey. Such power does the stone bestow upon man that his flesh and bone immediately acquire youth. That stone is also called the Grail.

Today a message will appear upon it, for therein lies its highest power. Today is Good Friday, and therefore they can confidently expect a dove to wing its way from Heaven. To that stone it will take a small white wafer. On that stone it will leave it. The dove is translucently white. It will make its retreat back to Heaven. Always, every Good Friday, it takes the wafer to that stone, as I tell you; by this the stone receives everything good that bears scent on this earth by way of drink and food, as if it were the perfection of Paradise – I mean, all that this earth is capable of bringing forth. Furthermore, the stone is to grant them whatever game lives beneath the sky, whether it flies or runs or swims. To that knightly brotherhood the Grail's power gives such provender.

As for those who are summoned to the Grail, hear how they are made known. At one end of the stone an epitaph of characters around it tells the name and lineage of whoever is to make the blissful journey to that place. Whether it relates to maidens or boys, no-one has any need to erase that script. As soon as they have read the name, it disappears before their eyes. As children they arrived in its presence, all those who are now full-grown there. Hail to the mother who bore the child that is destined to serve there! Poor and rich alike rejoice if their child is summoned there, if they are to send him to that host. They are fetched from many lands. Against sinful disgrace they are forever guarded, and their reward will be good in Heaven. When life perishes for them here, perfection will be granted them there.

Those who stood on neither side when Lucifer and the Trinity began to contend, all such angels, noble and worthy, had to descend to the earth, to this same stone. The stone is forever pure. I do not know if God forgave them or whether he condemned them from that time forth. If He deemed it right, He took them back. The stone has been tended ever since by those appointed by God to the task, and to whom He sent His angel. Sir, this is the nature of the Grail.'[14]

We learn a little more about 'how matters stand regarding the Grail' in another romance by Wolfram which was to remain unfinished. The fragments are generally known as the *Titurel*, because they open with an account of the history of the Grail given by its first keeper, Titurel, whom Parzival saw lying before the Grail.

'When I received the Grail by the message which the exalted angel sent me, by his high authority, there I found written all my order. That gift had never been given, before me, to human hand. The Lord of the Grail must be chaste and pure. Alas, Frimutel, my gentle son, I have retained only you, of my children, here by the Grail! Now receive the Grail's crown and the Grail, my fair son!'[15]

Trevrizent now turns to the story of Anfortas, the present Grail king and Frimutel's son, as an example of the punishment of pride: for pride is Parzival's besetting sin, the pride which has led him to defy God. The Fisher King in the early French romances is a mysterious figure, and it is only here that we learn what his injury is: as king of the Grail, he has transgressed its rules by serving a lady 'beyond the bounds of wedlock':

'One day the king was out riding alone – that was greatly to the grief of his people – in search of adventure, seeking joy with Love's guidance, compelled to it by Love's desire. He was wounded in the joust by a poisoned spear, so that he has never regained his health, your gentle uncle – pierced through his genitals. It was a heathen who fought there and who rode that joust against him – born in Ethnise, where the Tigris flows forth from Paradise. That same heathen was convinced that his courage would win the Grail. Its name was engraved in the spear. He sought chivalry far afield. It was solely for the sake of the Grail's power that he traversed water and land. By his battle joy vanished from us.'[16]

When Anfortas returned, he was carried before the Grail, and desperate efforts were made to find a cure for his wound, all of which failed.

'We fell in genuflection before the Grail. There we once saw written that a knight was destined to arrive. If his question was heard on that occasion, then our anguish would be at an end. Whether it be child, maid or man, if anyone gave him warning at all about the question, then the question would be of no help, but the affliction would remain as before, and hurt even more intensely. The inscription said: "Have you understood this? Your warning him may lead to disaster. If he does not ask on that first night, then his question's power will disappear. If his question is put at the right time, then he shall possess the kingdom, and our anguish will be at an end, by the authority of the Highest Hand. Anfortas will be cured thereby, though he shall never more be king." Thus we read on the Grail that Anfortas's torment would come to an end if the question were put to him.'[17]

Parzival learns next that the lance which he had seen at the beginning of the Grail procession is the one which had wounded Anfortas: only by placing it in his wound can his pain be temporarily relieved until the question is asked. And Trevrizent also explains about the fellowship of the Grail: how they send out knights to be rulers of lands which have lost their lord, who go anonymously and in secret; and how kings and noblemen ask for the hands of the women who serve the Grail in open marriage.

As Wolfram puts it in *Titurel*, 'All the Grail company are elect, ever blessed here and destined for unfailing fame hereafter. Now, Sigune [Parzival's cousin] was also of that same seed which was strewn abroad in the world from Munsalvaesche and received by those capable of salvation. Wherever any of that seed was brought from that land, there it unfailingly bore fruit, and it also fell as a hailstorm upon wrongdoing.' Herzeloyde herself had been one of the servants of the Grail, and the bearer of the Grail, Repanse de Schoye, is her sister and thus Parzival's aunt. Titurel is his great-grandfather.

The conversation with Trevrizent is the high point of Wolfram's involvement with the nature of the Grail, and occupies most of one of the sixteen books into which his poem is divided. His preoccupation is the Grail itself, followed closely by the idea of a dynasty which serves the Grail and rules through its power, and Parzival's place in this dynasty is now clear. This dynastic vision also explains the first two books which recounted the history of his father Gahmuret.

Wolfram is still following in Chrétien's tracks, however, for he now returns to the adventures of Gawain, which occupy the next five books, and are an elaboration of the episode in the French version of Gawain and the proud lady who scorns his service, even though Gawain is still nominally in search of the Grail.[18] Parzival only reappears at the end of book fourteen, where he fights a duel with Gramoflanz, Gawain's enemy: and Wolfram once more turns to the audience at the beginning of book fifteen, to offer an apology for having delayed the end of the story. But from here onwards, Wolfram is now writing, as far as we can tell, entirely from his own imagination. The next episode brings us back to the theme of Parzival's dynasty. Feirefiz, his parti-coloured half-brother, has arrived in the West in search of adventures, and he encounters Parzival as he rides alone in the forest. A fierce contest ensues, for Parzival has at last met his match. His sword breaks on Feirefiz's helmet,[19] and he is at the stranger's mercy. Feirefiz calls a halt to the combat, even though, as he says, it is clear that Parzival would go on fighting without his sword. He names himself as 'Feirefiz Angevin', and Parzival quickly realizes that this is the half-brother of whom Cundrie had told him long ago when she reproached him for betraying his family honour. Feirefiz and Parzival are reconciled; Parzival's prowess is matched by his half-brother's magnanimity. Feirefiz is brought to Arthur's court, and as they feast in celebration of the newly arrived guest, Cundrie reappears:

'Praise be to you, Gahmuret's son! God desires to grant you grace now! I mean him whom Herzeloyde bore . . . Now be at once chaste and joyful! Hail to you for the high lot that has befallen you, you crown of man's salvation! The epitaph has been read: you are to be the Grail's lord! . . . In your youth you reared sorrow. Coming joy has deceived you of that. You have fought and won the soul's rest, and awaited in anxiety the body's joy.[20]

Parzival, Cundrie and Feirefiz set out for Munsalvaesche, after Parzival has told everyone that ' "no man could ever win the Grail by force, except the one who is summoned there by God". The news spread to every land that it was not to be won by force, with the result that many abandoned the Quest of the Grail, and all that went with it, and that is why it is hidden to this day.' When they reach Munsalvaesche, Anfortas's torments have become more intense than ever; but the question is soon asked, and Anfortas is at last healed. Order is restored and re-established: Parzival is reunited with Condwiramurs, Anfortas yields his place as ruler of the Grail to Parzival, Feirefiz falls in love with the Grail bearer, Repanse de Schoye, and is baptised so that he can marry her. Wolfram concludes with a brief account of the story of Loherangrin, Parzival's son, who is sent as ruler to Brabant, as husband of Elsa, its duchess. As a condition of their marriage, he makes her promise never to ask who he is: but she breaks that promise, and he returns to Munsalvaesche 'into the keeping of the Grail'. And Wolfram ends with a final word as to the authenticity of his tale:

If Master Chrestien of Troyes has done this tale an injustice, Kyot, who sent us the true tidings, has reason to wax wroth. Definitively, the Provençal tells how Herzeloyde's son won the Grail as was decreed for him when Anfortas had forfeited it. From Provence into German lands the true tidings have been sent to us, and this adventure's end's limit. No more will I speak of it now, I, Wolfram von Eschenbach – only what the master said before. His children, those of high lineage, I have correctly named to you, those of Parzival, whom I have brought to where Fortune had, despite all, intended him to go.[21]

The high heroic tone of the ending sharply underlines the difference between Wolfram's version of the Grail and that of the French writers. For this is not a vision of angels, a mystical striving towards the highest religious experience, but the working out of the destiny of an individual within an ordered, ideal society, a society which is a far cry from the civil wars of the Germany of his own day. The Grail is the warranty of Parzival's 'high lineage', the divine symbol of the authority by which his dynasty rules, but the focus is on Parzival himself; he finds fulfilment both in a spiritual goal and in the accomplishment of his ordained fate. The greatness of Wolfram's romance lies ultimately in its warm humanity, his portrayal of the depths of Parzival's despair or the joy and tenderness of his reunion with Condwiramurs and his sons at the end of the tale; it is these images that remain with us at the end of our reading. We began with a portrait of Wolfram the poet as idiosyncratic and highly individual; and his version of the Grail is precisely that.

Epilogue to Part One

These, then are the stories of the Grail as recorded by writers in the half-century between 1190 and 1240. If I have retold and quoted from them at some length, it is because this is the essential documentation for our understanding of how the Grail was envisaged by the authors who created it, and I have tried to do so as impartially as possible, without laying emphasis on points which would favour one interpretation over another. Nor, except in broad terms, do I believe that we can rely on the precedence of one author's version over another.* We must try to stand back and look at the romances as a group, and draw conclusions from the ensemble rather than singling out individual details.

Even in summary and paraphrase, the sheer richness and diversity of the material is impressive: furthermore, it has been claimed, with justice, that the origins of the prose romance itself, and hence – distantly – of our modern novel, lies in these tales:

... the Perceval adventures of the *Conte du Graal* [*The Story of the Grail*] ... give rise to Arthurian prose romance, which is a genre derived in its entirety from the Grail material. Thus soon after 1200 a clear differentiation of purpose is already becoming visible. The prose romances adopt the character of religious quests for which the seeds were sown in the *Conte du Graal*, while the contemporary verse romances avoid any reference to the search for the Grail and the quests are completely devoid of transcendental overtones. The change of direction is symbolized by the use of prose with its reputation for greater truth, which renders it a more fitting medium for treating questions of salvation; it should also be seen as a formal echo of the historical chronicles from which the romances evolved.[1]

These are large issues: why should the new genre of romance aspire to take on the great problems of theology and the highest moments of

---

* A possible but tentative chronology is outlined in Appendix 1.

mystical experience? But they must remain in the background while we turn first to ask our own version of Perceval's Grail question: 'What is the Grail?'

PART TWO

The Nature of the Grail

Apocrypha, Theology, Romance

7

The Grail

All the romances we have examined so far were produced in a relatively short period of time, between 1190 and 1240. These divide into three groups of works and two single romances. The three groups are *The Story of the Grail* of Chrétien de Troyes and his continuators, the work of Robert de Boron, and the anonymous *Lancelot-Grail* cycle. The two individual romances are *Perlesvaus*, also anonymous, and Wolfram von Eschenbach's *Parzival*. We have seen that we have virtually no information about the authors other than what they themselves tell us, and that it is almost impossible to establish a positive chronology, or to say definitely how the different works relate to each other. The results of our quest – for that is the most suitable name for what follows – are therefore going to be hedged about with reservations and qualifications, and there will be few, if any, positive conclusions. Our visits to the Grail castle will be in the role of Gawain or Lancelot, and the certainties of Perceval or Galahad will elude us.

Why was the Grail such an exciting topic for these writers? Clearly there was something about the subject which was both fascinating and inspiring to unleash such creative activity, and if we can shed any light on this we may start to understand what the Grail represents. So let us begin at what is probably the beginning, with Chrétien's version of the story.

In Chrétien, the Grail is first mysterious, and then '*tante sainte chose*', such a holy thing. The initial aura of mystery has been the source of immense speculation, and a huge literature has been created over the years devoted to reading this riddle, and unlocking the 'secret' behind it.* In a sense, what follows is only another such solution. I would argue that the Grail in Chrétien is no more and no less than what he himself says it is. There are no hidden meanings here, no agenda of ritual or symbol or allegory. The

---

* See Chapter 10 below.

most convincing argument for this is that the whole tone of the romance is no different from that of Chrétien's other works, where there is no question of a spiritual or religious dimension, and this scene could be inserted into the adventures recounted in his other tales, *Erec* or *Yvain* or *Lancelot*, with little adaptation. *The Story of the Grail* differs from these earlier romances in that Chrétien is dealing with the psychology of growing up rather than the psychology of love. But it is not a radical new departure, and should be read in the same way as his earlier works, for which no one has proposed a concealed agenda.

Let us try, then, to simply read what the text says. When we first see the Grail, Chrétien makes us see it through Perceval's eyes. Because the procession is a mystery to Perceval, it remains a mystery to us, the readers; we have exactly the same information as Perceval himself, as the brilliant images pass before us. Chrétien dazzles us deliberately by his technique, as Perceval is dazzled by the light of the candles borne before the Grail. At the end of the scene, we are not meant to have recognized anything arcane or symbolic, religious or ritual, in what has happened, but to have seen and not understood, just as the hero of the tale has seen and not understood.

Again, the scene between Perceval and his uncle the hermit is a formidable obstacle for those who would have it that there are arcane meanings in the original Grail procession. The explanations offered by the hermit are straightforward, and those who propose such readings have put forward long arguments to show that this scene is not Chrétien's work but an addition after his death, designed to obscure the original inspiration and meaning of the first Grail scene. There are, indeed, some distinct problems with the explanations given by the hermit: why should there be no discussion of the bleeding lance, and why, if the Grail is so holy and contains the Host, is it borne by a girl when women were allowed no part in the Church's rituals? We can give some sort of answer to the first problem, because the adventure of the bleeding lance is specifically allocated to Gawain. We would therefore expect any explanation of it to be given to him, as indeed happens in the *First Continuation*. The second problem is much more difficult: we can argue that Chrétien does not say that the Grail contains the Host when the girl carries it through the outer chamber. It is therefore merely the receptacle for the Host, and Chrétien may have envisaged a service within the inner chamber at which the Host was consecrated. Such an argument, however, is a perfect example of the special pleading to which most scholars are reduced when confronted with the mystery of Chrétien's Grail.

Let us go back and look at what we are told, rather than what we are not told. The Grail is a dish of some size: the girl uses both hands to carry it, and the hermit, by telling Perceval that it does *not* contain 'a pike or lamprey or salmon' confirms the definition of it as a large dish. A brilliant radiance comes from it, and it is made of gold and decorated with the richest of precious stones. A single Host, by which the Fisher King's father is sustained, is carried in it, and because of this Chrétien calls it 'such a holy thing'.

The key to both scenes seems to me to be imagination. Chrétien's concern in the first scene is to show us how an innocent might misunderstand the conventions of society, as Perceval mistakes Gorneman's instructions not to be inquisitive as an absolute ban on the asking of questions. There must therefore be a scene which demands that a question be asked, and Perceval must fail to ask it. The more striking and mysterious the scene, the more forcefully we will feel Perceval's misinterpretation of Gorneman's words, because we, the audience, are longing for an explanation ourselves; and Chrétien imagines to perfection the kind of apparition which will tantalize and impress the reader. The Grail procession has a very definite function within the narrative of Perceval's education.

In *The Story of the Grail*, despite its title, the Grail is not necessarily, as we have seen, the central point of the story, which has other ends in view. But the combination of the sacred and the mysterious aroused the curiosity of listeners or readers, and ultimately fired someone else's imagination. When we next encounter the Grail, its context has changed dramatically: it no longer figures as an object of mystery in a mysterious romance, but it has become part of the central drama of the Christian faith – the Crucifixion of Jesus. Three voices, each with a very different accent, tell us that Joseph of Arimathea was the Grail's guardian, and that it was the dish from which Christ ate at the Last Supper. Yet, despite their differences, all three accounts stem from the same cultural and geographical area as Chrétien himself, the north-east of France and the borders of Flanders. All three witnesses seem to have had religious connections, though two have secular lords as patrons and dedicatees of their work. And they are all in broad agreement on the description of the Grail.

What we cannot even guess is when and where this sudden change came about. It is remarkable in terms of the general pattern of development of the Arthurian romances, for Chrétien's work was held in the highest regard, and 'he was admired on all sides'.[1] One possibility must therefore be that this vision of the Grail is Chrétien's own, and that he had told the rest of the tale to his friends or followers, and this was to be the crowning revelation and culmination of *The Story of the Grail*. The Grail in this next avatar is indeed 'such a holy thing': but why would a story of this kind strike a particular chord in contemporary society?

First of all, however, we need to look at what we learn about the Grail in the generation after Chrétien. Our first witness – not necessarily in chronological order – is Hélinand, a former poet and frequenter of chivalric society, who became a monk at the Cistercian monastery of Froidmont near Beauvais, and later preached against the Cathars in southern France.[2] As a monk, he did not abandon his poetry, and wrote a powerful condemnation of contemporary society, not in Latin, but in French verse, entitled *Vers de la mort* (Poem of death). This may have been one of the works which made the leaders of the Cistercian order formally condemn 'monks who make rhymes' as the first item of business at their chapter at Cîteaux in 1199. The condemnation was repeated in 1202, but it seems that it was no longer a matter of concern by the time of the next general chapter in 1220. Hélinand turned instead to the writing of history, and provides us with almost the only reference in all medieval scholarship to the Grail, in his chronicle of world history under the year 718:

At this time in Britain a certain miraculous vision of the decurion St Joseph who took down our Lord's body from the cross was shown to a certain hermit by an angel, and of the dish or paropsis from which our Lord supped with his disciples. The hermit wrote down a description of this which is called the story of the Grail. Gradalis or gradale in French means a broad dish, not very deep, in which precious meats in their juice are customarily served to the rich, one morsel after the other in different orders. In the vernacular it is called 'graalz' because men are grateful for it and pleased to eat from it; also because of the container, which is usually silver or some other precious material; and because of the contents, that is, the multiple array of precious foods. I have not been able to find this story written in Latin; but it has been written in French by certain masters, nor is it easy to find it complete, or so they say. I have not been able to obtain it anywhere in order to read it carefully. As soon as I am able to do so, I will translate it into Latin more accurately and usefully.[3]

This incomplete romance – 'nor is it easy to find complete' – could well be Chrétien's own work, except that Chrétien does not mention Joseph of Arimathea. It is only the later group of romances which introduce this idea, and all the accounts associate the dish with Joseph of Arimathea.[4] Hélinand, Robert de Boron, *Perlesvaus* and the *Continuations* of *The Story of the Grail* all agree that the Grail – never defined by Chrétien – is a dish (*vaissel*). Except for *Perlesvaus* and the *First Continuation*, they further identify it as the dish of the Last Supper; Hélinand does not mention it as the receptacle

94

of the holy blood.[5] But what kind of *vaissel* are we dealing with? What exactly is a Grail? Its nature seems to have puzzled an early reader of Chrétien, Wolfram von Eschenbach, whose imaginative description of the Grail we shall study separately, since it is so radically different. In the context of the romances that we are examining, the word is almost always attached to one specific dish, kept at the castle of the Fisher King. But what of its origins as a word? Do these shed any light on its nature?

The word 'grail' is relatively rare in twelfth-century French, but it is not an invention of Chrétien. In the *First Continuation*, it appears in a secular context, when Gawain comes to the Proud Castle and finds there a feast set out, with 'a hundred boars' heads on grails of silver'.[6] Similarly, when Gawain arrives at the Grail castle, he does not immediately realize that the grail which he sees there is *the* Grail for which he is seeking, just as he does not at first recognize the lance which accompanies it, and which is the specific object of his quest.[7] The grail is simply a kind of large platter, in a perfectly normal context, that of a meal or feast, and the word is found in other romances as well as in records of the period, which show that it was in current use. Chrétien's use of the word carries no magical or religious connotation.

The origin of *graal* is disputed. One school of thought derives the word from the Latin *gradale*, which can be found as early as the ninth century, when Bernhard von Werden wrote to the German emperor Lothar II, describing an 'excellent *gradale* from Alexandria',[8] in a context which makes it clear that this is a dish or a cup. The Latin may, in turn, be derived from the Greek word 'krater', a two-handled shallow cup; alternatively, it may come from *garalis*, a receptacle in which the Romans kept *garum*, a fish sauce made from anchovies, which was a basic ingredient of their cookery. *Garum* was expensive, and the *garalis* may have been of glass, with a foot and handles. Other scholars trace *graal* back to *cratis*, a woven basket, which gradually came to mean a dish.[9]

Whatever its ultimate origin, the earliest examples in the vernacular come from Catalonia, whose language is related to that of the south of France. There are references in wills and accounts to *gradals*, which are evidently a kind of dish or cup from the context in which they are mentioned. In the will of Ermengarde, daughter of count Borell of Barcelona, dated 1030, there are 'gold and silver vessels, that is five *hanaps*, two *gradales*, two cups and five spoons'. It also occurs as a French version of the word *gradale*, a gradual or service book containing sung responses or anthems; a *graal* could be a service book, which gives the word another set of resonances.

The word survives in modern French dialect, and it has been suggested that it may have first appeared in French in the area around Troyes, Chrétien's home.[10] Its use for ordinary domestic utensils implies that it is not a memory of Chrétien's 'rich Grail', but derives from an independent source. For our purposes, however, what is important is the clear existence of the word 'grail' outside the courtly context of romance, and there is evidence for its usage from medieval Gascony, Languedoc and Aragon.[11] It is an unusual word, perhaps, but certainly not (as it is sometimes made out to be) the unique creation of the author of *The Story of the Grail*.

There is a list similar to that in Ermengarde's will in one of the *chansons de geste*, *Girart de Roussillon*, written in the southern French dialect in about 1150: here the booty which a knight anticipates from a besieged castle includes 'gold and money, *enabs* and *grasals* and candelabra'.[12] *Enabs* are *hanaps*, a kind of cup, and *grasal* is the dialect form of *graal*. Elsewhere in the romance the same two items are described as 'beaten from gold'. In the *Roman d'Alexandre*, written in Poitou in about 1170, a pilgrim says to his host that 'yesterday I ate with you from your grail', which implies a dish of some size from which at least two people can eat.[13]

On balance, the evidence is that the early usage of the word implies an object of value, even luxury, made from precious metal, its shape being that of a large dish. Chrétien's description of it implies that it is large enough to hold a salmon; this corresponds with the definition in Hélinand de Froidmont: 'a broad dish, not very deep, in which precious meats in their juice are customarily served to the rich, one morsel after the other in different orders', and is confirmed in the *First Continuation*, where two manuscripts substitute dish (*tailloirs*) or platter (*platiaus*) for *graal* in passages where the word *graal* is used for any dish, rather than the Grail which is the object of Perceval's quest.[14]

The Grail in our romances only gradually comes to be called the 'Holy Grail'. Two manuscripts of the *First Continuation* use this phrase when Gawain sees the Grail on his first visit to the castle, but they may have been influenced by later texts.[15] Although at the very outset Chrétien had called it '*tante sainte chose*', it is only in *Perlesvaus* and the *Lancelot-Grail* that the phrase is used regularly. By the time we come to the *History of the Holy Grail* it is almost invariably prefaced by 'holy'. Robert de Boron does not use the phrase, and in the majority of romances, it is far more frequently called 'the rich Grail', from the description in Chrétien's original text, where it is portrayed as studded with the most precious jewels.

The Grail as Chalice

When we come to the work of Robert de Boron, the Grail becomes the dish in which Joseph of Arimathea gathers the blood that flows from Christ's wounds after the body is taken down from the Cross. Could this Grail be a cup rather than a dish? Robert de Boron calls it 'a noble vessel in which Christ made his sacrament'. The Gospel accounts refer to both a cup and a dish at the Last Supper, and *veissel* means vase or vessel; in *The Story of the Grail*, *vaisselemente* is used to mean plates or platters. But the Vulgate or Latin version of the Gospels speaks of the cup as a *calix*. If Robert de Boron had wished to indicate the cup of the Last Supper, he would probably have used the word *calice*.

There is evidence of a changing concept of the Grail in the *Perlesvaus*, most strikingly in Gawain's first visit to the Fisher King's castle, when he thinks that he sees in the Grail 'a chalice, which at that time was a rare sight indeed'. He then has two further visions of figures within the Grail, 'the shape of a child', and, when 'the Grail was high up in the air', a crowned king nailed to a cross with a spear thrust in his side;[16] both of these images, as we shall see, are among the visionary attributes of the chalice of the Mass.

Similarly, the chalice is central to the crucial passage in which the Grail appears to king Arthur when he comes on pilgrimage to visit Perlesvaus after the latter has retaken the Grail castle:

Then the holy and glorious service began. Now, the story tells us that at that time there was no chalice in the land of King Arthur. The Grail appeared at the consecration in five forms, but they should not be revealed, for the secrets of the sacrament none should tell save he whom God has granted grace. But King Arthur saw all the changes,[17] and last appeared the chalice; and the hermit who was conducting the mass found a memorandum upon the consecration cloth, and the letters declared that God wanted His body to be sacrificed in such a vessel in remembrance of Him.[18]

The fact that the final transfiguration of the Grail is the chalice confirms that it cannot have been a chalice at the outset.

In the *History of the Holy Grail*, the author follows Robert de Boron in describing the Grail as a bowl or dish (*escuele*, from the Latin *scutella*); but when we turn to the *Lancelot-Grail*, it is a *vaissel*, and we are told that it is 'in the form of a chalice' (*en samblance de calice*).[19] This almost certainly reflects the different sources of the two stories, for the *History of the Holy Grail*, as we have seen, is among the later romances, while the *Lancelot-Grail* is closer in date to *Perlesvaus*, which also has this ambivalence between a dish and a chalice. In the climactic scene in the *Quest*, when Christ himself gives the knights communion, the author specifically explains that the Grail is 'the dish from which Jesus Christ ate the lamb with his disciples at Easter', changing from the word *vaissel* back to *escuele*. And what is in the Grail is not the communion wine but the Host; the description of the scene is quite explicit about this. We have come full circle, back to Chrétien: the Grail contains the Host. Yet if the Grail can be 'now the chalice, now the patena, now the ciborium', it is always intimately related in form to the sacred vessels of the Mass.[20]

So the Grail evidently has powerful religious connotations, but what are its actual functions? In *The Story of the Grail*, as we have seen, it is simply a temporary container for the sacred Host; but from this ambiguous beginning it actually becomes part of the Mass and the centre of its own religious service. In *Perlesvaus*, Gawain encounters 'the service of the Holy Grail' before the Grail is even described, and the Grail in this romance is always associated with a chapel within the Fisher King's castle; even when it appears at a feast, it is brought from a chapel which adjoins the hall.[21] Yet it is not a relic kept in a shrine to be worshipped at will: the Grail comes and goes of its own accord, and only when Gawain sees it in the hall is it carried by a girl. Even this scene, with its attendant angels, is liturgical in tone. Likewise, in the *Lancelot-Grail*, there are scenes with liturgical overtones: Bors' nocturnal visit to the Grail begins with the appearance of 'a white-haired man dressed like a priest but without any chasuble' who carries the lance, and when he sees the Grail itself: 'upon the silver table was the Holy Grail, covered with a piece of white samite, and before the table was a kneeling man, dressed like a bishop'.

These hints of a special liturgy of the Grail anticipate the climax of the *Quest*, the last appearance of the Grail at Corbenic and the final scene in the 'spiritual palace' at Sarras. As we would expect, these concluding images are foreshadowed in the *History of the Holy Grail*. Josephus puts on his vestments and goes before the holy vessel to celebrate Mass, 'as he was accustomed to', before king Mordrains is blinded for looking into the Grail; and at the end of the *History*, king Alphasan sees 'the Holy Vessel sitting on a silver table; in front of it was a man he did not know, who looked like a priest when he is saying Mass'.[22]

Even in the *Quest* itself, until we reach the achievement of the adventures, the description of the liturgy is always qualified and uncertain, because the final vision has not been attained: in Lancelot's partial revelation at Corbenic, he sees 'an aged man in priestly vestments' in front of the Grail, who is 'engaged to all appearance in the consecration of the mass'.[23] It is only when Galahad, Perceval and Bors reach Corbenic that the full liturgy and the mysteries are revealed. Josephus celebrates Mass using the Grail and the Holy Lance; the blood from the lance runs down into the Grail, and from it Josephus takes a Host, which gradually becomes flesh. He returns it to the Grail, and completes the Mass, before telling the knights to sit at the Grail table. He vanishes, and the liturgy is concluded by a naked man who emerges from the Grail, and gives communion to Galahad and the others. He is not named as Christ, but he speaks of 'My mysteries and My secrets'. The Grail liturgy is therefore represented as the ultimate celebration of the Mass, in which Christ Himself, rather than his surrogate, the priest, recreates his own sacrifice.

A striking feature of the Grail ceremonies in the *Quest* and in the *History of the Holy Grail* is that they are always carried out by attendant angels; only the celebrant is human. The theme is also found in *Perlesvaus*, where Gawain sees first two and then three attendant angels before he has his dramatic vision of the Crucifixion within the Grail.[24] This may simply be a creation of the writer's imagination, but there are distinct parallels in the liturgy of the Eastern Church, where the hymn which is sung as the Host is prepared for consecration is called the *Cherubikon*, and refers to 'the King of the world who comes escorted by unseen armies of angels'.[25] It is perhaps an echo of this which lies behind the story told by Martin, a Cistercian abbot, who brought back precious relics from Constantinople in 1205, a year after the Western crusaders had seized the city, for his abbey at Pairis in Alsace. On his journey back, he had a vision which he later recounted to a fellow-monk:

He was not asleep, but was most certainly awake, and saw two angels where the sacred relics were kept ... These angels seemed to perform the divine office with marvellous devotion around the reliquary in which the holy gifts of God were kept, and praised God with all reverence ...[26]

The 'holy gifts' certainly included a fragment of the True Cross, but possibly also one of about a dozen relics of the Holy Blood which were looted at this period.[27] The idea of the presence of angels at Mass is very unusual in Western Christianity, and is only rarely mentioned. Guillaume Durand, a French bishop who wrote the classic text on the 'rationale of the divine offices' in the late thirteenth century, notes that the congregation does not say 'Amen' at a certain point; he says that this is because 'the angels, who always assist [at Mass] reply'.[28] Visual images of the angelic liturgy are almost unknown in the religious art of the West; the most striking example is in fact an illumination in a copy of the *Quest* written and decorated by Pierart dou Tielt at Tournai in 1351 (Plate 10, p. 107 below).[29]

The Grail as Source of Healing

The Grail does not always appear in a religious context, of course: in *The Story of the Grail*, it ambiguously contains a holy object but in the context of a secular feast. It can be both an agent of healing and a provider of food in these secular scenes. In the *Lancelot* section of the *Lancelot-Grail*, before the adventures of the Grail have really begun, the Grail appears three times as an instrument of healing. After Gawain's disastrous night in the Palace of Adventures, he sees the Grail again: its arrival is heralded by a violent storm, and it is accompanied by sweet odours and 'voices which sang together more sweetly than a human heart can imagine, or earthly language describe'. He is dazed from the wound he has received from a magic lance and from a fight with a mysterious knight; but when the song ends and the Grail is taken back by the girl who bears it, 'he felt as strong and healthy as if he had never had any pain or injury'.[30]

Towards the end of the *Lancelot*, there are two further instances. Perceval does battle with Ector, Lancelot's brother, because they fail to recognize each other, and both nearly kill each other. Severely wounded, they have not even the strength to reach a nearby hermitage for the last rites; but

when they were in such danger and anguish that they thought they would truly die, they saw a great brightness coming toward them, as if the sun were descending upon them, and they were mystified as to what this might be. They looked and saw a vessel made like a chalice and covered with white samite; it was preceded by two censers and two others followed it, but they could not see who carried them or who was holding the vessel. Nevertheless, the vessel seemed to be a holy thing, and they hoped for so much virtue from it that they bowed down to it, despite all the pain they were suffering. And immediately such a wondrous thing befell them that they felt hale and hearty, recovered from their wounds.[31]

Ector tells Perceval that what they had seen was the Holy Grail; 'Our Lord has revealed many great miracles for its sake.'

Likewise, when Lancelot goes mad after discovering that king Pelles' daughter, once again disguising herself as Guinevere, has tricked him into sleeping with her for a second time, he is healed by the Grail:

... the king had him taken to the Palace of Adventures; they left him there all alone, thinking that, as soon as he came into the palace, Lancelot would be cured by the power of the Holy Grail and would regain his memory. And it happened just as they thought, for when the Holy Grail came into the palace, as was its wont, Lancelot was cured at once ...[32]

This healing power of the Grail is evoked once in the *Quest*, in the strange episode in which a knight is healed at a remote chapel in a deserted land, while Lancelot is unable to move throughout the appearance of the Grail.

If the Grail can restore life, it can also sustain it: the Grail is a miraculous source of nourishment, as its secular meaning, a serving-dish, implies. The question which comes to Perceval's mind, seeing it for the first time – but which he fails to ask – is 'Whom does the Grail serve?' It feeds the ailing king in Chrétien's version, on a single Mass wafer. But then we come to the *First Continuation* of *The Story of the Grail*, which has given rise to a great deal of scholarly speculation. The Grail performs a miracle when Gawain comes to the Grail castle, and feeds the assembled company. In two of the three versions of this text, the Grail supplies bread and wine:

Then he saw the rich Grail enter through a door, which served and put bread swiftly before the knights everywhere. Then it put wine in great cups of fine gold, as a butler should serve it according to his duty, and set them on the tables before the lords and their followers.[33]

When this is done, the Grail serves the feast to the assembled knights, moving among them of its own accord to do so. It is possible that the idea was taken from Chrétien's original account of the Grail feast, which tells us that each time a course was served, Perceval saw the Grail pass back through the room; the presence of the Grail was misread as being the source of the food, when, in fact, the text makes no such connection. If anything, the implication is that the mysterious recipient of the contents of the Grail is served by the Grail each time more food is brought to the diners in the hall. The constant reappearance of the Grail also reinforces the picture of Perceval's refusal to ask about it.

Yet this is only one aspect of the Grail's powers, for when Gawain tells his son Guinglain of his adventures in the Grail castle in the *Second Continuation*, he omits this magical feeding, and recounts only the procession of lance, sword and Grail, which comes and goes as the knights are at table.[34] But Gawain also tells Guinglain that the sight of the Grail 'greatly comforted me' (*molt me reconfortoie*).

The first appearance of the Grail in the *Lancelot-Grail* again takes up the idea of the Grail's ability to provide food magically. In a scene which echoes the *First Continuation*, Gawain comes to the Grail castle and sees the procession; but here he is distracted by the beautiful girl who bears the Grail and thinks only of her, without revering the Grail itself. When it distributes its miraculous favours, everyone save Gawain is provided 'with all the delightful nourishment that one could describe. The hall was filled with delicious odors as if all the spices in the world had been scattered there.'[35] The Grail feast is repeated for Lancelot and Bors when they come to Corbenic; both pay due reverence to the Grail and are fed with 'all the fine foods in the world'.[36] The feast is no longer a simple marvel, but a kind of preliminary test, distinguishing between the sinful and the pious. Lancelot can only be distracted from piety by the thought of Guinevere, and Bors is one of the chosen Grail knights; but Gawain is unable to resist the temptation of indiscriminate lust.

In the *Quest*, the Grail appears at Arthur's court at the Whitsun feast, and feeds the assembled company without making any distinction between them. But the atmosphere is quite different: there is no Grail bearer, and before it appears, there is a brilliant radiance and 'the people inside seemed to have been illumined by the grace of the Holy Spirit'. The Grail enters and fills the room 'with fragrance, as if all the spices of the earth had been spilled abroad';[37] the phrase is an echo of the biblical 'Song of Songs'. And the Grail provides the food that each of the company 'most desired'.

There are two interwoven strands of thought here: the Grail as provider of earthly food, and the Grail as a spiritual presence, rejecting sinners and providing grace. Only in the *First Continuation* is there no spiritual element at all to the feast when Gawain reaches the Grail castle; and yet later in this scene Gawain learns that the lance which appears as soon as the feast has ended is the one used at the Crucifixion. The scene at Arthur's court in the *Quest* has strong echoes of the Grail's appearance in Robert de Boron, where it is a provider of grace: it does not feed the followers of Joseph of Arimathea, but the contemplation of its presence eliminates the need for physical food. When Joseph institutes the Grail table and places the Grail on it, it offers spiritual comfort – 'the sweetness and the fulfilment of their hearts' – just as the sight of it had offered '*reconfort*' to Gawain. And the Grail 'will allow no sinner in its presence'; those who have sinned are excluded from participation, just as Gawain is not fed by the Grail in the *Lancelot-Grail*. At the achievement of the quest, the two themes merge into one: when the Grail knights receive communion at Corbenic, the Host becomes 'the holy food, which they found so honeyed and delectable that it seemed as though the essence of all sweetness was housed within their bodies'.[38]

The role of the Grail as a source of food is therefore not merely magical and material. Only in the *First Continuation* does it fulfil this function without any associated spiritual overtones, and even there the context is one in which Gawain learns of the spiritual background to his personal quest for the bleeding lance. The usual portrayal of the Grail is as both a source of material food and of spiritual comfort, and is closely associated with the gift of divine grace. In most cases, those who lack divine grace and are in a state of sin are not allowed to participate in its feasts or to approach it; the extreme case is in *Perlesvaus*, where the Grail does not even appear to Lancelot because of his sinful love for Guinevere. The Grail may provide for physical needs, but it only does so for those who are pure in spirit.

8

The Setting of the Grail

Arthurian romance contrasts the ordered world of the castle with the mysterious forest of adventures outside it; the Grail clearly belongs within the castle. It almost always appears in the hall of a castle, usually when a feast is taking place. It is usually taken into an adjoining room, which has all the characteristics of a chapel, though we can never be sure whether this is really consecrated ground. Exceptionally, it appears outside these contexts as part of an adventure: at the chapel in the deserted land when Lancelot cannot rouse himself when it appears, and in the forest when it heals Perceval and Ector. Mysterious and brilliant lights reveal its presence in the forest when Perceval is in search of it, and it is present in a deserted chapel where a huge black hand appears and extinguishes all the candles.

Within the castle, the Grail appears in one of two ways. It is either carried in procession, or it moves of its own accord: 'no mortal hand was seen to bear it'. The Grail in procession occurs primarily in Chrétien's poem and the *Continuations*. Here, it is always carried by a girl, usually described as being of exceptional beauty. It is accompanied by the lance which bleeds from its tip, carried by a boy or squire, by a girl carrying a silver *tailleoir* or carving-dish, and by boys bearing candlesticks. These details vary only slightly; in one instance the lance is carried by a girl, and in another there are two silver dishes. The images so brilliantly depicted by Chrétien are preserved intact to the end of the *Continuations*, but there are additions, related to new adventures associated with the Grail: after the Grail procession in the *First Continuation*, a dead knight on a bier and a broken sword are carried through the hall, and the broken sword alone reappears within the procession in the *Second Continuation*.

When the Grail procession is described in other romances, the details are remarkably similar. In *Perlesvaus*, the Grail and lance appear when Gawain is at the Fisher King's castle, carried by two girls but accompanied by angels with candles, and none of the other accoutrements. The *Prose Perceval* has an unexpected variation, in that the Grail is carried by 'uns vallés', a boy, accompanied by another boy with the lance and a girl with two *tailleoirs*; and one manuscript, which calls the Grail 'the vessel in which our Lord's blood was placed', describes it as being accompanied by 'the worthy relics', implying that both the lance and the dishes have a sacred history. The Grail itself is totally different in *Parzival*, and will be discussed separately for this reason: but the Grail procession is not so radically different, though Wolfram gives us a far more lavish description of the event: the lance is present, but the function of the procession is to set up the tables and to light the hall where the feast is to be held. The *tailleoirs* are transmuted into *mezzer*, two keen-edged knives, and the half-dozen figures of Chrétien's procession are replaced by twelve girls on either side of the Grail-bearer herself.

In *Lancelot*, by contrast, the procession is reduced to the single figure of the beautiful girl, who comes and goes alone on the three occasions when the Grail appears in the hall at Corbenic, to Gawain, Lancelot and Bors in turn. At the beginning of the *Quest*, however, when the Grail appears at Arthur's court, it is self-moving, and the atmosphere is not that of a simple feast, but has strong overtones of religious visitations: there is a clap of thunder, a brilliant light, and the participants are struck dumb. Similar echoes recur in the scene at Corbenic, when a fiery wind, like that at the first Pentecost in the 'Acts of the Apostles', precedes the Grail's appearance.

9 *The Holy Grail appears at Pentecost at Arthur's court. Although the text clearly says that it was covered in white samite, and that no one could see who carried it, the artist has only observed the first detail; the monk who is the Grail-bearer is his invention. From an early fourteenth-century Flemish manuscript.*

As the story progresses, so the signs and marvels that accompany the Grail increase in grandeur.

In almost every case where the Grail appears in procession, it is accompanied by the lance which bleeds from the tip. The two objects are inextricably associated, and it is only in Robert de Boron's *Joseph of Arimathea* and in the *Lancelot-Grail* that the Grail appears alone. In the scenes at Corbenic, the lance is part of the liturgy of the Grail. Since Gawain and Lancelot, as sinners, can only see this ceremony imperfectly, it is not until Bors has a clearer vision of it that the lance appears. Bors is told that it is the 'avenging lance', but that Galahad alone will be able to discover its secrets. And in the final scene at Corbenic, when the full liturgy of the Grail is celebrated, lance and Grail appear together. The Grail procession in these romances is reduced to a single figure, perhaps to heighten the focus on the Grail itself; but even so the lance is still a vital element in the ceremonies of the Grail. The presence of the lance, and the identification of the Grail as a relic of the Passion, are the two most consistent features of the central ritual. The two objects are so inseparable that even in Wolfram von Eschenbach's radically different version, the lance survives, despite the total transformation of the Grail itself.

Adventures Associated With the Grail

Although the achievement of the Grail is the supreme adventure in itself, there are other adventures associated with it. When a sword is given to Perceval by the Fisher King at his first visit to the Grail castle in *The Story of the Grail*, Perceval's cousin prophesies that it will break at a crucial moment. Two writers actually tell us that Perceval broke the sword: in Wolfram, it fails him in his battle against his half-brother at the end of *Parzival*, and Gerbert de Montreuil describes how he shatters it on the gates of the Earthly Paradise. But the idea of a broken sword as one of the keys to the achievement of the Grail remains a leitmotif. It appears in the *First Continuation*: here, after the Grail procession has passed, ending with the dead knight and the sword, the king has the sword fetched and challenges Gawain to mend the blade. If he can do so, he will learn the secrets of what he has just seen. His failure to do so means that he 'has not yet achieved enough as a knight to be able to know the truth about these things'. The test of the mending of the sword is applied to Perceval at the end of the *Second Continuation*: he is more successful, but 'just by the join there remained a very small notch'. Although Perceval is the best knight living in combat or in battle, he is not yet endowed with all the necessary qualities to learn the secrets. The sword is finally mended at the end of Gerbert de Montreuil's *Continuation*, and at the opening of the *Third Continuation* Perceval learns what he desires to know.

The adventure of the broken sword is a theme originally introduced by Chrétien, who probably intended it as a symbol of Perceval's imperfections as a knight. But in the *Continuations* it is used as a narrative device, to delay the conclusion of the story and to allow the storyteller to embark on a new series of adventures. In the *Third Continuation*, once Perceval has been told about the mysteries, the story is linked back to the dead knight whom Gawain had seen at the end of the Grail procession. This leads to a new topic – that of avenging the dead knight's slayer, on whom the sword had been broken. In Gerbert's version, the notch shows that yet again Perceval is not ready to learn the story of the Grail, and the adventures continue as before.[1]

10 *The chosen knights behold the service of the Grail, conducted by bishop Josephus. At the right, two angels bear in the covered Grail and the spear. In the following central scene the Grail is revealed as a chalice, with the naked Saviour emerging from it; the spear is beside it. From a manuscript written at Tournai in 1351.*

The association of a sword with the Grail reappears in *Perlesvaus*, where Gawain is told that he can only take part in the Grail service if he is able to acquire and bring to the Grail castle the sword with which John the Baptist was beheaded. This leads to a relatively brief and self-contained quest on Gawain's part, in which he is eventually successful. The sword is seen as an addition to the collection of relics kept at the Grail castle, and may also reflect Gawain's role in the story as the forerunner of Perceval, just as John the Baptist was the herald of the coming of Christ. This is an imaginative addition to the story in line with the strong religious element in *Perlesvaus*.[2]

Likewise, in *Lancelot*, which is primarily a romance of adventures, the Grail becomes the focus for a set of such events. At the Grail castle itself, adventures are given a much more important role with the addition of the Palace of Adventures. Most of the episodes are in the style of the supernatural encounters in the *Continuations* of Chrétien, such as the story of the deserted chapel lit by a single candle which is suddenly extinguished by a huge black hand, or the mysterious tree in the forest illuminated by a thousand lights, which are extinguished when Perceval approaches it. In *Lancelot*, the Palace of Adventures contains the Bed of Marvels: when Bors sits on it, he is first wounded by a flaming lance which moves of its own accord, and then, in his weakened state, is forced to do combat with an unknown armed knight, who renews his strength by retreating into the chamber where the Grail is kept. He is then bombarded by arrows and crossbow bolts, and attacked by a lion. This is the last of Bors' trials; he watches a combat between a leopard and a dragon, and meets a harper, who sings the 'Lay of Tears' which tells of Joseph of Arimathea's coming to Britain. Finally, the Grail service begins, and Bors is healed of his wounds. Gawain's adventures are similar, and in both cases the Palace of Adventures represents a kind of test: Bors emerges with honour, even though he is prevented from approaching the Grail, while Gawain, who has failed to honour the Grail at the feast on the previous evening, is dragged out by unseen hands and tied to a cart, on which he is carried out of the castle. Spiritual failure leads to physical punishment.

The Grail Question

The most crucial of all the Grail adventures is, however, not a physical challenge, but a test of a very different kind. When Perceval comes to the Grail castle in *The Story of the Grail*, the crux of the scene is his failure to ask about the mysterious procession which he witnesses. Afterwards, he learns from his cousin that he should have asked why the lance bled and where the Grail procession was going; later in the romance the hideous messenger rephrases this as 'nor did you ask what worthy man was served from the Grail that you saw'. This question is reshaped in the *Continuations*, but the gist of it remains the same – that the answers concern, not the nature of the Grail (to which Chrétien provides an answer in the scene between Perceval and the hermit) but its purpose and destination. Likewise Gawain, whose story runs parallel with that of Perceval, must ask about the ceremonies because he is in search of the lance. When he is told that he has not yet achieved enough to know about these things, the king promises information about 'the Grail and the lance and the bier', so that the question must include all these elements. In the *Second Continuation*, where the bier is absent, Perceval asks about 'the Grail which has passed before us twice, and also about the lance that bleeds . . . tell me as well about the broken sword . . .' In the *Third Continuation* Perceval says, 'let me not be deceived about the lance and the Holy Grail and the trencher that I've seen: if you will, tell me first who is served from them, and where they come from . . .'

The service of the Grail – 'whom does the Grail serve?' – is the abiding question in the other romances, in the *Prose Perceval*, *Perlesvaus* and *The Elucidation Prologue*. In the *Prose Perceval*, the question concerns all the elements of the Grail procession: 'who is served by these things which I see carried here?'[3] In *Perlesvaus*, the question is apparently limited to the Grail. The most curious comment is from *The Elucidation Prologue*, where Perceval 'asked by whom the Grail is served, but did not ask why the lance bled nor about the sword of which half was missing . . . nor about the great disappearance'.[4] Finally, in *Parzival*, the question is initially undefined – Wolfram insists simply on Parzival's failure to *ask*, to put the *question*: 'sît ir vrâgens sît verzagt!' (since you refrained from asking), repeating constantly the word *vrâge*, question. When we at last come to the final scene, Parzival simply asks Anfortas, 'oeheim, waz wirret dir?' (Uncle, what troubles you?).[5] The question is not about mysteries or objects, but is a straightforward declaration of human sympathy; Wolfram has elaborated the significance of the question in Chrétien, where Perceval's failure to ask it is due to the selfishness he has not yet outgrown: his concern is with what others will think of him if he breaks what he believes to be the rules of polite society. Here, the same self-centred attitude leads Parzival to quell any interest in the sufferings of his host.

So the original question is not a single question: there are at least two questions to be asked, one about the Grail, the other about the lance. If we remember that Chrétien has two heroes, one seeking the Grail and one seeking the lance, this fits the plot perfectly. It also implies that the Grail's role in the story is not unique, and it reminds us how difficult it is to read *The Story of the Grail* without some degree of hindsight. There is one other aspect which points to the fact that Chrétien's imagination is the driving force here. There are many stories in folklore and literature which revolve round the finding of an answer to a question, but stories where the crux is the *asking* of the question in the first place are rare in the extreme. I have not as yet been able to find any satisfactory parallel for this daring leap of invention, for such it must be.[6]

It is from the Grail question that the Grail quest develops. When Perceval first comes to the Grail castle, he is not looking for the Grail; his quest for it begins when he realizes what he has lost, and what he has failed to do. *The Story of the Grail*, *Perlesvaus*, the *Prose Perceval* and *Parzival* all have this in common: Perceval is in search of a place he has once found, and a situation which he has once experienced. In the *Lancelot-Grail*, the quest is very different. It is external, announced by divine powers, as part of the grander scheme of the fortunes of the kingdom of Logres. Arthur's creation of an almost ideal earthly kingdom is recognized by heaven when the Grail appears in his court, but the intrusion of the spiritual world destroys earthly harmony instead of co-existing with it. The quest is a search for the experiences which the Grail offers; the knights treat it as another adventure, but quickly realize that there are spiritual dimensions to it which lie beyond the bounds of earthly chivalry. But it is nonetheless an archetypal chivalric quest – a vow to leave the safety of the castle walls and to undertake the search for a physical object or person through whatever hardships may befall. The concept of a chivalric quest is far from unique to the Grail, and in *The Story of the Grail* the lack of any spiritual dimension at the outset is underlined by the parallel of Gawain's quest for the spear. Perceval may have the spiritual qualities of an innocent, but Gawain is entirely worldly, and undertakes his quest for worldly motives, to defend himself against an unjust accusation of murder.

The Spiritual Journey to the Grail

In *The Quest of the Holy Grail* and the last chapters of *Lancelot* which form a prelude to it, we have left behind the orthodox world of chivalric romance. The tone of the story is beginning to change with the appearances of the Grail. In the normal course of the events of a chivalric quest, marvels and wonders may befall the hero, but they are, so to speak, part of the scenery of romance, designed to captivate an audience, and with no greater significance than to underline the heroic stature of the protagonist. Once the Grail enters the story, another register becomes apparent, since the episodes centred on the Grail carry both a literal and a spiritual meaning. Since this meaning is deliberately obscure and veiled, the meaning – *significatio*, to use the medieval term – must be explained; and this is usually done by the hermits who come to populate the story almost as much as the knights. Immediately after Gawain's visit to the Grail castle, he arrives 'at the abode of a hermit who was called Hermit Segre', an appropriate name for the first of the line of holy men who expound the secrets of the tale.

Segre explains the significance of part of his experiences: interestingly, given that Gawain is the least spiritual of those who come to the Grail castle, he only learns the meaning of the vision of a serpent attacked first by a leopard and then by small serpents, which is a foreshadowing of king Arthur's death. This is not religious, but is a parallel to Arthur's own symbolic dream of the wheel of fortune and of his own death in the English romances. And at the end of *Lancelot*, it is a hermit who tells Arthur that Galahad will come to court at Whitsun, and 'will put an end to the adventures of the Holy Grail'.

When we come to the *Quest* itself, Gawain is told by another hermit that 'the adventures which are happening now are the meanings and manifestations (*senefiances et demostrances*) of the Holy Grail; these signs will never appear to sinners or men surrounded by sin'.[7] The Grail began as part of the story of a knight's progress to maturity, in Chrétien; it was reinvented as a journey to the achievement of worldly perfection in Wolfram; and in its final avatar, it stands as the symbol of the ultimate spiritual perfection. But Perceval, as a recognized figure in the Arthurian stories, with his history of failure in the original Grail quest and his early sins, was not seen as a suitable hero for this new story. So Galahad is introduced to supersede, but not to replace, him; and again this entails a shift in the emphasis of the story. The strength of the earlier romances was that their heroes were fallible, even though they might triumph in the end. Here, Galahad is the predestined hero, a less sympathetic and somewhat ethereal figure, who appears and disappears throughout the story so that the tale often becomes a quest, not for the Grail, but for Galahad, the Grail hero.

If our interest and sympathy is often with Bors, Perceval, or Lancelot, whose encounters are much more human, and frequently more dramatic, Galahad too has to pass the tests placed in his way. Interestingly, Galahad's tests are largely physical, such as the moment when he sits in the empty seat at the Round Table, the Siege Perilous, and is not destroyed like the knights who have previously essayed this test. It is Perceval and Bors who bear the brunt of the spiritual tests, because Galahad is beyond temptation. These are dramatic temptations, in the shape of a fine black horse which appears when Perceval is in need of a mount, but carries him off in a wild charge until he remembers to make the sign of the cross; or of a beautiful girl who tempts him into her bed in a rich tent, from whom he only escapes by seeing his sword on the ground which reminds him to cross himself – at which the tent vanishes and the devil flies off, crying and roaring. Other adventures are more subtle in their imagery, and have to be explained by the ever-present hermits. But throughout all this, the concept of a spiritual quest has entirely replaced that of the secular quest. Failure is possible, and powerfully portrayed, as in the case of Lancelot, whose love for Guinevere debars him from the last stages, even though his secular prowess carries him further than any other knight save the three elect. We hesitate as to whether Perceval and Bors will make their way through the devil's entrapments to fulfil their destiny; but there is never any doubt about Galahad.

Just as the story has moved from a secular to a spiritual plane, the Grail is no longer a mere relic, a physical object with sacred associations, but a symbol of spiritual powers. It is a sign in the definition of St Augustine: 'that which shows itself to our outward senses, and which shows beyond that something to the spirit'. What, then, does it signify? Ector, Lancelot's brother, has a vision in which he sees Lancelot trying to drink from 'the most beautiful spring he had ever seen', which disappears before his eyes. He learns (from a hermit) that Lancelot, as a sinner, cannot drink from it even though the 'waters of this spring will never fail, however much one draws from it: it is the Holy Grail, it is the grace of the Holy Spirit'.[8] The Grail is thus raised to the pinnacle of the spiritual world. But it has been claimed that the symbolism goes further than this: 'immaterial, omnipresent, surrounded by celestial beings, it is all powerful and possessed of miraculous grace: it is the symbol of God'.[9]

Within the Grail

So far we have been looking at the external aspects of the Grail. We know that, according to most of our authors, the Grail originally held the blood of Christ; but what does it now contain? Chrétien tells us that it holds a single Host; but what lies within it is not physical, but spiritual. The Grail is a gateway to the spiritual world, a physical focus for the metaphysical. In *Perlesvaus* a succession of images present themselves to Gawain as the Grail procession passes through the hall. As he gazes at it, he 'thought he saw therein a chalice, which at that time was a rare sight indeed'. He sees two angels bearing candlesticks, who become three; and when the Grail returns, he thinks he can see a child in it. It passes before him for a third time, and 'it appeared to him that the Grail was high up in the air. And above it he saw, he thought, a crowned king nailed to a cross with a spear thrust in his side.' These are specific images of the Mass and the Crucifixion, even though none of the events takes place in a chapel, but in the hall where the knights are at table. Later in *Perlesvaus*, Arthur sees the Grail itself go through a series of transformations, the 'five forms' which are the secrets of the sacrament, 'and last appeared a chalice'. Similarly, at the end of the

Quest, Christ himself appears to the twelve Grail knights: 'Then the companions, raising their eyes, saw the figure of a man appear from out of the Holy Vessel, unclothed, and bleeding from his hands and feet and side . . .'

These are external visions, and in a sense the appearance of the Grail as a self-moving, unsupported object, which is one of its most frequent attributes, must also count as a form of vision. Its nocturnal appearances in the *Lancelot-Grail*, accompanied by angels and mysterious hieratic figures, are also visionary, but these are visions of the outward mysteries of the Grail. Lancelot approaches the Grail too closely, and is punished for his presumption, but although he later describes what he sees as 'no earthly but a spiritual vision', what the romance tells us is that he has seen the Grail ceremony, but not its mysteries.

The object of the quest, the knights' dearest wish, is to see the Grail itself, openly and in plain view. From the beginning, the Grail is mysterious, veiled: on its first appearance in *The Story of the Grail*, we are told that Perceval sees it 'entirely uncovered', as if it was normally concealed from men's eyes. The sight of the Grail is a blessing in *The Romance of the History of the Grail*. It is because the Grail is covered when it appears to Arthur's knights at Whitsun that the quest begins, with Gawain declaring his intention never to return to court 'until I have looked openly upon the mystery we have glimpsed this day'. And it is the sight of the Grail that is forbidden to sinners, both to Lancelot in *The Quest of the Holy Grail* and to Nasciens and Mordrains in *The History of the Holy Grail*. At the very end of the story, most versions lay emphasis on the Grail's withdrawal from this world in words similar to those of *The Quest of the Holy Grail*, 'that no man since has ever dared to say he *saw* the Holy Grail'.[10]

Yet there is one last ultimate vision, foreshadowed in the *History of the Holy Grail*: Mordrains, converted from paganism, is desperate to see what lies *within* the Grail, and despite a voice which warns him not to go any closer, 'he had already gone so close that no tongue could name what he saw nor mortal heart conceive it'. He is punished for his temerity by being paralysed, but in answer to his prayer he is granted life until 'the good knight, he who is to see the marvels of the Holy Grail' comes to him. When Galahad, 'the good knight', has indeed come, and has healed Mordrains, he rules as king of the spiritual palace at Sarras for a year. At the end of that year, he and his companions go to the Grail, where the Mass of the Virgin is celebrated by a man in the vestments of a bishop, who proves to be Josephus, son of Joseph of Arimathea. At the climax of the Mass, Josephus calls Galahad to come forward, and uncovering the Grail chalice, says:

11 Christ (robed as a bishop) gives the sacrament to Galahad at Corbenic, at the end of the Grail quest. From a northern French manuscript of The Quest of the Holy Grail, c. 1290.

'Come forward, servant of Jesus Christ, and look on that which you have so ardently desired to see.'

Galahad drew near and looked into the Holy Vessel. He had but glanced within when a violent trembling seized his mortal flesh at the contemplation of the spiritual mysteries.[11]

Words falter and fail: '. . . now I see revealed what tongue could not relate nor heart conceive. Here is the source of valour undismayed, the spring-head of endeavour; here I see the wonder that passes every other!' Galahad prostrates himself before the Grail, and dies; the Grail itself vanishes heavenwards. This is a revelation that transcends and ends mortal things.

We have reached the *ne plus ultra* of our explorations, and it is time to turn back, to the physical attributes of the Grail. These, in summary, are as follows: in shape it is a dish or chalice, and only the words *graal*, *vaissel* or *calice* (or their equivalent forms) are used to describe it. It is called 'rich', and, more rarely, 'holy'. It may be embellished with precious stones, and emit a brilliant radiance. It is either carried by a girl or moves of its own accord. In Chrétien, it holds a single Host; it is subsequently treated as having contained the blood of Christ, and as being a relic of the Crucifixion. It is accompanied by other objects – a platter and a lance which bleeds. In some instances, it is a magical source of food. It is a focal point of adventures, adventures which are either in the orthodox mould of chivalric romance or which carry a symbolic and religious meaning. We can describe the Grail;

but what do we know of its history? The paradox for us is that the Grail romances are not religious works, but secular and chivalric: they do not pretend to be devotional. To the agnostic Western mindset of the twenty-first century, it is difficult to envisage a world where the secular and religious merge so easily; but if we are to understand the origins of the Grail, it is precisely this world that we must explore.

9

Obscure Histories, Dubious Relics

The Biblical Background: Joseph of Arimathea and Longinus

For the medieval reader, both Grail and lance had biblical origins. All the romances insist on this, with just one exception: Chrétien himself. Grail and lance are clearly described as relics of the Passion, and there is nothing to contradict the possibility that this lack of identification in Chrétien's text is simply the result of his failure to finish his story.

The prologue to *Perlesvaus* neatly sums up the central facts about the Grail and lance and their place in the story of the Crucifixion.

Joseph . . . for seven years had been a soldier of Pilate; and he asked no reward for his service but permission to take the body of Our Saviour from the cross . . . Pilate granted Joseph the body of Our Saviour, supposing that when he had taken it from the cross he would drag it shamefully through the city of Jerusalem and leave it in some foul place outside; but the good soldier had no such intention: rather did he honour the body as highly as he could, laying it to rest in the sacred tomb; and he kept the lance with which Christ's side had been pierced and the holy vessel in which those who believed in Him and feared Him gathered the blood which flowed from His wounds when He was nailed to the cross.[1]

We learn in the *Prose Perceval* and the *First* and *Third Continuation* that the lance was wielded by a soldier named Longinus;[2] although he is usually anonymous, we shall see how details of his legend are reflected in the depiction of the lance.

The romance versions of the Crucifixion story rest on a fairly slender biblical basis. When we turn to the Gospels themselves, the role of Joseph of Arimathea is modest. He appears briefly in the three Gospels which give a similar account of Jesus' death, the 'synoptic' Gospels, where he is called 'an honourable counsellor' (Mark 15:43) or 'a rich man of Arimathea'

(Matthew 27:57). Matthew tells us that 'he also himself was Jesus' disciple'. John, who gives a different version, adds that Nicodemus helped Joseph of Arimathea to bury the body in traditional Jewish fashion. That is all that we learn. The spear figures in John's Gospel: 'one of the soldiers with a spear pierced his side, and forthwith there came out blood and water. And he that saw it bare record, and his record is true' (John 19:34–5).

The Christians of later centuries were not satisfied with this simple narrative, and a number of elaborated versions of the Gospel began to circulate.[3] The New Testament as we know it evolved over a period of time; at one point even the Gospel of John and the 'Book of Revelation' were rejected, while at another moment we find in some of the earliest surviving bibles books included which are almost entirely forgotten today, such as the *Epistles of Barnabas* and *Clement of Rome*, and the *Teaching of the Apostles*. Among the less authoritative works were the extended narratives of the Passion, such as the very early *Gospel of Peter* (c. AD 150) and the *Acts of Pilate* or *Gospel of Nicodemus*, written towards the end of the fourth century.[4] This was a hugely popular book, translated into every language in Europe from a Latin translation made in the fifth century: one such translation was incorporated entire into the late Arthurian romance known as *The Book of Arthur*.[5] The Latin text itself exists in over four hundred manuscripts and in three main versions; the translations were often free, and incorporated both new, imaginative material and details drawn from the Gospels. It was highly regarded, and it was still occasionally taken as authentic: a bible made for Richard II places *Nicodemus* after St John's Gospel and before the 'Acts of the Apostles'.[6] It is with the *Gospel of Nicodemus* that we are chiefly concerned, as it relates the events after the Crucifixion in much more depth.

The story it tells is as follows: the Jews seize Joseph of Arimathea after he has buried Christ when he reproaches them for having him put to death. Joseph is thrown into prison in a windowless house, the doors of which are sealed. But when the Jews open the seals the next day, proposing to kill him, there is no sign of Joseph. Nicodemus (who is portrayed as one of the leaders of the Jews but at the same time a secret disciple of Christ) suggests that they send messengers in search of both Joseph and Christ, since there are reports that Christ has been seen in Galilee. Joseph is found, but not Christ, and when Joseph returns to Jerusalem, he gives an account of how Christ had appeared to him in prison, and had released him. The *Gospel of Nicodemus* ends with the questioning of three rabbis who have witnessed the ascension of Christ into heaven; they are examined by Annas and Caiaphas, the high priests, who assert that they have seen Christ crucified at the place of a skull and two criminals with him; and he was given vinegar and gall to drink, and Longinus the soldier pierced his side with a spear. Our honourable father Joseph asked for his body . . .[7]

This is the first time that Longinus is named, and the popularity of the *Gospel of Nicodemus* made his story a familiar one. It was well established by the ninth century in ecclesiastical tradition, and was to be found in writers of the time such as Bede, Rabanus Maurus and Notker.[8] Furthermore, it was cited by the poets of the *chansons de geste*, the half-historical poems about famous deeds of war which preceded and overlapped with the early romances of chivalry in the mid-twelfth century. In six instances, these texts insist on a detail which exactly corresponds to Chrétien's description of the Grail procession: the blood which issues from the tip of the spear runs right down to the hand of the person who carries it. Longinus and the boy who appears in the procession share the same experience.[9] This comes from a version of the legend of Longinus in which Longinus is blind: he is given the spear by a Jewish onlooker, who guides him as he strikes Christ in the side. When the blood runs down the spear to his hand, he puts his hand to his eyes, and is cured of his blindness, only to realize the enormity of what he has done.[10] This motif is taken up in the twelfth-century religious play *Resurrection du Sauveur*, probably written in England or Normandy. It is difficult to avoid the conclusion that Chrétien was thinking, consciously or unconsciously, of the Holy Lance of this legend.

Robert de Boron derives most of his material on Joseph of Arimathea from the *Gospel of Nicodemus*,[11] but he then continues to use the same text or group of texts. He tells the story of the emperor Titus' son, Vespasian, who is cured by the sight of an image of Christ belonging to a poor woman named Verrine, or Veronica, which Pilate sends to Rome. This derives from a work often found as a continuation of the *Gospel of Nicodemus*, the *Healing of Tiberius*. Veronica had encountered Christ on his way to the Crucifixion, and had lent a cloth for Christ to wipe his face; when she took it home, she found a miraculous image of Christ on the cloth. The story has little to do with Joseph of Arimathea and the history of the Grail, though it motivates Vespasian's attack on the Jews as a result of which Joseph and his followers leave Jerusalem.[12] Its importance lies in the fact that this is the history of yet another relic of the Crucifixion. In effect, two-thirds of *The Romance of the History of the Grail* is taken up by the legends surrounding two of the great relics of the Crucifixion.[13]

In *Perlesvaus*, two other such relics are invoked: the Crown of Thorns appears in the guise of the Circle of Gold, which is worshipped in the castle of that name. When Lancelot asks 'What golden circle is that?', he is told that it is the 'crown of thorns . . . which the Saviour of the world wore on His head when He was nailed to the cross. The queen of this castle has set it in gold and precious stones . . .' It will be won by the knight who first saw the Grail, i.e. Perlesvaus.[14] And at the Perilous Cemetery, Perlesvaus' sister obtains a portion of Christ's winding sheet, without which Perlesvaus cannot reconquer the Grail castle.[15]

The crucial difference between the story of Joseph of Arimathea in the *Gospel of Nicodemus* and in Robert de Boron's version is the addition of the Grail to the account of Joseph's burial of Jesus, and its description as the vessel in which he collected Christ's blood. We know that no source actually names the Grail as a vessel with these sacred associations before Robert de Boron (leaving aside Chrétien de Troyes and the question of the Host contained in the Grail); but was there perhaps an intermediate version of the story of the burial of Christ, which introduced the theme of the collection of the holy blood without specifically describing the vessel in which it was gathered? There is no written evidence of this, but if we look at the visual imagery of the period, it seems very likely that such a tradition existed.

12 *Joseph of Arimathea collects Christ's blood in the Holy Grail when Christ's body is taken down from the cross. From a manuscript finished by Arnulf de Kai at Amiens on 27 August 1286.*

Visual Images of the Crucifixion

The archetypal image of the Crucifixion, even at the end of the Middle Ages, is that of Christ on the cross flanked by the Virgin and St John.* But as the apocryphal stories gained in popularity, so we find a more complex composition, with a number of figures surrounding the cross, and here the spear or lance with which Christ's side was pierced became an important visual element. The figure of Longinus piercing Christ's side with the spear is balanced by the soldier offering a reed with a sponge soaked in hyssop to relieve the agony; and there are other additions to the traditional scene. Origen, writing a commentary on Matthew's Gospel in the fourth century, interprets Longinus' blow as equally merciful, intended to put an end to Christ's suffering, and the piercing of Christ's side with the spear therefore represents the moment of His death. A series of ivory tablets adopt this iconography, which may go back as far as the fifth century. It is particularly prevalent in Irish depictions of the Crucifixion, and with the spread of Irish artistic influence on the Continent, it became popular in Carolingian art. It is found in later miniatures as well: it becomes one of the standard representations of the Crucifixion. Sometimes, indeed, there are only three figures shown, and Longinus and the second soldier, known in apocryphal stories as Stephaton, replace the Virgin and St John.

This brings us to a second theme of vital importance to our investigations: images of the Crucifixion which show a chalice in which blood is collected. Before these versions, we find the Crucifixion portrayed with a chalice which is often simply on the ground at the foot of the cross; it is often impossible to tell whether the cup of the Last Supper is intended, or whether it is the container for the draught of gall offered to Christ before the Crucifixion – or even for the vinegar which he is later given. Once the artist shows Christ's blood flowing into the cup, which either floats unsupported or is on the ground, we can be certain that the chalice of the Mass is intended. Examples of this image occur from the ninth century onwards.[16] We also find the 'chalice of salvation' held up by an unidentified figure (possibly King David), as in the Utrecht Psalter illustration to Psalm 115, from Reims in the mid-ninth century; in this case he is holding the paten or chalice cover in the other hand.[17]

But there is a further stage in this iconographical trail. In the next version, there is a symbolic figure, often labelled *Ecclesia* (The Church), standing next to Longinus or appearing alone, who collects Christ's blood as it flows from

---

* See Appendix 2 for a discussion of the visual images.

13 The Crucifixion, with a small unidentified figure at the foot of the cross holding a cup, into which Christ's blood flows: a typical late example of this visual theme. From a mid-thirteenth-century missal from Westphalia.

14 One of the earliest known illustrations of the collection of Christ's blood at the Crucifixion. A miniature from the mid-ninth-century Utrecht Psalter in which an unidentified figure holds out a chalice into which the blood flows.

the wound into a cup which she holds up. The figure of *Ecclesia* is fairly widespread, appearing in late Carolingian art, particularly in the eleventh century, and may have origins in Byzantine art. The surviving examples imply that it was an accepted part of the iconography of the Crucifixion.[18]

One highly unusual representation shows neither *Ecclesia* nor Longinus;

15 A more developed form of the theme of the Crucifixion and the holy blood,
with symbolic figures instead of the usual group of Mary and the disciples.
Ecclesia, representing the Church, holds a banner in one hand and the chalice in
the other, while the Synagogue, symbol of the law of the Old Testament, is shown
blindfolded at the right. Enamel plaque from Hildesheim, c. 1170.

instead, there is a small female figure with a halo at the foot of the cross,
with a dish into which Christ's blood flows. It is difficult to relate this
personage to any known narrative or iconography of the Crucifixion; the
nearest parallel is the symbolic depiction of Christ crucified by the virtues,
which occurs in later medieval art. It does, however, echo the account in
two of the *Continuations*, in which Joseph collects the blood which runs
down from Christ's feet as he hangs on the cross.[19]

A final stage reverts to the simpler three-figure Crucifixion; but instead of
Mary and John, we have *Ecclesia* on the left with her cup, and *Sinagoge*,
the synagogue, a blindfold figure representing the Jewish faith, turning away
in confusion on the right. These two figures are the New Law and the Old
Law in person, of which *Perlesvaus* has so much to say. And the last
metamorphosis of this image is to be found in the Romanesque art of
Catalan churches, where *Ecclesia* and the Virgin Mary have become the
same person, and the Virgin herself holds up the mystic cup.

The importance of these images for our present purpose is that we have in
them a woman holding a cup or dish in which Christ's blood is being
collected, and the figure of Longinus. Both figures have close parallels in the
Grail procession. This is not to argue for a simplistic equation of the girl

bearing the Grail with the figure of *Ecclesia* in the Crucifixion scenes; it merely points to a visual source which could have been familiar to the writers who were elaborating on Chrétien's original imagery. Equally, this is visual evidence for the alternative Grail tradition, found in the prologue to *Perlesvaus*, in which the blood of Christ is not collected by Joseph of Arimathea at the Deposition, but is gathered by anonymous hands at the time of the Crucifixion.

. None of these images of the Crucifixion from religious manuscripts shows Joseph of Arimathea himself. It is only the illuminators of the manuscripts of the Grail stories who add him to images of the Crucifixion and Deposition, which otherwise rely closely on the orthodox iconography. He is portrayed collecting the blood from Christ's feet at the Crucifixion in a chalice in three instances, and in other images the dish of the Last Supper is used for the same purpose (Plates 12–16).

However, there is one surviving manuscript which seems to relate very closely to the legend of Joseph in the *Gospel of Nicodemus*. It is from the abbey of Weingarten, near Lake Constance in South Germany, and it is based on a splendid gospel book from England, which was given to the abbey by Judith of Flanders soon after 1100. The magnificent images in the English gospel book inspired the creation of other manuscripts in the same style at the abbey, and it is one of these manuscripts, another gospel book written perhaps twenty-five years after Judith's gift, which contains an illumination of the Deposition. This miniature is the first evidence in Western Europe of a tradition that the blood of Christ was collected when his body was taken down from the cross. It shows the Deposition (Plate 16), with two men taking Christ's body down from the cross, while a figure to the right collects the holy blood in a chalice. It is possible that this figure is St John, and that the image derives from the verse in St John's Gospel in which John asserts that he himself had seen the blood and water come out of Christ's side.[20] The attributes are not those normally associated with St John, and it may be that Longinus is intended. It is unlikely to be Joseph of Arimathea, since he and Nicodemus would almost certainly be the figures in the centre supporting the body and removing the nails.

This is as close as we get to a link between the *Gospel of Nicodemus* and the Grail itself, repeatedly described in the romances as the receptacle into which Christ's blood was gathered at the Deposition. Because of the date of the miniature, this must represent an earlier tradition, independent of the Grail romances. As we have seen, the Grail is intimately linked with the Crucifixion and its relics, but it is chiefly identified with the relic depicted in the scene from the Weingarten gospel book, that of the Holy Blood. For the

16 Miniature from an early twelfth-century Gospel book from the abbey of Weingarten, south Germany, showing the Deposition from the Cross. To the right, an unidentified figure collects Christ's blood in a chalice. This is the first evidence for the tradition that the blood was collected at the Deposition; it pre-dates Robert de Boron's story by nearly a century, and comes from an abbey with a special interest in the Holy Blood, which was one of its most precious relics.

actual blood of Christ was believed to survive in medieval Europe, and it is to the cult of relics, and especially those of the Holy Blood, that we now turn.

Relics of the Crucifixion

The power of religious relics is difficult for us to understand today; they lie in the dusty recesses of cathedral treasuries, in hideously elaborate containers displaying almost invisible fragments of this or that saint. Today, most relics are part of a lost past, revered only by a handful of the faithful. But in the Middle Ages relics were immensely powerful images, for which a king's ransom might literally be paid.[21] In the early Christian Church, relics were physical reminders of the deeds of saints and martyrs: in particular, the bodies or ashes of the early Christian martyrs were venerated as memorials of their sacrifice for the faith. There was also a belief that a spiritual power emanated from such objects, which helps to explain why they were so eagerly sought after: a text survives which is said to have been written by a group of martyrs before their execution, begging that their remains should not be scattered throughout the world.[22]

From attributing spiritual power to relics, it was a short step to endowing them with the power of physical healing; and this was – and is – one of the principal motives for religious pilgrimage: to seek a miraculous cure at the tomb of a saint when all else has failed. To some extent, relics of the saints became the focal points for the local pagan worship which Christianity had swept aside: the saints dispensed the same favours as the pagan deities, healing the sick, granting prayers through their intercession with Our Lord, striking down those who questioned or challenged their authority.

Relics were keenly sought after by both religious institutions and lay patrons, not only for their intrinsic power, but for the benefits in terms of pilgrims or prestige which they could bring.[23] When the distinguished historian William of Malmesbury wrote his account of the abbey of Glastonbury in about 1135, he not only described its foundation and past, but was at pains to record the vast quantity of relics which the abbey possessed. He goes on to list about thirty saints, and concludes:

Many relics too, [were] carried from the kingdom of Northumbria at the time the Danes were waging war there. Others were brought from Wales, when it was being persecuted, to Glastonbury, as though to a storehouse of saints.[24]

The most spectacular example of the acquisition of a relic by a lay patron is that of the Crown of Thorns, which St Louis brought from Constantinople in 1239, by paying off the debts which the Byzantine emperor owed to the Venetians. For this he built the Sainte-Chapelle in Paris, which was part of his royal palace, and is one of the masterpieces of early Gothic architecture, a casket in stone to house the precious trophy.

The beginnings of the cult of relics dates back to the third century AD. The early pilgrims to Palestine had been shown the sites of the Gospel and Old Testament stories, and were soon bringing back relics associated with the Gospel and particularly with the Passion. The mother of the emperor Constantine, Helena, is said to have gone to Palestine in search of the True Cross in about 326, and later legends say that she did indeed find it. This, the greatest of all relics, was very much in the public eye when the Grail romances were being written. The fragment of the True Cross belonging to the kings of Jerusalem had been lost in spectacular fashion to the Saracens at the disastrous defeat at the Horns of Hattin in 1187. It had been a tradition of the royal house that the True Cross was carried into battle; it was used as a talisman at the battle of Ramleh in 1103, within two years of the establishment of the Christian kingdom of Jerusalem after the First Crusade. In almost every major engagement in the following decades the

Christian army was blessed by its presence. But when Saladin overwhelmed the largest force the crusading kingdoms had ever assembled at Hattin, the True Cross fell into his hands. The recovery of the True Cross was one of the main themes of the preachers who sought to inspire the launching of a new crusade in 1189–90.

The lance of Longinus played an even more dramatic role in the history of the Frankish expeditions to the East. It was at a desperate moment in the fortunes of the First Crusade in 1099 that this lance was found during the siege of Antioch: St Andrew appeared in a vision to a poor crusader, Peter Bartholomew, and showed him its hiding place in the cathedral. Bartholomew's story was received with some hesitation, but after further visions, an excavation took place, and he was able to produce the spear triumphantly from the trench. The effect on the crusaders' morale was crucial, and an unexpected victory over the Turks followed.

But there were also cooler heads who did not take such events at face value, notably the leader of the expedition, Adhémar, bishop of Le Puy.[25] He had very probably seen the Holy Lance, clearly identified by its owners as that used by Longinus, in the possession of the Byzantine emperors. This lance was kept in the imperial palace chapel of the Virgin of the Pharos, with the other great relics of the Passion, including pieces of the True Cross discovered by St Helena, a phial of the Holy Blood, and the Crown of Thorns. Constantine Porphyrogenitus, the Byzantine emperor who wrote a treatise on the ceremonial of his court in the mid tenth century, tells us that the lance was venerated on Good Friday.[26] The Greeks referred to this as a lance while the weapon found at Antioch was described by them as a spear, which might be used for throwing as well as thrusting.

In the following days, other crusaders recollected having seen it at Byzantium, and the outcome was disastrous for Peter Bartholomew. When the authenticity of the lance was questioned, he offered to undergo an ordeal by fire. Holding the lance, he walked through a narrow passage of flaming logs, but emerged so burnt that he died of his injuries. This finally discredited the lance as a relic in the eyes of all but a handful of crusaders. The whole episode, with its plethora of attendant saints appearing to different members of the First Crusade, underlines their eagerness to believe in the relic. In doing so, they ignored not only the lance at Byzantium, but also the existence of yet another holy lance among the regalia of the Holy Roman Empire. The emperor Heinrich II had acquired this relic from Rudolf of Burgundy in 926; it was regarded with such reverence that one of the great lords of the imperial court was deputed to guard it.[27] And further to the east, the Armenians claimed to have the holy lance at Echmiadzin, near Erivan at the foot of Mount Ararat, though this is not recorded until the thirteenth century.[28]

One of the Grail romances has a positive obsession with relics. *Perlesvaus* may omit the lance of Longinus, but it brings in two other major Crucifixion relics: the shroud of Turin and the crown of thorns. The crown of thorns ranked with the fragment of the True Cross in importance, perhaps because the holy lance was a contested relic. It was of course pledged by Baldwin to the Venetians in the 1230s, and finally acquired by St Louis, who built the Sainte Chapelle to house it. There is however a discrepancy between the actual relic and the desciption in *Perlesvaus*. St Louis' crown of thorns was encased in crystal, while in the romance the crown is generally referred to as 'the Circle of Gold' because, as the author explains, its owner has had it 'set in gold and precious stones'. Perceval is crowned with it towards the end of the story. Such gold crown-reliquaries containing a thorn or thorns from the crown of thorns were relatively common in Flanders.

The other relic which is specified in *Perlesvaus* is the shroud in which Christ is wrapped, and the writer probably had in mind the famous shroud imprinted with Christ's image, now at Turin. The shroud was almost certainly at Byzantium in 1204, because Robert de Clari describes the cloth kept at the imperial chapel as bearing the imprint of Christ's features, and no other shroud of this type is recorded. The episode of the Perilous Cemetery is unusual in that it is Perceval's sister, not a knight, who undertakes the adventure. She tells Perceval that she must obtain a piece of the cloth which covers the altar in the chapel of the Perilous Cemetery if her enemies are to be vanquished. 'It is a most holy cloth, for it was the sheet that shrouded God in the sacred tomb, when he returned from death to life on the third day.' The relics in *Perlesvaus* are the major relics of the Crucifixion, and they also correspond to the famous collection of such relics in the imperial palace at Byzantium.

The Cult of the Holy Blood

The Grail is presented in the romances as the most charismatic of all the relics of the Crucifixion. Robert de Boron describes it as both the dish of the Last Supper, and the vessel used by Joseph of Arimathea to collect Christ's blood at the Deposition. Other writers, notably in the *Continuations* of Chrétien, take a simpler view and make it only a dish in which our Lord's blood was collected at the Crucifixion, either by unknown hands (as in the *First Continuation* and *Perlesvaus*), or by Joseph himself. All are agreed that the relic subsequently comes into Joseph's possession.

In the *Lancelot-Grail*, although the *History of the Holy Grail* gives the full version of the story, the Grail is usually regarded simply as the dish of the Last Supper, and there is only one isolated reference to its role as a receptacle for Christ's blood.[29] In the *Quest*, where the spiritual inspiration is at its greatest, the Grail becomes less and less a material object, and it is only in the climactic scene at Corbenic that we learn from Christ himself that it is 'the dish in which Jesus Christ ate of the paschal lamb with his disciples'.[30]

The Grail is, therefore, consistently identified with either the relics of Christ's blood or with the vessel used by Christ at the Last Supper, or with both. The cult of the Holy Blood is one of the major influences on the Grail stories, and it is to this that we now turn.[31]

One of the earliest records of a relic of the Holy Blood comes from Mantua, where a relic was discovered in 804. This is reliably recorded in a contemporary imperial chronicle, but it seems to have been lost again, as it was rediscovered in 1048.[32] An account of how the relic came to Mantua was written around 1200, and tells us that it was Longinus who brought it to that city. Part of the relic was given to the emperor Heinrich III after its rediscovery, and he in turn gave it to count Baldwin V of Flanders. It was inherited by his daughter, Judith of Flanders, who gave the relic of the Holy Blood to the abbey at Weingarten at the beginning of the twelfth century.[33] Such at least was the tradition at the end of the twelfth century; Judith's will makes no specific mention of the relic, though she certainly bequeathed four 'shrines', as well as the great gospel book which we have already mentioned.* Hence the earliest illustration of the Holy Blood being gathered in a cup at the Deposition comes from an abbey which housed a relic of that same blood.

Another early relic of the Holy Blood was nearby, at Reichenau on Lake Constance, reputedly sent to Charlemagne by Azan, prefect of Jerusalem; the relic survives, with a Greek inscription: 'Lord, help Hilarion Tzirithon, deacon and abbot of your monastery'. The Tzirithon family are recorded among the Byzantine nobility in the ninth century, and the relic was certainly at Reichenau by the time of the emperor Otto the Great, who endowed lights and lamps for the shrine where it was kept.[34] Although the Reichenau relic was much revered, there do not appear to be any substantial medieval legends associated with it.

The opposite is true of the Holy Blood at Fécamp in Normandy, where there is a multiplicity of often conflicting stories. These are again of great

* See p. 123 above.

interest to us, in that they are all securely dated before the Grail romances. Around the beginning of the twelfth century, the monks composed the *Liber de revelatione* (Book of Revelation) in order to claim exemption from the jurisdiction of the archbishop of Rouen; this document claimed that the abbey was founded before the existence of the archbishopric, and was therefore entitled to privileged status. In the *Liber de revelatione*, a miracle of the Holy Blood is recorded, which tells how the priest of a neighbouring parish, named Isaac, saw the wine that he had just consecrated turn into blood; the blood was preserved at Fécamp.[35]

At some later date, possibly as early as 1120, Baudri de Bourgueil, bishop of Dol in Brittany, refers to the presence of this relic at the abbey: '*custodia sanguinis Domini Iesu, humati à Nicodemo, ut testatur B.Ioannes, de membris recollecti*' ('guardian of the blood of Lord Jesus, buried by Nico-demus, as the blessed John bears witness, collected from his limbs').[36] Once again this is crucial evidence for a tradition that the collection of Christ's blood was associated with the Deposition and Entombment before the Grail romances were written. It is difficult to tell from this reference whether Baudri is merely elaborating in reverent fashion on the description of the Holy Blood, or whether he knows a different version of the legend. However, later in the century, just such a version appears. According to this, Nico-demus, when he helped Joseph of Arimathea to place Christ's body in the tomb, collected the clotted blood from his wounds and preserved it carefully. When he died he gave it to his nephew Isaac; a voice from heaven told him to seal it in lead, and put it in the trunk of a fig tree, which he was to throw into the sea. The fig tree was washed up in Normandy, and the place was called *Ficus campus* (the field of the fig tree), which became Fécamp in Norman French. The abbey was founded at the place to which the fig tree was brought, and the relics were rediscovered by Richard I, duke of Normandy, who had them concealed in a round pillar near the altar of the Holy Sacrament.

This version of the legend evidently post-dates the year 1171, for it would have been extraordinary for the duke to *conceal* relics of such importance rather than displaying them for general admiration. In 1171, however, the abbot of Fécamp, Henri de Sully, announced the rediscovery of the relics, and they were put on public view. It is reasonable to date the new version of the history of the relics to the years just after this 'rediscovery', probably between 1187 and 1200.[37]

The whole story has its echoes on the other side of the Channel, and there are some very surprising points of contact. After the Conquest, Glastonbury Abbey was put under the charge of a Norman abbot, who caused a riot, in which several monks were killed, by replacing the traditional Gregorian chant with that of William of Fécamp. In 1126, Henry of Blois was appointed abbot, and it was he to whom William of Malmesbury dedicated his history of Glastonbury, a document whose purpose was to prove that Glastonbury was such an ancient foundation that it owed no duty to later foundations such as Canterbury. The purpose of the book, and the spirit behind it, was very similar to that of the monks of Fécamp when they composed their treatise thirty years earlier. More interesting still, Henri de Sully, abbot of Fécamp when the rediscovery of the relics was announced, was the nephew of Henry of Blois. And another, apparently unrelated, Henry of Sully was abbot of Glastonbury in 1191 when the bodies of king Arthur and Guinevere were discovered there. The tactics of the two monasteries are remarkably similar; perhaps there were, after all, personal connections.

Although neither the legend from Fécamp nor the Weingarten miniature specifies that it was Joseph of Arimathea who collected Christ's blood, there is a striking element in both which is absent from the original apocryphal gospels, but present in the work of Robert de Boron: the idea that the Holy Blood was collected at the time of the Deposition.

The relic of the Holy Blood which has most often been associated by scholars, albeit tentatively, with the history of the Grail is the most famous of all, that at Bruges. Traditionally, the Holy Blood relic at Bruges was brought from the Holy Land by Philip of Flanders' father, Thierry of Alsace.[38] A late medieval inscription on his tomb at Watten recorded that he 'visited the Holy Land four times, and on his return brought with him the Blood of our Lord . . .',[39] and late medieval chronicles give a precise date for this event, either 1148 or 1150. However, the earliest evidence of the presence of this important relic at Bruges is no earlier than 1256, and despite the loss of the early records of the chapel of St Basil where it was housed, it is clear that the story about its acquisition by Thierry is a later invention. Even though we would expect the acquisition of such an important relic to have left some record in the Flemish annals, we know nothing of its history. There is just a possibility that if the story of the origin of the Holy Blood at Weingarten is correct, part of the relic belonging to Baldwin V of Flanders was retained by Baldwin VI, and that Judith of Flanders inherited only part of the original, which she then bequeathed to Weingarten. This is plausible; but since we cannot even prove for certain that the Weingarten relic did indeed come from Judith, it must remain a speculation, particularly in the absence of any mention of the relic at Bruges before 1256. If we could prove it, it would then mean that Philip of Flanders, Chrétien's patron, had a strong interest in a topic that was later to be central to the Grail stories; and it might explain why the *Continuations*, also written for the house of Flanders, refer to this aspect of the legend.

The Bruges Holy Blood is much more likely to have been one of the many relics of the Holy Blood which came to the West following the conquest of Byzantium by the Fourth Crusade. In the first decade of the thirteenth century, a vast number of relics had found their way to the West when the crusaders brought back their booty from the sack of that city; among the pillagers were no fewer than six Cistercian abbots. It is not beyond the bounds of possibility that one of the motives for diverting the crusade to Byzantium was the acquisition of the rich holdings of relics preserved there.[40] These are emphasized in contemporary descriptions of the capital of the Eastern Empire: the Byzantine emperors had been masters of Palestine since the days when Christianity first became the official religion of the Roman Empire, and most relics of interest which could be procured there found their way to Byzantium. However, the relic of the Holy Blood at Byzantium has an obscure history. It was almost certainly acquired by the emperors at some time between 1099 and 1150, but its origins are unknown. Once it was installed in the palace chapel of the Virgin of the Pharos, its presence there was widely advertised by the imperial court. So we find both the Holy Blood and the Holy Lance in the same chapel at the same time. Robert de Clari, describing the conquest of Byzantium in 1204, was astonished by the wealth of relics to be found in this one place. The pillagers of the imperial city seem to have multiplied the relic of the Holy Blood successfully: the doge of Venice, Enrico Dandolo, sent back such a relic almost immediately, and other relics reached Soissons, Pairis (in Alsace), Halberstadt, St Aubain in Namur, and the monastery of Clairvaux, centre of the Cistercian order. In succeeding years, relics of the Holy Blood appeared elsewhere in Flanders, north-eastern France, and Paris itself.[41]

The Cult of Joseph of Arimathea at Glastonbury

Glastonbury, the most famous of all medieval Arthurian sites and 'store-house of relics', was modest in its claims when it came to relics of its supposed founder, Joseph of Arimathea. The early twelfth-century chronicler William of Malmesbury was unaware of any legend connecting him with the abbey, but by the thirteenth century, a new version of the abbey's foundation had been created: and William of Malmesbury's work appeared in a new edition, in which Joseph played a prominent part.[42] By the mid-fourteenth century, John of Glastonbury actually used the Grail romances to supply material for his history of the abbey.

Whether the new foundation story preceded or followed the Grail romances, we do not know, but there are two romances which offer possible connections to Glastonbury, which might have been the germ of an imaginative development of the stories on the part of the monks.

Towards the end of *The Romance of the History of the Grail*, Joseph of Arimathea, who is about to give the Grail into the keeping of Bron, 'the rich fisher king', foretells that his other lieutenant, Petrus, will go to the *vaus d'Avaron* to report that the Grail has been handed to a new guardian, and a few lines further on, Petrus himself says 'I shall go to the land in the west, which is wild and harsh, to the *vaus d'Avaron*'. These are the only two mentions of the vale of Avaron in the poem,[43] and we cannot be certain that they refer to Glastonbury. For a start, the monks themselves had called Glastonbury '*insula Avallonia*' (the isle of Avalon) on the cross supposedly found with Arthur's body in 1191,[44] and the phrase 'vale of Avalon' does not seem to occur in Glastonbury sources. Furthermore, Avallon in Burgundy is not far from the home of Robert de Boron and Gautier de Montbéliard, and stands on a granite peak above two ravines, perhaps a better match for the vale or valley of Avaron.

If Robert de Boron's contribution in *The Romance of the History of the Grail* is indecisive, that of *Perlesvaus* is much more positive. The colophon of *Perlesvaus* tells us in flowery language that 'The Latin text from which this story was set down in the vernacular was taken from the Isle of Avalon, from a holy religious house which stands at the edge of the Lands of Adventure; there lie King Arthur and the queen, by the testimony of the worthy religious men who dwell there, and who have the whole story, true from the beginning to the end.'[45] Now a Latin version of the opening story of the *Perlesvaus* survives, the so-called 'St Augustine's chapel' episode: it is an extraordinary tale of a squire who robs a church in his dream, and awakes, dying, with a dagger in his side, saying that he was stabbed, again in the dream, by a knight guarding the treasure. It is to be found in John of Glastonbury's chronicle, written in the mid-fourteenth century, and as a separate story in a manuscript anthology compiled at Glastonbury.[46] There may well have been a copy of *Perlesvaus* at Glastonbury, albeit an unusual possession for a monastic library, as fragments of an early copy have been found in a binding from nearby Wells Cathedral.[47] Furthermore, the author of another romance, *Fouke Fitz Waryn*, who wrote in Shropshire in the late thirteenth century, borrows the story, and acknowledges that he has taken it from the book of the Grail.[48]

All this looks like good evidence for a connection between the Grail stories and Glastonbury at the beginning of the thirteenth century, and

Perlesvaus has two other important references to the abbey in the text of the romance itself. It is the place where the head of Arthur's murdered son is buried; and Lancelot comes to the Lady Chapel later in the romance to find that Guinevere, of whose death he is ignorant, is buried beside her son. Arthur later visits the graves, declaring that it ought to be the place on earth which he holds most dear. This detail would point to the context of the 1191 discovery of Arthur's grave, as Lancelot is told that the other tomb in the chapel has been prepared for Arthur.[49]

Perlesvaus is different from the other Grail romances in that Arthur plays a large part in the action, and the focus of the story is as much on his court and his wars as on Perlesvaus and his adventures; indeed, the second part is mostly concerned with his war against Brian of the Isles. It seems probable that it represents a reworking of Robert de Boron, who had united the themes of the Grail with the story of Arthur, though the uncertainty about the dating of the romances makes it impossible to be sure. If this is the case, then the appearance of Joseph of Arimathea at the beginning derives from Robert, and he is therefore ultimately responsible for the association of Joseph and Glastonbury, even though he himself never suggests that Joseph came to Britain. In fact there is nothing to suggest that this connection was made before the author of the *Perlesvaus* wrote, and it seems to have been an embellishment of the stories about Glastonbury's foundation. William of Malmesbury attributes this event to a mission sent by Pope Eleutherius in the second century AD to a mythical king Lucius, a story found in accounts by Anglo-Saxon historians. This was then elaborated into a story that the missionaries Phagan and Deruvian found a church already established at Glastonbury, and that this had been founded by the disciples St Philip and St James in AD 63. The final addition to the story of the beginnings of the abbey, in around 1250, was the name of Joseph of Arimathea.[50]

Yet the monks did little to emphasize the presence of Joseph until the very end of the fifteenth century, when the abbot, Richard Bere, encouraged the cult of 'St Joseph of Glastonbury', and changed the abbey's coat of arms accordingly. Until then, there had been a tradition that Joseph was buried in the old church, which had burned down in 1184, and that he had brought two cruets containing the blood and sweat of Our Lord to the abbey, where they had been hidden. This was attributed to an otherwise unknown writer called Melkin, who prophesied that when Joseph's body was found, 'it will be visible, whole and undecayed, and open to the whole world'. The first mention of this prophecy is in John of Glastonbury's chronicle[51] but, despite its huge political potential – if Joseph was the founder of Glastonbury, the abbey could claim to be on a par with Rome, as an apostolic foundation –

the idea was never developed. The English rulers had encouraged the monks to search for Arthur's remains in the 1180s, and twice in the succeeding centuries, royal initiatives were launched to find Joseph of Arimathea's tomb. We know little more about the first such attempt than that Edward III encouraged a mystic to seek the grave in 1345.[52] In 1419 Henry V, wishing to emphasize the independence of the English church, encouraged the monks to excavate in search of Joseph of Arimathea's tomb. A carefully worded report, from which the king might infer that Joseph's body had been found, even though the abbot did not say so directly, was sent back. But it seems that the death of Henry V, and the end of the gathering of ecclesiastics, the Council of Constance, at which the claim that the English church had been founded by Joseph was of great importance, led to the abandonment of this attempt to establish the legend.[53] The abbey was remarkably reticent about a story which had the potential to make it one of the great shrines of Christendom, and Glastonbury never claimed to have the Grail. Ironically, it was only in Protestant England that a relic said to be the Grail was given a Glastonbury provenance.*

We have mapped some of the specific links between the relics of the Holy Blood and the Grail, but in doing so we must not lose sight of the broader parallels between the way in which the legends surrounding these relics were created, and the writing of the Grail romances. As we look at the varieties of sacred writings, the lines between these and the prose romances blur, and they begin to merge imperceptibly into one another. We began with the New Testament itself, apparently inviolable and authoritative; yet the boundary between it and the Apocrypha was once fluid, and the existence of these largely forgotten alternative versions of the story of Christ is an important element in the creation of the Grail stories. Furthermore, the apocryphal stories were not only current in the twelfth and thirteenth centuries, but they were rewritten and translated into the vernacular. Both belong in the margins of the orthodoxies of the Church, extending and reaching out to a new audience, inventing new literary techniques to do so if necessary. At the heart of the Grail romances, however, is one of the crucial theological debates of the late twelfth century, and it is to this that we now turn.

---

* See p. 300 below.

IO

The Eucharist and the Grail

The Grail of the romances is not to be found in cathedral treasuries or among the possessions of the great monasteries. It is too holy an object for this sinful world: at the end of *Perlesvaus*, Perlesvaus is told that 'the Holy Grail will appear here no more, but you will soon know where it is to be'. Shortly thereafter, Perlesvaus himself embarks on a mysterious ship, and is never seen again by earthly man. At the end of the *Quest*, on Galahad's death, a hand comes down from heaven: 'it proceeded straight to the Holy Vessel and took both it and the lance, and carried them up to heaven, to the end that no man since has ever dared to say he saw the Holy Grail'.[1]

Yet in another shape, the Grail remained ever-present in medieval life. Robert de Boron and the authors of *Perlesvaus* and the *Quest* envisage the Grail as the precursor of the chalice of the Eucharist. The relation of Grail and Eucharist, and the relation of popular devotion to the theological debates of the early medieval period, are a crucial key to the romances, and to the image of the Grail in the minds of contemporary readers. The Eucharist is the central moment of the Mass, which in turn was the central ceremony of the medieval Church, an inheritance from the earliest days of Christianity. By the early thirteenth century, it carried both the weight of long tradition and a surprising degree of innovation and debate.

To understand this paradox, we need to trace, briefly, the history of the Eucharist. In the early Christian Church, the Eucharist was an act of remembrance, recalling Jesus' last supper with his disciples. St Paul, writing to the Corinthians, tells his audience that Jesus instructed the disciples to break bread and drink wine 'in remembrance of me'.[2] This breaking of bread seems to have been the earliest ritual of the newly founded religion, a feast which bound the members of the Christian community together. But from being a commemoration and a thanksgiving, it quickly acquired a deeper, mystical meaning. From the fourth century onwards, as Christianity emerged from the shadows of persecution, the Eucharist was no longer a ceremony which strengthened the resolve of its participants to resist a hostile world, but became a symbol of the union of the individual Christian with the risen Saviour. The emphasis moved from commemoration and the solidarity of communion to worship and adoration; from Paul's words to those of Matthew:

Jesus took bread, and blessed it, and brake it, and gave it to the disciples, and said, Take, eat; this is my body. And he took the cup, and gave thanks, and gave it to them, saying, Drink ye all of it; for this is my blood of the new testament which is shed for the remission of sins.[3]

The presence of Christ in spirit among his followers became the belief on which the Eucharist centred, and slowly the doctrine emerged that this was not merely a spiritual phenomenon, but a real and physical fact. The bread and wine which had at first been symbols of Christ now became, for the believers, Christ's actual flesh and blood.[4] This doctrine, propounded among the theologians of the Eastern Church, reached the West through the writings of Ambrose of Milan in the fourth century. The original mystical impulse became a matter for doctrinal debate in the course of the following centuries, even if the form of the Mass continued to emphasize the community of worshippers as much as the object of worship.

The first formal statements of the Church's teaching about this aspect of the Eucharist belong to the reign of Charles the Bald, grandson of Charlemagne; two monks from the great Benedictine abbey at Corbie, near Amiens in north-east France, wrote treatises on the Eucharist. One of them was the abbot, Paschasius Radbertus, who argued strongly for the real presence of Christ in the sacrament; Ratramnus, one of his monks, took a very different view, and made no connection between the bread and wine used in the ceremony and the body and blood of Christ. These divergent views might be seen as a controversy, but in the ninth century this was not an issue on which there were passionately held beliefs. Both views were possible within the current teaching of the Church, and it is perhaps only with hindsight that the differences seem so emphatic, because we now know how later theologians were to develop the arguments here presented for the first time.

But diversity could lead to heresy, and Paschasius himself speaks of heretics who disagreed with his views. The secular authorities were as anxious as the leaders of the Church to foster unity, and what had been a topic for discussion among scholars soon became a major test of orthodoxy, the orthodoxy which both Church and State strove to enforce. In the ninth century, the great philosopher John Scotus Eriugena was accused by the archbishop of Reims of teaching, contrary to the faith, that the sacraments of the altar were only a remembrance of the true body and blood of Christ, while a radical monk named Gottschalk argued that if the real presence of Christ was true, his worshippers were practising a rite bordering on cannibalism.

This might have remained an obscure if lively theological controversy, had it not been for the Church's use of the ritual of the Eucharist to assert its authority. The trend within the Church was towards a new power structure which centred on the papacy, at the expense of the local communities. Mass was no longer simply a gathering of believers in a common cause; it was also a rite which could only be performed by a priest consecrated by a bishop, who in turn derived his authority from the pope himself. Consecration was the delegation of the power granted by Christ to St Peter, and was the exclusive prerogative of the Church authorities. Only they could exercise this power, and the faithful could only obtain consolation and salvation by adhering to the rites approved by the Church and administered by its priests.

This process of replacing local rites and local theologies with a centralized and unified doctrine and practice moved forward under Charlemagne in parallel with the political unification of Europe; the Frankish rulers saw promotion of the unity of the Church as an important element in the creation of the imperial state: 'the liturgy was one of the most crucial elements in the shaping of Frankish society'.[5] The papacy reformed and repositioned itself in the tenth and eleventh centuries, and as their power and status increased, the popes attempted to claim universal jurisdiction; the most extreme proponents of papal rights insisted that the pope was the overlord of all secular rulers. Even at the local level, there were striking changes: churches which had once been the property of the local lords who founded them became parish churches, part of the grand scheme of Christian order which saw the creation of a central administrative system which would encompass the whole of Western Christendom.

The Eucharist as Drama

The clergy, like the pope, enjoyed an enhanced status as a result of these developments, set apart from the laity and bound by different laws. It was their power to administer the sacrament which was the badge of their new position. To demonstrate their authority, and that of the Church as a whole, the ecclesiastical authorities reinvented the Mass. The ceremony became the product of religious imagination; it was conceived as a theatrical occasion, with an emphasis on splendour, light and richness in the candles and robes which were an essential part of its setting, and on mystery, in the half-seen acts of the priest around the altar at the distant end of the apse. In a Romanesque church, this would have been lit almost entirely by candles; the new light of Gothic architecture was only just beginning to relieve the darkness in which much church ritual took place. Ceremonial gestures such as the raising of the Host after its consecration by the priest are mentioned for the first time at the end of the twelfth century, and the ringing of bells to emphasize the solemnity of the moment was also a relatively new practice. In *Perlesvaus*, when king Arthur witnesses the Mass of the Grail, he is not watching an age-old ceremony whose power lies in its customary reiteration of the familiar yet awesome mysteries, but a new and dramatic occasion, striking in its novelty: the emphasis is on the strangeness of bells and chalices, which are essential elements in the ritual. In this the anonymous author echoes the attitudes of his contemporaries, seeing the Mass as a dynamic, sometimes controversial service.

Furthermore, in the twelfth century, the elevation of the Host during the Mass so that the congregation could see and worship it had often taken place before the consecration; because the unconsecrated elements of bread and wine were not worthy of adoration, the bishop of Paris, Eudes de Sully, issued a canon instructing the priests of his diocese not to elevate the Host until it had been consecrated. The congregation would then be worshipping not the unconsecrated bread, but the body of Christ, redoubling their fervour for a sight of the sacred object.[6] For Gerbert de Montreuil, author of the last of the continuations of *The Story of the Grail*, Mass was

the most glorious of mysteries, and the most precious. There you can see the very body of Jesus Christ when the priest makes the sacrament and holds it in his hands . . . If you believe truly and hear mass willingly, I tell you on my soul that you will . . . learn all the secrets of the lance and the Grail.[7]

Even in the ordinary chivalric romances there is other evidence of this enthusiasm: there are occasional references to hearing Mass as part of the duties of a knight, or simply as an accepted ritual before a trial of prowess. But in *The Story of the Grail* the number of mentions of attendance of Mass is vastly increased, and this is true of all the Grail romances.

Adherence to these rituals became the touchstone for testing true belief: acceptance of the doctrine of the Eucharist and of priestly authority separated the orthodox from the heretic. The first point of dissent of many heretical sects was precisely the denial of priestly authority, and with it the power of the Mass. Hence to define the nature of the Eucharist became a crucial question in the struggle against the rival creeds proclaimed by the Cathars and the Waldensians, as well as many lesser heresies. So in the twelfth century, there was renewed emphasis on defining the nature of the sacrament, and the physical constituents of the central ritual of the Mass. On the one hand were the proponents of the idea that the real presence of Christ in the Host and the wine led to a physical union of the believer with the Saviour, qualified only by the proviso that the recipient must be in a state of grace for this physical miracle to take place. Against this, those who took the approach that the Eucharist was primarily commemorative declared that, though Christ was really present at the altar, any union was spiritual rather than physical. With the new subtleties of thought developed by the philosophers of the schools of Paris in the twelfth century, a third approach was tried: although the Lord was present in the sacrament, salvation was not related to physical contact: rather, it was the operation on the believer of his reception of the sacrament, the virtue and effect of it, which was crucial.

All this may seem learned and remote, not unlike the famous question of how many angels could dance on the head of a pin which served to mock medieval philosophers in later ages. But what was being discussed and defined was a ceremony witnessed by most of the population of Western Europe at least once, and officially three times or more, in the year: a rite at once familiar and mysterious, arousing curiosity as much as outright belief. It was the most theatrical event which ordinary men and women would experience, and one which attracted fervent devotion.[8] The sight of the consecrated Host was regarded with awe and wonder; and when Innocent III, at the Fourth Lateran Council in 1215, sought for the most effective weapon with which to defeat the spread of the Cathar heresy, he did so by reaffirming the real presence of Christ at the climax of the Mass, using the word 'transubstantiation' to describe the process of transformation of the bread and wine: a word which, first used in the mid-twelfth century, was to become the focal point of controversy when, at the Reformation, these ideas were once more challenged and debated.

Joseph of Arimathea and the Eucharist

At the heart of the Church's own imagery of the Mass was the figure of Joseph of Arimathea. When in about 850, Amalarius of Metz wrote one of the first Latin commentaries to analyse the Mass in allegorical terms, he compared the deacon who helped the priest to raise up the chalice at the moment of consecration to Joseph. The theme was taken up by later writers and finds its fullest statement in the *Jewel of the Soul* of Honorius[9] in the first quarter of the twelfth century:

The deacon who places the covered chalice on the altar signifies Joseph of Arimathea, who took down Christ's body, covered his face with a cloth, laid the body in the sepulchre, and closed the tomb with a stone. The covering of the chalice represents the *sindonem mundam* [clean linen cloth] in which Joseph wrapped Christ's body; the chalice is the sepulchre; and the paten is the stone closing the tomb. The acolyte who holds the paten prefigures Nicodemus.[10]

It was a theme which was officially approved by the authorities: pope Innocent III, writing on the same theme, adopts these images.[11] And Alcuin, who was Amalarius' teacher, wrote in the late eighth century that 'the chalice with which the catholic priest celebrates mass is none other than that which our Lord gave to the apostles';[12] not only does the bread and wine become the body and blood of Christ, but the chalice itself is that used by Christ. For the devout, time and space are abolished, and the real presence is revealed. The images of Joseph and the Grail are one version of this vision, and it lies at the centre of Robert de Boron's poem. For in *The Romance of the History of the Grail* the poet devotes two long sections to an explanation of the symbolism of the Eucharist and to portraying the grace which it offers the true believer. When Christ gives the Grail to Joseph, he explains the ceremony of the Mass in terms which are very close to those found in the *Jewel of the Soul*. The altar represents Christ's sepulchre, the cloth on which the consecrated bread and wine are placed is the shroud in which Joseph wrapped Christ's body, the Grail is the chalice, and the stone which was rolled in front of the sepulchre is the paten on which the Host is served. Robert de Boron sets the Eucharist at the centre of his story from the very beginning.[13]

Later, Joseph preaches the faith to his followers at Christ's commandment: those who are chosen are allowed to witness the ceremony of the Grail, which is a form of the Eucharist. When their less fortunate brethren ask them what they have received, they try to describe the grace granted by the Grail, a delight beyond all imagination, which is conferred by Christ himself through the agency of the cup of the Last Supper. When the sinner Moyses deceives Joseph into admitting him into the company of the elect, he is swallowed up by the earth.[14]

The Eucharist as Source of Nourishment

The single Host which, according to Chrétien, feeds the father of the Fisher King, is paralleled by the nourishment which the Grail provides for Joseph of Arimathea in prison in *The Romance of the History of the Grail*. Both episodes derive from the tradition of miracles associated with the Eucharist, which is frequently portrayed as sustaining life *in extremis*. Within the circle of northern France and Flanders where the Grail romances originated, we can point to two contemporary stories of this kind, both recorded by Jacques de Vitry, one of the most redoubtable preachers of the time. At Vernon, on the borders of France and Normandy, a girl was said to have lived for forty years on nothing except the Host, brought to her by a dove each Friday, and received by her from the priest each Sunday.[15] A similar miracle was recorded by a number of chroniclers about a woman at Cudot, near Sens, who lived for thirty years only on the Host which she received at communion.[16] This story was known in England, where a similar tale was told of a recluse at Leicester, whom St Hugh of Lincoln placed under close observation for a fortnight, and found that she had indeed taken no other nourishment.[17] Examples could be multiplied from other regions.[18] This was clearly part of current belief about the Eucharist at exactly the time the romances were written.

There was also a wider tradition in the Bible of the magical provision of food. The most famous instance is that of the manna from heaven which sustained Moses and his people in the desert. The apocryphal Old Testament book of 'The Wisdom of Solomon' describes manna as 'angels' food', 'bread prepared without ... labour, able to content every man's delight, and agreeing to every taste',[19] in other words producing what each person wished to eat. In the *Quest*, this identification of the Grail food with manna is made quite specifically: Bors is told that 'the food of the Holy Grail' is 'the sweet food with which [Christ] has filled them, and with which he sustained the people of Israel for so long in the desert'.[20] In the context of the New Testament, this was transformed into the *panis angelicus*, the 'bread of angels', and the Eucharist was described in these terms by Peter the Venerable in the early twelfth century as 'the bread and life of men ... which is for ever the bread of the blessed and the food of angels'.[21] It is worth noticing that when the Grail provides its miraculous food in the *Continuations*, it serves first bread and wine, with obvious eucharistic overtones. In other descriptions of feasts in twelfth-century French Arthurian romances, the fact that bread and wine are served before the meal is never mentioned.[22]

There is a further link between the Grail and the Last Supper which is of

17 An early twelfth-century illustration of the Last Supper, showing the fish as the one item of food (other than bread) on the table. This kind of image would have been familiar to Robert de Boron, who first introduces the fish as part of the Grail ritual. From a manuscript written for a monastery near Paris, Saint-Maur-des-Fossés.

considerable interest. In *Joseph of Arimathea*, Joseph is told by Our Lord to recreate the Last Supper when he inaugurates the table of the Grail, the link between the table of the Last Supper and the Round Table itself. But there is one strange element: Bron, Joseph's brother-in-law, is told to go fishing, and to bring the first fish that he catches. This is very strange, and might at first simply seem to be a clumsy attempt to explain Bron's later title 'the Rich Fisher', which links him to the Fisher King in *The Story of the Grail*. But, as with the Grail itself and the Crucifixion, visual imagery gives a clue to what is going on: fish figure prominently in a number of illustrations of the Last Supper from this period.[23] The Last Supper is, of course, the Passover meal, and in Jewish tradition, the priestly caste ate fish on this occasion – lamb being the food for ordinary people. Furthermore, in Christian iconography, the fish represented Christ, and is a common symbol for Him in early Christian art. Hence the presence of fish at the Last Supper is easily understood, and artists from the late Byzantine period onwards placed fish prominently on the table, as in the mosaics at Ravenna. The tradition was certainly current in the twelfth century, as examples from northern France and from Hildesheim show (Plate 17); representations of the Last Supper are relatively uncommon, but this appears to be the standard iconography. And in one of the religious dramas on the Passion of the period, Judas steals a fish from the table when no one is looking. So the presence of the fish at this moment in the Grail's story is easily explained. This episode is also a way of linking the title of 'rich fisher', which Bron henceforth bears, with Christ's injunction to Peter to become a 'fisher of men'.

What is more interesting, but must remain highly speculative, is why Chrétien should categorically deny that the Grail contains a fish of any kind, when it is clear that the standard image of the dish of the Last Supper specifically shows it to contain a fish. It may be coincidence; it may simply be that Chrétien's reference was one of the points that led to Robert de Boron's imaginative connection of the Grail with the Last Supper. But it does also raise the intriguing possibility that Chrétien is actually saying that this is the dish of the Last Supper, which *should* contain a fish, but in fact contains the Host instead.

The Grail as Spiritual Solace

The sight of the Grail as a spiritual solace is a consistent theme in the romances, culminating in the episode in the *Quest* where Lancelot, conscious that his sinful love for Guinevere debars him from full participation in the Grail ceremony, obtains sight of the sacred vessel, and is both rewarded by the vision and punished for his temerity. Equally, William of Auxerre in his *Summa Aurea*, written around 1215–20, deals with the question of whether sinners profane the Host merely by looking at it, and declares that while a sinner may not touch the Host on pain of severe punishment, he is entitled to look at it, for from it he will derive the desire to see God, and lead a better life.[24] This is exactly what happens to Lancelot; he is struck down when he attempts to approach the Grail, and when he recovers, he insists on wearing a penitential hair shirt in recognition of his years of sinful desire.

This is not the warrior Christianity of *Perlesvaus* with its conversions by force, but a subtler theological exposition of themes central to the Christian faith. If the idea of an often abstruse religious debate as inspiration for secular literature seems strange to us, we have only to look at the boundaries between the laity and the clergy in the late twelfth century. Many of the leading figures in secular administration were in religious orders, and even if power remained in the hands of the great feudal lords, they needed clerks to help them in an increasingly literate age: our word 'clerk' derives from 'clericus' and has the same root as 'clergyman'; for much of the Middle Ages the two were identical. Thomas Becket, the flamboyant and luxury-loving head of Henry II's civil service who became the ascetic archbishop of Canterbury, is the most spectacular example of the interplay between the two worlds: at a humbler level, there were many men at home in both. Without being experts in theology, their religious background would make them receptive to the new ideas and lively debates within the Church. It is a moot point whether Robert de Boron's real title was the secular 'messire' or the clerical 'meistre'.[25] Such men moved as easily in one world as the other, just as the Grail stories cross from romance to theology with no apparent feeling of contradiction.

The Grail and Heresy

To assert the power of the Eucharist was to raise a standard against the heretics, and it is possible to read the Grail romances as a kind of call to arms to the chivalry of Europe against the forces threatening the Church. Philip of Flanders was famous as a scourge of the heretics, and Chrétien's work has been read as a kind of *roman à clef* with Philip's campaigns against heresy at its centre.[26] But to set up Perceval as the model of an orthodox Christian against the Cathar distortions of the faith is excessive: what we see in *The Story of the Grail* is the development of the hero from an almost agnostic state to that of a virtuous, devout but normal Christian knight. The point about the Grail romances, if heresy is to be mentioned in this connection at all, is that they are quintessentially orthodox in their presentation of the Christian faith. Robert de Boron has been portrayed as a sympathizer with the heretics, but his depiction of the Trinity and his views on marriage – a particular dislike of the Cathars – are entirely in concordance with the teachings of the Church.[27]

The Grail romances do not conceal a secret – they reveal the attitudes of the time. The philosophers and theologians debated the nature of the Eucharist for the same reason that these romances were written. From the tenth century onwards, there was an increasingly intense focus on the Eucharist.

In the ninth century, a church council held at Chelsea regarded the physical elements of the Eucharist, in particular the Host, as a kind of inactive relic, to be regarded like other relics, and suitable for placing in the foundations of a newly built church or in an altar.[28] The theological debate about the real presence not only changed this attitude completely, but moved the focus of the Church's liturgy from a commemoration of Christ and the saints to a celebration of Christ as an active force in the everyday life of every member of the Church. The Eucharist was in a sense Christ himself, and this explains the desire of the congregation to see the Host when it had been consecrated. 'By the thirteenth century, the Eucharist was universally accorded an extra-ordinary, unique reverence.'[29]

The highly technical debates among theologians about the Eucharist reached the congregations who gathered to hear and see the celebration of Mass through the preaching and teaching of parish priests, for whom summaries of the scholarly arguments were provided by bishops such as Robert Grosseteste of Lincoln, who had been at Paris and Oxford and who wrote his *Templum Dei* (Temple of God) in the 1220s. This is a sophisticated work, using the image of the Temple as a simile for the Christian faith, but it is paralleled by dozens of texts in the same vein, written by the Church's administrators to ensure that the priests in their charge were able to expound the divine mysteries to the best of their ability. These texts begin to appear at the beginning of the thirteenth century, and are part of a concerted effort to improve the understanding of religious mysteries by the laity. There are poems specifically devoted to the Mass, such as Gonzalo de Berceo's *El sacrificio de la misa* from early thirteenth-century Spain, which are intended for an audience which was not at ease in Latin, and who could well have been educated and pious lay men and women. The symbolism of the chalice and paten as representing the tomb in which Christ was laid by Joseph of Arimathea and the rock which covered it occurs in this poem, showing how erudite theological similes could reach a much wider audience.[30]

In a different vein, but also of use to preachers, was the collection of miracles made by Caesarius of Heisterbach, a Cistercian monk who wrote in the 1220s. His book is apparently directed at novices, new entrants to the monastery; but the tales he tells reflect the popular culture of the time, and he devotes an entire section, a twelfth of his book, to stories about the Eucharist. Miracle stories of this kind had a long-established tradition, going back to Gregory of Tours in the sixth century and to Paschasius Radbertus' treatise on the Eucharist in the ninth century; the miracle stories supported his argument for the physical reality of the Eucharist. In many cases, these tales come very close to scenes in the Grail romances, such as the vision of the infant Christ in the chalice, which is a consistent theme from *Perlesvaus* to the *Lancelot-Grail* cycle.[31] This is a story which is found occasionally in earlier sources, but which becomes very popular in the thirteenth century: Matthew Paris, in his biography of Edward the Confessor, says that it happened when Archbishop Wulfstan celebrated Mass in front of the king; and Eleanor, sister of Henry III of England, was said to have had a similar vision.[32]

The tradition represented by Caesarius' work has more to offer in terms of the atmosphere of the Grail romances. There are stories of the healing power of the Eucharist which parallel the episodes in *Lancelot* where Bors, Ector, Perceval and Lancelot are all cured by the simple presence of the Grail.[33] And the fifth book of *The Dialogue on Miracles*, 'Of demons', has descriptions of the devil in his various guises which find an echo in the adventures of Perceval and Bors in the *Quest*, particularly in the physical descriptions of the apparitions. Caesarius' work is interesting because it is on the borders of religious and secular writing; ostensibly designed for novices in his monastery, it records the type of story used by the Cistercian preachers to enliven their sermons and to engage the attention of their audience. He tells of the priest who would not trust in God, but carried a sword for his own protection as he rode to Mass along a lonely road:

... when he came to a certain wood, so great fear and horror seized upon him that all his hair stood on end, as men say, and a cold sweat broke out on every limb. The cause of this horror did not long lie hid, because as soon as he turned his eyes to the wood he saw a man of hideous aspect standing near a tall tree. And as he looked, this man grew suddenly so vast in size that his height was equal to that of the tree, and round him all the trees were crashing and there were fearful blasts of wind . . .[34]

This is an encounter that would not be out of place in any of the Arthurian romances, and shows how the imagery which we assume to be fundamental to such tales finds its way into a much wider range of material.

Even the great festivals of the Church, and its central beliefs, could be touched by the influence of devout members of the laity. One of the most striking instances concerns the feast of Corpus Christi,* which specifically commemorated the Eucharist. This was inspired by a lay worshipper, Juliana of Cornillon, who belonged to a religious community in Liège in the first decades of the thirteenth century. The vision which began the process of the creation of the new feast probably occurred around 1208, in other words

* I.e. 'the body of Christ'.

at the same time and in the same area as the Grail romances.[35] Juliana's community, the Beguines, were the most prominent of a number of similar movements in which lay people sought to lead a life ruled by the precepts of the Gospel without entirely sequestering themselves from secular life, a *via media* or middle way which had its roots in early Christian practices. In effect, this is a variant on the context we have suggested for the Grail itself: instead of devout individuals within the knightly society of north-west Europe, we have a more formal devout bourgeois society in the cities of the same area.[36]

If the Grail owes much to the popular devotion to the Eucharist, and to the debates and images surrounding it, Grail and Eucharist are by no means one and the same. The Grail is both more and less than the central icon of the Mass, beginning as a mysterious container for the Host, and ending as a transcendent vehicle for the highest of all visions. The theology of the Grail and the 'secrets' to which the Grail romances often refer need to be explored to complete the missing elements in our picture of the Grail.

11

The Holy Grail

When, in *The Story of the Grail*, the hermit explains the Grail to Perceval, he tells us very little about it, other than that it is 'such a holy thing'. His concern is not with inanimate objects, but with the sinner before him. The homily is directed at Perceval: it is a simple lesson in Christian worship and Christian behaviour, such as any twelfth-century preacher might have set out in a sermon for a secular audience. The hermit emphasizes the importance of penitence, and of attending Mass, which is his main theme: through regular attendance at Mass – 'stay there until the priest has said and sung everything', he insists – 'you may come to redeem yourself and win honour and a place in Paradise'. All this is orthodox and simple; Perceval has never been properly instructed in the Christian faith, and by remedying this, the hermit is helping him forward in his spiritual development, which, as we have seen, is the driving force behind the story. Only for a moment is there a hint of something less familiar, when the hermit teaches Perceval a prayer. 'Many of the names of Our Lord appeared in this prayer, including the greatest ones, which the tongue of man should never utter except in fear of death.' We shall return to this strange comment, but otherwise the scene is familiar and uncomplicated in its ideas.

The continuations of *The Story of the Grail* offer little more in the way of theological ideas. The account of the lance and of Joseph of Arimathea is presented as a narrative, with little comment, and the identification of the Grail as a relic of the Passion is done in a factual way; there is no attempt to expand on the implications behind its existence. Both Grail and lance are simply presented as most precious relics; we are looking at them from a layman's standpoint, with all due reverence but perhaps rather too little in the way of understanding.

When we come to the work of Robert de Boron, we are in very different territory. From the opening of *Joseph of Arimathea*, it is evident that theology is one of his interests, and is the main reason for the writing of the poem. The opening lines summarize in a broad sweep the redemption of mankind through Christ by 'the Father and by the Son and by the Holy Spirit, and these three beings are one . . . Much could be said of this, for the fountain of His goodness is inexhaustible. So I must digress now, and turn to this work of mine, in which I pray He may by His grace direct my thought and understanding.'[1]

The prime purpose of *Joseph of Arimathea*, in both verse and prose versions, is to recount the missionary activities of Joseph's followers, how they dispersed throughout the world and how, wherever they went, they 'recounted the story of the death of Jesus Christ'. The Grail is the symbol of the authenticity of their mission, but it is also the test of true belief and of a virtuous life. In the early scenes its history is established, and the first miracle that it brings is the feeding of Joseph in prison; Joseph is sustained both spiritually and physically, through the Grail, by his faith. It is only in the scene when Joseph establishes the table of the Grail that its wider powers come into play. The table itself is part of the overall structure of the poem and its sequels – the Grail originates from the table of the Last Supper, the table of the Grail is made 'in its name', and it appears at the Round Table. The latter is made in the time of Uther Pendragon, in memory of both the earlier tables and as a symbol of the Trinity.

When Christ instructs Joseph on how to establish the table of the Grail, it is because some of his followers have sinned and, as a result, the harvests have failed. Christ tells Joseph that 'you will give your people a great sign, testing the power of my flesh and blood against those who have sinned'. The rest of Joseph's followers are summoned 'to see the cause of their distress' and those 'who have true faith in the Trinity of Father, Son and Holy Spirit' are told to take their seats at the table. Those who come forward sense 'the sweetness and the fulfilment of their hearts', and ask the others, who have remained standing, whether they can feel this too. When the others say that they feel nothing, they are declared to be guilty of sin, and to be the cause of the famine. The Grail company are represented as the elect, and the Grail has the power of rejecting sinners; this is a common theme of the miracles of the Eucharist, where those who attempt to take communion in a state of sin are punished in a variety of ways.

Robert de Boron also introduces directly the analogy between the celebration of Mass and the actions of Joseph of Arimathea found in Amalarius of Metz: Christ tells Joseph 'the sacrament shall never be made without remembrance of your good work by those who recognize it'. He goes on to make the same analogies as those found in Amalarius: the vessel 'in which you put my blood when you gathered it from my body'[2] shall be called the chalice, and represents the tomb; the paten or cover is the stone with which the tomb was closed, and the corporal or cloth on which the chalice is placed is the winding sheet.

Robert de Boron is clearly at home with the ideas of the greatest Cistercian writer of the age, Bernard of Clairvaux, as well as the theology of the Eucharist which we have already explored. Two central themes are embedded in *The Romance of the History of the Grail*: the idea of redemption and the concept of faith as essential to salvation. We have noted how Robert lays particular emphasis on belief in the Trinity: he repeatedly insists on this doctrine, one of the central tenets of medieval theology, and anathema to many of the heretical sects of the period. He raises a more difficult question in the scene we have just quoted, where some of Joseph's followers are admitted to the Grail ceremony while others are excluded: that of election or predestination and of grace. The debate over whether God is all-powerful and therefore predetermines our fate, or whether by divine dispensation mankind has free will and is therefore responsible for his own destiny, is as critical an issue as that of belief in transubstantiation. Indeed, these two topics were the chief grounds for Protestant dissent at the Reformation. Again, Robert's theology seems to be entirely orthodox, for when Joseph's followers beg him to admit the dissembling Moyses to the holy table, Joseph's reply is entirely in line with the Church's teaching as set out by St Augustine: 'Our Lord God gives it [grace] as He wishes to any person.' What is also clear is how divine grace operates: grace is 'of God our Father, Jesus Christ and together with the Holy Spirit', and it is conferred through the presence of the Grail.[3] But Robert does not tackle the thorny question of sin and its relation to grace. Are those excluded from the table condemned to sin because they lack grace? If their sin precludes them from a state of grace, it contradicts the statement that 'our Lord . . . gives it to any person', which implies no such condition. While *Joseph of Arimathea* is ready to embark on serious theological matters, the deeper subtleties of such arguments lie outside its range, and rightly so, for it is presented as a straightforward narrative, not a debate.

The author of *Perlesvaus* writes in a very different vein. If the adventures are wild and strange, the thinking behind them is also highly unusual, and is difficult to place within a clear religious context. The opening sentences are much more direct than Robert de Boron's prologue:

Hear the story of that holy vessel which is called the Grail, in which the precious blood of the Saviour was gathered on the day when He was crucified to redeem mankind from Hell; Josephus recorded it at the behest of an angel, so that by his writing and testimony the truth might be known of how knights and worthy men were willing to suffer toil and hardship to exalt the Law of Jesus Christ, which He had aimed to renew by His death and crucifixion.[4]

He then invokes the Trinity, and gives a summary account of the story of Joseph of Arimathea, before describing how the knights of Perlesvaus' family and of king Arthur's court had 'advanced the Law of Jesus Christ' by their deeds.

And deeds are what the ensuing story is about. If, broadly speaking, the conflict of the Old Law and the New Law is the crux of the tale, the author is more concerned with portraying dramatic events, the sheer excitement of knightly activity driven by a belief in the all-conquering righteousness of the New Law, than in setting out a consistent doctrinal position. His images are vividly pictorial and show a powerful imagination: he draws in particular on the 'Book of Revelation', and figures such as the Black Hermit, whom Perlesvaus defeats at the end of the book, are worthy of St John's vision of the apocalypse. Some of the adventures are specifically charged with meaning, as Gawain learns when he comes to the Castle of Enquiry. The relationship of the events he has witnessed to the story of the fall and redemption of mankind is made plain: ' "Sire," said the priest, "the good hermit explains the meaning of these things for us for the sake of the New Law, with which most people are poorly acquainted, and he wishes to remind us of it by relating events which provide examples." '[5] The key word is perhaps 'remind'; these are not literal analogies, and *Perlesvaus* is not a *roman-à-clef*, even if the dazzling array of mysterious episodes tempts us to search for a solution to so many puzzles. The author is capable of combining religious and profane ideas in startling juxtapositions: in the same scene, Gawain is told that the bald girl who drives the cart bearing the heads sealed in gold, silver and lead signifies Fortune, whose wheel controls the world; Arthur has a vision of Fortune's wheel just before his final battle with Mordred in later romances, and it is a well-known concept from the writings of Boethius, a fourth-century pagan philosopher. But this is immediately associated with the shield with a red cross, which signifies 'the holy shield of the cross for which none but God ever dared pay the price'. And a succession of secular and religious scenes which Gawain has witnessed are interpreted in similarly striking fashion, ending with a terrible episode which proves to be a parallel to the Eucharist:

'Sire,' said Sir Gawain, 'I wish to ask you about a king I saw who took his dead son and had him boiled and cooked, and then gave him to all the people of his land to eat.' 'Sire,' replied the priest, 'he had brought his heart to the Saviour and wanted to make a sacrifice to Our Lord with his son's blood and flesh, and so he gave him to be eaten by all his people, wishing them to share his belief. And he has so cleared his land of all wrongful religion that none now remains.'[6]

Note that we do not get the expected interpretation, which would be that the king represents God, and the dead son who is eaten represents Christ in the Mass; it is an imaginative reworking of the idea of redemption through sacrifice, with a similarly beneficial result. What the author is doing is using a process familiar to medieval commentators on the Old Testament, where events prior to the coming of Christ heralded those of the New Testament – 'coming events cast their shadow before'. Thus, looking at Perceval's combat with the Black Hermit, the Harrowing of Hell, in which Christ freed the souls of the righteous who had died before His time,

is adumbrated in [this] event, which thus speaks of it, reminds men once more of its message of hope or salvation or terror – *but does not portray or represent it* . . . [It is] an archetypal deliverance mirrored in some sort by all deliverances since . . .[7]

Perlesvaus, more than any of the other Grail romances, is an exhortation to action, to achieving the work of redemption begun by Christ by assisting in the triumph of the New Law. At the outset, we see Arthur fallen into lethargy, failing to hold court for his knights, and recalled to his high purpose by the vision at the chapel of St Augustine. It is Arthur who has the vision of the Grail as chalice, and it is he, not a priest, who is charged with introducing the chalice, until then unknown in Britain, into his kingdom. The New Law is to succeed through the efforts of the knights – even through the deeds of Lancelot who, as a sinner, cannot see the Holy Grail. For those knights who are able to behold the Grail, it acts as both a reward and a renewal of their zeal: Arthur, when he undertakes the pilgrimage to the Grail, is told that 'when he returns his belief will be twice as great'.

Whereas in the other romances, the mission of the seekers of the Grail is either the healing of the Fisher King or individual spiritual achievement, here the author creates the dark antithesis of the Grail castle, the 'Castle Mortal' (*Chastel Mortel*), whose king is brother to the Fisher King but is his deadly enemy. There is therefore a physical enemy who must be conquered: the king of Castle Mortal succeeds in taking the Grail castle, but Perlesvaus reconquers it and the king of Castle Mortal commits suicide, the most heinous of all sins, by stabbing himself with a sword and falling from the battlements.* The mood of the romance is that of the crusades: force of arms can be a weapon in the redemption of the world, by physically defeating evil, and by the conquest and conversion of the heathen.

The author of *The Quest of the Holy Grail* took the physical history of the Grail as described by Robert de Boron, and turned it into a spiritual history, the history both of the Grail and of the three knights who 'achieve' the quest. In so doing, he picked up one of Chrétien's major themes – the moral and spiritual development of a knight. Furthermore, he provided a new hero, Galahad, descended not only from the lineage of David and of the guardianship of the Grail, but from Lancelot, the peerless secular knight. The new hero has Lancelot's baptismal name, Galahad. The name Galahad occurs in the 'Song of Songs' ('mount Galahad'), and a Cistercian commentary says of it, 'This mountain is the head of the church.'[8] We are in a world where the haphazard excitements and adventures of the earlier romances are replaced by carefully orchestrated symbols. Where *Perlesvaus* offers types and analogies, the *Quest* offers signs that are much more direct and systematic. And where it is difficult to place the author of *Perlesvaus*, it seems reasonably certain that the author of the *Quest* had strong Cistercian connections. On the face of it, it is unlikely that he was actually a Cistercian monk, yet we have evidence that Cistercians strayed from the strict ideals of their founder, St Bernard, and went as far as 'making rhymes'.† Even though any religious writer could, on the face of it, have reworked the romance in this symbolic vein, there are good reasons which argue for a Cistercian author, or at least a writer who was very close to the order. At the most obvious level, the order itself – whose habit was white – is prominent in one respect. As the knights pursue the Grail quest and come to different abbeys, those which are identified as belonging to a specific order are always named as being houses of white monks.

More important, however, is the demonstrably Cistercian element in the theology behind the *Quest*. Etienne Gilson analysed the ideas put forward in the romance, and showed that the crucial doctrine of grace is couched in terms used by the Cistercian theologians of the period.[9] In his words, 'we acknowledge that the *Quest* is an abstract and systematic work, to the extent that we can hardly promise to find ten consecutive lines written simply for the pleasure of telling a tale'.[10] There are none of the gratuitous

---

* As always in *Perlesvaus*, it is tempting to read meanings into this, and to make of the king of Castle Mortal a dualist heretic, with the two castles parodying the belief of Cathars and others in the near-equality of good and evil in the world.

† See p. 94 above.

adventures found elsewhere in the romances – of which the first appearance of the Grail itself in Chrétien is a prime example. Each scene in the *Quest* is composed as a symbol, and the whole romance is infested by hermits, whose function is to explain both to the protagonists and the reader the spiritual import of the events that unfold before them.

In Chrétien's romance, Perceval moves from untutored simpleton to some degree of self-knowledge and maturity before the text breaks off. In the *Quest*, by contrast, any odyssey is purely spiritual, and even then Galahad does not progress from innocence to a state of grace so much as lead the way for his companions, Perceval and Bors, the two other heroes of the story. Galahad is perfect from the start, and possesses spiritual qualities which both set him apart and enable him to guide the others. The quest adventures merely set the seal on what we already know: that he is perfect, and is indeed a type of Christ himself. But this does not mean that there is nothing to be learnt from his example. Gilson argues that the *Quest* is about approaching God through feeling (sentiment) rather than intellectual knowledge, and that the keynote of the adventures is grace and its action on the soul. We have already touched on the concept of the Grail as the symbol of grace in the *Quest*, and noted that it is directly stated to be 'the Holy Grail . . . the grace of the Holy Spirit'.[11]

The Cistercian doctrine of grace provides the dramatic tension of the romance, because, in Bernard of Clairvaux's analysis, free will can co-exist with grace: although in a sense Galahad, Perceval and Bors are predestined to achieve the Grail, and there are signs and symbols to remind us of this, each is ultimately a free agent, possessing free will. As another hermit tells Bors, who has likened a man's heart to the helm of a ship, 'At the helm . . . there stands a master who holds and governs it . . . and turns it where he would; so is it too with the human heart. For a man's good works proceed from the grace and guidance of the Holy Ghost, the evil from the enemy's seduction.'[12]

The adventures, therefore, are seen as a series of tests, in which the Grail knights must accept the action of grace if they are to succeed. The dramatic tension lies in the choice: whether the hero will perform the right action. This fits well with the traditional adventures of chivalric romance, but substitutes a moral choice for the often arbitrary key to the secular versions of such episodes.

But to portray the *Quest* as a relentless sermon by example is to do it an injustice. The author is by no means rigid in his approach: a theologian would detect the operation of grace in an episode such as Perceval's escape from the temptress. As he gets into bed with the lady, it happened by chance that he caught sight of his sword, which the servants had laid on the ground when they unbuckled it. As he went to place it against the bed, his glance fell on a red cross which was inlaid in the hilt. Directly he saw it he came to his senses. He made the sign of the cross on his forehead and immediately the tent collapsed about him and he was shrouded in a cloud of blinding smoke, while so foul a stench pervaded everything that he thought he must be in hell.[13]

Equally, there is direct divine intervention, as when God prevents Bors from fighting his brother Lionel; and we have already touched on the way in which Galahad is shown as a kind of Christ figure. On the other side there are varying degrees of sinfulness, from Gawain's refusal to repent and Lionel's obdurate violence against his own brother, to Lancelot's efforts to free himself from Guinevere.

The author of the *Quest* is not simply using the framework of romance to put across a religious viewpoint. His grounding is in Cistercian theology, and in some ways both the weakest and strongest passages in the book stem from this: at one extreme are the sometimes laborious expositions of the meaning of the knights' adventures, and at the other the mystical vision of the scenes at Sarras when the Grail is finally achieved. His methods are original, even if rooted in the long tradition of scholarly commentaries on the Bible, and he often creates images with multiple echoes of Biblical and allegorical topics; it is this multiplicity of meaning that gives the story much of its richness. We can read the story as a romance, and accept the literal interpretations of the knightly episodes expounded by the hermits, but we can also look below the surface and find further layers of transformation. Just as in *Perlesvaus*, Arthur's vision of the Grail undergoes a series of changes (*muances*), shifting its shape, so the events of the *Quest* seem to come into focus as they are described and decoded, only to dissolve into another range of images if we look at them closely.

In *Perlesvaus*, the implication is that the *muances* are physical forms with spiritual overtones, ending in a chalice. In the *Quest*, the shape of the Grail is constant, but the facets of the spiritual forms change: it is never exclusively to be identified with one specific aspect or attribute, and to try to 'identify' it is to misunderstand its nature. It is not a question of whether it 'is' the dish of the Last Supper, the Eucharist, a symbol of grace or indeed of God itself: it is all of these, and yet no single one of them. Nor is this a question of evading the issue, of hedging one's scholarly bets. The style of the author of the *Quest* works exactly in these indefinite yet precise ways, and the layering of identity, meaning and symbol which can be found even in minor episodes applies a fortiori to the pivot and centre of his story.[14]

The knights who set out on the Grail quest are in search of a physical object. But when Gawain, who, for all his sins, is the initiator of this search, declares that his aim is to see it 'openly', he does not want to know exactly what this object looks like. 'But we are so blinded and beguiled,' he says, 'that we could not see it plain: rather, its true appearance (*vraie semblance*) was hidden from us.'[15] The knights are therefore in search of a metaphysical truth rather than a simple physical presence, and we shall return to this when we come to look at the question of the 'secrets of the Grail'. But the physical objects surrounding the Grail reinforce its sacred and special nature: the table on which it is placed recalls the table of the Ark of the Covenant, the candlestick which accompanies it in Lancelot's and Gawain's vision the sacred six-branched candlestick that is found on that table. And Galahad, when he becomes king of Sarras, builds an ark in which the Grail is to be housed. Again, the spices and scents which accompany the Grail's appearances at Camelot and elsewhere echo the language of the 'Song of Songs'. The imagery and language of the *Quest* are deeply imbued with scriptural tradition, which is used, not in any artificial and didactic way, but as an entirely natural mode of discourse, with no hesitation as to whether it is appropriate to a secular romance. It is this that gives the *Quest* its added dimension.

The theology of the *Quest*, given the demands of the narrative and the fact that it is a work of the imagination, is never precise, and just as too simplistic an approach to meaning and symbolism is dangerous here, so the identification of a particular theological tenet is equally difficult. There are echoes, not direct statements, and the author uses theological concepts as another weapon in his artistic armoury. We can detect a particular devotion to the idea of the Trinity, but this was a commonplace of thirteenth-century belief, and its absence would be more surprising: it is not emphasized as strongly as in the opening pages of Robert de Boron's work. By contrast, the final Mass at Sarras is said to be 'the Mass of the glorious Mother of God'; and yet there is very little evidence of a specifically Marian devotion in the romance before this point.

Galahad's final vision is deliberately left to the realms of things beyond imagination and description. Its nature can be traced to the ideas of St Bernard on the possibility of seeing God face to face, the so-called Beatific Vision. At the heart of this is the famous passage of St Paul: 'for now we see through a glass darkly; but then we shall see face to face'.[16] The Latin, *per speculum in aenigmate*, refers not to the loss of light that the translation of the King James Bible implies, but to riddles and mysteries, the *aenigmate somniorum*, riddles of dreams, of Cicero's Latin: William Tyndale's version of 1534 talks of 'a darke speakynge'. Clarity of vision is not simply a question of more light, but of revelation, of the discovery of mysteries. So the word used consistently of the desired vision of the Grail is not 'clearly' but 'openly', *apertement*. The knights who are privileged to see the Grail are never certain of what they see until the final scenes at Corbenic and at Sarras – until, at Corbenic, Christ himself explains the identity of the Grail and one of its symbolic meanings, as the centre of the ritual of the Eucharist.*

But the mystery within the Grail is greater than the mystery of the Real Presence at Mass; Galahad senses this, and at Sarras he alone attains the personal vision for which he has sought. The Beatific Vision is also the climax of the other medieval masterpiece which treats of divine matters in a secular framework: Dante's *Divine Comedy*. According to the theologians, the true Beatific Vision, the revelation of the face of God, can only be achieved in the life hereafter, and although the language and context evoke the Beatific Vision, which was a subject dear to the Cistercian mystics of the time, and much discussed by them, what Galahad sees may be clear to him, but to us lesser mortals remains *aenigmata*, a riddle and a mystery:

'For now I see openly what tongue cannot describe nor heart conceive. Here I see the beginning of great daring and the prime cause of prowess; here I see the marvel of all other marvels.'[17]

Galahad describes the ultimate vision not in the vocabulary of mysticism, but in essentially chivalric terms, 'daring' (*hardemenz*) and 'prowess' (*proeces*): the *Quest* is, above all, a glorification of idealized knighthood, for here neither the monks nor the kings attain the final vision. It is as if 'the Grail is the relic which Christ himself has destined for chivalry, the fief with which he has invested it'.[18] We may be able to read the story in a multiplicity of ways, but in the end it is a secular romance, not a sermon or a moral tract. And this is why it is such an astonishing work: it is as if the entire hierarchy of the spiritual world had been put at the service of the highest secular ideals.

The *Quest* is carefully integrated into the cycle of romances, yet, as Sir Thomas Malory sensed when he came to translate it, it does not confront entirely the problems that this causes, notably in the case of Lancelot. Galahad's birth is wrought by magic, and he is illegitimate; and at the end

---

* Although the reader is aware of this identification, the knights themselves do not learn of it until this scene.

of the *Quest*, Lancelot goes back to his old sin. This makes the *Quest* seem like a journey into a different world, and the problem of the relationship of this highly religious and symbolic text to the rest of the cycle has not yet been satisfactorily analysed. The disciplined world of the *Quest* reflects closely both the spiritual world of the Cistercians and their links with the secular aristocracy, and enshrines the supreme vision of the Grail itself as a moment which is the spiritual climax of the Arthurian stories.

The *History of the Holy Grail* forms a 'prequel' to the *Quest*; it is almost certainly by another, later hand. Whereas the *Quest*'s narrative is essentially within the norms of romance, the *History* reads more like an attempt by a religious writer – once more, probably a Cistercian – to mould a secular form to his own ends. To some extent, it provides the pre-history of later adventures central to the Grail quest, such as the ship of Solomon which carries the chosen heroes on their journey towards Sarras, the Grail castle, at the end of their journeys, and sets up spells and enchantments which only the knights who are to achieve the Grail will be able to bring to a close. But its function is also to provide a kind of Old Testament to the New Testament of the *Quest*, in that its narrative prefigures the events of the *Quest* in the same way that medieval theologians read the Old Testament as a foreshadowing of the New. It provides the history of some of the objects. In terms of prefiguration, we find Josephus wounded in the thigh, like the Fisher King; Nascien undergoes a version of Perceval's temptation by the devil in female form; and there is a spiritual version of the love of Lancelot and Guinevere.[19]

The concept of prefiguration is a commonplace of medieval theology, but there are other theological concerns. Much play is made of the virginity of Mary, and Lucian, a pagan philosopher who denies the possibility of the virgin birth, is struck dead. This emphasis on the role of Mary in the preaching of Joseph and his followers when they attempt to convert pagans to Christianity could arguably be due to Cistercian influence. Bernard of Clairvaux and other writers from the order were ardent champions of the Virgin. The vision of Josephus when he opens the ark containing the Grail* might also indicate something of the author's background: it belongs to a mystic and apocalyptic tradition, and it has been argued that this is related to the writing of Joachim of Fiore, the Cistercian visionary of the late twelfth century.[20] The *History* also contains an account of the first Eucharist, celebrated by Joseph of Arimathea, and the description of the service includes details which imply some degree of special theological knowledge.

* See p. 67 above.

But the opening of the *History* is in one sense deeply indebted to the conventions of romance. The book containing the history of the Grail is given to a hermit by an angel. Almost at once, it mysteriously vanishes, and the hermit sets out like a knight errant in quest of the book, guided by a strange creature, part sheep, part dog, part fox, with a lion's tail, and his adventures are typical of a knight-errant's adventures.[21] Likewise, when Josephus is instituted as the first bishop, the text echoes the speech of the Lady of the Lake on knighthood when Lancelot is knighted, and the instruction given by Merlin to Arthur when he is crowned.

In the *History* and the *Quest*, the knightly conventions of the romances are transmogrified into something as hybrid as the strange beast of the hermit's adventure; we are left wondering if we are reading the work of a monk with a lively secular imagination, or that of a devout layman wishing to adapt his favourite reading to a higher purpose. Perhaps the latter is not such a remote possibility; the mystical tradition which inspires the pages relating the culmination of the Grail quest was one in which the laity partook, and which, like the legend of the Grail, was often at one remove from the official teachings of the Church. Equally, the Cistercians were the one monastic order with a special involvement in secular knighthood, and whether we are looking for a monk or a layman as author, it is to this milieu, at once chivalrous and religious, that he is most likely to have belonged. And it is arguable that the right way to read the *Quest* is not as an intrusion of theology into literature, but as an extension of the scope of the history of Arthur. We should perhaps see the *Quest* as the work of a chivalric enthusiast bold enough to add a spiritual dimension unparalleled in any other romance.[22]

The Grail and Its Hero

This dual legacy of spiritual and knightly perfection means that the Grail hero has to represent the ideal of both earthly and heavenly chivalry, and the situation is complicated by the question of whether he is predestined to win the Grail. In Chrétien's version, the Grail is simply Perceval's personal adventure, just as the lance is assigned to Gawain. Each quest is a kind of allocated task, which only a particular knight is obliged to achieve – Perceval because of his failure to ask the question on his first visit, Gawain because he has to undertake it to clear himself of an accusation of murdering a fellow-knight. There is nothing special about Perceval's status as seeker of the Grail, and the same is true in *Perlesvaus*. It is Robert de Boron, the writer of theological romance, who introduces the idea of predestination, as we have seen earlier in this chapter. From this evolves the picture of Galahad as the predestined hero who is, from the outset, chosen to achieve the Grail; this is also part of his role as an image of Christ, chosen to achieve the redemption of mankind.

Christ, in medieval imagery, was shown as a knight fighting for this redemption; the Grail knight remains quintessentially a knight, and may win his way to the Grail by knightly prowess. True, Galahad's prowess consists more in resisting temptation than in physical fighting; but the concept of fighting for the Grail returns in Wolfram's *Parzival*, where it is harnessed uneasily with the idea of predestination, and is complicated by Parzival's hereditary claim to the Grail.[23] All these elements occur in the French stories, where much is made of Galahad's descent from the lineage of Joseph of Arimathea. But in Wolfram, Parzival is not descended from a biblical ancestor, but from the first keeper of the Grail, a knight chosen for his purity of life. So we find contrasting references to the ways in which the Grail may be won: 'whoever aspired to the Grail had to approach fame with the sword'; 'no one, indeed, can gain the Grail except he who is known in Heaven to be appointed to the Grail'; 'with God's favour I have inherited the Grail'.[24] Two of these concerns are the paramount driving forces of feudal society – warlike skills and inheritance of status; the third, divine election, is what sets apart the Grail knight from all other romance heroes.

12

The Secrets of the Grail

Robert de Boron talks of the 'secrets of the Grail', and this has led many modern writers to pursue the idea of a lost source or a secret tradition concerning the Grail. It can be traced back to the beginnings of the history of the Grail, but when we come to examine the evidence closely, the references to books and secrets are not quite what they seem. Even in *The Story of the Grail*, Chrétien twice mentions a book given to him, and in the first instance, in the prologue to the story, he specifically implies that this was his source: 'It is the story of the Grail of which the count gave him the book.'[1] The second mention appears in the description of the hideous messenger who comes to reproach Perceval for his failure to ask the Grail question. Here Chrétien lends authority to his vivid portrait by appealing to his source: if 'the words are true which the book sets out' (*devise*). At other points, he uses the phrase 'as the story (*estoire*) says'. *Estoire* was frequently used by historians writing in French, and had acquired, in addition to its original meaning of 'story' or 'narrative', the more precise meaning of a 'true narrative', and it implied a specifically historical text.[2] The word *estoire* occurs at the end of the description of a knight whom Perceval has conquered, whom Chrétien calls 'the finest knight in the world'; in the description of the Grail castle, when a table of solid ivory is brought in; it is used when Perceval is said to have lost his memory, and when Gawain arrives at a splendid castle.[3] In every case, the appeal to a source occurs when something superlative or beyond belief is introduced. The *estoire* is a fictional device which is used to suspend our disbelief by appealing to a higher authority.

Twelfth-century writers were particularly sensitive to the charge that they were inventing stories for which there was no 'authority'. The philosopher Adelard of Bath complained that if he had something new to say, he was 'constrained by the prevailing conservatism of the day to conceal it under a pseudonymous author who can act as an authority'.[4] If we turn to Chrétien's other romances, we find in each case a declaration that what follows comes from a written source of some kind; only in *Lancelot* is there any doubt as to whether it was a book: Chrétien says that the matter and treatment of it came from Marie, countess of Champagne. In *Cligés*, which is primarily drawn from his imagination, in that both characters and situation are unknown elsewhere, he makes greatest play with the idea of a higher authority: this tale comes from a book in the library of the church of St Pierre at Beauvais.

We cannot positively identify a single one of Chrétien's source books,[5] and the way in which he handles them in the narrative, either to whet the appetite or to suspend disbelief, makes it reasonably certain that this is a literary device. The books, like the stories, stem from Chrétien's fertile imagination: there may have been written tales that inspired him as far as details were concerned, part of whatever learning and reading he had done, but none of these books contained anything remotely like the whole of one of his romances. There will never be any certainties where the Grail is concerned, but my reading of Chrétien is that the idea of an earlier Grail book is a chimera, an authority invented by the writer. What Chrétien had imagined, however, was to have an extraordinary future.

We have argued thus far that the Grail romances are orthodox, in their various ways, and that they have nothing to do with an esoteric or heretical tradition. But there is one problem which must be faced to justify this interpretation: the consistent references to the 'secrets' of the Grail. In Chrétien, there is no 'secret' about the Grail, other than his imaginary book. But what is 'secret', because the romance is unfinished, is Perceval's presumed asking of the question and the answer that he receives. If we look more closely, however, this information is clearly set out by Chrétien: Perceval learns first from his cousin what the question should be, and then, from his uncle the hermit, what the answer is. So the Grail's secrets are fully revealed, and all that Perceval has to do is to find the Grail castle again, and fulfil his appointed task. The nearest to a mystery that we come is in the scene in which the hermit tells Perceval about the Grail, and few commentators have explored its implications: Perceval is taught a prayer which contains the names of Our Lord, which may not be uttered except in dire peril. But this is not the central issue, and Chrétien's Grail is not a secret.

It is only in the *First Continuation* that the idea of secrecy first appears: when Gawain approaches the Grail castle by night, he encounters a terrifying storm. In the long version of this section, the marvels of the night are said to be such 'that they should not be told to anyone; he who does so will suffer for it, for they are among the secrets of the Grail, and those who set out to tell them other than they should be told will be punished for their pride'.[6] Later, Gawain is told that he can learn about the lance, but the Fisher King says that he cannot reveal anything else for the moment, because Gawain has failed to mend the broken sword, 'the rest is so secret that I dare not tell you about it'. So the Grail becomes a secret, not for the reader, who already knows about it from Perceval's uncle, but for Gawain, because he is not yet worthy of such knowledge. The same rule of secrecy is applied to Perceval in the *Second Continuation*, when he is searching for the Grail castle, and sees a marvellous tree burning with light in the forest; the girl on the white mule explains to him that the lights are those of the Fisher King's company, who have the Grail with them. He begs her to tell him more about the Grail, but she refuses: 'for it is a most secret thing'. No one should speak of it unless they are a priest in holy orders, or a man who leads a holy life. Only such men can speak of the Grail and recount the marvels 'which no man can hear without shivering and trembling, changing colour and going pale with fear'.[7]

Towards the end of the *Second Continuation*, four out of ten of the manuscripts speak of the 'precious Grail, about which no man should talk, even if he has all the wealth in the world'.[8] The idea that the secrets can only be revealed when a knight has repaired the broken sword is taken up again at the beginning of Gerbert de Montreuil's *Continuation*, where Perceval is told that if he can mend the broken sword perfectly – there is still a small notch in the blade – 'truly then, you may be sure, you would know the profound truth, the secrets and the divine mystery'.[9] Finally, *The Elucidation Prologue*, which is an exercise in obfuscation, lays heavy emphasis on the secret: 'this [romance] is about the Grail, whose secret no one should tell or relate; for if the tale were fully told many men might be the worse for it who would not otherwise have suffered. Wise men leave it alone, and pass on, for master Blihis does not lie when he says that no one should tell the secret.'[10] Yet in the context of Chrétien's poem – to which all the *Continuations* and *The Elucidation Prologue* are of course inextricably linked – there is no secret, except within the framework of the story, in that the protagonists themselves are kept in ignorance of the meaning of their experiences.

Robert de Boron, by contrast, insists that there is a secret surrounding the Grail, and this has given rise to all sorts of attempts to identify what this secret might be, or to what it might relate. The crucial passage comes just after Jesus has appeared to Joseph of Arimathea in prison, and has instructed him in the celebration of Mass and in its symbolism. At the end of Christ's speech, Robert turns to his audience to reassure them that he tells this story on good authority, before Christ gives Joseph the Grail. He says:

I would not dare to tell this tale, nor could I do so even if I wanted to, if I did not have the great book in which these histories are written down, dictated and made by the great clerks. There are written the great secrets which are named and called the Graal.[11]

What we have to consider is the context: Christ has just instructed Joseph in the central mystery of the Church, the Mass. The prayer at the consecration of the Eucharist was called the 'secreta' in the early Middle Ages.[12] It is the Mass itself that constitutes the 'secrets', particularly the interpretation of the vessels used in it, which corresponds to that in Amalarius of Metz and the texts which derive from him. It could be argued that the 'great book' to which Robert refers is one of these texts, such as Honorius' *Jewel of the Soul*. Robert's 'secrets', as with Chrétien's claim to have used another text, and the extreme case of the *History of the Holy Grail*, where the source-book is said to have been written by Christ himself, are a way of validating the story and reassuring the reader as to the truth of what he is being told.

This reading is confirmed by the subsequent references to this episode, both in *The Romance of the History of the Grail* and in the prose versions. Towards the end of the poem, Joseph names Bron, the Rich Fisher, as his successor: an angel commands him to tell Bron 'the holy words which are sweet and precious, gracious and full of pity, whose proper name is to be called the secrets of the Grail'; Joseph does so, and also writes them down. He then demonstrates the secrets to Bron 'very privately'.[13]

The fact that Joseph 'demonstrates' the secrets implies that there is a ritual at the heart of the matter; and this confirms our view that Robert has the Mass in mind.[14] As to the words, they are exactly those to which Robert has already referred in his description of the 'great book': there is no deeper level of significance. The prose version supports this view, and moves from 'secrets' to 'consecration': '*secré*' becomes '*sacre*' in two instances,[15] and in the *Prose Perceval* Bron passes on to Perceval the 'sacred words' which Joseph had taught him.[16] It is only in the second manuscript of the *Prose Perceval* that the 'sacred words' become once more 'the secret words',[17] but the two are effectively interchangeable. In *Perlesvaus*, the idea of secrets associated with the Grail appears only once, when Arthur goes on pilgrimage to the Grail; the Grail appears at the consecration of the Host in the Mass in five forms, 'but they should not be revealed, for the secrets of the sacrament none should tell save he whom God has granted grace'.[18]

In the *Lancelot-Grail*, we find a combination of both aspects of the secrets of the Grail. In the Grail scenes in *Lancelot*, knowledge of the Grail is denied to all the knights concerned, to Lancelot and Gawain because they are unworthy, to Bors because the quest has not yet been undertaken. And the reader knows that the Grail is the dish of the Last Supper long before Christ reveals this to the assembled knights at Corbenic almost at the end of the story. The saintly old man who announces the quest to Arthur at the beginning of the *Quest* moves our expectations on to a different plane, however:

For this is no search for earthly things but a seeking out of the mysteries and hidden sweets of Our Lord, and the divine secrets which the most high Master will disclose to that blessed knight whom He has chosen for His servant from among the ranks of chivalry: he to whom He will show the marvels of the Holy Grail, and reveal that which the heart of man could not conceive nor tongue relate.[19]

Marvels and mysteries, but the secrets of Robert de Boron have vanished, for if we turn to the beginning of the *History of the Holy Grail*, the scene in which Christ teaches Joseph about the sacrament of the Mass while he is in prison has been removed. Instead, a very different account of the institution of the Mass is given after Joseph's son Josephus has been consecrated as the first bishop of the Christian Church. This harks back to the Eucharistic miracles we have already discussed; it derives from the stories of the transmutation of the Host into the form of actual blood and flesh, and then into the form of a small child, which offer a dramatic visual image of the theological concept of transubstantiation. Again, there are no secrets: indeed, quite the reverse, for the sacrament is to be celebrated 'so that all My people will see it clearly'. In the least secular of all the romances, we should not be surprised to find that the ideas echo so clearly the central issues of the debate over the celebration of Mass and of what its central act entails.

If there is a hidden tradition here, it is not very deeply hidden: the author of the *History of the Holy Grail* is simply returning to the theological sources which Robert de Boron used for his account of the institution of the Mass, and using them in a different way. In other words, the writer of the *History of the Holy Grail* recognized the tradition from which Robert had drawn his inspiration and returned to it for a new approach to the same subject. In the same way the author of *The Book of Arthur* returned to the *Gospel of Nicodemus*, another of Robert's sources, for additional details of the history of Joseph of Arimathea.

The combination of these two books, the apocryphal gospel and the work which drew its allegory of the Mass from it, constitute Robert de Boron's book of the 'secrets of the Grail'; the writers who took up his story and elaborated it were well aware of the identity of that book. The supposed 'secrets' of the Grail are the hidden meanings within the ritual of the Mass, explained by Christ to Joseph, and relate to the symbolic interpretation of the unfolding of the sacrament. In these works, intensely orthodox in their theology, the central ritual of the Church, which was the subject of keen discussion and interest on the part of both laity and clergy at the time, is the focus of the chivalric world, and the secular order of knighthood becomes the means of attaining the highest religious experience within that ritual. What is unorthodox is the history that they relate: but these are romances, works of the imagination, which we would expect to go beyond a simple retelling of the Church's own account of its history. The emphasis on the primacy of Joseph of Arimathea in the preaching of the Gospel, and on Josephus as the first bishop, may point to a milieu which was unsympathetic to the claims of Rome to be the first see of Christendom, but this is a question of ecclesiastical politics, not of heresy or orthodoxy in terms of belief.[20]

13

The Grail Outside the Romances

The romances of Arthur were hugely popular among educated laymen from the thirteenth century onwards. We know that many noble families treasured luxurious manuscripts of them, and the Grail quest was therefore widely known. The romances unequivocally identified the Grail as the cup or dish of the Last Supper, and it was, as we have seen, associated with the relics of the Crucifixion. There were at least three major medieval relics which were said to be the chalice used by Christ at the Last Supper.[1] The earliest of these relics to be recorded appears in the account of Arculf, a pilgrim who travelled from the British Isles to Palestine in the seventh century and described in some detail his experiences there. According to him,

> between the basilica of Golgotha and the *Martyrium*, there is a chapel in which is the chalice of the Lord, which he himself blessed with his own hand and gave to the apostles when reclining with them at supper the day before he suffered. The chalice is silver, has the measure of a Gaulish pint, and has two handles fashioned on either side ... After the resurrection the Lord drank from this same chalice, according to the supping with the apostles. The holy Arculf saw it, and through an opening of the perforated lid of the reliquary where it reposes, he touched it with his own hand which he had kissed. All the people of the city flock to it with great veneration. Arculf saw the soldier's lance as well, with which he pierced the side of the Lord when he was hanging on the cross. This lance is in the porch of the basilica of Constantine ...[2]

This is the only mention of the chalice in the Holy Land, and the only occasion on which it appears as a silver vessel. Nothing is heard of it after the seventh century, though there is a reference in the late thirteenth century to a copy of the Grail being at Byzantium. This occurs in Albrecht's *Later Titurel*,* which says:

* See p. 192 below.

A second costly dish, very noble and very precious, was fashioned to duplicate this one. In holiness it has no flaw. Men of Constantinople assayed it in their land, [finding] it richer in adornment, they accounted it the true *grâl*.[3]

This dish of the Last Supper was said to have been looted from the church of the Bucoleon during the Fourth Crusade and sent from Byzantium to Troyes by Garnier de Trainel, the then bishop of Troyes, in 1204. It was recorded there in 1610, but it disappeared at the French Revolution.[4]

Two vessels of the Last Supper survive to the present day. One is at Genoa, in the cathedral, and the other in Valencia, also in the cathedral. The Genoa vessel is known as *il sacro catino*, the holy bowl or basin, traditionally carved from emerald; it is in fact a green hexagonal Egyptian glass dish, about eighteen inches across.[5] It was sent to Paris after Napoleon's conquest of Italy, and was broken when it was returned to Genoa after his defeat; the breakage showed that it was indeed glass rather than emerald. Its origin is uncertain; according to William of Tyre, writing in about 1170, it was booty from the First Crusade, found in the mosque at Caesarea in 1101:

In this same chapel was found a vase of brilliant green shaped like a bowl. The Genoese, believing that it was of emerald, took it in lieu of a large sum of money and thus acquired a splendid ornament for their church. They still show this vase as a marvel to people of distinction who pass through their city, and persuade them to believe it is truly an emerald, as its color indicates.[6]

An alternative story in a Spanish chronicle[7] says that it was found at Almería in southern Spain when Alfonso VII captured the city from the Moors in 1147 with Genoese help, and that among the booty was '*un uaso de piedra esmeralda que era tamanno como una escudiella*', 'a vase carved from emerald which was like a large cup'. The Genoese said that this was the only thing they wanted, and that it would be sufficient payment for them. The identification of the *sacro catino* with the Grail is clearly made by Jacopo da Voragine (the author of *The Golden Legend*) in his chronicle of Genoa, written at the end of the thirteenth century. He discusses the dish, saying that Christ and his disciples ate from a golden or emerald dish at the Last Supper. According to certain English books, Nicodemus then used a certain emerald vessel to collect Christ's blood at the Deposition, and 'that vessel the aforesaid English call "Sangraal" in their books'.[8]

The equation between the *sacro catino* and the Grail depends simply on the claim that it was the dish used at the Last Supper; if the identification was genuinely made, it must be no earlier than Robert de Boron, and is unlikely to have been introduced much after the mid-thirteenth century, when, as we shall see, the Grail was generally regarded as a cup or chalice. The *sacro catino* seems to have been regarded as precious more because of its apparent intrinsic value as a huge emerald; there is little sign of any local cult attached to it as a relic with a specific history as the dish of the Last Supper.

Much more publicity has surrounded the *santo caliz* of Valencia Cathedral.[9] This may well be a genuine artefact of the Graeco-Roman period from the Near East, though it is extremely difficult to date a fairly simple agate cup, which is what the *santo caliz* essentially consists of. The mount is medieval, and the foot is an inverted cup of chalcedony, perhaps worked in the twelfth to fourteenth centuries; again, dating is extremely difficult. There is an Arabic inscription, whose exact meaning is disputed. The mounts are in the style of fourteenth-century Spanish jewellery.

The history of the Valencia chalice is difficult to trace. It certainly came from a monastery in Catalonia, at San Juan de la Peña. But a reference to the chalice as being there in 1134 is almost certainly a later invention, while a document of 1135 which mentions a chalice being exchanged by San Juan de la Peña for a charter from the king simply reflects a customary transaction of the period, and does not specifically refer to the Valencia chalice.[10] The earliest certain reference is in 1399, when it was given by the monastery of San Juan de la Peña to king Martín I of Aragon in exchange for a gold cup.[11] By the end of the century a provenance had been invented for the chalice at Valencia, by which St Peter had brought it to Rome, and in around 256 it was supposedly given by Pope Sixtus II to St Laurence, who took it to his native city of Huesca.[12] No word of Joseph of Arimathea, no association with the Holy Blood; this is a different tradition altogether. In all these documents, the chalice is simply called *caliz*, even though the word *grial* is found most frequently in the Hispanic- and Catalan-speaking area.

There are hints that the kings of Aragon were particularly interested in the chalice of the Last Supper. Jaime II of Aragon, in a letter to the sultan of Egypt dated 1322, asks the latter to send him the chalice used by Christ at the Last Supper, which is among the treasures owned by the sultan.[13] However, nothing seems to have come of this. A century later, there is possible evidence that Alfonso V of Aragon associated the Valencia chalice with the Grail. A drawing by Pisanello shows a jousting helmet designed for Alfonso. It has a fashionably elaborate crest, which represents the Siege Perilous, the seat in which Galahad sat at the beginning of the Grail quest. A similar design was described on his armour.[14] But when he apparently pawned the chalice to the cathedral at Valencia to help to pay for his wars in 1437, his clerks described it by its usual title, 'the chalice in which Jesus Christ consecrated the blood on the Thursday of the supper'.[15]

So, despite Robert de Boron's description of the Grail as among the most important relics of the Crucifixion, and despite the appearance in Western Christendom about this time of other similar relics – of Christ's blood, of the Crown of Thorns, of the Holy Lance – there is little or no evidence that anyone claimed in the thirteenth century to possess the Grail. At some time in the early fourteenth century, the kings of Aragon claimed to possess the chalice of the Last Supper, without calling it the Grail; and only in the fifteenth century is there tenuous evidence to suggest that the king wished to make the identification between the Valencia chalice and the Grail.

If the custodians of the dish of the Last Supper were reluctant to identify their treasures with the Grail, they were only following the normal attitude of the Church to the stories about the Grail, which was to studiously ignore them. Yet in two cases distinguished churchmen showed that they knew the romances, or at least stories very similar to them.

In the light of the possible association made by Alfonso V between the Valencia chalice and the Grail, it is an interesting coincidence – but perhaps nothing more – that the only work of sacred literature to mention the Grail is the Catalan *Libre de Gamaliel*, written by Pere Pasqual, bishop of Jaén; he was martyred in 1300 by the Moslems as he was saying Mass. In the *Libre de Gamaliel*, the association of the Grail with the *Gospel of Nicodemus* actually leads to the crossing of the division between romance and sacred literature. There was an early apocryphal *Gospel of Gamaliel*, narrated in the first person, which is related to the stories about Pilate, dating from as early as the fifth century, and of which only fragments survive.[16] Pasqual's source was a variant on the *Gospel of Nicodemus*, written in Occitan, the language of southern France, whose anonymous author created a new apocryphal narrative attributed to Joseph of Arimathea, Nicodemus and Gamaliel; the latter was a historical figure who was St Paul's teacher. It included the version of the story of Longinus, in which Longinus is blind, and the blood running down the lance on to his hand restores his sight. However, Pasqual adds at this point:

Then Joseph of Arimathea took a *gresal* in which he put the blood of Jesus Christ, and he kept the lance [which Longinus had used]; and they all returned to the city, save for the relatives of the mother of Jesus Christ and the others who were with her, St John the Evangelist and Joseph of Arimathea.[17]

This is the single instance of the use of the word *gresal* by an ecclesiastical writer. One other author, the distinguished theologian Robert Grosseteste, also knew a variation on the *Gospel of Nicodemus* in which Joseph played a part very similar to that in Robert de Boron's romance. When Henry III acquired a relic of the Holy Blood for Westminster Abbey from Jerusalem in 1247, Robert Grosseteste wrote a tract to glorify the relic. In it, he describes how Joseph washed Christ's body after taking it down from the cross. Joseph preserved the water which he had used, which was mingled with blood, 'in a most pure vessel. The pure blood that had flowed from the wounds in His hands and feet he placed more reverently, with the greatest respect and honour, in a most noble vessel . . . like a treasure beyond price, keeping it for himself and his successors.'[18] This echoes Robert de Boron, but does not name the Grail itself.

Other writers, who were probably not clerics, were aware of the link between the *Gospel of Nicodemus* and the romances: the insertion of a French translation into the so-called 'Livre d'Artus', part of a lengthier version of the *Lancelot-Grail*,[19] is evidence of this. A very different approach was taken by Jacob van Maerlant, who in about 1260–65 translated Robert de Boron's work into Dutch. Instead of treating the *Gospel of Nicodemus* as an extension of the romance text, he used it to correct what he saw as egregious errors in the original from which he was working.[20] Even as he worked through the French text, he inserted critical comments about the authenticity of the story he was retelling, and reduced the story of Pilate giving the cup to Joseph and the collection of Christ's blood to two brief passages.[21]

Two decades later he wrote a rather different work – a history based on part of the Latin encyclopaedia of Vincent of Beauvais, which was called, like the original, *The Mirror of History* (*Spiegel Historiael*). It seems that the Grail still troubled him, for although it has no place in Vincent's work, on three occasions he inserts critical comments about the Grail romances. In the prologue he declares

Whomever the silly fiction of the Grail, the lies about Percival and many other false stories annoy and fail to please, should prefer this *Spiegel Historiael* . . . for here one finds in particular truth and many wonders, wisdom and beautiful instruction . . .[22]

He is contrasting the idle amusement afforded by the romances with his serious purpose in presenting a translation of real history to much the same audience. But it is odd to single out the absent Grail, and this can only be ascribed to his earlier discovery of the discrepancies between romance and scripture. He adds another comment to this effect when he comes to relate Joseph of Arimathea's part in the Crucifixion:

About this Joseph of Arimathea the liars of the Grail compose their nonsensical stories which I consider to be altogether nothing.[23]

Maerlant is a historian who happened to choose for his first major commission a subject to which he was unsuited temperamentally, and he clearly regretted his encounter with fiction. There is no ideological programme behind his attacks, merely an incorruptible view of historical truth. But even so, in general terms, Maerlant was far from alone in his hostility to the Grail. The Church was deeply suspicious of the world of romance, and sermons attacking idle fables were a commonplace; yet Maerlant is the only writer to specifically criticize the Grail romances. Elsewhere in ecclesiastical circles the response seems to have been a studied or contemptuous silence. The Grail was destined to remain outside the Church's ken, cherished only by the poets who had created it and the enthusiastic readers of their work.

14

'There is a thing that's called the Grâl'

One name has been missing from our analysis of the concepts and theology surrounding the Grail: Wolfram von Eschenbach. His view is so radically different that there are hardly any points of contact, and the problems that his poem raises are so intractable that the only possible approach is to take him in relative isolation.

Wolfram's Definition of the Grail

Wolfram's description of the Grail procession which Parzival sees on his first visit to Munsalvaesche is the most elaborate to be found in any version of the story. Chrétien had depicted a simple, swift and mysterious image which imprinted itself indelibly on the mind of the young Perceval. Wolfram gives us instead a ceremonial occasion: the procession does not simply pass through the hall of the Fisher King's castle, but uses it as the stage for an extended, choreographed ritual, which he describes in his usual luxuriant style. If we strip away the layers of Wolfram's colourful imagery and look simply at the personnel and objects involved in the procession, this is what we find:

> the bleeding lance, carried by a page who runs into the hall and out again; this
>   is a prelude to the Grail procession, and is not part of it
> two girls carrying lights
> two ladies carrying ivory trestle-tables
> four ladies carrying candles
> four ladies carrying a table-top made of a garnet-hyacinth cut thinly, which is
>   placed on the ivory trestles
> two ladies with silver knives
> four ladies with lights
> six ladies with lights of balsam
> the princess with the 'grâl'

Wolfram has assembled a cast of twenty-five to present the 'grâl' to the Fisher King, and the first part of the scene ends when the princess, surrounded by her attendants, places the 'grâl' on the table; they all stand in formation, twelve on each side of the princess, while the knights are seated at table, served by chamberlains and pages. In the second part of the scene, the 'grâl' provides food and drink for the assembled company. Once the feast is over, the attendants of the 'grâl' come forward and the procession is reversed as they bear away the 'grâl' and its attendant objects. Wolfram gives us this description once only; after Parzival returns to ask the crucial question, the 'grâl' is once again brought out, and the ceremony is repeated. But the account of the procession centres on Repanse de Schoye, the Grail-bearer, with whom Parzival's half-brother Feirefiz falls in love, and the rest of the ritual passes unmentioned.

On the surface – particularly as the surface is a glittering embroidery of verbal decoration – the scene in which the Grail first appears in Wolfram is a very different event from that created by Chrétien. But if we look more closely, it is nonetheless recognizably the same occasion, if we take into account the description of the Grail feast in the *First Continuation*, which would have been present in many of the manuscripts of *The Story of the Grail*. These two passages contain all the basic material for Wolfram's version; the only essential difference, apart from the numbers of attendants, is the presence of the mysterious silver knives, to which Wolfram makes no further reference. The brilliant lights, the lance and the Grail itself all come from Chrétien's original procession: the second part of the scene corresponds to Gawain's Grail visit in the longer version of the *First Continuation*, where the details of how the Grail feeds the assembled company are very similar. The two romances, *Parzival* and the *First Continuation* of *The Story of the Grail*, are undoubtedly talking about the same events.[1]

But what about the Grail itself? Neither Chrétien nor the *First Continuation* author actually *describe* it. Chrétien's audience knew – unless we are totally misinformed – that the Grail was a kind of dish, and that its nature was implicit in the word itself: it did not require further description. Wolfram does not initially describe it either. At its first appearance, he presents it in splendid terms, but we are none the wiser as to what it might be.

Upon a green achmardi she carried the perfection of Paradise, both root and branch. This was a thing that was called the Grail, earth's perfection's transcendence.[2]

This reticence is all the more striking when the rest of the scene is described with the greatest of detail and precision. It is only later, when Parzival comes to the hermitage on Good Friday and meets his uncle Trevrizent that, as in

Chrétien, both he and we, the readers, learn anything more. Chrétien's phrase *sainte chose*, 'a holy thing', would still describe Wolfram's 'grâl' – and it is worth noting that in the earlier scene Wolfram calls the 'grâl' 'a thing'. But the context is totally different: Wolfram declares that Parzival is 'about to learn matters about the Grail that have been hidden', and offers as his excuse for the delay in revealing these secrets an assertion that such matters should not be related 'till the story itself reached that point expressly where it *has* to be spoken of'. What Wolfram tells us, however, is far from clear; indeed, there is an air of deliberate obfuscation. Meister Kyot, whom he claims as his informant, found the tale 'in heathenish script', yet 'it helped him that he was a baptized Christian – otherwise this tale would be still unknown. No infidel art would avail us to reveal the nature of the Grail and how one came to know its secrets.' Yet it is precisely the heathen Flegetanis who 'wrote of the marvels of the Grail', and who

saw with his own eyes . . . occult mysteries in the constellation. He said there was a thing called the Grail, whose name he read immediately in the constellation – what it was called: 'A host abandoned it upon the earth, flying up, high above the stars. Was it their innocence drew them back? Ever since, baptised fruit has had to tend it with such chaste courtesy – those human beings are always worthy whose presence is requested by the Grail.'

Thus Flegetanis wrote of it.[3]

Kyot's own contribution was to embark on 'a search for this tale in Latin books in order to discover where there may have been a people suited to keep the Grail and follow a disciplined life'. What he found enabled him to tell the history of the Grail dynasty, Parzival's kin, and of their guardianship of the Grail.

Is this all in Wolfram's imagination, or did Kyot really exist?[4] If we answer the latter question in the affirmative, we accept the existence of a lost Grail tradition of great importance; if we deny Kyot's existence, we have to be able to show that Wolfram could have imagined *Parzival* on the basis of existing French tradition. Medieval authors are usually vague about their fictitious sources. Wolfram tells us a good deal more about Kyot than is usual with such a source: he says that he came from Provence, wrote in French, and that he had lived in Toledo and could read Latin and Arabic. The connection with Toledo, the great centre of intellectual contact between Christian and Moslem scholars, ties in with Wolfram's keen interest in astronomical lore and abstruse natural history, but not with the actual story of Parzival as Wolfram tells it.[5] Wolfram first invokes the name of Kyot quite suddenly, in the eighth book, as assurance that he has named a minor character correctly: Kyot found Parzival's adventures written in the heathen tongue, and translated them into French.[6] He is cited in the same way at the end of book eight, but it is only in the account of the Grail we have just quoted that his full story emerges. The implication is that he translated Flegetanis' work, but found it unsatisfactory or incomplete, and searched elsewhere for the story of the Grail dynasty. Wolfram briefly cites him once more as an authority before the conclusion of the tale, but as he ends, he insists that Chrétien has told the story wrongly, and that Kyot's version is the correct one:

If Master Chrestien of Troyes has done this tale an injustice, Kyot, who sent us the true tidings, has reason to wax wroth. Definitively, the Provençal tells how Herzeloyde's son won the Grail as was decreed for him when Anfortas had forfeited it. From Provence into German lands the true tidings have been sent to us.[7]

This is the only time that Wolfram names Chrétien, showing that he knows of the French poet's work; and he immediately conjures up Kyot in order to deny that he is dependent on the famous master of Arthurian romance. This relationship, of French original and German reworking, would have been the norm for German romances on Arthur at this time: Hartmann von Aue and Gottfried von Strassburg both used French or Anglo-Norman material, and Hartmann acknowledges his debt to Chrétien. Wolfram has to be different: *he* has found the original that lies behind the French story, and knows better than to follow the French slavishly.[8] Furthermore, the ending of the story is not to be found in the romances which he has followed so far, and he therefore needs a new 'authority' to authenticate his tale, even though he increasingly puts himself forward as the creator of the work in the later books.[9]

This scenario seems to offer a plausible sub-text to Wolfram's protestations. We can support it by showing, as we shall do, his probable dependence on the French poems, and by pointing out inconsistencies in his description of Kyot: a Provençal writer of the time would have written in Occitan, not French. This points to what may be a solution: knowing Wolfram's delight in playing with names, he has taken the name of the perfectly respectable Guiot de Provins, a real contemporary author, and has turned him into a Provençal rather than a native of Provins, to the south-east of Paris.*[10] The real Kyot

---

* Interestingly, Guiot does seem to have studied in Provence; and he could be said to be '*der meister wol bekant*', 'the well-known master', but in all other respects he fails to match Wolfram's description.

never existed; the Kyot in the poem is, in effect, another of Wolfram's characters, and as such has to be provided with a history of his own. His role is a familiar one, and just as the medieval versions of the story of Troy were ascribed to the fictitious Dictys the Cretan, who took the side of the Greeks, and Dares the Phrygian, who favoured the Trojans, so Kyot is the 'authority' for Wolfram's reworkings of Chrétien.[11]

There are large tracts of Wolfram's romance which have no counterpart in Chrétien or his continuators, notably the first two books telling of Gahmuret, Parzival's father. Wolfram's source may well have been a romance similar to the Anglo-Norman dynastic poems such as *Beves of Hampton* and *Guy of Warwick*; in particular, Beves, the hero of the former, has Eastern adventures which are not dissimilar in tone to those of Gahmuret. Such a story had no connection with the Grail; but its introduction into the history of Parzival was an essential part of Wolfram's plan. Wolfram changes the key in which the whole story is composed, reverting to Chrétien's theme of the chivalric development of the hero; the spiritual element is only part of the chivalric whole, but because Parzival's destiny is to guard the Grail, it is an essential part. So the religious family of Joseph in Robert de Boron is replaced by a secular dynasty; but dynastic matters loom large throughout both Robert's and Wolfram's poems. The concept of a family whose allotted task is to guard the Grail is the common factor.

There are other points which imply that Wolfram knew Robert's work. There is much less theology in Wolfram, but when Trevrizent teaches Parzival about the love of God, many of the themes are echoes of the scene in which Joseph instructs the emperor Vespasian in *Joseph d'Arimathie*. Wolfram, like Robert, insists on the secrets of the Grail, even though he dramatically re-imagines these, setting them in the context of heathen learning, which, mysteriously, only a Christian can interpret correctly. Robert was writing in a strictly orthodox Christian context; Wolfram is writing in the light of an interest in or knowledge of the kind of scientific learning that had come from Arabic Spain in the twelfth century. This reintroduced the thinking of the Greek philosophers to the West, but also provided access to the Arabs' own discoveries. In this field, the figures of Flegetanis, the learned heathen, and Kyot, the Christian interpreter, have many parallels, but in order to attribute this interest to Wolfram himself, and not to an unknown source, we have to refuse to believe Wolfram's own declaration that he was not a learned man. There are many reasons for thinking that this declaration is an example of Wolfram's ironic playfulness; he is evidently knowledgeable about astronomy, the lore of precious stones, and he is prepared to venture into obscure corners of theology.[12] But the

Grail itself does not stem from this lore, or represent some hidden tradition of necromancy; Wolfram uses his arcane knowledge to add to the mystery of the Grail, not to define the object itself. Furthermore, the idea of '*die verholnen maere umben grâl*', 'the hidden stories of the Grail', seems to be another case where Wolfram has picked up a phrase or idea from his source, in this case Robert de Boron's '*li grant secré escrit qu'en numme le Graal*', 'the great secrets of the Grail', and used the alchemy of his imagination to transmute it into something quite different, for which the original phrase is simply the starting point.[13]

As with everything about this extraordinary writer, the argument over the nature of his text and its meaning continues to rage; there is not space to rehearse the complex arguments here, but we shall proceed on the assumption that we are dealing with a formidable intellect and imagination, widely read but ultimately eclectic – we come back yet again to Gottfried von Strassburg's description of him as 'friend of the hare'. Just as a hare will jink and circle when hunted, unlike the fox or deer, which will run in a straight line, so with Wolfram nothing is straightforward, and his train of thought is often unexpected. He will pick up a name from an earlier poem and subtly change it, or he will make a dramatic alteration: Blancheflor becomes 'Condwiramurs', the bringer of love (*conduire amors*),[14] and the Proud Knight of the Heath, *Orgueilleus de la Lande*, is transformed in the opposite direction – pride becoming the proper name Orilus. Wolfram's name-play has been extensively studied. The problem is that we cannot tell how far the changes are due to oral misunderstandings, or to visual misreadings, or to sheer exuberant invention. Compared to other poets, his work is full of names, a total of over six hundred in *Parzival* and *Titurel*; they are evidently a kind of extension to his poetic vocabulary, adding to the qualities of richness and mystery which characterize his style. He loves lists of names, whether of countries and people as when Parzival and Feirefiz describe their exploits and followers to Arthur when Feirefiz first comes to the king's court;[15] or of the exotic gems to be found decorating Anfortas' sickbed.[16] The first and last lists occupy exactly one strophe of thirty lines each, as if to underline their importance in the poem. Such lists are not unknown in epic poetry, from Homer's list of the ships in the *Iliad* onwards, and Wolfram's contemporary, Hartmann von Aue, has a similar list of Arthurian knights in his *Erec*, even though the names in Hartmann's list are familiar where Wolfram's are exuberant invention.

But nothing in all this can prepare us for Wolfram's concept of the Grail itself when it is finally revealed. Parzival, when Trevrizent has calmed his rage against God, asks to be told about the Grail. In response, Trevrizent seems to answer obliquely, for he describes Munsalvaesche and its warriors, who continually ride out in search of adventure, and then says, 'I will tell you how they are nourished.' The source of their sustenance is 'a stone whose essence is most pure', named 'lapsit exillis', by virtue of which the phoenix is able to die and be born again. It has the power to prolong youth, and to delay death. Only at the end of the description does Trevrizent add, 'That stone is also called the Grail.' He goes on to explain that 'today a message will appear upon it [the Grail] and therein lies its highest power': each Good Friday a dove brings a small white wafer from heaven and places it on the stone, ' by this the stone receives everything good that bears scent on this earth by way of food and drink, as if it were the perfection of paradise'.[17] The method of selection of the members of the company at Munsalvaesche is revealed: an inscription appears on the Grail, naming the chosen child and their lineage, for all members of the Grail company go as children, and to be named is regarded as the highest honour. And finally, Trevrizent associates the Grail with the neutral angels, those who sided with neither God nor Lucifer after the rebellion of the latter and his fall from heaven; they were forced to descend to earth to the Grail. Thereafter the Grail had been in the keeping of the dynasty to whom it had been entrusted. It is housed in a temple,[18] and its keepers are called 'templeise';[19] this word has often been translated as 'Templars' and it has been argued that Wolfram had the Order of the Knights Templar in mind.* Typically, he simply uses the word, which is not found elsewhere, without explanation. But there are good reasons why the Templar identification does not work, particularly in the light of evidence that in the late Middle Ages German nobles did not think that the templeisen and the Templars were the same. The Templars had a very low profile in the Germany of Wolfram's day, and the first master of the Templars' handful of German houses was only appointed in 1227, a century after the Order was founded.[20] A century and a half later, Otto von Habsburg, duke of Austria, founded a knightly society of the 'Templaist' or 'Templois',[21] a clear echo of Wolfram's templeisen, which has nothing to do with the Templars and shows that the two were regarded as quite distinct; to have refounded anything to do with the Templars three decades after they had been suppressed would have been extremely foolish in political terms.

The conditions which bound the guardians of the Grail owe much more to Wolfram's imagination than to any actual military order of knighthood. The most obvious objection to the identification with the Templars is the presence of the women who serve the Grail, and who seem to be the most

---

* The Templars are usually Tempelherren in German.

important figures at Munsalvaesche, saving only the king himself.[22] There is also the question of the marriage of the Grail knights, which, while it does not happen at the Grail castle itself, is a frequent occurrence when they are sent out into the world. To use the word 'utopia' is an anachronism,* but the imagined structure of the Grail society is a daring stroke, to say the least. It is a society subject to a rule, dictated by the Grail itself: Titurel tells his son that 'when I received the Grail by the message which the exalted angel sent me, by his high authority, there I found written all my order'.[23] Yet it is not a monastic society as such, and there is no mention of a priest; its purpose is both religious – if the service of the Grail can indeed be counted as such – and secular. Because the members of the society are both chosen by the Grail and directed by it, the Grail company is a means by which God can intervene directly in human affairs.

All this raises a host of difficult questions. We can only begin to see something of Wolfram's vision of the Grail if we read him slowly and cautiously; as one critic has said, he 'writes in symbols'.[24] First, the Grail is unequivocally a stone; there is no ambiguity in the German text. It has magical powers, and can provide food, but these powers are conferred on it by a divine providence. The symbol of the Grail knights is the turtle-dove, and this was an accepted symbol for the Holy Ghost, taken from the biblical account of Christ's baptism when 'he saw the Spirit of God descending like a dove'.[25] The Grail's own powers derive ultimately from the Holy Ghost, which descends to the Grail each Good Friday in the form of a dove, and the white wafer which it bears can only be intended as the Mass wafer. It is therefore the medium through which the Eucharist acts on the anniversary of Christ's crucifixion.

But Wolfram's chief concern is not with the theology of the Grail; its function in his tale is to represent a mysterious, supernatural power whose guardianship is the highest of earthly honours. This guardianship is, in turn, Parzival's destiny, and it is his struggle to achieve his destiny which is the central topic of the poem. Hence the Grail need not be fully explained to fulfil Wolfram's purpose, and we should not see it as the key to understanding the poem: Wolfram's work has rightly become known as *Parzival*, and the Grail has never been part of its title, unlike the French romances. Hence the enormous debate over the alternative name of the Grail: 'lapsit exillis' is probably a huge red herring, which Wolfram would have enjoyed. More ink has been spilt over these two words than any other comparable phrase in the whole of Arthurian romance. For a start, 'lapsit' is simply not Latin,

---

* It was, of course, coined by Sir Thomas More some three centuries later.

though many scholars ignore this and translate it as if it read 'lapsavit', 'it fell'.[26] The first scribes who copied Wolfram's poem seem to have been baffled by them, and other copies read 'lapis exilis' and 'iaspis exillis'. Any theory constructed round the interpretation of these two words is therefore on very shaky foundations, particularly as Albrecht von Scharfenberg, who completed Wolfram's *Titurel* at the end of the thirteenth century, envisaged the Grail as 'jaspis', a jasper.[27] Albrecht was therefore working within a century of the writing of the original; the reading 'jaspis', which most modern scholars disregard, fits in very well with Wolfram's evident predilection for precious stones and the lore surrounding them. Interpretations of the phrase always involve correcting the text, and suggesting a better reading, and almost all the scholars who have attempted such an interpretation opt for the reading 'lapis', a stone, with 'exillis' as the corruption of an adjective – hence we have 'the stone from heaven' (*ex celis*), the 'elixir stone' of the alchemists and hermetic philosophers,[28] 'the stone of exile' (*exilii*) or even 'the stone of asbestos' (*textilis*).[29] My own suggestion, for what it is worth, is that it could be one of Wolfram's notorious twistings of French words: '*grail*' in French is an adjective meaning slender, for which *exilis* is the Latin equivalent: philologists may demur that the French words '*graal*' and '*grail*' are not related, but Wolfram's playfulness with sounds is no respecter of precise definitions.

But why should the Grail be a stone? The list of suggestions as to the origins of the Grail stone is extremely varied. It has been suggested that it should be envisaged as a small portable altar, of a type found in Carolingian Europe, which would consist of a large semi-precious stone in a metal mount; this would be a suitable receptacle for the Mass wafer brought by the dove each Good Friday. Other writers have proposed the altar found in the Ethiopic ritual, or even a borrowing from Islam; some writers have invoked the Kaaba, the sacred stone at Mecca. More to the point, perhaps, are the magical or wonder-working stones to be found in the Bible or in alchemy; there are possible parallels in the 'Book of Revelation', particularly in the fourth chapter, where St John describes 'him that sat upon the throne' and the twenty-four elders: jasper and emerald figure prominently here.[30] Wolfram, like most medieval authors, is very familiar with biblical texts, and the resemblances are not so precise that they seem deliberate; rather, they are echoes of ideas which would be reasonably commonplace for the time. They belong to a wider cultural background, not to a specific use of the apocalypse as a model for the Grail and its ceremonial.

It is possible to find a huge list of faintly plausible parallels for this or that aspect of the Grail by scouring Eastern tradition about precious stones, from the stories of the Jewish mystical writers in the *Kabbalah* to the Iranian traditions: the biblical Urim and Thummim, the Chvarenah, the Chechina and the Goral can all offer analogues and precedents, but their contributions to Wolfram's poem amount at most to a distant echo here and there.[31] Ultimately, however, we return to Wolfram's curious relationship with the French texts from which his story ultimately derived. In Chrétien, the Grail is made 'of fine, pure gold; and in it were set precious stones of many kinds, the richest and most precious in the earth or the sea: those in the Grail surpassed all other jewels . . .'[32] This is Wolfram's starting point, but did he misunderstand it, or was it the inspiration of his own flight of fancy? The problem is the same as that of Wolfram's names: we have to weigh his intellectual playfulness against his protests that he is unlettered. Once again, imagination comes into play: Wolfram seized on the idea of the Grail as surpassing all other jewels, and transformed the brilliant variety of gems on it into a single stone.[33] The possibility of a misunderstanding is strengthened by the likelihood that the two mysterious silver knives, which seem to serve no function at all in the story, are a misreading of Chrétien's *tailleoir d'argent*, a silver platter or dish on which food is cut up. Another possibility is that Wolfram was drawing on a text like the prose version of *Joseph d'Arimathie* where we are told that the 'vessel [i.e. the Grail] signifies the stone', meaning the stone at the entrance of the tomb of Jesus.[34] This uncertainty about the nature of the Grail would account for the fact that Wolfram never actually ventures on a physical description of it; but the absence of such a description may equally be dictated by a desire to preserve a degree of mystery about the Grail's nature.

And so we come back to 'lapsit exillis': whatever it did once mean to Wolfram, we can be certain that it was not the password to a secret world, which, if we construe it aright, will admit us to the presence of the Grail. It is part of the imprecise and therefore intriguing nature of Wolfram's vision of the Grail: the magic is in the mystery.

The Grail, because of its qualities, is described on several occasions as the '*wunsch*', literally, 'perfection', of this world and of paradise, but why and how it is perfect remains a mystery, perhaps deliberately so. The other attributes of Wolfram's Grail belong, by and large, to the world of natural miracles reflected in the bestiaries, herbals and lapidaries of the time. He draws the legend of the phoenix from the bestiary, but it is difficult to see how the power of the stone burns the phoenix to ashes as Wolfram relates.[35] The phoenix is present to emphasize the power and unique nature of the Grail: it is the rarest and most splendid of birds, just as the Grail is the rarest and most splendid of precious stones. Beyond that it is difficult to construct any kind of symbolic argument, since the phoenix is interpreted in the bestiary as a token of the resurrection of the dead, which has no obvious relation to the Grail's function. The next theme, that of the power to delay death, is a commonplace of eucharistic legend, and therefore relates easily to the eucharistic nature of the Grail which is represented by the dove and Mass wafer. Other attributes are less easy to place: the idea that the Grail can confer continued youthfulness is more of a puzzle, for it is only found elsewhere in *Perlesvaus*, which Wolfram does not seem to have known. Equally, the Grail has properties which belong to the realm of magical stones: it can only be carried by the chosen virgin, for whom it is light and easy to handle. For a sinner, it would be impossibly heavy. And when Parzival's half-brother, Feirefiz, comes to the Grail while he is still a heathen, it is entirely invisible to him; only when he is baptised is he able to see it.

In the very first scene in which the Grail appears, after the hieratic ceremony that accompanies its entrance into the hall, we learn that the presence of the Grail provides the assembled company with food:

whatever anyone stretched out his hand for, he found it all in readiness – hot food, cold food, new food and old too, tame and wild. 'Never did anyone see the like!' – someone or other is about to say, but he'll have to eat his words, for the Grail was bliss's fruit, such sufficiency of this world's sweetness that it almost counterweighed what is spoken of the Heavenly Kingdom.[36]

This is Wolfram at his most playful and ironic; first, he puts forward a marvellously unbelievable story, and then anticipates his audience's reaction before reiterating what he has said in a different vein. The implication is that his audience ought to know that the Grail is a provider of food, a detail which he borrows from the early continuations of *The Story of the Grail*, and he is teasing them as to the magnificence of its feasts. It also serves to underline Parzival's unnatural restraint in refusing to ask any questions about such an extraordinary scene.

The description of the Grail as a source of nourishment is reiterated in Trevrizent's dialogue with Parzival, and its power to feed the brotherhood who serve it is ascribed to the Mass wafer which the dove lays on it each year. Here Wolfram is echoing the idea that the Eucharist is by itself sufficient to sustain life, but linking it back to his earlier portrayal of the Grail feast. In Chrétien, the Grail nourishes the father of the Fisher King; here it is the entire company of Grail knights whom it supports, and it has moved from providing sumptuous feasts to being the source of their everyday sustenance, though it still only appears at solemn occasions.[37] Wolfram goes on to describe how this company is chosen by the Grail itself: the emphasis is on the idea of a dedicated community, membership of which is a high honour and a cause for rejoicing: 'They are fetched from many lands. Against sinful disgrace they are guarded for evermore, and their reward will be good in Heaven.'[38] The function of this chivalric brotherhood is not only to guard the Grail, but to maintain order in lands where the succession was in doubt because there was no male heir: knights were sent secretly from the Grail to marry the heiresses of the lands and restore peace. Girls chosen to serve the Grail were given openly in marriage, and Herzeloyde, Parzival's mother, had been one of the servants of the Grail before she married her first husband. The Grail company acts as a stabilizing influence in an unstable world – Wolfram himself was only too aware of the troubles that could result from weak rule, having lived through a decade of civil war in the Holy Roman Empire, when Otto IV and Philip of Swabia vied for the imperial crown. *Parzival* was probably written in exactly this period of turmoil, from 1198 to 1208. Like Sir Thomas Malory writing his Arthurian epic during the Wars of the Roses, Wolfram used *Parzival* to appeal from his present woes to an image of ideal society.

Before Wolfram turns from the Grail to the story of the Grail king, Anfortas, he has one more element of its history to recount, the strangest of all: he tells us that when Lucifer rebelled against God and was hurled from heaven, 'those who did not take sides, worthy, noble angels, had to descend to earth to that Stone which is forever incorruptible. I do not know whether God forgave them or damned them in the end: if it was His due He took them back.' The story of the fallen angels is told in Robert de Boron,[39] where a third of the angels fall to hell, a third to the earth, and a third remain in the air. It is possible that this passage is a garbled recollection of Robert's account; it might have attracted hostile comments when the poem was first read – Wolfram's work seems to have been circulated before it was completed – for when Trevrizent meets Parzival again just before he succeeds to the kingship of the Grail, he tells him that he had lied to him 'as a means of distracting him from the Grail', and that what he had said about the neutral angels was not true: they too were damned, for they had not sided with God when Lucifer rebelled. One argument is that Wolfram had created one mystery too many, and that the disapproval of the Church had been made plain; but a more plausible reading is that this is all part of Wolfram's deliberate mystification of the Grail. Even Trevrizent, who seems to know more about the Grail than anyone else, is not sure of his ground when discussing its history and secrets.

Scholars have seized on this passage to search eagerly for secret heretical threads in Wolfram's work, and have tried to portray him as sympathetic to the Cathar and Waldensian heresies.[40] It is true that, unlike the French romances, there is no direct reference to the Church and its ceremonies, but this has more to do with his exaltation of secular chivalry than any heretical credo. Wolfram is too individual to follow a specific programme of this kind; if there is heresy, it stems from his own inventiveness, and is accidental rather than intentional. His backtracking over the neutral angels reads like a throwaway line designed to correct a problem caused by his own exuberance of imagination rather than a deliberate retraction of a sincerely held belief.

The Grail itself is undeniably more secular in Wolfram than in the French romances, and it is notable that the lance is disassociated from it. This is not a holy relic, but simply the lance with which Anfortas was wounded; and it does not appear as part of the procession. On Parzival's first visit, a page runs in with the lance, which bleeds as in Chrétien, carries it round the hall and disappears again: 'this rite was to evoke grief', and the assembled company break down in tears at this reminder of the disaster that has befallen their king. On his second visit, there is no sign of the lance, for Anfortas is healed, and grief is banished. But the function of the lance, despite the brevity of its appearance, is crucial to Wolfram's completion of Chrétien's story. In Chrétien, Gawain, who is searching for the lance, is told that

it is written that the time will come when the whole kingdom of Logres, which was once the land of the ogres, will be destroyed by that lance.[41]

Chrétien does not take up this theme in the remaining part of his poem, and this leaves the field clear for Wolfram to elaborate on it. He identifies the lance with the 'javelot' which wounds Chrétien's Fisher King, and it becomes the poisoned spear which is the cause of Anfortas' incurable wound. Furthermore, it also becomes the sign of Parzival's achievement of the Grail kingship. In *The Story of the Grail*, Perceval's question about the Grail, 'Whom does the Grail serve?' is a kind of riddle in reverse, which can only be asked when he has qualified himself to do so. We do not know what subtleties Chrétien might have added if he had finished the poem, but Wolfram takes an altogether bolder approach: the question now shows that Parzival is worthy of the Grail because he has become sensitive to the woes of others, and by asking 'Uncle, what troubles you?' he cures Anfortas and restores order to the kingdom of the Grail. For the Grail is not to be won by physical force, by simple knightly achievements, but by a spiritual struggle. Wolfram uses the word *strîten*, which means both physical fighting and debate or argument. The latter best describes the process by which Parzival attains his goal, for although he undertakes three great contests – against Gawain, Gramoflanz and Feirefiz – his real struggle is against despair, and even, in his bleakest moments, against God himself. The scene with Trevrizent is hence crucial, for before he reveals the secrets of the Grail, Trevrizent shows him the error of his ways. Parzival cannot succeed until he resolves his quarrel with God, and diverts his energy into making himself worthy of being summoned to the Grail. Trevrizent confirms this in the final scene: he tells Parzival that 'it has ever been uncustomary that anyone, at any time, might gain the Grail by fighting. I would gladly have deflected you from that purpose'.[42]

Wolfram is therefore completing and bringing together the themes set out by Chrétien; but he does so with a free hand, and creates both a different world, a different Grail and a higher set of values. For Wolfram's central concern is not with the spiritual alone, but with the place of the spiritual within the chivalric world, as the guiding light of the truly chivalrous. The Grail functions as the link between the spiritual and the physical worlds, for through it God makes his wishes known to the Grail company, and is thus able to intervene directly in human affairs. This is an altogether bolder concept of the chivalric world than anything that has gone before: Arthur's court, the nearest equivalent to the Grail company in French romance, is the background for the exploits of individual knights, and Chrétien and his continuators are concerned with the fortunes of Perceval as an individual, not as part of a divine scheme of things. Robert de Boron and the *Lancelot-Grail* move away from the chivalrous world until the ethos of the Grail and that of the knights who seek it are in opposition, and the resulting conflict is only resolved with difficulty. Wolfram, on the other hand, gives a picture of the development of the individual within society: Parzival's rebellion against God is also an unconscious rebellion against his destiny as Grail king, and a betrayal of the society to which he and his family belong. For Wolfram is deeply conscious of dynasty and heredity: Parzival can only find himself by achieving the task which has been laid upon him from birth. If he can recognize his own true nature and be reconciled to God through confession and penance, he will come again to the Grail, find Condwiramurs again, and heaven and earth will move once more in harmony. It is a rich vision, told in ambitious if eclectic style, and ultimately perhaps the greatest of all the Grail poems.

15

The Adventures of the Grail:
The Later German Romances

Heinrich von dem Türlin: an anti-Parzival

Parzival was an immediate, if controversial, success; there are more surviving copies of it than of any other medieval German romance. Its popularity, in a sense, invited a response, an alternative view, and this was provided by Heinrich von dem Türlin in his poem called *The Crown*. The title implies that it was to be the best of all Arthurian romances, and it reads as a kind of anti-*Parzival*.[1] It is bold in its concept: the emphasis is on the events narrated and not on the inner significance of the tale, its hero is a kind of secular rival to Galahad, and it deliberately strips all religious connotations from the Grail itself. *The Crown* dates from about 1240, just the time when the main group of French Grail romances comes to an end; but it stands as an isolated work, without predecessors or followers. It is about adventures, adventures of the most extraordinary kind, involving magic, chivalry and humour in almost equal parts. Heinrich was very widely read in Arthurian romance: while Wolfram's knowledge is esoteric, not to say eccentric, Heinrich comes across as a researcher into the Arthurian legends, reading widely in the earlier romances as Malory was to do. But he badly lacks Malory's skills as a writer; his story becomes stifled in fantasy, despite his attempts to relieve it by flashes of humour. The list of texts which he seems to have known is substantial;[2] this is interesting in that it shows us that all the Grail stories circulated widely and quickly. Heinrich chooses, however, to strike out in a totally different direction from most of them in making Gawain his hero, and treating other knights of the Round Table as distinctly his inferiors. Perceval becomes a kind of anti-hero, a real fool, who genuinely fails to achieve the Grail.

In *The Crown*, the Grail quest is simply another adventure: Gawain has to undertake it in order to pacify Angaras. Gawain kills Angaras' brother accidentally, but falls into Angaras' hands. Angaras makes him 'swear to discover the manifold wonder of the mysterious Grail'.[3] This echoes

Gawain's quest for the lance in Chrétien's *The Story of the Grail*, which he undertakes to appease Guigambresil, whose lord he has killed.[4] Heinrich presents the Grail quest as the last and greatest of Gawain's adventures: it forms a self-contained episode of some 2,000 lines at the end of a poem of 30,000 lines. It is quite unlike any other version of the story; a reinvention rather than a retelling. In brief, it describes how Gawain sets out on the quest but is distracted for a long while by other adventures. He comes to a castle where he meets the sister of a magician who has previously helped him. It is she who tells him how to achieve his object. The way to the Grail is filled with fantastic and terrifying mysteries: he encounters a fiery man who drives a crowd of beautiful naked women before him with a whip, but when the man sees him, he runs up and kisses Gawain's foot, and the figures sink into the earth. Next he sees a knight and a girl fleeing from an old woman, who hurls a glass at a tree; the surrounding forest bursts into flames and burns the knight and the girl to death. This is followed by the appearance of a monster to which an old knight is bound by golden fetters: he holds a box with a fragrant salve, the scent of which revives Gawain and renews his strength. Then Gawain comes to a castle, richly furnished, where a feast is set out, but there is no one to be seen. He eats his fill, and finds the table renewed when he does so; even when he spends the night there, he sees no one. Lancelot and Calogrenant meet him, and they come to the Grail castle, where they are invited to join the Grail feast. The other two knights drink the wine they are offered and fall asleep; but Gawain, forewarned by the magician's sister, refrains, and witnesses the Grail procession, which begins with two girls bearing candlesticks, two squires carrying 'a highly ornate spear' and two more girls who hold a golden bowl adorned with precious stones.

Behind them, stepping very lightly, walked the most beautiful lady God had created since the beginning of the world: her form and her dress were perfect. On gold-embroidered silk she held something that looked like a small gridiron of red gold, on which was as splendid an object as has ever been wrought, made of a single jewel and the finest gold; it resembled a reliquary on an altar. The lady wore a golden crown. As the last, walking gracefully, came a lovely maiden who was quietly weeping and lamenting; all the others were silent. Surrounding the old lord, they bowed and curtsied to him with great decorum.

Gawein's eyes did not deceive him: he knew the lady. It was she who had told him about the Grail and warned him to be ready with the question wherever he might see her and her five companions. Now that this had happened, he was eager to ask. At the moment he remembered, the four with the spear – the squires and the maidens –

together placed the spear on the table and the bowl under the spearhead; this was the wish of their lord. A miracle occurred before Gawein's eyes: through the power of God three drops of blood fell from the spear into the bowl. The old lord took them.

The squires and the maidens then moved back and the elegant lady stepped forward with the grieving maiden, lifted the lid from the reliquary, and set it on the table. Gawein, who was watching everything, saw that the reliquary held a small piece of bread. When his host broke off a third of the bread and ate it, the knight waited no longer with his question. 'For the sake of God and His majesty, lord, tell me the meaning of this large assembly and this miracle!' he exclaimed. As soon as he said this, all the knights and ladies in the hall sprang up noisily from the tables with cries of joy . . .[5]

The lord explains that this is the Grail, but will tell him no more about it, except that they had hoped that Parzival would learn the secret, 'but he left like a coward, without daring to ask . . . this calamity came about because Parzival's uncle murdered his own brother to get the latter's land. Because of this treacherous deed, God vented his stern wrath on him and on his clan, so that they were all lost.' Furthermore, he and his company are not living beings, but dead, and Gawain's question has released them from the spell by which they were bound. The Grail will now disappear, never to be seen again. With these words, the lord and his company vanish.

Although Heinrich takes some details from Gawain's visit to the Grail castle in the *First Continuation*, there is a dramatic difference in the context of the story. Gawain's quest is merely another mystery, another adventure. The supernatural prevails, and the Grail company become the living dead of folklore. The Grail ceremony retains the outward forms of the Mass, but there is no reference whatsoever to any religious element. In an earlier section of the romance, Heinrich reworks Gawain's second visit to the Grail castle from the *First Continuation* in similar fashion, totally omitting the Grail, though the lance appears in a chapel within the castle. His concern is with the appurtenances of romance, not with the substance of the tales. Similarly, Gawain is presented from the outset as the perfect knight, a secular Galahad. While Galahad's predestination has a religious aspect, in that he is a type of Messiah, chosen of God, once this role is translated into secular terms, the point of the adventures is lost. They are no longer tests of Gawain's character, but simply proofs of his pre-eminent rank as a knight.[6] The Grail has become meaningless, a mere name without a function. We are left with the feeling that Heinrich von dem Türlin only included the

Grail in his story because of its newly established fame as the defining moment of the supernatural aspect of Arthurian romance.

Fifteenth-century German Writers and the Grail

The same delight in chivalric adventure is the hallmark of the late fifteenth-century Bavarian poet and painter Ulrich Füetrer. His first work was a translation of the *Lancelot* which he later versified: it is an abbreviated version, and condenses the story of the Grail quest drastically, completely omitting Galahad's final vision, and cutting back the descriptions of religious ritual in the earlier Grail scenes. Although the sequence of events and many details are changed, the ideology is still the same: Füetrer's changes tend to make the story more logical and realistic. For example, the bleeding lance only appears at the end of the Grail ceremony, and the blood is immediately used to heal the maimed king; and the Grail does not mysteriously transfer itself to Solomon's ship after the healing of the maimed king, but is taken to the seashore 'with a most beautiful procession'.

Füetrer's second account of the Grail story is to be found in *The Book of Adventures*, which includes not only a wide range of Arthurian material, but also parts of the history of the Trojan war. Füetrer was extremely well read, and combines details from different versions of the story of Perceval. His patron, Albrecht IV of Bavaria, was an enthusiast for chivalry, particularly for tournaments, and Füetrer's work reflects this. He uses the German rather than the French versions, *Parzival* and *Later Titurel*, combining the Grail scenes from the two skilfully, while at the same time recasting them in a different form, so that the healing of Anfortas becomes a lengthy dialogue between Parzival and his uncle, in which the latter explains the virtues of the Grail.[7] The Grail itself is described as '*ain masse*', literally a lump of metal, which is 'called the noble, rich Grail'; this was evidently derived from a manuscript of Wolfram's *Parzival* which read 'lapis exillis', and was as obscure to Füetrer as it is to us today. The girl who bears it sets it on four supports, each resplendent with precious stones and gold,[8] which are perhaps an echo of the Grail table in the French romances.

In the hands of lesser poets and in popular belief the Grail undergoes some strange transformations in Germany. During the course of a fictional poetic debate between Wolfram von Eschenbach and Klingsor (another poet, who was to provide Wagner with the name of his magician) in the late thirteenth century, we learn that the Grail was once a jewel which graced Lucifer's crown; after he had rebelled against God, St Michael tore the crown from his head and broke it in two. The Grail fell from the crown to earth, where Titurel found it.[9] And in the later stories about Lohengrin, Parzival's son, the Grail kingdom became confused with that of Arthur: Arthur was supposed to have sent Lohengrin to rescue Elsa of Brabant, so that the Round Table and the company of the Grail seemed to be one and the same. The strangest juxtaposition comes in the romance of Lorengel, where we find Parzival fighting Attila the Hun, known as 'könig Etzel' in the German sagas. Etzel conquers most of Europe, and it is only when Parzival 'leads the army with the Grail in his hand to help him' that Etzel is defeated.[10] The Grail has in a sense returned to its source: Parzival uses it in the same way as that other relic of the Crucifixion, the True Cross, was used by the kings of Jerusalem against the Moslems.*

It seems that the muddled version of the Grail company in the Lohengrin story was at the root of another strange avatar of the Grail as a kind of cross between an earthly paradise and limbo, in which knights remain alive until the Last Judgement, and indulge meanwhile in sensual pleasures. Legends in which a great ruler does not die but lives on in a cave in the mountains to await the summons to return to the aid of his former realms, are told of Charlemagne and Frederick Barbarossa as well as Arthur. In the late versions of the Lohengrin story, Lohengrin is sent 'from the Grail' by Arthur; he was therefore believed to have come from Arthur's place of concealment, and 'the Grail' became a synonym for Arthur's retreat in a hidden cave. A German writer in 1410 places 'the Grail' in the numinous countryside near Pozzuoli, where three famous sites of classical antiquity, the Phlegrean Fields, Virgil's tomb and the cave of the Cumaean Sibyl, were also to be found:

... four miles from Pozzuoli is the mountain of St Barbara, a round hill that rises from a level plain, which many deluded Germans call in their language the Grail, declaring that ... there were many living men in it, who would live until the day of judgement, who were nonetheless given over to dancing and other delights, and all kinds of diabolical lusts.[11]

The Grail becomes the twin of the setting of another great medieval German legend, the Venusberg or court of Venus. This is at the centre of the story of Tannhäuser, who repents of his sins and goes as a pilgrim to Rome. But the pope refuses to pardon him, saying that for his sojourn in the court of Venus, he is damned until a pilgrim's staff shall flower. The miracle occurs, and Tannhäuser is saved. Indeed, in a German translation

* See p. 125 above.

of Rabelais in 1575, the mountain near Pozzuoli is actually called 'the Gral or Venusberg'.[12]

The riotous living in the Venusberg Grail is an echo of another use of the word *gral*, which in northern German meant a confused noise; it became associated, however, with knightly sports, combining the rowdiness of a tournament with its other chivalric meaning. The most famous example is the 'Grail' held by Brun von Schonebeck at Magdeburg in 1280. According to the town chronicler of Magdeburg, Brun von Schonebeck, one of the constables of the town – 'he was a learned man' – presented a joyous entertainment. He 'made a Grail', and wrote courtly letters to Goslar, Hildesheim, Brunswick and other places, inviting all those who wished to practise knightly skills to come to Magdeburg. He and his fellow-constables found a beautiful woman, of doubtful morals, whom they called 'Frau Feie' and who was to be given to the victor in the jousts. This aroused great enthusiasm in the surrounding towns, and the various contingents arrived, each in their own colours. The 'Grail' was set up on the marshes outside the town, and two of the constables took up their station in it; outside was a tree on which the constables' shields hung. Any would-be challenger rode up and touched one of the shields, and its owner came out to joust with him. But the end was pure anticlimax: 'an old merchant from Goslar' won the hand of 'Frau Feie', married her off with a good dowry and persuaded her to abandon her wild ways. The chronicler notes that 'a whole book in German was made about this', and that Brun von Schonebeck wrote a number of works in German, including religious treatises and many good poems.[13] So was the whole episode a literary exercise, perhaps even a satire on the knightly aspirations of the young bloods of the city? If it had survived, we might have been able to discover what was really behind this strange episode, but all we have is a puzzle and a curiosity. To complicate matters even further, there was also a popular tradition which saw the Grail as a holy place: prayers in German from Bremen and Lübeck speak of 'Mary in the heavenly Grail', and 'the Grail of paradise'.[14]

Albrecht: The Later Titurel

Heinrich von dem Türlin imagines a mysterious, threatening but ultimately supernatural rather than religious context for the Grail. When a poet whom we know only as Albrecht took as his starting point the fragments of Wolfram von Eschenbach's *Titurel*, the centrepiece of his poem was at the opposite pole of the imagination: a loving recreation, in obsessive detail, of the richest imaginable temple. The *Later Titurel*, as Albrecht's work is usually called, sets the romance of Sigune and Schionatulander within an opening and closing framework. This framework deals with the Grail, its early history and its removal to India, where Titurel dies – passages which mirror in a distant way the structure provided by the *History* and *Quest* of the French *Lancelot-Grail* cycle. The beginning is set in the early days of Christianity, and the conclusion removes the Grail from the eyes of Western Christians. Titurel enjoys the same longevity as the biblical patriarchs, abdicating his kingship of the Grail at the age of 450, and dying when he is 500. He is fifty when an angel entrusts the Grail to his keeping, and he at once sets about establishing the Grail kingdom at Munt Salvatsch, in the land called Salvaterre: these are the Munsalvaesche and Terre de Salvaesche of *Parzival*. Albrecht describes Munt Salvatsch as surrounded by impenetrable forest, the Foreist Salvasch, and ringed by thirty miles of mountains: no one could find their way there, unless the angels so wished, and the castle itself was fortified against all comers.

The opening section of the romance, as in *Parzival*, deals with the hero's ancestry. Titurel is descended from the Trojans and the emperor Vespasian, and his grandfather Parillus converts to Christianity. After Parillus' death, Titurel is born to Parillus' son, Titurison, and his wife, Elizabel. Titurel's upbringing and education are described, his education in letters and in knighthood. His mother seeks to keep him from all knowledge of love, but then a tutor acquaints him with the distinction between secular and divine love. Titurel opts for chastity.

An angel announces that the chaste Titurel is called to be the Grail king. He leaves his tearful parents, and is taken by angels to Foreist Salvasch and to the mountain in its midst, Munt Salvasch, the home of the Grail, in the land of Salvatierre. There Titurel decides to build a temple for the Grail. The description of the Grail temple follows. Its design and execution were so lavish that its construction could not have been attempted if the Grail itself had not 'sent the king guidance in writing. Whatever was needed was found before the Grail, according to the master builders' every desire.'[15]

Like Wolfram, Albrecht delights in brilliant images: lists of precious stones and descriptions of paintings and elaborate musical automata are all part of his account of the building, an account so detailed that it has given rise to voluminous papers attempting to reconstruct its appearance or to identify it with existing buildings. Some of these efforts, as we shall see, belong to the wilder shores of scholarship, but this is hardly surprising in the light of the original. This excerpt from Albrecht's survey of the Grail temple gives some idea of his eclectic vision: his language abounds in words which are found nowhere else:

Wherever the choir turned outwards there was the altar, so that the priest could turn his face correctly to the Orient when he desired to increase the bliss of Christians and God's praise in the Mass.

The greatest of the choirs pointed to the Orient. Two entire galleries were given to this direction, for it was dedicated to the Holy Ghost in all elegance of ornamentation, enriched at special expense, since he was the patron of the whole temple.

The one next to it was dedicated to the Virgin, who is the mother of that child who has both Heaven and Earth in His power and their population. John was the name of the lord of the third choir. The rest of the twelve disciples were housed close by.

The inside of the temple had such rich craftsmanship, built in beauty for the love of God and the Grail, everywhere equally so, save that the choirs lacked such ornament as was bestowed upon the rest of the temple. The whole work was completed in thirty years.

There was only one single sanctified altar there, the choirs around it were empty. Such a wonder of wealth was invested in it. In front of the belfry stood rich ciboria with images of the saints. Each carving told its own story there.

This same rich temple was devoted to the Grail, so that it could be kept there every day and when it was raised on high a broad and radiant sacristy was visible below . . .

High above one of the gates, elegantly facing the Occident, was an organ, a construction with a clear, sweet note, a great pleasure to hear; it accompanied the office on feast days, as is still the case all over Christendom:

A tree of red gold, equipped with all desirable foliage, twigs and branches, with birds perched everywhere of those kinds whose sweet voices are praised. Wind went in from a bellows, so that every bird sang in its fashion,

One high, the other low, depending on the manipulation of the key. Laboriously the sound was conducted back down into the tree. Whichever bird he wished to press into action, the master was well acquainted with the key according to which the birds sang. Four angels were perched on the ends of the branches in immaculate pose, each holding a horn of gold in his hand; these they blew with a great din, whilst with their free hand they beckoned as if to say 'Rise up, all ye dead!'

There was the Last Judgment, cast, not painted. The simplicity of the design was intended to reinforce the warning that bitterness ever follows after sweetness, and so when a man is happy he should ever think upon that same sadness.

Two most exquisite doors led into each choir there. Between them stood an altar, over which hung chancels, vaulted, supported by two spindle columns, each forming a circle of some six feet, with the area between them filled with special ornament.

The doors in front of all the choirs had railings of rich gold, so that people could see and hear better from all directions. The walls by the doors also all had rich railings, closed with clasps, and everything was studded with precious stones.[16]

Through the thickets of highly coloured language, the underlying intention of the poet is clear: to evoke the image of an incomparable building,
far beyond the experience of his audience. Albrecht's temple rises around
the central miracle of the Grail. For Albrecht, the Grail is the centre of an
ordered and harmonious state, and its temple not only symbolizes that order
and harmony, but also the religious function of the Grail as a mediator of
salvation. To the extent that this is a symbolic building, like Chaucer's
'House of Fame' or Lydgate's 'Temple of Glass' – to name but two examples
of a longstanding medieval tradition of descriptions of such allegorical
buildings – if we try to draw its groundplan, we fly in the face of the writer's
intentions. Even the texts hinder us: we cannot be sure whether Albrecht
intended the temple to have twenty-two or seventy-two choirs or surrounding chapels.[17] It is much more probable that 'if Albrecht's building has a
rational plan, it is not based on architectural principles'.[18] Albrecht himself
says later in the poem:

I have constructed the temple elegantly for the instruction of noble Christian people,
that they may desire to look with loyalty to God, guided by the temple's design.[19]

The Grail for which this is the extraordinary setting is also an original
concept. Albrecht agrees with Wolfram that it is a stone, brought to earth
by a host (presumably of angels). It is called 'jasper and flint' (*iaspis et silix*)
and the phoenix rises from its ashes through the power in the stone. But he
tells us, probably following Robert de Boron as his authority, that 'people
decided to fashion a dish from it', a dish which was later used by Jesus
Christ 'for his sublime Eucharist of which His disciples partook with him'.
This dish was preserved by Joseph of Arimathea and was brought to Titurel
by an angel to be preserved in the Grail kingdom.[20] When it was first given
to him, the Grail moved of its own accord, and at the time of the building
of the temple, had never been carried by any mortal being; it hovered in
the central sacristy. We learn that the Grail named its bearer, Tschosian
(Wolfram's Schoysiane*), by writing which appeared on the Grail itself.
Albrecht intends it to remain a mystery: 'No one can describe the Grail or
its meaning with mouth or tongue.'[21]

The end of the story of the Grail tells of the withdrawal of the holy vessel,
but instead of vanishing into the Western fastnesses of Sarras, it is taken to

---

* Schoysiane appears in Wolfram, but is not, of course, herself the Grail-bearer; she is the sister
of the Grail-bearer, whom Wolfram names as Repanse de Schoye. For Wolfram, she is the
mother of Sigune, and dies giving birth to her; why Albrecht should change her role is a mystery.

the East. Salvatierre, the domain of the Grail, is surrounded by hostile realms, and to avoid the evil that would come about if the Grail fell into impious hands, Parzival and Titurel set out with the Grail to find a new home for it. They travel far afield, and eventually come to Marseilles, guided by the Grail in their wanderings: they embark, and voyage to India, where the legendary Prester John rules; he is both priest and king, and his empire, which embraces the whole of Asia, is a fitting resting place for the holy vessel. His palace stands near the Earthly Paradise, and is even richer than the Grail temple. Much of this is drawn from travellers' tales and from tales about Prester John, a great Christian emperor in the East, who would ally himself with Western crusaders and retake Jerusalem. It is to Prester John that Titurel recounts the story of the Grail; when he has finished, he begs that it should be concealed from him, so that he may die. This comes to pass, and he is buried in a splendid tomb: thenceforward the Grail no longer provides food, and the names that appear on it are those of sinners who are to be punished.

Albrecht's poem was once thought to be the work of Wolfram himself, a pretence that Albrecht uses until the very end. But once the deception was discovered by scholars, the poem was dismissed as of little value. Yet it does have its own idiosyncratic power, and it is an important witness as to how an intelligent reader understood Wolfram's poems some sixty or seventy years after his death, and it was much admired during the next two centuries. In 1491, Graf Gerhard von Sayn commended it to his sons as the 'most godly lesson to be found in German books, for all virtue and honour are in it which princes and lords should possess and by which they should rule'.[22]

There are hints in Wolfram's original poem of a vision of the Grail kingdom as both an ideal earthly state and as the means by which God works his will on earth: the sending of Grail knights to kingdoms in need of leadership, as in the story of Lohengrin, is one example of this. Albrecht retells this story, but, more important, he develops the idea of the Grail kingdom as a utopia; its mission is to protect the Grail company from sin, and to assure their salvation. Through them the rest of mankind will also be saved. *Tugend*, virtue, is the key to this; the 'virtue' of the Grail must be matched by the virtues of those who serve it, and this theme is emphasized in the description of the Grail temple.[23] Titurel is given custody of the Grail because of his 'many virtues'.[24] In place of Wolfram's highly individual and unorthodox world view, Albrecht offers us an orthodox reading of salvation through spiritual virtue: his poem has devotional elements, with a lengthy opening prayer to God. In some copies the Grail temple is presented as a symbol of the worship of the Virgin.[25] Apart from the long central portion dealing with Schionatulander and Sigune, the tone of the work generally is much more religious, but in a very different way from the religion of the *Quest of the Holy Grail*: there is little of chivalric values in Albrecht's approach, and his symbols and moralizing are addressed to Christian laymen in general. It is hardly surprising that for most medieval German readers, *Parzival* remained the classic account of the Grail story.

16

The Adventures of the Grail:
The Last Flowering

In the room, a woman is reading. The manuscript that lies open before her on a little ivory and wood reading desk with a candle on each side is richly decorated, a match for anything in the great library of Jean, duc de Berry, prince of France.[1] That library was unrivalled in Western Europe for its size and the magnificence of its volumes; the text on the reading desk, its miniatures brilliant with blue and scarlet and gold and its paragraphs sumptuously decorated, is in an equally splendid style, as befits one of the greatest of all love stories, that of Tristan and Iseult. Interspersed with the story of their adventures are the poems which express their love, complete with the music to accompany them so that a minstrel could recreate the famous harping of Tristan and his songs as the reader paused to look at the artist's vision of their adventures.[2] Such an exotic experiment in multimedia presentation belongs only to the most luxurious surroundings, and the tapestries and furnishings of the room testify to a secular, pleasure-loving ambience.

Yet within the volume on the reading desk are to be found the adventures of the Grail, presented as an integral part of the vast romance which we know as the *Prose Tristan*. To discover how the extremes of religious chivalry and romantic love came to be combined in one work we have to return to the origins of the prose stories and the material from which they sprang, and to consider the reaction of the audience to these relatively novel stories. Once again, the sheer speed with which the romances developed is remarkable, as the *Prose Tristan* may be as little as fifty years later than the first surviving Arthurian romance.

Tristan and the Round Table

The earliest romances had centred on a single hero; Chrétien's tales are often known simply by the name of their protagonist. When the individual stories were interwoven into the history of Arthur's kingdom in the *Lancelot-*

Grail, there was an inherent tension between the different aspects of the story the cycle told: Arthur's tale was of kingship and conquest, Lancelot's of love and knightly exploits, Galahad's of a spiritual quest. What was a delight to one audience might be wearisome to the next, and as new writers took up the stories, the established themes of conquest and heroic deeds on the one hand and religious piety on the other gave way before an insatiable demand for adventures. The audience wanted stories and marvels, not ideals, and the elaborate allegories of *The Quest of the Holy Grail* were abandoned in favour of more miracles and mysteries, while new variations on the tournaments and knight-errantry of the secular stories were all the rage. In the hands of inexperienced or over-enthusiastic writers this could lead to disaster – an inextricable tangle of disconnected episodes – but in skilful hands it could work well enough. Indeed, the best of the later writers not only control their own contributions carefully, but also attempt to tie up the many loose ends offered by the earlier romances, ensuring that episodes which had been left without an ending in previous versions were brought to a successful conclusion.

The audience also wanted to hear stories of their favourite heroes within the broader context of the story of the Round Table. So it was that Tristan was drawn into the Arthurian cycle; indeed, within the *Prose Tristan* itself, there is a reflection of this enthusiasm. We are told that Charlemagne himself found Tristan peerless among knights, preferring him to Galahad. The story is apocryphal, for Charlemagne could not have known of either hero, but it conveys accurately the intense loyalty with which audiences followed their favourite characters.

The romance of Tristan was originally an independent tale; unlike the Grail stories, it was demonstrably Celtic, and was set in Cornwall, where a standing stone which may mark Tristan's burial place is still to be seen. The story probably had nothing to do with Arthur, but like a number of lesser tales was drawn into his orbit by the pull of his great renown in the twelfth century. Even then it remained at a distance from the central stories of the Round Table until the middle of the thirteenth century, for the ethos of the story is at odds with the accepted chivalric ideals of courtly love, where the relationship between knight and lady has an element of self-denial and chastity, deriving from the troubadour poetry of southern France. Tristan and Iseult are deeply and passionately in love, in defiance of the conventions, and particularly in defiance of Tristan's loyalty to his uncle king Mark, who is also Iseult's husband. No matter that Tristan has a prior claim on Iseult's affections, having won her in Ireland on Mark's behalf and fallen in love with her on the voyage home, whether through magic or pure passion; the triangle of torn loyalties lies at the heart of their story. The relations of Lancelot, Guinevere and Arthur may well be a more subtle and complex echo of the primeval force of the Cornish story.

As with the Grail story, when this stark tragedy of divided love and divided faith was transmuted from poetry to prose, probably in the second quarter of the thirteenth century, it was overlaid with chivalrous adventures and the deeds of knights-errant. The author of the *Roman de Tristan en Prose* (*Prose Tristan*) saw his tale – which he claimed to have taken from 'the great Latin book, the very one which tells openly the history of the Holy Grail' – as the pinnacle of knightly stories and Tristan as the exemplar of chivalrous love. He transferred much of the action to Arthur's court, and made Tristan's exploits one of the central reasons for its fame: Tristan becomes a knight of the Round Table for the first time, and we are told that

he was the most renowned [*soveriens*] knight who ever lived in the realm of Great Britain, whether before or after king Arthur's day, save only for the excellent knight Lancelot du Lac. And even the Latin of the history of the Holy Grail declares openly that there were only three knights in the time of king Arthur who excelled in chivalry: Galahad, Lancelot and Tristan.[3]

For the same reason, the author included most of the story of Arthur's kingdom within the framework of his romance. So it was that the story of the spiritual achievements of chivalry, the quest for the Grail, was integrated into the passionate world of Tristan and Iseult. Tristan, as the greatest lover of his time, is also one of the greatest knights, and shares with Lancelot and Galahad the same descent from the family of Joseph of Arimathea.[4] When he vies with Lancelot and Galahad for superiority, their combats are inconclusive.

While most of the text is original, large parts of the *Lancelot* from the *Lancelot-Grail* are incorporated, most notably the final section leading up to the Grail quest, and Tristan is absent from the action for many pages. But when it comes to the Grail quest itself, the author reintroduces his hero, and radically alters the tone and content of the *Lancelot-Grail* story. At the outset of the quest for the Grail, Tristan comes to court after Galahad has sat in the Siege Perilous, destined for him alone; it is Tristan's arrival that means, for the first and only time, all the knights of the Round Table are assembled. In the adventures which follow, Tristan's exploits are interwoven with the more serious deeds of the Grail knights. What we witness is no longer a single-minded pursuit of an ideal, but a series of knightly adventures which are only occasionally interrupted by reminders of the higher purpose of the Grail. Tristan has little to do with the quest, but is occupied by thoughts of Iseult, and with his rivalry with Palamedes, a Saracen knight who is also in love with her. Palamedes is a new character,[5] a heathen who steadfastly refuses to be baptised, preferring the service of love, but who is otherwise a match for any Christian knight. Galahad appears from time to time, but simply as another 'knight adventurous', riding in the company of different members of the Round Table. This contrasts with his character in the *Quest of the Holy Grail*, where he is a solitary figure obsessed with the achievement of the Grail and rarely seen by the other knights, who spend much time searching for him.

But at the climax of the story, the Grail quest at last interacts with the fates of Tristan and Iseult. Because Arthur's knights have departed from the court, king Mark invades Logres, intent on conquering the kingdom. He is able to seize Iseult and carry her back to Cornwall, but he is defeated in battle by the intervention of Galahad and Tristan, who return just in time to help Arthur. Tristan, badly wounded, goes back to Cornwall to recover, but is treacherously slain by Mark with a poisoned spear: Iseult dies of grief, and Mark, at last repentant and heartbroken, raises a rich shrine, a temple of love, to their memory.[6]

Palamedes now forms a vital link between the world of Tristan and the world of the Grail. So far we have only seen him in the context of his rivalry for Tristan; but he now accepts baptism at Arthur's insistence, and joins the Grail quest; he is one of the twelve knights who come together to Corbenic. But at this point the story takes a surprising turn. Galahad goes alone into the castle, at the bidding of two knights sent by the maimed king:

The two knights took Galahad straight to the room where the Maimed King lay, and told him to enter. He went in and saw a most handsome bed on which there lay the Maimed King, his grandfather. 'God's blessing on you, sire!' said Galahad when he saw him. And the king replied, 'You are welcome; thanks be to God, who has led you here.' Then he said, 'Galahad, my son, go into the Holy Chamber, take the lance that you will find there, and bring it to me.' 'I will,' said Galahad. He went into the room, where he had the impression that all the balms and perfumes of the world were gathered. He saw the lance with which Our Lord was pierced in the side as He hung on the Holy Cross; he took it, left the room and returned to the Maimed King. Then the king said: 'Galahad, my son, take the blood which is on the tip of this lance, and rub my legs and thighs with it.' And Galahad devoutly and piously took the blood and rubbed his legs and thighs. And at once the king was healed.

The king said, 'My son, let us go into the Holy Chamber; bring the lance.' A thin and pallid man appeared, more dead than alive, and said, 'Ah, lord Galahad, for

God's sake free me from the torment which I endure!' He had two snakes hanging from his neck which bit him in front and behind. Galahad seized the snakes and pulled them from his neck; and the man was cured. But he only lived for a month afterwards. Then twelve girls, clad in miserable rags, weeping hot tears, came to Galahad, saying, 'Lord, for God's sake free us from the great torture which we endure!' 'What do you want me to do?' he said. 'Lord, lead us out of this room.' He agreed to do this, and took them by the hand and led them out of the room. 'Lord, we are saved!' Galahad told them to thank God, and they did so. Then the king said, 'Galahad, my son, there is a marvellous test in which you must succeed.' 'Show me what it is,' replied Galahad. The king led him into another room and showed him the broken sword which had broken when it was used to wound Joseph of Arimathea in the thigh. Galahad grasped the two fragments, joined them together, and the sword was whole and better than ever before; later, it worked many other miracles.

'Galahad, my son, let us return to the Holy Room!' said the king. They heard several voices singing sweetly, and all the instruments imaginable playing together, harp, rote, viol, gigue, bells; the most melodious instrument could not compare to the beauty of these songs. And the voices said, 'Blessed be the hour in which Jesus Christ was born! Welcome to Galahad, the servant of Jesus Christ, the true and perfect knight! Now the supreme adventure begins which God has destined for you, and for Bors and Perceval.' Then the king said, 'Did you hear that voice?' 'Perfectly!' 'Let us go into the room.' 'Go first, in God's name,' said Galahad. They entered the room and saw the brightest light that you could imagine; and Galahad truly believed he was in Paradise. If all the spices and perfumes of the world had been gathered there, they would have been nothing compared to the scent of that room. And every bliss of the soul became reality there. Galahad said, 'Ah, Lord, I beg you, do not take me from this bliss!' But a voice replied: 'Galahad, that is not the will of God himself; you and your companions will carry the Grail to the spiritual palace. There you will receive what you have asked of Our Lord, for you have served him well.' 'If that is the will of my Lord,' said Galahad, 'I bow before it.' Then he said to the king, his grandfather: 'Sire, I beg you, tell me what the Holy Grail is, and the lance from which there flowed the three drops of blood which cured you!' 'My son, I will tell you. I know that you already know it, but I will tell the story, for no one knows it perfectly.

'When the Jews had crucified Jesus Christ – and this is the truth – a Jew came up to the Cross with a lance in his hand, and buried it in the side of Jesus Christ. The blood spurted out at once, and three drops remained on the lance, as you have seen. The blood was running down the side of our Lord, when a lady arrived who was blind, carrying in her hands a vase in the form of a chalice. She came so close to the Cross that the blood of the Creator fell into her eyes; at once she was cured and recovered her sight. She placed the chalice under the Cross to gather the blood of the Crucified. And when the vase was full, she hid it in her house. I will not tell the story of the resurrection of the true God, because the four evangelists tell it in the story of the Passion, but I will tell you the truth about the Holy Grail.'[7]

The king goes on to tell the story of Joseph of Arimathea and of the Grail's arrival in Britain, but he also explains the history of the man with the serpents and the girls dressed in rags. Three men and twelve girls among the followers of Joseph mocked the service of the Grail, and were sentenced to eternal damnation. Only Joseph's pleas obtained a lesser punishment for them: two of the men, Moyses and Simeu, were condemned to burn until Galahad's arrival, while the rest were to remain in the Palace Adventurous to await his coming. The author of the *Prose Tristan* thus resolves a mystery which *The Quest of the Holy Grail* had left in the air, the mysterious harper whom Bors encounters during his night of trial at Corbenic.* Before Galahad leaves, he is taken to see his mother: they greet each other affectionately, but Galahad refuses to allow her to embrace him, as he does not wish to be touched by a woman in view of the great task that lies ahead of him – the transport of the Grail to Sarras. He rejoins his companions, and with Bors and Perceval carries the Grail on its silver table to the waiting ship, which is sent on its way by a favourable wind.

Before the final scenes at Sarras, we learn of the death of Palamedes, treacherously killed by Gawain after he had sustained serious wounds during a joust with Lancelot. It is a strange scene, at a strange moment in the story, as if the author was intent on rounding off the story of all those involved in the deeds of Tristan and Iseult, and it is rendered even more horrific by the suicide of Palamedes' father Esclabor when he learns of his son's death. It can only be seen as a counterpoint to the achievement of the Grail – a reminder that the adventures of the Grail are cursed with misfortune, and that evil as well as good comes from the quest. When Arthur learns of these tragic events, he expresses the wish that Gawain will never show his face at Camelot again.

The arrival of the Grail at Sarras is taken, in an abbreviated form, from the *Lancelot-Grail* again; but the ecstasy of the final scene is at odds with all that has gone before, and indeed with what follows. Bors returns to Arthur's court, and tells Arthur of the ending of the quest; but Gawain also returns, and Arthur accuses him of murdering many of the fifty-four knights who had died in the search for the Grail. Gawain admits that he has killed

* See p. 108 above.

thirty-two of them, but attributes it to '*malheur*', misfortune. And with this the romance closes abruptly:

> The story ceases to speak of the adventures of the Holy Grail, for they have come to their conclusion, and anyone who wanted to say more would only be lying. Thus ends the history of sir Tristan and the Holy Grail, so complete that no one could add anything to it.[8]

The *Prose Tristan* represents a new departure in terms of the Grail romances, in that it tries to include all the great Arthurian heroes in one narrative; and this is probably the ultimate reason for the presence of the Grail, which, despite the fact that it frames the story at the beginning and the end, is actually a relatively minor element in the tale. Adventures come to the fore throughout the long narrative, and the principal focus of the narrative is on the combats between knights, which are sometimes merely verbal rather than physical. There is a kind of running debate on knighthood, to which Tristan's companions Dinadan and Palamedes contribute in different ways, Dinadan cynical and mocking, Palamedes a heathen who nonetheless holds the highest knightly ideals. (It is tempting to see in Palamedes an echo of Feirefiz in *Parzival*, but the figure of the noble Saracen is to be found in other French romances.) The Grail could be seen as representing the spiritual side of knighthood, but it is handled with little enthusiasm, even though the author claims to have 'read and reread it [the story] many times',[9] and the theme of the misfortune which accompanies the quest is very much more to the fore than its religious implications for the knights who seek it.

A New Version of the Lancelot-Grail

The process by which adventure dominates the action is taken a stage further in the so-called *Romance of the Grail*.* As with the earlier romances, it is difficult to establish the priority of one text over another, and the *Romance of the Grail* has been regarded as the source for material in the *Prose Tristan*. Although there are good arguments for the *Prose Tristan* being the original, the two romances seem to some extent to have developed side by side. There are numerous complete or nearly complete copies of the *Tristan*, but the *Romance of the Grail* is another matter. It is a highly problematic work,

---

* Scholars usually refer to this by the cumbersome title 'Post-Vulgate Cycle'. I have used *Romance of the Grail* to avoid confusion with earlier works with similar titles.

because we have nothing approaching a complete text, and it has to be reconstructed from fragments of the French original and from versions which survive in Spanish and Portuguese. We can tell that it was widespread, because some of the French fragments have been found in northern Italy. Most of the text can be plausibly restored, and the result shows a work that tries to bring together the warring elements that different hands contributed to the original *Lancelot-Grail*. This *Romance of the Grail* is also called the 'pseudo-Robert de Boron' cycle, because the unknown editor and rewriter attributed his version to Robert, whom he recognized as the great authority on matters Arthurian, and he used a similar title for the whole work, *The History of the Grail*.[10] At times we can see the patches in the *Lancelot-Grail*, where the ending of the Lancelot section, probably once an independent romance with its own conclusion, has been reworked to lead into the adventures of the *Quest*. In this new version, such transitions are smoothed out, and the whole cycle is welded into 'the epic of Arthur – the story of the rise and fall of the *roiaume aventureus*'.[11]

In some ways, it is a much more single-minded work than its predecessor: instead of the history of the Grail, the overarching frame is that of the tragedy of the kingdom of Logres and its knights, brought down by two great sins, which are punished by *malheur* and *mescheance*, misfortune and mishap. One is the familiar theme of Arthur's incest with his half-sister, the begetting of Mordred; the other is relatively novel.

The Waste Land and the Dolorous Blow

The Waste Land has become, thanks to T. S. Eliot's use of the image, one of the most famous associations of the Grail. In the earliest Grail stories the desolation of the land is not magical: it is simply a consequence of the illness of the Grail King, who can no longer lead his men into battle and therefore defend his kingdom. Chrétien does not couch his description of the consequences in terms of a natural disaster but entirely in human terms: we need to look at what the hideous messenger actually says to Perceval:

And do you know what will happen because that king will not now rule his land or be healed of his wounds? Ladies will lose their husbands as a result; lands will be lost;* and girls who will be left orphans, will be without guardians;† and many knights will die because of it.[12]

* Literally, *escillies* = 'exiled'.
† Literally, *desconseillies* = 'without advice'.

This is a straightforward picture of the consequences of the loss of a leader, particularly acute in a feudal society such as that of Chrétien's day. If our close reading of the text is correct, the problems are depicted in specifically feudal terms: lands are lost because they are 'exiled' from their rightful owners, and where women inherit because of the death of the menfolk of their family in war, there is no one left to defend them. Nor is there any magical transformation of the lands of the Grail king when Perceval leaves the castle on the morning after the feast at which he has failed to ask the question: the castle is deserted, and there is no one to be seen, but there is no change in the landscape. Again, in the *First Continuation*, when the Grail king shows Gawain the broken sword, he speaks of the destruction caused by the blow which broke it in the same terms as Chrétien.

In *Perlesvaus*, the king's weakness is caused directly by Perlesvaus' failure to ask the crucial question: he is not an invalid until this happens. But the consequences are the same, for 'all lands were engulfed by war; whenever a knight met another in a forest or glade they would do battle without any real cause'.[13] There are many references to the desolate state of the kingdom of Logres; however, there is no magic about this desolation, for it is the simple consequence of this disorder: we only have to recall the words of the *Anglo-Saxon Chronicle* about the anarchy of Stephen's reign in England – 'you could easily go a whole day's journey and never find anyone occupying a village, nor land tilled'[14] – and it is clear that what the author of *Perlesvaus* is portraying is a land ravaged by civil war.

There is, however, another passing remark in Chrétien which may have led to the creation of the story of the waste lands. Gawain, on his quest for the lance, is told that 'it is written that the time will come when the whole kingdom of Logres, which was once the land of the ogres, will be destroyed by that lance'; but because the romance is unfinished, this reference, like the end of Perceval's quest, remains unresolved. Such destruction is also associated with the lance in the *First Continuation* and in *The Elucidation Prologue*. There is a tremendous storm, through which Gawain rides to the Grail castle; and when he has achieved partial success by asking about the lance, the land is restored; but it is not clear whether the restoration refers to the destructive effects of the storm or to an earlier devastation. Given the curious wording which tells us, not that the rivers flow again, but that they are restored to their former courses, as if the storm had been such that they had burst their banks, and that the trees are once again clothed in green, as if they had been stripped of their leaves by the wind, there is a case to be made for reading this simply as a description of the return to normality after the great storm.[15] So the Waste Land is a peripheral motif in the *Continuations*, associated with the lance rather than the Grail.[16]

In the *Romance of the Grail*, an imaginative writer has once again seized on a detail, and recreated the heart of the story by using it skilfully to give a new perspective on the accepted version of the tale. The crucial episode comes about when Balin, a knight who has a justified quarrel with Garlon, brother of king Pellehan, arrives at the latter's court, where the Grail is kept. He learns that Garlon can make himself invisible when he is armed, and realizes that he must act quickly, during the feast to which he has been welcomed, if he is to find him without his armour. On the pretext of an insult offered to him by Garlon, he kills him; Pellehan attacks him to avenge his brother's death, and breaks Balin's sword. Weaponless, Balin runs through the castle until he comes to a richly furnished room where a voice warns him not to enter. Despite this, he rushes in.

In one part of the room was a silver table, broad and tall, supported on three silver legs. On the table, right in the middle, was a vessel of silver and gold, and standing in this vessel was a lance, the point up and the shaft down. And whoever looked long at the lance wondered how it stood upright, for it was not supported on any side.

The Knight with Two Swords looked at the lance, but he did not recognise it. He headed that way and heard another voice, which cried loudly to him, 'Do not touch it! You will sin!'

In spite of this warning, he took the lance in both hands and struck king Pellehan, who was behind him, so hard that he pierced both his thighs. The king fell to the ground, severely wounded. The knight drew the lance back to himself and put it back in the vessel from which he had taken it. As soon as it was back there, it held itself as erect as before. When he had done this, he turned quickly toward the palace, for it seemed to him that he was well avenged, but before he got there the whole palace began to shake; all the rooms did the same, and all the walls shook as if they would instantly fall down and disintegrate. Everyone in the palace was so dumbfounded at this marvel that there was no one brave enough to remain standing . . . they thought that the end of the world had come and that they must now die.

Then came among them a voice as loud as a wild man's, which said clearly, 'Now begin the adventures and marvels of the Kingdom of Adventures, which will not cease until a high price is paid . . .'[17]

The object of the Grail quest is as much the release of Logres, 'the Kingdom of Adventures', from the effects of this 'Dolorous Blow', as the achievement of the Grail itself. Once the spiritual climax of the tragedy of Arthur, the Grail becomes – as in the *Prose Tristan* – merely another cause for knightly confrontations with the mysteries and dangers of the world outside the castle. 'Adventures' are the driving force of the romance, even if the author takes a critical view of other knightly values. 'Fin' amors', the knight's love for his lady, and particularly the love of Lancelot for Guinevere, receives short shrift, and indeed the bulk of the adventures of Lancelot are cut on the grounds that they would make the book too long. What replaces them are numerous individual 'adventures and marvels'; even the descriptions of great tournaments are shortened. The tone is set at the beginning, at the first court held by Arthur, when a squire rides into the hall where he and his knights are feasting, bringing with him the body of his lord, who has just been slain. Merlin says:

This is the first adventure that has happened at your court, and it displeases me greatly that they are beginning in this way, for it is a bad and troublesome sign. Have this put in writing and others after it, just as they occur in the kingdom of Logres. And know that, before you depart from this world, so many of them will have occurred that the written record that will be made of them will make a large book.[18]

Adventures are associated with both the Grail and Arthur's kingdom in general. Gawain kills a girl by mistake when she throws herself between him and his opponent, who was her lover. He is condemned to return to court carrying her body before him on his horse, with her head tied around his neck. Merlin tells the assembled company: 'Know that you may hold this adventure as one of the adventures of the Holy Grail, and from now on you will often see them happen, crueller and uglier than this.' He then delivers a great speech in which he expounds the meaning and purpose of the adventures, declaring that Arthur himself was

begotten by adventure, and by adventure you received your crown, for thus it pleased our Lord. Know that so many and such marvelous adventures have not happened for nothing but are signs and beginnings of those that are to come in your household and in many other places under your rule. Therefore, I say that you should be called the King of Adventures, and your kingdom the Kingdom of Adventures. Know that just as adventure gave you your crown, so will it take it away ... Many will put themselves to trouble to seek chivalric adventures, whose efforts will often miscarry, and many times they will suffer disgrace and ugliness and villainy, and they will often be overcome at arms.[19]

These ideas are remembered by Arthur in his last words to Girflet before he departs in the mysterious ship: 'if they ask you for news of me, answer them that King Arthur came through God's adventure, and by God's adventure he departed, and he alone was the King of Adventures'.

The texture of the romance is dominated by sequences of adventures, one episode leading into the next, and although the author is deft at weaving together the narrative so that there are no loose ends – and indeed at tying up the loose ends left by his predecessors – the great ideas of the earlier versions of the Arthurian epic tend to become submerged under this endless coming and going of combats and marvels, mistaken identities and unexpected encounters. As in the *Prose Tristan*, the Grail is diminished to little more than another marvel in a compendium of marvels. For example, the way in which Lancelot is cured of his madness is typical of the way in which it has become just another relic, rather than a *ne plus ultra* of the spiritual. Lancelot's madness is attributed to a devil which possesses him, and when he comes to king Pelles' castle where the Grail is kept, a girl appears bearing the Grail. 'As soon as Lancelot saw her, he could not bear her coming, for the demon that had entered his body and held him in this frenzy could not stay where such a sacred thing as the Holy Grail was about to come.' Lancelot flees, but returns when the Grail is withdrawn. However, Pelles recognizes him and has him bound hand and foot; he is carried to the Palace of Adventures. When the Grail appears, he cannot move; the demon leaves him, unable to endure the Grail's presence, and he is cured. It is a tale told in honour of many a medieval saint and his shrine; the much simpler version in the original *Lancelot-Grail* is far more powerful in its understatement.[20] This is not to deny that the holiness of the Grail is in any way diminished: when the disaster of the Dolorous Blow occurs, Merlin does not dare to enter the Grail chamber himself, but searches for a priest, and tells him to put on his vestments – 'the arms of Jesus Christ' – before the priest can go in and rescue Pellehan and his attacker.[21] But any spiritual message which this sanctity implies is diluted by the context of adventure and marvel in which the Grail is set.

This emphasis on adventure is a reflection of the way in which knightly culture in general was developing. The earliest roots of chivalry were in training for war, a corporate activity, which gave rise to the tournament in its earliest form: of bodies of knights in warlike formation attacking each other with often realistic ferocity. This developed gradually into a quest for individual prowess, the institution of coats of arms as a means of recognizing the individual jouster, and eventually to the newer form of tournament which consisted primarily of single combats. The focus in these later romances is on the knight as competitor for fame and honour; the Round Table functions perfunctorily as a badge of honour, but its mythical status, like that of the Grail, has also diminished. In the *Lancelot-Grail*, the crowning moment of the Round Table is when Galahad sits in the Siege Perilous, which swallows up any knight not worthy of occupying it. In the Post-Vulgate, the same events occur, but as in the *Prose Tristan*, it is only with the arrival of Tristan that all the knights of the Round Table are gathered for the first and last time, and the Holy Grail appears to the assembled company.

The focus of the action is on the individual heroes, and on their encounters with each other. The story is built up and developed by a lengthy chain of motives and circumstances, and here the author of the Post-Vulgate version is adept at rationalizing and organizing the sequence of events: if an episode in the *Lancelot-Grail* lacks motivation or if there is no sequel to an otherwise significant event, he provides the missing element and uses it to structure his narrative. In the case of the Grail, however, the new motif of the Dolorous Blow detracts from the integrity of the Quest and much of its spiritual context is absent. Where the *Lancelot-Grail* provides symbolic adventures, whose meaning is expounded by the hermits of the wild forest, the Post-Vulgate continues as in its earlier sections, with adventures whose causes and consequences are carefully worked out but which have no inner significance. Such sections of the *Lancelot-Grail* as it retains are overpowered by the continuing adventures, and these adventures are dark and dismal – *mescheance*, mishap or mischance, predominates: the same *malheur* which beset Gawain and other knights in the *Prose Tristan*. Knights kill innocent girls by mistake; best friends fight each other to the death; a promise rashly given leads to a knight beheading his sister.

The atmosphere is not so much of spiritual redemption as that of the working out of a curse imposed by the *Haute Mestre*, the High Master, who appears as an Old Testament deity bent on revenge. As Girflet and Kay tell Yvain, who has been wounded in an adventure, 'the marvels of this land – even those of the Holy Grail – won't fail to happen for you or for any knight, as long as it pleases Our Lord for them to happen. For thus Our Lord pours out his vengeance on the just and unjust according to his will.' And vengeance it is indeed: the new version of the *Quest* has several suicides in addition to the mishaps already described, as well as death from an invisible sword. Gawain's evildoing in the *Lancelot-Grail* becomes a catalogue of crimes: at the outset of the quest a girl foretells that he will kill 'a good eighteen of these companions of yours, such that they are better knights than you'.

It is these events that occupy the foreground: even though many episodes are taken over from the *Lancelot-Grail* version, for much of the romance we are only dimly aware of Galahad and Perceval moving to accomplish the quest. And when they eventually reach Corbenic it is as much in order to heal Pellehan and cancel out the Dolorous Blow as it is to achieve the Grail. Perhaps because of his recent and dramatic conversion, Palamedes replaces Bors as their companion; though, as Palamedes is killed by Gawain soon after the visit to Corbenic, it is Bors who figures in the final episode at Sarras, as in the *Lancelot-Grail*. At the Mass celebrated at Corbenic, the identity of the priest is never given, so that Joseph of Arimathea becomes an anonymous figure; his face 'was of such brightness that mortal eyes could not look at it, but fell humbly, so that no one's eyesight could look at this celestial marvel'. The vision of the real presence in the Eucharist which is ecstatically described in the *Lancelot-Grail* is reduced to a much simpler level: 'But know that each one of them thought he was putting a living man in his mouth.' The vision of eternal things has been closed off, and a darker vision of divine wrath and its expiation replaces it.

The great versions of the Arthurian romances continued to be copied and reread for the next two centuries, though the *Prose Tristan* was by far the most popular. They were translated, adapted and recycled into new stories, such as the extraordinary *Perceforest*, which tells the pagan pre-history of the kingdom of Arthur. Some of the ideas about the Grail which are found in their pages are distinctly odd. In one instance, the whole court of the Fisher King goes out on a spring day for a holiday in the forest, and at lunchtime the Grail appears punctually to distribute everyone's favourite food, just as at the feasts at Corbenic.[22] And in the *Prophecies of Merlin*, when fish have been caught by mistake in a magic river, the Grail prevents any resulting disaster: 'from the direction of the palace there was such a noise and shouting that it was one of the great marvels of the world. And everyone looked in that direction: the Grail came like thunder with the fish, which were cooked underneath, and they threw themselves in the water, and the Grail returned to dry land.'[23] Odd fragments of the old stories have been shuffled into a new order: the lights seen in the forest by Perceval when the Grail accompanies the Fisher King in the *Second Continuation* may have inspired the first scene, and the fish which are specifically said *not* to be in the Grail in *The Story of the Grail* could be the source of the comic second episode.

A similar confusion of half-remembered aspects of the Grail story is responsible for a strange episode in *Sone de Nausay*, a late thirteenth-century romance which has no Arthurian connections.[24] Sone, the hero of the story, comes to Norway on his travels in search of pagan enemies, and stays at a monastery where the Grail is kept; it was brought there from Syria by Joseph of Arimathea, who was wounded by God for his sin in marrying a heathen princess after he had seized the kingdom, and was known as the Fisher King. Logres – not Norway, as one would expect – was barren from the day on which he was wounded. The Grail is used at a service in the abbey, and is a 'vessel of ivory, carved with many stories'; the weapon used by Longinus to wound Christ is kept there too, and a drop of blood hangs from its tip. Joseph of Arimathea and his sons Adam and Josephus are buried there. It has been claimed that this muddle reflects early traditions,[25] but it is much more likely to be a corrupt version of details from the *Lancelot-Grail* cycle, with some echoes of *The Story of the Grail*.

But as time went on, there was a demand for shorter, more coherent versions of the stories, in the face of conflicting versions. In the mid-fifteenth century, several shortened versions of the *Prose Tristan* were produced: in one of these, which became the basis for the early printed editions, there is evidence of a kind of antiquarian curiosity as to what the true story might be. The writer seems to have had access to a copy of the *Prose Perceval*, from which he takes a scene in which Perceval attempts unsuccessfully to occupy the Siege Perilous. Perceval escapes unscathed, and a voice foretells that the Maimed King can only be cured by a knight of the Round Table, who will ask him about the lance and the Grail, and 'who is served with them'. Once this question is asked, the adventures of the Grail will end. The phrasing of the question is almost exactly that of Chrétien, which is otherwise only quoted in *The Story of the Grail* and its continuations.[26]

This same desire to know the true story of Arthur was, at least in part, the inspiration for the greatest English version of the acts of Arthur, that of Sir Thomas Malory, usually known as the *Morte Darthur*, completed in 1470.* His first exploration of the possibilities of the Arthurian material may have been a version of the English poem with a similar title, *Morte Arthure* (*The Death of Arthur*), whose language and style were already archaic, and which he modernized into prose. What is certain is that he read widely in the books on Arthur and his knights, both in French and English, and was aware of the variety of versions of the main story. By the end of his work, he was something of an expert in the field, able to display the results

---

* The only surviving manuscript lacks the opening leaves; the title is William Caxton's, from the version he printed in 1485.

of his antiquarian researches into the tales of '*rex quondam rexque futurus*', 'the once and future king'; Malory quotes this as the epitaph on Arthur's supposed tomb at Glastonbury.[27]

The result is that Malory moves easily from one source to another, retelling the often long-winded and philosophical French texts in his inimitable direct style; in the process he abbreviates drastically, usually to good effect, but sometimes to the detriment of the thread of the story, and he does not always succeed in joining the various versions which he uses in a seamless fashion. Knights reappear many pages after their death has been reported, and important themes are begun but never brought to a conclusion. Thus the Grail first appears in Malory's work in a section where he is translating from the Post-Vulgate version of the story. Merlin prophesies that the magic tapers around the tombs of the twelve kings killed by Arthur will cease to burn 'after the adventures of the Sankgreall, which will come among you and be achieved'.[28] And a little later Malory refers to another adventure which reaches its conclusion 'in the SANKGREALL'.[29] Malory either did not know or rejected in its entirety for the purposes of his book the history of Joseph of Arimathea and his wanderings as told in *The History of the Holy Grail*. As a result, the first episode involving the Grail is the crucial story of the Dolorous Blow, which appears early in the Post-Vulgate, before Arthur's marriage to Guinevere and the institution of the Round Table. It seems as if Malory is setting up the same overarching motif of sacrilege and divine vengeance that drives the action of the *Romance of the Grail*; and he depicts the events leading up to the blow in a brief but intense narrative. Balin kills king Pellam's brother, who is a sorcerer, and Pellam seeks his revenge, breaking Balin's sword with his first blow. The story of the lance follows, as in the Post-Vulgate,* but Malory then adds three sentences of his own:

And king Pellam lay so many years sorely wounded, and could never recover until Galahad the High Prince healed him in the quest of the Sankgreall. For in that place was part of the blood of Our Lord Jesu Christ, which Joseph of Arimathea brought into this land. And he himself lay in that rich bed. And that was the spear with which Longinus smote Our Lord to the heart.[30]

This is our first glimpse of Malory's own entirely distinctive view of the Grail and the spear. For the Grail had never been associated in the romances with a relic of the blood of Our Lord, even though it was the vessel in which

---

* See p. 207 above.

that blood had been collected. What these added sentences offer us is a layman's understanding of the Grail and its associations: for Malory, the context is unequivocally that of the Crucifixion as related in the *Gospel of Nicodemus*. He does not actually call the Grail a reliquary of the Holy Blood, but merely tells us that such a relic was present in the chamber. The presence of Joseph of Arimathea in the bed is also unusual: the nearest parallel in earlier romances is king Mordrains, who survives to see his descendant Galahad before he achieves the Grail. Malory very probably wrote this passage before he translated his version of the Grail quest, and it is an intriguing insight into his original perception of the story.[31] For Malory, as we shall see, the holy vessel is an intimate part of the Crucifixion, and it is inextricably entwined with the Eucharist: we are back at the roots of the Grail story in the twelfth century.

Furthermore, Malory defines the Grail as an object much more closely than does the French original; in the *Quest*, the aim of the knights in setting out in search of the Grail is to find out more about it; the reader is likewise held in suspense as to its appearance and nature. In Malory, the knights may be in ignorance, but the reader knows exactly what the object for which they are searching is like.[32]

Malory moves away from the Post-Vulgate version of Arthur's story at the end of the first tale, and he does not return to it: the theme of the Dolorous Blow is abandoned, and there is only a brief and tentative reference to Balin's sword at the beginning of the *Tale of the Sankgreal*.[33] Instead, he uses first brief extracts from the *Lancelot*, and then takes the largest portion of his text from the *Prose Tristan*. This in turn borrowed large sections of the *Lancelot* when it came to the adventures which form a kind of prelude to the Grail quest,[34] and so Malory's account of the begetting of Galahad comes at second hand from the *Lancelot-Grail*. It seems that Malory was also familiar with the *Lancelot-Grail* itself, for instead of following the unusual version of the Grail quest found in the *Prose Tristan*, he announces firmly 'but here is no rehearsal of the third book', and proceeds to offer instead 'the noble tale of the Sankegreall, which is called the holy vessel and the signification of blessed blood of Our Lord Jesu Christ, which was brought into this land by Joseph of Arimathea'. These are Malory's own words, not found in the original, and, crucially, he reiterates the connection with the Holy Blood and with Joseph of Arimathea.[35]

In the same context, we need to look at the name which Malory uses for the Grail; it is rarely called the 'Grail'[36] and is almost always the 'Sancgreal' or some variant of that word. This seems to have been an English tradition: the Irish translation of the *Quest*, a faithful rendering of the French, calls it consistently the 'Holy Vessel', *Soidheach Naomhtha*, while the Welsh version makes it 'the Holy Greal', *y seint greal*.[37] Henry Lovelich, who translated the *Lancelot-Grail* versions of the *History of the Holy Grail* and *Merlin* into English verse within a decade of Malory, says that 'the people called this vessel "the Sank Ryal" or "Seint Graal" ',[38] keeping the French name and inventing a new meaning for it, 'royal blood' or 'holy Grail'. The same theme of the blood-relic reappears in *Joseph of Arimathie*, a much earlier verse translation of the *History of the Holy Grail*, where the author introduces into Josephus' vision of the ark containing the Grail 'an altar clothed with very rich cloths; on one end lay the lance and the nails, and on the other end, the dish with the blood, and a gold vessel between them'.[39] The original describes 'three nails dripping with blood and a bloody lance-tip', but the presence of blood in the dish is not asserted.[40]

In *Morte Darthur*, when Perceval and Ector are healed by the Grail, the definition of the Grail given by Ector is completely changed: in the French, it is 'the vessel in which Our Lord ate the lamb on Easter Day with his disciples',[41] but this becomes 'an holy vessel that is borne by a maiden, and therein is a part of the blood of our Lord Jesu Christ'.[42] Perceval, who is pure in mind and body ('a parfyte maiden') can vaguely discern the vessel and the girl, but Ector cannot, even though it is he who is able to say what it is. The power of the Grail to detect and confer spirituality is confirmed when it appears at Arthur's court: Malory adds the detail that the knights 'either saw other, by their seeming, fairer than ever they were before', transfigured by the Grail.[43]

Yet when Malory begins to tell the story of the quest for the Holy Grail, he treats the French original respectfully, and the emphasis on the Holy Blood largely disappears. He offers a close recreation of the events recounted in the French book, though he abbreviates substantially.[44] The original *Quest* was by no means the longest of romances, but he reduces it by about a third. This is in line with the tendency of writers throughout Europe who deal with the Arthurian romances in the fifteenth century to offer abbreviated versions of the stories, but where other authors simply condense the narrative in the same general style, Malory transforms it into a new experience, direct and powerful in its approach. He is a master of narrative and dialogue, and uses the vivid precision of English to great advantage. Where the French original tends towards the language of scholarship, with lengthy sentences which are full of reservations and qualifications, Malory's chosen style is much closer to speech. Nor does he translate as a form of copying into another language, but rethinks his material as he works on it. His preference is for the brilliant image over the oblique descriptions of the original. The most dramatic instance of this is at a crucial point in the narrative of the Grail Mass at the castle of Corbenic. After Joseph of Arimathea has celebrated the Eucharist, the French book, as Malory calls it, says: 'Then the companions, raising their eyes, saw a man appear from out of the Holy Vessel, unclothed, and bleeding from his hands and feet and side . . .' Malory substitutes for this elliptical but immediately recognizable figure: 'Then they looked and saw a man come out of the Holy Vessel who had all the signs of the Passion of Jesus Christ, all bleeding openly . . .'[45]

The effect of Malory's approach is both to highlight the adventures of the Grail in line with the emphasis on action in the later French tellings of the Grail story, and also to return to the simplicity of the original story. What Malory gives us is the story of the Grail as it had been told two hundred and fifty years earlier. For as soon as he sets aside the idea of the Grail as a reliquary for the Holy Blood, he puts in its place a clear concept of the Grail as the vessel of the Eucharist, which after consecration also contains Christ's blood, but as part of the living faith, rather than as a relic. The connection with the consecrated wine which becomes blood is reinforced when Bors has a vision of the pelican, the bird which in medieval bestiaries fed its young by drawing blood from its own breast. This was the symbol of Corpus Christi, of the body and blood of Christ,[46] and where the French writer refers simply to the shedding of Christ's blood at the time of the Crucifixion, Malory adds that 'there was the token and the likeness of the Sankgreall that appeared before you'. Again, when Lancelot sleeps through the appearance of the Grail to a sick knight, the knight prays: 'Fair sweet Lord who art here within the holy vessel . . .',[47] implying that Christ's blood is within the Grail; and when Lancelot reflects on his adventures, he bemoans the fact that he 'had no power to stir nor speak when the holy blood appeared before me'; the content of the Grail is more important than the vessel itself.[48]

There is an intriguing link here with the most famous of all the relics of the Holy Blood in England, that at the abbey of Hailes in Gloucestershire. This was a mere thirty miles from Malory's estate at Newbold Revel, and was renowned as a place of pilgrimage throughout the fifteenth century: Margery Kempe, the East Anglian mystic, went there, and John Myrc, whose *Instructions to a Parish Priest* was the most popular handbook of its kind, refers to the Hailes relic and its power to heal the sick. In the early sixteenth century Richard Pynson printed a tourist pamphlet about the miracles, which implies a continuing pilgrimage to, and interest in, the relic.[49] A poem contemporary with Malory tells how the Holy Blood of Hailes was collected by Joseph of Arimathea in a vessel, and how it sustained him in prison, echoing the Grail versions of his legend.[50] And we have seen

18 Lancelot sleeps while the Grail appears to a sick knight. North Italian miniature of about 1380–1440, from The Quest of the Holy Grail.

how the anonymous author of the alliterative *Joseph of Arimathie* shows the same insistence on the contents of the Grail rather than the vessel itself. The only surviving copy of the poem seems to come from the West Midlands, not far from Hailes. The writer of this text avoids naming the Grail altogether, and refers only to 'the blood' or 'the dish with the blood'.[51]

Hailes and its relic seem the most likely source of Malory's insistence on the Grail's association with the Holy Blood; it would have been a familiar part of his religious experience, and, given his preference for concrete images, it would have presented an obvious model on which to base his picture of the Grail. This would fit well with Malory's general approach to the Grail, which is that of a layman, concerned with the outward and visible signs of religion, not with its intricate depths.

But Malory learned from his French source that the Grail is more than the container for the Holy Blood: it is the original of all chalices in which the miracle of the transformation of wine into blood occurs. It is the dish of the Last Supper, and it is for this reason that it becomes the focal point of the knights' quest. It is the most precious of all relics, tangible evidence of Christ's sacrifice for mankind.

Malory's rendering of the whole of the closing scenes of the quest intensifies the fervour of the French tale by the directness of his style. His style is not unlike that of the contemporary English mystics, such as Richard Rolle and Nicholas Love, who share a way of using language which values an immediate and personal dialogue more highly than esoteric and theological discourse. His attitudes are common to what we know of the devotional practices and beliefs of English laymen in the mid-fifteenth century.[52] The celebration of Mass was an occasion for adoration, not participation, and the remoteness and inaccessibility of the Grail are paralleled by the remoteness of the Eucharist for the ordinary worshipper, who might take part in communion once a year. The chalice of the Mass contained the consecrated wine, which was withheld from the lay congregation in Malory's lifetime, despite papal edicts to the contrary. If a layman or laywoman received Mass, it was in the form of the wafer of the Host only; and as a result the chalice became an object of almost superstitious reverence. The worship of the Eucharist as an object is typified by the continued popularity of the cult of Corpus Christi, with its lavish processions on the feast day of that name and the numerous pious fraternities dedicated to it. Furthermore, this was a devout society: we can tell from the books and manuscripts that survive from the period that not only were texts offering religious instruction to the layman produced in huge quantities, but laymen were associated with some of the leading figures among the mystical writers, such as Richard Rolle, who, although he lived as a hermit in Yorkshire, was famed for his instruction of lay people and wrote for them rather than his fellow-religious.

Where Malory differs from his predecessors is in the qualities by which his knights succeed or fail in their search for the Grail. The *Quest* insists that it is the religious virtues that determine the fate of the knights; earthly deeds have no place here. For Malory, earthly fame is not without its merits, and at one moment Bors even says of the quest that 'he shall have much earthly worship who may bring it to an end'. The hermit to whom he is speaking replies: 'Certainly that is true, without fail, for he shall be the best knight of the world and the fairest of the fellows.' Malory has neatly turned the French conversation, which talks of 'such honour as the heart of mortal man cannot conceive', and 'the most loyal serjeant and the truest of the whole Quest',[53] deliberately ignoring the implied religious overtones and stressing '*earthly* fame' and 'the best knight of the *world*'. The Grail adventure is one more of the marvels of Arthur's time, even if it does lead to a wholly spiritual conclusion: and when Lancelot attempts to achieve the Grail, Malory emphasizes his relative success rather than his complete rejection at the last and crucial moment. When Lancelot recovers from the coma by which he is punished for his attempt to enter the chamber, he is told by the people of the castle that his part in the quest is at an end, and that he will see no more of the Grail than what has already passed before his sight. In the French, they add, 'May God send us others who ought to see more of this.'[54] Malory suppresses this, and makes Lancelot say, 'Now

I thank God for his great mercy and for that which I have seen, for it suffices me. For, as I suppose, no man in the world has lived better than I have done to achieve what I have done.'[55]

But this change of emphasis does not in any way diminish the Grail itself. In the scenes in which the Grail appears, Malory follows the French original very closely. In each of the ceremonies of the Grail, beginning with Lancelot's vision of the service which ends so disastrously, Malory follows the French almost word for word, abbreviating slightly but never interfering with the central theological imagery:

(Malory) Then he looked up into the middle of the chamber and saw a table of silver, and the holy vessel covered with red samite, and many angels around it, whereof one held a candle of wax burning and the other held a cross and the ornaments of an altar. And before the holy vessel he saw a good man clothed as a priest, and it seemed that he was performing the consecration of the Mass. And it seemed to sir Lancelot that above the priest's hands were three men, two of whom put the youngest in appearance between the priest's hands; and so he lifted him up very high, and it seemed that he did so to show this to the people.[56]

(French *Quest*) So he let his gaze run round the room and observed the Holy Vessel standing beneath a cloth of bright red samite upon a silver table. And all around weret ministering angels, some swinging silver censers, others holding lighted candles, crosses and other altar furnishings, each and every one intent upon some service. Before the Holy Vessel was an aged man in priestly vestments, engaged to all appearances in the consecration of the mass. When he came to elevate the host, Lancelot thought he saw, above his outstretched hands, three men, two of whom were placing the youngest in the hands of the priest, who raised him aloft as though he were showing him to the people.[57]

(Malory) And then the bishop acted as though he would have begun the consecration of a Mass, and then he took a host which was made in the likeness of bread. And at the lifting up there came a figure in the likeness of a child, and his visage was as red and as bright as any fire; and he smote himself into the bread, so that they all saw that the bread was formed of a fleshly man. And then he put it into the holy vessel again, and then he did what a priest should do to celebrate mass.[58]

(French *Quest*) Next Josephus acted as though he were entering on the consecration of the mass. After pausing a moment quietly, he took from the Vessel a host made in the likeness of bread. As he raised it aloft, there descended from above a figure like to a child, whose countenance glowed and blazed as bright as fire; and he entered into the bread, which quite distinctly took on human form before the eyes of those assembled there. When Josephus had stood for some while holding his burden up to view, he replaced it in the Holy Vessel.[59]

Only in the final scene does Malory abbreviate the rituals, and in so doing he appears deliberately to obscure the nature of Galahad's vision, perhaps because this was still dangerous ground, and the nature of the Eucharist was a contentious issue, particularly in England, where the reformist Lollard movement had once again questioned the orthodox teaching, and men had been burnt for their beliefs about the central act of the Mass.* Everything Malory has written so far is impeccably orthodox, but the last scene presents him with a problem. When, in the French, Galahad looks into the holy vessel after the moment of consecration, what he sees could be construed as offering an interpretation of the very essence of the Grail itself. In the French, Grail and Eucharist are associated but distinct up to the point of the final ceremony. Because Malory chose to identify the Grail so closely with the Eucharist, if he had followed the French closely, the vision in the last scene could have been understood as an interpretation of the Eucharist. This was not ground on which anyone, least of all a layman, should venture.[60] In the French version, there is no question but that Galahad's vision lies within the Grail:

When the year was up and the self-same day that had seen Galahad crowned came round again, the three companions rose at crack of dawn and went up to the palace which men termed spiritual. Looking towards the Holy Vessel they saw a noble-looking man in the vestments of a bishop kneeling before the table reciting the Confiteor. After a long moment he rose from his knees and intoned the mass of the glorious Mother of God. When he came to the solemn part of the mass and had taken the paten off the sacred Vessel, he called Galahad over with the words:

'Come forward, servant of Jesus Christ, and look on that which you have so ardently desired to see.'

Galahad drew near and looked into the Holy Vessel. He had but glanced within when a violent trembling seized his mortal flesh at the contemplation of the spiritual mysteries. Then lifting up his hands to heaven, he said:

'Lord, I worship Thee and give Thee thanks that Thou hast granted my desire, for now I see revealed what tongue could not relate nor heart conceive. Here is the source of valour undismayed, the spring-head of endeavour; here I see the wonder

---

* For example, William Sawtrey in 1401, the first victim of a new statute which condemned heretics to be burnt at the stake.

that passes every other! And since, sweet Lord, Thou has fulfilled my wish to let me see what I have ever craved, I pray Thee now that in this state Thou suffer me to pass from earthly life to life eternal.'[61]

In Malory, the mysteries are not specifically linked with the Grail itself; nor does Galahad describe the essence of the mysteries, merely saying that his wishes have been fulfilled, for he deliberately omits the phrases which tell us where Galahad saw the vision. For a writer whose imagination is primarily visual, it is as if Malory recognizes that this is the point at which both words and earthly sight must fail.

Now at the year's end, and on the same Sunday on which sir Galahad had borne the crown of gold, he arose up early, and his fellows, and came to the palace, and saw before them the holy vessel, and a man kneeling on his knees in the likeness of a bishop, who had around him a great fellowship of angels, as if it was Jesu Christ himself. And then he arose and began a mass of Our Lady. And so he came to the consecration, and when he had finished, he called sir Galahad to him, and said,

'Come forth, thou servant of Jesu Christ, and thou shalt see that which thou hast much desired to see.'

And then he began to tremble very hard when mortal flesh began to behold spiritual things. Then he held up his hands towards heaven and said: 'Lord, I thank Thee, for now I see that which hath been my desire many a day. Now, my Blessed Lord, I do not wish to live in this wretched world any longer, if it might please Thee.'[62]

Yet if the vision itself is veiled and mysterious, we learn a moment later that Galahad has indeed seen the 'marvels of the Sankgreall'.

For Malory, then, the Holy Grail and the Eucharist were closely linked, and both the images of the Trinity and of transubstantiation were understood by him. It should not surprise us that as a layman he has nothing to add to these scenes; but unlike other writers who translated or reworked the story told in the original French *Quest of the Holy Grail*, he has kept the sacred character of 'the tale of the Sankgreal . . . which is a tale chronicled for one of the truest and the holiest that is in this world'.[63] In the power of his language and the sharp focus of his narrative, he has created the supreme version of the medieval portrayal of the Grail.

Epilogue to Part Two

For the writers whose works we have explored, the Grail is indeed the Holy Grail; there is only the merest whisper of dissent. The Holy Grail exists in the borderland between orthodox doctrine and lay devotion, and it reflects the religious enthusiasm for relics, and for the Eucharist as the living relic of Christ and object of intense desire and adoration. What Galahad sees in his final vision, we lesser mortals can only envisage 'through a glass darkly', because it is beyond the powers of human language: yet there can be no doubt that the image which the authors had in mind was the central mystery of the performance of the Mass.

In the hands of the most imaginative of Arthurian poets, Wolfram von Eschenbach, the Grail is recreated as the means through which God works on earth. If Wolfram makes the Grail mysterious so that he can emphasize Parzival's striving towards the achievement of full humanity rather than the divine vision, the Grail nonetheless owes its powers to the Mass wafer laid on it by the heavenly messenger each Good Friday. Readers and interpreters of Wolfram's poem seem to have been in no doubt of its sacred nature. But that sacred nature, initially inspired by the Eucharist, and still recognized two and a half centuries after it was first envisaged, was recreated by secular imagination, and it is the encounter between the great poets and writers of the age and the central symbol of their faith that gives the Grail its extraordinary power. We shall never know how Chrétien de Troyes would have ended his tale; but take the closing pages of *Perlesvaus*, *The Quest of the Holy Grail*, Wolfram and Malory, and in each instance they are masterly: the spiritual aura of the deserted castle in *Perlesvaus*, the apotheosis of the Grail in the *Quest*, Parzival's achievement of spiritual and emotional maturity, and the intensely personal vision of the Eucharist in Malory.

But the religious beliefs at the heart of the Grail stories were dramatically challenged in the early sixteenth century. The belief in the real presence at the consecration of the Mass, with which the Grail was intimately linked, was bitterly contested by devout Christians who sought to re-establish a faith free of what they saw as idolatry and superstition; and in response the reformers within the Church, while affirming the traditional doctrines, preferred to challenge their critics on new ground, and frowned on the excesses of popular enthusiasm. The coming of the Reformation was the moment at which the Grail vanished from the poetic imagination: 'and since then there was never a man so bold as to say that he had seen the Holy Grail'.[1]

I. Perceval watches the Grail procession. The Grail is shown as an elaborate vessel surmounted by a cross. From a manuscript of *The Story of the Grail* written in France in about 1330–1340.

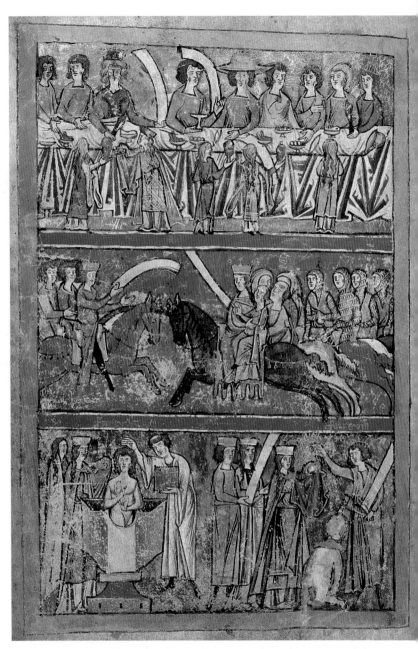

II. The Grail feast, the reunion of Parzival and Kondwiramurs, and the baptism of Feirefiz. From a manuscript of *Parzival* written in Strassburg around 1250–1275.

III. Lancelot's vision of the Grail at a wayside cross. The Grail is a crowned cup borne by angels. From a manuscript of *Lancelot* written in France in the mid-fifteenth century.

IV. The Grail appears at Arthur's court at Pentecost. The Grail image has become standardized as a cup carried by angels, as in Plate III. From a manuscript of *Lancelot-Grail* written at Tournai by Michel Gantelet, priest, and finished on 4 July 1470.

V. Dante Gabriel Rossetti, *How Sir Galahad, Sir Bors and Sir Percival were fed with the Grael: but Sir Percival's sister died by the way* (1864). Here the Grail is depicted as a communion chalice.

VI. James Archer, *La Mort d'Arthur* (1861). This version of Arthur's death includes the traditional figures of Morgan le Fay and the three queens; in addition, Merlin appears in the background, and a shadowy angel bearing a simple Grail hovers at the right.

VII. Sir Edward Burne-Jones, *The Achievement of the Grail* (1891–94), based on *The Quest of the Holy Grail*. Galahad is shown in the centre, with Bors and Perceval to the left. Angels worship the Grail, but there is no sign of Josephus or Christ as in the original romance.

VIII. *The Grail*, centrepiece by Anton Seder, 1899, for the Paris Exhibition of 1900. This spectacular piece echoes medieval jewellery in its detail, while still being entirely of its period.

PART THREE

New Grails for Old

Secular Images of the Grail

Interlude

The medieval Grail was intensely religious in nature, even though it had never been part of the official belief of the Church. The Protestant reformers of the sixteenth century were especially hostile to popular and unsanctioned cults, and the Grail, with its elaborate fictional history, was hardly likely to appeal to Puritan tastes; they did not trouble to separate the Grail stories from the general condemnation of Arthurian romances as a whole, which they saw as a pernicious influence. The Puritan preacher Nathaniel Baxter, regretting that Malory's work had been recently reprinted, complained that among other immoral matter it contained 'the vile and stinking story of the Sangreall'.[1] Nor was the Catholic Counter-Reformation, with its attempts to return to a stricter faith, inclined to make room for such marginal fantasies.

Even before the Reformation, there had been authors who saw the Grail as a more-or-less secular institution, or who criticized the books about it. John Hardyng, a contemporary of Malory, starts his account of the Grail in a similar way, with the appearance of the holy vessel at the Round Table, which is the signal for the quest to begin. Galahad finds the 'sank roiall' in Wales after four years' search. Hardyng, like Henry Lovelich at about the same period, uses the misreading 'sang real' for 'san greal', so that the Holy Grail becomes the 'royal blood'.[2] Hardyng then turns the end of the Grail quest into a crusading expedition. After his discovery, Galahad rides to Palestine 'through God and holy inspiration' and becomes king of Sarras, where he founds an order of the 'sanke roiall', whose twelve members reflect the number of the apostles.[3] The order has a chivalric oath not dissimilar to those found in secular orders of knighthood of the period. But Hardyng's real interest is in Galahad's shield, the red cross shield which had once belonged to Joseph of Arimathea, and in which he sees the origin of the arms of St George and of England. It is this which Perceval reverently brings back after Galahad's death, and it is hung above the place at Glastonbury where Galahad's heart is buried.[4] All this is less to do with the spiritual quests of knighthood than with the glorification of an England in decline, and more particularly the defence of Arthur's reputation against attacks on his name by Scottish historians such as John of Fordun. The Scots were especially hostile to the Arthurian histories, which had been used by Edward I to prove his claim to overlordship of Scotland. Hardyng was anxious to re-establish Arthur's reputation, and his account of Galahad's crusade is an attempt to outdo the story of the death of Robert Bruce, whose heart was similarly brought back from Palestine. It is a strange, muddled episode in the story of the Grail, but also a reminder that not all writers in the fifteenth century treated the theme with reverence.

Although much of our discussion of the medieval Grail has been concerned with its historical background, the Grail was ultimately a literary concept, and its fortunes were entirely bound up with the changing fashions in literary taste. For the Renaissance audience, medieval romances were deeply uninteresting, and were to remain so for the next two centuries. There was a brief respite, however, as the invention of printing brought the stories to a new audience.

The earliest printed Arthurian romance was Wolfram's *Parzival*, in 1477, but because this was, unfashionably, in verse, it does not seem to have been much read.[5] In France, the *Lancelot-Grail* version of the *Quest* was printed eleven years later, as part of a trilogy comprising the *Lancelot, Quest* and *The Death of Arthur*.[6] These two handsome folio volumes were evidently a commercial success and the text was reprinted six times between 1494 and 1533, usually as a three-volume set, which meant that they would have been very expensive. The first English printed version of the Grail was in Caxton's edition of Malory's *Morte Darthur* in 1485, which was reprinted by Wynkyn de Worde in 1498, and again in 1529; it remained in demand longer than any of the other printed versions, as the last issue was that of Robert Stansby in 1634. The Grail story was also to be found in the *Prose Tristan* of 1489, which was reprinted seven times, the last being in 1533. *The History of the Holy Grail*, the remaining part of the *Lancelot-Grail* version, had to wait until 1514–16 before it was published, and the second of the two volumes in the set was made up by an adaptation of *Perlesvaus*, since the printer was evidently reluctant to duplicate the Grail text in the *Lancelot* but wanted to complete the story. Lastly, Chrétien's *Perceval*, with three of the continuations and versions of both the prologues, appeared in 1530. However, the classic Arthurian romances of the thirteenth century fell into disfavour from 1530 onwards. In France, only the 1488 version of the *Lancelot-Grail* was reprinted after 1533, in an abbreviated version in 1591. Instead the pastoral romance, whose heroes and heroines were shepherds and shepherdesses or their equivalents, became hugely popular, with an average of one new title a year from 1509 to the end of the century. Readers of chivalric romance demanded the more fantastical later stories, and it was *Amadis of Gaul* and *Tirant lo Blanc* that Don Quixote read, not *Lancelot* or *Tristan*, and certainly not the Grail stories. Even Rabelais, that arch-mocker of all things fusty and medieval, has only the merest hint of a parody of the Grail in Pantagruel's search for *la dive bouteille*, the sacred bottle. For two centuries, the Grail was destined to oblivion rather than obloquy.

17

The Scholars and the Grail

J'ai seul la clef de cette parade, cette parade sauvage   Arthur Rimbaud

*I ignore entirely the pseudo-problems raised by reading which regards
symbols as a sort of quarry or game, to be pursued, shot down, bagged
and brought in, inducing chiefly a feeling of achievement on the part of
the hunter*   Rosemond Tuve, *Allegorical Imagery*[1]

In the room a man is copying a manuscript. Between the dramatic visions
on the baroque ceiling and the exuberant patterns of the floor, balconies and
pillared bookshelves dazzle the eye; everything here is new and appointed in
the rich style that befits the oldest and greatest of the Swiss abbeys, that of
St Gall.[2] The scholar is Christoph Heinrich Müller, who studied under the
late professor of Helvetic history at Zurich, J. J. Bodmer, and he is engaged
in copying a text. This text is in verse, in a relatively modest manuscript
with red and blue initials and the occasional touch of gold. As so often with
medieval manuscripts, the first page is worn, but thereafter the words,
written by three different scribes, are tolerably clear. Most of the visitors to
the library come to see historical texts or illuminated manuscripts; what is
unusual is that Müller has before him neither of these, but a work of fiction,
Wolfram's *Parzival*, one of the long-neglected Grail romances. The results
of his labours at St Gall appeared in 1784: this was the first printing of
an accurate text of a medieval Arthurian romance. But the manuscripts
themselves had lain largely undisturbed since the early sixteenth century.

Why were scholars now turning their attention to medieval literature for
the first time as a suitable subject for their researches? Why, in this supposed
age of reason, were they hunting out the old fantastic tales again? To
understand this, we have to look briefly at the history of European scholarship in the preceding decades:

The seventeenth century, or more exactly the period from about 1630 to 1730, was a golden age of scholarship. The great and absorbing theological controversies of the Reformation, in which almost all the great minds of the age had been engaged, were now near spent, and a period of relative peacefulness began; throughout Europe a generation of highly educated and civilized men, full of curiosity and appreciation of the history and writings of the distant past, was able to review the treasures, printed and unprinted, that had been assembled in the great libraries and collections of Europe. The spirit of the age, which witnessed so many triumphs of mathematical discovery and the first great advances in natural science, showed itself in the humane disciplines as an influence in the direction of criticism and analysis.[3]

Historians turned from their ecclesiastical controversies to national histories. The old scholarly world, in which Latin was the universal language and what was written in Stockholm could be read with ease in Seville or Siena, came to an end as the new authors wrote in their native tongues; but the new scholarship was pursued with enthusiasm and energy.

Literature, which had remained largely beyond the province of scholars, was drawn into the sphere of learned discussion by the same interest in national history. Literary works were often the earliest evidence of national identity, and the works of the medieval poets were used to wage modern polemics. In the case of J. J. Bodmer, his preoccupation was to overturn the influence of French classicism on German literature. French was the language of polite German society, and French culture was its accepted norm; the professor at Leipzig, Johann Christoph Gottsched, argued that German writers should follow the approach of the Académie Française in the form of their works, and respect the supposed three unities of Greek literature – unity of action, unity of space and unity of time – as found in the masterpieces of the ancient theatre. Form and discipline were valued above imagination and the picturesque. Bodmer, by contrast, argued for the freedom of the imagination, in works such as On the Marvellous in Poetry of 1740, and what could better fit that title than the flights of fancy and ornate descriptions of Parzival? In 1753, he produced an abbreviated version of the poem based on the printed edition of 1477, which was itself a reworking. The result was to make something of the substance of Wolfram's work available to the curious. More important, Bodmer inspired the production of Müller's new transcription of the original poem.

Initially, the attraction of Parzival for German readers was not its subject, but the treatment of the subject. The brothers Schlegel, the most influential critics in the Romantic movement at the end of the eighteenth century, admired Wolfram's poem, if with reservations. A. W. Schlegel, famous as co-translator with Ludwig Tieck of Shakespeare's plays, called *Parzival* 'a highly bizarre, but great and rich composition', and attacked the only available version of the French Grail romances, in the *Universal Library of Romances* by the comte de la Vergne de Tressan, as being 'miserable excerpts', tasteless and lightweight. The contrast could hardly be more extreme: Tressan had tried to turn the stories into eighteenth-century light reading, using the early printed editions as his basis. His volumes are illustrated with curious engravings of the Arthurian heroes as eighteenth-century gentlemen, with the ladies similarly transmogrified.

For German scholars, therefore, Wolfram's Grail romance represented the potential of native German inspiration, untrammelled by artificial rules – a prelude to the 'holy German art' praised by Wagner in *The Mastersingers of Nuremberg*. *Parzival* appeared in a definitive edition by Karl Lachmann in 1833 (which, even today, in its seventh edition, is still unchallenged), and when Wagner came to read Arthurian romance in the 1840s, he had a wide range of material to explore, as the surviving contents of his library at Dresden show: they include copies of editions and translations of *Parzival* by Lachmann, Simrock and 'San Marte' (Albert Schulz).[4]

In France, by contrast the romances were either trivialized, as we have seen, or forgotten. Inquiring readers, among them the German writer Lessing in the mid-eighteenth century, might turn to the 1516 printing of *The History of the Holy Grail*, with its curious mixture of different romances.[5] In 1841, the poems attributed to Robert de Boron were privately printed at Bordeaux, but the work of Chrétien and his continuators did not appear in print until 1865, in a vast but unreliable edition by Charles Potvin. The same was true in the field of translations: the first modern French version of the *Lancelot-Grail*, that of Paulin Paris in 1868–77, was free, often lively, but scarcely faithful to the original. Although Chrétien's *The Story of the Grail* was part of Potvin's 1865 edition, it was only properly edited in 1932.

This neglect of the romances in France was due to the preference of nineteenth-century French medievalists for the *chansons de geste*, roughly contemporary with the early romances, depicting the world of Charlemagne and his barons rather than the realm of Arthur, in which the courtly values played little, if any, part. The feudal bond between lord and vassal is the central motif, and there are set-piece battles in place of jousts and challenges. These were regarded as the masterpieces of the French literature of that period. Léon Gautier declared – in capital letters – 'LA CHANSON DE

ROLAND VAUT L'ILIADE',*[6] and the Arthurian romances were regarded as obscure and decadent, a falling away from the vibrant energy of the stories of Roland and his peers, of Guillaume d'Orange and the feudal barons. Just as *Parzival* had been used to invoke a German national identity in imaginative literature against French influence, so the French medieval epics – denied the very name of epic by the classical critic Amaury Duval in the *Histoire littéraire de France* in 1838 – were now held up as the model for loyal French writers.

But even as this new orthodoxy was proclaimed, there were dissenting voices. Edgar Quinet,[7] in his essays in the *Revue des deux mondes* in 1837, echoed Bodmer's enthusiasm for the imaginative in literature, declaring that the Carolingian epics belonged to a materialist Germanic tradition, and that 'Arthur, who has nothing to do with the warriors of Germanic origin, is king of the dreams of the conquered people.' Quinet's interest is not in the sources and transmission of the stories; for him the romances represented a natural outpouring of a new literary form, derived solely from the imagination of the poets.

As a scholar, Quinet stands at the crossroads of the careers of the man of letters and that of the professional academic. He began as an essayist, and rose to become professor of the literatures of Southern Europe at the Collège de France: after he lost the chair because of his political views in 1846 and went into exile, he wrote a major novel on the Grail.† His interest, like that of Jules Michelet the historian, was in the way in which French genius had been formed: for him, *The Story of the Grail* was part of a magnificent age of poetry in France which had flourished in the twelfth century, a half-Celtic, half-French art which was to be the way forward for French authors of his own time. Michelet, on the other hand, found courtly love unsatisfactory and spiritually unrewarding as an ideal, and saw the Grail cycle as a clerical antidote to the romances which celebrated secular love.

The Search for Sources

So far we have looked at scholars who were interested in the substance of the romances. We now turn to the topic which has obsessed much scholarship about the Grail in modern times: the question of sources. Essentially, so long as discussions of literary texts are focused on the text itself, like the medieval commentaries on Dante's *Divine Comedy*, the pursuit of sources

---

* 'The *Song of Roland* is equal to the *Iliad*.'
† See p. 261 below.

was of minor interest. It is only with the emergence of literary history that the problem of origins, and of which author first conceived a particular idea, becomes a crucial question. This is exactly what happens when literature is drawn into the arena of national history. French writers from the Romantic period onwards championed regional cultures as formative influences on the literature of their country; and it was in this context that the question of sources was first raised, when Claude Fauriel, the first professor of foreign literature to be appointed in France (in 1830), suggested that the Arthurian tales had their origins in Provence, since only a highly developed literary culture such as that of the troubadours could have given rise to sophisticated works of this kind.[8] This generalized approach was quickly superseded by the exploration of the Celtic parallels for the French romances.

Too little attention is paid to the historical, political and even cultural context of scholarship. On the one hand, we need more books such as Eric Stanley's magisterial *Imagining the Anglo-Saxon Past*, which shows how a political agenda shaped an image of a struggle which never existed – of pagan bard versus Christian monk – for such agendas underlie interest in medieval texts from the beginning of the renewal of interest in such works in the early eighteenth century. Behind Bodmer's enthusiasm for *Parzival*, Fauriel's championing of Provence and Gautier's dismissal of the romances, lies a common enthusiasm for the promotion of national literature, whether French or German. On the other hand, we need a clear view of the material available to scholars, for it is easy to forget that many of the early writers who shaped the arguments about the Grail simply did not have all the texts in front of them. Apart from the first editing of Wolfram von Eschenbach in 1784, it was only in the early nineteenth century that literary scholarship became a widely respected pursuit and the editing of texts began in earnest. In 1816, Sir Thomas Malory was reprinted for the first time since 1634, but the argument about the origins of the Grail was well under way before the most important of all the Grail texts, Chrétien's *The Story of the Grail*, was first edited in 1868. Equally, the *Lancelot-Grail* appeared in a limited edition in England in 1864,[9] and was not readily available until the 1890s.

The Publication of The Mabinogion

This meant that those texts which were in print assumed a disproportionate importance. The combination of availability of material and an ardent nationalist agenda is nowhere better seen than in the publication of Welsh medieval literature. The defining moment of the exploration of these texts was the publication in 1801–7 of *Myvyrian Archaiology of Wales*, edited by Owen Jones, Iolo Williams and William Owen Pughe: this collection aimed to print all the hitherto unpublished Welsh poetry up to 1370, as well as historical texts and documents and other literary material from this period. Other publications by the editors of *The Myvyrian Archaiology* included, somewhat surprisingly, a periodical called *Y Greal*, which first appeared in London in 1805 under the auspices of two learned societies devoted to the study of the Welsh past. The reason for the choice of name is obscure; the prospectus gives no clue, but it may have been because of the Grail's reputation as a rarity in medieval Welsh literature.[10] William Owen Pughe, in his *Dictionary of the Welsh Language* (1803), defines 'Grëal' as follows, though his entry owes as much to his imagination as to his researches:

It was the name of a celebrated book of Welsh stories, long since lost, extolled by different writers. *Gwlad y Grëal*, the elemental world or world of the spirits.

The periodical was short-lived, as was another publication put out by the Baptists in Wales, *Greal y Bedyddwyr*, but what all this does imply is that the idea of the Grail was current in Wales, though it is difficult to decide how it was conceived.

Algernon Herbert in 1836 saw the Arthurian material as part of the repository of bardic lore, correctly pointing to the Welsh origin of much of the romance material. But his view of the Grail was, to say the least, unorthodox:

The great work, and as I may say, the Alcoran, of Arthurian Romance, was the Book of the Saint Greal. In truth, it is no romance, but a blasphemous imposture, more extravagant and daring than any other on record, in which it is endeavoured to pass off the mysteries of Bardism for direct inspirations of the Holy Ghost.[11]

The real revival of interest in Welsh prose literature of the early medieval period was initiated by Lady Charlotte Guest. Her major work was *The Mabinogion, from the 'Llyfr Coch o Hergest' and other ancient Welsh Manuscripts*, which appeared between 1838 and 1849, and included an English translation. This unlocked the riches of the Welsh material for a wide readership, and it attracted the attention of scholars across Europe. It was published at a time when there was also renewed interest in Celtic religion, and this was treated as new grist to the mill in the process of elucidating the mysteries of the pagan past of Wales.

It was evident to readers of *The Mabinogion* that there was some kind of a relationship between the Welsh stories and the Arthurian romances.

However, in the absence of proper texts of the French romances to which the Celtic tales were supposed to relate it was difficult to carry out any extensive analysis, and the idea that the French books had Celtic origins was accepted without any firm foundation in textual analysis. This came later, and although it provided a good deal of evidence to show that episodes and characters, as well as the atmosphere of the narratives, from *The Mabinogion* were indeed to be found in the later retellings, it does not follow that the Celtic romances are the major source of Arthurian romance. But the ardent advocacy of the Welsh scholars made it difficult to argue that these contributions were no more than a part of a larger cultural context, and that other elements were far more important.

Peredur

The problem is at its most acute when we look at the Welsh prose romance of *Peredur son of Efrawg*. The earliest complete text dates from the end of the thirteenth century, but a Welsh scholar claims that 'close examination of the orthography suggests the existence of a written version probably from the early twelfth century, predating *Perceval*'.[12] Now it is impossible for mere mortals to argue with this kind of statement, relying as it does on knowledge of the medieval forms of one of the more difficult of the Indo-European languages. The writer goes on to claim that 'the strong oral tradition in Celtic culture and the nature of the material in the romance suggest that it existed in pre-Roman times . . .' Here we are clearly in the realms of speculation, and we had better turn to the story itself.

Peredur is the youngest of seven sons; all his brothers and his father have been killed in tournaments or wars, and his mother has brought him up in the remote forest to prevent him from pursuing the knightly career which has brought disaster to the family. However, one day he encounters three knights, and is immediately seized with a desire to become a knight. Despite his mother's entreaties he sets out, and, after a series of misadventures due to his failure to understand her advice, he comes to Arthur's court. A strange knight rides in and insults the queen, carrying off her goblet. Peredur goes after him, and kills him with a javelin; he takes his armour, and his knightly adventures begin.

He comes to a castle where there is an old man sitting by a lake watching youths fish; he goes into the castle, and the old man is there, seated on a cushion. He reveals himself as Peredur's uncle and tells him how to conduct himself as a knight. The next day Peredur rides on, and comes to another castle; before they go to dine, Peredur is given a sword, and told to smite an iron column in half; he does it twice and the sword and column rejoin when broken. The third time they stay broken. The lord reveals himself as another uncle.

Thereupon he could see two youths coming into the hall, and from the hall proceeding to a chamber, and with them a spear of exceeding great size, and three streams of blood along it, running from the socket to the floor. And when they all saw the youths coming after that fashion, every one set up a crying and a lamentation, so that it was not easy for any to bear with them. The man did not, for all that, interrupt his conversation with Peredur. The man did not tell Peredur what that was, nor did he ask it of him. After silence for a short while, thereupon, lo, two maidens coming in, and a great salver between them, and a man's head on the salver, and blood in profusion around the head. And then all shrieked and cried out, so that it was hard for any to be in the same house as they. At last they desisted therefrom, and sat as long as they pleased, and drank.[13]

Peredur's next journey takes him to the mountain-top castle of the witches of Caer Loyw; he defeats one of them, and in return she takes him to learn how to handle a horse and arms. He spends three weeks with them, and sets off again. He comes to a hermit's cell; here he sees two drops of blood in the snow where a hawk had killed a duck, and a raven nearby, which reminded him of 'the hair of the woman he loved best, which was as black as jet, and her flesh to the whiteness of the snow, and the redness of the blood in the white snow to the two red spots in her cheeks'.[14]

He eventually returns to marry his beloved, and rules with her for fourteen years. After that he goes to Arthur's court, where a hideous messenger appears, and accuses Peredur of failing to ask about the spear and other marvels, bringing ruin on his uncle's kingdom. Peredur wanders for a long while, and meets a priest, who reproaches him for bearing arms on Good Friday, but then tells him how to find the Castle of Wonders. He stays at a castle where he is imprisoned on suspicion of seducing the lord's daughter, but she persuades her father to let him fight their enemies; he defeats them, and is freed, but refuses her hand and asks again for the Castle of Wonders. He comes to the castle of the magic chessboard, which plays against him and defeats him; he throws it in the lake. The hideous messenger reappears and tells him it is the empress's board, and that to recover it he must fight a black man at a nearby castle, whom he kills. He then slays a magic stag which is laying waste the nearby forest, but a lady appears and tells him he has slain the fairest jewel in her domains. To regain her friendship, he strikes a stone slab on a nearby mountain, and a black man in huge rusty armour on a bony horse jousts with him. Each time he is unseated he leaps back into the saddle, until Peredur dismounts and draws his sword, when he vanishes and Peredur's horse with him. He walks along the mountain and comes to the Castle of Wonders where he finds his horse again. His uncle welcomes him, and a yellow-haired youth kneels to him:

'Lord,' said the youth, 'I came in the guise of the black maiden to Arthur's court, and when thou didst throw away the board, and when thou slewest the black man . . . and when thou slewest the stag, and when thou didst fight against the black man of the slab; and I came with the head all bloody on the salver, and with the spear that had the stream of blood from its tip to the handgrip along the spear. And the head was thy cousin's, and it was the witches of Caer Loyw that had slain him. And 'twas they that lamed thy uncle. And thy cousin am I, and it is prophesied that thou wilt avenge that.'[15]

Peredur summons Arthur, and they attack the witches, whom Peredur kills. 'And thus is it told of the Castle of Wonders.'

This tale obviously belongs to the context of the medieval Grail romances we have already discussed, but it is not a Grail romance. Some of this is familiar; some of it is totally unexpected. There are two important things to note: Peredur's adventures depend crucially on the concept of knighthood as an exclusive caste, both in terms of the overall pattern of the story and in the details. It would be difficult to imagine a version with any literary pretensions that worked outside the confines of the chivalric world. So the existence of an early twelfth-century version, if it has to include the chivalric detail which is at the heart of the story, seems very improbable: it would mean that the Welsh, whose culture was virtually untouched by chivalry, were the first to write a chivalric romance. It is, in terms of the substance of the story, much more plausible that this is a Welsh retelling of a late version of Chrétien's The Story of the Grail, using material from the Continuations as well. But just as the attraction of the Celtic stories to French writers was the new imaginative world which they were able to combine with the chivalric world, so, when the Welsh writer reworked Chrétien's tale, he did so in the context of the marvels and mysteries of his own traditional culture.[16] Why the Host contained in the Grail should become a bloody head is indeed a problem, but the simplest explanation is that they are unrelated, and that another story has been merged with that of the Grail. This new story clearly has a relationship with the pagan Celtic cult of the head, which does seem to date back to pre-Roman times, but it could also be an echo of the story of John the Baptist. The central theme of the new tale is also quite different, as it is a simple story of a question for vengeance for the murder of Peredur's cousin, into which the severed head fits naturally. The ending of the tale, too, with its destruction of the workers of magic, is typical of the style of the other Welsh romances, where the main action takes place on another plane, and is brought back to reality in the closing pages. This is in sharp contrast to the Grail romances, where no such resolution, no lifting of the magic spells, occurs.

Claims for the primacy of *Peredur* over *The Story of the Grail* have become bound up with questions of national pride. At best, there is a possibility that some kind of tale about Peredur/Perceval may have provided Chrétien with an element of his material, perhaps the idea of the hero who begins as a fool. But as far as the Grail is concerned – and that, not the character of Perceval, is the point of our present inquiry – the bloody head on the platter is not a precursor of the dish in Chrétien's mysterious procession. It requires an improbable series of speculations to reconstruct such a transition.[17]

The Celtic Origins of the Grail

Interestingly, the earliest attempts to show that the Grail had its origins in Celtic myth made no mention of *Peredur*. Theodore de La Villemarqué wrote in his *Contes populaires bretons* of 1842:

The most ancient of these traditions [i.e. of the bards of Wales] speak in effect of a vase which has the name and characteristics of the Grail. The bards of the sixth century use the word *per* to describe it, a word which a Welsh vocabulary of 882 translates as *basin*, and of which a more modern dictionary says that it signifies 'a household utensil in which are served or cooked dishes of all kinds'. Now this is exactly the meaning of the word *graal* . . . Taliesin places the bardic basin in the temple of a goddess whom he calls the patron of bards: 'This vase,' he says, 'inspires poetic genius; it confers wisdom, it reveals to its worshippers the knowledge of the future, the mysteries of the world, the entire treasury of human knowledge . . .' The graal provides some of these advantages. As for the basin itself, its rim is decorated, like that of the graal, with a row of pearls and diamonds.[18]

And it was the Breton poets who inspired the French romances, by way of Provence:

The authors of the French poems which form the Arthurian cycle evidently found in Celtic literature their precursors and models.

The Breton cycle on Arthur gave birth to a Provençal cycle on the Round Table, contemporary with the French cycle. A similar movement to that in the west arose simultaneously in the south of Europe; the heroes of the Round Table were celebrated simultaneously by the trouvères and the troubadours ... The epic movement produced by the Breton fables of the Arthurian cycle did not encompass French and Provençal literature alone, but extended to English, Germanic and even Scandinavian literature ...[19]

La Villemarqué championed the cause of Breton literature with enthusiasm, and his detractors claimed that his work on Breton folktales was creative and imaginative, rather than scholarly: he invented more than he actually found. In this he was not unlike the Scottish author Macpherson, whose collection of Gaelic poems ascribed to Ossian had enchanted a previous generation of literary enthusiasts for folklore. The demand for Breton and Gaelic material, and for discovering the 'originals' of themes supposedly taken up later by the early French poets, outstripped the supply. There was in fact little evidence for his insistence on the primary role of the Breton poets in transmitting the Arthurian stories, yet the Celtic origins of Arthurian romance were generally and quickly accepted as the new orthodoxy. The influential critic Ernest Renan, in an essay on 'La poésie des races celtiques', considered *Peredur* to be a less developed predecessor of Chrétien's Perceval, but saw the Grail as a version of the cauldron of Brân the Blessed, and Perceval's reticence in asking the crucial question as a reference to the secrets of bardic initiation: 'the Grail in its primitive form appears as the password of a kind of freemasonry which was preserved in Wales long after the preaching of the Gospel'.[20] He was aware, however, that French writers must have set aside this bardic and pagan beginning, for they envisaged the Grail quite differently, as a form of the Eucharist, and

Perceval became the model of a spiritual knight. This was the last of the metamorphoses which that all-powerful fairy called the human imagination made him undergo, and it was fair that after running the gauntlet of so many dangers, he should find rest from his adventures beneath a monastic habit.[21]

Perhaps because there was no major version of the Grail story in English before Malory, English scholars were less interested in the Grail romances than their continental counterparts. Even though the one medieval English poem entitled *Sir Perceval* contains no mention of the Grail, J. O. Halliwell, in his edition of 1844, affirmed that it was derived from Chrétien and his continuators, and argued that *Peredur* was also derived from the same source. But other writers were less restrained in developing their own theories. The translation of Wolfram's *Parzival* by San Marte, which appeared in 1842, was prefaced by an extensive essay on the origins of the legend, in which the translator accorded *Peredur* the pride of place as the original source of the story of Perceval. However, he regarded it as totally distinct from the tradition of the Grail. According to San Marte, who accepted as genuine Wolfram's claims that Kyot was his source, the Grail story originated in Provence, and was intimately linked with the rise of the Templars. It was part of 'the exploits of the Knights of the Round Table', and 'we must be deceived upon every point, if Arthur and the Sangraal did not first meet half way in France about 1150, coming from the North and the South'.[22]

But such speculative theories were easily demolished. The next translator of *Parzival*, Simrock, denied that Wolfram's 'Kyot' was a historical figure; instead he centred the Grail around the cult of St John the Baptist, claiming that in the eleventh century the relic of the Baptist's head was used to keep one of the Byzantine emperors from dying, since, like the Grail, no one who saw the relic would die on the day on which he saw it. Simrock argued that the Grail derived ultimately from the archetypal myths of the dying and reviving god, and found echoes of these stories in Germanic folk-tradition. Wolfram was merely the interpreter of an existing German tradition.[23] Even the usually sober J. F. Campbell, in *Popular Tales of the West Highlands* (1860), seems to have claimed that Gaelic folktale held the key to the stories. Writing of the 'Lay of the Great Fool' he says

I am inclined ... to consider the 'Lay' as one episode in the adventures of a Celtic hero, who in the twelfth century became Perceval le chercheur du basin. He too, was poor, and the son of a widow, and half starved, and kept in ignorance by his mother ... in the end, he became possessed of that sacred basin le Saint Graal, and the holy lance, which, though Christian in the story, are manifestly the same as the Gaelic talismans which appear so often in Gaelic tales, and which have relations in all popular lore – the glittering weapon which destroys, and the sacred medicinal cup which cures.[24]

In 1896, Alfred Nutt, avowedly a pupil of J. F. Campbell, elaborated this thesis and provided the map for the numerous twentieth-century scholars who have followed this path. Despite his painstaking analysis of the literary evidence, by now including Chrétien's *The Story of the Grail*, which he recognized as the earliest of the Grail poems, he worked on the underlying assumption that romance literature owes very little to the imagination, and a great deal to lost folktales. In his view, a common oral tradition stretched from Brittany to northern Scotland, and from Ireland to the Welsh border, and was conveyed by bilingual poets to the audiences of Anglo-Norman England and northern France. Here it was to re-emerge in literary form in the romances of Chrétien.[25] In studying the relationship of literature to oral tradition there was no need to look at the date at which a story or an idea had first been recorded, or their manuscript context: the fact that the source was an oral tradition guaranteed that it pre-dated any such written record. The best warning I know against such assumptions is to be found in Thomas Hardy's comment in the introduction to the 1919 reprint of his *Wessex Tales*:

An experience of the writer in respect of the tale called 'A Tradition of Eighteen Hundred and Four' is curious enough to be mentioned here. The incident of Napoleon's visit to the English coast by night, with a view to discovering a convenient spot for landing his army of invasion, was an invention of the author's on which he had some doubts because of its improbability. Great was his surprise several years later to be told that it was a real tradition.[26]

This is a classic instance of a literary invention becoming a folktale, something which occurs perhaps more often than is generally admitted.* I do not mean to imply that the case for oral transmission should be dismissed out of hand, merely that it should be treated with the greatest caution. In parallel with this devotion to the pre-eminence of oral literature went the idea – beloved of early twentieth-century scholars in this field – that *any* episode in a later romance formed part of a jigsaw which, if correctly completed, would lead to the discovery of the 'original', of which all subsequent versions were 'corrupt' images.

The History of the Grail Romances

The excesses of those who sought historical authors and documented contacts between them could be equally alarming. Hucher, who printed for the first time much of the prose version of the pre-history of the Grail, the *History of the Holy Grail* and *Joseph of Arimathea*, presented an elaborate biography of Robert de Boron in his introduction, which depends on a couple of documents and a great deal of conjecture.[27] According to Hucher, Boron was lord of a domain near Fontainebleau in the 1150s, and travelled

---

* Parallel examples could be cited from Restoration ballads, which have become folksongs, and from modern urban myths, which can be shown in some instances to have literary origins.

to England around 1169, where Walter Map taught him the secrets of the Grail. On his return, he wrote the prose *Joseph d'Arimathie* and *Merlin* for Gautier de Montbéliard, before going back to England to write the *Lancelot-Grail Quest* with Walter Map. Chrétien, in Hucher's view, was a mere imitator of these two literary giants.

The first major scholarly survey of the Grail literature was undertaken by A. Birch-Hirschfeld in *The Saga of the Grail*.[28] He concluded that Chrétien's version depended on that of Robert de Boron, but that *Peredur* was later, and realized that Walter Map was unlikely to have written large parts of the *Lancelot-Grail*. His conclusions, based on a sensible mixture of literary and historical criticism, have largely stood the test of time, with the exception of his central hypothesis that Robert de Boron preceded Chrétien. He also argued for Wolfram's dependence on Chrétien, and the non-existence of the elusive 'Kyot' whom Wolfram claims as his source. His work is essentially a model of orthodox literary criticism, staying scrupulously with the texts and the scraps of historical evidence about the authors and their milieu. He does not invoke later folklore or other parallel legends, and this was the ammunition which his opponents deployed against him – arguing that weight must be given to the ambience of Celtic culture, not merely to the text and its historical authors.

Anthropology, Comparative Mythology and the Grail

In this Birch-Hirschfeld's critics were following the other great development of late nineteenth-century scholarship: the emergence of anthropology and of writers such as Sir J. G. Frazer, whose massive work *The Golden Bough* set the tone for a whole school of followers. Here analogues carry as much weight as the evidence of the text itself, and the possibilities of speculative solutions are therefore vastly increased. Furthermore, the basic premise of the anthropological school of interpretation is that legends such as that of the Grail are inherently pre-Christian: in Alfred Nutt's words, a theory which claims that 'this vast body of romance sprang from a simple but lofty spiritual conception' and 'postulates a development of the legend which is the very opposite of the *normal* one'.[29] I emphasize *normal*, as it betrays a determination to impose a preconception on the analysis of the romances: normality is the pagan past, Christianity the aberration.

Any analysis based on this assumption must, however, reconstruct that pagan past; and here the problems begin. What we know about Celtic mythology is difficult to substantiate, as with all oral traditions. In the words of Proinsias MacCana, 'There remains ... a considerable body of residual evidence, but, since by its very nature it is allusive rather than descriptive, or else is reported at second hand, the modern student is frequently in the uncomfortable position of working from the ambiguous to the unknown.'[30] With due caution, much can be derived from this difficult material; but in the case of the Grail, the path has been all too often from ambiguity to pure imagination. The problem for scholars looking for Celtic originals for the Grail itself is that all the evidence we have points to the Grail being a platter or serving dish in its first appearances in the romances. Celtic legend has little to report that even vaguely resembles the Grail in this form, and appeal is usually made to the very different magic cauldrons which have a prominent place in the stories. But this is a leap not of logic, but of imagination: both are capable of containing food, but shape and function are different, as one is a serving dish, while the other is an implement for preparing the food. Yet the assumption that the original of the Grail is a vessel like that of Brân the Blessed in the *Mabinogi* of 'Branwen daughter of Llyr' has persisted into recent scholarship; its transition into a Christian sacred cup feebly explained by such statements as 'if the original of this vessel . . . was a possession of Celtic sea gods like Manannan and Bran, it is easy to see why an atmosphere of sanctity should have surrounded it'.[31] And this line of argument leads us to confident conclusions such as that of Glenys Goetinck, for whom 'the origin of the Grail becomes perfectly clear'. She explains that it is

one of the talismans found in the dwelling of the otherworld God; it was of great significance in the ritual of conferring sovereignty upon the hero upon the occasion of his visit to the otherworld. The Grail in its original form was the vessel offered to the hero by Sovereignty: it was itself a symbol of sovereignty. The quest for the Grail was originally the hero's quest for sovereignty.[32]

The archetypal Celtic enthusiast among the twentieth-century scholars was R. S. Loomis, hugely diligent and learned, who elaborated the parallels already established by earlier writers. But in the end, his zeal for Celtic origins outran the material on which he was working, and his arguments rely on a series of assumptions and analogues which scarcely hang together. And his reading of the French romances is often selective: in his analysis of the Grail, he emphasizes its function as a dish, and the attribute of providing food, which are indeed important characteristics, but, as we have seen, far from the only aspects of the Grail: its role as a cup and as a sacred vessel are set aside. The theme of the Waste Land, which is only of real importance in the very late romances, is seen as an essential part of the Grail story. In the closing pages of his study of the Grail, he propounds a typical theory to account for the problems which his own insistence on Celtic origins created:

We have strong reason to believe that one misinterpretation, frequently repeated, had momentous consequences for the development of the Grail legend. The words *cors beneïz* or *benoiz*, meaning 'blessed horn', and referring to the food- and drink-providing horn of [the Welsh hero] Brân, must have occurred frequently in association with the words *sains graaus*, referring to the holy dish of the same Brân . . . Now the word *cors* in the nominative case could have several meanings besides 'horn', and the French were not any too familiar with holy drinking horns. On the other hand they were constantly hearing and talking about the wonders wrought by . . . the body of Christ in the form of the consecrated host. Since the word *cors* meant 'body', is it any wonder that under these circumstances the words *cors benoiz* or *beneïz* were regularly interpreted as the Blessed Body of Christ . . . ?[33]

There are many problems with this train of thought, not least that there is no known translation into French of the exploits of Brân, and the Anglo-Normans at least were just as familiar with drinking horns, holy or otherwise, as the Welsh. This is, at best, an example of a powerful imagination at work on the Celtic tradition; though not perhaps as powerful as that of a certain Chrétien de Troyes.

The Grail from the East

The proponents of the Celtic Grail rely on Chrétien as their starting point. There are equally ardent enthusiasts for an Oriental Grail, for whom the crucial text is Wolfram's *Parzival*.[34] They point to the pervasive references in *Parzival* to Eastern words and to the kind of luxury associated with the East in the early thirteenth century. The mysterious *achmardi* on which Repanse de Schoye bears the Grail is an example of this vocabulary; the 'brocade of Araby' which she wears echoes the wealth of the East. There are analogues for the Grail in Eastern legend, such as the Jewish *schamir*, the stone of Solomon: both originate in Paradise, both give power over a kingdom, both can only be won by the person predestined to do so, both radiate light, both have names written on them. Other scholars point to the jewel called *Chvarenah* in Iranian myth, and to the 'pearl' sought by Gnostic adepts in the Christian culture of fourth-century Alexandria.

The case for the Grail's origins in Iran was put forward in great detail in a monograph issued by the Royal Historical Academy in Stockholm in 1951.[35] Its author, Lars-Ivar Ringbom, identified the home of the Grail as

Shiz, the birthplace of Zoroaster and the national shrine of the great Sassanian empire from the second to the sixth centuries A D. Its buildings, so he claims, correspond to Munsalvaesche and to the descriptions of the Grail temple in *Later Titurel*. The problem with this approach, even discounting the fact that Wolfram tells us virtually nothing about the physical appearance of Munsalvaesche, is that the description of the Grail temple in *Later Titurel* is confused and often hard to interpret, but clearly envisages a Gothic building. It is described with enough detail to convince us that the building's appearance and plan could be recreated from the text; however, close examination shows that the author is more concerned to evoke the magnificence of the setting than to describe the overall shape and purpose of the building. He tells us that it is circular, and the impression that he gives is of an imagined enlargement of a jewelled shrine made to house a precious relic, such as could be seen in the treasury of most Gothic cathedrals. It is a gigantic Gothic reliquary in stone. Ringbom admits that the temple could be a poetic fantasy, but pursues his hunt for a series of real sources undeterred.

As for the Grail itself, Ringbom links it to the Gohar, the pearl contained in a chalice; this is the *ur*-Grail, for the Gohar rests in its vessel 'like the pearl of the host in the chalice of blood, the globe of the earth in the world-ocean', linked to the life-force of Zoroastrian belief.[36] Apart from the distinctly unorthodox liturgical idea of a chalice containing the Host, this begs the question as to how all this might have come to Wolfram's attention; as usual, 'Kyot' is invoked as the answer to all such mysteries.

Even more radical are the arguments of two American scholars, C. Scott Littleton and Ann C. Thomas, who believe that the legends of the Caucasian people known as the Ossetes, in what is present-day Georgia, are 'an epic tradition that almost certainly dates back to the pre-Christian period'.[37] These stories were collected in the late nineteenth and early twentieth centuries, and were analysed by the French mythologist Georges Dumézil. They include a parallel with the death of Arthur, and the return of Excalibur to the lake before he dies, which is striking enough; there are also tales of a sacred cup, the 'Amonga', which have much vaguer parallels with the Grail. This all leads to a theory that Arthur himself was descended from the Sarmatians, the predecessors of the Ossetes, who were sent by the Romans to serve in Britain. These soldiers, we are told, 'were in fact the immediate source of what later became the core of the Arthurian and Holy Grail legends'. But the arguments are tenuous, and it would probably be just as easy, with a similar use of ingenuity and general analogies, to prove the reverse: that the Arthurian stories had reached the Caucasus in the late Middle Ages and were the origin of these heroic narratives.

On a more serious note, we are faced by the ultimate conundrum which all students of folklore eventually encounter: why do similar stories or traditions emerge in cultures that are highly unlikely to have been in contact with each other at the time? A favourite example of this phenomenon is the *immram* of the Celtic saints, a voyage to sea in a boat without oars or sail, at the mercy of God's dispensation. This is closely paralleled in the stories of the Buddhist monks of Japan. In both cultures, the same imagination is at work: in trying to show their complete resignation to the divine will, two separate cultures at the extremities of the Eurasian landmass have reached the same solution. There is no common source, only a common mode of existence at the edge of an unknown and terrifying ocean. So with the Grail: these widely separated avatars of cups and stones are united not by one text or one tale, but by a common imagination.

In a sense, the opposite to the schools of Celtic and Oriental source-hunters is that represented by the argument of the present book, that the Grail's sources are to be found in Christianity. But, although scholars have argued for a secret Christian tradition – and we shall return to this theme – the point at issue is that the Grail does not have 'sources' as such; it is a product of a certain time and a certain place, and the most powerful argument for this is the way in which the major romances were written within a surprisingly short time span. The 'source' of the image is less important than our understanding of its context, and again there have been huge scholarly labours in this direction.[38] Beneath the arguments over theological subtleties and differences of emphasis, this view does at least allow that stories can grow organically and naturally, despite the medieval convention that everything had to be derived from an 'authority' – an idea which indirectly gave us the word 'author'. The central inspiration may be Christian imagery, but that does not mean that the result is exclusively Christian. To take just one point: the idea that the Grail can sustain life by its spiritual properties, as with the story of Joseph of Arimathea in prison, and later with his disciples in the wilderness, inspires Wolfram and other writers to endow it with the purely secular power of producing meat and drink at feasts. The secular image derives easily enough from the Christian original.

The Search for a 'Key'

The problem that many of the essentially folkloric approaches to the identity of the Grail encountered was that they were looking for a solution which would embrace all aspects of the Grail. The search was for an *ur*-Grail, which would explain its diversity and make of it a unity. In the words of Jessie Weston,

no theory of the origin of the story can be considered really and permanently satisfactory, unless it can offer an explanation of the story as a whole . . . and of the varying forms assumed by the Grail: why it should be at one time a Food-providing object of unexplained form, at another a Dish; at one moment the receptacle of streams of Blood from a Lance, at another the Cup of the Last Supper; here 'Something' wrought of no material substance, there, a Stone; and yet everywhere and always possess the same essential significance; in each and every form be rightly described as The Grail?[39]

Jessie Weston's answer to this question was famously enshrined in From Ritual to Romance as a survival of pagan fertility rites, drawing heavily on The Golden Bough. She emphasizes the Waste Land, which, as we have seen, is a minor theme in all but the very late romances, and even in these romances it becomes important only because the writer was anxious to tie up the loose ends left by his predecessors. Weston takes it as crucial evidence for the Grail's origin in the ritual of death and rebirth through which the land was revived each year. The procession of the Grail is therefore reinterpreted as symbolic of that fertility, with cup and spear representing female and male sexuality. It is an interpretation which has haunted twentieth-century literature to a degree quite disproportionate to its basis in fact; and the other side of Jessie Weston's scholarship, her immense and detailed knowledge of the text and her recognition that the final version of the legend owed as much, if not more, to Christianity as to the pagan past, has been overlaid by the powerful images which she unleashed.

Other scholars believed that the succession of images presented by Chrétien as the lance and then the Grail are brought through the hall of the Fisher King's castle reflected a ritual of some kind, but offered very different solutions. Richard Heinzel tentatively suggested in 1892 that there was a connection with the ritual of the Orthodox church;[40] later scholars asserted that the procession had its origins in the Byzantine liturgy, notably the ceremony of the 'great entry' in the liturgy of St John Chrysostom, in which symbolic objects which resemble those in the Grail procession are used.[41] While Byzantine influence on some aspects of the story remains a possibility, as we have already seen, the actual details of the ritual simply do not correspond that closely to the Western romances.[42]

More radically, Eugene Weinraub, in Chrétien's Jewish Grail,[43] argued that there were close parallels with the seder feast at the Passover, in which symbolic objects were brought in, and the youngest person present asks questions about them which lead to the recounting of the Passover story. There is a possible analogy with the girl who bears the Grail, in that, in modern Jewish usage, the first question is prompted by the removal of the *seder* plate before the meal by a girl of marriageable age, and the candelabra are familiar images from Jewish ritual. But the logic of the importation of Jewish imagery into a romance where the Grail is called 'such a holy thing' with evident *Christian* connotations – it contains a single Host – remains inexplicable. It seems even more far-fetched to make of Perceval the Jewish Messiah, and to argue for 'the centrality of Jewishness to the original Grail story', when the whole point of the Jewish ancestry of the Grail hero is that he, like Christ, is 'of the lineage of David': it is the Christian parallel, not the underlying Jewish origin, that is intended.[44]

Even more dramatic is the hypothesis put forward by Leo Olschki, for whom the Grail ceremony is meant to echo the ceremonies of the heretics of whom Philip of Flanders, Chrétien's patron, was a notable scourge. The unconsecrated Host and the secular setting of the procession, according to Olschki, are reminders of rites in which no priest took part, characteristic of the anti-clerical movements in the Low Countries and of the Cathars in southern France. Chrétien 'wished to bring into play, discreetly and yet with sufficient emphasis, the religious aberrations that menaced the orthodoxy of courtly society'.[45] Again, the problem is that this reading sits ill with the romance itself; the Grail ceremony is portrayed in positive terms, not in the negative way which such an approach would require. Even discounting the dangers of interpreting Chrétien in the light of the way in which his story was developed, it is clear that the Grail ceremony is a test which leads to Perceval's spiritual awakening, and to make of it something that he must later reject is to strain the meaning of the text beyond credible limits. Michel Roquebert's reading in *Les Cathares et le Graal* seems much more plausible: he sees Chrétien's work as a key anti-Cathar text which celebrates the power of the Eucharist, denied by the Cathars.[46]

Joseph Campbell, in his wide-ranging exploration of mythology in *The Masks of God*, avows his debt to Jessie Weston's 'bold and learned study'[47] and attempts to relate the Grail to as many mythologies as possible. His theme is that 'each individual is the centre of a mythology of his own'[48] which may well be the best way of reading his work. Immensely learned and wide-ranging as it is, it is essentially Campbell's personal creed, and it is the individual nature of the Grail quest that appeals to his way of thought. You have to believe in his methods, where the figure of Orpheus as fisherman on a fourth-century Romanian bowl used in the Orphic rites evokes the comment 'one thinks . . . of the Fisher King of the legends of the Grail'. That one image can evoke another is enough to show that there must be a connection; by such chains of evocation, he arrives at an intensified version of the sexual interpretation of the Grail, linking it to the sexual images of Eastern religion, and declaring that it is representative of the life force.[49]

Campbell is applying the theories of C. G. Jung to mythology in a detailed way, working back from Jung's idea that behind mythology, and indeed much of human thought and behaviour, lies the world of the archetype. Jung himself believed the Grail to be 'a thoroughly non-Christian image', but seems not to have studied its origins closely. But he does provide a view of symbols which has a good deal of truth in it in relation to the Grail:

To be effective, a symbol must be by its very nature unassailable. It must be the best possible expression of the prevailing world-view, an unsurpassed container of meaning; it must also be sufficiently remote from comprehension to resist all attempts of the critical intellect to break it down; and finally, its aesthetic form must appeal so convincingly to our feelings that no argument can be raised against it on that score. For a certain time the Grail symbol clearly fulfilled these requirements, and to this fact it owed its vitality . . .[50]

Though Jung himself touched on the Grail only in passing, there is a notable Jungian interpretation of the whole myth by Emma Jung, C. G. Jung's wife, and Marie-Louise von Franz, a leading Jungian analyst, in their book *The Grail Legend*. Here scholarly argument is of no avail; if Jungian analysis is accepted as valid, then the argument of the book has its own value. For my part, I can accept that, in broad terms, this approach does shed some light on the way in which the Grail has been envisaged by readers, and on its symbolic and psychological implications. Where I hesitate is when the devotees of Jungian analysis try to support the broad thesis with detail. To take, briefly, two examples: at the end of *The Grail Legend*, the authors propose, as a key conclusion, the idea that Merlin is 'the spirit of the Grail stone', and that the *esplumoir* to which he retreats at the end of the *Prose Perceval* is a stone, 'the alchemical stone itself, and *Perceval's real quest is to find it* [authors' italics]'.[51] This story is only found in one text, the Didot version of the *Prose Perceval*, which offers an unorthodox ending, and to lay such emphasis on this unique instance is perhaps taking too much for granted.

Similarly, Campbell has to misread Wolfram's perfectly orthodox religious attitudes in order to make his argument work. He sees the pilgrims, who, in their conventional but devout piety, bring Parzival back to his senses on Good Friday, as a parody – that convenient device for getting rid of awkward points in the text. And he makes much of Feirefiz's baptism as mystical and non-Catholic because the Grail, which provides everything within the Grail kingdom, also fills the baptismal font with water. He too can make mountains out of molehills: the peacock feathers in the 'bonnets' of Gramoflanz and the Grail king become a means of declaring that the two are counterparts, one lord of the spiritual realms, the other lord of the realm of nature. But a quick look at contemporary German miniatures would have shown that they were a common ornament for knights' crests, a perfectly normal part of a knight's parade armour.[52]

The Grail and Alchemy

Jung was deeply interested in alchemy, and alchemists proper have, of course, found rich material in the Grail legends. There have been numerous attempts to relate the Grail to alchemy, mostly based on Wolfram's *Parzival*; the encyclopaedic curiosity for which Wolfram was notorious in his own time extended particularly to the lore of precious stones, and the Grail is of course a stone in his version of the story. Once again, we are in deep water: alchemy is still a subject, even at a scholarly level, for the initiated, and I can only speak as a rank amateur in such territory. To find actual alchemical lore in the stories, however, has proved less easy than proponents of the alchemical influence might have wished, and theses such as that of Paulette Duval on *La pensée alchimique et le Conte du Graal* have tended to take refuge in arguments about the structure of alchemic philosophy which seem remote from what is actually on the pages of the text.

The argument for alchemical meanings in Wolfram is not very different from that which sees hermetic or esoteric meanings behind *Parzival*; both rely on setting aside Chrétien as a traducer of the real story, and taking Wolfram's comments about him literally. Kyot then becomes the key figure in the transmission of the story, and its origins are placed firmly in Mozarabic Spain, specifically in the schools of Toledo. All this is a perfectly tenable reading – Wolfram is marvellous in this respect, in that his very richness of style and imagery offers endless leads for speculation – but it does in a sense divide the medieval Grail story into two: the philosophical *ur*-Grail and its hidden tradition, and the debased Christian allegory subsequently derived from it. There is material in the Grail stories which can be read as redolent of a hidden tradition similar to that of the hermeticists, such as the comments in Robert de Boron and in the continuators of Chrétien about the unknowability of the Grail story, the sacred origin of the story, and the penalties for revealing it to the wrong audience. All this has encouraged readings such as that of Henry and Renée Kahane in *The Krater and the Grail*.[53] They see Kyot as an identifiable figure, namely William (*Guillot*) of Tudela, author of the *Song of the Albigensian Crusade*, with contacts with the Jewish community in Tudela who were intermediaries for the hermetic lore handed down from Greek sources to Arab philosophers. The hermetic tradition was essentially pagan, centred on the legendary figure of Hermes Trismegistus; it drew on a variety of religious and philosophical systems, which it attempted to harmonize, and is well described as a pagan version of Gnosticism. The *krater* is a vessel which contains the knowledge sent down from Heaven by God, in which the initiates are baptised. Once again, the difficulties arise when too large a part is ascribed in Wolfram's work to the influence of hermetic beliefs: we are presented with 'Wolfram's Key', as if one single source unlocked the entire meaning of *Parzival*.

This is a crucial feature of a whole group of scholarly – and not-so-scholarly – approaches to the Grail: the assumption that there is a key which, once found, will explain everything. This applies not only to the 'secret knowledge' theorists, but also to a number of other approaches, both historical and archaeological. A good example is the work of André de Mandach, in the two versions of his book on the 'original' romance of the Grail.[54] He traces the Grail story back to Spain, following a similar line of reasoning to the Kahanes, but reaches very different conclusions. His line of inquiry leads to the monastery of San Juan de la Peña in Aragon, and to the royal house of Aragon, who are identified (on the flimsiest of evidence) as the personnel of Wolfram's romance – Alfonso I is Anfortius, Anfortas; Ramon Berenger IV is Guiot; the niece of Alfonso I, Peroniella, somehow becomes Schoysiane, Parzival's aunt. From San Juan de la Peña the trail leads us to the relic preserved in the cathedral of Valencia, centre of an ardent local cult, as the chalice of the Last Supper.* Mandach tells us that this is the real Grail, with its Arabic inscription representing the letters which, Wolfram tells us, appear on it with divine messages for the Grail knights.

The same search for a *roman-à-clef* has led to the idea that the Grail romances are a commentary of some kind on contemporary political circumstances. Perhaps the most curious of these readings is that of Sebastian Evans, the first translator of *Perlesvaus* into English, who read that romance as a version of the events of the reign of king John; he also brought in the *Elucidation Prologue*, in which king Amangons represented king John, and

---

* See p. 169 above.

the disappearance of the wells and their attendants was an allusion to the ban on church services imposed by the pope when John refused to recognize the newly elected archbishop of Canterbury.[55]

The problem with any approach which treats the romances in this way is that it would make the Grail stories unique in medieval literature: no other romances have been shown conclusively to have this kind of historical key. There is, indeed, a perfectly respectable tradition of poems which address their subject indirectly, such as Chaucer's *Book of the Duchess*. This was written in memory of Blanche, duchess of Lancaster, but the text never mentions her name. The 'key' is, however, undisputed, fitting in with Chaucer's own circumstances. Romances are a different genre. If we try to interpret *The Story of the Grail* as a political diatribe intended to relate to the crusading activities of Philip count of Flanders, Chrétien's patron, or Wolfram's *Parzival* as connected with the unsuccessful efforts of Otto of Brunswick, the Holy Roman Emperor of the time, to go to the Holy Land, the difficulties are immense. Some of the figures may seem to bear a possible relationship to historical personages: for example, the maimed lord of the Grail is equated with Baldwin IV, the leper king of Jerusalem who died in 1185. But however ingeniously these identifications are made, the crucial question is never resolved: how does either poem relate to the people who are supposed to be depicted in them? Is the object an exhortation to go on crusade? Is either poem a criticism of their failures? Neither of these ideas really works and, without a purpose, the argument must fail. It is difficult to read any kind of exhortation into the texts, unless we lay extraordinary stress on the idea that Perceval/Parzival is predestined to achieve the Grail. The texts simply do not support this kind of reading. If there are references to the crusades, it is because these were in everyone's mind at the time, and several of the patrons or possible patrons for whom the romances were written were indeed crusaders. This, rather than an elaborately concealed agenda, is a much more plausible reason for any parallels with contemporary history. And there is one last question: what, if these interpretations are, after all, correct, does the Grail stand for? The scholars who put forward these arguments avoid the issue, with one exception, and the Grail does not figure in their schemes. Only Helen Adolf has argued for a precise identification for the Grail, namely the Holy Sepulchre, which is at least distantly related to the Grail of the romances, in that both it and the Grail belong to the story of the Crucifixion.[56] But the moment we try to take the identification further, the theory fails: how can the Holy Sepulchre be represented by a platter or cup, particularly when that cup is given a very precise history and provenance? There seems no precedent for this kind of allegory; in the last analysis, the romances simply do not lend themselves to these historical parallels.

At the beginning of this chapter stand two quotations. Against the scholars who search for Jessie Weston's 'explanation of the story as a whole', 'the key to this savage parade', we have the source-hunters whom Rosemond Tuve so eloquently demolishes. It is true to say that the Grail is not a single concept whose meaning has been lost, but a literary symbol which has developed over the years. Here the danger is that scholars place far too much emphasis on the sources behind this development. For those who pursue this path, each stage in the development must be susceptible to documentation; there must be sources and analogues: nothing can be created *ex nihilo*. But this, in my view, is the arch-heresy of literary criticism, and its greatest danger: to deny the imagination. It is this that scholars need to remember as they try to interpret and illuminate. We are dealing with imaginative literature, and I come full circle, demanding with J. J. Bodmer in *On the Marvellous in Poetry*, that we must allow imagination pride of place. Poets and writers are creators; the Grail is the creation, not of mysticism, not of pagan religion, not even of Christian tradition, nor of the scholars themselves, but of the poetic imagination working on and with all these materials.

18

The Revival of the Grail

In the room, a sick child asks his mother, 'Where is the big book? I want to look at pictures.' 'Which one?' 'The one with golden covers, with the great gold shields and pages in it which show, in bright bold colours yet softly, Parcival's deeds. You often told me about him. I liked him.' The book cannot be found, and the child wonders if he has dreamt it. His mother encourages him to remember, or perhaps imagine, what he can of it, and helps him to recreate the missing pictures. First, the child sees Parcival coming to a great castle, where he is welcomed by his host and dressed in a rich cloak. Then Parcival quarrels with a squire, and the next scene shows him in a splendid room, where a feast has been set out; and yet, despite the brilliant lights reflected in the marble walls and the music of harps, the company seem sad. The following page shows a squire who runs in with a bleeding lance, and the general sorrow at this sight. Finally, the child says: 'Then I saw another splendid picture appear, the picture of a queen, richly clothed, with smiling eyes, though clouded with weeping, who held a vessel of light that sparkled like a thousand jewels, no, like all the fire in heaven, and yet it only gave out light, and did not burn.' She sets it beside the host, who seems to be comforted by the sight of it. Parcival watches all this, and says nothing. The child is angry with Parcival for keeping silent, but quickly falls asleep, leaving his mother to hope that in later life he will learn to ask 'never too much, and never too little'.

This is how one of the first writers to recast the Grail story in modern form chose to set out the crucial scene of Parcival's first visit to the Grail castle. The idea of putting it forward as a scene from a picture book – or from a child's imagination – is intriguing, as it grasps the essence of the scene in the medieval original, whether in Wolfram's *Parzival* or *The Story of the Grail*: it is essentially a visual episode, where what is seen is all-important. When this modern version was written, colour printing, in particular lithography, was coming into its own, so such images in a book would be an exciting novelty. But the subject matter, too, was a novelty in a different way, and to discover what lies behind this we must go back to the scholars and their exploration of the Arthurian texts.

When scholars explored the surviving remains of the medieval libraries of Europe in the eighteenth century, poets and novelists turned away from the prevailing classical models which dominated literary fashion, and the 'Gothick' became all the rage, its supposed natural wildness set against the formalities of Greek and Roman literature. Chivalry and the world of knightly exploits were once again the material for storytellers, but much of this new literature was an imaginative rather than historical reconstruction of the Middle Ages. Even a writer like Sir Walter Scott, who edited the medieval English version of the legend of Tristan, did not think of retelling the old romances in modern terms, but invented instead the new genre of the historical novel. In Germany, and later in France, enthusiasm for Shakespeare led to a rash of historical plays, and from the mid-eighteenth century onwards the English Royal Academy was full of massive canvases representing the great moments of the historical past.

These were reinventions, but on historical themes. Only the labours of the scholars could make medieval literature familiar once more, and enable authors to take up the themes of medieval romance as the basis for genuinely original works. Modernizations and translations of the medieval texts, as well as editions, were needed before Arthurian themes could become the basis of new works. Malory might be relatively easy for an English author to read in the original, and two editions appeared in 1816 and 1817. But Wolfram's *Parzival* is formidably difficult in the original, and the French works were only available in the black-letter editions of the early sixteenth century until modern editions began to appear in 1841. The tentative beginnings of a renewal of creative interest in the legends of Arthur date from the early years of the nineteenth century, yet it is not until the 1830s that any major works on the Grail appear.

Even so, there were problems. The scene at the beginning of this chapter comes from the first serious attempt to produce a modern version of the Grail story, based on Wolfram's *Parzival*. The author was Friedrich de la Motte Fouqué, who, despite his name, was a Prussian aristocrat. He had had a huge success with a medieval romance, *Undine*, and similar titles, which appeared between 1803 and 1813. But with the ending of the Napoleonic wars, public taste moved on, and his star waned as a new generation of writers – whom he himself had encouraged – explored the themes which we now call Romantic. Fouqué, according to the poet Heinrich

Heine, 'immersed himself ever more deeply in his books of chivalry'.[1] In 1815, he conceived the idea of 'an epic of the Holy Grail', and in December he wrote to a friend that 'this work will become the peak of my whole poetic career'. However, the actual writing of it was delayed until 1831. He completed *Der Parcival (The Parcival)* in April 1832, by which time such things were wholly out of fashion. Furthermore, the form he chose was that of a drama in verse, designed for reading rather than performance. It was not that there was no interest in the original literature: the edition of Wolfram's *Parzival* by Karl Lachmann appeared the following year, and translations by Karl Simrock and 'San Marte' in the following decade. Fouqué's retelling, however, languished in manuscript. It was still unpublished at his death, and finally appeared in print in 1997.[2]

The Parcival is far from being an orthodox retelling of the story. Technically, it is very interesting: Fouqué plays with different narrators and different perspectives on the tale. He himself appears as 'Master Friedrich' and there is a running commentary on the poem in the form of a dialogue with 'Master Wolfram', who is of course Wolfram von Eschenbach: the two form at times a kind of Greek chorus to the action as the story of Parcival is read, or told, or imagined, by a whole cast of characters, who also form the audience. Even by the standards of the German Romantic writers, for whom the device of differing narrators or of stories within a story were familiar, this is a bold and complex approach, and it may be that it was rejected by publishers as too difficult, even avant-garde, rather than because it was an old-fashioned 'book of chivalry', as Heine would have it. To a modern reader, it seems 'a work of impressive virtuosity and surprising individuality'.[3]

Fouqué's concept of the Grail is somewhat hesitant. It appears first as 'a vessel of light', in the scene we have already recounted. The explanation of the Grail given by Trevrizent in Wolfram's *Parzival* disappears, and a rather different story emerges. In medieval accounts of natural history, the phoenix, when it sensed that death was approaching, built a pyre and burnt itself to death: from the ashes a new phoenix arose. Wolfram had enrolled this story in his version of the Grail, and Fouqué makes this incidental episode the centrepiece of his Grail: a magic stone, whose name is too hedged about with magic for anyone to dare to write it down, is the means by which the phoenix lights its funeral pyre, and 'from such stones the Grail was formed'. But the Grail can only be guarded by the 'Christian order' and vanishes without trace if it falls into heathen hands. The poet Guyot, who learns about the Grail in Toledo, is not satisfied with this knowledge, and sets out in search of 'the light of the Grail'. In France they are silent about it; in

England, people seem to know of it, but are suddenly reticent when asked. In Ireland, old songs tell of it, but when they are performed the singer is interrupted by an angry cry. We never learn the outcome of Guyot's search, merely that a marvellous song could be written about his wanderings. The Grail becomes the object of a poetic as well as a chivalric quest.[4]

We learn a little more about the Grail in the scene where Anfortas begs for death: as in Wolfram, the sight of the Grail prevents him from dying. Again the emphasis is on its quality as a source of light, 'shining with divine light', and on its magical power to sustain life. In the final scene, Parcival asks the healing question; as the knights watch, 'in the writing of the stars there flames on the Grail "Parcival, keeper of the Grail"'.

Fouqué's skill lies in the presentation and in the colour of his story, rich in language and in images. He gives a narrative which is very like the splendid book that the sick child recalls, full of dazzling pictures. The tone is set in an exchange between Master Wolfram and Master Friedrich: 'Everything, people, their deeds, their fates – whatever has occurred to your spirit or to mine which is great and serious, or cheerful and childlike and attractive – let us be true to that . . . Whatever may have fluttered in from outside – let the men with passports and the official visitors of literature take on the task of putting it into order.'[5] What Fouqué aims to present is the spirit of the past, not its literal history, and to this end he uses colour and variety and anecdote rather than a direct narrative. And yet, for all his ingenuity, at the heart of the poem there are no overarching ideas, and no new avatar of the Grail for a new century. Indeed, he treats it somewhat more literally than Wolfram, while removing the specific Christian imagery and replacing it with a mixture of magic and bedazzlement. It is almost as if Fouqué hesitated to confront directly the problems which the Grail might pose.[6]

Carl Immermann, a friend and protégé of Fouqué, was also intrigued by the Arthurian legends, but he was more fortunate, and his work appeared in print just as Fouqué was finishing *The Parcival*. Although Immermann's poem is entitled *Merlin. A Myth*, its central section is headed 'The Grail'; and the Grail myth is interwoven with that of Merlin, not from any deep knowledge of the original scheme of Robert de Boron, which had shaped the medieval romances, but through Immermann's own imaginative re-creation of the story, which is more than a little indebted to Goethe's *Faust*, and perhaps also to Milton. Merlin is an ambivalent figure, acknowledging that he is Satan's son, but paradoxically defying him and wishing to save the world. Early in the poem he tells his mother's father, Placidus, about the Grail:[7] it is the blood of Christ, 'sanguis realis' as popular story would have it, gathered by Joseph of Arimathea at the Crucifixion in the cup used at the Last Supper. It sustains Joseph in prison, but Joseph is never released. Instead, when the emperor Titus storms Jerusalem, the tower in which he is captive collapses, burying Joseph in the rubble. As he dies, the Grail hovers over him, 'as a rose touches a girl's hair', and disappears heavenwards, 'returning to its own'. But Merlin knows that it has once again descended to earth: he declares that it is now imprisoned at Montsalvatsch, in the care of the 'stupid Titurel'. Merlin, declaring that he has been chosen by God, intends to provide the Grail with a guardian worthy of it: himself.

Arthur, too, knows of the Grail's return, which troubles him; when a minstrel sings of how four angels brought it to Titurel, who had sought it since he was a youth, he tells the singer to be silent. Gawain says that the song contains 'secret magic', and the knights never speak of the Grail and its guardians in Arthur's presence. Arthur dreams of leading the knights of the Round Table to the Grail, but the inscription on the temple which houses the Grail declares that only they whom the Grail seeks out can find it; those who seek it, cannot find it. Merlin offers to make Arthur king of the Grail, and says that he will lead him to it, for he himself is the Holy Ghost. But the Grail declares him to be the Antichrist, and tells Titurel that he and his companions must accompany it to the East, for 'that which cannot be compelled is emperilled by the uttermost evil'. The poem ends with Arthur and his knights dying of thirst in the wilderness surrounding the Grail castle, calling in vain for Merlin's help, for Merlin has, meanwhile, fallen under the spell of Niniana, who has imprisoned him. He is now powerless, and the knights perish. In an epilogue, Lohengrin mourns the dead, declaring that 'the black flag of destruction is flying'; Satan reasserts his power over the mad Merlin, who dies in despairing repentance, with a prayer on his lips.

Immermann had read Wolfram's *Parzival*, but his knowledge of the other romances of Arthur was largely second-hand, through the version of the French *Merlin* published by Dorothée Caroline Schlegel, wife of Friedrich Schlegel, in 1804. Other summaries of the romances had appeared in German between 1810 and 1820, in particular a modernized collection of texts of 'old German poems from the time of the Round Table'.[8] From one of these books Immermann acquired the version of the Grail story found in Robert de Boron; this included the idea that Merlin was engendered by the forces of evil as the Antichrist. In Robert de Boron, Merlin takes after his mother, and is redeemed; Immermann reverses this, and ultimately makes him an evil and disastrous figure, despite his apparent good intentions, whose redemption is uncertain. Immermann echoes many of the ideas of the original romances, but ultimately points the stories of Merlin and of the Grail in an entirely new direction. *Merlin. A Myth* is an intriguing, high-flown work, consciously echoing Milton and Goethe. Its achievements are considerable, but not as great as its ambitions.

Merlin was a highly attractive figure for nineteenth-century writers, combining the image of a 'free spirit' with his aspects as a magus, powerful through knowledge. In an age of great scientific discoveries and a literary cult of the individual, he was once more a character to be taken seriously. This new response to Merlin is also found in France, in the work of Edgar Quinet, whom we have met as an Arthurian scholar. His *Merlin the Enchanter* (1860) is a vast novel, a baroque hybrid of romance and political allegory. He treats the legends freely, and his main concern is with the relationship between Arthur, as symbol of the ideal ruler, and the people. Merlin creates the Round Table not only for the great heroic figures of every nation – Siegfried, Antar and Rustem take their places alongside Perceval and Lancelot – but also for all the peoples of the world. At the opening feast, the Grail is produced by Merlin, to the astonishment of both heroes and populace, all of whom have been seeking it. Archbishop Turpin* tells them all how it was 'sculpted by shepherds and kings' and 'given to the Man-God as he wept on the straw in the stable at Bethlehem'. Christ had quenched his thirst from it on the cross, and Joseph of Arimathea had found it in the sepulchre. It is passed round to all those present, and 'holy friendship entered into the heart of the most savage of men'.[9] The table grows as new nations come to it, but at last a solitary man, whom everyone regards with horror, appears: it is Ahasverus, condemned to wander eternally for having mocked Christ on the way to Calvary, and unable to end his life. He asks if drinking from the Grail will bring on death, but he is told that it will make him immortal. 'Then keep your hateful present,' he declares. Merlin asks that the table shall be left just as it is, eternally self-replenishing, to feed the hungry of the world. But, Quinet asks, 'men, what have you done with this round table?' All that remains of it are a few broken pieces, for the nations have demolished it, and shattered the cup of the Grail.

Quinet's Grail is unlike any other: it belongs to a political vision of a golden age which cannot be restored. According to Quinet's widow, it is the symbol of 'the brotherhood of nations, the civilising and hospitable mission of France, which has fed and watered all the proscribed people of the world and the nations which hungered and thirsted for justice'.[10] The

* A character from *The Song of Roland*.

old idealism behind the concept of the Grail is there, but in an entirely new guise. It is a double-edged allegory, because it was written as an attack on Louis-Napoleon, who as Napoleon III tried to present the Second Empire as a revival of the age of chivalry; Quinet's Round Table and Grail seem to be intended as an evocation of the virtues of the Republic which Napoleon III had overthrown. *Merlin the Enchanter* is perhaps most interesting for the very fact that Quinet chose the Arthurian material as a way of commenting on contemporary politics, implying that it was familiar enough to his audience to be adapted in this way.[11]

An equally idiosyncratic approach to the Grail is to be found in Victor de Laprade's *La Tour d'Ivoire*, a minor work by a minor poet, but perhaps unique in that the quest for the Holy Grail leads to the ivory tower which is the home of the last of the enchantresses of fairyland. The knight who seeks the Grail equates this with the search for a magical world, beyond that of ordinary humanity which, at the outset, a hermit declares to be extinct. But the unknown knight perseveres; he finds the ivory tower and falls in love with the lady, and returns to the world of mortals with the power to mete out justice and succour the weak.[12] Again, there is a political motif behind this curious treatment of the story, as it seems that Laprade, like Quinet, intended it as an allegorical attack on the Second Empire. The Grail has become – at least for these two French authors – some kind of abstract ideal of political perfection, which has little to do with its medieval origins.

The Victorian Grail

For English-speaking readers, the publication of three editions of Malory's *Morte Darthur* in 1816 and 1817 reopened the gates of the Arthurian legend. Two of them were based on a 1634 printing which was full of errors; the third, by the poet Robert Southey, was based on Caxton's original printing, but was a luxury edition of only 300 copies. Nonetheless, the book was once more freely available, and was eagerly seized on by an audience whose appetite for such literature had been whetted by Sir Walter Scott. In the early decades of the century it was poets and artists who seized on the romances as subject matter, but they knew that the public at large was not entirely familiar with them. Matthew Arnold's poem on Tristan appeared in 1852; when a second edition was needed, he added a preface giving a summary of the story for the benefit of readers, who, he had found, were evidently ignorant of it. Summaries of the Tristan story had appeared in three surveys of English literature between 1774 and 1814, and George Ellis's *Specimens of Early English Metrical Romances* was available in

Bohn's Library, a best-selling series of cheap editions which were the paper-backs of the day.

This renewal of interest in the Arthurian legends attracted not only poets but painters as well, and the stories themselves became a focal point of British national consciousness, an addition to the heroic past demanded by a self-confident age. Alfred Tennyson's *Poems* of 1842 included four poems on Arthurian themes, among them 'Sir Galahad'. This had been written as early as 1834, and is a simple, almost simplistic view of Galahad's character. There is more than an echo of Sir Walter Scott in the opening lines, and the atmosphere is that of Kenelm Digby's *The Broad Stone of Honour, or Rules for the Gentlemen of England*, which had been published in London in 1822 and had met with great success: it harked back to an ideal age of chivalry, and was partly behind the attempt to revive chivalric sports which culminated in the disastrous tournament at Eglinton in Scotland in 1839. The idea that chivalry was relevant to the mores of a Victorian gentleman is essential to the understanding of the immense appeal of Tennyson's poems. In 'Sir Galahad', Tennyson places the emphasis on Galahad's prowess, and above all on Galahad's chastity. This was crucial to Tennyson's view of Galahad; in 1833, he told a friend that his planned 'Ballad of Sir Lancelot' (which was never written) would end with Lancelot, riding with Guinevere to his castle of Joyeuse Garde, meeting Galahad: 'his own son (the type of

19 Arthur Hughes, Sir Galahad *(1870).*

Chastity) passes by; he knows his father, but does not speak to him, *blushes and rides on his way*.[13] Galahad keeps his heart 'fair thro' faith and prayer' and is rewarded by visions of 'some secret shrine' where invisible hands celebrate Mass. The Grail, too, is seen in visions, but in a different context:

> Sometimes on lonely mountain-meres
>   I find a magic bark;
> I leap on board: no helmsman steers:
>   I float till all is dark.
> A gentle sound, an awful light!
>   Three angels bear the holy Grail:
> With folded feet, in stoles of white,
>   On sleeping wings they sail.
> Ah, blessed vision! blood of God!
>   My spirit beats her mortal bars,
> As down dark tides the glory slides,
>   And star-like mingles with the stars.

But this is only dreaming: Galahad seeks the reality of the Grail, and the closing lines set his quest firmly in the context of the physical world:

> So pass I hostel, hall, and grange;
>   By bridge and ford, by park and pale,
> All-arm'd I ride, whate'er betide,
>   Until I find the holy Grail.

The Grail symbolizes the desire for the spiritual world – 'I yearn to breathe the airs of heaven' – but is carefully separated from the religious rituals to which, in Malory, it belongs. It is as if the poet, realizing he is on dangerous ground, retreats into a safe image of muscular Christianity.

The Grail presented similar problems for an American poet a decade later. James Russell Lowell, in *Sir Launfal*, a poem which rivalled those of Tennyson in popularity,[14] rewrites both the setting and substance of the legend. This was not out of ignorance of the original story; on the contrary, like Edgar Quinet, Lowell was a critic and essayist who became a distinguished professor. He had a long-standing interest in romance; his enthusiasm was such that he considered changing his name to Perceval. He was familiar with Wolfram's *Parzival* and the French romances.[15] Yet his attitude to romance as matter for modern poetry was distinctly ambivalent: when he came to write about the Grail, he rejected almost all the trappings of the story. He does set his poem in a vague medieval context, but insists that it is 'a period subsequent to king Arthur's reign'. The Holy Grail is initially seen as the object of a quest. Launfal, lord of a castle, is proposing to set out in search of it the next day, and the central action of the poem is the dream which he has that night. We never learn what his object is in searching for the Grail, and only its name implies that there is a spiritual aspect to his projected journey. He dreams that as he rides out, he scornfully tosses a coin to a leper begging at the castle gate. Many years pass; his search is in vain, and he finds himself at his own gate, where he has been given up for lost, and a new lord rules in his castle. As Launfal tries to shelter, a leper again begs alms: this time, he gives freely of his last crust and finds him a cup of water. The leper reveals himself as Christ, and tells Launfal that the cup from which he has just drunk is the true Holy Grail; and the moral of the tale is drawn:

> The Holy Supper is kept, indeed,
> In whatso we share with another's need, –
> Not that which we give, but what we share –
> For the gift without the giver is bare;
> Who bestows himself with his alms feeds three, –
> Himself, his hungering neighbour, and me.

Lowell's poem is no great masterpiece, and reads nowadays as a period piece both in its passages of nature-worship and in its message. Yet it is a carefully considered transformation of the legend, echoing the progress of Perceval towards understanding and sympathy for others. It clearly struck a chord, and if modern critics denounce it as bad poetry, it is how generations of Americans envisaged the Grail: nearly fifty editions or reprints appeared between its publication in 1848 and the end of the century.

When the Houses of Parliament were being rebuilt after the disastrous fire in 1834, the artist William Dyce was commissioned to paint a set of Arthurian frescoes for the Queen's Robing Room in the House of Lords. The commission had arisen because he had suggested to Prince Albert that Malory's *Morte Darthur* would be a suitable subject for the proposed decoration, and Albert had responded enthusiastically. Despite having suggested the subject, Dyce was reluctant to undertake the work himself, and it seems to have been on Albert's insistence, as chairman of the Fine Arts Commission, that he finally agreed. He researched the history and legends of Arthur carefully, and began to plan the seven frescoes, but soon realized that the idea was not such a happy one as he had thought, and that, in the words of Elizabeth I's tutor, Roger Ascham, Malory had written of 'open manslaughter and bold bawdry' as well as of chivalric ideals, and the two were difficult to disentangle: most of the proposed subjects involved moral or religious pitfalls. This was especially true of the Holy Grail. Each fresco symbolized a virtue – 'Generosity', 'Piety', 'Mercy' and so on – but the courtly scenes had caused offence because of the adultery of the pairs of lovers (Guinevere and Lancelot, Tristan and Iseult). The Grail story simply represented 'Religion', but the achievement of the Grail aroused a different and equally problematic set of sensibilities. Roman Catholics had only recently been allowed to practise their religion freely in England, to vote in elections and to hold public office, by an act of 1829. The appointment by the pope of Cardinal Wiseman as the first Roman Catholic archbishop in England since the Reformation had caused public riots in 1850. So Dyce was quite right when he wrote to Charles Eastlake, the President of the Royal Academy and a member of the commission, that 'it seemed to me wise to keep out of sight the particular adventures of the St Greal which . . . appeared to me to involve matter of religious and antiquarian controversy, which had better be avoided'. The difficulty was the clear association of the Grail in Malory with the doctrine of transubstantiation, which posed serious dangers, especially as Dyce himself was an Anglo-Catholic, and was indeed rumoured in 1847 to have converted to Roman Catholicism. He was very sympathetic to the Grail story, but realized that he could not let his enthusiasm show at a time when Anglo-Catholics were regarded by many churchmen and most of the population as a kind of fifth column within the Church of England. At first he tried to avoid the climax of the Grail story by showing the knights departing on the quest, but unfortunately the central image of the sketch was Lancelot kissing Guinevere's hand as they said farewell, and the adulterous connotations of this were unacceptable. In the end, Dyce solved the problem by illustrating the scene in which Galahad, Bors and Perceval (and Perceval's sister) have a vision at the climax of the Mass of Christ and the four evangelists, which signifies that they are the knights chosen to achieve the quest. Dyce's style also removed the image from its medieval context; his models were from the Renaissance, as was usual for the period.* So the Grail itself is carefully absent; the cup held by a priest to the left of the picture is a respectable and ordinary chalice, and the thoughts of the queen as head of the Church of England when she was robed for the highest ceremonial occasions would not be distracted by the least taint of heresy.

---

* This was exactly the artistic fashion against which the Pre-Raphaelites were to react.

The story of the Grail might pose difficulties for official artists, but it was taken up with enthusiasm by the members of the Pre-Raphaelite Brotherhood, who were dedicated to a return to medieval ideals in artistic matters. William Morris published his Arthurian poems in 1858, just after Dante Gabriel Rossetti and his friends had begun the murals on Arthurian themes at the Oxford Union, to which Morris contributed. Morris seems to have been the prime mover in introducing the group to Malory's *Morte Darthur*; although Rossetti had encountered the book before he met Morris, it was the enthusiasm of the latter and his friend Edward Burne-Jones that led Rossetti to choose it as the topic for the Oxford murals, which had been commissioned by John Ruskin. However, Morris's poem on the Grail, 'Sir Galahad: A Christmas Mystery', has echoes of Tennyson as well as Malory, and Rossetti had just helped to illustrate the new edition of Tennyson's poems commissioned by the publisher William Moxon. Art fed literature; literature fed art. Morris in particular saw himself not simply as a painter or a poet, but as a craftsman-artist who could turn his hand to whatever form was required.

In Morris's 'Sir Galahad', as in Tennyson's poems, his hero is very conscious of his chastity. But whereas Tennyson's Galahad is firm in his purpose, and seems a stranger to desire, Morris depicts Galahad thinking enviously of the warmth and pleasure that love brings, and contrasts it with the cold, lone emptiness of his quest. He is somewhat comforted by a vision of Christ, though his first emotion is that of sheer dread, and afterwards 'my face and wretched body fell upon the ground'. Angels and saints summon him to fulfil the quest by boarding the ship of Solomon, and for a moment we think that the ending will be that of Malory, as Bors and Perceval join him. But the conclusion is bitter and dark: the knights who set out on the quest are dead or wounded, and those who survive

> . . . everywhere
> The knights come foil'd from the great quest, in vain:
> In vain they struggle for the vision fair.

This is the most autobiographical vision of the Grail, reflecting a long struggle on Morris's part to decide between his ambitions for the priesthood and his ultimate rejection of holy orders in favour of an artistic career. It is almost as if he is trying to persuade himself through his dark vision of the tale that he has made the right choice, while confessing to the attraction of the spiritual calling.

The visual equivalent of Morris's poem is the work of Dante Gabriel

Rossetti, whose images of the Grail remind one irresistibly of Gawain at Corbenic in the *Lancelot-Grail*, distracted by the beauty of the girl bearing the Grail, and thus debarred from the spiritual and material comforts of the Grail itself. 'The Damsel of the Saint Graal', painted in the year of the Oxford Union murals, is on one level simply a portrait of a 'stunner', to use the slang term coined by the group to describe their ideal beauty. But Rossetti's involvement with the Grail theme went much deeper. His first illustration of a Grail poem was for Tennyson's 'Sir Galahad', showing the knight at the mysterious empty church where Mass was being celebrated. At the Oxford Union, he chose Lancelot's vision of the Grail as his subject, and it was Lancelot's partial vision and ultimate failure that haunted him. 'Launcelot's Vision of the Sangraal' is a highly original composition, drawing in themes which Malory scarcely touches on or positively rejects. Lancelot lies asleep on the right, while the Grail is held by a female figure on the left. Between them stands the languorous figure of Guinevere, dominating the composition, while the apple tree behind her and a snake that hovers above Lancelot evoke the biblical story of the fall of man. The

20 *Dante Gabriel Rossetti*, The Damosel of the Sanct Grael *(1857), watercolour. The dove is the symbol of the Holy Spirit, and the damosel bears not only the Grail, but the communion bread.*

guardian of the Grail looks pityingly at Lancelot, while Guinevere watches him, half-alluring, half-anxious, in case he wakes and chooses the Grail in preference to her.

The damsel of the Grail appears in a watercolour by Rossetti in 1865 (Plate V), based on a sketch for a possible mural at the Oxford Union. She holds out the chalice to Galahad, who approaches with Bors and Perceval, hands joined as if in a courtly dance, while ranks of red-winged cherubim look on: the Holy Spirit in the form of a dove hovers behind the damsel, while the lily of chastity springs at her feet, beside the body of Perceval's sister. The mood is hieratic and ritual: the knights move as if in a daze, eyes closed and heads bowed, towards the Grail. There is no sense of revelation or of splendour; if anything, the image is of hard-won achievement, of weariness and accomplishment of the quest.

Rossetti's last involvement with the Grail was literary: he moved away from Arthurian themes in his painting, but he wrote to Swinburne in 1870: 'If I do anything else . . . it will be "God's Graal", the Lancelot poem.' Soon afterwards he explained that this would be 'the loss of the Sangreal by Lancelot, a theme chosen to emphasize the superiority of Guenever over God'.[16] What survives of the poem combines the serried ranks of the cherubim of Galahad's achievement of the Grail with the images from the Oxford Union mural of the sleeping Lancelot and the apple tree. Rossetti's plan was to tell the story from Lancelot's point of view, and it is not difficult to imagine that if he had completed it, it would have shared Morris's dark vision of the Grail quest.

Rossetti's programme for the Oxford Union did not meet with general understanding: Max Beerbohm's cartoon of Benjamin Jowett, renowned for his liberal religious views which discounted mysticism, asking Rossetti: 'And what were they going to do with the Grail when they found it, Mr Rossetti?' neatly sums up the suspicion with which the Pre-Raphaelite penchant for the mysterious was viewed.[17] And the Grail lay on the borderlines of several worlds in which most Victorian writers were not at ease. If Galahad's purity had to be tempered by an evocation of the eroticism which defined that chastity, and the achievement of the Grail had to be set against the failure of Lancelot and the majority of knights, so the Grail as Eucharist in the medieval sense was beyond the permitted scope of poetry: yet the images crept back in. Tennyson only came to write of the Holy Grail in the *Idylls of the King* reluctantly. In 1859, he wrote to the duke of Argyll, who had urged him to work on the subject, which had been suggested by the historian Macaulay:

21 'The Sole Remark Likely to Have Been Made by Benjamin Jowett about the
Mural Paintings at the Oxford Union', cartoon by Max Beerbohm: 'And what
were they going to do with the Grail when they found it?'

As to Macaulay's suggestion of the Sangreal, I doubt whether such a subject could be
handled in these days without incurring a charge of irreverence. It would be too much
like playing with sacred things. The old writers *believed* in the Sangreal. Many years
ago I did write 'Lancelot's Quest of the Grail' in as good verses as I ever wrote, no,
I did not write, I made it in my head, and it has now altogether slipt out of memory.[18]

When the poem was eventually written, a decade later, Emily Tennyson
recorded that

I doubt whether the 'San Graal' would have been written but for my endeavour, and
the Queen's wish, and that of the Crown Princess. Thank God for it. He has had the
subject on his mind for years ever since he began to write about Arthur and his
knights.[19]

His hesitation about the subject is perhaps reflected in his pessimistic view
of the quest, though his ending is less dramatically dark than that of William
Morris. Tennyson's view does not stem from personal doubts or tensions,

but from a fear that the order and good government which Arthur's realm represented could not be sustained. The romances were, for an already huge audience, an allegory of the triumphs of Victorian Britain. Yet Tennyson presents us at the end of the poem with 'the summing up of all in the highest note by the highest of human men. These lines in Arthur's speech are the (spiritually) central lines of the Idylls.'[20]

> 'And some among you held that if the King
> Had seen the sight he would have sworn the vow.
> Not easily, seeing that the King must guard
> That which he rules, and is but as the hind
> To whom a space of land is given to plow,
> Who may not wander from the allotted field
> Before his work be done, but being done,
> Let visions of the night or of the day
> Come as they will; and many a time they come,
> Until this earth he walks on seems not earth,
> This light that strikes his eyeball is not light,
> This air that smites his forehead is not air
> But vision – yea, his very hand and foot –
> *In moments when he feels he cannot die*
> *And knows himself no vision to himself,*
> *Nor the high God a vision, nor that One*
> *Who rose again.* Ye have seen what ye have seen.'

The theme of service and honest labour, which is Arthur's view of his task as king and that of the knights as members of the Round Table, is introduced at the beginning of the poem: Perceval has withdrawn to a monastery after the quest, where one of the brothers, Ambrosius, asks him about his chivalrous past. As the story unfolds, Tennyson presents Ambrosius' own experience of life as a counterpoint to Perceval's high adventures: his simple existence as a monk and his pleasure in the ways of the village people whom he occasionally visits, 'small man, in this small world of mine'. Ambrosius' first reaction to Perceval's mention of the Holy Grail is that it is perhaps 'the phantom of a cup that comes and goes'. Perceval affirms the reality of the cup, and tells how Christ used it at the Last Supper, and how Joseph of Arimathea brought it to Glastonbury. There is no direct mention of Christ's blood, and the legend is carefully rooted in England, even though Glastonbury never claimed to have the Grail: it is a Grail for the Church of England, avoiding all difficulties of doctrinal controversy.

The Grail becomes a symbol of ascetic religion – religion in its aspect of withdrawal from worldly things. It is first seen by Perceval's sister, who is a nun: she attains the vision through prayer and fasting, to atone for the sins of Arthur's court, rumours of which have reached even the remoteness of her cell. Her confessor tells her of the Grail,

> . . . And when King Arthur made
> His Table Round, and all men's hearts became
> Clean for a season, surely he had thought
> That now the Holy Grail would come again.

She asks him if she can attain it by prayer and fasting. He is uncertain, but one night she attains the desired vision: in the moonlight

> Stream'd thro' my cell a cold and silver beam,
> And down the long beam stole the Holy Grail,
> Rose-red with beatings in it, as if alive,
> Till all the white walls of my cell were dyed
> With rosy colors leaping on the wall;
> And then the music faded, and the Grail
> Past, and the beam decay'd, and from the walls
> The rosy quiverings died into the night.

She tells Perceval of her vision, and he longs to achieve the same experience. When Galahad comes to court, Perceval's sister gives him a strange sword-belt woven of her own hair, and in a speech shot through with mystical-erotic overtones declares him 'my love, my knight of heaven'. He too believes 'in her belief', and when he sits in the Siege Perilous, the Grail appears to the whole court, save Arthur, who is absent redressing the wrongs of his subjects. When Arthur returns, the knights tell him of the vision: and because the Grail was 'all over cover'd with a luminous cloud', they had sworn to go in search of it to see it plainly and openly.

Arthur's response is blunt and sceptical, echoing the words of Christ to those who had gone into the desert to see John the Baptist:

> Lo, now, . . . have ye seen a cloud?
> What go ye into the wilderness to see?

He tells the knights that the vision is only for the few, and that they are acting like a herd, following their leader blindly: 'one hath seen, and all the blind will see'. He foresees that in their absence, noble deeds will go unaccomplished, 'while ye follow wandering fires / Lost in the quagmire.'

The knights depart, after one last great tournament, and Arthur's forebodings are proved right. The Grail, even if it is no 'phantom cup', leads to a land of phantoms; and hearing Perceval tell of his experiences prompts Ambrosius to celebrate the reality of his own 'small world', asking Perceval, 'Came ye on none but phantoms in your quest?' Galahad is the first to see the Grail, which, once found, never leaves him:

> . . . but moving with me day and night
> Fainter by day, but always in the night
> Blood-red, and sliding down the blacken'd marsh,
> Blood-red, and on the mountain top
> Blood-red, and in the sleeping mere below
> Blood-red . . .

Through its power Galahad has conquered pagan kingdoms, but when Perceval meets him it is time for him to go to his crowning in the spiritual city; and as a ship bears him away, Perceval in turn sees the Grail, hovering above the departing Galahad: 'the veil had been withdrawn'. Bors too sees the Grail, when he lies imprisoned by pagans who question his belief and tell him that he follows 'a mocking fire'. When Perceval and Bors return to Camelot, a shattered city and a remnant of Arthur's knights are all that they find. Lancelot tells how he approached the Grail at Carbonek, but was thrown back by a fiery blast when he opened the door of the Grail chamber, and had only glimpsed the holy vessel and the angels ministering to it. The 'reckless and irreverent' Gawain bitterly sums up the quest:

> . . . my good friend Percivale
> Thy holy nun and thou have driven men mad,
> Yea, made our mightiest madder than our least.

Tennyson ends with Arthur's defence of his decision not to take part in the quest, a speech in which he defines a spiritual path which is rooted in secular duty. The Grail still stirred uneasy memories in Victorian England, and echoed the current tensions between the Roman Catholic Church and the Church of England; Tennyson, despite his view that the Grail was no more than the chalice of the communion service,[21] insists on its 'blood-red' colour in Perceval's vision, raising the ghost of the medieval connection between the Grail and the Holy Blood which permeates Malory's account.

He himself said of the poem that 'Faith declines, religion in many turns from practical goodness to the quest after the supernatural and marvellous and selfish religious excitement. Few are those for whom the quest is a source of spiritual strength.' Yet he did not condemn those who achieved the quest, saying that the poem expressed 'my strong feeling as to the Reality of the Unseen', and according to his son 'he dwelt on the mystical treatment of every part of his subject, and said the key is to be found in a careful reading of Sir Percivale's vision.'[22]

'The Holy Grail' is therefore about the role of religion in the life of the individual and its relationship to the social order, as represented by Arthur. To see it as a commentary on the failure of the British Empire or as a reaction to the Indian mutiny and the re-examination of imperial ideals that followed, is to impose a twentieth-century perspective on it.[23] What did happen in the wake of 'The Holy Grail' was that Perceval and Galahad became bywords for the triumph of idealism over practicality, and their names were invoked by other authors when they wished to explore this problem.[24]

For a poem which treats the quest of the Grail as the mission of Arthur himself, we have to turn to Tennyson's acquaintance R. S. Hawker, the eccentric vicar of a small Cornish parish, who had some reputation as a poet and folklorist.[25] He published his unfinished *The Quest of the Sangraal* in 1863, very much in the shadow of Tennyson, even though Tennyson's idyll 'The Holy Grail' did not appear until six years later. He was dubious about the reception of his work in a materialist world: 'I fear that there will be a want of relish for such a theme and that those who do like the Subject would rather I had discussed the money value of the Vase and dealt with the Quest as a lucky speculation of Sir Galahad.'[26] He describes the history of the Grail very much as Tennyson does; however, it is Arthur himself who tells the knights of its existence, and Arthur who sends them out on the quest. It is Arthur's destiny to call this quest, but the purpose of the quest remains undefined, beyond that of plucking 'this Sangraal from its cloudy cave'.[27] The Grail seems to represent, by its absence from the world of Arthur, a land 'shorn of God':

> . . . Ah! loathsome shame
> To hurl in battle for the pride of arms:
> To ride in native tournay, foreign war:
> To count the stars; to ponder pictured runes,
> And grasp great knowledge, as the demons do,
> If we be shorn of God: – we must assay
> The myth and meaning of this marvellous bowl: . . .

Hawker offers a powerful vision of a world where 'giant-men arose, that seemed as gods', enabled by the use of armaments 'to hurl a distant death from some deep den', but from which 'The awful shadows of the Sangraal, fled'. In this he foreshadows the negative view of the Grail which we shall find in twentieth-century writers. Yet in the end his enthusiasm outruns his ideas and his skill as a poet: the banal opening, 'Ho for the Sangraal! vanish'd Vase of Heaven', sets the mood of the poem: exuberant but vague, and often obscure.

Hawker adapts the traditional story slightly to give Arthur a greater role, but the Scottish artist James Archer offers a much more radical innovation. He was haunted by the theme of Arthur's death throughout his career, and treated it in a manner akin to that of the Pre-Raphaelites, although he had no more than a passing connection with that group. His earliest version of 'La Mort d'Arthur' dates from 1861 (Plate VI), the latest from 1897. In the earliest version, the dying Arthur gazes at a shadowy figure of an angel bearing a chalice, scarcely visible to the onlooker, while he is tended by three queens and the Lady of the Lake. In the 1897 version, the Lady of the Lake has vanished, but the angel of the Grail now occupies a third of the picture, almost more than life-size and bearing a glowing, ornate vessel. The Grail does not figure in any of the literary accounts of Arthur's death, so Archer provided for the catalogue of the Royal Scottish Academy exhibition in which the 1861 version was shown a text which sounds like Malory, but is in fact his own invention. He begins by paraphrasing Malory's account, but then adds:

Right so there came by the holy vessell of the sanc greall, with all manner of sweetnesse and sorrow, but they could not readily see who beare that holly vessel.[28]

Archer's pictures present a highly unusual version of the Grail legend, for it implies that the Grail is not only visible to those who have achieved the ultimate in spiritual experience, but also to the great champions of chivalry and justice, to whom it appears as a healing vessel. The title for the missing 1863 version underlines this theme: *The Sancgreall, King Arthur, Relieved of his Grievous Wound in the Island-Valley of Avalon by the Application of the Contents of a 'Holy Vessel Borne by a Maiden, and therein Is a Part of the Holy Blood of our Lord'*. In the visual treatment of the Grail, there is perhaps also an echo of the 'vision' of Arthur in the closing lines of Tennyson's 'The Holy Grail', the passage which the poet called the spiritual centre of the *Idylls*.

But for a closer artistic equivalent of Tennyson's treatment of the Grail theme in *Idylls of the King* we turn to the work of Edward Burne-Jones, the youngest of the key figures of the Pre-Raphaelite group. The set of tapestries on the quest of the Holy Grail (Plate VII) were commissioned by a private patron in 1890, and Burne-Jones wrote his own description of the action depicted in the six scenes. This evokes the story in simple and direct language, and, as a reading of the Grail story at the end of the nineteenth century by an artist who had been deeply involved with the ideas for much of his life, it is an intriguing document:

The first subject is Pentecost morning, at the Round Table, when the damsel of the San Graal appears and summons all the knights to the adventure – and suddenly writing comes on the empty chair – the Siege Perilous set by Arthur – where no man may sit but the one who can achieve the adventure. Launcelot is opposite the chair, and points to himself as if asking if he is to sit there. Gawain and Lamorak and Percival and Bors are all there. Then in the second, the knights go forth, and it is good-bye all round. Guenevere is arming Launcelot. Then in the third and fourth are the subjects called the failing of the knights. Gawain and Ewain are kept from entering, eaten up by the world were they – handsome gentlemen set on this world's glory. Then comes Launcelot's turn in the fourth, eaten up, not by coveting glory, but eaten up he was, and his heart set on another matter. So he is foiled and dreams he comes to the chapel and has found it – but not a glorious one as he thought it would be, but a ruined and broken one – and he still cannot enter for one comes and bars the way. And then comes the ship – which is as much to say the scene has shifted, and we have passed out of Britain and are in the land of Sarras, the land of the soul, that is – and of all the hundred and fifty that went on the Quest three are chosen and may set foot on that shore – Bors, Percival and Galahad. And of these Bors and Percival may see the Graal afar off – three big angels bar their way – and one holds the spear that bleeds that is the spear that entered Christ's side, and it bleeds always. You know by its appearing that the Grail is near. And then comes Galahad who alone may see it – and to see it is death – for it is seeing the face of God.[29]

Burne-Jones lays the same emphasis on failure as Rossetti and Morris had done before him, but it is the personal failure of the individual knights: there is no wider symbolism here. It translates visibly in the tapestries as a haunted weariness, a feeling of the mortality of earthly passions. What is fascinating is the other side of the coin: he is unafraid to speak of the achievement of the Grail in dramatic theological terms. He defines the vision within the Grail as the 'beatific vision', the sight of God face to face by a living person, which is the culmination of Dante's *Divine Comedy*, and to which the medieval mystics aspired. Burne-Jones names it directly where his sources speak only of veiled mysteries. The tapestry itself portrays the Holy Spirit as a rushing fiery cloud that sweeps through the chapel where Galahad kneels in rapt adoration; the drops of blood that rain down into the chalice represent the actual moment of transubstantiation. Burne-Jones had been an Anglo-Catholic in his youth, and retained much sympathy for their position; a Roman Catholic might have shied away, as did the medieval writers, from such frankness about the central mystery of the faith. Burne-Jones actually goes beyond the previous definitions of the nature of the achievement of the Grail, and on the eve of a century which was to see the Grail transferred from Christian mysteries to pagan myths, gives us the most focused Christian image of it.

Richard Wagner and the Grail

The enthusiasm for all things medieval which had swept England after the republication of Malory's *Morte Darthur* owed its endurance to Tennyson and the Pre-Raphaelites. In Germany, on the other hand, after the first flush of Romantic celebration of the Middle Ages, the great masterpieces of German Arthurian literature inspired not artists and poets, but a composer: Richard Wagner. The controversy surrounding this extraordinary, highly talented artist and deeply flawed man rages unabated. Nowhere is the dictum 'You must separate the man from his work'[30] more hotly debated: surveying the vast array of literature about Wagner, we feel that we know too much about him to come to a conclusion, but the very richness of the documentation allows us to follow his thought processes in the finest detail. And nowhere is this more true than in the case of *Parsifal*, his last opera, in which his subject is the Grail story: we can trace its progress and see that, far from being a kind of afterthought, it was for many years his ultimate goal, the product of an almost lifelong involvement with the subject.

Wagner read medieval texts voraciously, and from an early age. He had encountered the Arthurian stories in the early 1840s, if not before, in both popular re-tellings and in scholarly editions. He first read Wolfram von Eschenbach's *Parzival* in 1845, and it was never far from his thoughts when, a decade later, he took up another Arthurian story, that of Tristan. Gottfried von Strassburg's *Tristan* and Wolfram's poem are the two great masterpieces of early medieval German literature: when we add to these Wagner's use of the story of Parzival's son, Lohengrin, as well as the story of the poet Tannhäuser and the early heroic poem about the Nibelungs, his expertise in medieval poetry is self-evident. It is in fact in *Lohengrin*, completed in 1848, that the Grail first appears:

In a faraway land, reached by paths unknown to you, lies a castle known as Montsalvat; in its midst stands a bright temple, more splendid than any known on earth; therein is a vessel of wondrous power which is guarded as a sacred treasure: it was brought down by an angel host to be tended by the purest of mankind; each year a dove descends from heaven to fortify its wondrous strength anew: it is called the Grail, and purest faith is imparted through it to its knighthood . . .[31]

This version of the story is largely taken from Wolfram, but the stone described in *Parzival* has already become a 'vessel'. The Grail remained constantly in his thoughts: while writing *Tristan*, Wagner thought of having Parsifal, searching for the Grail castle, encounter Tristan on his sickbed in the third act, and noted the similarity between the wounded Tristan and the wounded Amfortas. This was in 1855; a decade later, as he worked on *The Mastersingers of Nuremberg*, he broke off to spend four days writing the outline for *Parsifal*. The essentials of this outline barely changed when he returned to it in 1877.

Wagner approaches the story of Parsifal in a way which is both in harmony with that of Wolfram and yet quite distinct. The foolish youth of the opening of the story comes to maturity by virtue of his sympathy (*Mitleid*) for the sufferings of Amfortas. The surrounding details are much changed: it is only through the spear that Amfortas can be healed, and Parsifal's quest is for the spear, not the Grail. In Wolfram, the spear appears only as a momentary vision, when a squire runs through the hall with a lance from whose tip flow drops of blood, and all present break into loud laments. It then vanishes from his story. In Wagner, however, the spear is explicitly that of Longinus, and it is related to the story of the Dolorous Blow. But here the spear is not used against a blameless king; it becomes the instrument of divine retribution for Amfortas' unchastity, and Parsifal's quest is to find it and use it to heal the king's wound. We hear about the spear before we learn of the Grail, and Wagner's Grail performs a very different function. It is not the object of a quest, but the mid-point of the Grail kingdom, symbol of the faith which motivates the knights. The conjunction of the two is made at the very beginning of the action, as Gurnemanz awakens the two young Grail knights and they pray in answer to the sound of trombones from the Grail castle, which declare both the Grail theme and that of faith.

The Grail motif itself is based on the so-called 'Dresden amen' composed by J. G. Naumann in the late eighteenth century for the king's chapel at Dresden, where Wagner was *Kapellmeister* in the 1840s. The 'amen' at the end of a prayer is an affirmation of faith: Wagner again seems to be underlining the link between the Grail and faith. Gurnemanz relates how

Titurel was given the Grail 'when the cunning and power of savage enemies threatened the kingdom of pure faith . . . the Saviour's blessed messengers bowed before him one holy solemn night; the sacred vessel, the holy, noble cup from which He drank at the Last Supper, into which his divine blood also flowed on the Cross, together with the lance that made it flow – these symbols of most marvellous richness they gave into the care of our king'.[32] The brotherhood of the Grail are 'strengthened by the marvellous power of the Grail to carry out the highest works of salvation'. The Grail is the central focus of the kingdom ruled by Amfortas, and acts as both the inspiration and the source of strength of the Grail knights. The Grail itself is never sought by Parsifal. When the sight of Amfortas' agony awakes his sympathy, he seeks out the spear which will heal the king's wound. It is only when he has gained the spear that he goes in quest of the Grail castle; but again the object of his search is not the Grail, but Amfortas. The Grail for Wagner functions as a still centre, the centre of the kingdom of faith: in a sense Parsifal has lost his faith through Kundry's kiss at the very moment when he has won back the spear; and it is only when Gurnemanz challenges him for wearing armour on the holiest of days, Good Friday, that he regains both faith and Grail.

In the Grail ceremony itself, the choirs of boys and youths sing first of redemption: the sacrifice of his blood made by the 'redeeming hero'[33] should be matched by the Grail knights, who sacrifice their blood in his cause: from the heights, the boys' voices declare: 'The faith lives; the dove hovers, the saviour's loving messenger; the wine which flows for you, drink that and partake of the bread of life.'[34] Faith is at the heart of the Grail ritual. When the moment for the uncovering of the Grail comes, Amfortas despairingly sees a ray of light descend, and the 'divine contents of the sacred vessel',[35] the Saviour's blood, glow with radiant power. It is a visual image, close to Tennyson's glowing Grail descending in the moonlight to the cell of Perceval's sister. When bread and wine are distributed to the knights, their cry at the climax of the ceremony repeats the theme of faith:

> 'Blessed in faith.
> Blessed in faith and love.'

and the boys and youths reply

> 'Blessed in love,
> Blessed in faith.'

and as the ceremony ends, invisible voices repeat yet again 'Blessed in faith'.[36]

Gurnemanz has been watching Parsifal closely throughout the ceremony, and sees no flash of understanding in his behaviour. He now turns him away angrily, believing that he is merely stupid and foolish. But Parsifal's stillness is due to the depth of emotion which he feels on seeing the plight of Amfortas: the scene has aroused a fierce compassion in him. He determines to find the lost spear, and bring it back to heal the wounded Grail king. It is the spear which becomes the object of his quest, not the Grail itself. Indeed, the Grail does not figure in the second act, in which Parsifal resists the temptations of Kundry, now transformed into a beautiful woman by the magician Klingsor. Klingsor has achieved purity by force, by self-castration, and hopes to become master of the Grail when he has destroyed all the knights. He is, however, powerless against Parsifal's rejection of the lure of sexual love, and when he attempts to use the spear to destroy him, it hangs in mid-air: Parsifal seizes it and makes the sign of the cross, at which Klingsor's castle dissolves.

If there is a quest for the Grail in the opera, it is in the prelude to Act Three, depicting Parsifal's wanderings and doubts before he eventually finds the way back to the forests of the kingdom of the Grail. Here Wagner returns to Wolfram's poem, but extends the image of Parsifal's spiritual reawakening on Good Friday into some of his most ecstatic and beautiful music. This lengthy scene, in which Gurnemanz recognizes the stranger and the spear that he bears, and acknowledges him as the new lord of the Grail, leads to a relatively brief conclusion at the Grail castle. Amfortas refuses to unveil the Grail again and to celebrate the Grail ceremony, pleading the agony of his wound, which will be intensified by his remorse at the sight of the Grail; he longs for death, not the renewal of life which the Grail will bring. Parsifal enters with the spear; Amfortas is healed; and it is Parsifal who has the Grail shrine opened. He takes it from the shrine and kneels before it while the knights and youths sing the final cryptic lines:

> 'Miracle of highest salvation!
> Redemption for the redeemer!'[37]

Parsifal was an enigma and a challenge for its first audiences, and remains deeply controversial today. The music is generally admired, even by listeners who otherwise dislike Wagner's style; it inhabits a different world from that of his earlier operas. The text and meaning of the opera, however, have aroused very different passions. Is it a Christian opera, as many early listeners thought? In 1894, a Scottish clergyman wrote, after seeing it performed at Bayreuth: 'The directness of the impression of Christian truth made in "Parsifal" is heightened by the choice of subject of the drama.'[38] Others called it blasphemous, deploring the re-enactment of what seemed to them to be the ritual of communion in the theatre, for the theatre was an art form which still aroused deep moral suspicion among the devout. Friedrich Nietzsche, who had been a close friend of Wagner, was deeply shocked by what he believed to be Wagner's capitulation to orthodox Christian belief, and wrote a violent attack on Wagner as a consequence, in which he described how 'Richard Wagner, apparently most triumphant, but in truth a decaying and despairing decadent, suddenly sank down, helpless and broken, before the Christian cross.'[39] And in more recent years, the insistence on Parsifal as '*der reine Tor*', 'the pure fool', combined with the passages about the holy blood of the Redeemer and the sinful blood of Amfortas, was read as a precursor of the ideas of racial purity propounded by the Nazis. This at least is demonstrably nonsense: *Parsifal* was actually declared 'ideologically unacceptable' by the Nazis, and no performances were given at Bayreuth from 1939 until after the end of the war.[40] Attempts

22 *Set design for Act One of Richard Wagner's* Parsifal, *by Christian Jank (1879). It was prepared for Ludwig II of Bavaria four years before the opera's premiere.*

to portray the characterization of Kundry as anti-Semitic are equally mis-
guided; there is no indication that Wagner envisaged her as Jewish, even
though he invokes the legend of the Wandering Jew as the reason for her
endless, restless journey through the world: she says that she had laughed
at 'Him' in his agony, and for that is condemned to misery. Once again,
Wagner never even mentions the name of Christ: it is all oblique and
carefully unspecific.

For many years, *Parsifal* was only performed at Bayreuth, in accordance
with the composer's wishes, and even the 'pirate' American productions –
the work was not in copyright there – recreated the Bayreuth production.
Even after the First World War, the general reverence for the Bayreuth
original continued, and it was not until 1951 that a substantial reinterpretation of the staging took place, under the direction of Wieland Wagner at
Bayreuth itself. The naturalistic sets were replaced by open spaces and
symbolic minimalist scenery; but the core of the production was still traditional. Again, other opera houses followed suit, and it was not until the
second half of the twentieth century, with the rise of the director as artistic
protagonist rather than mediator of the composer's work, that drastic
reappraisals of *Parsifal* began to appear.[41] The first and most striking of
these was Hans-Jürgen Syberberg's film of 1978, which invokes all kinds
of cultural references as well as a radical re-reading of the hero. It is easy to
pick on the obvious bric-à-brac and to note the vast deathmask of Wagner
which fills the stage, the Nazi flag which appears for an instant, and the
Grail knights adopting the heraldry of the Teutonic Order. But these are in
a much wider context; the medieval English standard is shown near the
Nazi banner, and the deathmask is part of an element of late Victorian art
which predominates in the presentation of the choir of boys in the Grail
scenes; they become women looking at a huge book, in the style of decorative
engravings. Amfortas' wound acquires a separate existence, borne on a
cushion; and Parsifal himself separates into a male and female pair, whose
reunion at the end seems to be the climax of the film. And yet, despite all
these potential distractions, the power of the original is often well served by
Syberberg's vision and his intense theatricality. In particular, film – as
Syberberg has himself pointed out – is ideally suited to Wagner's emphasis
on precise gestures and movements, by the use of close-ups.[42] In all this, the
Grail retreats into a Victorian casket, from which it emerges as a glowing
vase not unlike its other film incarnations; unsurprisingly, it does not really
seem to interest Syberberg particularly.

Stage versions have been even more radical: at Frankfurt in 1982, Ruth
Berghaus portrayed the Grail community on the verge of disintegration, a

hierarchical male society rather like a school, into which the outsider Parsifal burst, bringing a new life but also a childlike sense of playing at his part. Other productions have offered the spear as a nuclear weapon (Rolf Liebermann in Geneva) and a science-fiction version by Götz Friedrich at Bayreuth itself, in which the Grail offered a life-giving liberation from the over-inventiveness of modern man. The most extreme version was that of Robert Wilson, who offered a production stripped of almost all the usual props: even the spear vanished, but the Grail survived, as a 'black box retrieved from a glowing pyramid of ice'.[43]

This plethora of interpretations is perhaps due in large part to the current enthusiasm for reworking rather than interpreting classic operas, but the variety of approaches does bring to the fore the extraordinary power of Wagner's vision, whether flawed or sublime, and the fascination that his chosen theme still holds for us.

But what was in Wagner's mind as he wrote both the libretto and the opera itself? There is no easy answer. The doctor who looked after him in Venice and who wrote an account of the physical causes of his death added at the end the following note:

It cannot be doubted that the innumerable psychical agitations to which Wagner was daily exposed on account of his particular mental outlook, his sharply pronounced attitude toward a whole series of burning problems in the fields of art, science and politics . . . contributed much to his unfortunate end.[44]

The enormous range of Wagner's interests, his wide reading in literature and philosophy, and his compulsive essay-writing in his later years, make it difficult enough to analyse his thinking, particularly when that thinking is not a consistent philosophy but is hugely influenced by whatever ideas he has just encountered, the latest concept that has caught his fancy. *Parsifal*, however, took shape long before Wagner's late essays, where his inconsistencies (and his anti-Semitism) are at their peak. When he wrote the outline in 1865, the dominant literary influence was still his enthusiasm for medieval literature, and the dominant philosophical figure in his life was that of Schopenhauer; Wagner continued to admire him even when his own ideas took increasingly opposing paths. Almost all the key points in *Parsifal* can be traced to these two sources.

If we look at two concepts which have, with hindsight, caused more problems than any others, those of blood and purity (*Reinheit*), both are rooted in the medieval texts which were Wagner's original sources. The 'divine contents of the sacred vessel' is the 'holiest blood': a theme familiar to us from the French romances which Wagner had drawn on for his image of the Grail. All the references in the libretto to blood – of which Nietzsche famously complained that there was too much in *Parsifal* – are within the context of this divine blood as the source of spiritual and earthly nourishment. Amfortas contrasts the sinful blood which pours from the wound in his side with the divine blood which flows from a similar wound to nourish the community. (Again, the reference to the Crucifixion remains oblique.) Wagner limits his use of this idea to this one point, and the contrast between divine and sinful blood arises naturally out of the parallel between the two wounds caused by the same spear: one redeeming, the other afflicting. In the same way, the idea of purity comes from the same French medieval sources; Parsifal has taken on the qualities of Galahad, and has become the chaste champion rather than the warm and human figure evoked by Wolfram von Eschenbach. Again, purity is only related to Parsifal himself, apart from a brief aside that it is a requirement for the Grail knights, which picks up an idea from the *Lancelot-Grail*: the Grail will only feed those who approach it in purity of heart: 'if you are pure, the Grail will now provide meat and drink for you'.[45]

There is a great deal of Christian imagery in *Parsifal*, and Wagner himself may have been closer to orthodox Christianity than many of his reported comments would lead us to believe. But there is a conscious avoidance of specifically Christian reference: apart from the absence of Christ's name, the Resurrection is never mentioned, and only the redeeming sacrifice of the Crucifixion is emphasized. The figure on the Cross is called 'the lord', 'the Redeemer', but remains a universal symbol, not the historical figure of Christ himself. Parsifal invokes 'the saviour' in his wild reaction to Kundry's kiss, but again the figure is shadowy, the mysterious lord of the Grail, who, it seems to Parsifal, begs him to rescue the holy vessel from the sinful hands of Amfortas. Wagner's original outline makes it clear that Amfortas feels this guilt also, and that Parsifal experiences it through his compassion for Amfortas.[46]

But just as the medieval Grail romances were outside the framework of official religion, so Wagner uses the outward forms of religion to convey an artistic message. He was quite aware that he was recreating the rituals of the Church – albeit the Lutheran rather than the Roman Catholic rite – and he had declared to Cosima that 'this scene of Holy Communion will be the main scene, the core of the whole work'.[47] Yet it is a highly unorthodox form of communion. Here the blood and flesh of the Redeemer – Christ is, of course, not named – become bread and wine in order to sustain the knights in their struggle to maintain the faith, an exact inversion of the doctrine of transubstantiation. The motif of the Grail as a source of nourishment for the pure in heart is given its most literal expression here. This is not a mere ritual, but a real and practical necessity for the continuance of the Grail community.

Parsifal is not a religious work in the accepted sense. Just as the medieval writers had introduced the contemporary concept of chivalry into the context of religion, so Wagner treads a similar path. He rejects the orthodoxies of established faith in favour of the syncretism that was beginning to become fashionable in the mid-nineteenth century. In his view, Christianity, Buddhism and Hinduism were the three genuine religions, and in their pure and primitive form they shared an emphasis on compassion for one's fellow-creatures which was the essential truth of religious feeling. This sympathy or compassion (*Mitleid*) is the central idea of *Parsifal*, and the rituals of Christianity are merely the framework against which the drama unfolds: the key is the development of Parsifal, from the uncaring youth who shoots swans to test his skill, into the man who dedicates himself to the alleviation of another's pain because of his compassion for his suffering. In this Kundry and her laughter are the anti-type of Parsifal; she is a human being who lacks all trace of compassion. Through compassion comes true knowledge of the human condition.

There is a strong Buddhist element in this, and Wagner did indeed talk for many years of an opera based on an incident from the youth of the Buddha, to be called *The Conquerors* because its hero and heroine overcame earthly desire. But the ideas which appealed to him had already been worked out to a large extent in *Tristan* and in *Parsifal*, and the idea never came to fruition, probably because Wagner had exhausted that particular philosophical vein once the outline for *Parsifal* was completed.

Another important element in Wagner's relation to religion was that he rejected the more developed forms of religion as aberrations from the original clarity of the thinking of the founders, and he particularly disliked the outward aspects of Catholicism: 'I come more and more to the conclusion that its continued existence is a scandal.'[48] Similarly, an essay written just after he had completed *Parsifal*, entitled 'Religion and Art', is prefaced with a quotation from Friedrich Schiller: 'I find in the Christian religion an inherent tendency towards the highest and most noble, and the different manifestations of it in real life seem to me repellent and tasteless precisely because they are failed representations of this highest original.'[49] In the essay itself he makes large claims for the role of art in the world of religion. Towards the end, he adopts Schopenhauer as his 'guide to the inexorable metaphysical problem of the human race' and declares that this can only be solved by suppressing our individual will, and attaining that self-knowledge which 'can be gained at last by Pity born of suffering – which, cancelling the Will, expresses the negation of a negative; and that, by every rule of logic, amounts to Affirmation'.[50] To achieve this, Wagner asks himself 'must a new religion first be founded?' But he has already declared that that is not the task of the artist:

One might say that where Religion becomes artificial, it is reserved for Art to save the spirit of religion by recognising the figurative value of the mythic symbols which the former would have us believe in their literal sense, and revealing their deep and hidden truth through an ideal presentation. Whilst the priest stakes everything on the religious allegories being accepted as matters of fact, the artist has no concern at all with such a thing, since he freely and openly gives out his work as his own invention.[51]

Parsifal is, therefore, a reinvention both of the medieval stories and of the religion which stands at the heart of those stories. It is not a religious work, but an opera about religion, and if Wagner puts into it his most sincerely and deeply held beliefs, he is not attempting to create a new faith or even a religious experience. The Grail is an ideal symbol for his purpose: it is both a mythical emblem created by artists of earlier centuries and a central example, in its avatar as the chalice of the Mass, of religious allegory presented as factual truth.

Compassion may be the central theme of *Parsifal*, but Wagner also explores other ideas, notably that of redemption: man, 'by perceiving the error of all existence, becomes the Redeemer of the world'.[52] The final words of the opera are an enigmatic echo of this idea: the knights and youths sing 'Redemption for the Redeemer!' I read this as meaning that Parsifal has both redeemed them and achieved his own redemption by overcoming the domination of the will through his compassion.[53] More enigmatic still is the insistence in the Grail scene of the first act on belief or faith (*Glauben*). As we have seen, the musical themes for the Grail and for belief are often found together in the score. If belief is so sacred and crucial – the words 'Blessed in faith' are the climax of the Grail ceremony – this surely runs counter to Wagner's standpoint on religion itself as something which comes between man and the divine: belief is the argument by which the invasion of reason is repelled. But Wagner is not arguing that religion itself is at fault: true belief in the primitive and pure forms of religion is what he urges. He had explored quite deeply the history of the early Church, partly because he found there writers who shared his own views, as well as forgotten legends which appealed to him, particularly in Gnostic writings. He admired Marcion, an early theologian who wished that Christianity would abandon the Old Testament and rely solely on the New. And it has been suggested that he may have known the apocryphal story of the son of God sent to redeem the Egyptian world of the spirits, who falls prey to its temptations, and becomes a redeemer who himself awaits redemption.[54]

Ultimately, we come back once again to the passage from 'Religion and Art': these religious scenes are the 'mythic symbols' of which Art reveals 'their deep and hidden truth through an ideal presentation'. His approach is very close to that of Goethe in the final scene of *Faust*: acknowledging the difficulty of depicting the final redemption and apotheosis of Faust's lover and victim Gretchen, Goethe wrote:

... dealing with such matters beyond the realm of the senses, which can scarcely be guessed at, I could easily have lost my way in vagueness, if I had not given my poetic intentions a well-defined form and firmness by using the sharply outlined figures and images drawn from the Christian church.[55]

Wagner is concerned to draw out the essence of Christianity, the idea of sin and redemption, of forgiveness and compassion, from the confines of the merely historical and the encrusting ritual of succeeding ages.[56]

The impact of Wagner's *Parsifal* was enormous. Quite apart from its electrifying effect on the musical world, it inspired artists to take up the Grail theme with enthusiasm. Wagner's young admirers, including the composer Humperdinck and the pianist Josef Rubinstein, formed a group called 'the Knights of the Grail' even before the completion of the opera:[57] they sent Wagner their artistic manifesto, which he approved of but would not endorse publicly. It was Wagner's patron, Ludwig II of Bavaria, who commissioned artists to provide a pictorial equivalent to the opera in the décor for his fantastic castle at Neuschwanstein. Ludwig had been an enthusiast for Wagner's work since attending *Lohengrin* in 1861 and had been involved in his plans and projects since the 1860s. His love of German medieval literature was equal to Wagner's own, and even before the completion of *Parsifal* images based on Wolfram's poem were being planned, alongside similar series from *Tannhäuser* and *Tristan und Isolde*. In the 1870s, during the building of Neuschwanstein, he commissioned Eduard Ille to paint designs of the Grail temple as described in *Later Titurel*. Ille showed this, not as a Gothic building as envisaged by the scholar Sulpice Boisserée some

23 *The Grail temple, as imagined by Edward von Steinle in 1884, two years after the premiere of* Parsifal. *The building is directly based on Sulpice Boisserée's drawing of the Grail temple as portrayed in* The Later Titurel, *and forms the centrepiece of an altar-like cycle of five paintings showing Parzival's story.*

thirty years earlier,[58] but very much in the Byzantine style, clearly inspired by Haghia Sophia in Constantinople, and this was to be the model for future versions, including the first stage sets for *Parsifal* itself. In 1877, Ludwig recreated the hermit's hut from which Gurnemanz emerges in Act Three of *Parsifal* at his villa at Linderhof, and wrote to Wagner: 'There I hear, full of premonition, the silver trumpets ring out from the Grail castle.'[59]

When it became clear that the plan for building a Byzantine palace, for which Ille's designs had been commissioned, would have to be abandoned, they became the basis for the throne room at Neuschwanstein. The final version of this owed more to later Byzantine church architecture than to Ille's fantasy, and it was in the frescoes at Neuschwanstein that the Grail theme was best represented. Despite Ludwig's enthusiasm for Wagner, he gave instructions that the programme of decoration should be based on the 'historic' versions of the stories, not on Wagner's reworkings of the medieval romances. In the Singers' Hall, which had been intended to commemorate the song contest in *Tannhäuser*, the scenes are from Wolfram's *Parzival*. They were executed in 1883–4, just after the premiere of *Parsifal*; Ludwig was so involved in reliving the romances that he insisted that the artist of the scene in which Parzival meets the pilgrims on Good Friday should complete his work on that precise day. Sadly, the paintings are little more than formal decoration and the whole ensemble is a monument to the obsession of the Bavarian king with the German past, and to his wild extravagance in pursuit of his ever-changing ideas as to how it should be recreated.

The same extravagant enthusiasm is reflected in the immensely elaborate table-piece created by a fashionable jeweller in Munich, which depicts the Grail castle and the Grail within its shrine, the whole surmounted by the fish, symbol of Christ and associated with the Grail in the earliest French romances.[60] This fantasy, together with the set of Grail tapestries by Edward Burne-Jones from Britain, was one of the outstanding attractions at the Paris World Exposition of 1900 (Plates VII–VIII). At the beginning of the twentieth century, the Grail had become a symbol of secular luxury, the first of the many changing and often inappropriate forms it was to take in the course of the next hundred years.

19

The Grail as Mirror

Until the end of the nineteenth century, the Grail remained a symbol rooted in religion, never moving far from its medieval origins. The poets and artists who took up the concept of the Grail accepted that it belonged in the context of medieval romance and medieval worship. Even Wagner came at the subject from its medieval standpoint, despite his contempt for the ritual forms of Christianity and his radical views on religious values. The twentieth century, however, offers a very different perspective, of which authors such as Immermann and Quinet were the precursors. The Grail becomes a mirror, reflecting the preoccupations of the individual writer and their intellectual milieu. It drifts free of its Christian connotations for all but a handful of writers; the general consensus declares that the old symbols need to be reinterpreted, whether in Jungian, pagan or philosophical terms. Nothing is taken as defined; everything in the old stories is questioned and reshaped according to the mood of the moment.

Secret Knowledge and the Occult

Wagner had demanded a return to the primitive purity of early Christianity. In the increasingly complex and industrialized society of the late nineteenth century, this was no more than a pious wish. But dissatisfaction with the rise of materialism and the dominance of capitalism, and the apparent acquiescence of the established churches with its principles, had already led to more radical alternatives. The concept of the 'occult' is one which arouses deep suspicion, if not outright hostility, but it was actually a respectable strand of Western philosophy for many centuries, and had its roots in the ideas put forward by admirers of Plato's thought in the late Greek civilization centred on Alexandria in the fourth century. The term itself was coined in Germany in 1533 by Cornelius Agrippa, who published three volumes on magic entitled *On Occult Philosophy*. He argued that magic exploited the invisible links between matter and spirit, and that spiritual powers could be invoked by means of their material counterparts, if the keys to these links were known. On this philosophical basis rested alchemy, astrology and divination or fortune-telling. When in the seventeenth century natural science emerged as a discipline, in which observation of physical results reigned supreme, these branches of knowledge were examined using the new procedures, and eventually found wanting in terms of scientific proof. But the 'scientists' of the period were steeped in the ideas of the Renaissance, where the late Greek learning of Alexandria and the world of the hermeticists, whose ideas derived from the secrets revealed (or concealed) in the writings of Hermes Trismegistus, were powerful intellectual influences. What could not be explained by science was now classified as 'occult' or hidden, because it defied rational investigation. Such areas of knowledge often bordered on the territory of orthodox religion, and were suspect to the established churches; and as science became increasingly dominated by rationalists, the scientists too grew wary.

This idea of secret knowledge is a major element in the twentieth-century image of the Grail, and in order to understand it we need to look at movements which deliberately cultivated an air of secrecy, in particular the Rosicrucians and the Freemasons. The origins of both are mysterious: the roots of Rosicrucianism can be traced back to around 1610, to a strange account of its reputed founder, Christian Rosenkreuz, who is said to have died in 1484, and who seems to have been entirely fictional. The author of the first work about him, *The Fame of the Brotherhood of R.C.*, published in 1614, was a Lutheran theologian, Johannes Valentin Andreae, who later declared that his pamphlet was intended as a *ludibrium*, variously translated as a farce or as a play. It seems likely that Andreae was thinking of the kind of instructive allegory that is found in court masques of the period, not of a satire on the contemporary fashion for occult studies; he is putting forward a serious viewpoint under the guise of entertainment.[1] The background to his publication is the attempt to reinstate a Protestant ruler in Bohemia at this time, in which Dr John Dee, the famous Elizabethan explorer of matters magical and astrological, had played a large part. The borders of alchemy and science, of philosophy and mysticism, were open for exploration by Protestants, freed from the restrictions and caveats of the Roman Catholic Church. The Rosicrucian manifestos draw heavily on this kind of material to create a Protestant equivalent of medieval prophecies, promising a new order in which disease and poverty will be conquered, the tyranny of the pope will be ended and a new page of enlightenment will dawn.

Despite the failure of the Protestant revival in Bohemia, Rosicrucian ideas survived this disappointment. It is possible that Freemasonry itself evolved from Rosicrucianism, though as Frances Yates says, 'The origin of Free-masonry is one of the most debated, and debatable, subjects in the whole realm of historical enquiry.'[2] There are links with alchemy, which in the mid-seventeenth century was turning respectable in the guise of chemistry; and the formation of the Royal Society in London in 1660 can be linked with both Freemasonry and Rosicrucianism. The penchant of the freemasons for secrecy and for a degenerate form of ancient symbolic images made their origins seem more mysterious than they probably are, and created a model for later secret societies with more exotic ends in view.

A further element in the miasma of mystical societies in the mid-nineteenth century was that of the followers of the Swedish scientist Emanuel Swedenborg, who in 1745 experienced a vision which led him to abandon science for the world of religion and theosophy ('knowledge of God'), arguing that all churches should unite to form a new religion. The first Theosophical Society was founded in London in 1783 to study his teachings and to pursue research into Eastern and Western mysticism alike. In the years of the French Revolution it faded, and the second Theosophical Society, which began in 1875, was only indirectly influenced by Sweden-borg's teachings, having much more to do with the new fashion for spiritual-ism and Egyptian religion: under the leadership of a Russian who had travelled in the East, Madame Blavatsky, the Theosophical Society aimed to replace the spiritualists' vaguely Christian activities with a revival of genuine occult practices.[3]

This necessarily brief and bald account of an often neglected area of Western intellectual history does lead us, eventually, back to the Grail. While Freemasonry, which pursued a rational and practical enlightenment behind the smokescreen of abstruse ritual, was the preserve of politicians and merchants, men of the world, artists and writers tended to prefer the Rosicrucian way, which offered spiritual enlightenment and the revelation of mysteries, and thus led to the exploration of the legacy of medieval occult practices. This was true both of the circle of William Blake in the early nineteenth century and of the French Romantic poets half a century later: an interest in the Rosicrucian mystical and spiritual ideas and in magic is found in the works of Victor Hugo as well as the 'decadent' poets such as Gérard de Nerval, Baudelaire and Rimbaud, or the symbolist Stéphane Mallarmé. In the 1890s, this circle widened to include artists and musicians, and a front-page article by the critic Maurice Barrès in *Le Figaro* on 27 June 1890, entitled 'The magi', described the new-found fashion for all things occult. The Rosicrucian order created by Joséphin Péladan, otherwise 'Sâr Méradock', under the title of the 'Ordre de la Rose + Croix, du Temple et du Graal'[4] was intended as a rejection of the original Rosicrucians, whom he regarded as heretical. The new order was to be Catholic, and, more important, aesthetic; and it became very much part of the artistic scene in Paris. Péladan's elder brother had been deeply interested in the occult, and had published extensively on the subject; Péladan himself had written on the Grail in 1883, eight years before the formation of his order.[5] He is the first of such enthusiasts whom we shall meet, and before we dismiss them as mere eccentrics or madmen, the attempt to involve the Grail in occult matters is an important element in its image in the twentieth century, with wide artistic repercussions. Despite his fondness for dramatic attire – preferably 'Assyrian' or medieval – and a flair for self-promotion, Péladan's activities attracted the attention of the artistic and literary world, including musicians such as Debussy and Satie, but the chief outward manifestation of Péladan's order was an annual art exhibition, 'Le Salon de la Rose + Croix', the first of which caused a considerable stir in the Parisian artistic world in 1892. Visitors to the opening of the first salon were greeted by the sound of a brass band playing the prelude to *Parsifal*, and paintings on themes from the opera appeared in several of the exhibitions. Rogelio de Egusquiza's etching of the Grail may have been the result of a meeting with Péladan on a visit to Bayreuth.[6] The Belgian artist Jean Delville was also a regular exhibitor, and his 'Parsifal' stems from the same Wagnerian enthusiasm.[7]

In the literary field, Paul Verlaine contributed to a periodical with which Péladan was associated, entitled *Le Saint-Graal*. It was edited by Emmanuel Signoret, and appeared at irregular intervals for twenty numbers from 1892 to 1899; the last numbers were written almost entirely by Signoret himself. Verlaine sent his good wishes for the first number on 20 January 1892:

The *Holy Grail*, what a word, what a name! A double meaning: the pinnacle of modern art, the summit of eternal Truth. Holy Grail, True Blood, the blood of Christ in incandescent gold; *Holy Grail, Lohengrin, Parsifal*, the triumphal and triumphant manifestation of the most sublime music, of what is perhaps the definitive poetic effort of our times![8]

Verlaine was an enthusiast for Wagner, and had already included in his collection *Amour* poems on *Parsifal* and on the Grail. '*Parsifal*' is an elegant summing up of Wagner's story in the space of a sonnet; 'Saint Graal' is in the heavily religious mode of the poet's declining years, a vision of Christ's redeeming blood flowing over France, 'torrent of the love of the God of love and gentleness', to become 'the salvation of our land, o blood that quenches thirst!'

Péladan himself was dedicatee of a strange reverie about Narcissus and the Grail in *Le Saint-Graal*.[9] In addition to *Le mystère du Graal*, he published a volume of prose poems extracted from his cycle of novels *La décadence Latine* under the title *La Queste du Graal* in 1892, though only the title evokes the Grail. His most important contribution was to revive, in a pamphlet of 1906, a suggestion that the Grail was associated with the Cathars. This slender publication was to have surprising and remarkable consequences.

The Rosicrucians also established themselves in England in the mid-nineteenth century, and the 'Societas Rosicruciana in Anglia' was a respectable offshoot of Freemasonry. In the meanwhile, the Theosophical Society had fallen into disrepute in 1883, when their leader, Madame Blavatsky, was shown to have used fraud in her spiritual seances, and was declared an impostor by the Society for Psychical Research. The president of the society, Anna Kingsford, founded a new group in 1884, the Hermetic Society, which continued with the original aims of the Theosophists. It concentrated on the mystical rather than the occult, rejecting claims to paranormal powers, and 'depending for guidance on no Mahatmas', a pointed rejoinder to Blavatsky's fondness for Eastern gurus of dubious origin. When another Rosicrucian order was founded in 1888, the 'Hermetic Order of the Golden Dawn', it attracted, among others, members of the recently discredited Theosophical Society. Its founder, William Westcott, claimed to have created it under the authority of a German order of the same name, which had a branch in France. Later, its most famous member, W. B. Yeats, was to write of its foundation that it

remains almost as obscure as that of some ancient religion . . . men who have come into possession of its rituals claim, without offering proof, authority from German or Austrian Rosicrucians. I add, however, that I am confident from internal evidence that the rituals, as I knew them, were in substance ancient . . . There was a little that I thought obvious and melodramatic, and it was precisely in this little, I am told, that they resembled Masonic rituals, but much that I thought beautiful and profound.[10]

Its objectives were described by the head of order, MacGregor Mathers, in a letter in 1901:

It is an association for the study of the Archaeology of Mysticism and the origin and application of Religious and Occult Symbolism. Its teachings are *strictly moral* and inculcate a profound respect for the truths of all Religions.[11]

By 1894 there were 'temples' in Edinburgh and Paris, and besides Yeats other literary figures had joined, including Arthur Machen and A. E. Waite. However, a major scandal engulfed the Order in 1901. A pair of American confidence tricksters, Frank and Editha Jackson, had used the rituals of the Golden Dawn to set up a false order, which was a cover not only for fraud but for the seduction or rape of three young women. The Order barely survived this episode, and various breakaway groups were formed. It was one of these groups, the Fellowship of the Rosy Cross, led by A. E. Waite and formed in 1915, that a young poet named Charles Williams joined in 1917.

The range of interests of these societies and orders was much wider than the discreet definition offered by Mathers. Some members, like Waite and Machen, had actually experimented with the rituals of black magic to be found in books like that of Cornelius Agrippa, albeit outside the activities of the order. Others were involved with the darker side of the *kabbalah*, the doctrines of the great Jewish religious thinkers, investigated the enigmas of the Tarot cards, or had dabbled in alchemy. This flirtation with the 'black arts' on the one hand was balanced on the other by scholarly research which explored these topics from a rational and sceptical standpoint. The two extremes of these often disorganized and quarrelsome groups are best represented by Aleister Crowley, called by the press 'the wickedest man in the world', a farcical and yet menacing practitioner of Satanic rites, who took the Rabelaisian dictum 'Do what thou wilt shall be the whole of the Law' as his philosophical motto, and by Charles Williams, poet, novelist and publisher, friend of C. S. Lewis, of whom T. S. Eliot said that he 'seemed to me to approximate, more nearly than any man I have ever known familiarly, to the saint'.[12]

In this world of symbols, mysticism and spirituality, it is not surprising that the Grail should have been a recurrent topic of discussion. A. E. Waite and Arthur Machen in 1903 'argued as fiercely as ever over the Holy Grail and all the other subjects that delighted them' and jointly wrote a verse drama, 'The Hidden Sacrament of the Holy Grail'.[13] Waite also recorded in his diary for 19 January 1903 that he had been to see Yeats, with whom he discussed the Grail legends.[14] And Charles Williams sent a copy of his first book to Waite after reading Waite's *The Hidden Church of the Holy Graal*, which had been published in 1909. But it would be wrong to position the Grail among the occult subjects studied by the members of these orders; it was a personal enthusiasm of Waite and one or two other members, rather than a central point of any hidden ritual or philosophy. Waite moved away from his early experiments with magic towards 'the possession of the

"Graces" of the Spirit, not of the "Powers"'.[15] His sequence of poems *The Book of the Holy Grail* (1921) could be read without offence by orthodox Christians and belongs firmly to the vein of late Victorian religious poetry.

A. E. Waite's work is often sound and scholarly, but he occasionally found parallels and meanings where there were none. He was the source of the link between the Grail and the Tarot cards, which has resurfaced at intervals in the wilder imaginings about the 'real' Grail, because he identified the four so-called 'Hallows of the Grail' – 'the Cup, the Lance, the Dish and the Sword' – with the four Tarot suites of cups, wands, swords and pentacles. By his own standards, the identification of pentacle and dish was far-fetched, and he added hints about occult rituals and fourteenth-century Tarot cards while at the same time mocking the 'fortune-telling rubbish' associated with the Tarot pack.[16] The best recent study of the history of the Tarot declares roundly that 'in the first three centuries of their existence, virtually the only purpose to which the Tarot pack was put was to play a certain type of card game';[17] the occult usage of the pack is bound up with eighteenth-century charlatans and nineteenth-century self-styled magicians. Its suits are simply a variation on the more familiar hearts, clubs, diamonds and spades, whose hidden meanings have never been thought worthy of investigation.

But the question of the Tarot and the Grail was small beer compared with Waite's main agenda, which he argues much more forcefully: the idea that there was a secret tradition within Christianity, '*The Hidden Church of the Holy Graal*' of his title. He argues here that

The Grail itself is in the root a Reliquary Legend. The Legend was taken over or invented and was connected with rumours of Secret Doctrine concerning the Eucharist and the Priesthood. It passed into Romance or was put forward therein, and it incorporated certain folk-lore elements which seemed adaptable to its purpose; they are naturally its hindrance . . . The Secret Doctrine reflected into the literature abode in a Secret School: it was a School of Christian Mystics and was of necessity Catholic at heart.[18]

He makes the connection between the Grail Mass and the Beatific Vision, but sees this, not as a stroke of genius of a literary imagination, but as a reflection of a real mystical practice, handed down outside the Church's teaching. 'Beyond all knowledge of the outside world, founded on faith and teaching, there is another knowledge; but it dwells in the hidden places of the mind . . .'[19] Waite cleverly avoids committing himself to the unveiling of a tangible, documented Secret Church; the final impression with which he leaves us is that the secret belongs to a group of like-minded individuals who 'know' instinctively about these mysteries. Waite was widely read, and knew the scholarly material; but his conclusions are of another order altogether:

All sacred symbols serve a need to open figurative gates and everlasting portals on the world's verge of emblems; and therefore sanctum mirabile can be said of each in definition. But that of the Holy Vessel, as it seems to me, is the 'Master Key' of all the Holy Treasures. It gives entrance into a Master Hall, and afterwards into an Inner Chapel, where Gloria in Excelsis Deo is chanted world without end.[20]

We are beyond the realms of orthodox methodology and experience; Waite quotes Elias Ashmole, the seventeenth-century scholar who explored the world of alchemy and spoke of that realm of experience of which he knew enough to hold his tongue but not enough to speak.

The Physical Grail

This insistence on the limitations of rational thought and on the value of personal mystical experience untrammelled by the bonds of ritual and doctrine was to be one of the main influences on Grail literature in England in the early twentieth century. It leads to Charles Williams' work;[21] it leads to the idea of a lost ritual of the Grail; and it leads to the New Age philosophy, which privileges personal experience over any formal or hidden knowledge. All, however, emphasize the superiority of the spiritual and its detachment from the material world, even if they sometimes secretly long to recover the physical Grail. The idea that the actual Grail, the dish of the Last Supper, might be found again was strengthened by the rise of archaeology and the spectacular discoveries of the late nineteenth century. If legendary cities such as Troy could be resurrected, why should the Grail be beyond reach? The Catholic relics which claimed to be the dish or chalice of the Last Supper were ignored, and new candidates emerged.

The first of these was linked with the occult movement, and the scene of this revelation was none other than Glastonbury, whose oblique and tentative association with the medieval Grail stories we have already discussed. At the end of the nineteenth century, Glastonbury was known as a small town with medieval ruins of some antiquarian interest, but it had lost its special place in the landscape of Britain's past. Romantic writers and artists had been inspired by the idea of Arthur's burial there. The ambiguous medieval monastic tradition, which never claimed that the Grail was at the abbey, was forgotten in favour of a version based on the romances. In 'The Holy Grail', Tennyson makes Arthur ask Perceval:

> . . . hast thou seen the Holy Cup
> That Joseph brought of old to Glastonbury?

It is impossible to pinpoint the origin of this statement; and it may well be that it is Tennyson's own invention, a half-remembered echo of the cruets of Christ's blood and sweat which were indeed preserved as relics by the monks. But once the idea was established as part of the popular folklore about Glastonbury, it was not long before it took a tangible form.

The story of the finding of the Grail at the 'Bride's Well' in Glastonbury in 1906 is a strange one, and indeed some of it may be fictional tradition.[22] The father of a West Country doctor, Dr Goodchild, acquired a small bowl of blue glass with a green surround, decorated with tiny crosses, on a visit to Bordighera in Italy in the 1890s. It was said to have been found in a cleft in a boulder, by a local peasant, and seemed old. His son, some years later, had a vision instructing him to take the bowl to the 'Women's Quarters at Glastonbury Abbey', and he did so when he inherited the bowl on his father's death in 1898, concealing it in the well there. The only person he seems to have told about this was William Sharp, otherwise known as the poet 'Fiona Macleod', author of romantic verses about the Hebrides.[23] By whatever means, the secret seems to have been passed on after Goodchild's death, and the bowl was retrieved in 1906 after another eccentric character, Wellesley Tudor Pole, had a vision in which he was given directions to send a messenger 'pure in the sight of God' to search a well at Glastonbury, which he also saw in his vision. He sent his daughter and a friend, and they identified the spot as Bride's Well. The glass cup was retrieved, and for a brief few months it was a sensation. Dom Aidan Gasquet, the distinguished Benedictine scholar, took it to Birmingham for examination; A. E. Waite and Annie Besant, president of the Theosophical Society, looked at it in London. Waite was cautious and a little sceptical, but Wellesley Tudor Pole had known Archdeacon Wilberforce, Canon of Westminster, for some thirty years. Wilberforce believed that Tudor Pole had always suffered from religious mania, but he was impressed by the change in his behaviour, and his account of the affair. It was Wilberforce who presented it to the world as the Grail on 20 July 1907. It was quickly picked up by the press, and was shown to visiting celebrities such as Mark Twain. Both the reaction of the *Daily Express*, on 26 July, and of Mark Twain are very interesting. The anonymous journalist is cool and detached:

It is good for the world to have really learned that 'there are more things in heaven and earth than dreamt of in our philosophy'. The science of the middle Victorian era was cock-sure in its materialism. It smiled loftily at the idea of miracles, it sneered at the existence of the mystic and unseen. But wisdom did not begin and end with the disciples of Darwin and Huxley . . . Certainly the more modern interest in the mystic has led to much folly and made easy much fraud. But in so far as we are moving away from a purely materialistic explanation of the universe, we are moving in the right direction . . . We express no opinion as to what the Glastonbury find may be, but it does seem to us both interesting and, in one sense, admirable, that the finding of an alleged 'holy relic' should stir the interest of a body of eminent men of widely differing opinions and culture. (*Daily Express*, 26 July 1907)[24]

Twain's account is much more highly coloured, conveying both enthusiasm and a level-headed assessment of what he was seeing:

I am glad I have lived to see that half-hour – that astonishing half-hour. In its way it stands alone in my life's experience. In the belief of two persons present this was the very vessel which was brought by night and secretly delivered to Nicodemus, nearly nineteen centuries ago, after the Creator of the Universe had delivered up his life on the cross for the redemption of the human race; the very cup which the stainless Sir Galahad has sought with knightly devotion in far fields of peril and adventure in Arthur's time, fourteen hundred years ago; the same cup which princely knights of other bygone ages had laid down their lives in long and patient efforts to find, and had passed from life disappointed – and here it was at last, dug up by a grain-broker at no cost of blood or travel, and apparently no purity required of him other than the average purity of the twentieth-century dealer in cereal futures; not even a stately name required – no Sir Galahad, no Sir Bors de Ganis, no Sir Lancelot of the Lake – nothing but a mere Mr Pole.[25]

The relic was returned to the West Country, and was kept at Clifton, in a room known as the Oratory, which was opened to visitors on request. In the absence of any real evidence as to its origin, interest gradually faded, and the 'Oratory' was closed. The cup was kept by the Pole family and is now the property of the Chalice Well Trust. It was shown to members of the Society of Antiquaries when they visited Wells in 1965, and the general opinion was that it was too well preserved to be ancient.[26]

The Glastonbury cup 'discovered' by Wellesley Tudor Pole was almost immediately challenged by another such discovery in Wales.[27] This was first discussed in a pamphlet published in Aberystwyth by an American visitor, Ethelwyn Amery, who disguised both the place where it was kept, and the name of the owner. The house was soon identified as Nanteos, the home of George Powell. Amery described how the cup had been brought from Glastonbury by seven monks, who had escaped in the nick of time, just before the arrival of the commissioners sent by Henry VIII to dissolve the abbey. They fled to the abbey of Strata Florida near Aberystwyth, where the owners gave them shelter even though the abbey had passed into private hands. When the last of the monks died, the cup passed to the family 'until the Church should claim its own'. In due course Strata Florida came by marriage to the Powells; the cup is not recorded before the middle of the nineteenth century, and was probably found at the abbey at some time during the previous hundred years. It was first seen in public in 1878, when it was described as having marvellous powers of healing. Recent archaeological analysis has shown it to be a mazer-bowl made of wych-elm, of late medieval date, a valuable but by no means uncommon piece; most monasteries would have owned a number of them.

How could a casual find of such a medieval wooden vessel be transformed into a new Holy Grail? The story of the flight from Glastonbury seems to have been deliberately invented using antiquarian accounts of the dissolution of the monasteries. No historical evidence has ever been offered for the story; the reputation of the cup grows by being repeatedly asserted. Such 'invented' legends are nonetheless extraordinarily resilient: the Nanteos story survived the criticism of Jessie Weston soon after it was first published, as well as the hostility of the supporters of the Glastonbury cup. It belongs to a similar genre to the 'urban myths' of modern folklore, where the eye-witness is always known to an acquaintance and the evidence is never direct. Such stories reveal more about the attitudes and aspirations of the society in which they were created than about any lost history. But the myth of the Nanteos Grail is alive and flourishing, as a search on the Internet will show.

Two archaeological discoveries in Palestine were briefly hailed as Grails, with a little more plausibility than the Nanteos cup. Both were called 'the Antioch cup'; the first was discovered in a cave near that city in the 1930s, and was exhibited in London in 1935. It was an intact Roman glass bowl with a stem, in a wooden case of later date, a fine example of its kind. A pamphlet of the time[28] identified it as one of the 'four cups of the Passover' and cautiously captioned the photograph of it 'reputed to be associated with the Holy Grail'. But an advertisement in *The Times* confidently declared that 'THE HOLY GRAIL' would be on show on 1 August at the Palestine and Bible Lands exhibition, earning a stiff rebuke from the editor of *Antiquity* who wrote: 'we should be glad to be told exactly how the adver-tiser knows that the "newly discovered cup" is the Holy Grail . . .'[29]

The second Antioch cup is in the Cloisters at the Metropolitan Museum in New York, and is part of the Antioch treasure, a collection of liturgical objects discovered outside the city in about 1910. Its outer silver-gilt framework supports a glass vessel which was supposed to be the cup of the Last Supper, on no better grounds than the London example. This was exhibited at the Chicago World Fair in 1933 by its then owners as the Holy Grail, and when it was displayed at Harvard in 1937, armed guards were posted round it, and visitors were not allowed closer than a yard from it. It was bought by the Cloisters in 1950; it is a spectacular piece, but the museum's website states cautiously that it 'is now assumed to be no earlier than the sixth century'. The idea that the Grail must be a glass chalice recurs in a lecture given in Manchester in 1927, where the speaker declared, after examining half a dozen examples of glass cups from the area of Palestine in the first century, that '*The Holy Grail was a glass cup with a Greek Legend on it*', the 'legend' being the words spoken by Jesus to Judas in St Matthew's Gospel.[30] The same certainty that the Grail could, and would, be found is once again to the fore.

In the last half-century the Arthurian legends have been transformed from an antiquarian curiosity and a topic for a handful of poets and artists into one of the most frequently revisited areas of a new type of popular culture. Arthur himself appeals to the public interest in historical mysteries, and to the increasing enthusiasm in Britain for local history. The trickle of scholarly efforts to identify Arthur as an actual figure, which began in the nineteenth century, has now become a spate; contributions may come from distinguished academics or from complete amateurs, but because there is so little material to work on, it is possible to create seemingly plausible theories which are difficult to refute. The only problem is that it is also impossible to go beyond mere theorizing. This, however, has encouraged rather than discouraged the audience; even better, the subject ties in very well with popular archaeology, which is always on the verge of producing the crucial hard evidence which will solve the mystery once and for all. Archaeology also provides the link with local history: claiming Arthur for a particular place is no longer merely a matter of local pride, but has potential real rewards in terms of attracting tourists. The use – and often misuse – of history as a sales pitch for a wide range of products outside tourism is another recent phenomenon, which underlines the insatiable public demand for identification with the past.

The latest discovery of the Grail belongs firmly in this context. It is *The Search for the Grail* by Graham Phillips, which localizes the Grail tradition on the border between England and Wales, and relies heavily on the slender but interesting connection between *Fouke Fitz Waryn*, a romance about one of the border lords, *Perlesvaus* and Glastonbury Abbey.* Phillips 'finds' an onyx cup of uncertain date which may or may not be the Grail, and which seems to have been placed in the base of a statue of the eagle of St John in a grotto at Hawkstone Park by the antiquary Thomas Wright in the 1850s. The result seems a feeble reward for the hype that surrounded the book; perhaps the author would have had a better story if he had realized that among Wright's publications was a pioneering edition of texts relating to sorcery and magic, which could have tied in with the Tarot and other occult topics which he explores in the course of his search.[31]

Of these five 'discoveries' of the real Grail the most significant was that at Glastonbury, which was part of the establishment of Glastonbury's image as a centre of ancient spiritual power. The development of the modern traditions associated with Glastonbury is far from clear; the name 'Chalice Well', with its obvious overtones of the Grail, seems to be eighteenth century, but many of the other stories that are now given as long-established are probably the result of this early twentieth-century enthusiasm. The extent to which this had spread is shown by the fact that when the abbey itself was put up for auction by private owners in 1907, it was very nearly bought by a group of Americans who intended to found a 'school of Chivalry' there. And occultists such as the writer Dion Fortune (Violet Firth) were attracted to Glastonbury; she was a member of one of the successors to the original Order of the Golden Dawn, and deeply involved in theosophy. Her book *Avalon of the Heart* was typical of the kind of enthusiasm that the Abbey and its surroundings now aroused, and in her writings she invoked not only its Christian past, but also 'the ancient faith of the Britons . . . its relics obliterated, its legends bent to a Christian purpose . . . shadowy and veiled'.[32] The idea of a literal Grail presence at Glastonbury resurfaces from time to time, as in Flavia Anderson's *The Ancient Secret* (1953) which offers us a Grail which is a crystal sphere used to generate fire, at the centre of mysteries celebrated in 'the British Hades', which proves to be none other than the famous caves at Wookey Hole.[33]

The Secret Tradition

At the opposite extreme to the searchers for a physical Grail are those who see the Grail as emblem of a secret tradition within the Christian Church. The kernel of the idea of a 'secret' about the Grail is, as we have

* See p. 132 above.

seen, part of the earliest Grail romances: but there it is a theological secret, the secret of the Mass of the Catholic Church. In effect, that secret is the Church's way of saying that the doctrines surrounding the Mass are too subtle for ordinary people to understand. But the Grail romances can also be read 'as a great attempt in the middle ages to combat the supremacy of Rome in the history of the propagation of the doctrines of the Church, and to substitute another authority for that of St Peter'.[34] How real this attempt may have been is very much open to question, but it has been argued by modern scholars that there were just such hidden or heretical trends which relate to the Grail.

One line of argument sees these trends as being within the Church itself. Behind the outward forms of faith and worship centred on the Eucharist, there was a second layer of initiation and secret knowledge, in which the Eucharist was represented by the Grail.[35] The first and outward layer is represented by the work of St Peter and St Paul; the second by St John and Joseph of Arimathea. In this scheme of things, Joseph, who is a minor, almost unknown figure in the Gospels, becomes the central figure in the hidden tradition, a tradition which persisted at least until the end of the seventeenth century. Joseph, as the 'secret disciple' of Jesus[36] and guardian of his body, is seen as the head of this alternative tradition, the record of which was deliberately suppressed in the Gospels. In St John's Gospel, he is said to have kept his adherence to Christ's teachings secret 'for fear of the Jews'; but this is seen as a later addition, making the secrecy of his belief the crucial point – John is indicating that the whole secret tradition, otherwise unrecorded, actually exists. The Grail, in this tradition, is a substitute – more direct than in the Mass – for Christ's body. The problem is that the evidence for such a hidden cult comes largely from two sources: the Grail romances themselves, which, as we have seen, are not a likely means of transmitting discussions about theology (let alone a secret and potentially highly controversial doctrine); and from selective reading among the huge mass of tracts on the vexed question of transubstantiation. This version of the 'secret tradition' is, at the end of the day, only what had once been orthodox belief, overlaid with the legendary history of Joseph of Arimathea.

A similar scheme for a secret doctrine of the Grail brings in as evidence Wolfram's *Parzival*, and with it a whole host of exotic elements; here we have a 'defined doctrine', either contained in a book, as in Robert de Boron, or explained by a master (such as Trevrizent in *Parzival*).[37] 'This doctrine concerns a Mystery present on earth, *in the fullness of its celestial power*, which can only be accessed through a path of qualification and in danger of death.' It is kept in a hidden centre (the Grail castle) and has its own special liturgy. But the presence of this doctrine can only be explained in terms of traditional esoteric teachings, which are self-referring, and cannot be subjected to normal scientific criticism. However, it has been argued that examination of the Islamic influences found in Wolfram reveals the sources of this tradition, which draws also on the Jewish esoteric lore. To validate this argument, we have to accept the reality of 'Kyot' as Wolfram's source: but we also have to accept connections between Kyot's Flegetanis, whom Wolfram calls a 'fisîôn', and the Order of the Knights Templar. Solomon was seen in Islamic tradition as a philosopher of cosmic sciences, to which 'fisîôn' seems to relate – it is a word coined by Wolfram, with overtones of both physician and philosopher – and the Templars were called the 'soldiers of the temple of Solomon'; so the two traditions can be loosely linked. But links like these are difficult to prove or to disprove, and the method of argument is all too often to add further assertions – Flegetanis is really the name of an Arab book, *Felek Thani* or the second sphere, he is associated with the evangelist's sign of the bull, and so forth. Any contradictory point in Wolfram's text is put down to the fact that he is protecting 'the secret of the transmission [of the story] which he was revealing against the horrible misunderstanding of ordinary people'. And so the readings and misreadings and speculations go on: the combat between Feirefiz and Parzival is a symbol of the 'essential unity of Christianity and Islam (and implicitly, at least, of Judaism)'.[38] Once the Celtic elements are brought in, the Grail becomes the 'repository, spiritual and doctrinal, of the primordial Tradition'.

This 'primordial Tradition' leads us back into the occult revival of the 1890s, and to the Theosophists. But it was a French writer, René Guénon, who regarded the Theosophical Society with deep suspicion, who developed this idea in relation to the Grail in his book *Le Roi du Monde* (*The King of the World*, 1925). Guénon argues that folklore may contain fragments, however distorted or reduced, of things which, 'far from being of popular origin, are not even human in origin'.[39] He sees in the symbols common to different cultures evidence for a body of pre-Christian learning based on initiation rites, which is neither Celtic, nor Oriental, nor pagan in origin, but stems from the lost universal 'primordial Tradition' in a specific and tangible way. This tradition stems from a 'universal revelation' in the earliest days of mankind from which all the great religions of the world stem. The Grail, cut from an emerald which fell from Lucifer's crown, was kept by Adam in the earthly paradise. But when he was expelled from Eden, he was unable to take it with him. Seth, his descendant, was able to re-enter paradise and recover the Grail. Its history was then unknown until it was used at the Last Supper; it may have been kept by the Druids, which would account for the Celtic stories about it. The 'blood of Christ' which it contains is a kind of *soma*, the draught which confers immortality in Hindu and Persian myth.[40] The quest for the Grail in Arthurian romance is a metaphor for the recovery of the lost tradition. The Grail itself is kept in a place invisible to all except initiates; it has its appointed guardians, whose main role is to preserve and hand on the primordial tradition. All this must be read on a symbolic rather than literal plane; and the traces of the myth which appear in medieval writers are not evidence that many knew and understood it, or were initiated into its rituals. They may have been chosen to retell the stories, and given hints and fragments of the knowledge of the Grail in order to do so. Nor should we imagine a formal structure to all this in terms of societies and rituals; the world of Guénon's Grail works on a spiritual rather than physical plane. Guénon postulates that the 'primordial tradition' remains oral, and that even its current forms are extremely ancient.

Guénon offers the most elaborate version of the Grail myth as such to have been put forward in the twentieth century. If it has indirectly influenced other writers, its impact generally has been slight; writers such as Patrick Rivière have restated his conclusions, declaring that 'the Graal myth by itself is the synthesis of the primordial tradition', and warning the unwary against false interpretations of the transcendent image.[41] One follower, however, needs to be recorded: this was Julius Evola, whose book *The mystery of the Grail and the Ghibelline tradition of Empire* appeared in 1937. Evola sees the Grail legends as being of specifically Celtic or, rather, Irish/Aryan origin, and as offering an image of a heroic society where an elite group pursues spiritual transcendence while at the same time defending the material world from the powers of chaos and darkness which threaten it. He discusses the Christian versions of the myths, which he sees as a dilution and distortion of the original ideas, and much of his thinking was influenced by his interest in Buddhism. He uses Guénon's ideas as a kind of universalist background, but also to argue his specific theme – that it is not the Church but the pagan Empire which is really the inheritor of the ancient spiritual powers. As a result, the 'king of the world' is no longer a spiritual figure, but the medieval Holy Roman Empire, whose Italian supporters were known as Ghibellines. Evola looks forward to the revival of this empire, in a right-wing form, though he avoids specific support for Fascist ideas on the new *imperium*. In the epilogue to the original Italian edition, he quotes the famous forgery of the 'Protocols of the Elders of Zion' (which he had translated into Italian) as evidence that the modern mind was seeking a new universal empire; whether the Protocols were true or not, they were evidence that such ideas were in circulation, albeit in a perverted, 'world

Jewish-masonic conspiracy', form. The ideal of the Grail was similarly being undermined by an 'intelligence' which directed its efforts into creating a kind of inverted image of the reality: 'the modern epoch . . . ends by turning the action on its head, into its opposite . . . on another level the concept of the nordic tradition and an Aryan super-race is asserted by some as zoological materialism and political mythology'.[42] The emperor and the hero of the Grail who vindicates and restores belong, not to a dead romantic past, but 'are the truth of those who today can alone legitimately call themselves alive'. Evola mixes rhetoric, prejudice, scholarship and politics into a strange version of the present and future, but in the process he brings together for the first time the interest in the esoteric and in conspiracy theory which characterize much of later Grail literature.

The Templars and the Grail

Both Guénon and Evola evoke the Templars and Cathars as guardians of this hidden spiritual tradition, and it is to the attempts to reconstruct in historical rather than esoteric terms the presumed Templar or Cathar Grail, and the hidden Christian tradition, that we now turn. The association of the Templars and the Grail, on the face of it, is extremely implausible. They were a practical military order, whose spirituality seems to have been that of the knightly class from which most of their members were drawn, highly organized and very disciplined but with absolutely no interest in mysticism or the higher levels of theology. There is no trace in any medieval source of an association between the Templars and the literature on the Grail, and the earliest suggestion of such a possibility comes from a very unexpected quarter, the great German critic Lessing, writing in the 1770s. Lessing, who was the librarian at the ducal library at Wolfenbüttel in Saxony, had certainly read the Grail romances,[43] and it was from him that Friedrich Schlegel got the idea of a possible connection between them and the Templars. In a lecture in Vienna in 1812 Schlegel said:

We can take it . . . that not only the ideal of a spiritual knight, as it was in men's minds in the time in which the pre-eminent religious orders of knighthood of the period arose and flourished, but also many of the symbolic concepts and traditions which some of these orders, especially the Templars, had among themselves, are set down in these poems. Lessing, who was the first as far as I know to remark on this and who examined the question very carefully, was in a good position to judge . . .[44]

Lessing had come to Templar history through his involvement with Free-masonry, and had read widely on the subject.[45] He knew not only a number of historical works which had recently appeared in Germany on the Order, but also that the Templars had been adopted as part of the Masonic past by eighteenth-century Scottish Freemasons. The connection between the crusading orders and the masons was made, apparently for the first time, by a Scottish mason, Andrew Michael Ramsay, in a speech to Freemasons in Paris on 21 March 1737, in which he said:

At the time of the Crusades in Palestine, many princes, lords, and citizens associated themselves, and vowed to restore the Temple of the Christians in the Holy Land, and to employ themselves in bringing back their architecture to its first institution. They agreed upon several ancient signs and symbolic words drawn from the well of religion in order to recognise themselves amongst the heathen and Saracens . . .

Sometime afterwards our Order formed an intimate union with the Knights of St John of Jerusalem. From that time our Lodges took the name of Lodges of Saint John.

Our Order therefore must not be considered a revival of the Bacchanals, votaries of Bacchus, drunken revellers, but as an Order founded in remote antiquity, and renewed in the Holy Land by our ancestors in order to recall the memory of the most sublime truths amidst the pleasures of society.[46]

This address is to some extent a reflection of Ramsay's other theories: he was a student of mythology, and regarded the pagan gods as representing aspects of the One God.[47] In the same way, the different civilizations have a common organization devoted to the 'most sublime truths'. The text was quickly adopted as part of Masonic history, and appears in an account of the order published in Frankfurt in 1742; it was frequently reprinted in Masonic handbooks for the rest of the eighteenth century.

The only problem is that Ramsay does not mention the Templars, but associated the Freemasons with the Knights of St John or Hospitallers. How the transition to the Templars came about is not clear, but it seems to have been in Germany, where around 1760 at least three versions of the Masonic/Templar connection were in circulation.[48] Lessing undoubtedly knew at least one of these myths, and was also interested in the Templars per se. He used a Templar as an important character in his play *Nathan the Wise*, though there are no Masonic connotations. He also wrote five dialogues, *Ernst und Falk*, between a Freemason and a layman who is curious about the Masonic orders and is thinking of joining them. At one point, Lessing describes the popular beliefs about the masons, particularly those who followed the Scottish rites: among would-be members 'one wants to make gold, another to summon up spirits, a third to reinstate the Templars'.[49] However, although Schlegel's comment seems genuine, I have not been able to track down any specific discussion of the Grail romances and their Templar associations in Lessing's work: so we are left, as so often, with an enigma. It seems that we cannot discover how the Grail first appeared in this context of secret knowledge, a secret knowledge which in turn had been spuriously attributed to the Freemasons; their secrets were more to do with passwords and rituals than any great secret tradition handed down from the past.

However, one connection between the Templars and the Grail itself as object was made very soon after Schlegel's lecture by the Austrian oriental expert Joseph von Hammer-Purgstall, in a huge folio volume which appeared in Vienna in 1818 as part of a series on Eastern source material. Hammer-Purgstall had some knowledge of Masonic lore, and believed, as did many conservatives, that the masons were at the centre of plots against the Austrian and other orthodox Roman Catholic governments. He suspected them of propagating 'Templar' doctrines as part of this scheme; since the Templars had been condemned for heretical practices and the Order had been dissolved in 1307, such doctrines must have been part of the masons' subversive efforts against Catholicism. He therefore set out to prove that the Templars had indeed been justly condemned, and his account was based on carvings, which, so he asserted, were really idols that showed there was a Templar cult of 'Baphomet'. The worship of such an idol had been one of the main accusations in the trial of 1307. He believed this cult to be a version of the Ophite form of Gnosticism, in which the serpent who tempted Eve to eat of the Tree of Knowledge in Genesis was revered for teaching mankind to become aware of its true condition – a heresy against which the Fathers of the Early Church had fulminated. He found twenty-four examples of heads of Baphomet, as well as vases, in the form of Greek two-handled 'kraters', which were associated with these heads. In describing the 'kraters', he suddenly announces, although nothing in the previous argument relates to it:

After this there can be no doubt that this is that most famous cup of the middle ages known under the name of Holy Graal, which signifies the symbol of the Templar community of gnostic wisdom.[50]

He goes on to refer to *Later Titurel*, describing briefly the temple at 'Monsalvaz' where the Grail was kept, and the fact that it was guarded by

Templeisen, which he translates as Templars. He goes on to argue that if the Grail is the symbol of Gnostic wisdom, the Round Table represents the twelve Templars who, according to him, ruled the Order, though the number of knights at the Round Table is never specified as twelve; these knights were the guardians of the Grail. He goes on to find another representation of the 'Gral' on a so-called statue of Baphomet, and proposes that GRAL is an acronym for a Gnostic motto in Latin, 'Gnosis Regit Animas Liberas' or perhaps 'Gnosis Retribuit Animi Laborem'. All this nonsense is overlaid with a veneer of learning, and Hammer-Purgstall was undoubtedly learned in his field. But here he was in uncharted waters, and ended by inventing his own maps. The conclusion of his work is that a pagan religion survived alongside Catholicism into the Middle Ages, and in the guise of Freemasonry remained a threat to the Church even in the early nineteenth century. This was the message his political masters wanted to hear – he was a diplomat under Metternich, the Austrian foreign minister – but behind this there was also the Romantic passion for the primitive, an appeal to primeval myths which had existed before Christianity.

The scenario created by Hammer-Purgstall has proved irresistible to many Grail enthusiasts since his day. The crucial link is provided by Wolfram's use of the word *Templeisen* for the guardians of the Grail, by which he almost certainly meant 'templar' with a lower case 't' rather than the Order of Knights Templar. But this is a matter of opinion, not susceptible to proof, and the field is therefore open to all sorts of speculative connections. San Marte (Alwin Schulz), who translated *Parzival* in 1842, repeated some of Hammer-Purgstall's ideas in his study of the Arthurian legends in 1841,[51] pointing out the parallel between the head on a dish in *Peredur* (which he identified with the Grail) and the Templar worship of Baphomet. He claimed that the Templars believed that Baphomet made trees and forests blossom, thereby providing a link to the vegetation myths later expounded in *The Golden Bough* and their implications for the Waste Land theme in the Grail romances. Jessie Weston, too, was tempted into speculation about the Templars. Having suggested that the Grail was connected with the rites of an obscure third-century Gnostic sect called the Naassenes, she then conjectured that the Templars were in contact with their twelfth-century successors, and that the Grail and its secrets were so dangerous and heretical that the Templars had to be suppressed.[52] In support of this, she pointed out that the creation of Grail romances ceases about the time that the Order was disbanded.

The Conspiracy Theory of History and the Grail

The Templar-Grail myth was not seriously revived until the last two decades of the twentieth century. It is at the heart of the most notorious of all the Grail pseudo-histories, *The Holy Blood and the Holy Grail*, which is a classic example of the conspiracy theory of history. For 'conspirators', history is not bunk, as Henry Ford famously described it, but in its orthodox form it is a vast deception practised by those in power to cover up the truth. Historical evidence is, of course, uncertain and susceptible to different interpretations, and when doubts surround even such recent events as the assassination of President Kennedy, it is easy to see why the certainties offered by an alternative version of history are so attractive. It would take a book as long as the original to refute and dissect *The Holy Blood and the Holy Grail* point by point: it is essentially a text which proceeds by innuendo, not by refutable scholarly debate. A crucial link in the story relies on an anonymous informant and the fact that a man named by him had been acquainted in Paris many years earlier with another character in the supposed sequence of events. Essentially, the whole argument is an ingeniously constructed series of suppositions combined with forced readings of such tangible facts as are offered. It is the framework of the book that is the real point of interest. It begins with a mystery: how did a parish priest in the Cevennes acquire a large enough fortune to spend adorning his church at Rennes-le-Château with mysterious inscriptions and paintings? In effect, the ingredients are those of a treasure hunt, in which 'the treasure' changes from financial wealth into a secret of world-shaking importance. Central to the inquiry are a supposed mass of documents in the Bibliothèque Nationale, consisting of pamphlets about the small village where the church in question stands. These, from the description given by the authors, seem to be the harmless fantasies which surface from time to time – all too familiar to any publisher remotely connected with historical publishing – from imaginative amateurs who believe that they suddenly hold the key to 'life, the universe and everything'. It is a genre, which, if it were not usually so tedious, would repay study as a manifestation of twentieth-century popular culture: a good folklorist would be able to classify it in the way that 'urban myths' have been studied. The usual source is a debased – or perhaps not necessarily even debased – form of the more extreme writings of eighteenth- and nineteenth-century Freemasons or their sympathizers. This is then combined with cryptography and the innuendo we have already mentioned, and an apparent case is built up: 'By means of cryptic asides and footnotes, each piece . . . enlarges on and confirms the others.'[53] This is the authors' own description of the material on which their argument rests, and it perfectly describes their procedures.

How does this lead us to the Grail? The authors describe the 'intrusion of the Grail into our inquiry' and wonder if there was a 'continuity under-lying and connecting them'. That continuity is provided by a series of statements based on eighteenth- and nineteenth-century inventions about the Grail: in three sentences we have the Cathars as owners of the Grail, the Templars as its custodians, and the Templar heads as parallels for the Grail.[54] On the way, they manage to read the symbolic scenes in romances such as *Perlesvaus* as obscure allusions to crimes of which the Templars are said to have been accused.[55]

This is the excuse for a rapid survey of the Grail stories, and we are told that 'modern scholars concur that the Grail romances ... refer to the Merovingian period', which may surprise readers of the present book some-what. At this point, there is an excursus on the 'need to synthesise', a thinly veiled attack on 'experts' and on the specialist nature of modern university research:

What is necessary is an interdisciplinary approach to one's chosen material – a mobile and flexible approach that permits one to move freely between disparate disciplines, across space and time. One must be able to link data and make connec-tions between people, events and phenomena widely divorced from each other. One must be able to move, as necessity dictates, from the third to the twelfth to the seventh to the eighteenth centuries ...[56]

And 'it is not sufficient to confine oneself exclusively to facts'. This is carte blanche to create an imaginary network of previously invisible links – which is precisely what the authors proceeed to do, in what they call 'our hypothesis'. The mistaken fifteenth-century etymology of the Grail as 'Sang real', John Hardyng's secularization of the Grail, is quoted as definitive: a misreading or whim of an English writer perhaps not entirely at ease with French becomes the key to the whole mystery. If the Holy Grail is not the 'sang real' or 'blood royal', the whole argument (such as it is) falls to the ground, and the splendidly imaginative construction of a 'bloodline' of Merovingian kings descended from a Jesus who was never crucified can have no connection with the Grail, or indeed anything else in the real world. Once again, the Grail's true function seems to be as a lodestar for imaginative creation, in this case disguised as history but in truth imaginative indeed.

There is a further element in the Rennes-le-Château affair. The origin of the book lies in a television documentary. Attractive television is exactly the antithesis of the sort of arena where complex subjects can be investigated reliably; it is inevitable, given that a script for a half-hour programme runs to perhaps 3,000 words of spoken dialogue – roughly seven pages of this book – that arguments have to be reduced to statements, and the problem of how one set of facts links to the next has to be ignored or indicated by a couple of sentences. The style of such documentaries means that an enormous amount of trust must be placed in the expertise and veracity of the presenter. There is no room for the detailed proof. *The Holy Blood and the Holy Grail* is, in effect, a book written in the style of a television programme. But instead of being based on the distillation of research, it is as if the script was written first, giving the main line of inquiry and the solution, and the proofs and links were filled in afterwards. We have in a way come full circle: we began at a time when oral culture was turning into written culture, and now we find that written culture is dominated by a new oral culture.

The methodology of *The Holy Blood and the Holy Grail* has become widely popular. Two other authors re-examined the supposed evidence, and concocted an equally wild theory, that the 'core of the treasure is a strange artifact, an inexplicable power source created by some ancient, long-forgotten technology, or brought to Earth in a starship . . .' whose qualities enabled its owners to accumulate a huge treasure.[57] At least they have the grace to admit that 'there is, of course, no proof for this theory'; we are in effect dealing with a new genre, fictional history. Another good example of it is Andrew Sinclair's work on the links between the supposed Scottish Templar tradition and the Grail, in which his own family, the Saint Clairs, figure largely. The trail leads from Rosslyn Chapel, once owned by the Sinclairs and allegedly full of secret Templar and Masonic symbols, to a supposed Venetian account of a Scottish expedition to America in 1400, and ends in a Masonic lodge at Kirkwall whose 'secret scroll' is the key to all mysteries.[58] The Grail supposedly lies concealed in a secret vault in Rosslyn Chapel.

This genre is perhaps best described as 'selective history'; historical facts which favour the argument are adduced as proof that the whole is true, ignoring their context and any contrary evidence. Sometimes the result is, on the surface, well-documented and referenced, and involves genuine historical research. A good example is Noel Currer-Briggs' attempt to link the Holy Shroud of Turin, the Holy Grail and the Templars in *The Shroud and the Grail*. Here the Grail becomes the casket in which the Shroud of Turin, imprinted with Christ's image and soaked in his blood and sweat, is housed. The tradition which connects the Grail so intimately to the concept of Christ's redeeming blood is dismissed because 'the very idea [of collecting blood as a relic] is revolting'.[59] Perhaps this is true for modern sensibilities, but not for the relic-hungry medieval believers, who longed for tangible contact with their Saviour.

The Cathars and the Grail

Another treasure-hunt leads us to the Cathars. On the face of it, the Cathars are as unlikely to be connected with the Grail as the Templars; the Grail represents exactly those aspects of Christianity which they rejected – the essentially Christocentric rituals of the Church. For them Christ was not the central figure in their worship, but merely the messenger, bearer of the new gospel of love. The Crucifixion and Resurrection were not part of their belief. So the Grail, which meant nothing without these two central tenets, could mean nothing to them. We have seen how in terms of the medieval romances such an association is unlikely. But, as we have also seen, the idea that Arthurian literature might have originated in the south of France was put forward in the early nineteenth century by Claude Fauriel; he had suggested that Munsalvaesche was in the Pyrenees, observing that the romances almost never called a place by its real name.[60] A variant of this idea was offered in 1858 by E. Aroux, in *Mysteries of Chivalry and of Platonic Love in the Middle Ages*, which sets out to show that the chivalric literature of the Middle Ages centred on courtly love was the creation of the Albigensians (Cathars), as a way of spreading their doctrines in a disguised form. Courtly love was outwardly a form of platonic love; in fact, it was the code for the Albigensians' insistence on love rather than the formalities of religion. It was in order to preserve and propagate these ideas that what Aroux calls 'la Massenie du Saint-Graal' was founded, a mysterious society the objective of whose members was 'to recover the vessel of truth with luminous characters wherein was received the Precious Blood of the Saviour; in other words, to bring back the Christian church to the time of the apostles, to the faithful observation of the precepts of the Gospel'.[61] The Round Table was composed of *perfect* knights (corresponding to the *perfecti* of the Albigenses). A knight was only admitted to it after a series of trials; 'we may get an idea of the manner in which a knight was received and of the precautions taken against indiscretion through the practices of freemasonry today, which is only a continuation of *massenie*'. Their squires were the companions (*socii*) who, according to Aroux, accompanied the Albigensian *perfecti*. And the object of their devotion was their lady-church, their parish or diocese; the jealous husband, theme of so much troubadour poetry, represents the established clergy whose authority the Albigensians rejected. 'Chivalry, invented and set to work by Albigensian protestantism, is only a symbol.'[62]

Aroux seems to have been the inspiration for a much more influential work half a century later. This was the work of none other than our old friend Sâr Méradock, Joséphin Péladan, whose pamphlet on the subject appeared in 1906, and whose elder brother is said to have known Aroux through Rosicrucian circles.[63] Its title was *The secret of the troubadours: from Perceval to Don Quixote*, and it was really a general study of medieval chivalric literature. The 'secret' was no more than the continuity between medieval literature and the age of Rabelais and Cervantes:

Before seeking the oracle of the *dive bouteille* [in Rabelais], our naïve ancestor sought the Holy Grail. In defeat, he is called Don Quixote: this is *the secret of the troubadours*.[64]

He goes on to draw a parallel between the historical Templars and 'the order of the Grail', which does not actually exist in medieval literature, and between Monsalvat and Montségur, claiming that 'the Albigensian soul, whatever the somewhat vague meaning of this may be, is the soul of Parsifal, a manifestation of the esoterism of the Middle Ages from which the Renaissance emerged'.[65]

He links, somewhat tentatively, Cathar beliefs and the Arthurian romances, saying that

around the Round Table . . . and at the foot of the Grail, a relic entrusted by angels to the purest of men, you will find, with a little attention, a belief which, well before the Reformation, endangered Catholic unity, and which alone makes sense of the literary and artistic work of the west . . . between the year 1000 and the end of the sixteenth century.[66]

It was this pamphlet which came to the attention of a young German scholar, Otto Rahn, who intended to write a thesis on the links between mysticism and twelfth-century poetry, and their influence on the German medieval mentality. As part of this project, he undertook research on the Cathars, and when he found himself in a position to travel to the Pyrenees and to visit Montségur, he was inspired to do so by the work of Maurice Magre, who in *Magicians and Illuminati*[67] had linked Hindu philosophy with the Cathars, whom he called 'the Buddhists of the West'. On his way to Provence, Rahn worked at the Bibliothèque Nationale in Paris, where he found Péladan's pamphlet. In the south, he met a local historian, Antonin Gadal, who had similar ideas, and who pressed on Rahn his book *On the Track of the Holy Grail*, which localized the final resting place of the Grail at Ussat. It seems to have been Maurice Magre who first identified the legendary Cathar treasure as the Holy Grail.[68] This treasure, according to evidence from members of the Cathar garrison at the time, was taken from Montségur, the site of their last stand against the forces of orthodoxy, just before it fell in 1244.[69]

Rahn took up the story with enthusiasm, and his book *Crusade against the Grail* (1933) is the text in which the story of the Cathar Grail came to general attention. His thesis depends on identifying 'Kyot', the supposed source of Wolfram's *Parzival*, with Guiot de Provins, and, by using the sparse physical descriptions of places given by Wolfram, finding their equivalents in the Cathar homeland. The identification of Munsalvaesche with Montségur, for instance, is based on a line in *Parzival* which says 'Never was a dwelling so well fitted for defence as Munsalvaesche', which supposedly corresponds to 'safe mountain', said to be the meaning of the name Montségur.[70] Wolfram's phrase is simply a way of praising the strength of Munsalvaesche, and the explanation of the name Montségur is at best doubtful. An equally dubious etymology turns Parzival into Trencavel, surname of one of the Cathar leaders, and this leads to yet more identifications of leading characters in the poem with Cathar lords.[71] A further confirmation of the identity of Montségur as the Grail castle is the idea found at the end of the Middle Ages, that the Grail is the Venusberg, home of the pagan goddess of love; Montségur is claimed as a pagan site.[72] What the Grail itself actually is remains undefined: it is identified with the treasure of the Cathars, mentioned in documents of the Inquisition at Carcassonne: four of the Cathars are said to have escaped from the siege of the castle with 'the treasure of the heretics'.[73] But what became of this 'treasure' is uncertain, and Rahn is wisely vague about it, claiming only that they saved 'the desire of Paradise, as Wolfram calls it, symbolised by a shining stone, the Grail!'[74] Certainly, nothing in the last chapter of his book implies that he thought it was a physical object hidden in the cave where the last Cathar followers met their death, at Sabarthès: this story was put about by local enthusiasts.

But Rahn's next book, *The Courtiers of Lucifer* (1937), recounted his travels in the Cathar lands and elsewhere in Europe in search of the Cathars and their philosophy, and of the troubadours, whom, like Péladan, he regarded as closely connected with the Cathars. In the course of his travels, he develops his thesis in terms all too familiar from Nazi propaganda of the period. The Cathars were said to be Aryans who worshipped the morning star, Lucifer.[75] Christianity was invented by the Jews, who tried to make men worship a Jew, Jesus of Nazareth.[76] The Grail was the symbol of

Lucifer, and was the great treasure of the Cathars for that reason, while the Church had invented the story of the Grail as the cup of the Last Supper to discredit the Cathar relic, which they knew to be the true Grail.[77] Because Rahn was an ardent Nazi, stories began to circulate that the Nazis had mounted a search for the Cathar Grail. Rahn was supposed to have had a double identity, and to have been acting on the highest orders.[78] Similarly, he was supposed to have sent a package of his 'finds' at Montségur to Heinrich Himmler; these 'finds' were said to include something which 'Rahn believed was the true Grail'.[79] Other sources say that members of a French right-wing society conducted a dig in Cathar territory in search of 'the runic tablets which according to certain rumours were at the root of the text of Wolfram . . .'[80] Alfred Rosenberg, whose book *The Myth of the Twentieth Century* is one of the key texts of Nazi doctrines, is said to have started a kind of pagan Nazi religion; it is reputed that a gold cup on the lines of the Grail was made for him.[81] He was also meant to have started a kind of pagan order in which Himmler was involved, and the latter was said to have made Wolfram's *Parzival* his bedside reading. When local people gathered at Montségur on the exact day of the 700th anniversary of its fall a German aircraft is said to have flown over the ruins, tracing a Celtic cross in the sky. But none of those present seem to have made a formal statement to this effect; even more improbable is the suggestion that Rosenberg was on board. Since Rosenberg devotes a bare four or five lines to Catharism in *The Myth of the Twentieth Century*, the story is little more than a later embroidery on the story of the pilgrimage of 1944.[82] But all these stories turn out to be mere assertions, with no hard evidence behind them.[83] They belong to the world of the Nazi quest for the Grail in Steven Spielberg's film *Indiana Jones and the Last Crusade* (1989), and they have been the basis for a number of novels, including Pierre Benoit's *Montsalvat* (1957), which had considerable local success, and Marc Augier's *Nouveaux cathares pour Montségur* (1969), published under the pseudonym Saint-Loup, which has a splendid array of extreme right-wing myths. The problem is that fiction has spilled over into history, and apparently historical books and television programmes have been based on this heady mixture, in which, as so often when dealing with the Grail, imagination plays a much greater part than reality.[84]

One last fable deserves a brief airing. It is seriously suggested that the Nazis wanted to find the Grail, in case its powers would be of use to them. The organization entrusted with this search was said to be the *Ahnenerbe*, better known from the Nuremberg trials for a series of gruesome scientific experiments connected with racism. The *Ahnenerbe* was indeed involved in archaeology and prehistory, but with the object of proving that the Aryan race was the precursor of all civilization; the excavations under its aegis were generally conducted in a scholarly manner, but the interpretation of the finds was falsified to suit propaganda purposes. There were no treasure hunts; indeed, one of the organization's positive actions was to protect German prehistoric monuments from destruction by the military. And they were far more interested in resurrecting the remains of a supposed Germanic religion than in pursuing the Grail, as scholars who have worked on the surviving documents make clear.[85]

If we are to look for a connection between the Grail and Nazi ideas, we must go back to the cultural background from which National Socialism arose – the popular philosophers and literature of the first two decades of the twentieth century. Here we will find the Grail invoked in a variety of ways. An idealistic nationalism in Germany seized on Wagner's imagery, and proclaimed the emergence of a new elite: it was not the masses but this elite who were concerned with 'the holy Grail, this jewel set apart . . . remote from the day's idle gossip'. The elect will search in spirit for the 'serene temple mount, where the divine jewel gleams'.[86] The same strain is found in Austria, where a 'Grail union' (*Gralsbund*) was founded by provincial Catholic writers to resist the sophisticated aestheticism of Vienna. Among the writers who had once been the admirers of Wagner under the banner of the Grail, the idea of a Germanized religion was linked to the ideals of Parsifal and the Grail, as in the 'Templeisen' order founded by a former monk during the First World War, Jörg Lanz von Liebenfels. Hitler is known to have read his book *Ostara*, and it is perhaps from this source that the one reasonably certain Grail reference associated with Hitler stems: Hermann Rauschning wrote in 1940 that Hitler had spoken of a 'brotherhood of Templars around the Grail of pure blood'.[87]

A Local Grail

Normandy has also been claimed as the homeland of the Grail by a group of writers from that area. The arguments for this proceed from local patriotism rather than any hard evidence, and tend to rely heavily on etymology, the analysis of the original form and meaning of place-names. Unfortunately, the strict rules by which scholarly work on such derivations are governed are largely ignored in favour of general similarities, and the Norman Grail is more notable for the enthusiasm of its proponents, led by René Bansard, than for any evidence to support it. A good example is Philippe Lavenu's *L'ésoterisme du Graal* (1989), which revisits all the occult disciplines – astrology, the Tarot cards, ley-lines (in this case zodiacal axes) – to make

Mont Saint-Michel the focal point of the Grail romances, and to show that astrology lies at the heart of Arthurian romance. It is a remarkably ingenious and imaginative book, but ingenuity and imagination do not necessarily lead to the truth. To take the Tarot as anything other than a set of playing cards is to declare one's hand immediately. And zodiacal lines of influence seem to be a novelty even in occult astrology.

We are not far – spiritually, though not geographically – from the world of the flying saucer enthusiasts and alien visitors. Despite the title of John Michell's book, *The Flying Saucer Vision: the Holy Grail Restored* (1967), the author has only a brief passage at the end on the Grail, in which he identifies 'the central object of British mythology, the cauldron or Grail' with the flying saucer, and continues:

It belongs to another world, and sometimes itself stands for the unearthly country: it inspires man with wisdom, and reveals to them great secrets, raising them to the level of gods; it heals wounds, bestows immortality, gives everyone what he wants most . . . The Grail was the sacred vessel, once known on earth, but now removed to another world from which it may occasionally reappear to be glimpsed by men until the day when it is finally attracted to earth again. It was the vehicle by which all benefits first came to men, the flying disc of the gods.[88]

These are the farther shores of the madness which can overtake Grail-seekers.

New Age Grail Enthusiasts

Mention of the Tarot leads us to the activities of the New Age Grail enthusiasts, for whom an 'Arthurian Tarot' has been designed. The Grail has become a focal point for the practices and belief of a section of the New Age community, for whom 'the Self itself is sacred'.[89] The search for the authentic self, the real nature of one's own being, is achieved by harnessing a wide variety of spiritual traditions: the theoretical syncretism of theosophy and its kindred cults is replaced by an attempt to weave together actual mystical and spiritual practices from many religions and beliefs. The Grail looms large as a non-specific symbol of the quest for interior truth, stripped of its Christian overtones, and, given the New Age fondness for a return to a more primitive religious state on the grounds that it leads us closer to the natural world and therefore brings us into harmony with our environment, it is not surprising that the supposed Celtic Grail figures largely in their writings.

One of the most ardent advocates of the search for the spiritual Grail is John Matthews, who has written extensively on the subject. Some of his work is a more or less orthodox account of the development of the Grail legends seen from his own particular viewpoint. Other essays take up themes we have explored, such as the links between Rosicrucianism and the Grail. The problem is that all too often closer examination of his statements simply does not relate to the medieval stories: in 'The Grail and the Rose', he describes the Grail temple as usually set on a mountain-top surrounded by impenetrable forest or deep water, accessible only by a perilously narrow bridge; the castle that houses it may revolve to prevent entry. As the texts we have quoted in the first part of this book show, none of this is strictly true: in particular, the revolving castle belongs to a quite different strand of romance. It is the image of the Grail temple as he would like it to be, 'a temenos, a place set apart, where an invisible line shows that here divinity lives . . .',[90] and much of what he has to say is a re-imagination of the material to suit his own purposes, which are not simply scholarly or instructive: the Grail is seen as a path to the achievement of spiritual self-healing and a heightened spiritual awareness. Two of his books contain a series of exercises to this end: in *Elements of the Grail Tradition*, each chapter concludes with exercises connected with the part of the Grail history retold in the preceding text. These are a series of suggested meditations built round highly coloured imagery drawn from the romances, from symbolism and from astronomy, which allow the self to become a crucial force in the cosmic order, as in this passage concerned with the spear of Longinus:

. . . you now face true North, where you find the constellation of Piscis Australis, the great Cosmic Fish, in whose mouth glows the bright star Formahalt. Below the outline of the fish is the shape of a great Spear, the weapon which, in the story of the Grail was used to wound, but which now sends forth healing light towards you. You capture and distil it forth again from your heart centre, through your feet and into the earth, where the crystal Grail, the final shape it assumes in the mystery of the Five Changes,[91] waits to catch, and then send forth again, the light you perceive as passing through the earth . . .[92]

In *Healing the Wounded King*,[93] this is developed further to treat cases of mental trauma, 'the wounded soul', through meditation on images from 'archetypal stories', a procedure for which Matthews claims some remark-able successes. This is not territory for the sceptic, but it seems that this new religion, too, has to have its miracles.

For this is in many ways a new faith based on belief in the overriding importance of the self, of the individual. It contrasts sharply with the self-denying Eastern tradition from which it borrows some of its procedures. The Western idealization of the individual is taken to its extreme, and the Grail, once symbol of a universal redemption, is the means only to individual self-fulfilment. It is a romantic obsession with the self shared with the occult practitioners of the early twentieth century, who are the shadowy forerunners of many elements in the New Age version of the Grail, and whose work is eagerly scanned for revelations by New Age enthusiasts.[94] The Grail takes its place in the 'hermetic tradition', and Matthews envisages a continuity of tradition down the centuries, embracing the Druids, the Gnostics, the Cathars, Atlantis and the nineteenth-century occult societies among others.[95]

The Grail itself becomes the object of worship and belief: a telling passage in *At the Table of the Grail* describes the varied forms the Grail may take, 'chalice or stone, dish or womb', and continues

Yet much as these views differ, they are at one in their belief in the Grail as guide, counsellor, helper, and as gateway to the interior life, the inner journey we must all travel to its end, beset by danger and doubt, fear and loss of faith. And, so long as our goal is a true one, and carries no taint of evil, the Grail remains always at hand like a light in the wilderness.

You may learn much from these pages, yet if you learn nothing more than to recognize the Grail within your own being you will have discovered a truth that will never desert you, that will shine forth on the path before you and show you the way to self-realization.[96]

If we substitute 'Christ' or 'Buddha' for 'the Grail', the passage still makes perfect sense. Ironically, a symbol with a very precise Christian origin and context has become a means of escaping from established religion into a world where everything has a voice. Instead of Christianity, we have the 'Western Mystery Tradition' which invents a new mythology for today, of which the Grail is one of the central images. A New Age has reimagined the Grail, this time as a self-sacred cult object. This new Grail can embrace a huge range of concepts, including those we have already touched on, but extending to feminism, the Shakers, Taoist teaching, until we feel that everything, somewhere, somehow, must be a Grail.[97]

20

The Grail Today

Mark Twain's *A Connecticut Yankee at the Court of King Arthur* succeeds in making fun both of the world of medieval romance and of nineteenth-century American society, by introducing a modern American into Arthur's court by an accidental piece of time travel. The satire works well enough on a social and cultural level, but there is a problem when it comes to the spiritual side of chivalry, and Twain neatly sidesteps the issue of the Grail:

The boys all took a flier at the Holy Grail now and then. It was a several-years' cruise. They always put in the long absence snooping around in the most conscientious way, though none of them had any idea where the Holy Grail was, and I don't think any of them actually expected to find it, or would have known what to do with it if he had run across it . . . Every year expeditions went out holy Grailing and next year relief expeditions went to hunt for them. There was worlds of reputation in it, but no money.[1]

He turns the quest for the Grail into a kind of Victorian voyage of exploration, but wisely avoids any jest at the expense of the Grail itself.

His view of the subject, however, might stand as a good description of what we find when we start to look at the literature of the last half of the twentieth century on the Grail. With a few honourable exceptions, it feels as if there are too many expeditions out there, chasing something that they have only half-defined, through the jungles of fantasy, historical fiction or the esoteric. What is certain is that the Grail now assumes a chameleon-like character; or perhaps it simply multiplies its forms until we are hard put to find a common denominator among all its avatars.

If we have to map out some kind of path for our expedition, it would be fair to say that there are very few modern examples of Grail literature where Christian belief is at the centre of the action. French and German authors tend to look at the Grail from an individual and philosophical viewpoint, while the predominant emphasis in English and American writers is all too often a kind of warmed-over neo-paganism which owes a great deal to the scholarly ideas circulating in the early twentieth century, taking the Grail as a symbol of the pagan past. Other writers have chosen to elaborate on a particular medieval version in their own style, and there are a handful of more original and eclectic works.

A good starting point for our exploration – and we can only map a handful of the books on the Grail produced in the twentieth century – is a novel in which the multiple aspects of the Grail become a central motif, Naomi Mitchison's *To the Chapel Perilous* (1955). Mitchison, herself a journalist, makes her protagonists two rival reporters, in a medieval world which, like that of Mark Twain, is intertwined with modern ideas: Camelot has its own newspaper industry, and the world of journalism is overlaid on that of chivalry. Her hero and heroine work for rival papers, and report on the Grail from their different standpoints, dictated by the press barons and the editors: the novel is in one sense a witty diatribe on the craft of the journalist. What they find when they are sent to investigate the strange happenings at the Chapel Perilous is not just one Grail, but five, with the possibility of more. The three traditional Grail knights, Bors, Perceval (here called Peredur) and Galahad, each carry off their own private Grail; even Gawain, usually the anti-hero of the Grail quest, gets one for himself, and Lancelot has a Grail which is quite distinct from that of his son Galahad. All the Grails are different, and are derived either from the original romances or from scholarly theory. Each reflects one aspect of the Grail. If this sounds ponderous, Mitchison's touch is deft: as one of her characters says, 'Even when it's something you really care about, keep it light if you want to get it across', and this is just what she succeeds in doing. So Gawain takes home a cauldron of plenty, and a pagan orgy ensues. Lancelot's Grail is a healing relic, echoing his miraculous healing of Sir Urry in Malory's *Morte Darthur*. Peredur has a shining stone, as in Wolfram's poem, but this stone is the centrepiece of obscure Celtic rites. Bors, the virtuous husband in the romances, has a fertility symbol connected with harvest rituals and the well-being of his family and estates, while Galahad's spiritual Grail consoles those who are pure spirit, the dead who gather in the church on All Souls' Night. The question, of course, for the journalists is 'Which is the real Grail?' There is no answer to this, for there are only 'different patterns that people can make themselves into. Or be made into if they aren't strong and knowledgeable. And each pattern uncovers a different aspect of the heart: a different means of wisdom. That's the nearest I can get. And each pattern is dangerous to the other patterns and must seem hateful to their followers. Unless to the very wise and tolerant people.'[2] And there may be more Grails to be found, more patterns to be uncovered: as the hermit who watches over the Chapel Perilous says at the end, 'It would be sad beyond all telling if the finding of the Grail were to happen once for all.'[3]

It is not surprising that one of the first novels about the Grail was by a member of the Order of the Golden Dawn, A. E. Waite's close friend, Arthur Machen. *The Secret Glory* (1915) is a strange mixture of the physical and the mystical. It portrays the brutality of life at a public school through the eyes of a schoolboy, Ambrose Meyrick, and contrasts his existence there with his experiences in his Welsh home. One day his father takes him to a farmhouse set deep in the countryside, where an old man keeps the Grail, 'a veiled and splendid cup':

All the hues of the world were mingled on it, all the jewels of the regions seemed to shine from it; and the stem and foot were encrusted with work in enamel, of strange and magical colours that shone and dimmed with alternating radiance, that glowed with red fires and pale glories, with the blue of the far sky, the green of the faery seas, and the argent gleam of the evening star.[4]

The two adults begin a ritual in 'pure Welsh', at the end of which Ambrose has a vision which he recognizes as Corbenic; here, in his vision, he witnesses the ancient rite of the Grail being enacted, and sees 'in unendurable light the Mystery of Mysteries pass veiled before him'. But Meyrick's subsequent life is romantic and squalid by turns, as if Machen wanted to write a picaresque novel as well as a spiritual fantasy. The ending, in which Meyrick takes the Grail to the East to give it to a mysterious keeper in accordance with unspecified instructions, and is martyred as a Christian, seems forced and at odds with the rest of the book.

We have seen how Glastonbury was involved in the fringes of the occult movement and in the search for the physical Grail at the beginning of the twentieth century. A different vision, that of the town as an artistic centre, was behind the proposal in 1913 to create a 'National Festival Theatre for Music and Drama' at Glastonbury, invoking the example of Bayreuth;[5] this too was to have its share of mystical material. The festival itself had been started by the composer Rutland Boughton, who had embarked on a cycle of Arthurian operas; it was supported by leading lights in the fields of drama and music, Galsworthy, Shaw, Beecham and Elgar among them. The reality that emerged was rather different: the first Glastonbury festival was held in August 1914, overshadowed by the beginning of the First World War and consisting of performances with a piano and amateur chorus rather than the professional forces that had been envisaged. But the event was deemed a success, and was the first of a series which was to run until 1927; the festivals included performances of Boughton's Arthurian operas as he finished them. However, it was not until 1943 that Boughton reached the Grail section of the romances; Galahad owes more to his Communist politics than to the ethereal spirituality of Glastonbury, and instead of achieving the elitist Grail, he emerges as the champion of the oppressed.

This heady mixture of mysticism, romantic nostalgia, Arts and Crafts liberalism and general eccentricity may, to the casual visitor, still seem to pervade Glastonbury today. And it is from this fertile ground for the imagination that there sprang the most massive work of fiction centred on the Grail ever to be written. John Cowper Powys' *A Glastonbury Romance* outdoes even the medieval romances in sheer length. It is a vast assemblage of different ideas and observations, veering from the Rabelaisian to the numinous within the space of a couple of sentences. At the heart of the story is

the immemorial Mystery of Glastonbury. Christians had one name for this Power, the ancient heathen inhabitants had another, and a quite different one. Everyone who came to this spot seemed to draw something from it, attracted by a magnetism too powerful for anyone to resist, but as different people approached they changed its chemistry, though not its essence, by their own identity, so that upon none of them it had the same psychic effect ... Older than Christianity, older than the Druids, older than the gods of Norsemen or Romans, older than the gods of the neolithic men, this many-named Mystery had been handed down to subsequent generations by three psychic channels; by the channel of popular renown, by the channel of inspired poetry, and by the channel of individual experience.[6]

'The traditional name of this identity' is the Holy Grail, and Powys' purpose is to depict a world where the spiritual and mystical are intimately interwoven with the stark physical reality of everyday life. It is on one level a realistic novel in the tradition of Dickens or Eliot, with the same vast canvas and proliferation of characters; these characters use the religious and the spiritual as a means to practical ends. Some of the characters are close to the real-life Glastonbury enthusiasts whom we have already met, fired up by the idea of a festival or of a new spiritual dimension; others are materialists, factory-owners and strike leaders. There are elements of autobiography, in the antiquarian Owen Evans whose self-confessed sadism corresponds to Powys' own obsession with that vice, and in the figure of Matt Dekker, a clergyman like Powys' father. Even the central figure, Johnny Geard, a lay preacher of highly unorthodox opinions with a silver tongue, seems in part a self-portrait. He resembles J. B. Priestley's image of Powys as 'a gigantic half-comic character, a clown . . . but a wise clown',[7] and Geard's rhetorical gift was also shared by his creator. Geard is also a 'mystical realist': the central plot revolves round his inheritance of an unexpected fortune, which he proposes to spend on a Religious Fair which will be a non-denominational revival of the ancient mysteries of Glastonbury. The battle is between him and those attracted by the Grail, that 'magnet-gatherer of all the religions that had ever come near Glastonbury', and the forces of materialism, who meet 'in a great mêlée of warring dreams, tossing and heaving, with the gonfalon of the Grail on one side, and on the other the oriflamme of Reason', the reason that drives both the industrialist Philip Crow to exploit the town and its natural resources and the anarchist Dave Spear and his allies to set up a commune in opposition to him.

The people of Glastonbury both use and are used by the magic power which is concentrated there, and which Powys regards as very real. Comparing Glastonbury to Jerusalem, Rome, Mecca and Lhasa, he claims: 'Generations of mankind, aeons of past races, have – by their concentrated will – made Glastonbury miraculous.'[8] It is this effect that he regards as intimately linked to the Grail, as he explains in his preface:

What, in fact, does this long book attempt to describe in its somewhat tumultous and chaotic manner?

Nothing more and nothing less than the effect of a particular legend, a special myth, a unique tradition, from the remotest past in human history, upon a particular spot on the surface of this planet . . . What has made the tradition of the Grail so absolutely different from all other Christian Legends and Myths is that it is so near, so close, so vibrantly akin to eating and drinking and love-making and even to voiding our excreta. In its long history in contact with our heroic pitiful human life it has succeeded in establishing itself both as a reality touched by the miraculous and as a miracle based on reality . . .

There are intimate correspondences between it and the traditions that reach us from both the extreme East and the extreme West. It changes its shape. It changes its contents. It changes its aura. It changes its atmosphere. But its essential nature remains unchanged; and even that nature is only the nature of a symbol.[9]

To describe and encompass such unbounded concepts requires a canvas of heroic proportions and a throng of characters, and Powys uses these to portray a wide range of visions of the Grail, from outright disbelief to the vision of a blood-filled chalice, in which there swims a fish, symbol of Christ. This is seen by Sam Dekker, the vicar's son, an innocent at heart who loves all natural things, and thinks that he recognizes the fish as a tench, which in folklore has the power to heal: his question to himself, 'Is it a Tench?' voices at the same time his hope that it will bring spiritual healing. Powys mocks the enthusiasts for the idea of Celtic origins by having these theories recounted breathlessly at night by a girl to her friend: 'her esoteric whisperings with burning cheeks and eyes growing brighter and brighter'. Yet he does not discount the idea of the Grail as a fertility symbol, but sees it as one more aspect of the same immense principles and powers for good. When two cousins fall in love, and are quivering with unfulfilled desire for each other, they 'come to the very brink of this floating Fount of Life' and 'approach the invisible rim of that wind-blown mystery'. The Grail is not what its name seems to imply:

Names are magical powers. Names can work miracles. But the traditional name of this entity – the Holy Grail – might easily mislead an intelligent historian of our planet. The reality is one thing; the name, with all its strange associations, is only the outward shell of such reality.[10]

Of this reality and its cosmic power there is no doubt: the Grail and the power that it represents are constantly at work among the affairs of men. And it is this, rather than the distant echoes of the older stories, which is Powys' contribution to the modern image of the Grail. He sees it as magical as much as religious, a focal point for the mysterious forces we call divine. Its origins, as we have seen, lie far back beyond Christianity, in the primal world of the creation, but with the passing of time it has acquired an inherent power which makes it independent of the laws of nature. Johnny Geard, the lay preacher, working 'the interior cogs and pinions of his mind', defines it to himself as the magnet which attracts thought – thought which can create and destroy and exist independently of the thinker:

'For a thousand years the Grail has been attracting thought to itself, because of the magnetism of Christ's Blood. The Grail is now an organic nucleus of creation and destruction. Christ's Blood cries aloud from it by day and by night. Yes, yes,' so his thoughts ran on, 'yes, and bugger me black!' – this was a queer original oath peculiar to Mr Geard – 'I know now what the Grail is. It is the desire of the generations mingling like water with the Blood of Christ, and caught in a fragment of the Substance that is beyond Matter! It is a little nucleus of Eternity, dropped somehow from the outer spaces upon one particular spot!'

Here Mr Geard stretched out his head, like a mud-turtle, and peered down at the crack in the floor, through which he had heard the old couple in the room below relieving Nature.[11]

The last sentence gives perfectly the extraordinary juxtaposition of the mystical and the Rabelaisian in Powys' work, his mixture of the ethereal and the earthy.

In the final apocalyptic scene, when Glastonbury is overwhelmed by the sea that floods across the Somerset Levels, Geard seeks death by drowning of his own accord. As he sinks into the waters,

Bloody Johnny's body danced, in fact, its own private death-dance, in brute defiance of the spirit that had brought it to this pass.

For the last time he came up to the surface. Again his black eyes opened; opened so wide that anyone would have thought their sockets must crack. He was staring frantically at Glastonbury Tor, but what he was seeing up there now will never be known.

The books say that Arthur saw the Grail in five different shapes; and that what the fifth shape was has never been revealed. Perhaps it was this fifth shape now that caused the black demonic eyes of Bloody Johnny to start out of his head.[12]

A page or so later we learn that this is indeed what he had seen, 'the Grail under its fifth shape – upon the top of Gwyn-ap-Nud's hill'.

In *A Glastonbury Romance*, the Grail, although taken up by Christians and made into a symbol of their faith, does not belong to them. Christian thought and belief have enhanced its power, but it exists before all religions, and will survive them. It belongs to the world of the First Cause, a creative force which Powys sees in dualist terms, composed of good and evil whose struggle is the essence of existence. This is syncretism on the grand scale, going far beyond the ideas of the late nineteenth-century mythologists or of *The Golden Bough*. Powys' headlong enthusiastic narrative bears up these vague ideas as it rushes onwards; but perhaps they do not bear too close a scrutiny. This is a novel which arouses either huge enthusiasm or a sceptical antipathy. But its cosmic view of the Grail was to be deeply influential, and its realistic passages do indeed invoke something of the curious mixture of commerce and high idealism that seems to characterize the recent history of Glastonbury.

The Influence of From Ritual to Romance:
The Waste Land *and Pagan Rites*

If *A Glastonbury Romance* is about the presence of the Grail, the most famous of all Grail poems of the twentieth century is about the absence of the Grail. This is T. S. Eliot's *The Waste Land*, which borrows its central image from the work of Jessie Weston. In *From Ritual to Romance*, she had argued that the Grail was derived from an ancient, forgotten initiation rite, and that the story of the 'dolorous blow' by which the land was laid waste was central both to this ritual and to the Grail romances. We have seen why there is reason to believe that this idea was an invention of a later poet trying to tidy up the loose ends which he found in his original,* but the vision of sin and retribution and eventual redemption in her version of the tale is hugely powerful. T. S. Eliot, as befits a poet writing just after the First World War, offers sin and retribution, but no redemption. The 'Waste Land' of the title stands for a spiritual desert, not the physically barren fields of the romances and of Jessie Weston's rituals. The actual references to the legends in the poem are slight: the Fisher King appears twice, once fishing 'in the dull canal/on a winter evening round behind the gashouse'[13] and once 'upon the shore/Fishing, with the arid plain behind me/Shall I at least set my lands in order?'[14] He is only one of a host of characters from both Eastern and Western myth and literature who haunt the poem, which is also a patchwork of quotations from literature of all kinds. Some allusions are so subtle that we would not recognize them if it were not for Eliot's own notes to the text: this is the case with the Perilous Chapel, which would be hard to identify as such from the verses alluding to it. There is one direct, brief reference to *Parsifal*, but even this is a line from Verlaine's poem inspired by the opera:

Et O ces voix d'enfants chantant dans la coupole![15]

Attempts to find other Grail images in the text have usually been far-fetched. It is the concept of the Waste Land which interests Eliot, the Waste Land from which the Grail is absent; nor does anyone seek to find it. To read significance into absence is always dangerous, but here it would seem apt that a poem about the sterile secularity of the post-war world should have at its heart an empty space where the expected and ultimate religious symbol should be.

This negative view of the Grail is taken up by other twentieth-century writers. Six years after Eliot published his poem, Mary Butts made the Grail the centrepiece of her novel *Armed with Madness*.[16] She wrote in 1927: 'T. S. Eliot . . . the only writer of my quality, dislikes me and my work, I think. But what is interesting is that he is working on the Sanc-Grail, on its negative side, the Waste Land.'[17] *Armed with Madness* is set in a remote house overlooking the English Channel where a group of unorthodox artistic

* Above, pp. 205–8.

friends are gathered, with an American visitor who is uneasy in their company. One of them, a sculptor, steals an ancient jade cup from his father, a collector of rare and mysterious objects; he hides it, and the resulting quest for the cup and its true meaning redefines the complex relationships between the group. Here, too, there is the barrenness of a world in which the Grail no longer has a place; however, Butts looks not at absences and desolation, but at spiritual alienation, the madness of her title. The Grail for her is 'an ancient, a not yet exhausted event, in the most secret, passionate and truthful part of the spiritual history of man'. If it belongs anywhere in secular history, it is part of the ancient Celtic church, and its ritual may be the real, primitive Eucharistic rite which has been forgotten and exists only in spiritual terms. There is more than a hint of Arthur Machen here, and of A. E. Waite's *The Hidden Church of the Holy Graal*.

But the object which is the centre of the novel and of the twists and turns of the plot is never positively identified as the Grail. It could be any one of a number of things, from an antique jade cup, 'Early English altar vessel. From the collection of Christopher Tracy Esq.', to an oriental physician's means of detecting poison (as jade is said to do); and it may be that the enigmatic artist Picus is the only one to name it as the Grail – ' "Why did he pretend it was the cup of the Sanc-Grail?" ' asks his father.[18] What matters is the movement of the figures around it. The old vicar whom they consult about the cup conveys the atmosphere of this strange book in staccato sentences that are typical of its style:

This story as I see it is true Sanc-Grail. The cup may have been an ash-tray in a Cairo club. But it seems to me that you are having something like a ritual. A find, illumination, doubt, and division, collective and then dispersed. A land enchanted and disenchanted with the rapidity of a cinema. Adventures. Danger and awe and love.[19]

Mary Butts herself is an interesting and neglected figure, who knew Eliot, Cocteau, and Charles Williams, explored the occult with Aleister Crowley at his notorious 'abbey of Thélème' at Cefalù in Sicily, and knew many of the important British artists of the period. She was also a writer haunted by the Grail, which she first mentions in her *Journals* in 1918, after a visit to Glastonbury, and was still pondering its mystery a year or so before her death in 1937.[20] For her, it is a real presence: in a storm, she writes: 'It is a wild night. Come out, Grail. Slide down the wind & rain to that house.' Or struck by the beauty of the Cornish landscape, she sees it as 'dim holy place after another, hill & woods soaring. "Mysterious, beautiful", the Grail

Country.'[21] Elsewhere she speaks of the Grail as sustaining her, or thinks that it might be seen in Cornwall that winter. And she instinctively turned to the Grail for the theme of the book which followed *Armed with Madness*, only to realize that she could not continue in the same vein.

Armed with Madness is negative in its depiction of the lives of its protagonists: the quest gets nowhere; there is no conclusion, only an evocation of the past; the characters insist that life is 'complicated, violent, inconclusive'. And yet there is a hint of a positive side, for the Grail is 'not yet exhausted', and there is a feeling – however distant – that a new spiritual force may yet be at hand.

The idea of 'finding' the Grail is at the centre of a silent film starring Lon Chaney, Sr, *The Light of Faith* (1922). This seems to have existed in three versions, of which only one has survived. Two lovers, Elaine and Warburton, separate after a misunderstanding: she hides in a humble boarding house and searches unsuccessfully for work, while he goes to England. She falls ill from hunger and heartbreak, and Tony, a rough diamond who lodges in the same house, tries to restore her to health. Meanwhile, while Warburton is out shooting, his dog finds the Grail in the ruins of an old abbey; and he decides to return with it to America. The story of his discovery comes to Elaine's attention, and she tells Tony the story of the Grail and its healing powers: the account is based on Tennyson, and the vision of the Grail descending on a moonbeam to Perceval's sister is filmed almost exactly as Tennyson describes it. Tony steals the Grail in order to cure her; its healing powers work, but he is arrested. The lovers come face to face in court, where Warburton denies that he recognizes Tony, who is set free; Warburton and Elaine are reconciled. A trite enough tale, which was shown to Christian groups across the United States, it had begun as an altogether blacker story, *Light in the Dark*, in which the Grail is stolen from Elaine; it is artificial, and is made to give off light by filling it with a special mixture. It is as if this earlier version was too irreverent, too disrespectful of an emblem which had a powerful hold on the popular imagination.

Curiously, the same idea of the theft of the Grail in order to cure someone *in extremis* reappears in Terry Gilliam's film *The Fisher King* (1991), which also reworks in modern terms the archetypal situations embodied in the medieval romances. Both the main characters, Jack and Parry, are in effect psychologically lamed by horrors, and also show compassion: they are the Fisher King and Perceval to each other. Jack, a radio show presenter, is the indirect cause of a shooting at a restaurant, in which Parry's wife dies: Parry, who was with her, goes mad. Jack loses his job, and becomes a misanthropic recluse, while Parry joins the homeless on the New York streets. Jack makes his initial approach to Parry to assuage his own guilt by helping him in material terms, but Parry needs friendship, not money, and a superficial friendship grows up between the two men. It is only after Parry is attacked and beaten unconscious that Jack realizes the strength of his compassion for Parry. Parry's madness has been in the form of an Arthurian fantasy based on the scholarly research he had once worked on: he is pursued by a fantastical and monstrous red knight in his moments of horror, and he also believes that a cup he has seen in a newspaper is the Holy Grail. It is this that Jack steals from a millionaire's mansion in the hope that it will heal him, because Parry has told him about it and about the story of the Fisher King. Jack sees the relevance of the story to his own situation, but until now has not been able to act accordingly. When Parry recovers consciousness, he is able to face his tragic situation; we never know whether the myth or the physical injury has healed his mind, but in a sense the myth has indeed worked for Jack.

Parry's version of the story of the Fisher King is unusual: the Grail appears, surrounded by fire, to the boy who is destined to be the Grail king, but he rejects it, preferring the possibility of power and luxury to the Grail which heals the hearts of men. The boy tries to seize the Grail so that he can possess it, and is burned; the wound grows as he gets older. He becomes king, and seeks for a cure; a fool sees him and asks what is wrong with him, and he replies that he is thirsty. The fool gives him a drink of water, and he is healed; but when he asks the fool how he could find the answer when everyone had failed, the fool says that he only knew that the king was thirsty. The film hovers uneasily between the comic and the portentous, but in its best moments Gilliam offers a subtle interplay between literature, myth and modern life: the waste land of the streets of New York is an urban landscape similar to that which inspired T. S. Eliot.

The idea of the waste land put forward by Jessie Weston has an even more powerful influence on John Boorman's *Excalibur* (1981). Here the Grail, instead of distracting the fellowship of the Round Table from their task of maintaining the good governance of the kingdom, becomes the means by which that kingdom is saved at a critical juncture. Arthur is struck down by the witchcraft of his sister Morgana, ambitious that her son Mordred should succeed to the throne. When Arthur is stricken, the country suffers from plague, famine and disorder; through scenes of terror and misery the knights ride in search of the lost secret of the Grail, at Arthur's command: 'only the Grail can redeem us', he says. Many of the knights perish, lured by Morgana's magic. Perceval resists her temptations, and achieves a vision of the Grail, which he approaches fully armed; the chalice, as in Tennyson, descends on a shaft of light, but it pours out blood, and when an invisible voice asks him 'What is the secret of the Grail?', Perceval flees in terror. He meets Lancelot, who is leading the people in revolt against Arthur and his knights, who have failed them; they beat him and throw him in a stream. Stripping off his armour to survive, he emerges to find himself back at the Grail castle. He approaches almost naked: and this time he answers the questioning voice, which he recognizes as that of Arthur. As the chalice descends again, the voice asks whom the Grail serves, and Perceval replies, 'You, my lord.' The secret of the Grail, Perceval realizes, is that 'the land and the king are one'. Perceval takes the Grail to Arthur, who drinks from it and is roused from his half-living, half-dying state to ride out against Mordred, to his last and fatal battle.

The Grail itself, for Boorman, is a symbol of the king's power which makes the land prosper. It is a healing cup, its role as a fertility symbol subsumed in the link between the king's well-being and that of his kingdom: Christian overtones are absent. The Grail is successfully reimagined in a new role and in a new context, with a different set of attributes: we never learn what it is or where it comes from, but only what its powers and functions are. It is a refreshingly different view, even if its point of departure is clearly the work of Jessie Weston.

Christian Relics and Pagan Vessels

A similar fusion of Christian relics and pagan vessels has been popular in fiction. The most ambitious – and the most popular – of these recreations of the religious past is Marion Zimmer Bradley's *The Mists of Avalon* (1982), which combines the ideas of the 'New Age' writers with Celticism and feminism. The bulk of the narrative is Morgaine's autobiography, which recounts the history of Arthur within the framework of a duel between the old religion of the priestesses of Avalon and the new Christian worship. In all this the Grail plays a relatively small but crucial part. Avalon is located at Glastonbury; it was here that Joseph of Arimathea brought Christ's blood; but this, as in the abbey's medieval tradition, was contained in a flask, and Joseph did not bring the Grail with him. Instead, the Grail is one of the talismans of the mysteries of the ancient religion tended by the priestesses of Avalon, the Holy Regalia; there are four of these, and they are all objects which appear in the Grail procession as described in medieval romances. They are to be used for the service of the gods, 'by whatever name men called them'; but if they were used by any religion which claimed to be exclusive, this would profane them. The Christians come to Glastonbury, and proclaim their faith as the one true creed, and 'the Merlin' removes the regalia to Camelot. Morgaine, as priestess of the Goddess, interrupts the ceremony at which the Grail is being used for a Christian Mass, and raises the cup herself. Although the Christians see the Grail as Christ's chalice, the other worshippers recognize it as the 'cup of the Goddess'. Morgaine's action precipitates the Grail quest which ultimately destroys Camelot, and is the Goddess's revenge for the attempt to seize the regalia.

Bradley's ideas draw on the figure of the Great Mother in ancient cults and on the modern concepts of witchcraft as a religion put forward by the anthropologist Margaret Murray, as well as the twentieth-century humanist disavowal of any religion which claims a monopoly on revelation. Within this context the Grail becomes all things to all men, a vague benevolent source of spiritual – and physical – nourishment. The result is a heady mixture of feminism, New Age ideas, modern witchcraft and Arthurian myth, which has ensured *Mists of Avalon* a considerable following.

Other writers see the Grail as an invention designed for religious or political reasons, whether with good or bad intentions. In Catherine Christian's *The Pendragon* (1979), king Pelles creates a new religion 'that, so he believed, could bring inspiration to Britain, and through Britain, to the whole troubled, broken Empire'. In it the knowledge of the Druids and the meditations of the desert hermits of Eastern Christianity are combined; Pelles was convinced that no man who had not 'reached enlightenment in his soul was fit to govern others'. The symbol of this new faith is chosen by Merlin and Arthur: the cup is a 'symbol all faiths could share, and sharing, bind themselves in brotherhood ... drinking together from the one Cup sacred to all'. But the quest, which is launched by Pelles' emissary, Lancelot's daughter, and is encouraged by Peredur, who persuades the knights to take an oath to seek the Grail, ends in disaster: instead of providing new governance, the realm is left defenceless.

Philosophical Approaches to the Grail

Claude Debussy wrote in his *Proses lyriques*, 'The knights are dead on the road of the Grail',[22] and this negative attitude to the Grail is almost a commonplace in twentieth-century literature: it becomes in the hands of French and German writers a vehicle for dark reflections on human nature. Even Jean Cocteau, whose magical recreations of ancient myths in the cinema are largely optimistic in outlook, takes a dark view of the Grail in his play *The Knights of the Round Table* (1937). As the first act opens, Arthur and his court are drugged by a mysterious force, and his castle is shrouded in mist: Lancelot feels that 'the castle is asleep on its feet, and we are its dreams'. Some of the knights blame the Grail, 'a mysterious taboo, a relic of Christ which enchants or disenchants Britain', as Cocteau puts it in his preface. The advent of Galahad, legitimate son of Lancelot and the fairy Melusine, leads to the lifting of the spell; but the spell is not due to the Grail. The culprit is Merlin; he has further confused matters by transforming his familiar spirit Ginifer into different members of the Round Table, and throughout the play these doubles appear and disappear. Only Galahad can resist Merlin's power, and the false knights vanish when he is present. So Galahad offers the truth: but truth is hard to bear, and Lancelot and Guinevere commit suicide. But nonetheless the sun returns, the mist vanishes, and the Grail appears:

GALAHAD: Arthur, do you see it?

THE KING (ecstatic): I see it.

GALAHAD: What shape is it?

THE KING: It has no shape . . . I can't describe it.

GALAHAD: Blandine, do you see it?

BLANDINE (ecstatic): I see it.

GALAHAD: What colour is it?

BLANDINE: All colours . . . You couldn't paint it! . . . oh!

GALAHAD: Segramor, Gawain, do you see it?

GAWAIN and SEGRAMOR (together): I see it.

GALAHAD: What is its scent? Where is it?

GAWAIN: It smells of balm.

SEGRAMOR: It is shining . . . it is nowhere . . . it is everywhere . . . it moves of its own accord . . .[23]

Arthur asks Galahad why he wants them to describe the Grail, and Galahad replies that he himself cannot see it; he will never see it, but he is the one who enables others to see it. Galahad, who reveals the truth and unveils mysteries, identifies himself as the poet, condemned always to 'search for the great adventure' and to move on. His quest is for Corbenic and the poet's vision of the Grail, as opposed to the Grail quest which took place as soon as he arrived at Arthur's castle. This was another of Merlin's deceptions, an attempt to lure Galahad and Arthur's knights from the castle, so that Merlin's magic would again be in control.

Cocteau's Grail regains its medieval attributes at the end of the play; it is the shining, self-moving, perfumed Grail of the French medieval romances; but for much of the time we are unsure whether it is the Grail's magic that is responsible for the lethargy of Arthur and his court. In the final scene, Cocteau rebuilds the myth in a new shape, not so far from Wagner's vision of art replacing the forms of worn-out religions; here the poet replaces the priest of the Grail Mass, and becomes the mediator between the Grail and the knightly world.

A decade later, Julien Gracq, whose subtle novels touch on a different set of myths from those used by Cocteau, also chose the theatre for his exploration of the Grail. The Grail is to be found in the background of his other work, but it is in *The Fisher King* (1948)[24] that he directly confronts the Grail story. Whereas Cocteau uses the medieval French versions as his basis, Gracq's play is based firmly in the world of Wolfram and Wagner, and he specifically names Wagner as one of his inspirations.[25] We are at Montsalvatge, and we see Perceval/Parzival arrive to witness the Grail ceremony and failing to ask the question which will heal Amfortas. But the nature of the Grail and the events surrounding his visit are not at all what we might expect. The Grail is 'light, music, nourishment', Amfortas tells us;[26] but it is also dangerous, laying waste, not lands, but the lord of the Grail, Amfortas himself. Gracq sees it as a pre-Christian force, symbol of man's aspiration to overcome the limits of his human existence, which is uneasily cloaked in a Christian guise. Trevrizent the hermit tells Perceval to leave the Grail alone: 'I mistrust this old leather bottle which has been strangely filled with new wine. I see traps, a badly cleaned-down symbol, a temptation, older than the world, of redemption.'[27] For Clingsor, the Grail will not work either as the dark counterpart to Christianity: Amfortas tells him that 'the Grail was not born with Christ, and it is not the Grail that will separate your shadow and your light. The ways of the Grail are closed to you.'[28] And in the Grail castle, things are not as we expect them: Clingsor and Kundry are at Montsalvatge, the magician in disguise and Kundry caring for her victim Amfortas. Clingsor tempts Amfortas to retain his power as lord of the Grail castle by turning Perceval away.

When Perceval arrives, Amfortas tries to dissuade him from staying by describing how he has accomplished the same quest as Perceval and has seen the Grail; but in his loneliness he became Kundry's lover, and his disease stems from their love-making. The quest has brought him sickness and misfortune. Perceval is shocked, and tries to leave, but Kundry calls him back to witness the Grail procession, telling him that 'Montsalvatge is inhabited by phantoms' whom only Perceval can bring back to life.[29] The Grail ceremony takes place offstage, and is described to Kundry by a page watching through a window high in the wall.

After the ceremony, Amfortas confronts Perceval once more. Gracq sees the Grail as the 'temptation of possessing the divine while still on earth',[30] for to find it is a kind of living death. Amfortas tells Perceval that if he does achieve the vision he desires, he will strip himself of humanity, and 'bathe in certainty':[31] it will be the end of adventures. And he will always be alone; even the pure in heart cannot be his friends, for they will only be able to worship him, and Kundry cannot live in the presence of the Grail, which withers up anything impure. The outcome is that Amfortas persuades Perceval not to ask the question, and not to take his place as Grail king – but he does not do so out of a love of power. Perceval has come to him driven by his own vision, and by Clingsor and Kundry; Amfortas accuses Kundry of 'pushing him towards the Grail, blindfold, like some glorious beast of sacrifice. I preferred to treat him as a man.' Amfortas affirms the values of the human condition, with its terrors and uncertainties, over the sterile absolutes of mysticism. It is both a bleak image of the Grail and a brave affirmation of man's resolve in the face of existence. At the end Amfortas settles down to await the next would-be saviour: 'The folly of the Grail is not yet at an end . . . another will come,' he tells Kundry.[32]

For Gracq, Amfortas is the central character; his ambiguous relationship to the Grail, which both gives him his power and makes him vulnerable to the arrival of the 'Most Pure' dominates the action. At the end, we cannot be sure that Amfortas is not reproaching himself for having let Perceval go. But Amfortas can confront the Grail precisely because of his wound, because he cannot approach it in its absolute form. Instead, he has hidden it, so that 'poor mankind will not burn itself on it' and it has become 'the dream of the world' as a result.[33]

Gracq uses the Grail story to study the problem of the sacred in an age where Christianity, represented by Trevrizent, and its twin the occult, represented by Clingsor, are 'two old worm-eaten allegories of good and evil,'[34] which have renounced all attempts to confront the divine in its absolute form: and he imagines brilliantly the fate of the man who is bold enough to come face to face with that absolute, to achieve the quest. His reward is not bliss, but a solitary desert of the spirit. In this state of mind, Amfortas falls for Kundry's temptation; but he cannot accept deliverance at Perceval's hands, for that means death, and at the end only hope is left.

The human condition is at the heart of Christoph Hein's play *The Knights of the Round Table* (1989), but in a very different context. Gracq is unhappy with the moral code and faith required by Christianity; Hein is dismayed by the results of Marxist idealism. Written in the declining days of the German Democratic Republic, *The Knights of the Round Table* depicts Arthur and his companions as the weary old guard, who, having established what they believe to be an ideal society, no longer know how to manage it. Mordret, Arthur's son, represents the new order, which will sweep away the old conventions, which have become mere superstitions. The Grail is both part of these and the one element in the old order which offers something for the future. It is a spent force for Arthur's knights; Gawain gives up the Grail quest because he no longer believes in the Grail and resigns from the Round Table to live with the ladies of Chastel Merveille. When this news reaches the Round Table, Mordret claims that no one has ever seen the Grail, but another knight, Orilus, contradicts him: many people have seen it, but their descriptions of it differ. It is a huge shining jewel; the sun-table of the Ethiopians which provides magic food; the site of the earthly paradise; the hill of Venus; God himself; the Virgin Mary; the beloved. But everyone agrees, he says, that man once had the Grail and has now lost it. His wife says that this sounds like a fairytale, to which Orilus responds that the Grail is really peace, and if that isn't a fairytale, then what is? Arthur reproves them, saying: 'The Grail is not foolishness. Only animals can do without it, because they don't know that they are going to die. Our mortality compels us to search for the Grail. The knowledge of our death makes us restless, and makes us stir ourselves and seek.' For him, the Grail is an essential part of human nature, 'a hunger for hope . . . which we must try to quell', and 'even if the Grail became unattainable for us, we must seek out other ways which no one has seen, in order to reach it'.

Lancelot returns from the Grail quest, saying that if it existed on earth, he would have found it: perhaps it has crumbled to dust, perhaps it is only an idea. Arthur tries to comfort him by saying that through the quest the knights have come closer to the Grail, even if they have not found it. He knows that the world outside thinks that the Round Table knights are fools, but he still insists that 'if we give up the Grail, we give up our selves, because without the Grail there is no hope'. At the end of the play, he admits that the Round Table has fallen apart, but says that the search for the Grail must go on, even if it means handing over to Mordret, who wants to sweep away everything his father has created. Alone with Arthur, Mordret half-accepts Arthur's challenge to continue the search, but declares that he will put the Round Table in a museum. Arthur says that Mordret will destroy many things; and Mordret agrees.

Hein uses the Round Table and the Grail as symbols in a subtle discussion of the interaction between ideologies (the Round Table) and ideals (the Grail). Even if ideologies become obsolete and have to be replaced, the ideals remain, and the very fact that they are unattainable is all the more reason to cherish them. If an ideology which promises a better world cannot deliver it, it does not mean that we cannot at least hope to achieve that better world. Behind the satire on the entrenched autocracy of the German Democratic Republic, portraying them as a bunch of quarrelsome elderly idealists who have lost their way, and can only relive the great exploits of their past, Hein has larger themes in view, and his image of the Grail as the sum of all that is utopian is an apt and powerful one. Out of a profound pessimism about the present and the potentially destructive future, he raises up the Grail as a small emblem of hope.

If Christoph Hein offers a possibility of meaning and hope, other German writers use the Grail stories to put across an almost entirely dark view of the human condition. Tankred Dorst focuses on Parzival the questioner. He works on an epic scale: his drama *Merlin* would run for nearly twelve hours on the stage. *Parzival* (1990) offers part of this in a form that can be readily staged. The question that Dorst's Parzival asks is simply 'How should one live, how should one act?' and receives many answers.[35] Parzival is a child in a man's body, violent and innocent at the same time: and the Grail plays almost no part in his history. If there is a quest, it is for the lost innocence of the child's union with nature, a mystical bond which represents a golden age. But this is implicit, and is not the physical object of his search: he wants to serve God, because he has been told that God is the mightiest of lords, and he asks where he can be found, what his address is. But he destroys what he cannot understand: when told that God is everywhere, his reaction is that he will destroy everything 'until He alone is left', so that he can enlist in his service. However, he takes up with a hermit, and for a time lives peacefully, until he realizes that his companion is a fraud. But he has learnt something in the hermit's company: he must try to put the world to rights by whatever means. He rescues a fish from a heron, and, miraculously, the fish follows him wherever he goes. He comes to Trevrizent, who uses violence on himself in the form of self-flagellation: Parzival pities him, and is at last able to recognize his own guilt. It is precisely his certainty that God exists that has shielded him from the recognition of his own sins: he can now become a social human being. He has to lose God in order to find mankind and himself: 'I look up into the empty heaven with the eyes of humanity.'[36] There is hope here; but the final scene is darkness once more. Parzival and Blanchefleur stand in the snow, on one side of an abyss: Galahad stands on the other. We know from earlier scenes that Galahad is raving mad: according to Dorst, he has no ego, and is therefore untouched by whatever happens to him.[37] Above the abyss hovers the Grail: Parzival too is mad and he believes that he can reach the Grail because God will bear him up on a twig of broom. The way of belief means abandoning reason:

he must either listen to reason and lose the Grail, or follow his belief and die. The play ends before he has made his choice: an earlier scene depicts Parzival and Blanchefleur trying to remember the 'moment that cannot be recalled', and although Blanchefleur thinks that she knows what happened, Parzival denies all her memories, though he does admit to having seen a marvellous light, and Galahad dissolving into that light. He cannot bring to mind the image of the Grail: Blanchefleur prompts him by saying that they have had thousands of images of it made; the greatest artists have painted it, and cheap copies are sold in the street.[38] Ultimately, however, Parzival goes on his way, and the questions remain unanswered: what is this Grail towards which a wild youth from the forest strives, and what is his fate?

Dorst offers one powerful image of the Grail:

On the highest peak of a desert mountain massif stands the glittering Grail: it is gigantic. High on the slopes of the mountain men are climbing; they hang minute against the rock. You can see them moving, but they seem to make little progress upwards.[39]

Dorst's *Parzival* is presented as part of an ongoing obsession with the central character, as unfinished work in progress, and as a paradigm of uncertainty; the questions go unanswered, the certainties elude us.

The only recent writer working in English to come near the imaginative power of these German treatments of the legend is perhaps Jim Hunter, in a much simpler and shorter piece, the novel *Percival and the Presence of God* (1978). We meet Perceval as a battle-hardened warrior who is searching for Arthur's court; the novel opens violently, with a brutal account of a fight between two groups of knights, at the end of which Perceval is victorious; he has been defending a castle, whose lady, Whiteflower, becomes his lover. He has had two tutors: the warrior Mansel, who has been killed in an ambush a year previously, and an old abbot, who appealed to his latent sense of spiritual things and tried to teach him patience in the face of the insoluble problem of pain, of which Perceval is acutely aware. His advice is: 'Wait: accept: keep silence'; and it is this that Perceval has in mind when he comes to the court of Henged, the Fisher King. Here, in the midst of a feast, two figures enter, a girl bearing a silver cup and a boy with a spear: Henged is at once overcome by agonizing pain. He holds the spear over the cup, and blood flows from it. Perceval keeps silent, but is deeply troubled and leaves the hall. Henged cries out in despair, realizing – and accepting – that his pain cannot be transferred by the asking of a ritual question; the cup is overturned in the confusion, and the blood pours on to the floor. The next morning, the castle is deserted. Perceval continues to search for Arthur, but can only find the ruins of a great castle which might have been his. As he explores it, he is trapped by a falling beam in what might have been the chapel, and he is rescued by the men from a nearby castle, who shelter him while he recovers from his injuries. In his own pain, he reflects that he might have ended Henged's pain if he had asked the question instead of keeping silent, but he also realizes that he was silent because 'even now I do not know what questions, what form'.[40] The novel ends as he continues his search, which is now not for Arthur's court but for that of the Fisher King, but he is resigned to not finding it.

This is a quiet, low-key version of the story which, nonetheless, has powerful undercurrents. The problem is not compassion but involvement. Perceval is capable of feeling, but is held back by the quietist philosophy of the abbot, which is not the misunderstood conventional politeness of Chrétien's tale, but a decided philosophical, almost religious, stance.

Renewing the Religious Image of the Grail

For an unequivocally religious treatment of the Grail theme, we turn to Charles Williams, whom we have met as a friend of A. E. Waite and explorer of the fringes of the occult. Something of this world is reflected in his first venture into the world of the Grail, the novel *War in Heaven* (1930). It reads now as something of a period piece, a 'thriller' in the style of Dorothy Sayers, but in it he betrays his knowledge both of the Grail legends and of magical rituals such as those studied by Waite in his scholarly work. But it is one of the first of the genre to invoke the powers of good and evil in wider terms, and to make the struggle between the characters one of universal significance. The Grail appears as an ancient chalice of unknown origin, with immense powers for good, which is identified by the forces of evil and used by them in magic rituals intended to destroy its potential threat to their activities. At the opening of the story, it belongs to a small country parish; the archdeacon who is the priest there discovers its identity through an accidental sight of uncorrected proofs when he visits a publisher's office. The paragraph in question should have been deleted on the author's instructions, for he and a friend are anxious to lay hands on the Grail for their own purposes.

Sir Giles Tumulty, the author, is an equivocal figure, knowledgeable and curious about the occult, but loath to become directly involved in black magic; there is perhaps an echo of Waite himself here. Gregory Persimmon, who instigates the attempts to gain possession of the Grail, is entirely in the thrall of evil; the novel opens with the discovery of the body of a man he has just murdered. The Grail itself operates on two planes: it is in material terms simply a physical relic, on another it is an object which over time has become a focal point for spiritual powers, through the veneration which has been accorded to it. And it is also a gateway to the invisible world of the spirit which co-exists with the material world, a point where the forces of good and evil can be concentrated through the belief of their worshippers. Williams portrays the machinations of evil, and its power, as vividly as that other master of horror, M. R. James: the terrible emptiness and the strength of rejection and the negative are perhaps more strongly depicted than the triumph of the Grail itself, which for all its 'terrific and golden light' and 'blast upon blast of trumpets' seems to overcome evil for no very obvious cause, spiritual or rational, other than its mere existence. And the appearance of its keeper, Prester John, the mythical priest-king of the East of medieval legend, simply happens, without explanation – as do the final Mass and disappearance of the Grail.

War in Heaven is certainly still readable, but its real interest lies in the way that it reveals the Grail in a new context. It is no longer the object of a spiritual quest, but the focal point of the highest and best of religious experience. In one scene, the archdeacon and his two allies contemplate the Grail, and under their 'concentrated attention the vessel itself seemed to shine and expand'.[41] To each of them, it represents something different. For the Duke of North Ridings, the scion of an ancient Catholic family, 'the great tradition of his house stirred within him': it is the sense of religion as an inherited responsibility, an inexorable duty. For Kenneth Mornington, the publisher who had accidentally revealed the secret, the quality of the Grail is both as a symbol and as a focus for the imagination, an inspiration for the future created by past literature. He thinks of the heroes of knightly romance, and of Malory's great portrayal of the Grail at Corbenic, but also of 'a grave young God communicating to a rapt companionship the mysterious symbol of unity'. And for the archdeacon, it represents the heart of all religious experience, to which all creation yearns and responds.

It is this intense religious experience which informs and inspires Charles Williams' poetry. If *War in Heaven* is an enjoyable but somewhat dated book, his poems are intellectually powerful and sometimes abstruse. In them, he created a purely Christian Grail, perhaps the most challenging of all modern versions of the myth. His work is rooted in a deep knowledge of the Arthurian legends, and his purpose was to restore the Grail to what he saw as its rightful standing within the pattern of those stories:

The problem is simple – is the king to be there for the sake of the Grail or not? It was so the Middle Ages left it; but since then it has been taken the other way. This may still be so, but it can no longer be accidentally so. Tennyson, in that sense, was right; he meant to make the Grail an episode, and he did. He said it was only for certain people, and he modified the legend accordingly. If it is to be more, it must take the central place. Logres then must be meant for the Grail . . . This indeed must be the pure glory of Arthur and Logres . . . It is the central matter of the Matter of Britain.[42]

Williams works out this idea in his two volumes of linked poems, *Taliessin through Logres* and *The Region of the Summer Stars*.[43] He intended to write further poems which would offer a complete account of the major aspects of the Grail story, and was moving towards longer narrative poems; he left fragments of these at his death. What he did not treat in full were the key elements which he identified in the introduction to *The Region of the Summer Stars*:

. . . the argument of the series is the expectation of the return of Our Lord by means of the Grail and of the establishment of the kingdom of Logres (or Britain) to this end by the powers of the Empire and Broceliande. Logres, however, is distracted by its own sins, and the wounding of King Pelles . . . by the Lord Balin the Savage was the Dolorous Blow which prevented the union of Carbonek and Logres and therefore the coming of the Grail.[44]

Instead, the enchantments of Broceliande engineer Galahad's birth; if the Grail cannot come to Logres, then the best of Logres – Galahad, Perceval and Bors – can go to the Grail in Carbonek. Williams did not feel himself ready to write of the Dolorous Blow itself and the 'Achievement in Sarras',[45] yet the scheme of the poems does not really suffer by the absence of these moments of high drama. There is a blazing power of purpose and language about Williams' mature verse, but it is couched in a deliberately hieratic style which is not easy to approach. Furthermore, he presents us with a geography of secular and spiritual power which is complex and sometimes distracting. This is defined early in *Taliessin through Logres*, in 'The Vision of the Empire'. The image is that of a reclining female figure. The 'skull-stone' is the rocky outer edge of Britain/Logres, which stands as the Empire's soul and brain. The breasts are in Gaul, where the schools of Paris, famous in the Middle Ages, provide the nourishing milk of learning. On Rome the hands lie clasped: here the pope says Mass with its 'heartbreaking manual acts'. Jerusalem is the womb, from which Adam, fallen man, came. Caucasia is the 'fool's shame', the bottom of the figure. Lastly there is Byzantium, the navel, in which all the 'dialects' arise and re-echo. These are the 'themes' of the Empire, which are related in the same way as the body.

There is an antithesis to the Empire, on the other side of the world, in P'o-lu, where the headless Emperor of the Antipodes walks. This is the consequence of the Fall: bodies become shameful instead of a glory of creation, and so here the 'feet of creation' walk backwards. For in P'o-Lu are the feet of the Empire, and they are feet of clay. It is from here that the failure of Arthur's mission springs.

At the opposite extreme, beyond Logres, lies the Wood of Broceliande – a sea-wood, Williams calls it – and beyond a certain part of it, Carbonek, the castle in which the Grail is kept. Beyond this and a stretch of open sea, is Sarras, the home of the Grail. It is towards this that Arthur's mission and the whole feeling of the poems tend, reflecting Williams' deep religious and mystical attitudes.

Through Broceliande lies the way from earth to heaven – as witness the Grail city and castle. But Williams insists that these last lie beyond only a certain part of it. If one goes far enough the Antipodes may be reached through these same regions. C. S. Lewis explains this apparent contradiction as follows:

In a writer whose philosophy was Pantheistic or whose poetry was merely romantic, this formidable wood ... would undoubtedly figure as the Absolute itself ... All journeys away from the solid earth are equally, at the outset journeys into the abyss. Saint, sorcerer, lunatic and romantic lover, all alike are drawn to Broceliande, but Carbonek is beyond a certain part of it only. It is by no means the Absolute. It is rather what the Greeks called the Apeiron – the unlimited, the formless origin of forms.[46]

Against this background Arthur, Taliessin and Merlin start their mission.[47] The divine purpose begins to work itself out, but it requires the co-operation of man. Nimue, lady of Broceliande, sends her children, Merlin and Brisen, to perform the great task of perfect union. They meet Taliessin, the pagan poet of Wales, as they go to create the kingdom of balanced humanity, an earthly kingdom parallel to the holy kingdom of Carbonek, in which the Empire and Broceliande, the physical, the intellectual and the spiritual, shall meet. Arthur is to be their instrument; they depart for Logres, and Taliessin, now converted, for Byzantium.

Taliessin's part in the mission is not immediately clear, but we learn that on his return from Byzantium he bears with him the vision of the Empire, standing for order, which he must impose on the as yet chaotic Logres; this must be accomplished before the Grail can come to dwell there. He is also the type of the poet, which is bound up in his personal task. The poet, in Williams' view, cannot inspire love for himself, yet can inspire others to it; this is illustrated in 'Taliessin's song of the unicorn', where the poet is likened to the legendary unicorn, attracted to a virgin; she will not love him, and her lover will come and kill the creature out of jealousy. And it is around Taliessin, not Arthur, that the company who will enable the achievement of the Grail gather. The Round Table is present, dimly, as the image of secular order, but it is in the household of the poet that the purposes of the Grail are set forward.

Taliessin's mission is a success, and the Golden Age of Logres ensues. The lyric pieces which describe this involve various philosophical concepts, but centre on the nature of love. The last of these is 'The Coming of Palomides'; Palomides, learned in Arabic science, looks on Iseult and admires the geometrical beauty of her form. But at the end of the poem as he dreams of the first kind of love, physical consummation, the Questing Beast

> . . . scratched itself in the blank between
> The Queen's substance and the Queen.

He must find the answer to the connection between the flesh and the spirit before he can find intellectual love.

But the plan as a whole is doomed to failure: the actual deeds which prevent Logres from becoming the kingdom of the Grail are Arthur's unwitting incest with Morgause, and Balin's equally unconscious slaying of his brother and giving of the Dolorous Blow. Both pairs act blindly; it is not their individual fault that these things are done, but the fault of human nature, of fallen man, operating deep below the surface of Logres.

Yet out of this failure springs a measure of success. The Grail cannot come to Logres; but the uncorrupted part of Logres may reach the Grail. It is again Taliessin's task to prepare the way. The company of his household are his instrument; at the base of their efforts lies salvation worked through poetry and the senses, Taliessin's own special task. It is Taliessin as head of this 'Company of the Redeemed' who greets the first of the future Grail band to arrive at court, Perceval and his sister Blanchefleur. By the machinations of Merlin and Brisen, Galahad is born, at the cost of the sanity of his father Lancelot, for which Galahad later atones. He is delivered into Blanchefleur's care, and the space of his youth is filled by one poem only: 'Palomides before his Christening'. Palomides has failed in his quest; intellectual love is not for him. But through disillusionment comes his conversion to Christianity, if only as a belief in disbelief.

'The Coming of Galahad' takes place on the evening of Palomides' christening, and we hear of his appearance at Camelot from Taliessin, Gareth and a slave as they discuss it afterwards, a discussion so intense and poetic and abstruse that even C. S. Lewis confessed that there were passages in it which he simply did not understand. We can, however, grasp the most important image here: the union of flesh and spirit which was to have been Logres has been fulfilled in one man only. None save three will succeed, and reach Carbonek; the rest will sink into Britain. The forces of Broceliande depart.

Palomides finds the answer to his problem: what he had seen as ends in themselves, love, fame, irony, were only paths to a greater end, and, happy in this knowledge, he dies.

The climax and, simultaneously, the anticlimax are now reached. The Grail is achieved at the expense of the Round Table. So triumph on the one hand, in 'Percivale at Carbonek' and 'The Last Voyage', are balanced by the implied disaster of 'The Meditation of Mordred' and 'The Prayers of the Pope'. Mordred sees egotism replacing idealism in the crumbling kingdom, and declares 'I will have my choice and be adored for the having'; for him, the Grail is meaningless or merely a mythical cauldron of plenty:

> My father dwelled on the thought of the Grail for his luck,
> but I can manage without such fairy mechanism.
> If it does prove to be, which is no likely thought,
> I will send my own dozen of knights to pull it in.
>
> My cooks would be glad of such a cauldron of Ceridwen
> to stand by their fires . . .[48]

But Mordred is wrong, and Mordred dies; instead, the best part of Logres comes to Carbonek, and the Grail is achieved. As the Grail is withdrawn to Sarras, Logres sinks into the chaos out of which it had risen. Taliessin dissolves his company, but they gather for the last time, in flesh or in spirit, at the Mass performed by Lancelot. The mission has reached its end; all that could or can ever be achieved has been achieved. Lancelot's voice singing 'Ite; missa est' is the signal for the irrevocable dispersal, and 'that which was once Taliessin' rides slowly away.

The poems are symbolic and not a little opaque, but rich in concept; the poet in Williams struggles, sometimes unsuccessfully, with the philosopher. But the verse itself is brilliant in its incantation, and the words flow in a rich music. Here are two contrasting examples. Taliessin comes to Lancelot's Mass at the end of *Taliessin through Logres*:

> I came to his altar when dew was bright on the grass;
> he – he was not sworn of the priesthood – began the Mass.
> The altar was an ancient stone laid upon stones;
> Carbonek's arch, Camelot's wall, frame of Bors' bones.
>
> In armour before the earthen footpace he stood;
> on his surcoat the lions of his house, dappled with blood,
> rampant, regardant: but he wore no helm or sword,
> and his hands were bare as Lateran's to the work of our Lord.[49]

The measured simplicity of words and scene are very different from the following passage, the climax of Taliessin's mission: Merlin's and Brisen's incantations at the launching of the Mass. Splendour is part of the Grail's inherent attributes, and in this passage Williams evokes it with all the power that language can command, in images that 'once known, become for us one of the means by which we touch reality':[50]

> The stars vanished; they gone, the illumined dusk
> under the spell darkened to the colour of porphyry,
> the colour of the stair of Empire and the womb of woman,
> and the rich largesse of the Emperor; within was a point,
> deep beyond or deep within Logres,
> as if it had swallowed all the summer stars
> and hollowed the porphyry night for its having and holding –
> tiny, dark-rose, self-glowing,
> as a firefly's egg or (beyond body and spirit,
> could the art of the king's poet in the court of Camelot,
> after his journeys, find words for body or spirit)
> the entire point of the thrice co-inherent Trinity
> when every crown and every choir is vanished,
> and all sight and hearing is nothing else.[51]

Williams has used the Arthurian legend as the mould for his individual and intensely Christian philosophy. While the matter and events of the old tales are retained, characters and values are totally different. Yet this, in its mystical way, is one of the great works of Arthurian literature, where for once, as C. S. Lewis pointed out, poet and subject are at one:

It is in one way a wholly modern work, but it has grown spontaneously out of Malory and if the king and the Grail and the begetting of Galahad still serve, and serve perfectly, to carry the twentieth-century poet's meaning, that is because he has penetrated more deeply than the old writers themselves into what they also, half consciously, meant and found its significance unchangeable as long as there remains on earth any attempt to unite Christianity and civilization.[52]

For Charles Williams, the Grail is symbol of the possibility of the perfect union of earth and heaven; not simply the encounter of the individual soul with God, as in the medieval romances, but a great, more humane vision, defiant in its challenge to the darkly contrary evidence of history.

Retellings

Charles Williams recreates the Grail stories almost entirely, making his own new myth. Other writers have preferred to follow the medieval originals closely, while inventing their own variations on the stories, and introducing their own ideas, even though they do not change the line of the original narrative.

Adolf Muschg in *The Red Knight* (1993) gives us a set of variations on one version of the story, Wolfram's *Parzival*. He follows Wolfram's story, not only in outline but often in fine detail, and as storyteller adopts a persona similar to that of Wolfram himself in the original, commenting on the action, digressing and acting as an extra character within the story. The tale itself is massively expanded, into a novel of nearly a thousand pages, and is recast in an entirely modern way: Arthur is malicious and mocking, the Round Table a place of endless formalities and conventions. And some of the episodes take on a much darker tone: for example, the ecstatic reunion of Parzival and Condwiramurs becomes a tense argument, and Condwiramurs later questions whether Kundrie really exists, and Parzival furiously denies that he has imagined the creature who has led him 'into hell', the hell of spiritual despair. Parzival's achievement of the Grail does not bring enduring happiness: the Grail kingdom proves to have echoes of a totalitarian state, where the knights answer only to numbers, and Parzival recognizes its dark side by changing the emblem of the Grail knights from a dove to a magpie. He is crowned as king of the Grail, but at the feast which follows, the Grail provides only a revolting thin soup instead of the expected plenty.

The Grail kingdom dissolves: Feirefiz and Repanse de Schoye lead the knights to eastern lands on a kind of crusade, bearing the Grail with them. Parzival and his family watch them depart; when they turn back towards Munsalvaesche, it has vanished. A last visit to Arthur's court reveals only how deeply Arthur and his knights have misunderstood Parzival, and indeed chivalry itself. The remaining characters go their way; only Parzival, Condwiramurs and their children are left, making their way back to Parzival's birthplace. And at the very end, the hundredth chapter, in which, according to the table of contents, 'the main characters of this book reveal its secret, and the hundred is completed', is simply absent. Here there are no solutions, no happy endings; or perhaps there are, but we are not to be told about them.

The Grail itself is largely absent: Trevrizent, instead of explaining it to Parzival, delivers a virtuoso sermon on his failings, and discourses on the seven deadly sins, before he at last turns to his expected subject:

'Young sir, the Grail allows itself neither to be sought nor found. You are either summoned to the Grail or not. I haven't asked who you are; but now I fear that you are a fool, or what would be even worse, half a fool – and my beautiful monologue to myself was completely wasted on you. I will give you a book to read tomorrow, so that you can learn what one can know about the Grail; and it is much more digestible to read about the Grail than to seek it, believe you me.

'*You can't read?* Now you are joking, young man.'[53]

And with this dig at Wolfram's protestation that 'he did not know a single letter' Muschg launches into an alphabet, with which Trevrizent proposes to teach Parzival to read:

You can't read, and want to seek the Grail! Know then: anyone who can't read won't even know if he is summoned to the Grail. The Grail summons through the writing that appears on it. It is nothing else but a piece of writing which fell from heaven like a stone. And he who would guard it, must guard himself, or the stone will fall on his head, and the writing which he does not understand will fall on his soul and flatten it.[54]

The alphabet which follows, set out in alliterative definitions, shows Parzival what his relationship with his family and the rest of the world, including the Grail, should be.

The tension between writing and reading tales is at the heart of Muschg's style: he is telling 'a story of Parzival', not necessarily 'the story of Parzival'.

It is at once playful and exceedingly self-conscious, a set of variations and cadenzas on the original *Parzival*. Muschg sees the Grail as enormously powerful, controlling lives much more directly than in Wolfram; or rather, he imagines a culture where 'the stone' is invoked as the reason for all the customs that have developed over time. Of the Grail itself, he says:

Lord Tyturel had inherited the vessel in which Joseph of Arimathea, owner of the Holy Sepulchre, had gathered up the blood of our Lord. When the grave was empty he had to conceal the dish full of blood, and it was handed on in secret down the ages. It contained a dreadful secret.

The dish changed not only those whom it fed, but also itself. It was the stone which had fallen from heaven from Lucifer's crown, in his war against the Lord of Hosts. The fallen jewel was caught up by the angels who had not fought on either side. After his victory God made them guardians of the stone, in eternal penance for their lukewarm behaviour. The place where they kept their secret could never be hospitable or companionable. So it was called the Hidden Heights.[55]

This is Wolfram's text, but seen in a mirror which brings out a different set of features. The description of the Grail procession is similarly an oblique reworking of the text; it ends, not with Wolfram's ironic comments on the food provided by the Grail, but with a cornucopia that bursts out like a flood: Repanse de Schoye brings in the Grail,

... The Thing, the wish of wishes. It trembles before the guests' eyes. She puts it down on the table, at his feet. There it stands, and hardly stands still, for it is beginning to flow already.

It flows continually and yet stands still; it has no form and plays with all forms. It is the black fire that dances behind a child's eyelids when it has looked at the sun. It is the Book of Creation in Lîâze's hands, the curl in Condwîr amûrs' castle. It is the bird on its soundless flight into pure disappearance.

It flows and overflows. It falls, drop by drop, as water and wine, as sinôpel, pomegranate juice and mulberry wine. It falls as quails' breasts and smoked eel onto the table, as saddle of venison and frogs' legs, calves' liver and pieces of duck. It pours out gravy afterwards, and provides fruit sauce as well.[56]

The Grail is seen through the eyes of ordinary mortals, as a magical source of food. It has many names, 'a work of love' being one of them: but the women who carry it called it simply 'the thing': 'they should have been able to say what it was: kettle, giblet, stone or magic table. But they were precisely the ones who did not know. You could almost have said that they didn't even see it.'[57] 'But the main thing was that it worked.' Muschg brings to the fore the idea, present but only obliquely stated in Wolfram, that it is the Grail which is the driving force of the kingdom, so effective that it ensures the cohesion and security of the society of the Grail companions.[58]

A simpler reworking of Wolfram's *Parzival* is Lindsay Clarke's *Parzival and the Stone from Heaven*,[59] which is essentially Wolfram von Eschenbach's poem stripped of its obscure, rich vocabulary and set out in plain English. Subtle shifts of emphasis are used to make the story reflect the concerns of the modern world, and the author's reading of the meaning of the original is set out in an appendix. But something of the power of the story has gone: he diminishes rather than enriches the image of the Grail in the closing scene, when it appears as a human heart, a womb containing twins and finally as a glass in which Parzival sees reflected himself and Blanchefleur/Condwiramurs. The new vision is not powerful enough to bear the weight of the old myth. And this problem of a reverent approach to the original, which disallows all changes to the content of the story while attempting to reshape its ethos in modern terms, is perhaps why such new-old versions do not figure more largely among the major works of twentieth-century Grail literature.

One of the most restrained and striking retellings of a medieval version of the Grail story is Eric Röhmer's film *Perceval le Gallois* (1978), based on Chrétien de Troyes. A series of simple images, closely based on medieval illuminations – even down to the chequered pattern of the background – illustrate the tale as told by Perceval himself. The hero becomes an impersonal narrator, viewing his own deeds from a distance: but at the end he undergoes a more dramatic transformation, and doubles as Christ himself. Röhmer, having treated the scenes at the Grail castle with scrupulous fidelity,* carefully avoids any invention of a new conclusion to Chrétien's unfinished poem. Instead, he focuses on the hermit's teaching in the last scene in which Perceval appears, and on the words 'Thus Perceval came to recognize that God received death and was crucified on the Friday',[60] a re-enactment of the Crucifixion in the form of a medieval passion play begins. The actor who plays Perceval now plays the part of Christ. In creating this new finale, Röhmer acknowledges the deeply religious nature of the original, and produces an ending which is in harmony with the spirit of Chrétien's work, while avoiding the need to create a new episode in the style of the original in order to complete the text.

---

* Except that the Grail is a bowl which glows from within.

Irreverent Grails

A very small handful of writers have decided that in a world that seems constantly to mock traditional ideals, reverence towards the Grail is no longer the right approach. As a cultural point of reference, one of the traditional markers of Western civilization, it is fair game for a lighter approach. David Lodge's *Small World* (1984) satirizes academic society and its obsession with research while at the same time sending the main characters on a Grail quest of sorts: Persse McGarrigle pursues the elusive and beautiful Angelica who, like himself, studies medieval romance. Early in the novel, Persse says in conversation, 'I suppose everyone is looking for his own Grail. For Eliot, it was religious faith, but for another it might be fame, or the love of a good woman.'[61] Lodge plays skilfully with the traditional motifs and characters: the Fisher King is Arthur Kingfisher, an impotent elderly scholar who mysteriously recovers his energy, and the Siege Perilous is a coveted university chair. Other romance elements appear: Angelica has an identical twin Lily, and it is to her that Persse finally makes love, just as Lancelot makes love to Elaine thinking she is Guinevere; and an American Express card becomes a kind of enchanted weapon, 'a magic green and white card' which enables Persse to follow Angelica's endless travels on the academic lecture circuit. Both the world of scholarship and its subjects of research are neatly parodied, but it is an affectionate parody nonetheless.

In *Monty Python and the Holy Grail* (1974), just about anything is a target for humour, and general anarchy reigns. Even film-making itself is sent up – the budget will not run to horses, so a character with the two coconuts traditionally used for horses in sound effects stands in – and the knightly quest ends ignominiously with Arthur's arrest by the police. The Grail does actually figure (which is perhaps surprising), firstly when a cartoon God sends Arthur and his knights in search of it, and also when Galahad reaches the Grail castle. The Grail maidens have accidentally lit their Grail-shaped beacon, which Galahad sees; but when he enters the castle, he is beset by a bevy of enthusiastic and delighted beauties. After some initial reluctance, he is about to succumb to their temptations with an air of happy resignation, when Lancelot sweeps in and 'rescues' him, much to his annoyance. It is all good fun, contrasting an easy 1970s hedonism with the priggish attitudes of those who see evil temptresses everywhere. Galahad, dragged outside, is told by Lancelot that he has been rescued from terrible peril, but Galahad proclaims that it is his duty to 'sample as much peril as I can', and tries to return. The joke is at the expense of knightly adventures; as to the Grail itself, perhaps one can read the lascivious Grail maidens as a version of the Grail as the feminine principle, a fantastic gloss on Jessie Weston's ideas in *From Ritual to Romance*. But that is probably too weighty a view of an essentially light-hearted film.

Satire is not enough for some writers, however, who take a downright iconoclastic approach. Galahad, who does indeed come across in the medieval romances as a somewhat inhuman figure, if not a straightforward prig, is a particular target. John Erskine's *Galahad: Enough of his Life to Explain his Reputation* (1926) actually removes the Grail from the story until the last page. Erskine sets out to 'tell the story as it happened in our world, to people like ourselves or only a little better – the story, that is, as it was before poets . . . used it as a language for remote and mystical things'. Galahad's only quest until the end is the ordinary chivalric topos of rescuing a lady from two evil knights. It is Guinevere who tries to instil idealism into him, much to Lancelot's mistrust, trying to make of him a knight without physical desire, as if to atone for her sin with his father. When Galahad finds out about their affair, he cannot find a way of reconciling his idealistic principles with the world about him: the last we hear of him is that he is devoting himself 'to the search for the holiest treasure in the world'. The Grail has become a refuge to compensate for the failure of his relations with other people, who have 'larger hearts and more generous thoughts'.

In Godfrey Turton's *The Emperor Arthur* (1986), the Grail is simply a fraud, a fraud perpetrated by none other than the monks of Glastonbury under their abbot Illtyd. Illtyd is an old rival of Arthur, and is jealous of his newly acquired power. By proclaiming the holiness of the Grail and making Galahad their figurehead, he and the monks hope to overthrow the emperor, and put Galahad in his place. But the ceremony at which Galahad is to be proclaimed as emperor goes horribly wrong: the lady Ettard, his mistress, appears at his side, and the voice of Viviane the sorceress is heard, proclaiming that Ettard is to be Augusta, the empress. Galahad flees, dropping the Grail: the monks have made him out to be a chaste knight, and he has been unmasked as an impostor. Despair drives him to commit suicide. This is the blackest view of the Grail since the Puritan denunciations of the sixteenth century: it has become a pious forgery used for political ends.

Eclectic Grails

Italo Calvino specializes in tales which touch on folklore and tradition while offering a very individual view of the world. The Grail knights appear in *The Non-Existent Knight* (1959) as an order who have apparently reached 'complete communion with the all',[62] but who turn out to be tyrannical and vicious towards the peasants whose tribute of food sustains them. The Grail is an abstract ideal to which they are devoted; their king is 'so rapt by love of the Grail that he no longer needs to eat or move or do his daily needs, or scarcely to breathe. He neither feels nor sees . . .' Yet this abstracted figure presides over military parades – ''Tis a rite of the Grail' – and when the knights attack the peasants who beg to be forgiven their tribute because of famine, they claim that ''tis the Grail moving us! Abandon yourself to its burning love.' The knights are strange automata, moving in a trance; they are as empty of reality as the central character of the story, a knight who is only an empty suit of armour.

Calvino plays with the image of the Grail in another story, *The Castle of Crossed Destinies* (1969), which is one of the rare occasions when an association between the Grail and the Tarot pack actually surfaces. But this is entirely fictional, a fiction within a fiction, because the stories are predetermined by the Tarot cards which are dealt, which can be interpreted in different ways depending on which character's story they are telling. At one point the Ace of Cups – which in the accompanying images of the cards does indeed look somewhat like late medieval depictions of the Grail, but is in fact simply a splendid cup – takes on aspects of the Grail, as an alchemist and a knight compete to tell their tales using the same hand of cards:

If you look carefully, the destination for both the alchemist and the knight-errant should be the Ace of Cups, which, for the one, contains phlogiston or the philosopher's stone or the elixir of long life, and for the other the talisman guarded by the Fisher King, the mysterious vessel whose first poet lacked time – or else was unwilling – to explain it to us; and thus since then rivers of ink have flowed in conjectures about the Grail, still contended between the Roman religion and the Celtic. (. . . There is no better place to keep a secret than in an unfinished novel.)[63]

Another eclectic – and underrated – writer is Peter Vansittart, whose *Parsifal* (1988) is a virtuoso, individual version of the story. In this book, Vansittart's lifelong enthusiasm for myths and history results in a hero who embodies the different images of Parsifal in different cultures, with the Grail as a shadowy presence in the background. The fifth-century Peredur inhabits a Celtic world where there is a ritual human sacrifice in place of the king who should be killed each year, and Peredur's quest is for a 'summer princess' in the depths of winter. The first section ends with the culmination of the Celtic mysteries, in which Peredur has a vision of a 'vast, blue, airy cup tilting to drench the earth with dew',[64] before being renamed Perceval, and healing the wounded lord. We are then transported to fifteenth-century Burgundy, where Perceval is hailed as Knight of the Grail; but the Grail is dangerous territory, 'anathema to the Pope and proscribed by the Black Brothers'.[65] The Black Brothers condemn the Grail stories as fantasies and wickedness; the court believe that it has to do with alchemy and orgies, while 'Perceval remarked, rather too casually, that the Grail was too bright to actually exist.'[66] The Duke creates a masque in which all the Grail myths come together, as Perceval is questioned by the Black Brothers; he is rescued by a troop of children, who are devoted to him because of his skill in storytelling. The wheel of history moves on to the Thirty Years War, to a commune whose simple Christianity eventually gives way to outside pressures, and, after Perceval's disappearance in search of Kundry, to the last days of the Nazi era, where the narrator is questioned by Himmler about Parsifal. Through all this, the Grail is no more than a shadow, 'conceivably a simple hope, a device to cherish lost existences, purged of the animal, moulded to a shape inviolate in perfection'.[67]

And the Grail continues to fascinate novelists. Even as this book was in progress, Umberto Eco gave us a new account of a fantastical Grail quest in *Baudolino* (2000). Eco is best known for *The Name of the Rose*, and the same mixture of ingenious plotting and immensely erudite knowledge of the medieval world is presented here, with a typical playful handling of modern critical theory thrown in. The protagonist, Baudolino, is a self-proclaimed liar; how much of his story is true, particularly when his tale is a heady mixture of history and of the wonders of the East, with its marvels and monsters? Into the story of the death of Frederick Barbarossa, mysteriously drowned on crusade in 1189, and the sack of Constantinople by the crusaders in 1204, the quest for the Grail is intertwined. Readers of this book will at once recognize two of the six companions: Boron and Kyot. They set out with Baudolino to seek the 'Grasal' in the kingdom of the fabled Eastern ruler, Prester John. The other three companions have their own desires and ambitions which the Grasal may fulfil. The Poet, whose verses Baudolino claims to have written, secretly longs to obtain the Grasal for himself and to rule Prester John's kingdom. There are two non-believers, who have different ideals in mind. Abdul hopes to find the distant beloved whom he has never seen, like his half-historical counterpart, the troubadour Jaufré Rudel, who claimed to have fallen passionately in love with the countess of Tripoli on hearing of her astonishing beauty. Rabbi Solomon hopes to discover the lost ten tribes of Solomon.

On their travels they acquire a simple wooden bowl, which they decide must be the Grasal, and it is for possession of this that they eventually come to blows, in a fatal confrontation between the Poet and Baudolino, Kyot and Boron. Baudolino kills the Poet; Boron departs to write the history of the Grail, while Kyot, who cannot write, seeks someone to whom he can tell the story. As he leaves, he tells Baudolino to hide the Grail, and it is eventually concealed in a statue in Baudolino's native town. What counts is that the search for the Grail must be kept alive, for it 'has the power of moving men only when it can't be found . . . What counts is that nobody must find it, otherwise the others would stop seeking it.'[68] There speaks the poet; but at the end, when the historian to whom Baudolino has told his story wonders whether to include it in his book, he is advised to leave it out: 'would you like to put into the heads of your future readers the notion that a Grasal exists . . . ? Who knows how many lunatics would start wandering endlessly, for centuries and centuries?'[69]

To attempt to catalogue or to classify all the avatars of the Grail in modern literature begins to feel like trying to keep track of Eco's 'lunatics'. What I have tried to do is to offer some idea of how modern authors have used the legend, and the patterns into which their re-imaginings of the Grail fall, while keeping to a relatively strict criterion of what might constitute a representation of the Grail. Other pundits take a much wider view: Andrew Sinclair, for example, discovers Grails in the New World by the most casual and unfounded analogy: 'Just as there had been material Grails in the hanging ornamental bowls of the sixth century . . . so there were in Mexico and Peru when the conquistadors reached those American empires.'[70] Robert Baudry, looking for literary images of the Grail, would include among its manifestations the 'blue flower' of the German novelist Novalis, the golden cup of his contemporary E. T. A. Hoffmann, key to initiation into the secrets of the universe; and the vase cut from a single emerald in which the narrator of Jan Potocki's Gothic masterpiece *The Manuscript found at Saragossa* drinks a magic elixir which leads to ecstasy and realms of black magic. Its forms and attributes multiply, in Baudry's view (and he catalogues them enthusiastically) until 'almost everywhere . . . you can detect the supreme breath of the Grail (*le souffle suprême du Graal*)'.[71] I would beg to disagree: authors since the eighteenth century seem to have had many other things on their minds, and it is the handful of exceptions whose work we have just explored who have turned consciously to the Grail for inspiration.

21

The Question Answered?

> '... *In conclusion, a letter promising a work in eight volumes on the*
> *Grail and the Sacred Heart.*'
> '*What's its thesis? That the Grail is an allegory of the Sacred Heart or*
> *that the Sacred Heart is an allegory of the Grail?*'
> '*He wants it both ways, I think ...*'
>
> (Umberto Eco, *Foucault's Pendulum*)

Perhaps there is a solution after all, the missing key to the mystery of the Grail ...

In the room, a man is lying on the floor. It is a simple cell, such as might be found in a monastery, but it seems more like a hermitage than part of a larger building, as if it were a deliberately secluded place. In the corner of the room is a flask of water and the stale remains of a loaf of bread; the rest of the room is spotless, and completely empty except for a couch of hay in the centre. Around the couch there are ashes strewn on the floor, and in the ashes there is writing, which is evidently a series of names separated by the sign of the cross. The ashes surround the bed entirely, as if to encircle it and guard it. The man is clad in black, and is reading prayers from a small manuscript in a low voice; snatches of the words are familiar:

> Holy, Holy, Holy, Lord God of Sabaoth
> Heaven and Earth are full of thy glory

but these are mingled with strange incantatory names – 'Occynimus, Elyorem, Theloy, Archima'. The movements of the praying figure are weak, as if he had been fasting for a long time; he turns the pages eagerly but with difficulty until he comes to the final lines of his recitation, when he raises his voice in exultation:

Look upon me and hear my prayers, that through Thy grace and the power of Thy Holy Names, Thou wouldst vouchsafe to deliver my soul from the darkness of my body and the filthiness of my sins, for in Thee do I end my life.

O my God, ✝ *Stoexhor* ✝ *Ablay* ✝ *Scyystalgaona* ✝ *Fullarite* ✝ *Resphiomona* ✝ *Remiare* ✝ *Baceda* ✝ *Canona* ✝ *Onlepot*, Who said on the Cross,
It is finished![1]

At these words, he closes the book, and prepares to sleep; sleep comes quickly, for he is weary with hunger and the intense concentration on his ritual. Who knows what he sees? Is it what the great mystics sought so avidly, the Beatific Vision?

The ritual of which this is the culmination had exactly this end in view. It comes from one of the very rare books of so-called 'white magic' to survive from the Middle Ages, books where magic becomes an extension of Christian practice rather than a dark force ranged against it. It is known as *The Sworn Book*, and is supposedly by Honorius of Thebes.[2] What it aimed to provide was a way which led to the divine outside the restraints imposed by the Church. The power of the Church depended on its ability to restrict such access to those who faithfully followed its doctrines. By using *The Sworn Book*, the individual could achieve direct contact with the ultimate secrets of creation. It offered a way of doing this which circumvented the recognized routines. Instead of the long years of exceptional personal piety or of slow advancement within the church hierarchy, the possessor of *The Sworn Book* could invoke powers which gave immediate fulfilment of the desired end. It attained this by harnessing powers for good by exactly the same means that powers for evil might be constrained in the pursuit of black magic.

The visionary sleep is the culmination of a ritual which required a mere twenty-eight days to perform instead of a lifetime's devotion. However, the ritual lays great emphasis on orthodox prayer and fasting, as well as cleanliness of body. It also requires entirely orthodox attendance at Mass, but with the help of a priest who is prepared to add certain prayers to the service, from the text of *The Sworn Book*. This is not simply required once, but involves the insertion of different prayers into separate celebrations of Mass over a period of twenty days. At the end of the first three days, the first intimation of success or failure will come, because an angel will reveal 'whether you will obtain your petition or not'. If the first vision does not materialize, the opening rites must be repeated with greater care. If, on the other hand, the rites are successful, on the twenty-first day a new set of prayers is used, most of which invoke a different name of God. The names of God are a key element in *The Sworn Book*; they 'seem to be in Hebrew, Aramaic or Greek', but no detailed study of them has yet been carried out. Not only do they appear in the prayers, but it is these names which must be written in the ashes on the floor before the final prayers are said. The whole procedure is designed to create a rising sense of intensified consciousness and excitement, as the full panoply of divine names is deployed, and the effects of fasting take hold.

As Robert Matthiesen points out in his essay on *The Sworn Book*, this ritual may have appeared to work, whatever its theology and whatever the sources of its magic. He cites in support of this proposal work by neurobiologists showing how ordinary individuals, by performing 'patterned, repetitive acts' can manipulate their own bodies, using the normal reactions of the nervous system to such stimuli, to arrive at a state of 'ritual trance'. If it were indeed possible to do this in the Middle Ages, outside the formalities and structures of the Church, it would have profound implications. The Church could understand and sympathize with – indeed deeply revere – individual mystics who might achieve similar visions through their own prolonged devotions. But *The Sworn Book* undercut the teaching of the Church, which insisted that such visions were a reward for exceptional devotion and holiness. It offered a means by which the Beatific Vision, supposedly restricted to the saints in the next life and a handful of privileged devotees in this, could be attained by a mere month of ascetic practice.

It seems that the Church was aware of the threat: in 1398 and again in 1402 the faculty of theology at the university of Paris, traditionally the most learned and authoritative in matters of rooting out heresy, condemned the idea 'that by certain magical arts we can come to a vision of the Divine Essence or of Holy Spirits'. We know too that such books were not extraordinarily rare. A thirteenth-century library catalogue has thirty-six 'secret books' which the compiler does not wish to describe because they contain deep secrets and should be kept from the eyes of the public. So we are dealing with a text which does not stand alone; rather, it is part of a tradition which we can trace. It is not the tradition of black magic, but a parallel practice of magic within the Church which was evidently successfully restricted, or even entirely suppressed.

What does all this have to do with the Grail? Arguably, a great deal. We have seen how the Beatific Vision, the precise object of the ritual in *The Sworn Book*, is at the heart of the Grail romances. It is a vision achieved after rigorous spiritual self-discipline, by a knight whose spiritual cleanliness is one of his chief characteristics. Nowhere else, save in *The Sworn Book*, is it suggested that a layman can achieve such a vision. There are traces in the earlier Grail literature of a lost ritual associated with the Grail, and there are other lesser points of contact: *The Sworn Book* belongs to the magical school which invokes Solomon as one of its principal patrons, just as it is in Solomon's ship that the knights reach the Grail castle.

But *The Sworn Book* also solves one of the real mysteries of the Grail material. In the first account of the Grail story, Perceval's interview with the hermit in Chrétien's *Story of the Grail*,

the hermit whispered a prayer in his ear, repeating it to him until he had learnt it. Many of the names of Our Lord appeared in this prayer, including the greatest ones, which the tongue of man should never utter except in fear of death.[3]

The 'secret names' of Our Lord is a highly unusual idea, certainly at the end of the twelfth century. I came across *The Sworn Book* by chance, having previously asked a number of scholars – theologians as well as literary scholars – what they knew about the subject of these secret names, and had been unable to find anything definitive on the subject in a Christian context. True, there were examples of something like this in later texts, after the Jewish mystical learning known as the *kabbalah* was translated into Latin, but these were never remotely associated with the Beatific Vision, as in the Grail stories and *The Sworn Book*.

It is clear that this hypothesis makes sense of the various elements of the Grail tradition which have so far perplexed us. It also offers a solution as to how Chrétien's unfinished poem would have ended, an ending which is only preserved in *The Quest of the Holy Grail*. The Grail is about a body of secret lore within the Church, a tradition of ritual magic which was known to a select few, and which represented a kind of non-apostolic tradition. Chrétien – whose name means 'Christian', and which might perhaps be a nom de plume[4] – realized that this knowledge could safely be presented as a romance which only initiates would understand, and which would read as a chivalric story with a strong moral element to those outside the charmed circle. The book which Philip of Flanders gave him was a text similar to *The Sworn Book*, perhaps already embedded in the form of a Latin allegorical poem. The ending of his poem would have shown Perceval finding the answer to the question 'Whom does the Grail serve?': the response would have been, 'Those who know its true nature.' The 'secrets of the Grail' which Robert de Boron is so careful not to reveal, and which re-emerge disguised as orthodox Christian mysticism in the *Quest*, would have been preserved.

In support of this – and 'secret traditions' are of course notoriously difficult to establish – the later history of *The Sworn Book* provides an extraordinary thread through the maze of the Rosicrucian and Templar myths of the seventeenth and eighteenth centuries. There are six copies of *The Sworn Book* in existence. All of them are in the British Library, and five of these belonged to its founder, Sir Hans Sloane. Of these, one of the two medieval copies bears the distinctive ownership mark of Dr John Dee, whose explorations of mysticism and magic were, as we have seen, the major source of the Rosicrucian movement. This copy subsequently passed to the playwright Ben Jonson, whose interest in such matters led him to write *The Alchemist*.

One of the other manuscripts also dates to the fourteenth century, but the rest were copied in the sixteenth and seventeenth centuries, indicating a renewed curiosity about such matters now that the Church no longer had a universal grip on censorship. The other fourteenth-century copy was the property of one of the Jekyll family, whose name was so famously borrowed by Robert Louis Stevenson in connection with a different kind of magic in *The Strange Case of Dr Jekyll and Mr Hyde*. All that we know about *The Sworn Book* before it reached the library of Dr Dee is that Thomas Erghome, who left a large number of books to the friars at York in the late fourteenth century, had a copy of it in one of the seven volumes of magic in his collection.

Pursuing the link with the Rosicrucians, the movement takes its name from a 'rosy' or 'red' cross, and although the Cross of St George has been suggested, as well as the 'Red Cross Knight' of Spenser's *The Faerie Queene*, both of these are nationalistic and English and do not have the right connotations. Once we set the Grail within the context of Dee's circle through the link with *The Sworn Book*, the mystery of the 'rosy cross' is easily resolved. If you look at any Arthurian armorial,[5] the first shield is that of Galahad, whose arms are a scarlet cross on a white field. Furthermore, the scarlet cross has its own history: during a battle, the figure of a crucified man had appeared on the cross, but afterwards, by another miracle, the shield became blank, and was repainted by the guardian of the Grail with his own blood. So the Rosicrucian use of this symbol could be taken to imply the revival of the secret tradition of the pre-Reformation Church.

However, the tradition remained a secret, and is therefore difficult to trace. Even A. E. Waite, who gave the fullest account of it within the framework of Masonic and Rosicrucian thought, was careful not to betray the knowledge of the connection between the Grail and ritual magic, though at different times he wrote about both: indeed, he was the first modern scholar to discuss *The Sworn Book*. Instead, he chooses the description of the secrets of the Grail given by Robert de Boron at the end of his book *The Hidden Church of the Holy Graal*, entitling his conclusion 'The Secrets of the Grail'. The language is high-flown, in contrast with Robert de Boron's simplicity, but the message is the same:

Now the Secret Tradition in Christian times is the rumour of the Secret Sanctuary, and this tradition has many voices. The voice of spiritual alchemy, succeeding that of the Graal, is the voice of the Graal literature under another veil, but it says He is there . . . The voice of the Temple, reflected in its later revival, says that He is risen and gone away. The voice of Masonry says that the old Temple was not built according to the true and original plan. The voice of the Rosy Cross says that in places withdrawn, He, being dead, yet testifies . . . The Hidden Voice of Christ is in the Secret Literature, and I have therefore written this book as the text-book of a Great Initiation.[6]

Is *The Sworn Book* the hidden text of the Grail?

Creating a Grail Theory

We have not yet looked at Umberto Eco's *Foucault's Pendulum*, in which a modern publishing firm sets out to create a library of occult books, and the protagonists become deeply, indeed fatally, involved in their subject, although their motives at the outset are entirely cynical and commercial. Bombarded with eccentric theories and lunatic texts by would-be authors, they are finally ensnared by an enthusiast, Colonel Ardenti, who produces a fragmentary medieval text which, so he claims, was found in a secret vault in a French provincial town. He offers them an interpretation of it which involves, in quick succession, the Templars, magical code-breaking, and then the Grail, which, according to Ardenti, he first identified as an immense treasure-hoard, then as radioactive material, before discovering that it was a power source of such magnitude that mastery of it would enable the Templars to rule the world. The Druids and Tibetan religion are quickly sucked into the maelstrom of ideas, followed by Stonehenge. Ardenti leaves, but the next they hear of him is that he has vanished, apparently murdered. Eco takes us on a grand tour of the occult and the conspiracy theory of history, from Brazilian *candomblé* to characters who claim to have lived for many generations, from Druid rites to the satanists' parodies of Catholicism, and, inevitably, into territory which he himself describes elsewhere, in more serious mode:

The Middle Ages of so-called Tradition, or of occult philosophy . . . an eternal and rather eclectic ramshackle structure, swarming with Knights Templar, Rosicrucians, alchemists, Masonic initiates, neo-Kabbalists, drunk on reactionary poisons sipped from the Grail, ready to hail every neo-fascist Will to Power, eager to accept as a visual ersatz for their improbable visions all the paraphernalia of the Middle Ages [as a barbaric age], mixing up René Guénon and Conan the Barbarian, Avalon and the Kingdom of Prester John.[7]

Eco seems to have read everything and to have woven it all into a picaresque novel, whose subtleties and allusions only emerge if you are well versed in the panoply of eccentric beliefs and literature which he parodies. The three editors, more to amuse themselves than to make money, decide to use Ardenti's document to create a Plan which will draw all these diverse elements together; it will lead the seeker to a map, which, combined with the movement of Foucault's pendulum at a critical moment in time, will reveal the great source of hidden power which offers world domination. The narrator continues:

'The challenge isn't to find occult links between Debussy and the Templars. Everybody does that. The problem is to find occult links between, for example, cabala and the spark plugs of a car.'
    I was speaking off the top of my head, but I had given Belbo an idea. He talked to me about it a few mornings later.
    'You were right. Any fact becomes important when it's connected to another. The connection changes the perspective; it leads you to think that every detail of the world, every voice, every word written or spoken has more than its literal meaning, that it tells us of a Secret. The rule is simple: Suspect, only suspect . . .'[8]

Eco puts it another way in *Faith in Fakes*, writing of today's imaginary version of the Middle Ages:

Anti-scientific by definition, these Middle Ages keep going under the banner of the mystical weddings of the micro- with the macrocosm, and as a result they convince their adepts that everything is the same as everything else and that the whole world is born to convey, in any of its aspects, the same message. Fortunately the message got lost, which makes its Quest fascinating . . .[9]

If *Foucault's Pendulum* is Umberto Eco's demonstration of how to create a mystical message in this 'proof-tight, philology-resistant' universe, the first part of this chapter is an exercise in conjuring up just such a Plan in relation to the Grail, on a rather humbler level. I have restricted myself in one way: all the information used is genuine and verifiable, in contrast to many of the books which propose 'secret histories', where the actual details do not stand up to closer examination; but the technique is the same. Let us call it 'argument by false association': because two acknowledged facts appear to have something in common, they must be connected. We started by connecting the prayer in Chrétien's *Story of the Grail* with *The Sworn Book*. Now that prayer is indeed one of the more mysterious elements in the Grail texts. It is a prayer specifically containing 'many of the names of Our Lord',[10] rather than of God, and it is not a ritual using the names of God. There is an analogy with *The Sworn Book*, but no connection. A much better parallel is to be found in the similar prayers recorded in fourteenth-century manuscripts,[11] with a prologue saying that 'he who names them will not die that day of an evil death [*male mort*]'. This echoes a superstition associated with the taking of communion in the Middle Ages, and brings us back into the much more probable context of the Mass. This is relatively unexplored territory, and research may well reveal other texts associated with the names of God.

Furthermore, *The Sworn Book* is very probably later than Chrétien's poem: it has been argued that there is a reference to it in a work written in 1247, but other scholars believe it to be as late as the mid-fourteenth century. One of the problems is precisely that the Jewish *kabbalah*, from which the names are partly drawn, and from which the idea of the multiple names of God and their power is derived, was not accessible in the West until the late thirteenth century, and while it is possible that Chrétien and 'Honorius of Thebes' might both have had knowledge of it direct from Jewish sources, this would be quite exceptional, and the dating further undermines our constructed argument.

Next, we have to assume that Chrétien and Robert de Boron both know, but do not tell us, that the story of the Grail is connected with the Beatific Vision. Now we have no proof of this, and it is much more likely that the theme of the vision within the Grail belongs, not to ritual magic, but to the perfectly orthodox circles of Cistercian mysticism. The visionary elements in *Perlesvaus* are quite independent of the Beatific Vision, and show that there is no one accepted tradition about the nature of the Grail; our supposed argument requires that there is just such a unique and self-contained tradition. It is far more likely that the connection between Grail and Beatific

Vision is an imaginative leap by a later author, developing the theme of the Grail as archetype of the Mass chalice. Ultimately, we have to acknowledge that the identification of Galahad's vision with the Beatific Vision is convincing, but by no means absolute.

Let us assume for the moment, however, that the medieval connection of *The Sworn Book* and the Grail is a tenable idea, and look again at the suggested modern history of our tradition. John Dee's ownership of *The Sworn Book* is interesting, but the missing element, until the nineteenth century, is the Grail itself. Dee's magic has no element of ritual Catholicism about it, which would be present if the tradition of *The Sworn Book* had been part of his repertoire. He probably collected the manuscript as part of his general research into magic; the same would apply to Ben Jonson who, after all, satirized practitioners of the mysterious arts in *The Alchemist*, which would make him an unlikely follower of the secret tradition. Equally, the suggestion that Galahad's red cross shield is the origin of the Rosicrucian emblem is plausible in itself, but probability is against it, given the very low level of readership of the medieval romances when the Rosicrucian texts were written. In view of its great popularity, Spenser's *The Faerie Queene* is a much more likely source if we admit a connection with Dee and English intellectual circles. And A. E. Waite's work on the Grail and *The Sworn Book* was, despite his occult activities, largely scholarly: it is only in the conclusion of his book that he moves into the speculative and occult aspects of the Grail, and what he is seeking is 'the books concerning the Secret Words of the Eucharist or the text of the Secret Ordination', neither of which relate easily to *The Sworn Book*. And if he already knew the text which he was looking for – his work on *The Sworn Book* appeared in 1898, *The Hidden Church of the Holy Graal* in 1909 – the passage would be a very elaborate double-bluff. In short, our little excursion into the world of 'answers' to the question of the Grail is of no more value than any of its predecessors in the genre.

The Grail is, in one of its aspects, a mystery, a historical and literary puzzle; and there is an insatiable appetite for solutions to such mysteries and puzzles. It is as if, living in an uncertain age, we are desperate to eliminate the mysteries of the past, and to remove the doubts that may surround them. Another element is the need to reassure ourselves that scientific investigation is capable of solving such enigmas, and that simple answers can be found to the most complex questions: which brings us back to the conspiracy theory of history, which offers concrete solutions instead of the shifting kaleidoscope of knowledge which is all we can really grasp about the past.

In keeping with this need for clear-cut solutions, the books which purport to 'solve' mysteries such as the Grail appear to use scholarly procedures and well-documented evidence, and this is the point of our little fantasy above. There is no one 'truth' about the Grail. All we can do is suggest how it may have arisen, and what it may mean, because, I would argue, the force that shaped it is not history, but imagination, the creative thought that subtly built on an unfinished story, and invented the Grail. All we can do is to offer a possible account of its history; there are many other such accounts, and perhaps this is not the right one. In the end, it can only be the version which I believe to be right. So we end on the central themes of this book – the interplay between imagination and belief.

Epilogue

The last and most unexpected imaginative transformation of the Grail has largely come about in the last half-century. In literature, it has always been the legendary vessel of Arthurian romance, but if you open a newspaper today, you are very likely, in the course of a week's reading, to come across two or three references to 'the holy grail'. But it is not simply 'the Holy Grail', it is the 'holy grail of . . .' a particular line of commercial or scientific development, or of a competitive sport, or of a type of product – in other words, something entirely material. The idea of the Grail as an unattainable object of desire is implicit in the medieval romances: Wolfram von Eschenbach calls it 'earth's perfection's transcendence',[1] and as early as the fifteenth century the Welsh poet Dafydd ap Gwilym uses the expression in a secular context: 'I have travelled to find thee as if for the Grail.'[2] But with the retreat of the Grail romances in the sixteenth century, it is not surprising that the Grail disappears from common speech, and Gwilym's comment is a lone premonition of the Grail's future.

For in the twentieth century, 'the holy grail' has come to represent an abstract perfection, the idea that somewhere a perfect solution or object can be found. This image of the Grail depends on the original image of it in literature as being the ultimate object of a prolonged search. The earliest example that I have found is in Stead's *If Christ came to Chicago* in 1894, which is a splendidly materialist specimen of the usage: 'The quest of the Almighty Dollar is their Holy Grail.' In 1896, the architect Edwin Lutyens, wooing his future wife Emily Lytton against her family's wishes, could write, 'If only like that knight of old I could have some hope – some Grail – how I would fight', and when she gave him that hope, he wrote back that he had 'seen the Holiest Grail'.[3] It is an image that turns up again in a much less idealistic context in F. Scott Fitzgerald's *The Great Gatsby*: Gatsby ponders his relationship to Daisy, whom he has casually seduced, and realizes that 'it didn't turn out as he had imagined. He had intended, probably, to take what he could and go – but now he found that he had committed himself to the following of a Grail . . .'[4]

But all this still has a strong literary resonance; it was only in the last decade of the twentieth century that the 'holy grail' metaphor had come to exist quite independently of any literary overtones. A survey of three French journals in the early 1990s revealed a fondness among scientists for the term 'holy grail' in relation to the more speculative and philosophical areas of research, such as particle physics and the origins of the universe. The idea of a 'unified theory' in physics was 'what researchers called the Holy Grail of physics'.[5] Interestingly, the French usage has tended to evolve towards 'grail' rather than 'holy grail', dropping the adjective. But many of the examples from this period still retain at least an overtone of the original image, either through a specific reference to the legend, or because they deal with the area where science invades territory usually regarded as belonging to religion, as in the origins of the universe. And in the world of computing, there are at least five languages or applications whose acronym is GRAIL, which once again testifies to the word's resonance.[6]

What is most striking is the way in which in the last decade, 'the holy grail' has become a usage entirely free of its historical associations. An excellent example is a French headline about Unilever's disastrous washing powder which produced exceptional results but destroyed the fabrics: 'The washing was so clean that we thought Unilever had rediscovered the Holy Grail.' This concept of the Grail, now normally reduced to lower-case letters, is extraordinarily frequent in today's press. I began to collect specimens of it when I embarked on this project in 1997. At first they were relatively few and far between, if sometimes bizarre. Prize finds included 'the Holy Grail that is the original and indestructible Tupper Wonder Bowl, its burp [when opened] bowdlerised to a whisper in the 1970s'[7]; ' "Nude" tights are something of a holy grail';[8] 'Pretty much the Holy Grail of foodstuffs, Marmite boasts an enormous range of vitamins',[9] and – somehow inevitably – 'the holy grail of the Modern Miss – an enormous willy'.[10] It is just possible to read the description of the Tupperware Wonder Bowl as a splendidly erudite and ironic evocation of the original concept of the Grail as a vessel, but it is clear that 'holy grail' has become a journalistic shorthand for the ultimate perfection that will always elude us. Research into newspaper archives seems to reveal a steep increase in the usage of the term in the mid-1990s (Appendix 4); the proportion of references to the original legend or to related works, such as the oft-cited *Monty Python and the Holy Grail*, is around 10 per cent of the total. Although the chosen samples are difficult to evaluate because neither the methods of the search engines nor the principles of selection for archiving are documented, the overall trend seems convincing enough. From a relatively infrequent occurrence in the 1980s and early 1990s, the phrase rapidly became commonplace from 1995 onwards, but now appears to be levelling off.

So yet again the holy Grail has been reimagined. From being a mythic and romantic version of the central act of one of the world's great religions, it is now some sort of Platonic archetype, the ideal primal version of whatever object or objective or concept is under discussion. It epitomizes Browning's couplet

> A man's reach should exceed his grasp,
> Or what's a heaven for?

Where our medieval forebears reached for the spiritual and intangible, our materialistic age reaches only for the top shelf in the supermarket.

This is not the book I expected to write when I started. I believed that I would be engaged with pagan myth and the marvellous Celtic stories on which much of Arthurian romance is founded, and that the first shape of the Grail would be dimly discernible in the remote past. Instead, I find myself offering a very different picture, deeply indebted to medieval theology and mysticism, driving forces which, as an agnostic, I can only approach from outside, like Lancelot at the door of the Grail chamber. And the modern image of the Grail in literature, scholarship and popular history has proved quite other than what I had imagined: a myth which is common ground for writers across Europe, yet reinterpreted in highly individual ways. The Grail encompasses great ideals and masterpieces of literature and music, from Chrétien de Troyes' original lesson in compassion, through Wolfram's reconciliation of heavenly and earthly chivalry, to the dazzling splendour of Malory's final Grail scene. If the image of the Grail had not been rekindled in the nineteenth century, its medieval forms would have been reason enough for this book. But the Grail also gives us Wagner's final masterpiece, and a whole range of modern reinterpretations which show how the concept behind it is extraordinarily persistent, and open to all kinds of new creative imaginings. True, there have been moments of dullness and banality and there have been other times when it seemed that there was nothing to be found save shadows flickering against the flames of the imagination, but as a whole our journey has been set among the highest and most challenging ideas of the human spirit.

Postscript

The Da Vinci Code

Since the present book appeared, the extraordinary publishing phenomenon of *The Da Vinci Code* has brought the Grail back into the public eye. It has spawned a host of books trying to fill in the background, very few of which have much factual element in them. Once there was imagination, and there was history: imagination was imagination, and history was history. Now, it seems, imagination is entitled to pass for history. The prologue to *The Da Vinci Code* is headed 'Fact' and assures us that 'The Priory of Sion – a European secret society founded in 1099 – is a real organization.' This is pure fiction, and has been shown to be fiction since the 1980s. The source of the fiction, like so much of the material in the book, is *The Holy Blood and the Holy Grail*, which I described on p.310 as fictional history. Dan Brown, the author of *The Da Vinci Code*, has realized that the thesis put forward in *The Holy Blood and the Holy Grail* is the ideal substance for a modern thriller, but his protestations in a television interview that everything in his book is historical are simply untrue. Imagination has become history, and history has become imagination.

The true story of the Priory of Sion cannot be stated too strongly or too often.* It centres on the forgery of the documents which later became known as the '*dossiers secrets*' (which Dan Brown amusingly describes as 'discovered *by* the Bibliothèque Nationale' in 1975). These documents were placed there in 1975, and were 'discovered' by Pierre Plantard, who had created them with the help of a journalist, Gérard de Sède and Philippe de Chèrissey. The two key pieces were a genealogy which showed the Merovingian kings of France as being descendants of Jesus Christ and Mary Magdalene, and a list of the masters of the supposed 'Priory of Sion'. Many of the ideas behind this dossier derive from our old friends 'Sâr Méradock' (p.292) and Julius Evola (p.305). The genealogy was taken from a French historical journal, *Les cahiers de l'histoire*, and was extended back from the real Merovingian kings to link with Jesus Christ. The list of the masters was pure invention, with a quite improbable sequence of well-known names.

---

* Even the exposés of the Plantard forgeries are not always in agreement: see Robert Richardson in *Gnosis* (No. 51, Spring 1999), pp. 49–55; Alain Jourdain in *Tribune de Genève*, 16 September 2004; and material on http://priory-of-scion.com.

The dossier was subsequently exposed as a hoax by Jean Luc-Chaumet. But this did not stop the authors of *The Holy Blood and the Holy Grail* from using the documents as authentic in their book, despite the fact that they were in touch with Chaumet, and had been warned by him of the true nature of the material on which they were relying. The myth was quickly established; it was sufficiently implausible to make an attractive idea for those who found ordinary history too dull or too inexplicable to make sense. Something like this was the key to all the problems that orthodox history offered. The production of evidence that the whole thing had been dreamt up by Plantard did nothing to deter the believers. Plantard was deeply involved in right-wing royalist fantasies, and wanted to show that he was of Merovingian blood and could therefore fantasize that he was rightful king of France. Although the details of the forgery have not been systematically researched, and the authors determined to unmask the hoax are not always in agreement on details, there is no doubt that we are dealing with something which is pure invention. In a recent television interview, de Sède's son described the whole affair, which he had discussed with his father after the latter had admitted that it was a hoax, as 'absolute piffle', a suitably colourful epitaph on a colourful affair.

It is relatively easy to demolish the Priory of Sion. The problem with the story of the marriage of Jesus and Mary Magdalene is that there is nothing substantial there in the first place; trying to demonstrate that this is nonsense is like taking a gun to a ghost. It is all innuendo and hints, and there are no errors because nothing definite is ever produced as evidence. The most tangible idea, that *Sam Greal* should be read as *Sang real* (which is any case royal, not holy, blood) stems from a single unreliable source, John Harding's reinterpretation in the 1460s, which may have been a deliberate attempt to secularize the Grail or just a straight misreading (p.227). No earlier writers even hint at this explanation, and no-one took it up again until the appearance of *The Holy Blood and the Grail*. The legends of Mary Magdalene contain nothing about the supposedly intimate relationship with Jesus, and it is only in the gnostic gospels, discovered at Nag Hammadi in 1945, that we find real evidence that there is more to her story than is told in the New Testament. But this does no more than show that she was possibly a more important figure in the early days of Christianity than the Gospels suggest, and that the misogynist streak that first emerges with Paul's leadership had suppressed accounts of her ministry and even the gospel she wrote. The gnostic gospels are difficult territory, the preserve of a handful of scholars; but they lead neither to the 'holy blood' of the Merovingians, nor to the Grail.

The Grail, as we have seen, is an ideal. It is ironic that its modern popularity owes much to its adoption by modern entertainers, to the comedy of *Monty Python and the Grail*, and the equally, if unintentionally, comic world of *The Da Vinci Code*.

I

The Major Grail Romances 1180–1250

Titles used in text are in **bold italic**; original titles are in *italic*. Dates in all cases are tentative.

Chrétien de Troyes and continuations	Robert de Boron	Lancelot-Grail (Vulgate cycle)	German romances	Other French romances
Perceval 1180–90 (*Le Conte du Graal*)				
First Continuation 1190–1200				
Second Continuation **Elucidation Prologue** **Bliocadran Prologue** All 1200–1210	**Romance of the History of the Grail** (*L'Estoire du Graal*) (verse) before **Joseph of Arimathea** (*Joseph d'Arimathie*) (prose) **Merlin** (prose) **Perceval** (Didot-*Perceval*) (prose) All 1200–1210			**High Book of the Grail** (*Perlesvaus*) before 1210
Third Continuation (Manessier) possibly 1210–20		**Lancelot** (Grail episodes) 1210–20	Wolfram von Eschenbach, **Parzival** 1210–20	
Fourth Continuation (Gerbert de Montreuil) 1226–30		**Quest of the Holy Grail** (*Queste del Saint Graal*) 1220–30		
		History of the Holy Grail (*L'Estoire del Saint Graal*) 1230–40	Heinrich von dem Türlin, **The Crown** 1230–40	
		Romance of the Grail (Post-Vulgate Cycle) 1240–50		

2

Visual Images Relating to the Medieval Grail Stories

The following list generally includes items which pre-date the earliest Grail romances, and which are therefore potential sources for the imagery in them. A few early thirteenth-century examples contemporary with the first romances are also included.

For what follows, see Rehm (1995) 31–9.

I. The Crucifixion
THE CHALICE AT THE CRUCIFIXION
Male figure holds up a cup, and has a paten in his other hand containing the host
Utrecht Psalter, Utrecht, University Library MS 32, psalm 115, f.67r.

Small crowned figure (?Ecclesia) holding chalice at foot of cross into which blood flows
Cambridge, Fitzwilliam Museum, Marlay Bequest, Cuttings no. 21 (G.1). See Jochen Luckhardt and Franz Niehoff, *Heinrich der Löwe und seine Zeit* (exhibition catalogue, Herzog Anton Ulrich-Museum, Braunschweig, Munich 1995) I, 214, item D35.

Christ crucified by the virtues: separate figures hold the lance (Sponsa) *and the chalice* (Fides)
Donaueschingen Psalter, Fürstl. Fürstenbergische Hofbibliothek MS 185, f.8 (Schiller (1968) 4, pl.451).

Standing figure of Ecclesia *holds chalice into which blood flows*
Ivory plaque on binding of *Perikopenbuch* of Heinrich II, Metz, c.860–870, Munich, Bayerische Staatsbibliothek, Clm 4452 (Burdach (1974) 258; Lasko (1972) pl.29; Chazelle (2001) 267).

Plaque on the *pala d'oro*, San Marco, Venice, made in 976 for doge Orseolo, incorporating fifth-century material, subsequently restored in 1102–1107.

Sacramentary of Drogo of Metz BN MS Lat. 9428, f.43v illuminated initial (Burdach (1974) 297; Chazelle (2001) 255).

Carolingian relief of Metz school used on binding of BN MS Lat. 9453 (Burdach (1974) 303; Lasko (1972) pl.62).

Tournai diptych in the treasury at Tournai Cathedral, late ninth century (Burdach (1974) 298).

Ivory panel of Bishop Adalbero, 984–1005, Treasury, Metz Cathedral (Burdach (1974) 303; Lasko (1972) pl.109).

Book cover of abbess Theophanu, 1039–56, Treasury, Essen Minster (Lasko (1972) pl.141).

French ivory, Museo Bargello, Florence, Collezione Carrand 32, eleventh century (Burdach (1974) 305).

Ivory panel c.1050, Brussels, Musées Royaux (Lasko (1972) pl.173).

Chest, c. 950–1000, Metz school, Brunswick, Herzog-Anton-Ulrich Museum, inv. MA 59 (Schiller (1968) 4, pl.373).

Enamelled plaque, c.1160–70, Paris, Musée de Cluny (Lasko (1972) pl.221).

Paten, Tremessen church, Poland, probably a gift of Henry the Lion c.1175 (Schiller (1968) 4, pl.424).

Enamelled portable altar, Meuse school, twelfth century, Augsburg, Städtliche Kunstsammlung (Schiller (1968) 4, pl.446).

Hortus Deliciarum of Herrad von Landsberg, late twelfth century (Burdach (1974) 324–5; reproduced in Roques (1955) pl.III).

Wall painting at Sigena, Catalonia, early thirteenth century (Walter Oakeshott, *Sigena: Romanesque Paintings in Spain & the Winchester Bible Artists*, London 1972, pl.66).

Crucifixion window from Bourges, thirteenth century (Roques (1955) pl.I).

The image is found as late as the fifteenth century: see Bodleian Library, Oxford, MS Douce 93 f.100v.

For further examples, see Malcor (1991) 135 ff.

Images in manuscripts of Grail romances

Paris, BN MS Fr 120, f.520; Amsterdam, Bibliotheca Hermetica Philosophica, MS.1, f.6d; Bonn, Universitätsbibliothek, MS 526, f.1.

The Virgin holding a chalice

Examples in Catalan art at Tahull, Encamp (Andorra), Anyós and Ginestarre de Cardós.

See Riquer (1960) 271–3 and pls I–IV.

Saint John (?) collects Christ's blood at the Deposition

Sacramentary, first quarter of twelfth century, Fulda, MS Aa 35, fol. 81r.

See Jakobi-Mirwald (1994) I, 189, 196.

THE SPEAR OF LONGINUS

Burdach (1974) 233–70, discusses the iconography of Longinus. Many of the items discussed by him are reproduced in Lasko (1972) and Chazelle (2001). Burdach's list is by no means exhaustive: for example, there is a fine example of the Crucifixion showing Longinus in the Winchester Psalter f.22, *c.*1140–60 (Francis Wormald, *The Winchester Psalter*, London 1973, pl.25), and a similar composition in the east window at Poitiers Cathedral, given by Henry II and Eleanor of Aquitaine *c.*1180 (Joan Evans, *Art in Medieval France 987–1498*, Oxford 1969, pl.98). For further examples see Schiller (1968) 4, pls 300 ff. The earliest example is a Palestinian chest, possibly seventh or eighth century, in the Biblioteca Apostolica Vaticana, and there are tenth-century examples from rural France, for example a carving in the museum at Chinon and a fresco at Saint Pierre-les-Églises in Poitou. On Irish art, see Ann Dooley, 'The *Gospel of Nicodemus* in Ireland', in Izydorcyzk (1997) 367–8.

II. The Last Supper

Depictions of the Last Supper showing a fish on the central dish are found from the eighth century onwards in Byzantium. (It is possible that the sixth-century Augustine Gospels* showed a fish in the Last Supper scene, but the image is difficult to read due to damage.) In Western art, the Last Supper is only infrequently illustrated, as compared with the Crucifixion; but the majority of examples up to the mid-thirteenth century show a dish, either flat or with a foot, which contains a fish. In one extreme version, each apostle has his own fish (St Julien de Jonzy, below). The following is necessarily only a list of what has come to my attention.

Psalter, Byzantium, *c.*856–7, Moscow, Historical Museum MS gr.129, f.3 (Schiller (1968) 2, pl.68).

Miniature in Stuttgart Psalter, 820–30, France, Stuttgart, Württembergische Landesbibliothek, MS.23, f.43r (Schiller (1968) 2, pl.81).

Paten, Byzantium, late-ninth–mid-tenth century, private collections, Switzerland (*The Glory of Byzantium* ed. Helen C. Evans and William D. Wixom, New York 1997, 67).

Miniature in *Perikopenbuch* of Heinrich II, 1007–1012, Reichenau (south Germany), Munich, Bayerische Staatsbibliothek, CI m lat 4452, f.105 (Schiller (1968) 2, pl.84).

Ivory relief, mid to late eleventh century, southern Italy, Salerno, Museo del Duomo (Schiller (1968) pl.70).

Reliquary casket in silver, niello engraved with copper enamel, *c.*1000, north German, Hildesheim Cathedral (G. Swarzenski, *Monuments of Romanesque Art: The Art of Church Treasures in North-Western Europe*, London 1954, rp 1974, pl.30 fig.74.

Miniature in Wys'schrader Coronation Gospels, 1085–1086, Bohemia, Prague, University Library, MS XIV A 13, f.38v (Schiller (1968) pl.86).

Mural, Panteon Real de S. Isidoro, late eleventh century (Antonio Viñayo Gonzalez, *Pintura romanica: panteon real de San Isidoro – Léon*, Léon 1971, pl.18).

* Corpus Christi College, Cambridge, MS 286, f.125.

Tympanum, church of St Julien de Jonzy, Burgundy, mid-twelfth century (Schiller (1968) pl.92).

Bas relief in chancel, Volterra cathedral, twelfth century (Schiller (1968) pl.93).

3

Theological Terms Used in Text

Discussion of the evolution of the idea of the Holy Grail inevitably involves some quite technical details of medieval Christian belief, and while these will be tolerably familiar to followers of the Roman Catholic Church, some explanation is needed for other readers.

The events of the *Mass* are closely related to the events surrounding the death and resurrection of Jesus in the New Testament, and centre on his death, which is seen by the Church as a sacrifice which redeems sinful mankind. His *crucifixion* becomes an offering of his body and blood, and is linked to his words to his disciples at the last meal they shared together (the *Last Supper*), when he took bread and wine, and gave it to them, telling them to do likewise in his memory. The sharing of *bread and wine* is believed by Roman Catholics to be so intimately linked with the sacrifice of Jesus' body and blood that at the Mass which commemorates this sacrifice, the bread and wine consecrated by the priest become the actual body and blood of Christ. The original substances are transformed into physically different substances; hence the term *transubstantiation*. The crucial moment in the Mass is the *elevation of the Host*, when the priest holds up the Host and the consecrated *chalice*, the cup containing the wine, for the congregation to worship; a bell is traditionally rung at this moment. The Mass *wafer* or bread, known as the *Host*, is usually placed on a paten; the paten and chalice together are the vessels associated with the performance of Mass. When the congregation partakes of the consecrated bread and wine, this act is called *communion*.

Devotion centred on the Mass was so intense in the medieval period that a feast-day dedicated to the Host evolved in the thirteenth century, the feast of the Body of Christ or *Corpus Christi*. Other words commonly used for the bread and wine of the Mass service are the *Eucharist* or the *sacrament*.

Other Terms Used

APOCRYPHA, APOCRYPHAL BOOKS

The text of the Christian Bible was not definitely established until the second half of the second century AD. Before that, a number of texts had been created which appeared to qualify for inclusion in the Old or New Testaments, and, once the definitive text was established, these were relegated to the second rank, but were not totally ignored. Some Old Testament books survived to become the Apocrypha found in the English King James Bible, but New Testament apocrypha were generally disregarded, though they continued to circulate and to be translated from Latin or Greek into French, German and other vernacular languages. It is these that served as sources for the Grail romances; their relationship to the established Gospels varies from being relatively close retellings of the story of Jesus to versions which are clearly legendary. For an English version of many of the texts, see M. R. James, *The Apocryphal New Testament* (Oxford 1953).

CHASUBLE

A sleeveless garment, usually richly embroidered, worn by the priest while celebrating Mass.

CIBORIUM

A receptacle in which the consecrated Host was placed if it was not to be used immediately, for instance if it was to be taken to a sick person at their home.

DEPOSITION

The taking down of Christ's body from the cross after the Crucifixion, a crucial moment in the Gospel story from the point of view of the Grail legends, since it is at this point that Joseph of Arimathea is mentioned by name in the Gospels. He is said to have begged Pontius Pilate to be allowed to bury Christ, and was therefore responsible for the removal of the body.

TRINITY

In Christian belief, God is three persons in one: God the Father, the God of the Old Testament; God the Son, the God of the New Testament; and God the Holy Spirit. The so-called 'throne of grace' Trinity is the best visual representation of this: it shows God the Father holding the crucified Christ, while the Holy Spirit in the form of a dove hovers above them.

4

Use of the Term 'Holy Grail' in Major Newspapers, 1978–2002

	2001 2002	1999 2000	1997 1998	1995 1996	1993 1994	1991 1992	1989 1990	1987 1988	1985 1986	1983 1984	1981 1982	1979 1980	1977 1978
Guardian	142	115											
The Times	171	171	124	85	71	59	33	23	14				
Daily Telegraph	27	21	10										
Independent	95	54											
New York Times	140	145	110	32									
Washington Post	96	91	91	55	53	51	38	44	26	25	23	20	15
Le Figaro	113	61	66										
*Frankfurter Allgemeine**	280												
La Repubblica	10	8	2										
El País	53	45	25	31	20	13	13	7	8	15	6	3	1

* Total number of entries on database; not possible to break down by year.

Bibliography

Achad, Frater, *The Chalice of Ecstasy; being a Magical and Qabalistic Interpretation of the Drama of Parzival* (Chicago 1923).

Adamnan, *De Locis Sanctis*, ed. D. Meehan, Scriptores Latini Hiberniae III (Dublin 1958).

Adolf, Helen, *Visio Pacis, Holy City and Grail* (University Park, PA 1960).

Albrecht [von Scharfenberg?], *Jüngerer Titurel*, ed. Werner Wolf (and Kurt Nyholm) (Berlin 1955, 1968, 1985, 1992).

Allaire, Gloria, *Modern Retellings of Chivalric Texts* (Aldershot and Brookfield, VT 1999).

Amalarius of Metz, *Amalarii Episcopi opera liturgica omnia*, ed. J. M. Hanssens, Studi e Testi 139, II: *Liber officialis* (Vatican City 1948).

Andersen, Elizabeth, 'Heinrich von dem Türlin's *Diu Crône* and the *Prose Lancelot*: an intertextual study', *Arthurian Literature* VII (1987) 23–49.

Anderson, Flavia, *The Ancient Secret* (London 1953).

Angebert, Jean-Michel, *The Occult and the Third Reich: The Mystical Origins of Nazism and the Search for the Holy Grail* (New York 1974).

Anitchkof, E., 'Le Galaad du Lancelot-Graal et les Galaads du Bible', *Romania* 53 (1927) 388–91.

Anitchkof, E., 'Le Saint Graal et les rites eucharistiques', *Romania* 55 (1929) 174–94.

Anitchkof, Eugene, *Joachim de Flore et les milieux courtois* (Paris 1931).

Anna Comnena, *The Alexiad*, ed. and tr. E. R. A. Sowter (Harmondsworth 1956).

Appel, Anne M., 'Dante: poet of the grail: a study in the relationship between the Commedia and the Queste del Saint Graal', *Dissertation Abstracts* 31:11 (1971) 6044A.

Aroux, Eugène, *Les mystères de la Chevalerie et de l'Amour platonique au Moyen Âge* (Paris 1858, rp Puiseaux 1994).

Baigent, Michael, Leigh, Richard and Lincoln, Henry, *The Holy Blood and the Holy Grail* (London 1982).

Baldwin, John W., 'From the Ordeal to Confession: In Search of Lay Religion in Early Thirteenth Century France', in *Handling Sin*, ed. Peter Biller and Alastair Minnis (York, Woodbridge and Rochester, NY 1998) 191–209.

Barb, A. A., 'Mensa sacra: Round Table and Holy Grail', *Journal of the Warburg and Courtauld Institute*, 19 (1956) 40–67.

Barber, Malcolm, *The New Knighthood: A History of the Order of the Temple* (Cambridge and New York 1994).

Barczewski, Stephanie L., *Myth and National Identity in Nineteenth-Century Britain* (Oxford 2000).

Bartoli, Renata, 'Galaad "Figura militis christiani" ', *Museum Patavinum*, IV (1987) 341–61.

Batley, Edward M., 'Lessing's Templars and the Reform of German Freemasonry', *German Life and Letters* n.s.52 (1999) 297–313.

Baudry, Robert, 'La vertu nourricière du Graal', in *Banquets et manières de table au Moyen Âge*, Senefiance 38, Centre Universitaire d'Etudes et de Recherches Médiévales d'Aix (Aix-en-Provence 1996) 435–50.

Baudry, Robert, *Graal et littératures d'aujourd'hui* (Rennes 1998).

Baumgartner, Emmanuèle, 'Les aventures du Graal', in *Mélanges de langue et littérature françaises . . . offerts à Monsieur Charles Foulon* (Rennes 1980) I 23–8.

Baumgartner, Emmanuèle, *L'Arbre et le Pain: essai sur la Queste del Saint Graal* (Paris 1981).

Baumgartner, Emmanuèle, 'Robert de Boron et l'imaginaire du livre du Graal', in *Arturus Rex: Acta Conventus Lovaniensis*, ed. Willy van Hoecke et al. (Leiden 1991) II 259–68.

Baumgartner, Emmanuèle, 'Le Graal, le temps: les enjeux d'un motif', in *Le Temps, sa mesure et sa perception au Moyen Âge*, ed. Bernard Ribémont (Caen 1992) 9–17.

Baumgartner, Emmanuèle, *Chrétien de Troyes: Le conte du graal* (Paris 1999).

Baumstark, Reinhold, *Der Gral. Artusromantik in der Kunst des 19 Jahrhunderts* (Köln 1995).

Bayer, Hans, *Gralsburg und Minnegrotte: die religiös-ethische Heilslehre Wolframs von Eschenbach und Gottfrieds von Strassburg*, Philologische Studien und Quellen 93 (Berlin 1978).

Bayer, Hans, *Gral. Die hochmittelalterliche Glaubenskrise im Spiegel der Litteratur*, Monographien zur Geschichte des Mittelalters (Stuttgart 1983) (and review by D. H. Green, *Modern Languages Review*, LXX (1985) 971–5).

Beaufils, Christophe, *Le sâr Péladan: biographie critique* (Paris 1986).

Beckett, Lucy, *Richard Wagner*: Parsifal, Cambridge Opera Handbooks (Cambridge 1981).

Beigg, Ean and Beigg, Deike, *In Search of the Holy Grail and the Precious Blood – a travellers' guide* (London 1995).

Beltran Martinez, Antonio, *Estudio sobre el Santo Caliz de la Catedral de Valencia*, 2nd edn (Valencia 1984).

Benham, Patrick, *The Avalonians* (Glastonbury 1993).

Bernadac, Christian, *Le mystère Otto Rahn (Le Graal et Montségur): Du Catharisme au Nazisme* (Paris 1978).

Berthelot, Anne, 'The Other-World Incarnate: "Chastel Mortel" and "Chastel des Armes" in the *Perlesvaus*', *Yale French Studies* Special Issue (1991) 210–24.

Berthelot, Anne, 'Le Graal nourricier', in *Banquets et manières de table au Moyen Âge*, Senefiance 38, Centre Universitaire d'Études et de Recherches Médiévales d'Aix (Aix-en-Provence 1996) 453–66.

Berthelot, Anne, '*Perlesvaus* ou la fin du Graal', *PRIS-MA*, XIV:2 no. 28 (1998) 99–116.

Berthelot, Anne, '«L'épée qui décolla saint Jean-Baptiste» dans *Perlesvaus: le Haut Livre du Graal*', in *Jean-Baptiste le Précurseur au Moyen Âge*, Senefiance 48, Centre Universitaire d'Etudes et de Recherches Médiévales d'Aix (Aix-en-Provence 2002) 17–28.

Bertin, Georges, *La quête du saint Graal et l'imaginaire: essai d'anthropologie arthurienne* (Condé-sur-Noireau 1997).

Bertoni, Giorgio, *San Gral*, Istituto di Filologia Romanza della R. Università di Roma, Testi e Manuali 19 (Modena 1940).

Besamusca, Bart and Brandsma, Frank, 'Jacob de Maerlant, traducteur vigilant, et la valeur didactique de son *Graal-Merlin*', in *Miscellanea Medievalia, Mélanges offerts à Philippe Ménard*, ed. J. Claude Faucon et al. (Paris 1998) I 121–31.

Biget, Jean-Louis, 'Mythographie du Catharisme (1870–1960)', *Cahiers de Fanjeaux*, 14 (1979) 271–342.

Birch-Hirschfeld, Adolf, *Die Sage vom Gral: ihre Entwicklung und dichterische Ausbildung in Frankreich und Deutschland im 12. und 13. Jahrhundert* (Leipzig 1877, rp Wiesbaden 1969).

Birks, Walter and Gilbert, R. A., *The Treasure of Montségur* (Wellingborough 1987).

Blank, Walter, 'Die positive Utopie des Grals: zu Wolframs Graldarstellung und ihrer Nachwirkung im Mittelalter', in *Sprache, Literatur, Kultur. Studien zu ihrer Geschichte im deutschen Süden und Westen Wolfgang Kleiber zum 60. Geburtstag*, ed. Albrecht Greule and Uwe Ruhberg (Stuttgart 1989) 337–53.

Bliocadran: A Prologue to the Perceval of Chrétien de Troyes: edition and critical study, ed. Lenora D. Wolfgang, Beihefte zür Zeitschrift für Romanische Philologie 150 (Tübingen 1976).

Bloete, J. F. D., 'Die Gralstelle in der Chronik Helinands und der Grand Saint Graal', *Zeitschrift für Romanische Philologie*, XLVIII (1928) 679–94.

Bloete, J. F. D., 'Nachträgliche Bemerkungen zum Gralpassus in Helinands Chronik', *Zeitschrift für Französische Sprache und Litteratur* (Wiesbaden) LV (1931) 91–6.

Bogdanow, F., *The Romance of the Grail* (Manchester 1966).

Bogdanow, Fanni, 'Le Perlesvaus', in *Le roman jusqu'à la fin du xiii* siècle*, in Frappier and Grimm (1984) ii. 43–52.

Bogdanow, Fanni, *La version post-vulgate de la Queste del Saint Graal*, Société des anciens textes français (Paris 1991).

Bohigas Balaguer, P., *Los textos españoles y gallego-portugueses de la Demanda del Santo Grial*, Revista de Filologia Española, Anejo VII (Madrid 1925).

Boisserée, Sulpice, 'Über die Beschreibung des Tempels des heiligen Grales in dem Heldengedicht: Titurel Kap. III', *Abhandlungen der philosophisch-philologischen Classe der königlich Bayerischen Akademie der Wissenschaften*, I (1835) 307–92.

Bollard, John K., 'Theme and Meaning in *Peredur*', *Arthuriana* 10 (2000) 73–98.

Bolton, Brenda M., 'Some thirteenth-century women in the low countries – a special case?', *Nederlands Archief voor Kerkgeschiedenis*, 61 (1981) 7–29.

Bond, F. Bligh, *The Glastonbury Scripts V, VI* (Glastonbury 1924–5).

Bonte, Michel, Fabiani, Daniela and Grandjean, Monique, eds, *La quête de graal chez les écrivains européens contemporains* (Nancy 1994).

Borchmeyer, Dieter, *Richard Wagner: Theory and Theatre* (Oxford 1991).

Borgnet, Guy, 'Parcival et le graal dans le Buch der Abenteuer d'Ulrich Fuetrer', in Buschinger and Spiewok (1994b) 39–69.

Bouchard, Constance Brittain, *Sword, Miter, and Cloister: Nobility and the Church in Burgundy, 980–1198* (Ithaca and London 1987).

Bouchard, Constance Brittain, *Holy Entrepreneurs: Cistercians, Knights, and Economic Exchange in Twelfth-Century Burgundy* (Ithaca and London 1991).

Boulton, D'A. J.D., *The Knights of the Crown*, 2nd edn (Woodbridge and Rochester, NY 2000).

Bourre, Jean-Paul, *La quête du Graal: du paganisme indo-européen à la chevalerie chrétienne* (Paris 1993).

Bouyer, Louis, *Les liens magiques de la legende du Graal* (Paris 1986).

Bradley, Marion Zimmer, *The Mists of Avalon* (New York 1982).

Brall, Helmut, *Gralsuche und Adelsheil: Studien zu Wolframs Parzival* (Heidelberg 1983).

Breyer, Ralph, 'Cundrî, die Gralsbotin?', *Zeitschrift für Germanistik*, n.s. 5:1 (1996) 61–75.

Bridel, Yves, 'Julien Gracq et le Graal', in *Zwischen den Kulturen: Festgabe für Georg Thürer . . .*, ed. Felix Ingold (Bern and Stuttgart 1980) 25–38.

Browe, Peter, *Die eucharistischen Wunder des Mittelalters*, Breslauer Studien zur Historischen Theologie, n.s. 4 (Breslau 1938).

Brown, A. C. L., *Origins of the Grail Legend* (Cambridge, MA 1943).

Brownlee, Kevin, *Romance: Generic Transformation* (Hanover, NH, and London 1985).

Bruckner, Matilda Tomaryn, 'Looping the Loop through a Tale of Beginnings, Middles and Ends: From Chrétien to Gerbert in the *Perceval* Continuations', in *'Por le soie amisté': Essays in Honor of Norris J. Lacy*, ed. Keith Busby and Catherine M. Jones (Amsterdam 2000) 33–51.

Bryant, Nigel, tr., *The High Book of the Grail, a translation of the thirteenth century romance of Perlesvaus* (Cambridge and Totowa, NJ 1978).

Budge, E. A. Wallis, *The Book of the Cave of Treasures* (London 1927).

Bullock-Davies, Constance, 'Chrétien de Troyes and England', *Arthurian Literature*, I (1981) 1–61.

Bulst-Thiele, Marie-Louise, *Sacrae Domus Militiae Templi Hierosolymitani*

Magistri: Untersuchungen zur Geschichte des Templerordens 1118/19–1314 (Göttingen 1974).

Bumke, Joachim, *Wolfram von Eschenbach*, 5th edn (Stuttgart 1981).

Burdach, K., *Der Gral: Forschungen über seinen Ursprung und seinen Zusammenhang mit der Longinuslegende*, 2nd edn (Darmstadt 1974).

Burgess, Glyn, *Two Medieval Outlaws* (Woodbridge and Rochester, NY 1997).

Burns, E. Jane, 'Quest and Questioning in the Conte del Graal', *Romance Philology*, 41 (1988) 251–66.

Busby, Keith, Nixon, Terry, Stones, Alison and Walters, Lori, eds, *Les manuscrits de Chrétien de Troyes*, Faux Titre 73 (Amsterdam and Atlanta, GA 1993).

Buschinger, Danielle, *Lorengel*, Göppinger Arbeiten zur Germanistik CCLIII (Göppingen 1979).

Buschinger, Danielle, 'L'utopie du Graal', in *Gesellschaftsutopien im Mittelalter / Discours et figures de l'utopie au Moyen Âge*, ed. Danielle Buschinger and Wolfgang Spiewok, Wodan: Greifswalder Beiträge zum Mittelalter 30 (Greifswald 1994) 29–37.

Buschinger, Danielle, 'Zum Rappoltsteiner Parzival', in Buschinger and Spiewok (1994b) 71–8.

Buschinger, Danielle and Spiewok, Wolfgang, *König Artus und der heilige Graal*, Wodan: Greifswalder Beiträge zum Mittelalter 32 (Greifswald 1994) [=1994a].

Buschinger, Danielle and Spiewok, Wolfgang, *Perceval – Parzival hier et aujourd'hui ... pour fêter les 95 ans de Jean Fourquet*, Wodan: Greifswalder Beiträge zum Mittelalter 33 (Greifswald 1994) [= 1994b].

Butts, Mary, *Armed with Madness* (London and New York 1928, rp London 2001).

Butts, Mary, *The Journals of Mary Butts*, ed. Nathalie Blondel (New Haven and London 2002).

Byles, C. E., *The Life and Letters of R.S. Hawker* (London and New York 1905).

Cackett, S. W. G., *The Antioch Cup* (London n.d. [1935]).

Caesarius of Heisterbach, *The Dialogue on Miracles*, tr. H. von E. Scott and C. C. Swinton Bland (London 1929).

Calvino, Italo, *The Castle of Crossed Destinies* (London 1977).

Calvino, Italo, 'The Non-Existent Knight', in *Our Ancestors* (London 1980, rp 1998).

Campbell, J. F., *Popular Tales of the West Highlands*, new edn (Edinburgh 1994).

Campbell, Joseph, *The Masks of God: Creative Mythology* (London 1968).

Campbell, Joseph, 'Indian reflections in the Castle of the Grail', in *The Celtic Consciousness*, ed. Robert O'Driscoll (New York 1982) 3–29.

Campbell, Mary Baine, 'Finding the Grail: Fascist Aesthetics and Mysterious Objects', in *King Arthur's Modern Return*, ed. Debra Mancoff (New York and London 1998) 213–25.

Carley, James P., *Glastonbury Abbey: The Holy House at the Head of the Moors Adventurous* (Woodbridge and New York 1988).

Carley, James P., ed., *Glastonbury Abbey and the Arthurian Tradition* (Cambridge 2001) [=2001a].

Carley, James P., 'A Fragment of *Perlesvaus* at Wells Cathedral Library', in Carley (2001a) 309–36 [=2001b].

Carley, James P., 'A Grave Event: Henry V, Glastonbury Abbey, and Joseph of Arimathea's bones', in Carley (2001a) 285–302 [=2001c].

Carley, James P. and Crick, Julia, 'Constructing Albion's Past: an annotated edition of *De origine gigantum*', in Carley (2001a) 347–418 [=2001d].

Carnegy, Patrick, 'Which Way to the Grail?' Programme book for Royal Opera House, Covent Garden Production of *Parsifal*, December 2001, pp. 44–51.

Cavendish, Richard, *King Arthur and the Grail* (London 1978).

Cazelles, Brigitte, *The Unholy Grail: A Social Reading of Chrétien de Troyes 'Conte du Graal'* (Standford, CA 1996).

Cérisy, Colloque de, *Graal et Modernité*, Cahiers de l'Hermétisme (Paris 1996).

Chandès, Gérard, 'La société de communication et ses graals: panorama', in Cérisy (1996) 151–67.

Chapman, Graham, Jones, Terry, Gilliam, Terry, Palin, Michael, Idle, Eric and Cleese, John, *Monty Python and the Holy Grail (Book)* (London 1977).

Charvet, Louis, *Des Vaus d'Avaron à la Queste du Graal* (Paris 1967).

Chazelle, Celia, *The Crucified God in the Carolingian Era: Theology and Art of Christ's Passion* (Cambridge and New York 2001).

Chrétien de Troyes, *Cligés*, ed. Wendelin Foerster (4th edn by Alfons Hilka) (Halle 1921).

Chrétien de Troyes, *Le Roman de Perceval ou le Conte du Graal*, ed. William Roach, Textes Littéraires Français, 2nd edn (Geneva and Paris 1959).

Chrétien de Troyes, *Perceval: the Story of the Grail*, tr. Nigel Bryant (Cambridge and Totowa, NJ, 1982).

Chrétien de Troyes, *Le Roman de Perceval ou le Conte du Graal: édition critique d'après tous les manuscrits*, ed. Keith Busby (Tübingen 1993).

Christian, C., *Pendragon* (London 1979; originally published as *The Sword and the Flame*, London 1978).

Die Chroniken der niedersächsischen Städte: Magdeburg I, Chroniken der deutsche Städte VII (Leipzig 1869).

Chrysostom, St John, *The Divine Liturgy*, ed. Placid de Meester (London 1926).

Ciggaar, Krijnie N., 'Robert de Boron en Outremer? Le culte de Joseph d'Arimathie dans le monde byzantin et en Outremer', in *Polyphonia Byzantina: Studies in Honour of Willem J. Aerts*. ed. Hero Hokwerda et al., Mediaevalia Groningana 13 (Groningen 1993) 145–59.

Clarke, Lindsay, *Parzival and the Stone from Heaven* (London 2001).

Cocteau, Jean, *Les chevaliers de la table ronde* (Paris 1937).

Combarieu, Micheline de, 'Voir Dieu ou l'Apocalypse du Graal', *PRIS-MA*, XI:1 (1995) II 55–74.

Constantine VII Porphyrogenitus, *Le livre des cérémonies*, tr. Albert Vogt (Paris 1935).

Conway, Sir Martin, 'The *Sacro Catino* at Genoa', *Antiquaries Journal*, IV (1924) 11–18.

Corley, Corin, 'Refléxions sur les deux premières Continuations de *Perceval*', *Romania*, 103 (1982) 235–58.

Corley, Corin, 'Wauchier de Denain et la Deuxième Continuation de *Perceval*', *Romania*, 105 (1984) 352–9.

Corley, Corin, 'Manessier's Continuation of *Perceval* and the Prose *Lancelot* cycle', *Modern Languages Review*, 81 (1986) 574–91.

Corley, Corin, *The Second Continuation of the Perceval*, Modern Humanities Research Association Texts and Dissertations XXIV (London 1987).

Cormeau, Christoph, >*Wigalois*< und >*Diu Crône*<: *Zwei Kapitel zur Gattungsgeschichte des nachklassischen Aventiureromans*, Münchner Texte und Untersuchungen zur deutschen Litteratur des Mittelalters 57 (Zurich and Munich 1977).

Cormier, Raymond, *Three Ovidian Tales of Love* (New York and London 1986).

Crawford, Deborah K. E., 'St Joseph and Britain: the Old French origins', *Arthuriana*, 11:3 (2001) 1–20.

Currer-Briggs, Noel, 'The Turin Shroud and the Holy Grail: A Genealogist's View', *Genealogists' Magazine*, 22:2 (1986) 125–38.

Currer-Briggs, Noel, 'The Turin Shroud and the Holy Grail: A Genealogist's View – 2.', *Genealogists' Magazine*, 22:3 (1986) 101–6.

Currer-Briggs, Noel, 'The Turin Shroud and the Holy Grail: A Genealogist's View – 3.', *Genealogists' Magazine*, 22:4 (1986) 143–6.

Currer-Briggs, Noel, *The Shroud and the Grail: A Modern Quest for the True Grail* (London and New York 1987).

D'Arcy, Anne Marie, *Wisdom and the Grail: The Image of the Vessel in the* Queste del Saint Graal *and Malory's* Tale of the Sankgreall (Dublin 2000).

Dahlhaus, Carl, *Richard Wagner's Music Dramas* (Cambridge 1979).

Damian-Grint, Peter, *The New Historians of the Twelfth Century Renaissance* (Woodbridge and Rochester, NY 1999).

Daniëls, Johannes Cornelius, *Wolframs Parzival, S. Johannes der Evangelist und Abraham bar Chija* (Nijmegen 1937).

Decker, Ronald, Depaulis, Thierry and Dummett, Michael, *A Wicked Pack of Cards: The Origins of the Occult Tarot* (London 1996).

Delay, Florence and Roubaud, Jacques, *Graal théâtre* (Paris 1977).

Delcourt-Angélique, Janine, '«Lapsit exillis»: le nom du Graal chez Wolfram von Eschenbach (Parzival 4697)', *Marche romane*, 27:3–4 (1977) 55–126.

Delcourt-Angélique, Janine, 'Le Graal de Chrétien de Troyes: pour Wolfram von Eschenbach "un objet non identifié au Livre V ..."', in Stiennon et al. (1984) 89–105.

Deschaux, Robert, 'Merveilleux et fantastique dans le Haut Livre du Graal: *Perlesvaus*', *Cahiers de civilisation médiévale X^e-XIIe siècles*, 26:4 (1983) 335–40.

Diverres, Armel Hugh, 'The Grail and the Third Crusade. Thoughts on *Le Conte del Graal* by Chrétien de Troyes', *Arthurian Literature*, X (1990) 13–109.

Domínguez Lasierra, Juan, 'Aragon legendario: el Santo Grial', *Turia*, 18 (1991) 140–59.

Dorst, Tankred, *Parzival: Ein Szenarium* (Frankfurt am Main 1990).

Dragonetti, Roger, *La vie de la lettre au moyen âge: Le conte du Graal* (Paris 1980).

Driscoll, Daniel J., ed. and tr., *The Sworn Book of Honorius the Magician* (Gillette, NJ, 1983).

Dubost, F., *Aspects fantastiques de la littérature médiévale (XIIème-XIIIème siècles): l'Autre, l'Ailleurs, l'Autrefois* (Paris 1991).

Dubuis, Roger, 'La première rencontre de Perceval avec le Graal, dans le "Conte du Graal" de Chrétien de Troyes et le "Parzival" de Wolfram von Eschenbach', *Germanisch-romanische Monatsschrift*, XXXII (1982) 129–55.

Duby, Georges, 'Les «jeunes» dans la société aristocratique dans la France du nord-ouest au xiie siècle', in *Féodalité* (Paris 1996) 1383–98.

du Monstier, Arthur, *Neustria Pia, seu de omnibus et singulis abbatiis et prioratibus totius Normanniae . . .* (Rouen 1673).

Dumoutet, Édouard, *Le désir de voir la hostie et les origines de la dévotion au Saint-Sacrement* (Paris 1926).

Dumoutet, Édouard, *Le Christ selon la Chair et la Vie liturgique au Moyen Âge* (Paris 1932).

Dumoutet, Édouard, *Corpus Domini. Aux sources de la piété eucharistique médiévale* (Paris 1942).

Dundes, Alan, 'The Father, Son and Holy Grail', *Literature and Psychology*, XII (1962) 101–12.

Durandus, Gulielmus, *Rationale divinorum officiorum*, ed. J. Beleth (Naples 1859).

Duval, Paulette, *La pensée alchimique et le Conte du Graal* (Paris 1979).

Eckermann, Johann Peter, *Gespräche mit Goethe in den letzten Jahren seines Lebens*, ed. Ernst Beutler (Zurich 1948).

Eco, Umberto, *Faith in Fakes*, tr. William Weaver (London 1986).

Eco, Umberto, *Foucault's Pendulum*, tr. William Weaver (London 1989).

Eco, Umberto, *Baudolino*, tr. William Weaver (London 2002).

Eliot, T. S., *Collected Poems 1909–1962* (London and Boston 1963).

Elliott, J. K., *The Apocryphal New Testament* (Oxford 1993).

The Elucidation Prologue, ed. A. W. Thompson (Chicago 1931).

Entwistle, William J., *Arthurian Legend in the Literature of the Spanish Peninsula* (London and New York 1925).

Ernst, Ulrich, 'Kyot und Flegetanis in Wolframs "Parzival": Fiktionaler Fundbericht und judisch-arabischer Kulturhintergrund', *Wirkendes Wort*, 35 (1985) 176–95.

Erskine, John, *Galahad: Enough of his life to explain his reputation* (Indianapolis, n.d. [1926]).

Evans, Sebastian, *In Quest of the Holy Grail* (London 1898).

Evola, J., *Il Mistero del Graal e la tradizione ghibellina dell'Impero* (Bari 1937).

Faivre, Antoine, 'Présence du Graal dans les courants ésotériques au xxe siècle', in *Graal et Modernité*, Cahiers de l'Hermétisme (Paris 1996).

Fanger, Claire, ed., *Conjuring Spirits: Texts and Traditions of Medieval Ritual Magic* (Stroud 1998).

Fanthorpe, Patricia and Fanthorpe, Lionel, *The Holy Grail Revealed; The Real Secret of Rennes-le-Château* (North Hollywood 1982).

Faugère, Annie, *Les origines orientales du Graal chez Wolfram von Eschenbach*, Göppinger Arbeiten zur Germanistik 264 (Göppingen 1979).

Fauriel, Claude, *Historie de la poésie provençale* (Paris 1846).

Fichtenau, Heinrich, 'Zum Reliquienwesen im früheren Mittelalter', in *idem.*, *Beiträge zu Mediaevistik* (Stuttgart 1975) I 108–44.

Fiedler, Leslie, 'Why is the Grail Knight Jewish? A Passover Meditation', in *Aspects of Jewish Culture in the Middle Ages*, ed. Paul A. Szarmach (Albany 1979) 151–69.

Fitzgerald, F. Scott, *The Great Gatsby* (London 1950).

Flood, John L., 'Early printed versions of the Arthurian romances', in W. H. Jackson and S. A. Ranawake, *The Arthur of the Germans: the Arthurian Legend in Medieval German and Dutch Literature*, Arthurian Literature in the Middle Ages III (Cardiff 2000).

Foerster, Wendelin, ed., *Kristian von Troyes Cligés*, 4th edn ed. Alfons Hilka (Halle 1921).

Folger, Herbert, 'Eucharistie und Gral', *Archiv für Liturgiewissenschaft*, V (1957) 96–102.

Fotitch, Tatiana and Steiner, Ruth, ed., *Les lais du roman de Tristan en prose*, Münchener Romanistische Arbeiten XXXVIII (Munich 1974).

Fouke Fitz Waryn, ed. E. J. Hathaway et al. (Oxford 1975).

Fourquet, Jean, *Wolfram von Eschenbach et le Conte du Graal* (Paris 1966).

Frantzen, Allen J., *Desire for Origins: New Language, Old English, and Teaching the Tradition* (New Brunswick and London 1990).

Frappier, Jean, *Chrétien de Troyes et le mythe du Graal* (Paris 1972).

Frappier, Jean, *Autour du Graal*, Publications romanes et françaises CXLVII (Geneva 1977).

Frappier, Jean, *Chrétien de Troyes: the man and his work*, tr. Raymond J. Cormier (Athens, OH 1982).

Frappier, Jean and Grimm, Reinhold R., eds, *Le roman jusqu'à la fin du xiiie siècle*, Grundriss der romanischen Literaturen des Mittelalters IV (Heidelberg 1978, 1984).

Freeman-Regalado, Nancy, '*La chevalerie celestiel*: spiritual transformations of secular romance in *La Queste del Saint Graal*', in *Romance: Generic Transformation*, ed. Kevin Brownlee (Hanover NH and London 1985) 91–113.

Frolow, A., *Recherches sur la déviation de la IVe croisade vers Constantinople* (Paris 1955).

Frolow, A., *La relique de la vraie croix* (Paris 1961).

Füeterer, Ulrich, *Prosaroman von Lanzelot nach der Donaueschinger Handschrift*, ed. Arthur Peter (Hildesheim and New York 1972).

Gallais, Pierre, 'Robert de Boron en Orient', in *Mélanges offerts à Jean Frappier* (Geneva 1970) I 313–19.

Gallais, Pierre, *Perceval et l'Initiation* (Paris 1972).

Gallais, Pierre, *L'imaginaire d'un romancier français à la fin du xiie siècle*, Faux Titre 33 (Amsterdam 1988).

Gavara, Joan J., ed., *Reliquias y relicarios en la expansión mediterránea de la Corona de Aragón: el Tesoro de la Catedral de Valencia* (Valencia 1998).

Gazay, J., 'Études sur les légendes de sainte Marie-Madeleine et de Joseph d'Arimathie', *Annales du Midi*, LI (1939) 225–84, 337–89.

Geary, Patrick J., *Furta sacra: Thefts of Relics in the Central Middle Ages* (Princeton, NJ 1978).

Gerbert de Montreuil, *La continuation de Perceval*, ed. Mary Williams and Marguerite Oswald, Classiques Françaises du Moyen Âge (Paris 1922–1975).

Gerritsen, W. P., 'Jacob van Maerlant and Geoffrey of Monmouth', in *Arthurian Tapestry. Essays in Memory of Lewis Thorpe*, ed. Kenneth Varty (Glasgow 1981) 368–88.

Gicquel, Bernard, 'Aux origines du Graal: quelques sources de Chrétien de Troyes et Wolfram von Eschenbach', *Recherches germaniques* 10 (1980) 3–17.

Giffin, Mary E., 'A reading of Robert de Boron', *Publications of the Modern Languages Association of America*, 80 (1965) 499–507.

Gilbert, R. A., *A. E. Waite, Magician of Many Parts* (Wellingborough 1987).

Gilbert, R. A., *The Golden Dawn Scrapbook* (York Beach, ME 1997).

Gilliam, R., ed., *Grails: Quest of the Dawn* (New York 1994).

Gilson, Étienne, 'La mystique de la grâce dans la Queste del Saint Graal' in *idem., Les idées et les lettres* (Paris 1932) 59–91.

Girart de Roussillon, ed. M. Hackett (Paris 1963).

Girouard, Mark, *The Return to Camelot* (New Haven and London 1981).

Glencross, Michael, *Reconstructing Camelot: French Romantic Medievalism and the Arthurian Tradition* (Cambridge and Rochester, NY 1995).

Godwin, Joscelyn, *The Theosophical Enlightenment* (Albany 1994).

Godwin, Malcolm, *The Holy Grail: its origins, secrets and meaning revealed* (London 1994).

Goetinck, Glenys, *Peredur: A Study of Welsh Tradition in the Grail Legends* (Cardiff 1975).

Goetinck, Glenys, 'The Quest for Origins', in *The Grail: A Casebook*, ed. Dhira A. Mahoney (New York and London 2000) 117–47.

Gogan, L. S., *The Ardagh Chalice* (Dublin 1932).

Göller, Karl-Heinz, 'From Logres to Carbonek: the Arthuriad of Charles Williams', in *Arthurian Literature*, I (1981) 121–73.

Golther, Wolfgang, *Parzival und der Gral in der Dichtung des Mittelalters und der Neuzeit* (Stuttgart 1925, rp New York 1974).

Golther, Wolfgang, *Parzival in den deutschen Literatur*, Stoff- und Motivgeschichte der deutsche Literatur 4 (Berlin and Leipzig 1929).

Gonzalo de Berceo, *El sacrificio de la misa* in *Obras completas V*, ed. Brian Dutton (London 1981).

Gossen, Carl Theodor, 'Zur etymologischen Deutung des Grals', *Vox Romanica*, 18 (1959) 177–219.

Gottfried von Strassburg, *Tristan*, tr. A. T. Hatto (Harmondsworth 1960).

Goulet, Denyse, 'Le role d'Arthur et du Graal dans *Lohengrin*', *Le Moyen Âge*, XC (1984) 39–63.

Gouttebroze, Jean-Guy, 'A quoi sert le repas du Graal? Remarques sur la liturgie du Graal dans le *Conte du Graal*', in *Banquets et manières de table au Moyen Âge*, Senefiance 38, Centre Universitaire d'Études et de Recherches Médiévales d'Aix (Aix-en-Provence 1996) 451–67.

Gouttebroze, Jean-Guy, *Le précieux sang de Fécamp*, Essais sur le Moyen Âge, 23 (Paris 2000).

Gowans, Linda M., 'New Perspectives on the *Didot-Perceval*', *Arthurian Literature*, VII (1987) 1–22.

Gowans, Linda M., 'The Grail in the West: prose verse and geography in the *Joseph* of Robert de Boron', *Nottingham French Studies*, 35:2 (1996) 1–17.

Gowans, Linda M., 'What did Robert de Boron really write?' [forthcoming]

Gracia, Paloma, 'El mito del Graal', in *Literatura de caballerias y origenes de la novela*, ed. R. Beltran (Valencia 1998) 63–76.

Gracq, Julien, *Oeuvres complètes* (Paris 1989).

Grand, A. C., 'Le Haut Livre du Graal, Perlesvaus: Jean de Nesle and the *terminus ad quem*', *Bulletin bibliographique de la Société Internationale Arthurienne*, XLIV (1992) 233–5.

Green, D. H., *The Beginnings of Medieval Romance: Fact and Fiction, 1150–1220* (Cambridge 2002).

Groos, Arthur, 'Dialogic transpositions: the Grail hero wins a wife', in *Chrétien de Troyes and the German Middle Ages*, ed. Martin H. Jones and Roy Wisbey, Arthurian Studies xxvi (Cambridge and Rochester, NY 1993) 257–76.

Groos, Arthur, *Romancing the Grail: Genre, Science and Quest in Wolfram's Parzival* (Ithaca and London 1995).

Grueb, Werner, *Wolfram von Eschenbach und die Wirklichkeit des Grals* (Dornack 1974).

Guénon, René, 'L'ésoterisme du Graal', in *Lumière du Graal*, ed. René Nelli (Paris 1951) 37–49.

Guénon, René, *Le roi du monde* (Paris 1958).

Gutman, Robert, *Richard Wagner: The Man, His Mind and His Music* (London 1968).

Haferland, Harald, 'Die Geheimnisse des Grals. Wolframs "Parzival" als Lesemysterium?' *Zeitschrift für deutsche Philologie*, 113:1 (1994) 23–51.

Hagen, Paul, *Der Gral*, Quellen und Forschungen zur Sprach- und Culturgeschichte der germanischen Volker LXXXV (Strassburg 1900).

Hamel, A. G. van, 'The Celtic Grail', *Revue Celtique*, XLVII (1930) 340–82.

Hamilton, Bernard, 'Montségur: the history and mythology of a Cathar fortress' (private communication).

Hamilton, W. E. M. C., 'L'interpretation mystique de *La Queste del Saint Graal*', *Neophilologus*, XXVII (1942) 94–110.

Hammer-Purgstall, Joseph Freiherr von, 'Mysterium Baphometis Revelatum seu fratres militiae templi, qua Gnostici et quidem Ophiani apostasiae, idolodulae et impuritatis convicti per ipsa eorum monumenta', *Fundgruben des Orients*, VI (Vienna 1818) 3–120.

Hardy, Thomas, *Wessex Tales* (London 1952).

Hardyng, John, *The Chronicle of Iohn Hardyng...*, ed. Henry Ellis (London 1812).

Harris, J. Rendel, 'Glass Chalices of the First Century', *Bulletin of the John Rylands Library Manchester*, 11 (1927) 286–95.

Harty, Kevin, *Cinema Arthuriana* (London and New York 1991).

Hawker, R. S., 'The Quest of the Sangraal', in *Cornish Ballads and other poems* (London and New York 1908).

Heelas, Paul, *The New Age Movement: the Celebration of the Self and Sacralization of Modernity* (Oxford 1996).

Hein, Christoph, *Die Ritter der Tafelrunde* (Frankfurt 1989).

Heinrich, G. A., *Le Parcival de Wolfram d'Eschenbach et la légende du Saint-Graal* (Paris 1855, rp Puiseaux 1990).

Heinrich von dem Türlin, *Die Crône*, ed. Gottlob Heinrich Friedrich Scholl. Bibliothek des Literarischen Vereins in Stuttgart 27 (Stuttgart 1852).

Heinrich von dem Türlin, *The Crown*, tr. J. W. Thomas (Lincoln, NE and London 1989).

Heinrich von Ofterdingen, *Der Wartburgkrieg und verwandte Dichtungen*, ed. Friedrich Mess (Weimar 1963).

Heinzel, Richard, 'Uber die französischen Gralromane', *Denkschriften der kaiserliche Akademie der Wissenschaften: Philosophische-historische Classe*, 40.iii (Vienna 1892).

Heinzelmann, Martin, *Translationsberichte und andere Quellen des Reliquienkultes*, Typologie des sources du moyen âge occidental 33 (Turnhout 1979).

Heinzle, Joachim, 'Gralkonzeption und Quellenmischung. Forschungskritische Anmerkungen zur Entstehungsgeschichte von Wolframs "Parzival" und "Titurel"', in *Wolfram-Studien III: Schweinfurter Kolloquium 1972*, ed. Werner Schröder, Veröffentlichungen der Wolfram von Eschenbach-Gesellschaft (Berlin 1975) 28–39.

Helinand of Froidmont, *Chronicon*, Patrologiae cursus completus. Series Latina, ed. J.-P. Migne (Paris 1844–1902) 212, 814–15.

Hempel, Heinrich, 'Die Ursprünge der Gralsage', *Zeitschrift für deutsches Altertum und deutsche Literatur*, 96 (1967) 109–49.

Herbert, Algernon, *Britannia after the Romans* (London 1836).

Hermand, Jost, 'Gralsmotive um der Jahrhundertwende', *Deutsche Vierteljahrsschrift für Literaturwissenschaft und Geistesgeschichte*, XXXVI (1962) 521–43.

Herval, René, 'En marge de la légende du Précieux-Sang – Lucques – Fécamp –

Glastonbury', in *L'abbaye bénédictine de Fécamp: ouvrage scientifique du XIIIᵉ centenaire 658–1958* (Fécamp 1959) 105–26, 359–61.

Hindman, Sandra, *Sealed in Parchment* (Chicago 1994).

Hobson, Anthony, *Great Libraries of the World* (London 1970).

Hoffman, Donald L., 'Re-Framing Perceval', *Arthuriana*, 10:4 (2000) 48–51.

Hoffman, Walther, *Die Quellen des Didot-Perceval* (Halle an der Saale 1905).

Hofstätter, Felix Franz, ed., *Altdeutsche Gedichte aus dem Zeit der Tafelrunde* (Vienna 1811).

Holtzmann, Walther, *König Heinrich I und die hl. Lanze* (Bonn 1947).

Horgan, A. D., 'The Grail in Wolfram's *Parzival*', *Mediaeval Studies*, 36 (1974) 354–81.

Horstmann, C., *Altenglische Legende: Neue Folge* (Heilbronn 1881).

Howe, Ellic, *The Magicians of the Golden Dawn: A Documentary History of a Magical Order 1887–1923* (London 1972).

Hucher, E., ed., *Le Saint-Graal, ou Le Joseph d'Arimathie, première branche des romans de la Table Ronde* (Paris 1875).

Huchet, Jean-Charles, 'Le nom et l'image. De Chrétien de Troyes à Robert de Boron', in Lacy, Kelly and Busby (1998) II, 1–16.

Hucker, Bernd Ulrich, *Otto IV* (Hannover 1990).

Hüe, Denis, *Polyphonie du Graal* (Orléans 1998).

Hunt, Tony, 'The Prologue to Chrestien's *Li Contes del Graal*', *Romania*, 92 (1971) 359–79.

Hunter, Jim, *Perceval or the Presence of God* (London and Boston 1978).

Huntley-Speare, Anne, 'The Symbolic Use of a Turtledove for the Holy Spirit', in Meister (1999) 107–26.

Hurd, Michael, 'Rutland Boughton's Arthurian Cycle', in *King Arthur in Music*, ed. Richard Barber, Arthurian Studies lii (Cambridge and Rochester, NY 2002) 91–104.

Huschenbett, Dietrich, 'Über Wort, Sakrament und Gral in Spruchdichtung, *Jüngerem Titurel* – und bei Wolfram?', in bickelwort *und* wildiue maere: *Festschrift Eberhard Nellmann zum 65. Geburtstag*, ed. Dorothee Lindemann, Göppinger Arbeiten zur Germanistik 618 (Göppingen 1995) 184–98.

Huyghebaert, N., 'Iperius et la translation de la relique du Saint-Sang à Bruges', *Handelingen . . . Société d'Emulation de Brugge*, 100 (1963) 110–87.

Hynes-Berry, Mary, 'Malory's Translation of Meaning: *The Tale of the Sankgreall*', *Studies in Philology*, 74 (1977) 243–57.

Ihle, Sandra Ness, *Malory's Grail Quest: Invention and Adaptation in Medieval Prose Romance* (Madison, WI 1983).

Imbs, Paul, 'Enygeus', *Bulletin bibliographique de la Société Internationale Arthurienne*, 6 (1954) 63–73.

Immermann, Carl L., *Merlin. Eine Mythe in Werke* I.2 (Leipzig [n.d.]).

Insolera, Manuel, *L'Église et le Graal: étude sur la présence ésotérique du Graal dans la tradition ecclésiastique* (Milan 1997).

Izquierdo, Josep, 'The *Gospel of Nicodemus* in Medieval Catalan and Occitan Literature', in Izydorczyk (1997) 133–64.

Izydorczyk, Zbigniew, ed., *The Medieval* Gospel of Nicodemus: *Texts, Intertexts and Contexts in Western Europe*, Medieval and Renaissance Texts and Studies 158 (Tempe, AZ 1997).

Jackson, W. H. and Ranawake, S. A., *The Arthur of the Germans: the Arthurian Legend in medieval German and Dutch Literature*, Arthurian Literature in the Middle Ages III (Cardiff 2000).

Jakobi-Mirwald, Christine, 'Kreuzigung und Kreuzabnahme in den Weingartener Handschriften des 12. und 13. Jahrhunderts', in Kruse and Rudolf (1994) I 185–205.

James, M. R., *The Apocryphal New Testament* (Oxford 1924).

Jefferson, Lisa, 'Tournaments, Heraldry and the Knights of the Round Table', *Arthurian Literature* XV (1996) 69–157.

John of Glastonbury, *The Chronicle of Glastonbury Abbey: An Edition, Translation and Study of John of Glastonbury's* Cronica sive Antiquitates Glastoniensis Ecclesie, ed. James P. Carley, tr. David Townsend (Woodbridge and Dover, NH 1985).

Johnson, L. P., 'The Grail-Question in Wolfram and elsewhere', in *From Wolfram and Petrarch to Goethe and Grass: Studies in Literature in Honour of Leonard Forster*, ed. D. H. Green et al., Saecula Spiritualia 5 (Baden-Baden 1982) 83–102.

Johnson, Sidney, 'Doing his own thing: Wolfram's Grail', in *A Companion to Wolfram's Parzival*, ed. Will Hasty (Rochester, NY and Woodbridge 1999) 78–93.

Jones, Martin H., 'Parzival's fighting and his election to the Grail', in *Wolfram-Studien III: Schweinfurter Kolloquium 1972*, ed. Werner Schröder, Veröffentlichungen der Wolfram von Eschenbach-Gesellschaft (Berlin 1975) 52–71.

Joseph of Arimathea: A Critical Edition, ed. David Lawton (New York and London 1983).

Jung, C. G., *Psychological Types*, tr. H. G. Baynes, rev. R. F. C. Hull, Collected Works 6 (London 1986).

Jung, Emma and Franz, Marie-Louise von, *The Grail Legend* (London 1971, rp 1998).

Kahane, Henry and Kahane, Renée, *The Krater and the Grail: the Hermetic Sources of the* Parzival (Urbana and Chicago 1965, rp 1984).

Karczewska, Kathryn, *Prophecy and the quest for the Holy Grail: Critiquing Knowledge in the Vulgate Cycle* (Frankfurt 1998).

Karnein, Alfred, 'Auf der Suche nach einem Autor: Andreas, Verfasser von "De Amore"', *Germanisch-romanische Monatsschrift*, XXVIII (1978) 1–27.

Kater, Michael H., *Das 'Ahnenerbe' der SS 1935–1945: Ein Beitrag zur Kulturpolitik des Dritten Reiches* (Stuttgart 1974).

Kay, Sarah, 'Who was Chrétien de Troyes?', *Arthurian Literature*, XV (1997) 1–36.

Kelly, Thomas E., 'Love in the *Perlesvaus*: Sinful Passion or Redemptive Force', *Romanic Review*, LXVI (1955) 1–12.

Kelly, Thomas E., *Le Haut Livre du Graal: Perlesvaus* (Geneva 1974).

Kennedy, Angus J., 'Punishment in the *Perlesvaus*: The Theme of the Waste Land', in *Rewards and Punishments in the Arthurian Romances and Lyric Poetry of Mediaeval France*, ed. Peter V. Davies and Angus J. Kennedy (Cambridge and Wolfeboro, NH 1987) 61–75.

Kennedy, Edward Donald, 'John Hardyng and the Holy Grail', in *Arthurian Literature*, VIII (1989) 185–206.

Kennedy, Elspeth, *Lancelot and the Grail* (Oxford 1986).

Kienzle, Beverly, *Cistercians, Heresy and Crusade* (Woodbridge and Rochester, NY 2001).

Kleiber, Wolfgang, 'Zur Namenforschung in Wolframs *Parzival*', *Deutschunterricht*, XIV (1962) 80–90.

Knapp, Fritz Peter, 'Der Graal zwischen Märchen und Legende', *Beiträge zur Geschichte der Deutschen Sprache und Literatur*, 118:1 (1996) 49–68.

Knowles, David, *Great Historical Enterprises* (London 1963).

Koechlin, Raymond, *Les ivoires gothiques français* (Paris 1924).

Koehler, Erich, *Ideal und Wirklichkeit in der höfischen Epik: Studien zur Form der frühen Artus- und Graldichtung*, Beihefte zur Zeitschrift für Romanische Philologie (Tübingen 1983).

Kolb, Herbert, *Munsalvaesche. Studien zum Kyotproblem* (Munich 1963).

Kolb, Karl, *Vom Heiligen Blut* (Würzburg 1980).

Kraemer, Alfred Robert, *Malory's Grail Seekers and Fifteenth Century English Hagiography* (New York 1999).

Kraemer, Gabriele, *Artusstoff und Gralsthematik in modernen amerikanischen Roman*, Beiträge zur Anglistik 8 (Giessen 1985).

Kruse, Norbert, 'Der Weg des Heiligen Bluts von Mantua nach Altdorf-Weingarten' in Kruse and Rudolf (1994) 57–107.

Kruse, Norbert and Rudolf, Hans Ulrich, *900 Jahre Heilig-Blut-Verehrung in Weingarten 1094–1994: Festschrift zum Heilig-Blut-Jubiläum am 12 März 1994* (Sigmaringen 1994).

Kühnel, Jürgen, '*Parsifal* "Erlosung dem Erlöser": von der Aufhebung des Christentums in das Kunstwerk Richard Wagners', in Müller and Müller (1989) 171–227.

Kunitzsch, Paul, 'Erneut: der Orient in Wolframs "Parzival"', *Zeitschrift für deutsches Altertum und deutsches Litteratur*, 113 (1984) 79–111.

La Motte Fouqué, Friedrich de, *Der Parcival*, ed. Tilman Spreckelsen et al. (Hildesheim, Zürich and New York 1997).

La Queste del Saint Graal: Roman du XIIIe siècle, ed. Albert Pauphilet, Classiques français du moyen âge (Paris 1923).

[*La Queste del Saint Graal*] *The Quest of the Holy Grail*, tr. Pauline Matarasso (Harmondsworth 1969).

La Rue, G. de, *Recherches sur les ouvrages des bardes de la Bretagne armoricaine au moyen âge* (Caen 1815).

La Rue, G. de, *Essais historiques sur les bardes, les jongleurs et les trouvères normands et anglo-normands* (Caen 1834).

La Villemarqué, T. de, *Contes populaires des anciens Bretons* (Paris and Leipzig 1842).

Lacy, Norris J., *The Craft of Chrétien de Troyes: an Essay on Narrative Art* (Leiden 1980).

Lacy, Norris J., ed., *The New Arthurian Encyclopedia* (Chicago and London 1991).

Lacy, Norris J., Kelly, Douglas and Busby, Keith, eds, *The Legacy of Chrétien de Troyes* (Amsterdam 1988).

Lagorio, Valerie, 'Pan-Brittonic Hagiography and the Arthurian Grail cycle', *Traditio*, XXVI (1970) 29–61.

Lagorio, Valerie, 'Joseph of Arimathea: Vita of a Grail Saint', *Zeitschrift für romanische Philologie*, 91 (1975) 209–31.

Lagorio, Valerie, 'The Glastonbury Legends and the English Grail Romances', *Neuphilologische Mitteilungen*, 79 (1978) 359–66.

Lancelot, ed. A. Micha, Textes Littéraires Français (Geneva and Paris 1978–1980) vols II, IV, V, VI.

Lancelot-Grail: The Old French Arthurian Vulgate and Post-Vulgate in Translation, ed. Norris J. Lacy (New York and London 1993–6).

Laprade, Victor de, 'Le temple d'ivoire', in *Oeuvres poétiques* [6] (Paris n.d. [1906]) 33–88.

Lasko, Peter, *Ars Sacra 800–1200*, Pelican History of Art (London 1972).

Lavenu, Philippe, *L'ésoterisme du Graal: Secret du Mont Saint-Michel* (Paris 1989).

Le Bossé, Michel, 'Le Graal, fiction ou réalité?' in *La Légende arthurienne et la Normandie (Hommage à René Bansard)*, ed. Jean-Charles Payen (Condé-sur-Noireau 1983) 191–201.

Le Goff, Jacques, *The Medieval Imagination* (Chicago and London 1988).

Le Rider, Paule, *Le chevalier dans le conte du Graal du Chrétien de Troyes*, 2nd edn (Paris 1978).

Lee, Sonia, 'The struggle between Cistercian and Cathar 1145–1220 A. D. and its possible influence on Holy Grail literature', *Dissertation Abstracts* 36:6 (1975) 3656.

Lejeune, Rita, 'Préfiguration du Graal', *Studi Medievali*, 17 (1951) 277–301.

Lemarignier, Jean-François, *Étude sur les privilèges d'exemption et de juridiction ecclésiastiques des abbayes normandes depuis les origines jusqu'en 1140*, Archives de la France monastique XLIV (Paris 1937).

Le Roman de Tristan en Prose, I, ed. Renée Curtis, Arthurian Studies xii (Cambridge and Dover, NH 1985).

Le Roman de Tristan en Prose, IX, ed. Laurence Harf-Lancner, Textes Littéraires Français (Geneva and Paris 1997).

Le Saint Graal Numéros 1 à 20 (Paris 1892–3, rp Geneva 1971).

Les Romans du Graal aux xiie et xiiie siècles, Colloques Internationaux du Centre National de la Recherche Scientifique III (Paris 1956).

L'estoire del Saint Graal, ed. Jean-Paul Ponceau, Classiques Français du Moyen Âge (Paris 1997).

Lessing, Gotthold Ephraim, *Sämtliche Schriften*, ed. Karl Lachmann, 3rd edn (Leipzig 1907).

Lessing, Gotthold Ephraim, *Ernst und Falk: Gespräche für Freimaurer in Werke* II (Munich 1969).

Leupin, Alexandre, *Le Graal et la Littérature: étude sur la Vulgate Arthurienne en prose* (Lausanne 1982).

Lewis, C. S., *Studies in Medieval and Renaissance Literature*, ed. W. Hooper (Cambridge 1966).

L'Hystorie du Sanct Greaal 1516, ed. C. E. Pickford (London 1978).

Littleton, C. Scott and Malcor, Linda A., *From Scythia to Camelot* (New York and London 1994).

Littleton, C. Scott and Thomas, Ann C., 'The Sarmatian Connection: New Light on the Origin of the Arthurian and Holy Grail Legends', *Journal of American Folklore*, XCI (1978) 513–27.

Lloyd-Morgan, Ceridwen, 'A Study of *Y Seint Greal* in relation to *La Queste del Saint Graal* and *Perlesvaus*', D. Phil. thesis, Oxford 1978.

Lloyd-Morgan, Ceridwen, 'Perceval in Wales: late medieval Welsh grail traditions', in *The Changing Face of Arthurian Romance. Essays on Arthurian Prose Romances in memory of Cedric B. Pickford*, ed. Alison Adams et al., Arthurian Studies xvi (Cambridge and Totowa, NJ 1986) 78–91.

Locke, Frederick W., 'A new approach to the study of the *Queste del Saint Graal*', *Romanic Review*, 45 (1954) 241–50.

Locke, Frederick W., *The Quest for the Holy Grail: A Literary Study of a Thirteenth Century French Romance* (Stanford 1960).

Lodge, David, *Small World* (London 1984).

Lofmark, Carl J., 'Zur Interpretation der Kyotstellen in "*Parzival*"', *Wolfram-Studien* 4 (1977) 33–70.

Loomis, Roger Sherman, 'The Head in the Grail', *Revue Celtique*, 47 (1930) 39–62.

Loomis, Roger Sherman, 'The origin of the Grail legends' in *Arthurian Literature in the Middle Ages*, ed. Roger Sherman Loomis (Oxford 1959) 274–94.

Loomis, Roger Sherman, *The Grail: From Celtic Myth to Christian Symbol* (Cardiff 1963, rp Princeton 1991).

Loomis, R. S., and Loomis, L. H. *Arthurian Legends in Medieval Art* (London and New York 1938).

Lorengel, ed. Danielle Buschinger, Göppinger Arbeiten zur Germanistik 253 (Göppingen 1979).

Lorgaireacht an tSoidhigh Naomhtha: an early modern Irish translation of the Quest of the Holy Grail, ed. and tr. Sheila Falconer (Dublin 1953).

Löseth, Eilert, *Le Roman en prose de Tristan*, Bibliothèque de l'École Pratique des Hautes Études 82 (Paris 1890 rp Geneva 1974).

Lot-Borodine, Myrrha, 'Autour du Graal: à propos des travaux récents', *Romania*, 56 (1930) 526–57; 57 (1931) 147–205.

Lot-Borodine, Myrrha, 'Les apparitions du Christ aux messes de *l'Estoire* et de la *Queste del Saint Graal'*, Romania, 72 (1951) 202–23 [=1951a].

Lot-Borodine, Myrrha, 'Les grands secrets du Saint-Graal' in *Lumière du Graal*, ed. René Nelli (Paris 1951) [=1951b].

Lot-Borodine, Myrrha, 'Le *Conte del Graal* de Chrétien de Troyes et sa présentation symbolique', *Romania*, 77 (1956) 235–88; 78 (1957) 142–3.

Lovelich, Henry, *The History of the Holy Grail*, ed. Frederick J. Furnivall, Early English Text Society Extra Series 20, 24, 28, 30, 95 (London 1874–1905).

Lovelich, Henry, *Merlin*, ed. Ernst A. Kock, Early English Text Society Extra Series 93, 112 (London 1904, 1913).

Lozac'hmeur, Jean-Claude, 'De la tête de Bran à l'hostie du Graal', in *Arthurian Tapestry. Essays in Memory of Lewis Thorpe*, ed. Kenneth Varty (Glasgow 1981) 275–86.

Lozac'hmeur, Jean-Claude, 'À propos de deux hypothèses de R. S. Loomis: éléments pour une solution de l'énigme de Graal', *Bulletin bibliographique de la Société Internationale Arthurienne*, 34 (1982) 207–21.

Lozac'hmeur, Jean-Claude, 'Recherches sur les origines indo-européennes et ésotériques de la légende du Graal', *Cahiers de civilisation médiévale X^e-XIIe siècles*, 30 (1987) 45–63.

Lupack, Alan and Lupack, Barbara Tepa, *King Arthur in America*, Arthurian Studies xli (Cambridge and Rochester, NY 1999).

The Mabinogion, tr. Gwyn Jones and Thomas Jones (London 1949).

MacCana, Proinsias, *Celtic Mythology* (London and New York 1970).

Machen, Arthur, *The Secret Glory* (London 1922).

Mackey, Albert, *Encyclopedia of Freemasonry*, rev. Robert I. Clegg (Chicago 1956).

McKitterick, Rosamond, *The Frankish Church and the Carolingian Reforms 789–895*, Studies in History 3 (London 1977).

Macy, Gary, *The Theologies of the Eucharist in the Early Scholastic Period* (Oxford 1984).

Magee, Bryan, *Wagner and Philosophy* (London and New York 2000).

Magre, Maurice, *Magiciens et Illuminés* (Toulouse 1930).

Mahoney, Dhira B., *The Grail: A Casebook* (New York and London 2000).

Malcor, Linda A., 'The Chalice at the Cross: A study of the grail motif in Medieval Europe', PhD thesis, University of California, Los Angeles, 1991.

Malory, Sir Thomas, *The Works of Sir Thomas Malory*, ed. Eugène Vinaver, rev. P. J. C. Field (Oxford 1990).

Mancoff, Debra, *The Arthurian Revival in Victorian Art* (New York and London 1990).

Mancoff, Debra, *King Arthur's Modern Return* (New York 1998).

Mandach, Andre de, *Le 'Roman du Graal' originaire: I Sur les traces du modèle commun*, Göppinger Arbeiten zur Germanistik 581 (Göppingen 1992).

Mandach, Andre de, *Auf den Spuren des heiligen Gral*, Göppinger Arbeiten zur Germanistik 596 (Göppingen 1995).

Mann, Jill, 'Malory and the Grail legend', in *A Companion to Malory*, ed. Elizabeth Archibald and A. S. G. Edwards, Arthurian Studies xxxvii (Cambridge and Rochester, NY 1996).

Marino, John, 'Twentieth Century Retellings of the Grail Legend' (Cambridge and Rochester, NY, forthcoming).

Markale, Jean, *Le Graal* (Paris 1982).

Martin, Ernst, *Zur Gralsage: Untersuchungen*, Quellen und Forschungen zur Sprach- und Culturgeschichte der germanischen Völker XLII (Strassburg 1880).

Marx, Jean, *La légende arthurienne et le graal* (Paris 1952).

Marx, Jean, *Nouvelles recherches sur la littérature arthurienne* (Paris 1965).

Mas-Latrie, L. de, *Histoire de l'île de Chypre sous le règne des princes de la maison de Lusignan* (Paris 1852–61).

Matarasso, Pauline, *The Redemption of Chivalry: a study of the* Queste del Saint Graal (Geneva 1979).

Mathiesen, Robert, 'A thirteenth-century ritual to attain the Beatific Vision from the *Sworn Book* of Honorius of Thebes', in Fanger (1998) 143–62.

Matthew Paris, *Matthaei Parisiensis . . . Chronica Majora*, ed. H. R. Luard, Rolls Series (London 1876) III, 101.

Matthews, Caitlin and Matthews, John, *The Western Way. A Practical Guide to the Western Mystery Tradition* (London 1986).

Matthews, John, *The Grail: Quest for the Eternal* (London and New York 1981).

Matthews, John, *The Grail Seeker's Companion* (Wellingborough 1986).

Matthews, John, *At the Table of the Grail* (London 1987).

Matthews, John, *Elements of the Grail Tradition* (Shaftesbury and Rockport, MA 1990).

Matthews, John, *King Arthur and the Grail Quest* (London 1995).

Matthews, John, *Sources of the Grail* (Edinburgh 1996).

Matthews, John, *Healing the Wounded King* (Shaftesbury and Rockport, MA 1997).

Matthews, John, 'The Grail and the Rose', in White (1999) 25–42.

Meister, Peter, ed., *Arthurian Literature and Christianity: Notes from the Twentieth Century* (New York 1999).

Méla, Charles, 'Pour une esthétique médiévale', *Le Moyen Âge: Revue d'histoire et de philologie*, 84:1 (1978) 113–27.

Méla, Charles, '«La lettre tue»; cryptographie du Graal', *Cahiers de civilisation médiévale X^e–XIIe siècles*, XXVI (1983) 209–21.

Méla, Charles, *La Reine et le Graal: conjointure dans les romans du Graal de Chretien de Troyes au* Livre de Lancelot (Paris 1984).

Mély, F. de, *Exuviae sacrae constantinopolitanae* III (Paris 1904).

Ménard, Philippe, 'Problèmes et mystères du "Conte du Graal": un essai d'interprétation', in *Chrétien de Troyes et le Graal*, ed. Stiennon et al. (1984) 61–76.

Ménard, Philippe, *Du Chrétien de Troyes au* Tristan en Prose, Publications romanes et françaises CCXXIV (Geneva 1999).

Menéndez Pidal, Ramón, *Primera Crónica General de España* (Madrid 1955).

Mergell, Bodo, *Der Gral in Wolframs Parzival: Entstehung und Ausbildung der Gralsage im Hochmittelalter* (Halle 1952).

Merlin: roman en prose du xiii siècle, ed. Gaston Paris and Jacob Ulrich, Société des anciens textes français (1886).

Micha, A., *De la chanson de geste au roman*, Publications romanes et françaises CXXXIX (Geneva 1976) [Collected articles].

Michell, John F., *The Flying Saucer Vision: the Holy Grail Restored* (London 1967).

Millington, Barry, ed., *The Wagner Compendium: A Guide to Wagner's Life and Music* (London 1992).

Mitchison, Naomi, *To the Chapel Perilous* (London 1955, rp Oakland, CA, 1999).

Molina, Réjane, 'La Chapelle royale de Saint-Frambourg de Senlis et le Graal', in *La Légende Arthurienne et la Normandie (Hommage à René Bansard)*, ed. Jean-Charles Payen (Condé-sur-Noireau 1983) 127–49.

Morris, Colin, 'Policy and Visions: the case of the Holy Lance at Antioch', in *War and Government in the Middle Ages*, ed. John Gillingham and J. C. Holt (Woodbridge and Totowa, NJ 1984) 33–46.

Mosse, George L., 'The Mystical Origins of National Socialism', *Journal of the History of Ideas*, XXII (1961) 81–96.

Muir, Lynette R., 'Villard de Honnecourt and the Grail', *Bulletin bibliographique de la Société Internationale Arthurienne*, 23 (1971) 137–41.

Müller, Ulrich, 'Gral '89: Mittelalter, Moderne Hermetik und die neue Politik der Perestroika: Zu den "Parzival/Gral-Dramen" von Peter Handke und Christoph Hein', in *Mittelalter-Rezeption IV: Medien, Politik, Ideologie, Oekonomie*, ed. Irene Burg, Göppinger Arbeiten zur Germanistik (Göppingen 1991) 495–520 [=1991a].

Müller, Ulrich, 'Blank, Syberberg and the German Arthurian Tradition', in Harty (1991) 157–68 [=1991b].

Müller, Ursula and Müller, Ulrich, ed., *Richard Wagner und sein Mittelalter*, Wort und Musik 1 (Anif/Salzburg 1989).

Muschg, Adolf, *Der Rote Ritter: eine Geschichte von Parzivâl* (Frankfurt am Main 1993).

Naef, F., *Recherches sur les opinions religieuses des Templiers et sur les traces qu'elles ont laissées dans la littérature et l'histoire* (Nîmes 1890).

Navarro, M., 'Pignora Sanctorum', in Gavara (1998) 95–133.

Nelli, René, ed., *Lumière du Graal* (Paris 1951).

Nellmann, Eberhard, '*lapsit exillis? jaspis exillix?* Die Lesarten der Handschriften', *Zeitschrift für deutsche Philologie*, 119 (2000) 416–20.

Newstead, Helaine, *Bran the Blessed in Arthurian Romance* (New York 1939).

Nicholson, Helen J., *Love, War and the Grail: Templars, Hospitallers and Teutonic Knights in Medieval Epic and Romance 1150–1500*, History of Warfare 4 (Leiden 2001).

Nietzsche, F., 'Nietzsche contra Wagner', in *The Portable Nietzsche* (London 1971).

Nitze, W. A., 'Sens et matière dans les œuvres de Chrétien de Troyes', *Romania*, 44, (1915–17) 14–36.

Nitze, W. A., 'Perceval and the Holy Grail: an essay on the romance of Chrétien de Troyes', *University of California Publications in Modern Philology*, 28 (1949) 281–332.

Nitze, W. A., 'Messire Robert de Boron: Enquiry and Summary', *Speculum*, 28 (1953) 279–96.

Nitze, W. A., and Jenkins, T. Atkinson, eds, *Le Haut Livre du Graal: Perlesvaus* (Chicago 1932–37).

Nutt, Alfred, *Studies on the Legend of the Holy Grail* (London 1888, rp New York 1965).

Nyholm, Kurt, *Die Gralepen in Ulrich Fuetrers Bearbeitung (Buch der Abenteuer)*, Deutsche Texte des Mittelalters LVII (Berlin 1964).

O'Gorman, R., 'Ecclesiastical tradition and the Holy Grail', *Australian Journal of French Studies*, VI.1 (1969) 3–8.

O'Gorman, R., 'La tradition manuscrite de Joseph d'Arimathie', *Revue d'Histoire des Textes*, 1 (1971) 145–81.

O'Gorman, Richard, 'Robert de Boron's angelology and elements of heretical doctrine', *Zeitschrift für romanische Philologie*, 109 (1993) 539–55.

O'Gorman, Richard, 'Robert de Boron's *Joseph d'Arimathie* and the sacrament of penance', in *Conjunctures: Medieval Studies in Honor of Douglas Kelly*, ed. Keith Busby and Norris J. Lacy (Amsterdam 1994) 375–85.

O'Gorman, Richard, *Joseph d'Arimathie: a critical edition of the verse and prose versions* (Toronto 1995).

O'Sharkey, Eithne, 'The Influence of Joachim of Fiore on some 13th century French Grail Romances', *Trivium*, II (1967) 47–58.

O'Sharkey, Eithne M., 'Punishments and rewards of the questing knights in *La Queste del Saint-Graal*', *Rewards and Punishments in the Arthurian Romances and Lyric Poetry of Medieval France. Essays presented to Kenneth Varty on the occasion of his sixtieth birthday*, ed. Peter V. Davies and Angus J. Kennedy (Cambridge and Wolfeboro, NH 1987) 101–17.

Oates, J. C. T., 'Richard Pynson and the Holy Blood of Hailes', *The Library* 5th series, 13 (1958) 269–77.

Obermaier, Sabine, 'Adolf Muschgs *Der Rote Ritter* im Kontext der deutschsprachigen Parzival-Rezeption des ausgehenden Jahrhunderts', in Raposo Fernández (2000) 253–67.

Ofterdingen, Heinrich von, *Der Wartburgkrieg und verwandte Dichtungen*, ed. Friedrich Mess (Weimar 1963).

Olef-Krafft, F., 'Œdipe au château du Graal', *Le Moyen Âge: Revue d'histoire et de philologie*, 101.2 (1995) 227–57.

Olmos y Canalda, Elias, *Como fue salvado el santo caliz de la cena: rutas del Santo Grial desde Jerusalen a Valencia* (Valencia 1946).

Olschki, Leonardo, *The Grail Castle and its Mysteries* (Manchester, Berkeley and Los Angeles 1966).

Owen, D. D. R., *The Evolution of the Grail Legend* (Edinburgh and London 1968).

Owen, William (Pughe), *A Dictionary of the Welsh Language* (London 1803).

Paden, William D., Jr, '"*De monachis rithmos facientibus*": Hélinant de Froidmont, Bertran de Born and the Cistercian General Chapter of 1199', *Speculum*, 55 (1980) 669–85.

Paine, Albert Bigelow, *Mark Twain: A Biography*, III (New York and London 1912).

Palgen, R., *Der Stein der Weisen: Quellenstudien zu Parzival* (Breslau 1922).

Paris, Gaston, *Histoire littéraire de France*, 2nd edn (Paris 1890).

Partner, Peter, *The Murdered Magicians: The Templars and their Myth* (Oxford and New York 1982).

Paryns, Marilyn Jackson, *Malory: the Critical Heritage* (London and New York 1988).

Pastré, Jean-Marc, 'Munsalvaesche ou l'utopie wolframienne du Gral', in *Gesellschaftsutopien im Mittelalter/ Discours et figures de l'utopie au Moyen Âge*, ed. Danielle Buschinger and Wolfgang Spiewok (Greifswald 1994) 29–37.

Pauphilet, Albert, *Études sur la Queste del Saint Graal* (Paris 1921, rp 1980).

Pedro Pascual, *Obras*, ed. Pedro Armengol Valenzuela (Rome 1905–7).

Peebles, R. J., *The Legend of Longinus in Ecclesiastical Tradition and in English Literature, and its connection with the Grail* (Baltimore 1911).

Péladan, Joséphin, *Le Mystère du Graal* (Paris 1883).

Péladan, Joséphin, *Le Queste du Graal* (Paris 1892).

Péladan, Joséphin, *Le Secret des Troubadours: De Parsifal à Don Quichotte* (Paris 1906).

Pennick, Nigel, *Hitler's Secret Sciences* (Sudbury 1981).

[*Perlesvaus*] *The High Book of the Grail*, tr. Nigel Bryant (Cambridge and Totowa, NJ 1978).

Peter the Venerable, *Petri Venerabilis contra petrobrusianos hereticos*, ed. James Fearns, Corpus Christianorum continuatio medievalis 10 (Turnhout 1967).

Petersen, Karen-Maria, 'Zum Grundriss des Graltempels', in *Festschrift für Kurt Herbert Halbach*, ed. Rose Beate Schäfer-Maulbetsch et al., Göppinger Arbeiten zur Germanistik 70 (Göppingen 1972) 271–306.

Petzet, Michael, 'Die Gralswelt König Ludwigs II.: Neuschwanstein als Gralsburg und die Idee des Graltempels', in Baumstark (1995) 63–86.

Peyrat, Napoléon, *Histoire des albigeois: Les albigeois et l'Inquisition* (Paris 1870–2).

Phillips, Graham, *The Search for the Grail* (London 1996).

Pickens, Rupert, '*Mais de Çou ne parole pas Crestiens de Troies*: A re-examination of the Didot-*Perceval*', *Romania*, 105 (1984) 492–510.

Pickens, Rupert, 'Histoire et commentaire chez Chrétien de Troyes et Robert de Boron: Robert de Boron et le livre de Philippe de Flandre', in Lacy, Kelly and Busby (1988) II 17–39.

Pickford, Cedric Edward, *L'Évolution du Roman Arthurien en Prose vers la fin du moyen âge d'après le manuscrit 112 du fonds français de la Bibliothèque Nationale* (Paris 1960).

Pickford, Cedric E., 'Les éditions imprimées de romans arthuriens en prose anterieures a 1600', *Bulletin bibliographique de la Société Internationale Arthurienne* 13 (1961) 99–109.

Pincus-Witten, Robert, *Occult Symbolism in France: Josephin Péladan and the Salons de la Rose-Croix* (New York and London 1976).

Poag, James F., 'Diu verholnen mære umben grâl (Parz. 452,30)', in *Wolfram-Studien* II, ed. Werner Schröder (Berlin 1974) 72–83.

Poirion, Daniel, ed., *Le livre du Graal I* (Paris 2001).

Ponsoye, P., *L'Islam et Le Graal: Étude sur l'ésoterisme du Parzival de Wolfram von Eschenbach* (Milan 1976) 101–39.

Poulson, Christine, *The Quest for the Grail: Arthurian Legend in British Art 1840–1920* (Manchester 1999).

Powell, Anthony, *The Fisher King* (London 1986).

Powys, John Cowper, *A Glastonbury Romance* (London 1933, rp 1975).

Powys, John Cowper, *Autobiography* (London 1967).

Pratelidis, Konstantin, *Tafelrunde und Gral: Die Artuswelt und ihr Verhältnis zur Gralswelt im "Parzival" Wolframs von Eschenbach*, Würzburger Beiträge zur deutschen Philologie 12 (Würzburg 1994).

Primera crónica general de España, ed. Ramón Menéndez Pidal (Madrid 1955) 661.

Prins-S'Jacob, J. C., 'The Middle-Dutch version of la Queste del Saint Graal', *De Nieuwe taalgids: Tijdschrift voor neerlandici*, 73.2 (1980) 120–32.

Quin, E. O., *The Quest of Seth for the Oil of Life* (Chicago 1962).

Quinet, Edgar, *Merlin l'Enchanteur*, Œuvres complètes 16 (Paris 1895).

Ragotzky, Hedda, *Studien zur Wolfram Rezeption: die Entstehung und Verwandlung der Wolfram-Rolle in der deutschen Literatur des 13. Jahrhunderts* (Stuttgart 1971).

Rahn, Otto, *La croisade contre le Graal* (Paris 1933).

Rahn, Otto, *Kreuzzug gegen den Gral*, ed. Karl Rittersbacher (Stuttgart 1964).

Rahn, Otto, *Leben und Werk*, ed. Hans-Jürgen Lange (Engerda 1995).

Ralph of Coggeshall, *Chronicon Anglicanum*, ed. J. Stevenson, Rolls Series (London 1875).

Ramsay, Alexander Michael, *Travels of Cyrus* (London 1727).

Ranke, F., 'Zur Symbol des Grals bei Wolfram von Eschenbach', *Trivium: Schweizerische Vierteljahresschrift für Literaturwissenschaft*, IV (1946) 20–30.

Raposo Fernández, Berta, 'Parzival ilustrado, Parzival romántico: Bodmer y Fouqué', in Raposo Fernández (2000) 185–202.

Raposo Fernández, Berta, *Parzival: reescritura y transformacion* (Valencia 2000).

Rehm, Ulrich, '»Daz was ein dinc, daz hiez der Grâl«: zur Ikonographie des Gral im Mittelalter', in Baumstark (1995) 31–39.

Reiss, Edmund, 'The Birth of the Grail Quest', in *Innovation in Medieval Literature: Essays to the Memory of Alan Markman*, ed. Douglas Radcliff-Umstead (Pittsburgh 1971) 20–34.

Renan, Ernest, *Essais de morale et de critique* (Paris 1859).

Rhys, Ernest, *The Masque of the Grail* (London 1908).

Riant, Paul E. D. *Des dépouilles religieuses enlevées a Constantinople au xiiiᵉ siècle par les Latins*, Extrait des *Mémoires de la Société nationale des Antiquaires de France* XXXVI (Paris 1875).

Riant, Paul E. D., *Exuviae Sacrae Constantinopolitanae* I (Geneva 1877).

Ribard, Jacques, *Du Philtre au Graal: pour une interprétation philologique du Roman de Tristan et du Conte du Graal* (Paris 1989).

Richey, M. F., *Studies of Wolfram von Eschenbach* (Edinburgh 1957).

Riddy, Felicity, *Sir Thomas Malory* (Leiden 1987).

Riddy, Felicity, 'Chivalric nationalism and the Holy Grail in Hardyng's *Chronicle*', in Mahoney (2000) 397–415.

Riddy, Felicity J., 'Glastonbury, Joseph of Arimathea and the Grail in John Hardyng's chronicle', in *The Archaeology and History of Glastonbury Abbey*, ed. Lesley Abrams and James P. Carley (Woodbridge and Rochester, NY 1991) 317–31.

Riddy, Felicity J., 'John Hardyng's chronicle and the Wars of the Roses', *Arthurian Literature*, XII (1993) 91–108.

Ringbom, Lars-Ivar, *Graltempel und Paradies: Beziehungen zwischen Iran und Europa im Mittelalter*, Kungl. Vitterhets Historie och Antikvitets Akademian Handlingar 73 (Stockholm 1951).

Ríquer, Martin de, 'Interpretación cristiana de li contes del graal', in *Miscelánea filológica dedicada a Mons. A. Griera*, 7 Congrès internationale de linguistique romane (Barcelona 1953) II 209–83.

Rivière, Patrick, *Le Graal: histoire et symboles* (Monaco 1990, rp 2000).

Roach, William, 'Eucharistic Tradition in the Perlesvaus', *Zeitschrift für romanischen Philologie*, 59 (1939) 10–56.

Roach, William, ed. and tr., *The* Didot *Perceval according to the Manuscripts of Modena and Paris* (Philadelphia 1941).

Roach, William, *The Continuations of the Old French* Perceval *of Chrétien de Troyes* (Philadelphia 1952–1983).

Robert de Boron, *Le roman du Graal: Manuscrit de Modène*, ed. and tr. Bernard Cerquiglini (Paris 1981).

Robert de Boron, *Le Roman de l'Estoire dou Graal*, ed. William A. Nitze (Paris 1927, rp 1983).

Robert de Boron, *Merlin and the Grail: Joseph of Arimathea . Merlin . Perceval*, tr. Nigel Bryant (Cambridge and Rochester, NY 2001).

Robert Grosseteste, *De sanguine Christo*, in Matthew Paris, *Chronica majora*, ed. H. R. Luard, Rolls Series 57 (London 1882).

Robert of Torigni, *Chronicles of the Reigns of Stephen, Henry II and Richard I*, ed. Richard Howlett, Rolls Series (London 1889).

Roberts, Brynley F., 'Peredur Son of Efrawg: A Text in Transition', *Arthuriana*, 10:3 (2000) 57–72.

Robinson, David W., *Deconstructing East Germany: Christoph Hein's Literature of Dissent* (Rochester, NY and Woodbridge 1999).

Roethlisberger, Blanca, *Die Architektur des Graltemples im juengeren Titurel*, Sprache und Dichtung 18 (Bern 1917).

Rohr, F., *Parzival und der Heilige Gral: eine neue Deutung der Symbolik der Graldichtungen* (Hildesheim 1922).

Roquebert, Michel, *Les Cathares et le Graal* (Toulouse 1994).

Roques, Mario, 'Le Graal de Chrétien et la demoiselle au Graal', *Romania*, 76 (1955) 1–27.

Roques, Mario, 'Le nom du graal', in *Les Romans du Graal* (1956) 5–13.

Roubaud, Jacques, *Graal fiction* (Paris 1978).

Rubin, Miri, *Corpus Christi: the Eucharist in late medieval culture* (Cambridge 1991).

Ruck, E. H., *An Index of Themes and Motifs in 12th-Century French Arthurian Poetry*, Arthurian Studies xxv (Cambridge and Rochester, NY 1991).

Ruh, Kurt, 'Der Gralsheld in der "Queste del Saint Graal" ', in *Wolfram-Studien* [I] ed. Werner Schröder (Berlin 1971) 240–63.

Runciman, Steven, 'The Holy Lance found at Antioch', *Analecta Bollandiana*, 68 (1950) 197–209.

Salmeri, Filippo, *Manessier: Modello simboli scrittura*, Universita di Catania, Collana di Studi di Filologia Moderna (Catania 1984).

Salmon, David, 'The Nanteos Cup', *Notes & Queries*, CLXXIX (1940) 295.

Saly, Antoinette, 'Le Graal et le Château du Graal dans le *Perlesvaus*', in Büschinger and Spiewok (1994a) 181–7.

Sangorrin, Damaso, 'El santo Grial en Aragon', *Aragon*, III (1927) 133–6, 153–5, 173–6, 194–7, 214–18; IV (1928) 25–6, 45–50, 165–9.

Sansonetti, Paul Georges, *Graal et alchimie* (Paris 1982).

Saul, MaryLynn, 'The unholy grail: recasting the Grail myth for an unbelieving age' in Allaire (1999) 51–66.

Scavone, Daniel, 'Joseph of Arimathea, the Holy Grail, and the Edessa Icon', *Arthuriana*, 9.4 (1999) 1–23.

Schaeffer, Albrecht, *Parzival. Ein Versroman* (Leipzig 1924).

Schäfer, Hans-Wilhelm, *Kelch und Stein: Untersuchungen zum Werk Wolframs von Eschenbach* (Frankfurt and Bern 1983).

Schäfer, Hans-Wilhelm, 'Wolframs Calix Lapideus', *Zeitschrift für romanische philologie*, 103 (1984) 370–77.

Schiller, Gertrud, *Ikonographie der christlichen Kunst: 2. Die Passion Jesu Christi* (Gutersloh 1968).

Schirok, Bernd, *Parzivalrezeption im Mittelalter*, Erträge der Forschung CLXXIV (Darmstadt 1982).

Schlegel, A.W., *Geschichte der alten und neueren Litteratur*, Gesammelte Werke I (Wien 1822).

Schmidt, Jochen, 'Parzifals Gralsfrage und Zweifel', in *Festschrift für Friedrich Beiáner*, ed. Ulrich Gaier and Werner Volke (Tübingen 1974) 370–90.

Schmolke-Hasselmann, Beate, *The Evolution of Arthurian Romance: The Verse Tradition from Chrétien to Froissart*, tr. Margaret and Roger Middleton, Cambridge Studies in Medieval Literature 35 (Cambridge 1998).

Schröder, Franz, *Die Parzivalfrage* (Munich 1928).

Schröder, Franz Rolf, 'Kyot und das Gralproblem', *Beiträge zur Geschichte der deutschen Sprache und Literatur*, 97 (1975) 263–311.

Schröder, Werner, *Die Namen im 'Parzival' und im 'Titurel' Wolframs von Eschenbach* (Berlin and New York 1981).

Schröder, Werner, 'Der Schluss des "Jüngeren Titurels"', *Zeitschrift für deutsches Altertum*, CXI (1982) 103–30.

Schulz, Albert, *An Essay on the influence of Welsh Tradition upon the Literature of Germany, France, and Scandinavia* (Llandovery 1841).

Schwietering, Julius, 'Wolframs Parzival', in *Mystik und Höfische Dichtung im Hochmittelalter* (Munich 1960) 37–70.

Scott, John, ed. and tr., *The early history of Glastonbury* (Woodbridge and Totowa, NJ 1981).

Sechelles, D. de, *L'origine du Graal* (Saint Brieuc 1954).

Séguy, Mireille, *Les romans du Graal ou le signe imaginé* (Paris 2001).

Séguy, Mireille, 'Naming and Renaming: On two Grail scenes in L'Estoire del Graal', *Arthuriana*, 12.3 (2002) 87–102.

Sinclair, Andrew, *The Discovery of the Grail* (London 1998).

Sinclair, Andrew, *The Secret Scroll* (London 2001) (revised edition of *The Sword and the Grail* (London 1993)).

Skeels, Dell, *The Romance of Perceval in Prose: A translation of the E Manuscript of the Didot Perceval* (Seattle and London 1966).

Skerst, Herman von, *Der Gralstempel im Kaukasus* (Stuttgart 1986).

Soboth, Christian, 'Parzival und die Kunst der Erlösung – Die Lyrik der Jahrhundertwende auf der Suche nach dem verlorenen Gral', in bickelwort *und* wildiue maere: *Festschrift Eberhard Nellmann zum 65. Geburtstag*, ed. Dorothee Lindemann, Göppinger Arbeiten zur Germanistik 618 (Göppingen 1995) 151–66.

Sommer, H. Oskar, *The Vulgate Version of the Arthurian Romances edited from manuscripts in the British Museum* (London 1908–1916, rp New York 1979).

Sone von Nausay, ed. Moritz Goldschmidt, Bibliothek des Litterarischen Vereins in Stuttgart CCXVI (Tübingen 1899).

Spitzer, Leo, 'The Name of the Holy Grail', *American Journal of Philology*, LXV (1944) 354–63.

Spotts, Frederic, *Bayreuth: A History of the Wagner Festival* (New Haven and London 1994).

Stanger, Mary, 'Literary patronage at the court of Flanders', *French Studies*, 11 (1957) 214–29.

Stanton, Amida, 'Gerbert de Montreuil as writer of grail romance', Dissertation, University of Chicago 1942.

Steiner, Rudolf, *Christus und die geistige Welt: Von der Suche nach dem Heiligen Gral* (Dornach 1925).

Stephens, Louise D., 'Manessier's Continuation of Chretien de Troyes' Perceval', Oxford D. Phil. thesis, 1993, BL D184686.

Sterckx, C., 'Les têtes coupées et le Graal', *Studia Celtica*, XX–XXI (1985–6) 1–42.

Sterckx, Claude, 'Perceval le Gallois, Bran le Méhaigné et le symbolisme du Graal', *Revue belge de philologie et d'histoire*, LXII (1984) 463–73.

Stevens, Adrian, 'Fiction, Plot and Discourse: Wolfram's *Parzival* and its narrative sources', in *A Companion to Wolfram's Parzival*, ed. Will Hasty (Rochester, NY and Woodbridge 1999) 99–123.

Stiennon, Jacques, 'Bruges et le Graal', in Stiennon (1984) 5–15.

Stiennon, Jacques, ed., *Chrétien de Troyes et le Graal*, Lettres medievales I (Paris 1984).

Straughn, Gregory, 'Wagner's Musical Quest: the "Grail" in Parsifal', *Arthuriana*, 11.1 (2001) 54–66.

Syson, Luke and Gordon, Dillian, *Pisanello: Painter to the Renaissance Court* (London 2001) 67–8.

Szkilnik, Michelle, *L'Archipel du Graal – étude de l'Estoire del Saint Graal* (Geneva 1991).

Talarico, Kathryn Marie, 'Romancing the Grail: Fiction and Theology in the *Queste del Saint Graal*', in Meister (1999) 29–59.

Tanner, Michael, *Wagner* (London 1996).

Taylor, Beverly and Brewer, Elisabeth, *The Return of King Arthur: British and American Arthurian Literature since 1800*, Arthurian Studies ix (Cambridge and Totowa, NJ 1983).

Tennyson, Alfred, 'The Holy Grail', in *The Poems of Tennyson*, ed. Christopher Ricks (London 1987) III 463–90.

Tennyson, Emily, *Lady Tennyson's Journal*, ed. James O. Hoge (Charlottesville 1970).

Tennyson, Hallam, *Alfred Lord Tennyson: A Memoir* (London 1897).

Thomas, Neil, *The Defence of Camelot: Ideology and Intertextuality in the 'Post-Classical' German Romances of the Matter of Britain Cycle*, Deutsche Literatur von den Anfängen bis 1700, 14 (Bern 1992).

Thomas, Neil, *Diu Krône and the Medieval Arthurian Cycle*, Arthurian Studies l (Woodbridge and Rochester, NY 2002).

Thornton, Alison G., *Weltgeschichte und Heilsgeschichte in Albrechts von Scharfenberg Jüngeren Titurel*, Göppinger Arbeiten zur Germanistik 211 (Göppingen 1977).

Traxler, Janina P., 'The use and abuse of the grail quest: ironic juxtaposition in the "Tristan en prose"', *Tristania: A Journal Devoted to Tristan Studies*, 15 (1994) 23–31.

Trendelenburg, Gudula, *Studien zum Gralraum im "Jüngeren Titurel"*, Göppinger Arbeiten zur Germanistik 78 (Göppingen 1972).

Tresize, Simon, *The West Country as a Literary Invention* (Exeter 2000).

Turner, Sharon, *The History of the Anglo-Saxons*, 6th edn (London 1836).

Turton, Godfrey, *The Emperor Arthur* (London 1986).

Tuve, Rosemond, *Allegorical Imagery* (Princeton 1966).

'Twain, Mark' (Samuel Langhorne Clemens), *A Connecticut Yankee in King Arthur's Court*, ed. Allison R. Ensor (New York and London 1987).

Two of the Saxon Chronicles parallel, ed. Charles Plummer and John Earle (Oxford 1892).

Uscatescu, Jorge, 'Fuentes arabes del Santo Griale', *Calamo: Revista de Cultura Hispano-Arabe*, 13 (1987) 8–9.

The Utrecht Psalter: Picturing the Psalms of David, CD-ROM, ed. Kort van der Horst (Utrecht 1996).

van den Oudenrijn, M.-A., *Gamaliel: Äthiopische Texte zur Pilatusliteratur*, Spicilegium Friburgense 4 (Freiburg 1959).

Vanhaecke, Louis, *The Precious Blood at Bruges* (London 1912).

Vansittart, Peter, *Parsifal* (London 1988).

Varagine, Iacopo de, *Chronica civitatis Ianuensis*, ed. Giovanni Monleone (Rome 1941).

Vendryes, J., 'Les elements celtiques de la légende du Graal', *Études celtiques*, 5 (1950–51) 1–50.

Vial, Guy, *Le conte du Graal: sens et unité. La première continuation: textes et contenu* (Geneva 1987).

Vinaver, E., *The Rise of Romance* (Cambridge and Totowa, NJ 1984).

Vincent, Nicholas, *The Holy Blood: King Henry III and the Westminster Blood Relic* (Cambridge 2001).

Waddell, P. Hately, *The Parsifal of Richard Wagner at Bayreuth, 1894* (Edinburgh and London 1894).

Wagemann, Anke, *Wolframs von Eschenbach Parzival im 20. Jahrhundert: Untersuchungen zu Wandel und Funktion in Literatur, Theater und Film*, Göppinger Arbeiten zur Germanistik 646 (Göppingen 1998).

Wagner, Cosima, *Diaries*, ed. Martin Gregor-Dellin and Dietrich Mack, tr. Geoffrey Skelton (London 1978–80).

Wagner, Richard, *Richard Wagner's Prose Works: VI. Religion and Art*, tr. William Ashton Ellis (London 1897).

Wagner, Richard, *Richard Wagner to Mathilde Wesendonck*, ed. and tr. William Ashton Ellis (London 1905).

Wagner, Richard, *The Diary of Richard Wagner 1865–1882*, ed. Joachim Bergfeld, tr. George Bird (London 1980).

Wagner, Richard, *Parsifal. Ein Bühnenweihfestspiel* (London, Paris and Brussels n.d.).

Waite, Arthur Edward, *Strange Houses of Sleep* (London 1906).

Waite, Arthur Edward, *The Hidden Church of the Holy Grail* (London 1909); revised as *The Holy Grail: the Galahad Quest in Arthurian Literature* (London 1933, rp New York 1961).

Waite, Arthur Edward, *The Book of the Holy Graal* (London 1921).

Waitz, Hugo, *Die Fortsetzungen von Chrestiens' Perceval le Gallois nach den Pariser Handschriften* (Strassburg 1890).

Wapnewski, P., 'Parzival und Parsifal oder Wolframs Held und Wagners Erlöser', in *Richard Wagner, Von der Oper zum Musikdrama*, ed. Stefan Kunze (Bern 1978) 47–60.

Wapnewski, Peter, *Wolframs Parzival: Studien zu Religiosität und Form* (Heidelberg 1955).

Watson, Derek, 'Wagner's *Tristan und Isolde* and *Parsifal*', in *King Arthur in Music*, ed. Richard Barber, Arthurian Studies lii (Cambridge and Rochester, NY 2002) 24.

Wechssler, Eduard, *Die Sage vom Heiligen Gral* (Halle 1898).

Weinraub, Eugene, J., *Chrétien's Jewish Grail: a new investigation of the imagery and significance of Chrétien de Troyes's Grail episode based upon medieval Hebraic sources* (Chapel Hill, NC 1976).

Welz, Dieter, 'Gedanken zur Genese des Gralromans', *Acta Germanica*, 15 (1982) 7–15.

Westernhagen, Curt von, *Richard Wagners Dresdner Bibliothek* (Wiesbaden 1966).

Weston, Jessie L., *Arthurian Romances unrepresented in Malory's 'Morte d'Arthur': VI. Sir Gawain at the Grail Castle* (London 1903, rp Llanerch 1995).

Weston, Jessie L., *Arthurian Romances unrepresented in Malory's 'Morte d'Arthur': VII. Sir Gawain and the Lady of Lys* (London 1903, rp Llanerch 1995).

Weston, Jessie L., *The Legend of Sir Perceval: Studies upon its Origin, Development, and Position in the Arthurian Cycle* (London 1909).

Weston Jessie L., *The Quest of the Holy Grail* (London 1913, rp New York 1964).

Weston, Jessie L., *From Ritual to Romance* (Cambridge 1920, rp New York 1957).

Weston, Jessie, L., *The Romance of Perlesvaus*, ed. Janet Grayson (Holland, MI 1988).

Westwood, Thomas, *The Quest of the Sancgreall* (London 1868).

White, Ralph, ed. *The Rosicrucian Enlightenment Revisited* (Hudson, NY 1999).

Whitman, Jon, 'The Body and the struggle for the soul of romance: *La Queste del Saint Graal*', in *Body and Soul in Medieval Literature*, ed. Anna Torti and Piero Boitani (Cambridge and Rochester, NY 1999) 31–61.

Whitworth, Charles W., 'The sacred and the secular in Malory's Tale of the Sankgreal', *Yearbook of English Studies*, 5 (1975) 19–29.

William of Tyre, *A History of Deeds done beyond the Sea*, tr. E. A. Babcock and A. C. Krey (New York 1943).

Williams, Andrea M. L., *The Adventures of the Holy Grail: A Study of La Queste del Saint Graal* (Bern 2001).

Williams, Charles, *War in Heaven* (London 1930).

Williams, Charles, 'Malory and the Grail Legend', *Dublin Review*, 214.428-9 (1944) 144-53.

Williams, Charles, *The Image of the City*, ed. Anne Ridler (London and New York 1958).

Williams, Charles, *Arthurian Poets: Charles Williams* (Woodbridge and Rochester, NY 1991).

Williams, Charles and Lewis, C. S., *Arthurian Torso* (Oxford 1948).

Williams, Harry F., 'The Unasked Questions in the Conte del Graal', *Medieval Perspectives*, II (1988) 292-302.

Williams, Robert, *Y Seint Greal: The Holy Grail* (London 1876, rp Pwllheli 1987).

Wilmotte, Maurice, *Le poème du graal et ses auteurs* (Paris 1930).

Wilmotte, Maurice, *Le poème du Gral: Le Parzival de Wolfram d'Eschenbach et ses sources françaises* (Paris 1933).

Wilson, R. M., *The Lost Literature of Medieval England* (London 1952).

Wittmann-Klemm, Dorothee, *Studien zum 'Rappoltsteiner Parzival'*, Göppinger Arbeiten zur Germanistik 224 (Göppingen 1977).

Wolf, Werner, 'Der Vögel Phönix und der Gral', in *Studien zur deutschen Philologie des Mittelalters Friedrich Panzer ... dargebracht*, ed. R. Kienast (Heidelberg 1950) 73-95.

Wolff, Ludwig, 'Das Magdeburger Gralsfest Bruns von Schoenebeck', *Niederdeutsche Zeitschrift fur Volkskunde*, V (1927) 202-16.

Wolfgang, Lenora D., 'Prologues to the *Perceval* and Perceval's father: the first literary critics of Chrétien were the Grail authors themselves', *Oeuvres et critiques*, V:2 (1980-1981) 81-90.

Wolfram von Eschenbach, *Parzival und Titurel*, tr. (into modern German) Karl Simrock (Stuttgart and Augsburg 1857).

Wolfram von Eschenbach, *Parcival*, tr. (into modern German) 'San-Marte' (Albert Schulz) 2nd edn (Leipzig 1858).

Wolfram von Eschenbach, *Parzival*, ed. Karl Lachmann, 7th edn rev. Eduard Hartl (Berlin 1952).

Wolfram von Eschenbach, *Parzival*, tr. Helen M. Mustard and Charles E. Passage (New York 1961).

Wolfram von Eschenbach, *Parzival*, tr. A. T. Hatto (Harmondsworth 1980).

Wolfram von Eschenbach, *Parzival, Titurel, Love Song*, tr. Cyril Edwards (Cambridge and Rochester, NY 2004).

Wolfram von Eschenbach, *Titurel*, tr. Charles E. Passage (New York 1984).

Wood, Juliette, 'The Holy Grail: from romance motif to modern genre', *Folklore*, III (2000) 169-90.

Wood, Juliette, 'Nibbling Pilgrims and the Nanteos Cup: A Cardiganshire Legend', in *Nanteos: A Welsh House and its Families*, ed. Gerald Morgan (Gomer 2002) 202-53.

Wrede, H., 'Die Fortsetzer des Gralromans Chrestiens von Troyes', Dissertation, Göttingen 1952.

Yamaguchi, Eriko, 'The "Defence of Lancelot": Rossetti's Quest for "God's Graal" ', *Studies in Medievalism*, IV (1992) 235–46.

Yates, Frances, *The Rosicrucian Enlightenment* (London and Boston 1972).

Yeats, William Butler, *Autobiographies* (London 1955).

Y Seint Greal, ed. and tr. Robert Williams (London 1876, rp Pwllheli 1987).

Zahlten, Johann, 'Der "Sacro Catino" in Genua. Aufklärung über eine mittelalterliche Gralsreliquie', in Baumstark (1995) 121–31.

Zambon, Francesco, *Robert de Boron e i segreti del Graal*, Biblioteca dell' «Archivum Romanum» 189 (Florence 1984).

Zambon, Francesco, 'Graal et hérésie', *Actes du XIV Congrès International Arthurien*, ed. Charles Foulon et al. (Rennes 1985) II 687–706.

Zambon, Francesco, *Romanzo e allegoria nel medioevo* (Trento 2000).

Zatloukal, Klaus, *Salvaterre: Studien zu Sinn und Funktion des Gralsbereiches im 'Juengeren Titurel'*, Wiener Arbeiten zur germanischen Altertumskunde und Philologie 12 (Wien 1978).

Abbreviations

Works in the notes are cited by author and date, as described in the bibliography. The following abbreviations are used for major texts:

Continuations of Perceval	William Roach, ed., *The Continuations of the Old French* Perceval *of Chrétien de Troyes* (Philadelphia 1949–1983).
Didot-*Perceval*	William Roach, ed. and tr., *The* Didot *Perceval according to the Manuscripts of Modena and Paris* (Philadelphia 1941).
Estoire del Saint Graal	*L'estoire del Saint Graal*, ed. Jean-Paul Ponceau, Classiques Français du Moyen Âge (Paris 1997).
Gerbert de Montreuil	Gerbert de Montreuil, *La continuation de Perceval*, ed. Mary Williams and Marguerite Oswald, Classiques Françaises du Moyen Âge (Paris 1922–1975).
High Book of the Grail	Nigel Bryant, *The High Book of the Grail: a translation of the thirteenth-century romance of Perlesvaus* (Cambridge and Totowa, NJ 1978).
Joseph d'Arimathie	Robert de Boron, *Joseph d'Arimathie: a critical edition of the verse and prose versions*, ed. Richard O'Gorman, Studies and Texts 120 (Toronto 1995).
Jüngerer Titurel	*Albrechts von Scharfenberg Jüngerer Titurel*, ed. Werner Wolf (and Kurt Nyholm), Deutsche Texte des Mittelalters XLV, LV, LXI, LXXIII (Berlin 1955, 1968, 1985, 1992).
Lancelot	*Lancelot*, ed. Alexandre Micha (Paris 1978–1983).
Lancelot-Grail	*Lancelot-Grail: The Old French Arthurian Vulgate and Post-Vulgate in Translation*, ed. Norris J. Lacy (New York and London 1993–6).

Malory	Sir Thomas Malory, *The Works of Sir Thomas Malory*, ed. Eugène Vinaver, rev. P. J. C. Field (Oxford 1990)*
Merlin and the Grail	*Merlin and the Grail:* Joseph of Arimathea, Merlin, Perceval: *the trilogy of prose romances attributed to Robert de Boron*, tr. Nigel Bryant, Arthurian Studies xlviii (Cambridge and Rochester, NY 2001).
Parzival	Wolfram von Eschenbach, *Parzival*, ed. Karl Lachmann, 7th edn rev. Eduard Hartl (Berlin 1952). The translations are from Wolfram von Eschenbach, *Parzival, Titurel, Love Songs*, tr. Cyril Edwards (Cambridge and Rochester, NY 2004)
Perlesvaus	*Le Haut Livre du Graal: Perlesvaus*, ed. William A. Nitze and T. Atkinson Jenkins (Chicago 1932).
PL	*Patrologiae cursus completus. Series Latina*, ed. J.-P. Migne (Paris 1844–1902).
Perceval	Chrétien de Troyes, *Le roman de Perceval ou le Conte du Graal*, ed. William Roach, 2nd edn (Geneva and Paris 1959).
Queste del Saint Graal	*La Queste del Saint Graal: Roman du XIIIᵉ siècle*, ed. Albert Pauphilet, Classiques Français du Moyen Âge (Paris 1923).
Quest of the Holy Grail	*The Quest of the Holy Grail* tr. Pauline Matarasso (Harmondsworth 1969).
Roman du Graal	Robert de Boron, *Le roman du Graal: Manuscrit de Modène*, ed. and tr. Bernard Cerquiglini (Paris 1981).
Story of the Grail	Chrétien de Troyes, *Perceval: the story of the Grail*, tr. Nigel Bryant, Arthurian Studies v (Cambridge and Totowa, NJ 1982).

* I have modernized all quotations from Malory for spelling and vocabulary, as sparingly as possible.

Notes

Translations not referenced in the footnotes are by the author.

INTRODUCTION

1 *High Book of the Grail*, 19.
2 These were Troy, France and Britain, the stories of Aeneas, Charlemagne and Arthur. Wilson 1952, 243.

PART ONE

Prologue

1 'La légende du Graal: origine et évolution', in Frappier and Grimm (1984) i, 292.
2 Lewis (1966) 39–40.

1. Imagining the Grail: Chrétien de Troyes

1 There is much discussion on the balance between reading and recital in the twelfth century; for a good summary see Green (2002) 35–54. Robert of Gloucester died in 1147.
2 See 'Philomena et Procne' l.734, in Cormier (1986) 232; the problem is whether the poet is Chrétien de Troyes or a namesake, quite apart from the meaning of *gois*.
3 Bullock-Davies (1981) 1–61.
4 Anna Comnena (1956) 326.
5 Karnein (1978) 1–20.
6 *Story of the Grail*, 32–7; *Perceval*, ll. 2976–3421.
7 *Story of the Grail*, 51; *Perceval*, ll. 4678–83.
8 *Story of the Grail*, 38; *Perceval*, l. 3509.
9 *Story of the Grail*, 51; *Perceval*, ll. 4728–40.
10 Perceval had in fact learnt of this earlier from his cousin; *Story of the Grail*, 39; *Perceval*, ll. 3593–5.

11 *Story of the Grail*, 67–70; *Perceval*, ll. 6217–518.

12 Busby (1993) ix–xxxix, for a description of the manuscripts.

13 *Continuations of Perceval*, I, xxxiv ff.

2. Completing the Grail: Chrétien continued

1 This attribution has been disputed, but see Corley (1984) 351–9, who confirms that the passage in which the author identifies himself is genuine.

2 See Salmeri (1984) 31–9, and Stephens (1993) 13–15.

3 Translation based on *Story of the Grail*, 302; *Continuations of Perceval*, V, 343.

4 Stanger (1957) 214–29.

5 Hindman (1994) 121–4.

6 See Frappier and Grimm (1984) 127.

7 The distinguished French critic Gaston Paris suggested that the writer was working from notes left by Chrétien, but this can scarcely be true of the whole of his story, which ends on a topic which Chrétien does not even hint at. See Gaston Paris, *Histoire littéraire de France*, 2nd edn (Paris 1890) 98.

8 *Story of the Grail*, 112; *Continuations of Perceval*, I, ll. 1357–71; II, ll. 3853–77. As always, the chronology of the Grail tradition is far from certain; only two of the twelve manuscripts of the *First Continuation* contain the words 'Holy Grail' (I, v. 1363), and these are the most likely to be influenced by other romances.

9 *Story of the Grail*, 158, *Continuations of Perceval* IV, ll. 25614–17.

10 *Story of the Grail*, 160, *Continuations of Perceval* IV, ll. 25783–801.

11 *Story of the Grail*, 191, *Continuations of Perceval* IV, ll. 32396–414.

12 See Séguy (2001) 70–76.

13 *Continuations of Perceval*, V, l. 41966 n. (MS T).

14 *Bliocadran* (1976).

15 *Elucidation* (1931).

3. Sanctifying the Grail Hero: Robert de Boron

1 Mas-Latrie (1852–61) i. 170–81.

2 Pierre Gallais (1970) I, 313–19; Imbs (1954) 63–73; Burdach (1974) 489–94.

3 Ciggaar (1993) 145–59.

4 It is possible that the whole work was to be called *The Book of the Grail*; see *Merlin* (1886) I, 47–8: 'Et tes livres ... si avra a non tous jours mais li livres dou graal ...'

5 This has been disputed by Gowans (1996) 1–17, but given that this would go against the almost universal pattern of verse romances preceding their prose versions, this seems unlikely without very strong evidence to the contrary.

6 *Joseph d'Arimathie*, 110–11; *Merlin and the Grail*, 22.

7 *Merlin and the Grail*, 22; *Joseph d'Arimathie*, 112–13.

8 *Merlin and the Grail*, 35–6; *Joseph d'Arimathie*, 254–63.

9 *Merlin and the Grail*, 70–1; *Roman du Graal*, 120–1.

10 *Merlin and the Grail*, 94; *Roman du Graal*, 161.

11 *Merlin and the Grail*, 113; *Roman du Graal*, 194–5.

12 *Merlin and the Grail*, 147; *Roman du Graal*, 255.

13 *Merlin and the Grail*, 141–2; *Roman du Graal*, 245–6.

14 *Merlin and the Grail*, 154; *Roman du Graal*, 269.

15 *Merlin and the Grail*, 155; *Roman du Graal*, 270.

4. The Old Law and the New Law: *The High Book of the Grail*

1 Mas Latrie (1852–1861) i.156.

2 *Perlesvaus*, II, 73–8.

3 Grand (1992) 233–5.

4 *High Book of the Grail*, 19; *Perlesvaus*, I, 23.

5 *High Book of the Grail*, 34–5; *Perlesvaus*, I, 26.

6 *High Book of the Grail*, 61–2; *Perlesvaus*, I, 91–2.

7 *High Book of the Grail*, 79; *Perlesvaus*, I, 118–20.

8 *High Book of the Grail*, 112; *Perlesvaus*, I, 171.

9 *High Book of the Grail*, 172; *Perlesvaus*, I, 269.

10 Bryant translates 'transsubstantiations', but the original has simply 'muances', which has no religious overtones.

11 *High Book of the Grail*, 195–6; *Perlesvaus*, I, 304–5.

12 *High Book of the Grail*, 264; *Perlesvaus*, I, 407.

5. Creating the Grail Hero: The *Lancelot-Grail*

1 Translation based on *Lancelot-Grail*, III, 100; *Lancelot*, II, 377.

2 *Lancelot-Grail*, III, 102; *Lancelot*, II, 387.

3 *Lancelot-Grail*, III, 163; *Lancelot*, IV, 206.

4 *Lancelot-Grail*, III, 271; *Lancelot*, V, 270.

5 *Lancelot-Grail*, III, 272; *Lancelot*, V, 273.

6 *Lancelot-Grail*, III, 328; Lancelot, VI, 204–5.

7 *Lancelot-Grail*, III, 333; *Lancelot*, VI, 224.

8 *Lancelot-Grail*, III, 338; *Lancelot*, VI, 244.

9 *Quest of the Holy Grail*, 43–4; *Queste del Saint Graal*, 15.

10 *Quest of the Holy Grail*, 162; *Queste del Saint Graal*, 147.

11 *Quest of the Holy Grail*, 84; *Queste del Saint Graal*, 60.

12 *Quest of the Holy Grail*, 262; *Queste del Saint Graal*, 255.

13 *Quest of the Holy Grail*, 269–70; *Queste del Saint Graal*, 268–70.

14 *Quest of the Holy Grail*, 282–4; *Queste del Saint Graal*, 277–9.

15 *Lancelot-Grail*, I, 4; *Estoire del Saint Graal*, I, 4.

16 *Lancelot-Grail*, I, 10; *Estoire del Saint Graal*, I, 24.

17 *Lancelot-Grail*, I, 15; 'arche de fust', wooden ark, *Estoire del Saint Graal*, I, 41.

18 *Lancelot-Grail*, I, 24; *Estoire del Saint Graal*, I, 72–4.

19 *Lancelot-Grail*, I, 51; *Estoire del Saint Graal*, I, 167.

20 1 Samuel 6. 19: the men of Beth-shemesh are smitten by the Lord 'because they

had looked into the ark of the Lord'. 2 Samuel 6. 6–8: Uzzah is struck dead for putting his hand on the ark.

21 *Lancelot-Grail*, I, 135; *Estoire del Saint Graal*, II, 473–4.

22 *Lancelot-Grail*, I, 159; *Estoire del Saint Graal*, II, 563.

23 *Lancelot-Grail*, I, 352; Sommer (1908–1916) II, 334.

6. Visions of Angels, Versions of Men: Wolfram von Eschenbach's *Parzival*

1 *Parzival*, 115, 27–30.

2 *Parzival*, 297, 20–3.

3 *Parzival*, 217, 1–5.

4 Gottfried von Strassburg (1960) 105–6; a reference to *Parzival*, I, 15–19, where Wolfram says that his images are so swift that they will rush past 'stupid people' like a swift hare.

5 Duby (1996) 1395–6.

6 *Parzival*, 231.15–30.

7 *Parzival*, 233.12–236.22.

8 *Parzival*, 238.2–240.6.

9 *Parzival*, 332.1–8.

10 *Parzival*, 447.20–448.7.

11 *Story of the Grail*, 68; *Perceval*, ll. 6333–6.

12 *Parzival*, 451.14–452.9.

13 *Parzival*, 452.29–455.12.

14 *Parzival*, 468.23–471.29.

15 *Titurel* in *Parzival*, I, 6–7.

16 *Parzival*, 479.2–24.

17 *Parzival*, 483.19–484.13.

18 *Parzival*, 503.21–6.

19 An echo of the prophecy in *Perceval* that Perceval's sword will break at a critical moment (*Story of the Grail*, 40).

20 *Parzival*, 781.3–16, 782.22–30.

21 *Parzival*, 827.1–30.

Epilogue

1 Schmolke-Hasselmann (1998) 14.

PART TWO

7. The Grail

1 Schmolke-Hasselmann (1998) 34.

2 For Hélinand's career and writings, see Kienzle (2001) 174–82.

3 *PL*, 212, 814–15. Questions of 'which goes after which' at once confront us:

the date 717 could come from *The History of the Holy Grail*, and the etymology for the Grail from Robert de Boron or from the *Lancelot-Grail*. Equally, both could derive from Hélinand; his work is after all a chronicle and a date is natural here, and his explanation of the word is typical of this kind of scholarly writing.

4 The key passages are the prologue to *Perlesvaus* (see p. 47 above), and the early part of *Joseph d'Arimathie* (vv. 396–400, 507–10, 551–72). The *First Continuation* of *Le conte du graal* (*Continuations of Perceval, Continuations*, II, 524, vv. 17567–777 and the equivalent passages at III. i, 480–90 (MS A vv. 7491–708, MS L vv. 7459–670) and Manessier's continuation (V, 5–7, vv. 32698–770) both have versions of the story. A variant version of the ending of the *Second Continuation* also includes it: *Continuations of Perceval*, IV, Appendix XI, 590–1.

5 The opening of *Perlesvaus* does not mention Joseph of Arimathea, but Perlesvaus is told by the master of the Grail castle that Joseph collected Christ's blood in the Grail: *Perlesvaus*, I, 390–1; *High Book of the Grail*, 252.

6 *Continuations of Perceval*, I, v. 9649.

7 *Continuations of Perceval*, II, vv. 3823–66.

8 Gossen (1959) 199. See also Lejeune (1951) 277–82.

9 Spitzer (1944) 354–63; while the philological arguments are beyond my scope, the sudden transition from 'woven basket' to 'silver bowl' which Spitzer posits seems inherently rather improbable.

10 Roques (1956).

11 Gossen (1959); Duval (1979) 291–5.

12 *Girart de Roussillon* (1963) 73.

13 *Roman d'Alexandre* v. 611. The mention of 'lanza ni ·l grazaus' by the troubadour Rigaut de Barbezieux, once thought to be from the 1180s and hence before Chrétien, is now dated to the early thirteenth century (*Lexikon des Mittelalters*, Munich and Zurich 1977–1997, VII, col. 849).

14 *Continuations of Perceval*, I, 262, v. 9649, MS V; the fourteenth-century German translation uses *teller*, a dish: and II, 404, v.13431, MS M. Both manuscripts are late thirteenth century, implying that the word had lost its common usage as dish.

15 *Continuations of Perceval*, I, v. 1363.

16 *High Book of the Grail*, 61; *Perlesvaus*, I, 91–2.

17 See note 10 to Chapter 3 above.

18 *High Book of the Grail*, 195–6; *Perlesvaus*, I, 304–5.

19 *Lancelot-Grail*, III, 163; *Lancelot*, V, 206.

20 Lot-Borodine (1951b) 152.

21 *High Book of the Grail*, 61–2; *Perlesvaus*, I, 91–2.

22 *Lancelot-Grail*, I, 135, 169; *Estoire del Saint Graal*, II, 473, 563.

23 *Quest of the Holy Grail*, 262; *Queste del Saint Graal*, 255.

24 *The High Book of the Grail*, 79; *Perlesvaus*, I, 119.

25 St John Chrysostom (1926) 51.

26 Riant (1877) I, 116.

27 Riant (1875) 188–9, 194–5, 210–11.

28 Durandus (1859) 284.

29 Loomis and Loomis (1938) 123–4.

30 *Lancelot*, II, 384–5.

31 *Lancelot*, VI, 204–5.

32 *Lancelot*, VI, 224.

33 *Continuations of Perceval*, II, vv. 17348–56; III.i, MS L, vv. 7276–83, MSS A S P, vv. 7240–7. Eight out of ten manuscripts have this reading. The other two (MSS T and V: I, vv. 13278–304) do not attribute the serving of wine to the Grail itself; instead, it is poured by butlers, and the bread is distributed apparently by servants. But the implication of the rest of the passage is that the Grail serves the dishes of the feast. This scene is the source of the description of the Grail feast in the *Elucidation* prologue (see p. 36).

34 *Continuations of Perceval*, IV, vv.31184–227.

35 *Lancelot-Grail*, III, 100; *Lancelot*, II, 377.

36 *Lancelot*, V, 255.

37 *Quest of the Holy Grail*, 44; *Queste del Saint Graal*, 15.

38 *Quest of the Holy Grail*, 276; *Queste del Saint Graal*, 270.

8. The Setting of the Grail

1 One manuscript does what might be expected at this point, and brings the story to a swift conclusion: *Continuations of Perceval*, IV, Appendix XI, 591–2.

2 Berthelot (2002) 17–28.

3 Didot-*Perceval*, 239.

4 *Elucidation* 248–55.

5 *Parzival*, 795. 29.

6 For further discussion, see Johnson (1982) 83–102.

7 *Queste del Saint Graal*, 160–1.

8 *Queste del Saint Graal*, 158–9.

9 *Queste del Saint Graal*, viii–ix.

10 *Quest of the Holy Grail*, 284; my italics.

11 *Quest of the Holy Grail*, 283; *Queste del Saint Graal*, 277–8.

9. Obscure Histories, Dubious Relics

1 *High Book of the Grail*, 19; *Perlesvaus*, I, 24.

2 *Perceval*, 240; *High Book of the Grail*, 155. First Continuation: *Continuations of Perceval* I, 13471 ('Longis'). Third Continuation: *Continuations of Perceval* V, 32660; *Story of the Grail*, 271. Also: Malory ('Longeus') I, 85.

3 James (1924) xvi–xvii.

4 See Izydorczyk (1997) for a wide-ranging survey of the work and its influence in the medieval West.

5 Sommer (1908–1916) VII, 247–61.

6 BL MS Roy.1.E.IX.

7 Elliott (1993) 184.

8 See Peebles (1911), especially 15, 166, 185–6.

9 *Story of the Grail*, 35; *Perceval*, 3200; Ríquer (1953) II, 231–4 for examples from the *chansons de geste*.

10 Peebles (1911) 185–6.

11 Micha (1976) 207–50.

12 *Joseph d'Arimathie*, vv. 981–2356; *Merlin and the Grail*, 27–34. The story is derived from the *Vita Pilati*, a separate work from the *Acts of Pilate*.

13 *Merlin and the Grail*, 8–9. *Perlesvaus* is similarly preoccupied with the Cruci-fixion, and two of the manuscripts open with a miniature of the Crucifixion (pl. 12–13).

14 *High Book of the Grail*, 131; *Perlesvaus*, I, 200–201.

15 *High Book of the Grail*, 143; *Perlesvaus*, I, 224.

16 Malcor (1991) 51 ff.

17 *Utrecht Psalter* (1996) Psalm 115. See pl. 14. Verse 13 speaks of 'the chalice of salvation'. See Chazelle (2001) 246–8.

18 Malcor (1991) 135 ff.

19 *First Continuation* (long version) *Continuations of Perceval*, II, 17586–91; *Third Continuation*, IV, 32698–716. *Story of the Grail*, 272.

20 See Jakobi-Mirwald (1994) I, 189, 196. I owe this reference to Dr Constance Sciacca.

21 On relics in general, see Fichtenau (1975) I, 108–44.

22 Heinzelmann (1979) 20.

23 See Geary (1978) 3–5, 20–21, on the medieval attitude to relics.

24 Scott (1981) 71.

25 Runciman (1950) 197–209; Mély (1904) 23–163; Morris (1984) 33–46.

26 Constantine VII Porphyrogenitus (1935) I, 168–9.

27 Holtzmann (1947) 19–20.

28 Mély (1904) III, 53–63.

29 *Lancelot-Grail*, III, 102; *Lancelot*, II, 377.

30 *Queste del Saint Graal*, 270.

31 Since this was drafted, Vincent (2001) has appeared, and is now the standard account of the cult.

32 Vincent (2001) 54.

33 See Kruse (1994) 57–61, and the edition of the texts 'De inventione' and 'De translatione', *ibid.*, 102–7.

34 Kolb (1980) 47–9.

35 Printed in du Monstier (1673) 207. See also Herval (1959) 105–26, 359–61.

36 Herval (1959) 227. See also Lemarignier (1937) 198–9.

37 Gouttebroze (2000) 79–82; the earliest date possible would be 1171, but the event is dated in the text to the abbacy of Henri of Sully, implying that it was written after his death in 1187.

38 For what follows, see Huyghebaert (1963) 110–87. Stiennon (1984) and other recent writers seem to have ignored Huyghebaert's findings.

39 Huyghebaert (1963) 115.

40 Frolow (1955) 55–9.

41 Vincent (2001) 67–9.

42 The manuscript of this is Trinity College, Cambridge MS R.5.33; see Scott (1981) 35–7.

43 *Joseph d'Arimathie*, 308, ll. 3122–4; 314, ll. 3219–22; *Merlin and the Grail*, 41.

44 References to *insula Avalloniae* in William of Malmesbury's history of Glastonbury were added after this discovery; see Scott (1981) 29.

45 *High Book of the Grail*, 265; *Perlesvaus*, I, 409.

46 *Perlesvaus*, II, 105–20; John of Glastonbury (1985) 76–9. As a separate tale: BL MS Cotton Titus A XIX, ff. 16–16v; Bodleian Library, Oxford, MS Bodley 622, f.7–10, and MS Douce 54, f.4–f.6v.

47 Carley (2001b) 309–36.

48 *Perlesvaus*, II, 205–6; *Fouke Fitz Waryn* (1975) 60, ll. 29–30, and Burgess (1997) 127, 182.

49 *Perlesvaus*, I, 274, 317, 325.

50 Scott (1981) 46–9, 187.

51 John of Glastonbury (1985) 28–31.

52 Carley and Crick (2001) 373.

53 Carley (2001c) 285–302.

10. The Eucharist and the Grail

1 *Quest of the Holy Grail*, 284; *Queste del Saint Graal*, 279.

2 1 Corinthians 11.25.

3 Matthew 26. 26–8; compare Mark 14. 22–4; Luke 22. 19–20.

4 See Macy (1984) 19 ff, for what follows.

5 McKitterick (1977) 154.

6 See Dumoutet (1926) 37–53, on the theology of the elevation.

7 Gerbert de Montreuil, I, 5160–77.

8 On this see Dumoutet (1942) 113–34.

9 Honorius is called *Augustodunensis*, which has been traditionally translated as 'of Autun', which would place him in Burgundy; but scholars now agree that his early career was in England, and later in Regensburg. See Macy (1984) 65.

10 *PL*, 172, 558, translated in Lagorio (1975) 63.

11 *PL*, 217, 895.

12 *PL*, 100, 203 ('Epistola ad Paulinum Patriarcham').

13 *Merlin and the Grail*, 22; *Joseph of Arimathea*, 110–11, ll.893–928.

14 *Merlin and the Grail*, 38; *Joseph d'Arimathie* (prose version only), 277–9.

15 Browe (1938) 49–55.

16 Ralph of Coggeshall (1875) 125.

17 Matthew Paris (1876) III, 101.

18 See for example Caesarius of Heisterbach (1929) I, 150.

19 *Wisdom of Solomon*, 16, 20.

20 *Queste del Saint Graal*, 163.

21 Peter the Venerable (1967) 124–5.

22 Ruck (1991) 45–6.

23 Schiller (1968) 2, 41–6. I have not been able to confirm her statement about the eating of fish at the Passover.

24 Quoted in Dumoutet (1926) 18.

25 He calls himself 'messires' in *Joseph d'Arimathie*, 3461, 'meistre', *ibid.*, 3155.

26 See Roquebert (1994) 49–50. Roquebert's work is generally level-headed and interesting, and it is only on this point that I disagree with his readings.

27 See O'Gorman (1993) 539–55.

28 Geary (1978) 39–40. The relic of the Holy Blood at Fécamp was placed 'in altari' after its initial appearance, according to Robert of Torigni (1889) IV 294.

29 Geary (1978) 29.

30 Gonzalo de Berceo (1981) 52, stanza 270.

31 Caesarius of Heisterbach (1929) II, 108–11, 145–6. Fanni Bogdanow (1984) has argued that *Perlesvaus* must be later than Caesarius on the grounds that the two accounts are so similar, but there is no reason why Caesarius should not have borrowed from *Perlesvaus* rather than the other way round, and, given the intense interest in eucharistic miracles at this period, there may well have been a common source.

32 Rubin (1991) 118.

33 Caesarius of Heisterbach (1929) I, 154.

34 Caesarius of Heisterbach (1929) I, 388–9.

35 Rubin (1991) 170.

36 On the social standing of the Beguines and, in England, of the audience for the *Ancrene Wisse* see Bolton (1981) 25–6.

11. The Holy Grail

1 *Merlin and the Grail*, 15; *Roman du Graal*, 18.

2 *Joseph d'Arimathie*, 110, ll. 905–13.

3 *Joseph d'Arimathie*, 2649–52.

4 *High Book of the Grail*, 19; *Perlesvaus*, I, 1–7.

5 *High Book of the Grail*, 73; *Perlesvaus*, I, 109–10.

6 *High Book of the Grail*, 74; *Perlesvaus*, I, 110.

7 Tuve (1966) 403.

8 Pauphilet (1921) 137.

9 Gilson (1932) 59–91.

10 Gilson (1932) 60–1.

11 *Queste del Saint Graal*, 159.

12 *Quest of the Holy Grail*, 178; *Queste del Saint Graal*, 165.

13 *Quest of the Holy Grail*, 129; *Queste del Saint Graal*, 110.

14 For an example of the narrow approach, see Hamilton (1942) 94–110, where he identifies it as the Eucharist *in opposition to* Etienne Gilson's argument that it represents divine grace. For what follows, I am indebted chiefly to Matarasso (1979) 180–204.

15 *Queste del Saint Graal*, 16.

16 1 Corinthians 13. 12.

17 *Queste del Saint Graal*, 278.

18 Baumgartner (1981) 146.

19 *Lancelot-Grail*, I, 49; I, 62–3; I, 162; *Estoire del Saint Graal*, I, 159–60; I, 218; II, 573.

20 *Lancelot-Grail*, I, 23–8; *Estoire del Saint Graal*, I, 72–7. Lot-Borodine (1930) 526–57, examines the arguments of Eugène Anitchkof (1929) who sees a strong Joachimite and Cathar influence; she admits that there are elements of Joachimite writings in the *Estoire*, but places the work in a more general Cistercian milieu. I would not go as far as she does in tentatively attributing the work to a Templar (p. 556), given that there is very little evidence of literary activity of any sort among the religious orders of knighthood.

21 *Lancelot-Grail*, I, 6–9; *Estoire del Saint Graal*, I, 13–15.

22 See Talarico (1999).

23 Groos (1995) 38–40.

24 *Parzival* 503.27–9; 468.2; 803.3.

12. The Secrets of the Grail

1 See Nitze (1915–1917) 24–36 for a discussion of Chrétien's possible use of written sources.

2 Damian-Grint (1999) 220–1.

3 *livre*: ll.67 (source), 4617 (hideous messenger); *estoire*: ll.2807 (finest knight), 3262 (ivory table), 6217 (loss of memory), 7681 (description of castle). *Story of the Grail* translates '*estoire*' as 'source-book'.

4 Green (2002) 80.

5 For an attempt to pin down (unsuccessfully) the book from the library of St Pierre at Beauvais, see Foerster (1921) xxvii–xxxiv.

6 *Continuations of Perceval*, III.i, 456–7, vv. 7083–9, 7051–8.

7 *Continuations of Perceval*, IV, 259–60, vv. 25818–34.

8 *Continuations of Perceval*, IV, 492, vv. 32060–6.

9 *Story of the Grail*, 194; Gerbert de Montreuil, I, ll. 37–42.

10 *Elucidation*, ll. 4–13.

11 *Joseph d'Arimathie*, 112, ll. 929–36.

12 See for example Amalarius of Metz (1948) 323: 'It is called *secreta* because it is said in secret.'

13 *Roman du Graal* 70; compare *Joseph d'Arimathie* 322, 328, ll. 3332–6, 3411–20.

14 See Baumgartner (1991) II 259–68.

15 *Merlin and the Grail*, 22, 42; *Roman du Graal*, 30, 68.

16 *Merlin and the Grail*, 155; Didot-*Perceval*, Modena MS ll.1864–70.

17 Didot-*Perceval*, Paris MS 1527–35; see p.151, where the same manuscript adds a note about 'the secret words' in the prediction of the end of the Grail quest (ll.189–93).

18 *High Book of the Grail*, 195; *Perlesvaus* 304, 7223–5.

19 *Quest of the Holy Grail*, 47; *Queste del Saint Graal*, 19.

20 Zambon (1984) 71. I disagree, however, with his assessment of the content of Joseph's teaching and the description of his followers as 'una sorta di comunità occulta, che si trasmette un insegnamento ricevuto direttamente da Gesù, superiore a quello pubblico e taciuto dalle Scrittura canoniche' (a sort of occult community, which handed down teaching received directly from Jesus, superior to that generally known, and passed over in silence by the canonical Scriptures).

13. The Grail Outside the Romances

1 Two other relics claiming to be the dish of the Last Supper were recorded in seventeenth-century France, at the abbey of L'Isle Barbe near Lyon, and at Brive-la-Gaillarde in Périgord. See Heinrich (1855) 214–15, quoting C. Le Laboureur, *Les masures de l'Abbaye royale de l'Isle Barbe les Lyon*, Lyon 1665, ch.2, paras 8 and 9.

2 Adamnan (1958) 51.

3 *Jüngerer Titurel*, III, 478, stanza 6295; tr. Wolfram von Eschenbach (1980) 48.

4 Riant (1875) 40, 190–1.

5 Conway (1924) 11–18; Zahlten (1995) 121–31.

6 William of Tyre (1943) I, 437.

7 *Primera crónica general* (1955) 661.

8 Varagine (1941) II, 311–12.

9 For what follows see Beltran Martinez (1984); Mandach (1995) 50–2; Schäfer (1984) 370–7; Schäfer (1983).

10 Beltran Martinez (1984) 37.

11 Domínguez Lasierra (1991) 141.

12 Domínguez Lasierra (1991) 141.

13 Beltran Martinez (1984) 38.

14 Syson and Gordon (2001) 67–8.

15 Navarro (1998) 126–7.

16 Elliott (1993) 159–60.

17 Pedro Pascual (1905–1907) I, 131; see Izquierdo (1997) 131.

18 Robert Grosseteste (1882) VI, 140.

19 Sommer (1908–1916), 247 ff.

20 Besamusca and Brandsma (1998) I, 121–31.

21 See Gerritsen (1981) 371.

22 Gerritsen (1981) 377.

23 Gerritsen (1981) 377.

14. 'There is a thing that's called the Grâl'

1 See Fourquet (1966) and Heinzle's response (1975).

2 *Parzival*, 235.20–4.

3 *Parzival* 454.19–455.1.

4 For an overview of the question, which comes down on the negative side, see Lofmark (1977). There is an excellent summary in Green (2002) 78–82.

5 A considerable literature has grown up on the possible identification of Kyot with Toledan alchemists, scholars of the Kabbalah and suchlike: see, for example, Ernst (1985); Daniëls (1937).

6 The references to Kyot are as follows: 416.20; 431.2; 453.5; 776.1; 805.1; 827.1.

7 *Parzival*, 827.1–11.

8 Compared with Hartmann and Gottfried, Wolfram is far more involved with his material: he does not conceal his evident sympathy for his characters, and frequently breaks off to comment on the action as if he was personally affected by it. See Schwietering (1960) 316.

9 See Lofmark (1977) 69, for examples.

10 See *Lexikon des Mittelalters*, IV 1787.

11 See Stevens (1999) 110–16.

12 As Arthur Groos puts it, 'Whatever we wish to make of Kyot and Flegetanis, Wolfram was clearly familiar with the massive influx of Arabic science into twelfth-century Latin culture; indeed, his narrative constitutes one of the primary documents of its reception' (1995, 204). By the end of the thirteenth century, *Zabulons Buch*, a fictional debate between poets found in the great manuscript anthologies of medieval German lyric poetry, portrayed Wolfram as an expert on astronomy: Ragotzky (1971) 68, 70.

13 452.29; *Joseph d'Arimathie*, 110, ll. 935–6. See Haferland (1994) 23–51.

14 See Kleiber (1962) (on Condwiramurs, 86) and Schröder (1982).

15 *Parzival*, 770.1–30; 772.1–24.

16 *Parzival*, 791.1–30.

17 *Parzival*, 469.29 ff.

18 *Parzival*, 816.15; this is the only time that Wolfram mentions the temple in which the Grail is kept, when Feirefiz and Repanse de Schoye are married before the Grail.

19 Wolfram uses the word sparingly: 444.23 ('the *templeis* from Munsalvaesche'); 792.21 ('many well mounted *templeis*'); 797.13 ('a *templeis*'), 805.22 ('a *templeis* from Patrigalt'); 816.18 ('the wise *templeisen*'); 818.26 ('any *templeis*').

20 Bulst-Thiele (1974) 211; Barber (1994) map, 252–3.

21 See Boulton (2000) 559–64.

22 The erotic undercurrent in the Grail procession culminates in Feirefiz's passion for Repanse de Schoye, which must be an echo of Gawain's inability to 'see' the Grail because of the beauty of its bearer in the *First Continuation*. See Pratelidis (1994) 99–100.

23 *Titurel* (in *Parzival*) 6, 1–3.

24 Ranke (1946) 20–30.

25 Matthew 3.16; see Huntley-Speare (1999) 107–26.

26 I am indebted to Professor Michael Lapidge for pointing this out (private communication).

27 *Jüngerer Titurel*, III, 477, stanza 6292, 3.

28 The alchemical/hermetic view is put forward by Kahane and Kahane (1965) and Palgen (1922) among others. The problem of how detailed knowledge of the hermetic texts came to Wolfram is crucial, and neither author gives a satisfactory explanation of how this knowledge fits with what we know of Wolfram from his work as a whole.

29 For a comprehensive review of the different readings and interpretations see Nellmann (2000) and Delcourt-Angélique (1977) 55–126.

30 Daniëls (1937) 125–58; Delcourt-Angélique (1977) 100.

31 See Faugère (1979) for a survey of the various suggestions.

32 *Story of the Grail*, 35; *Perceval* vv. 3232–9.

33 Fourquet (1938) 46.

34 Two of the manuscripts of the prose version of *Joseph d'Arimathie* mention writing on the Grail: *Joseph d'Arimathie*, 305, note to l.1291, MSS EH.

35 Wolf (1950) 73–95, ranges widely but inconclusively across a range of Oriental, Greek and Latin sources; in none is there a stone associated with the rebirth of the phoenix as in Wolfram.

36 *Parzival*, 238.14–24.

37 *Parzival*, 807.18.

38 *Parzival*, 471.9–12.

39 *Joseph d'Arimathie*, 216, ll. 2089–138; *Merlin and the Grail*, 32; *Roman du Graal*, 48–9.

40 See for example Bayer (1983) and the review by D. H. Green in *Modern Language Review*, LXXX, 1985, 971–5.

41 *Story of the Grail*, 66; *Perceval* 6168–71.

42 *Parzival*, 798.24–7; but see Martin H. Jones (1975) 52–71 for the argument for a literal, physical interpretation. This seems to me to involve some very tortuous arguments about Parzival's ability to change God's intentions by fighting (p.69).

15. The Adventures of the Grail: The Later German romances

1 See Thomas (2002) for a general study of the work.

2 Andersen (1987) 33.

3 Heinrich von dem Türlin (1989) 213–14; Heinrich von dem Türlin (1852) ll. 18896–932.

4 *Story of the Grail*, 66; *Perceval* 6183–91.

5 Heinrich von dem Türlin (1989) 327–8; Heinrich von dem Türlin (1852) ll. 29340–450.

6 Cormeau (1977) 143–55.

7 Nyholm (1964) stanzas 1293–1304.

8 Nyholm (1964) stanzas 982–3.

9 Heinrich von Ofterdingen (1963) 143, 145.

10 *Lorengel* (1979) 29, Str 78.

11 Dietrich von Niem, *De schismate libri tres*, quoted in Golther (1925) 252.

12 Golther (1925) 253.

13 *Chroniken Magdeburg* I (1869) 168–9.

14 Golther (1925) 262.

15 *Jüngerer Titurel*, I, 93, stanza 370.

16 *Jüngerer Titurel*, I, 96, stanzas 370–85, 391–7; translation by Cyril Edwards.

17 *Jüngerer Titurel*, I, 86, stanza 341; the editor prefers the reading twenty-two to the seventy-two given in the best manuscript.

18 Zatloukal (1978) 195: 'Wenn Albrechts Bauwerk ein Gesamtplan zugrunde lag, so ist er nicht aufgrund von architektonischen Prinzipien erstellt.' (If there is an overall plan behind Albrecht's structure, it is not derived from architectural principles.)

19 *Jüngerer Titurel*, I, 138, stanza 516.

20 Zatloukal (1978) 234–5 argues that Albrecht only learned of Robert de Boron's work after he had written the first section of the poem, but before he wrote the stanzas which describe the Grail and its history.

21 *Jüngerer Titurel*, I, 138, stanza 516.

22 *Jüngerer Titurel*, I, x.

23 *Jüngerer Titurel*, I, 83–153, stanzas 311–553; see Barber and Edwards (2003).

24 *Jüngerer Titurel*, I, 68, stanza 271.

25 *Jüngerer Titurel*, I, 111–17 ('Marien lob').

16 The Adventures of the Grail: The Last Flowering

1 For the reading desk, see the accounts of the duc de Berry; Jean Syme sold him 'palettes d'ivoire et de bois pour tenir chandelle a lire romanz' in 1378; Koechlin (1924) 13.

2 The manuscript described is Österreichische Nationalbibliothek, Vienna, MS 2542, which belonged to Jacques duc de Nemours, great-grandson of Jean duc de Berry; it was probably made in England in about 1450–1475. See Fotitch and Steiner (1974) 14–15.

3 *Le Roman de Tristan en Prose* (1985) 39.

4 Through Sador, nephew of Joseph of Arimathea; a prologue describing his adventures and descendants is provided, just as the *History of the Holy Grail* provided the prehistory of the Grail. *Le Roman de Tristan en Prose* (1985) 41–86.

5 Although a romance bearing his name, *Palamède*, may predate the *Prose Tristan*, its contents scarcely touch on his exploits. There is no modern edition of *Palamède*, but the bulk of the text was printed as two separate romances, *Meliadus* and *Gyron le Courtois*, in the early sixteenth century.

6 *Le Roman de Tristan en Prose* (1997) 201–3.

7 *Le Roman de Tristan en Prose* (1997) 252–5.

8 *Le Roman de Tristan en Prose* (1997) 285–6.

9 *Le Roman de Tristan en Prose* (1985) 39.

10 *Lancelot-Grail*, IV, 204; *Merlin* (1886) I, 280. The author of the *Prose Tristan* also uses this title for the book which he claims to have used as his source.

11 Bogdanow (1996) 203.

12 *Perceval*, 4675–83. The reading is confirmed by the Welsh translation in *Peredur*: 'But henceforth strife and battle, and the loss of knights, and women left widowed, and maidens without succour, and all because of thee' (*Mabinogion* (1949) 218).

13 *High Book of the Grail*, 35; *Perlesvaus*, I, 50.

14 Peterborough Chronicle s.a. 1137: *Two of the Saxon Chronicles parallel* (1892) I, 264; see Kennedy (1987) 61–75.

15 *Continuations of Perceval* I, 13560–72; II 17820–34; III, 7753–65 (MS L); III, 7716–29 (MSS A S P); *Story of the Grail*, 132–3; Gerbert de Montreuil, I, 312–24, *Story of the Grail*, 197.

16 See Vinaver (1984) 53–67 for a reconstruction of the evolution of the Waste Land theme, showing the process of literary creation behind it.

17 *Lancelot-Grail*, IV, 212; Bogdanow (1966) 245–6.

18 *Lancelot-Grail*, IV, 175; *Merlin* (1886) I, 174–5.

19 *Lancelot-Grail*, IV 233; *Merlin* (1886) II, 97.

20 *Lancelot-Grail*, III, 333; V, 75 (Post-Vulgate); *Lancelot*, VI, 224.

21 *Lancelot-Grail*, IV, 213; Bogdanow (1966) 248.

22 Bibliothèque Nationale MS Fr 24400, quoted by Berthelot (1996) 464.

23 Berthelot (1996) 464–5.

24 *Sone von Nausay* (1899) ll. 4555–938.

25 Loomis (1959) 279.

26 Didot-*Perceval*, 311.

27 The translation is T. H. White's; Malory III, 1242.

28 Malory I, 78. At this point in the French original, but not in Malory, Merlin foretells the Dolorous Blow and its consequences.

29 Malory I, 82.

30 Malory I, 84–5.

31 If he wrote it *after* his translation of the *Lancelot-Grail* version of the *Quest*, it is extraordinary that he offers an account here which scarcely corresponds to the Grail scenes in the latter; but we shall see that consistency is not one of his virtues.

32 Ihle (1983) 162–3.

33 Malory II, 863, where it is the sword that Galahad takes from the floating stone.

34 Most of the adventures summarized on pp. 55–8 above are incorporated into the *Prose Tristan*.

35 Lagorio (1978) 359–66.

36 *Graile* or *grayle* occurs only half a dozen times, largely when it appears at Arthur's court (Malory II, 865–71, four instances; there are two other isolated examples).

37 *Lorgaireacht* (1953) xxiv; *Y Seint Greal* (1987). Both translations are relatively close and faithful versions; the translation of the *Quest* in *Y Seint Greal* is followed by a version of *Perlesvaus*.

38 Lovelich (1904) l.4360.

39 *Joseph of Arimathea* (1983) 9, ll. 295–8.

40 *Lancelot-Grail*, I, 25; *Estoire del Saint Graal*, I, 75.

41 *Lancelot*, VI, 205.

42 Malory, II, 817.

43 Malory, II, 865.

44 No manuscript corresponds exactly to the text used by Malory: Malory, III, 1534–5.

45 *Quest of the Holy Grail*, 269–70; *Queste del Saint Graal*, 270; Malory, II, 1030.

46 It was a familiar image in the context of contemporary medieval religious poetry and instruction. See Miri Rubin (1991) 311–12.

47 Malory, II, 894.

48 Malory, II, 896; the French speaks of the miracles which God has performed through 'this holy vessel which I see here'.

49 Oates (1958) 269–77.

50 Printed in Horstmann (1881), 276; see ll. 61–84.

51 *Joseph of Arimathea* (1983) 9, l. 297.

52 See Riddy (1987) 113, 123–5, 130–1, for Malory's attitudes within the context of contemporary English lay devotional literature.

53 Malory, II, 955; *Queste del Saint Graal*, 162.

54 *Queste del Saint Graal*, 259.

55 Malory, II, 1018.

56 Malory, II, 1015.

57 *Quest of the Holy Grail*, 262; *Queste del saint Graal*, 255.

58 Malory, II, 1029.

59 *Quest of the Holy Grail*, 275; *Queste del Saint Graal*, 269.

60 I owe this suggestion to Professor Felicity Riddy.

61 *Quest of the Holy Grail*, 282–3; *Queste del Saint Graal*, 277–8.

62 Malory, II, 1034.

63 Malory, II, 1037; Vinaver rather misleadingly also prints it as the heading to the tale (II, 847) when neither the manuscript nor Caxton's edition does so.

Epilogue

1 Malory, II, 1035.

PART THREE

Interlude

1 Quoted in Paryns (1988) 59.

2 This reading is also found in a French armorial of the knights of the Round Table contemporary with Hardyng and Malory: see Jefferson (1996) 145.

3 Hardyng (1812) 134–5. The earlier, long version of the chronicle is unpublished; it is in BL, MS Lansdowne 204.

4 See Riddy (2000) 397–414. On the possible political reasoning behind Hardyng's version of the Grail story, see Kennedy (1989) 185–206.

5 Flood (2000) 296.

6 See Pickford (1961) 99–109.

17. The Scholars and the Grail

1 Tuve (1966) 219.

2 The library was rebuilt in 1758 to the designs of the younger and elder Peter Thumb. The *Parzival* manuscript was bought ten years later from a private collection formed in Zurich in the sixteenth century. Hobson (1970) 36.

3 Knowles (1963) 38.

4 Westernhagen (1966) items 163, 166 (p. 110) and p. 113.

5 Golther (1925) 285–6.

6 Quoted in Glencross (1995) 83.

7 On Quinet, see Glencross (1995) 90–106; the quotation is on p. 96.

8 Glencross (1995) 60, 124–7.

9 For the members of the Roxburghe Club, a bibliophile society which at this time printed 36 copies for members and up to 100 copies for sale. See Barker (1963) 21.

10 See p. 367 below. I am most grateful to Dr Ceridwen Lloyd-Morgan for translating the prospectus, and for pointing me to the references in medieval Welsh.

11 Herbert (1836) vi.

12 Goetinck (2000) 127.

13 *Mabinogion* (1949) 192.

14 *Mabinogion* (1949) 199.

15 *Mabinogion* (1949) 227.

16 See Roberts (2000) 57–72. A further complication is the existence of a short version of the tale which ends with Peredur's reign at Constantinople and omits the final section, making it a kind of 'rags to riches' story and leaving the wonders unexplained.

17 Goetinck (2000) 130.

18 La Villemarqué (1842) 192–4.

19 La Villemarqué (1842) 220, 222.

20 Renan (1859) 424.

21 Renan (1859) 426.

22 Schulz (1841) 52–4.

23 Wolfram von Eschenbach (1857) 776–9.

24 Campbell (1994) II, 341.

25 Nutt (1965).

26 Hardy (1952) viii. The note is dated 1919; the volume was originally issued in 1888.

27 Hucher (1875) 29–59.

28 Birch-Hirschfeld (1969).

29 Nutt (1965) 126.

30 MacCana (1970) 16.

31 Newstead (1939) 43.

32 Goetinck (1975) 275.

33 Loomis (1991) 273–4.

34 See Faugère (1979).

35 Ringbom (1951).

36 Ringbom (1951) 509–12.

37 Littleton and Thomas (1978) 513–27.

38 For a detailed study of a group of critics who study the subject from this viewpoint, see D'Arcy (2000) 165–223.

39 Weston (1964) 72–3.

40 Heinzel (1892) 7–9.

41 Anitchkof (1929) 181–5, 191–2.

42 See St John Chrysostom (1926); the same comment applies to the thesis put forward in Scavone (1999) 3–23.

43 Weinraub (1976) 50–6.

44 Fiedler (1979) 151–69.

45 Olschki (1966) 45.

46 Roquebert (1994).

47 Campbell (1968) 406.

48 Campbell (1968) 36.

49 Campbell (1968) 459.

50 Jung (1986) 237.

51 Jung and von Franz (1998) 392.

52 Heidelberg, Universitätsbibliothek, Manessische Liederhandschrift, ff. 52r, 82v, 162v, 178r.

53 Kahane and Kahane (1965).

54 Mandach (1992), (1995).

55 Evans (1898).

56 Adolf (1960) 106 ff.

18. The Revival of the Grail

1 Quoted by Raposo Fernández (2000) 192.

2 La Motte Fouqué (1997) The quotation is on p. 594.

3 La Motte Fouqué (1997) 607.

4 La Motte Fouqué (1997) 371–2.

5 La Motte Fouqué (1997) 44.

6 Raposo Fernández (2000) 198.

7 Immermann [n.d.] 65–8.

8 Hofstätter (1811).

9 Quinet (1895) I, 347–56.

10 Quinet (1895) 504.

11 Glencross (1995) 170.

12 Laprade (1906) 33–88.

13 Quoted in Tennyson (1987) I, 545.

14 Lupack and Lupack (1999) 13.

15 Taylor and Brewer (1983) 168.

16 Yamaguchi (1992) 235–46.

17 See pl. 21.

18 Tennyson (1897) i. 456–7.

19 Tennyson (1970) 292–3.

20 Tennyson (1897) II, 90. The lines are 912–14, italicized in the excerpt.

21 Poulson (1999) 64.

22 Tennyson (1987) III, 464.

23 Barczewski (2000) 218.

24 Barczewski (2000) 222–3.

25 Tresize (2000) 63–76.

26 Byles (1905) 449.

27 Hawker (1908) 180.

28 Quoted in Mancoff (1990) 196.

29 Burne-Jones to May Gaskell, Burne-Jones Papers 27: 43–27, Dept of MSS, Fitzwilliam Museum, Cambridge, quoted in Mancoff (1990) 240.

30 Clemens Krauss, *Capriccio* (music by Richard Strauss) Act I, scene ii.

31 Watson (2002) 24.

32 Wagner [n.d.] 13.

33 Wagner [n.d.] 21 ('Erlösungs-Helden').

34 Wagner [n.d.] 22.

35 Wagner [n.d.] 23 ('des Weihgefässes göttlicher Gehalt').

36 Wagner [n.d.] 26.

37 Wagner [n.d.] 62 ('Höchsten Heiles Wunder:/Erlösung dem Erlöser').

38 Waddell (1894) 11.

39 Nietzsche (1971) 676.

40 Spotts (1994) 166.

41 Beckett (1981) 87–102.

42 See Hoffman (2000); Müller (1991b) 157–68.

43 This account is based on Carnegy (2001).

44 Wagner (1978–80) II, 1013.

45 Wagner [n.d.] 20.

46 Wagner (1980) 57.

47 Wagner (1978–80) I, 977 (11 August 1877). In 1843, Wagner had written music for an oratorio entitled *The Communion of the Apostles*, which has at least hints of the Grail theme in *Lohengrin* and the voice from on high used in *Parsifal*. He described it as one of his failures, but could it have lurked in his subconscious mind?

48 Wagner (1978–80) II, 195 (10 November 1878).

49 Wagner (1897) VI, 211.

50 Wagner (1897) VI, 244–5, 246.

51 Wagner (1897) VI, 213.

52 Quoted in Magee (2000) 283.

53 For a contrary view, see Borchmeyer (1991) 388–91.

54 Kühnel (1989) 210.

55 Eckermann (1948) 504.

56 While admiring Lucy Beckett's analysis (Beckett 1981, 'A proposed interpretation', 128–49), I disagree with her on the way in which Wagner invokes Christianity.

57 Wagner (1978–80) II, 119 (24 July 1878).

58 See Boisserée (1835) and pl. 23. This engraving was reproduced on the cover of the manuscript known as 'Ludwig II's Diary' (Bayerische Verwaltung der staatlichen Schlösser KLM Res. Mü., F.V.III, Bd.VII, fol.1375. A 1145).

59 Quoted in Petzet (1995) 63–86, 71.

60 Anton Seder, Tafelaufsatz der Gral 1900, Bayerische Nationalmuseum, 93/983.

19. The Grail as Mirror

1 Yates (1972) 50 ff.

2 Yates (1972) 209.

3 Godwin (1994) 284–9.

4 The surviving documents of the order do not always include 'et du Graal', which may have been an afterthought. See the appendices in Pincus-Witten (1976) 205 ff. which reproduce the manifesto and rules relating to the art exhibitions which the order organized; here it is called the Order of the 'Rose+Croix du Temple'. It seems to have been the monthly bulletin of the Order which added 'et du Graal'.

5 Pincus-Witten (1976) 25–8; Péladan (1883).

6 Pincus-Witten (1976) 117.

7 Pincus-Witten (1976) 115.

8 *Le Saint-Graal* no. 1 (1971) 9.

9 *Le Saint-Graal* nos 7–8 (1971) 201–3.

10 Yeats (1955) 576.

11 Quoted in Gilbert (1997) 13.

12 Quoted in Williams (1958) xxviii.

13 Gilbert (1987) 74.

14 Gilbert (1987) 114.

15 Howe (1972) 255.

16 Waite (1961) 573, 574.

17 See Decker et al. (1996) 33.

18 Waite (1961) 507.

19 Waite (1961) 508.

20 Waite (1961) 534.

21 'Taliessin at Lancelot's Mass' is almost certainly related to the last paragraph of 'The Conclusion of this Holy Quest' in Waite (1909) 687.

22 Unpublished account by Col. Harold Mynors Farmar, dated 27 March 1909. I am most grateful to Robert Dunning for lending me a copy of this. A similar account is given in Benham (1993).

23 Benham (1993) 38.

24 Benham (1993) 76–7.

25 Paine (1912) III, 1388.

26 Benham (1993) 141.

27 See Wood (2002) 219–53.

28 Cackett [n.d.]

29 [O.G.S. Crawford], *Antiquity* IX (1935) 356–7.

30 Harris (1927) 286–95. The supposed quotation is from Matthew 22.50.

31 A much better approach to the topographical Grail is that of Deike and Ean Beigg (1995) who give a generally even-handed account of the stories attached to sites which are associated with the Grail and with relics of the Holy Blood. They manage to balance scepticism and enthusiasm in a commendable way, even if some of their historical connections and attributions are a little dubious; and they do highlight the sites with a genuine link to the development of the Grail stories, such as Fécamp and Valencia, as well as objects such as the Holy Lance at Vienna.

32 Benham (1993) 262.

33 Anderson (1953) 127.

34 Bertoni (1940) 7.

35 Insolera (1997) 9 ff.

36 John, 19.38.

37 Ponsoye (1976).

38 Faivre (1996) 81.

39 Guénon (1951) 39.

40 Guénon (1958) 41–6.

41 Rivière (1990) 199; his book is a splendid collection of the more eccentric versions of the Grail myth in modern times, most of which he denounces.

42 Evola (1937) 185. The French edition of 1967 contains a very different epilogue, adapted to new political conditions.

43 Letter to Johann Joachim Eschenburg, in Lessing (1907) XVIII, 114. There is no mention of the Templars in this discussion of the Grail.

44 Schlegel (1822) 294.

45 Batley (1999) 297–313.

46 Mackey (1956) II, 832.

47 See 'Discourse upon the Theology and Mythology of Pagans' in Ramsay (1727).

48 Partner (1982) 110–11.

49 *Viertes Gesprach*, in Lessing (1969) II 1096. Lessing was reasonably well informed about the Grail romances: see p. 233 above.

50 Hammer-Purgstall (1818) 24.

51 Schulz (1841).

52 Weston (1957) 187.

53 Baigent et al. (1982) 68.

54 Baigent et al. (1982) 245.

55 Baigent et al. (1982) 253; in *Perlesvaus*, the king who gives his son to be devoured by the people is, of course, an allegory of God sending Christ to redeem mankind in the context of the Mass, not an allusion to the Templars' 'roasting and devouring of children'.

56 Baigent et al. (1982) 273.

57 Fanthorpe and Fanthorpe (1982) 143.

58 Sinclair (2001).

59 Currer-Briggs (1987) 23.

60 Fauriel (1846) II, 438.

61 Aroux (1994) 73.

62 Aroux (1994) 76.

63 Beaufils (1986) 16.

64 Péladan (1906) 5.

65 Péladan (1906) 45–6.

66 Péladan (1906) 69.

67 *Magiciens et Illuminés* (Toulouse 1930).

68 Maurice Magre, *La Clef des choses cachées* (Toulouse 1935), quoted in Bernadac (1978) 438.

69 Peyrat (1870–2) II 361–2, 368–9.

70 Rahn (1964) 67.

71 Rahn (1964) 75.

72 Rahn (1964) 163.

73 Rahn (1964) 254.

74 Rahn (1964) 255.

75 Rahn (1995) 95–6.

76 Rahn (1995) 156–9.

77 Rahn (1995) 42.

78 See Bernadac (1978).

79 Pennick (1981) 164.

80 Rivière (2000) 170.

81 The *Guardian* 7 August 2002.

82 Biget (1979) 317–18.

83 See Sinclair (1998) 250–2, 278; a series of half-documented hints are used to demonstrate the Nazi involvement with the Grail.

84 For example, Angebert (1974).

85 Kater (1974) 53–7, 290–302.

86 Friedrich Lienhard, *Der Meister der Menschheit* (Stuttgart 1919–21) III, 33, quoted in Hermand (1962) 530; see also Mosse (1961).

87 Hermand (1962) 540–2.

88 Michell (1967) 162.

89 Heelas (1996) 2.

90 Matthews (1999) 35.

91 A reference to Perlesvaus, see p. 51 above.

92 Matthews (1990) 102.

93 Matthews (1997).

94 See Matthews (1990).

95 Matthews and Matthews (1986) II, 18.

96 Matthews (1987) 3–4.

97 A good example of this all-embracing approach is Godwin (1994).

20 The Grail Today

1 'Mark Twain' (1987) 49 (ch. ix).

2 Mitchison (1999) 202.

3 Mitchison (1999) 211.

4 Machen (1922) 96.

5 Hurd (2002) 95–6, 98–9.

6 Powys (1975) 125.

7 Powys (1967) xvii.

8 Powys (1975) 285.

9 Powys (1975) xi, xv.

10 Powys (1975) 125–6.

11 Powys (1975) 457–8.

12 Powys (1975) 1116.

13 Eliot (1963) ll. 189–90.

14 Eliot (1963) ll. 422–4.

15 'And, oh, these children's voices singing in the dome': Eliot (1963) 202.

16 Butts (2001).

17 Butts (2002) 275.

18 See also Butts (2002) 224, where she notes that the Grail motif is a 'fake' on the part of Picus.

19 Butts (2001) 140.

20 Butts (2002) 101, 449.

21 Butts (2002) 421, 430.

22 'Les chevaliers sont morts sur le chemin du Graal' ('De rêve', 1892).

23 Cocteau (1937) 209–10.

24 Gracq (1989) I, 325–96.

25 Bridel (1980), 25.

26 Gracq (1989) 391.

27 Gracq (1989) 358.

28 Gracq (1989) 352.

29 Gracq (1989) 383.

30 Gracq (1989) 329.

31 Gracq (1989) 392.

32 Gracq (1989) 396.

33 Gracq (1989) 378–9.

34 Gracq (1989) 352.

35 Obermaier (2000) 260–7.

36 Dorst (1990) 109.

37 Dorst (1990) 112.

38 Dorst (1990) 78–9.

39 Dorst (1990) 69.

40 Hunter (1978) 137.

41 Williams (1930) 151–2.

42 Williams and Lewis (1948) 83.

43 See Williams (1991) which includes both volumes and many further drafts and unpublished versions.

44 Williams (1991) 97.

45 Williams (1991) 7.

46 Williams and Lewis (1948) 100–101.

47 What follows is necessarily the barest outline of the poems. An excellent interpretation is provided in Taylor and Brewer (1983) 250–61. See also Göller (1981).

48 Williams (1991) 135.

49 Williams (1991) 90.

50 Anne Ridler in Williams (1958) lxxi.

51 Williams (1991) 110.

52 Williams and Lewis (1948) 200.

53 Muschg (1993) 647.

54 Muschg (1993) 648.

55 Muschg (1993) 205.

56 Muschg (1993) 497.

57 Muschg (1993) 208.
58 Pastré (1994) 29–37.
59 Clarke (2001).
60 *Story of the Grail*, 70; *Perceval*, 6509–11.
61 Lodge (1984) 12.
62 Calvino (1998) 367.
63 Calvino (1977) 91.
64 Vansittart (1988) 68.
65 Vansittart (1988) 98.
66 Vansittart (1988) 125.
67 Vansittart (1988) 186.
68 Eco (2002) 502.
69 Eco (2002) 521.
70 Sinclair (1998) 204.
71 Baudry (1998) 346.

21 The Question Answered?

1 Mathiesen (1998) 155.
2 Mathiesen (1998) 143.
3 *Story of the Grail*, 69; *Perceval*, ll. 6481–8.
4 Kay (1997) 1–36.
5 For example, Jefferson (1996) 145.
6 Waite (1961) 684–5.
7 Eco (1986) 71.
8 Eco (1989) 377.
9 Eco (1986) 71.
10 *Story of the Grail*, 69; *Perceval*, 6485.
11 I am grateful to Professor Maureen Boulton for references to these; a good example is in BL MS Harley 1260 ff 230a–231a; ten lines of sacred names in Greek, Hebrew and Latin are preceded by a note saying that these names will protect from misfortune.

Epilogue

1 *Parzival*, 235.24.
2 Owen (1803); on the rarity of texts about the Grail in medieval Wales see Lloyd-Morgan (1978) 48.
3 Girouard (1981) 215.
4 Fitzgerald (1950) 142.
5 *Sciences et Vie*, 921 (1994) 63, quoted in Chandès (1996) 160.
6 General Recursive Applicative and Algorithmic Language (GRAAL); Graphical Input Language; Gene Recognition Analysis Internet Link; GRAIL (a 'pre-language' for teaching programming); Galen Representation And Integration Language.

7 The *Guardian*, 4 December 1999.
8 The *Guardian*, 26 May 2001.
9 The *Guardian*, 4 January 2002.
10 The *Guardian*, 5 January 2002.

Index